The European Union

The European Union

Economics, Policies and History

Third edition

Susan Senior Nello

McGraw-Hill Higher Education

London Boston Burr Ridge, IL Dubuque, IA Madison, WI New York San Francisco St. Louis
Bangkok Bogotá Caracas Kuala Lumpur Lisbon Madrid Mexico City
Milan Montreal New Delhi Santiago Seoul Singapore Sydney Taipei Toronto

The European Union: Economics, Policies and History, 3rd Edition
Susan Senior Nello
ISBN-13 9780077129668
ISBN-10 0077129660

Published by McGraw-Hill Education
Shoppenhangers Road
Maidenhead
Berkshire
SL6 2QL
Telephone: 44 (0) 1628 502 500
Fax: 44 (0) 1628 770 224
Website: www.mcgraw-hill.co.uk

British Library Cataloguing in Publication Data
A catalogue record for this book is available from the British Library

Library of Congress Cataloguing in Publication Data
The Library of Congress data for this book has been applied for from the Library of Congress

Executive Editor: Natalie Jacobs
Development Editor: Kiera Jamison
Marketing Manager: Vanessa Boddington
Production Editor: Alison Davis

Cover design by Watermelon Creative
Printed and bound in the UK by Bell and Bain Ltd, Glasow

ISBN-13 9780077129668
ISBN-10 0077129660

Dedication

This book is inevitably dedicated to Paolo, Matteo and Caterina, and to the many friends I have made throughout Europe and elsewhere while studying and teaching EU integration.

Brief Table of Contents

Detailed Table of Contents

Guided Tour

An Introduction to European Integration: Definitions and Terminology

Learning Objectives

By the end of this chapter you should be able to understand:

- ☑ The difference in meaning of the terms 'European Economic Community', 'European Community' and 'European Union'.
- ☑ How and why the membership of the European Union has changed over the years.
- ☑ What we mean by integration, and its various stages.
- ☑ What is the *acquis communautaire*.
- ☑ What we mean by the term 'subsidiarity'.
- ☑ The importance of the EU in the world economy.

1.1 Introduction

Over the years teaching European integration certain key questions invariably come up during lectures. The aim of this chapter is to reply to these questions before they arise at a later stage in the course.¹ The first part of the chapter addresses issues such as the difference between the terms European 'Community' and European 'Union', and the changing membership of the EU. The chapter then deals briefly with certain theoretical aspects of integration before explaining some of the concepts essential to understanding the working of the EU. Many students will be familiar with these topics, but almost

¹ There is a great deal of jargon associated with the EU. For explanations of the various terms see the Europa Glossary of

Learning Objectives

Each chapter opens with a set of learning objectives, helping readers to quickly grasp the essentials to be learned in the chapter.

Key Terms

These are highlighted in the relevant chapters providing ease of reference.

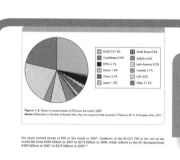

Figure 1.3 Share in inward stocks of FDI from the world, 2009
Source: Elaboration on the basis of Eurostat data, http://ec.europa.eu/trade [accessed 10 February 2011]. © European Union, 2011.

the main inward stocks of FDI in the world in 2007. Outflows of the EU(27) FDI to the rest of the world fell from €496 billion in 2007 to €274 billion in 2009, while inflows to the EU decreased from €400 billion in 2007 to €219 billion in 2009.

Table 1.2 Trade balance (€ billion)

	2007	2008	2009
EU(27) with extra EU(27)	–192.8	–255.1	–102.9
Canada	4.2	6.3	–40.5
USA	–600.7	–588.2	–467.5
China excluding Hong Kong	246.5	259.2	188.5
Japan	49.0	–4.3	6.5

Source: Eurostat data, http://ec.europa.eu/trade [accessed 10 February 2011]. © European Union, 2011.

Figures and Tables

Each chapter provides a number of figures and tables to help illustrate and summarize important concepts.

in to the requests of the steel lobby, knowing that consumers will be unlikely to organize any kind of effective resistance.

This type of political economy argument is very powerful in explaining the pervasiveness of protectionist measures. In the EU and USA, aside from steel, protection tends to be high in agriculture, textiles and clothing, and the automobile industry.

Summary of key concepts

- Many of our arguments in favour of free trade still owe much to the pioneering work of the classical economists **Adam Smith** and **David Ricardo** who illustrated that trade between two countries could be mutually beneficial thanks to the specialization of their production.
- The **Heckscher-Ohlin theorem** explains patterns of trade in terms of the endowments of factors of production of countries. For example, a country which has an abundance of cheap labour will specialize in the production of labour-intensive goods.
- According to the **Heckscher-Ohlin-Samuelson** theorem, under certain very restrictive assumptions, the liberalization of trade will bring about the equalization of relative and absolute returns to the factors of production between countries.
- **New trade theories** take into account aspects such as: imperfect competition, political economy arguments, new growth theory, the new economic geography, and open economy macroeconomics.
- Much trade between EU countries consists of **intra-industry trade**. This arises from product differentiation and means that each country (or producer) can specialize in a few varieties of the product and exploit economies of scale.
- **Static economies of scale** occur when the unit costs of production fall as the scale of production rises. Dynamic economies of scale are associated with the **learning process**.
- An import **tariff** is a tax or duty levied on a product when it is imported into a country. Tariffs can be ad valorem, specific or compound.
- Among the main **non-tariff barriers** are: quotas, voluntary export restraints (VERs), cartels, anti-dumping measures, trade facilitation measures (including customs procedures, measures to promote exports and so on), differences in standards and technical specifications, and lack of transparency in government procurement.
- The **effect of trade protection** for a particular product is to raise domestic prices. Producers in that country will benefit, while consumers will have to pay higher prices. However, the benefits to the producers can be very high, while the cost to consumers is diffused. Producers may have an incentive to lobby government to introduce protection in their favour, while consumers may feel that it is not worth their while to object.

Summary of Key Concepts

This briefly reviews and reinforces the main topics you have covered in each chapter to ensure you have acquired a solid understanding of the key topics.

Questions for Study and Review

These questions encourage you to review and apply the knowledge you have acquired from each chapter and can be undertaken to test your understanding.

Questions for study and review

1 What are the main arguments in favour of free trade?
2 Describe the main obstacles to trade and their use by the EU (see also Chapters and 18)?
3 Explain how non-tariff barriers have a negative effect on trade.
4 Illustrate how political economy reasons may help to explain the high levels of protection in sectors such as agriculture, steel or textiles.
5 Exercise on the effects of a tariff in a small nation (see Appendix 1 for an example of how to carry out the exercise). The quantity of a commodity supplied in a country is 24 tonnes, the quantity demanded (Qd) is 60 tonnes, and the world price (Pw) is €6/tonne. A tariff is introduced which raises the domestic price (Pd) to €7/tonne. The elasticity of demand is –0.3 and the elasticity of supply is 0.5. Calculate the effects of the tariff on: producer revenue, consumer expenditure, the trade balance and total welfare.[21]
6 Exercise on the effects of introducing a tariff in a large nation (see Appendix 2 for an example of how to carry out the exercise). It is assumed initially that in conditions of free trade the quantity supplied (Qs) by a country is 200 tonnes, the quantity demanded (Qd) is 400 tonnes, and the world price (Pw) is €4/tonne. A tariff is introduced which raises the domestic price (Pd) to €5/tonne and as a result the world price P'w falls to €3.5/tonne. The elasticity of demand is –0.5 and the elasticity of supply is 0.4. Calculate the effects of the tariff on: producer revenue, consumer expenditure, the trade balance and total welfare.

Appendices

Relevant chapters end with an appendix that aims to expand on themes explored in the chapter.

Chapter 4 Appendices

Appendix 1: A numerical example of the effect of introducing a tariff in a small nation

A simple numerical example can be used to calculate the effects of introducing a tariff.[13] It is assumed initially that the quantity supplied (Qs) by the country is 8 tonnes, the quantity demanded (Qd) is 30 tonnes, and the world price (Pw) is €2/tonne. A tariff is introduced which raises the domestic price (Pd) to €3/tonne (see Figure A4.1).

Figure A4.1 The introduction of a tariff in a small nation: a numerical example

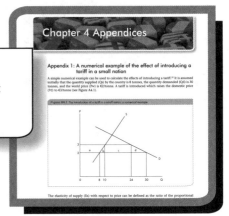

The elasticity of supply (Es) with respect to price can be defined as the ratio of the proportional

Supplements and Technology

Visit **www.mcgraw-hill.co.uk/textbooks/senior** today.

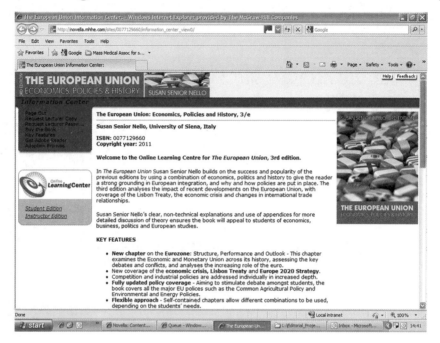

Online Learning Centre (OLC)

After completing each chapter, log on to the supporting Online Learning Centre website. Take advantage of the study tools and further reading offered to reinforce the material you have read in the text, and to develop your knowledge in a fun and effective way.

Resources for students include:

- Self-test questions
- Learning outcomes
- Useful web links
- Topical essays
- Guide answers to questions for study and review
- Additional exercises
- Chronology of enlargement
- Case Studies
- Chapters on Fisheries Policy and GATT/WTO

Also available for lecturers:

- Lecture outlines
- PowerPoint presentations

Let us help make our **content** your **solution**

At McGraw-Hill Education our aim is to help lecturers to find the most suitable content for their needs delivered to their students in the most appropriate way. Our **custom publishing solutions** offer the ideal combination of content delivered in the way which best suits lecturer and students.

Our custom publishing programme offers lecturers the opportunity to select just the chapters or sections of material they wish to deliver to t heir students from a database called CREATE™ at

www.mcgrawhillcreate.co.uk

CREATE™ contains over two million pages of content from:
- textbooks
- professional books
- case books – Harvard Articles, Insead, Ivey, Darden, Thunderbird and *Bloomburg BusinessWeek*
- Taking Sides – debate materials

Across the following imprints:
- McGraw-Hill Education
- Open University Press
- Harvard Business Publishing
- US and European material

There is also the option to include additional material authored by lecturers in the custom product – this does not necessarily have to be in English.

We will take care of everything from start to finish in the process of developing and delivering a custom product to ensure that lecturers and students receive exactly the material needed in the most suitable way.

With a **Custom Publishing Solution**, students enjoy the best selection of material deemed to be the most suitable for learning everything they need for their courses – something of real value to support their learning. Teachers are able to use exactly the material they want, in the way they want, to support their teaching on the course.

Please contact your local **McGraw-Hill representative** with any questions or alternatively contact Warren Eels e: **warren_eels@mcgraw-hill.com**.

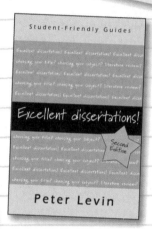

Preface

Many years ago when studying European integration at the College of Europe in Bruges, one of the professors organized a trip to the battlefields of Flanders of the First World War. The day seemed a little like a school outing, but with the relentless rain falling in the former trenches, the lesson was well taken. One of the main aims of integration was to render war in Europe not only inconceivable, but 'materially impossible'. Today, despite tensions in certain areas, in the EU we tend to take this success almost for granted. One of the aims now is to extend this achievement to other less stable areas of Europe such as the former Yugoslavia.

Of the many experts working on East–West studies, few predicted the collapse of the Eastern bloc from 1989. Right from the start of transition the Central and Eastern European countries wanted to join the integration process. At first the European Community seemed rather unprepared and overwhelmed at the prospect, but after a long and difficult process of preparation, between 2004 and 2007 much of Europe was again 'reunified'.

In 2007 there were celebrations of fifty years of European integration, and under the German presidency of the EU, Angela Merkel singled out environmental policy as a way of relaunching the integration process, announcing that the EU was at the vanguard of the battle against climate change. In recent years greater priority has also been given to increasing competitiveness, and the Europe 2020 strategy aims at smart (based on knowledge and innovation), sustainable (greener and more resource efficient) and inclusive (with higher employment and skills and less poverty) growth.

European integration has a strong political impetus, but the method of implementation has been primarily economic. The first successful initiative was the European Coal and Steel Community created in 1951, while in the early years of the European Economic Community (EEC) the main progress was in trade and agriculture (though the policy mechanisms chosen for the latter can be criticized). Numerous studies show that the Single Market Programme, introduced in 1985 and bolstered in many member states by the euro, has fostered trade and other closer economic ties between countries.

The recent international economic crisis has imposed severe strains on the EU and some of the member states that adopted the euro have had to request bail-outs. Faced with this situation EU institutions such as the European Central Bank have had to enter uncharted waters, but the turbulence seems likely to continue for some time, bringing political as well as economic consequences.

This book is aimed mainly at students of economics, European studies, business, political science and international relations. Though the approach is grounded in economics, the aim is to provide a multidisciplinary account of EU integration. The debate about whether the EU is primarily an economic or political entity is of long standing, but the view here is that in order to understand the process of integration a combination of economics, politics and history is necessary. The textbook is intended to have a strong policy orientation.

The objective has also been to organize the material in a flexible way so it can be directed at different audiences. For this reason the theory has been concentrated in Chapters 4 and 5 and in separate sections in other chapters. Omitting Chapters 4 and 5, and the theoretical sections, the book can and has been used in various courses where the students have little or no economics background. The aim has also been to write chapters that stand individually, and can be used independently from the rest of the book. A basic introduction to the EU could cover Chapters 1–3, 6, 7, 9–12 and Chapter 19. Those interested in individual policies can select from Chapters 13 to 18. A course on the external relations of the EU could use Chapters 1, 18 and 19. The intention has been to permit the use of different combinations of chapters depending on the needs or interests of the reader.

The EU is evolving constantly, and though every effort has been made to ensure that the text is up to date, more recent developments are necessarily covered by the Online Learning Centre (OLC) of this book. For reasons of the space the chapters on the EU Fisheries Policy and part of that on the EU and GATT/WTO have been moved to the OLC and updated.

Because each chapter has been written so that it can stand independently, the aim is also to provide a text that can be consulted by researchers or policy makers. For this purpose each chapter sets out references for further reading and relevant websites are indicated on the OLC.

Acknowledgements

Our thanks go to the following reviewers for their comments at various stages in the new edition's development:

Robert Ackrill, Nottingham Trent University
Etienne Bresch, London Metropolitan University
Norma Dytianquin, Maastricht University
Carmen Gebhard, University of Nottingham
Nigel Grimwade, London South Bank University
Matt Heckman, Maastricht University
Christer Karlsson, Uppsala University
Sangeeta Khorana, Aberystwyth University
Siobhan McCarthy, Dublin Institute of Technology
Stefania Paladini, Coventry University
Dr Anders Poulsen, University of East Anglia
Paul Roosens, University of Antwerp
Colin Simpson, University of Gloucestershire
Jean-Marc Trouille, Bradford University
Stefan Weishaar, Maastricht University

Thanks again to those who reviewed the first and second editions.

Few would be foolhardy enough to sit down and begin writing a textbook on the European Union these days. This book was never actually planned, but emerged as a result of teaching various aspects of EU integration over the years. As many of the courses were repeated, it seemed a good idea to keep a written record, and gradually the book emerged. My first thanks therefore go to the many students on whom (often inadvertently) the material was tried out. These include the students of the Faculty of Economics 'Richard Goodwin' and the Faculty of Political Science of the University of Siena, the Scuola Superiore Sant'Anna of Pisa, the California State University Florence Program and Cornell College, Iowa.

University work is invariably a combination of teaching and research, and this book has grown out of many years of research into European integration. I would therefore like to thank the many colleagues, in particular those at Siena University, the European University Institute and the European Commission, for offering opportunities for discussion of topics related to the book, including seminars, summer schools and conferences. Though I was helped by too many people to thank them all individually, I would like to mention the late Secondo Tarditi who provided help and advice over the years. I am also grateful to Alberto Chilosi, Pompeo della Posta, Massimo di Matteo, Tamara Evans, Jens Hoiberg, Alison McDonnell, Massimiliano Montini, Mario Nuti, Heikki Oksanen, Alessandro Sorrentino, Michael Tracy, Milica Uvalic, Alessandro Vercelli and Amy Verdun.

Recognizing that it would be difficult to pull together a final version of this text I hesitated some time before presenting the manuscript. The various members on the publishing team were invaluable in helping me to complete this final step. I am very grateful to those who helped with all three editions for their encouragement and assistance, in particular in organizing numerous reviews by the referees. These reviews have radically shaped the final version of this book, but any eventual mistakes that remain are, of course, my responsibility.

I would like to thank the following organizations and publishers for permission to reproduce material in this book:

Agricultural Policy Studies (APS)
CABI Publishing
Carocci editore, Roma
HarperCollins
IFPRI
IMD International World Competitiveness Centre
OECD
Official Publications Office of the European Communities
Oxford University Press
Palgrave Macmillan
Taylor and Francis, incorporating Routledge
UNHCR
John Wiley & Sons, Inc.
World Bank

List of Abbreviations

AC	average cost
ACED	Action Committee for Democracy
ACP	African, Caribbean and Pacific countries covered by the Lomé conventions and the Cotonou Agreement
ACTS	Advanced Communications Technology and Services
AENEAS	financial and technical assistance to third countries in the area of migration and asylum
AGEA	Agenzia per le Erogazioni in Agricoltura
AGOA	African Growth and Opportunity Act
AII	Adriatic–Ionian Initiative
AIMA	Azienda Italiana per i Mercati Agricoli
AR	average revenue
ASEAN	Association of Southeast Asian Nations
ASEM	Asia–Europe Meeting
BEREC	Body of European Regulators of Electronic Communications
BRICs	Brazil, Russia, India and China
BRITE/EURAM	Basic Research in Industrial Technologies for Europe/European Research in Advanced Materials
BSE	bovine spongiform encephalopathy
BSEC	Black Sea Economic Cooperation
CAP	Common Agricultural Policy
CARDS	Community Assistance for Reconstruction, Development and Stabilisation
CARE	Climate Action and Renewable Energy
CCP	Common Commercial Policy
CCCTB	common consolidated corporate tax base
CEEC	Central and Eastern European country
CEFTA	Central European Free Trade Area
CEN	Comité Européen de Normalisation
CENELEC	Comité Européen de Normalisation Electrotechnique
CFC	chlorofluorocarbon gases
CFP	Common Fisheries Policy
CFSP	Common Foreign and Security Policy
CGE	computable general equilibrium
CJ	Court of Justice
CJDv	Creutzfeldt-Jakob variant
CMEA or Comecon	Council for Mutual Economic Assistance
COPA	Comité des Organisations professionelles agricoles de l'Union européenne – Confédération générale des coopératives agricoles de l'Union européenne
Coreper	Committee of Permanent Representatives
CSCE	Conference on Security and Co-operation in Europe
CSDP	Common Security and Defence Policy
CSE	Consumer Support Estimate
DAC	Development Assistance Committee
DDA	Doha Development Agenda
DG	Directorate-General
DRC	Development Research Centre on Migration, Globalisation and Poverty
DSM	Disputes Settlement Mechanism

EAFRD	European Agricultural Fund for Rural Development
EAGGF or FEOGA	European Agricultural Guidance and Guarantee Fund
EAP	Environmental Action Programme
EBA	Everything but Arms
EBRD	European Bank for Reconstruction and Development
EC	European Communities
ECB	European Central Bank
ECCP	Europe Climate Change Programme
ECHO	European Community Humanitarian Office
ECJ	European Court of Justice
ECN	European Competition Network
Ecofin	Council of Economic and Finance Ministers
ECRE	European Council on Refugees and Exiles
ECSC	European Coal and Steel Community
ECU	European Currency Unit
EDC	European Defence Community
EDF	European Development Fund
EEA	European Economic Area, European Environment Agency
EEAS	European External Action Service
EEC	European Economic Community
EERP	European Economic Recovery Plan
EES	European Employment Strategy
EESC or Ecosoc	European Economic and Social Committee
EFF	European Fisheries Fund
EFSF	European Financial Stability Facility
EFTA	European Free Trade Association
EGTC	European Grouping for Territorial Co-operation
EIB	European Investment Bank
Eionet	European Environmental Information and Observation Network
EIT	European Institute of Technology
EMAS	Eco-Management and Audit Scheme
EMCF	European Monetary Co-operation Fund
EMI	European Monetary Institute
EMS	European Monetary System
EMU	Economic and Monetary Union
ENP	European Neighbourhood Policy
EP	European Parliament
EPA	Economic Partnership Agreement
EPC	European Political Co-operation
EQUAL	Community Initiative on transnational co-operation to combat all kinds of discrimination and inequalities in the labour market
ERA	European Research Area
ERASMUS	European Union Action Scheme for the Mobility of University Students
ERC	European Research Council
ERDF	European Regional Development Fund
ERM	exchange rate mechanism
ESA	European Supervisory Authority
ESCB	European System of Central Banks
ESDP	European Security and Defence Policy
ESF	European Social Fund
ESM	European Stability Mechanism
ESPRIT	European Strategic Programme for Research and Development in Information Technology
ESRB	European Systemic Risk Board

ETS	Emissions Trading System
ETSI	European Telecommunications Standards Institute
ETUC	European Trade Union Confederation
EU	European Union
Euratom	European Atomic Energy Community
Eureka	European Research Co-ordination Agency
EURES	European Employment Services
Eurogroup	Group of Economic and Finance Ministers of the euro area
EUSF	European Union Solidarity Fund
FAO	Food and Agricultural Organisation
FDI	foreign direct investment
FEOGA	European Agricultural Guidance and Guarantee Fund
FIFG	Financial Instrument for Fisheries Guidance
FRG	Federal Republic of Germany
FRONTEX	the EU agency responsible for managing operational co-operation at the EU's external borders
FSAP	Financial Services Action Plan
FTAA	Free Trade Area of the Americas
GAERC	General Affairs and External Relations Council
GATS	General Agreement on Trade in Services
GATT	General Agreement on Tariffs and Trade
GCC	Gulf Co-operation Council
GDP	gross domestic product
GMO	genetically modified organism
GNI	gross national income
GNP	gross national product
GSP	Generalised System of Preferences
ICES	International Council for Exploration of the Seas
ICT	information and communication technology
ICTY	International Criminal Tribunal on the former Yugoslavia
IDA	Industrial Development Agency Ireland
IEA	International Energy Agency
IFI	international financial institution
IFPRI	International Food Policy Research Institute
IGC	intergovernmental conference
IMF	International Monetary Fund
IMI	Internal Market Information System
INTERREG II	Community Initiative on cross-border, transnational and interregional co-operation
IPA	Instrument for Pre-Accession Assistance
IPCC	Intergovernmental Panel on Climate Change
ISPA	Instrument for Structural Policies Pre-Accession
ITO	International Trade Organization
LDCs	least developed countries
JET	Joint European Torus on thermonuclear fusion
JHA	Justice and Home Affairs
LEADER	Community Initiative on rural development
LINGUA	programme for the learning and teaching of European languages
MAGP	Multi-Annual Guidance Plan
MC	marginal cost
MCAs	monetary compensatory amounts
MDG	Millennium Development Goals
MEC	marginal external cost
MEP	Member of the European Parliament

MFA	Multifibre Agreement
MFN	most favoured nation
MGQ	maximum guaranteed quantity
MIFID	Markets in Financial Instruments Directive
MNPB	marginal net private benefit
MR	marginal revenue
MRS	marginal rate of substitution
NAFTA	North American Free Trade Agreement
NAMA	non-agricultural market access, National Assets Management Agency (Ireland)
NATO	North Atlantic Treaty Organization
NCB	national central bank
NGO	non-governmental organization
NIEO	New International Economic Order
NIS	Newly Independent States (of the ex-USSR)
NPAA	National Programme for the Adoption of the *Acquis*
NRA	New Regulatory Agency
NTA	New Transatlantic Agenda
NTB	non-tariff barrier
OCA	optimum currency area
OCTs	Overseas Countries and Territories
ODA	official development aid
OECD	Organisation for Economic Co-operation and Development
OEEC	Organisation for European Economic Co-operation
OLAF	European Anti-Fraud Office
OMA	orderly marketing arrangement
OMC	open method of co-ordination
OPEC	Organization of the Petroleum Exporting Countries
OSCE	Organization for Security and Co-operation in Europe
PCA	Partnership and Co-operation Agreement
PEA	Positive Economic Agenda
PHARE	Poland and Hungary Assistance for the Restructuring of the Economy
PJCCM	Police and Judicial Co-operation in Criminal Matters
PPF	production possibility frontier
PPP	purchasing power parity
PPS	purchasing power standards
PROGRESS	EU Programme for Employment and Social Solidarity
PSE	Producer Support Estimate
QMV	qualified majority vote
R&D	research and development
RAC	Regional Advisory Council
RACE	Research into Advanced Communications for Europe
RCC	Regional Co-operation Council
REACH	Registration, Evaluation, Authorisation and Restriction of Chemical Substances
RTA	regional trade agreement
SAA	Stabilisation and Association Agreement
SAARC	South Asian Association for Regional Co-operation
SAPARD	Special Accession Programme for Agriculture and Rural Development
SDR	Special Drawing Right
SDT	Special and Differential Treatment
SEA	Single European Act
SEE	South-Eastern Europe

SEECP	South East European Cooperation Process
SEM	Single European Market
SFP	Single Farm Payment
SGP	Stability and Growth Pact
SICA	Central American Integration System
SIS	Schengen Information System
SITC	Standard International Trade Classification
SOLVIT	the redress system for implementation of internal market rules
SME	small and medium enterprise
TABD	Transatlantic Business Dialogue
TACIS	Technical Assistance for the Commonwealth of Independent States
TEC	Treaty Establishing the European Community
TEN	trans-European network
TEP	Transatlantic Economic Partnership
TEU	Treaty on European Union
TFEU	Treaty on the Functioning of the European Union
TMT	technology, media and telecoms
TRIM	trade-related investment measure
TRIPs	trade-related intellectual property rights
UFM	Union for the Mediterranean
UN	United Nations
UNCTAD	United Nations Conference on Trade and Development
UNDP	United Nations Development Programme
UNECE	United Nations Economic Commission for Europe
UNFCCC	United Nations Framework Convention on Climate Change
UNFICYP	United Nations Peacekeeping Force in Cyprus
UFM	Union for the Mediterranean
UNHCR	United Nations High Commissioner for Refugees
UNMIK	United Nations Mission in Kosovo
UNSCR	United Nations Security Council Resolution
URAA	Uruguay Round Agreement on Agriculture
URBAN	Community Initiative on economic and social regeneration of cities and urban neighbourhoods
VER	voluntary export restraint
WEU	Western European Union
WHO	World Health Organization
WTO	World Trade Organization

Chapter 1

An Introduction to European Integration: Definitions and Terminology

Learning Objectives

By the end of this chapter you should be able to understand:

- ☑ The difference in meaning of the terms 'European Economic Community', 'European Community' and 'European Union'
- ☑ How and why the membership of the European Union has changed over the years
- ☑ What we mean by integration, and its various stages
- ☑ What is the *acquis communautaire*
- ☑ What we mean by the term 'subsidiarity'
- ☑ The importance of the EU in the world economy

1.1 Introduction

Over the years teaching European integration certain key questions invariably come up during lectures. The aim of this chapter is to reply to these questions before they arise at a later stage in the course.[1] The first part of the chapter addresses issues such as the difference between the terms European 'Community' and European 'Union', and the changing membership of the EU. The chapter then deals briefly with certain theoretical aspects of integration before explaining some of the concepts essential to understanding the working of the EU. Many students will be familiar with these topics, but almost

---

[1] There is a great deal of jargon associated with the EU. For planations of the various terms see the Europa Glossary of the EU at http://europa.eu/legislation_summaries/glossary, or the website of Baldwin and Wyplosz (2009) at www.mcgraw-hill.co.uk/textbooks/baldwin (accessed 10 February 2011). For additional information on these topics see the Online Learning Centre of this book at www.mcgraw-hill.co.uk/textbooks/senior.

always some are not. Depending on the knowledge and formation of the students this chapter can be used in a 'pick and choose' way, leaving the rest to background reading.

The second part of the chapter provides an overview of the position of the EU in the world indicating some of the main features of its trade and foreign direct investment, and comparing it with other major economic powers such as the USA, China and Japan.

1.2 Questions of terminology

The term 'European Economic Community' (EEC) dates from the Treaty of Rome (which came into force 1 January 1958, see Box 1.1). It was one of the then three European Communities, the others being the European Coal and Steel Community or ECSC, and Euratom, initially created to co-ordinate the civilian use of nuclear energy, (see Chapter 2). The institutions of the three Communities were fused from 1967 when the 1965 Merger Treaty came into force. In July 2002 the ECSC was formally wound up, and its assets and liabilities were transferred to the European Union (EU).

The widespread use of the term 'European Community' dates from a resolution of the European Parliament of 1975 when it was decided to drop the term 'economic' because the Community was considered to have extended its activities beyond the purely economic sphere. This term was confirmed formally with the Maastricht Treaty.

In the Treaty of Rome the founders of the original EEC laid the foundations for working towards 'an ever closer union'. According to the opening words of the Treaty of Maastricht (which came into force in 1993), this objective had been reached: 'By this Treaty, the High Contracting Parties establish among themselves a European Union, hereinafter called "the Union"'. With the Treaty of Maastricht the European Community was reinforced and flanked by two other 'pillars': the Common Foreign and Security Policy (CFSP) and Justice and Home Affairs (JHA). The three together formed the European Union.[2]

Box 1.1

The Main Treaties

Name of treaty	Year signed	Year came into force
Rome	1957	1958
Single European Act	1986	1987
Maastricht	1992	1993
Amsterdam	1997	1999
Nice	2001	2003
Lisbon	2009	2009

As a result of the Treaty of Amsterdam (which came into force in 1999), many aspects of JHA were brought under the Community pillar (which covered areas such as the Common Agricultural Policy, the Common Commercial Policy, the Single Market, Competition Policy and Economic and Monetary Union), and the name of the third pillar was changed to reflect its residual competences: Police and Judicial Co-operation in Criminal Matters (PJCCM). The Lisbon Treaty (which came into operation

---

[2] However, only the European Community pillar had legal personality.

on 1 December 2009) abolished the pillar structure. As a result the European Union replaced and succeeded the European Community, taking over all its rights and obligations. This meant that the EU (rather than the EC as was the case previously) has legal personality and can sign international treaties and participate in international organizations such as the World Trade Organization (WTO).

The reason for creating the pillar structure was that, at least initially on some sensitive issues, the member states were reluctant to give up responsibility. Decisions in the spheres of the second (CFSP) and third (JHA) pillars were taken using a form of inter-governmental co-operation, which involves direct negotiation between governments, and as a general rule unanimity was required in decision-making procedures.[3]

As described in Chapter 3, the Lisbon Treaty is composed of the Treaty on European Union (TEU), the Treaty on Functioning of the European Union (TFEU) and numerous protocols. The Treaty replaced the term 'Community' everywhere with 'Union' in the two treaties.

1.3 The Common Foreign and Security Policy

The Common Foreign and Security Policy (CFSP) covers what its name suggests and is one of the external relations instruments of the EU. According to the Lisbon Treaty (Article 25 TEU), the EU pursues the CFSP by: indicating general guidelines; adopting decisions defining joint actions and positions to be taken by the EU; and strengthening co-operation between member states. The Lisbon Treaty also created a High Representative for Foreign Affairs and Security Policy (Catherine Ashton from 2009) and a European External Action Service (EEAS) to back the High Representative and work in co-operation with the diplomatic services of the member states (see Chapter 3).

In 1992 at a meeting in Petersberg near Bonn the role of the EU was defined in what became known as the Petersberg tasks: humanitarian and rescue missions, peacekeeping and crisis management. In 1999 the EU agreed on the development of a common European Security and Defence Policy (ESDP) renamed the Common Security and Defence Policy (CSDP) in the Lisbon Treaty. The Online Learning Centre of this book describes the historical process of trying to develop the CFSP and the CSDP.

In terms of economic strength the EU is already a heavyweight international actor. The Common Commercial Policy was one of the first Community policies to be implemented (see Chapter 2), and the EU is a major trading bloc and generally (but not always) presents a united front towards the rest of the world on economic issues (see Chapter 18). However, a frequent criticism is that in practice the EU is essentially a civil power, and while it acts as an economic giant, the EU remains a political pygmy.

The EU member states have extreme difficulty in reaching common positions on foreign policy and defence issues, let alone imposing them. Differences between the member states on such matters frequently erupt, and countries often act unilaterally with little or no consultation. The EU proved largely ineffectual in halting the horrors on its doorstep that accompanied the disintegration of Yugoslavia. Difficulties were encountered in reaching common positions for example with regard to sending missions to Chad and Iraq, about what measures to adopt towards libya, and over recognition of the independence of Kosovo (see Chapter 18).

In recent years there have been various missions, such as those in Bosnia (see Chapter 19), the Congo, Palestine, Georgia, Indonesia, Sudan and the Somali Coast. However, the initiatives tended to be relatively small, were mainly civilian in nature, and often simply backed up NATO operations or UN peacekeeping missions.

The evolution of the EU on the international stage therefore appears lopsided. Margaret Thatcher, in her famous 1988 Bruges speech, argued that 'On many great issues Europe should try to speak with a single voice. Europe is stronger when we do so whether it be in trade, in defence, or in our relationship with the world.'[4]

---

[3] Decisions under the Community pillar were taken by the 'Community method', which generally involved the Commission proposing legislative acts, an active role for the European Parliament, the increasing use of qualified majority voting in the Council, and interpretation of Community law by the European Court of Justice (see Chapter 3).

[4] For the text of the speech see http://www.margaretthatcher.org/document/107332 (accessed 3 March 2011).

Part of the co-ordination difficulty arises because the various member states arrived at the integration process with very different historical baggage in terms of traditional alliances, geographical situation, perceived cultural interests and so on. Some member states (Austria, Denmark, Finland, Ireland and Sweden) have a tradition of neutrality. Britain emphasizes its 'special relationship' with the USA and until the late 1990s was reluctant to see the Community develop as a forum for foreign policy and defence issues. For many years French attitudes were shaped by the decision to leave the military structure of NATO in 1966. Until recently, Germany was reluctant to participate in military initiatives and, for example, was hesitant to take the lead in operations in the Congo (Giegerich and Wallace, 2010). Many of the new member states felt the legacy of the Cold War.

As Hill (1993) argues, there also appears to be a capability–expectations gap: not only does the EU often lack a common front on foreign policy questions but it also frequently seems unwilling or unable to supply the necessary means to deliver what is expected.[5]

1.4 From 'Justice and Home Affairs' to 'Freedom, Security and Justice'

With increasing tendency towards abolition of border controls between member states (see Chapter 6), there was a growing awareness of a need for more co-operation in combating transnational phenomena such as terrorism, organized crime and migration. The view was that freedom of movement of people within the EU should not be allowed to take place to the detriment of the security of the population, public order and civil liberties.

Over time national solutions to resolve such questions appeared increasingly inadequate. The collapse of the Soviet Union, the events of 11 September 2001, and the increase in immigration pressures, in particular with the unrest in Tunisia, Libya and elsewhere, added a new urgency to the question. However, governments are reluctant to sacrifice sovereignty on such sensitive issues, so common EU policies were slow to develop.

As set out in the Maastricht Treaty, Justice and Home Affairs involved co-operation between the police, judicial, immigration and customs authorities of the member states in order to jointly prevent and combat crime. The areas of co-operation covered both civil and criminal law.

The Maastricht Treaty also aimed at promotion of a European citizenship, setting out four special rights, which were reiterated in Article 20 (TEU) of the Lisbon Treaty:

1 Freedom to move and take up residence anywhere in the EU.
2 Any EU citizen living in another member state has the right to vote or stand in local and European elections.
3 Any EU citizen can use the diplomatic and consular activities of another EU country in any part of the world where their own country is not represented.
4 An ombudsman was to be attached to the European Parliament in order to address alleged cases of maladministration by EU institutions.

The Treaty of Amsterdam called for the development of the EU as an area of 'Freedom, Security and Justice'. This entailed a number of issues, including visas, asylum, immigration and other policies relating to the free movement of people being 'communitized' or brought under the first (or Community) pillar. The Tampere European Council of October 1999 attempted to render this area of 'Freedom, Security and Justice' operational. The Lisbon Treaty (Article 67 TFEU) spells out its main features: the absence of internal border controls for persons, and a common policy on immigration and asylum policy and external borders. The area of 'Freedom, Security and Justice' is to respect fundamental rights, and the different legal systems and traditions of the member states. There should be measures to combat crime, racism and xenophobia, and co-operation and mutual recognition of decisions in both criminal and civil law.

---

[5] Not surprisingly the head of the US Senate's Foreign Relations Committee, Jesse Helms, was reputed to have said that the EU could not fight itself out of a wet paper bag.

Chapter 8 deals with problems connected to the free movement of labour in the EU, and immigration from the rest of the world, while the Online Learning Centre of this book describes key features of the evolution of the EU as an area of 'Freedom, Security and Justice'.

1.5 The changing membership of the EU

There were six original members of the EEC, the ECSC and Euratom: Belgium, France, Germany, Italy, Luxembourg and the Netherlands. The various enlargements of the EU entailed the following countries joining:

- Denmark, Ireland and the UK in 1973;
- Greece in 1981;
- Spain and Portugal in 1986;
- Austria, Finland and Sweden in 1995;
- ten new member states in May 2004: Cyprus, the Czech Republic, Estonia, Hungary, Latvia, Lithuania, Malta, Poland, Slovakia, and Slovenia;
- Bulgaria and Romania in 2007.

As described in Chapter 19, Croatia, the Former Yugoslav Republic of Macedonia, Iceland, Montenegro and Turkey are candidate countries. Albania, Bosnia and Herzegovina, Serbia and Kosovo are potential candidate countries.

1.6 The definition of integration

Economic integration can be defined as the elimination of barriers to the movement of products and factors of production between a group of countries and the introduction of common policies.[6] Tinbergen (1954) made the distinction between negative integration (the removal of barriers to trade) and positive integration (the introduction of common policies, and building of common institutions). However, this distinction remains clear only when a state's intervention is limited to measures taken at the border, such as tariffs, import quotas and so on. If a state's more active role in the economy is considered, many measures with 'domestic' objectives will have repercussions for trade. For example, subsidies to domestic production in a particular country (such as those by the Italian government to Fiat) could constitute a barrier for foreign firms. As a result, in a modern, mixed economy with wide-scale state intervention, the effective elimination of barriers may require common policies.

1.7 The stages of integration

Following the pioneering work of Balassa (1961), the traditional literature on integration refers to different 'stages' in the process.[7] As explained below, these stages are: a free trade area, a customs union, a common market, economic and monetary union and political union. However, if the more active role of the state

---

[6] Examples of definitions of political integration include those by Deutsch (1968) who is associated with the so-called transactional theory of integration and refers to integration as 'the attainment within a territory of a sense of a community'. Haas (1958) defines integration as a 'shift of loyalties', expectations and political activities to a new centre whose institutions possess or demand jurisdiction over pre-existing nation states. Lindberg (1963) calls integration a process whereby nations seek to take joint decisions or to delegate decision making to a new central organ.

[7] See Chapter 18 for examples of integration initiatives, many of which also involve developing countries.

in the economy is taken into account, these should not be regarded as steps in an ascending scale since even complete realization of one of the 'lower stages' may require full economic, monetary and political union. None the less, the classification remains useful to indicate different forms of integration.

1.7.1 Free trade areas

The member states remove all barriers on trade between themselves but retain the freedom to implement different commercial policies towards third countries. In order to get around the problem of importing for re-exporting, free trade areas require rules of origin. In other words, when a good is traded it has to be accompanied by documentation stating where it was made. Rules of origin may be complex to administer, and the regulatory uncertainty to which they give rise means that market access is conditional.

An example of a free trade area is the EFTA (the European Free Trade Association), which was set up in 1960 by seven European countries as an alternative to joining the EEC (see Chapter 2).[8] A further example is NAFTA (the North American Free Trade Agreement), which came into operation between the USA, Canada and Mexico in 1994.[9]

1.7.2 Customs unions

The member states remove all barriers on trade between themselves and introduce a common external commercial policy (for instance a common external tariff) towards the rest of the world.

Examples of customs unions include the EEC, which had created a customs union by 1968 (see Chapter 2), and that between the EU and Turkey which came into operation from 1995, but which largely excluded agricultural products.

1.7.3 Common markets

These are customs unions, which also allow for free factor mobility. In other words, a common market entails the so-called four freedoms: freedom of movement of goods, services, labour and capital. During the early years the Community was sometimes called the 'common market', although this description was not very accurate as the then EEC was more like a customs union with certain sectoral policies (notably the Common Agricultural Policy) financed largely through a Community budget.

1.7.4 Economic and monetary union

An economic and monetary union should include the following elements: a common market; close co-ordination or central control of monetary and fiscal policies; a common money or complete convertibility among national currencies with no possibility of exchange rate adjustments; and a common authority which acts as a central bank. As will be seen in Chapters 9 to 11, in the case of the EU it was decided to introduce a single monetary unit (the euro), a common monetary policy, co-ordination of fiscal policy through the Stability and Growth Pact (though this was to prove inadequate, leading to a heated debate of reform of EMU governance), and a European Central Bank in Frankfurt.

1.7.5 Political union

The definition of political union in the literature is often imprecise and ambiguous, reflecting different conceptions of what it entails. In very general terms, political union involves a central authority that has supranational powers similar to those of a nation's government over various policy areas,

---

[8] The UK, Norway, Sweden, Denmark, Austria, Switzerland and Portugal.

[9] There was a proposal to create a Free Trade Area of the Americas, which would cover countries in North and South America, but negotiations stalled in November 2003 over differences similar to those encountered in WTO talks (see the Online Learning Centre of this book for a discussion of the WTO difficulties). Chapter 18 describes other examples of free and preferential trading areas.

including, for example, foreign policy and security matters, and is responsible to a directly elected central parliament.

1.8 Early views of approaches to integration

As will be shown in Chapter 2, early views about approaches or strategies to integration were influential in shaping the formation of the Community. The aim here is not to provide a comprehensive survey of these theories, but to indicate a few of the views of particular importance in influencing the early development of integration.[10]

The **federalist** approach calls for the immediate creation of a political union with transfer of many of the sovereign rights and obligations of the member states to a supranational federal authority.[11] Early US history offers many examples of the federalist approach. For instance, the Constitutional Convention of 1787 was concerned with wresting powers from the individual states in a way that was palatable to them. The various states had distinct histories, often dating back nearly two centuries, and were reluctant to relinquish their autonomy to an untried central authority.

Functionalists such as Mitrany (1966) advocated a form of integration that was pragmatic, flexible and technocratic. The functionalist approach maintains that in the modern world, technical, economic and social forces lead to interdependencies and shared problems for nation states. Individual countries acting in isolation cannot decide on issues such as the environment, the control of multinational enterprises, telecommunications and information technology. International co-operation is needed to deal with such matters. The potential gains of economic, functional and technical co-operation could be used to build international organizations. The function in question was to determine the appropriate level of integration (such as postal services at a global level, shipping at an intercontinental level and so on), regardless of national or political boundaries. The goal was not to create a 'superstate' above the member states, and Mitrany opposed European federalism considering that this would only change the arena or level of conflict and not avoid it. International integration between states would acquire its own internal dynamic as the benefits achieved would attract the loyalty of citizens and create mutual dependencies, making war unfeasible.

In contrast, the **neo-functional approach** developed, in particular, by Haas (1958), Lindberg (1963) and Schmitter (1970) brought the functionalism of Mitrany down from international spheres to the more concrete case of regional integration between a group of neighbouring countries. At the centre of the neo-functionalist approach is the idea of functional spillover, i.e. that integration in one sector will generate impetus for integration in other sectors. For example, integration of the defence effort will require democratic control, thus creating a spillover leading to integration in the political sphere. In this way, according to the approach, it should become possible to proceed with a strategy of 'integration by sector'.

Bache et al. (2011) identify another aspect of neo-functionalism as 'political' spillover, whereby both supranational actors such as the European Commission, and subnational actors such as interest groups become the drivers of integration. At the subnational level, interest groups in an integrated sector have to deal with the international organization responsible for their sector. The groups would therefore gradually transfer their activities and loyalties away from national governments towards the supranational authority. At the supranational level, organizations such as the Commission encourage such transfers of activities and loyalties. Clearly, this view was influenced the early experience of the Community with, for instance, the Common Agricultural Policy. As a result of sectoral and political spillovers the neo-functionalists predicted that the integration process would be self-sustaining. The neo-functionalist approach envisages a federal authority as the final stage in an ongoing process, whereas the federalist approach favours introducing that stage directly.

---

[10] For a more complete view of the various theories about approaches to integration (including later theories) see Wallace et al. (2010) or Pollack (2005).

[11] For early exponents of this theory see, for instance, Coudenhove-Kalergi (1926) or Spinelli (1972).

In contrast the **intergovernmental** approach maintains that the member states should retain their sovereignty, but should co-operate to achieve certain economic or political objectives, such as trade liberalization.[12] This is the idea of a *Europe des patries*, based on intergovernmental co-operation rather than transfer of power to a supranational authority.

1.9   The *acquis communautaire*

The *acquis communautaire* is literally 'what the Community has achieved'. It consists of the body (sometimes called 'patrimony') of EU legislation, practices, principles and objectives accepted by the member states. It is composed of:[13]

- the treaties, especially the Treaties of Rome, the Single European Act, the Maastricht Treaty, the Treaty of Amsterdam, the Treaty of Nice and the Treaty of Lisbon (signed and came into force in 2009, see also Box 1.1 above).[14] This is referred to as primary legislation;
- legislation enacted at the EU level and judgments of the European Court of Justice (secondary legislation);
- other acts, legally binding or not, adopted within the EU framework, such as resolutions, declarations, statements, recommendations and guidelines; and
- treaties of the EU with third countries.

Progress in EU accession negotiations depends to a large extent on the speed with which the candidate countries can take on and implement the *acquis communautaire*.

The *acquis* has been accumulating over the years and now amounts to about 12,000 legislative acts, and in 2007 debate exploded as to how long the *acquis* is. According to Open Europe, a UK organization, the *acquis* had reached 170,000 pages, but a Commission working group maintained that this also contained judgments of the Court of Justice, and that in effect there were 94,484 pages, of which 3,000 were international treaties. The Commission working group also maintained that, as part of the attempt to cut red tape, the *acquis* would be cut by 40,000 pages.[15]

1.10   Subsidiarity

In practice, difficulties may arise in deciding which is the appropriate level of government to take decisions on various policy areas. In other words, is a particular issue best decided at the EU, national, state, regional or local level? Subsidiarity is the principle that decisions should be taken at the lowest level that permits effective action.[16] The idea of subsidiarity is linked to that of taking decisions 'as closely as possible to the citizens'. It is also maintained that by limiting action at the EU level to where it is really necessary, the quality of EU legislation could be improved.[17]

---

[12] A basis for this approach was the claim by Hoffman (1966) that the nation state far from being obsolete had proven 'obstinate'. The intergovernmental approach was widely supported in countries such as the UK and Scandinavian countries such as Denmark, see Chapter 2.

[13] See the Commission website www.ec.europa.eu/enlargement, or Chapter 19 for a breakdown of the *acquis* by chapter.

[14] Unless stated otherwise, elsewhere in this book the dates given refer to when the treaties entered into force.

[15] *Financial Times*, 20 February 2007.

[16] The first reference to the principle was in the Papal Encyclical *Rerum Novarum* of 1891, and it was again taken up in the 1931 Encyclical *Quadragesimo Anno*. In this context the principle warned against the ever-increasing powers of the state (Bainbridge, 2002).

[17] As Jacques Santer, a former president of the Commission, stated in a speech to the European Parliament on 17 January 1995: 'I have a different notion of subsidiarity: it means not harmonizing every last nut and bolt, but stepping up our co-operation wherever this is really worth it. We should take as our motto "Less action, but better action".'

In the EU context the word 'subsidiarity' first appeared in the European Commission's submission to the 1975 Tindemans Report on European Union and the steps to be taken to create a more united Europe, closer to the citizens. However, the principle was not taken up in the final version of the report, partly because the proposals were less far reaching than the Commission had suggested, so there was less need to reassure those member states fearing a loss of their sovereignty.

Since the late 1980s the member states and regions wanting to limit the powers of the Community, in particular the UK, Denmark and the German *Länder* have frequently used the term. It was largely to assuage the fears of these countries that a subsidiarity clause was introduced in Article 3b of the Treaty of Maastricht. A protocol to the Amsterdam Treaty confirmed that Community actions should not exceed what is necessary to realize the objectives of the Treaty, and this has become known as the 'principle of proportionality'.[18] Article 5 of the Lisbon Treaty (TEU) indicates the main aspects of subsidiarity:

> *In areas which do not fall within its exclusive competence, the Union shall act only if and so far as the objectives of the proposed action cannot be sufficiently achieved by the Member States either at the central level or regional and local level, but can rather by reason of the scale or the effects of the proposed action, be better achieved at the Union level. ... Under the principle of proportionality the content and form of Union action shall not exceed what is necessary to achieve the objectives of the Treaties.*

In practice it is difficult to establish which measures should be centralized, and to what extent.[19] The standard Eurobarometer surveys of public opinion carried out each year assess which decisions EU citizens feel are best carried out at the national level and which at the EU level. The results vary little from year to year and, according to Eurobarometer (2010a), EU decisions were preferred in areas such as fighting terrorism, scientific and technological research, protecting the environment, defence and foreign affairs, energy, support for regions facing economic difficulties, immigration, fighting crime, competition, fighting inflation, the economy, and agriculture and fisheries. The policy areas where national decisions were favoured included pensions, taxation, social welfare, health, the education system and fighting unemployment.

1.11 The competences of the EU

The **principle of conferral** is a fundamental principle of EU law, according to which the EU is a union of member states, and all its competences are conferred upon it by its member states in the treaties (Article 5 TEU). The EU has no competences by right, and thus any areas of policy not explicitly agreed in treaties remain the domain of the member states. The treaties may allow for an extension of EU tasks if this is necessary to realize the objectives of the treaties. Over the years there has been a tendency towards 'competence creep', or an increase in the sphere of activities of the EU.

As shown in Table 1.1, the Lisbon Treaty (Articles 2 to 6 TFEU) classifies the policy areas of the EU according to:

- exclusive competence, where only the EU may legislate or adopt legally binding acts (member states may do so only if empowered by the EU);
- shared competence, where the competence to legislate and adopt legally binding acts is divided between the EU and member states; and

---

[18] The principle of proportionality seeks to set within specific bounds the action taken by the institutions of the EU. The extent of action must be in keeping with the aim pursued. When various forms of intervention are possible to achieve the same effect, the EU must opt for the approach that leaves greatest freedom to the member states and citizens.

Another principle with relevance to the delimitation of activities between the EU and member states is that of additionality. Additionality aims at ensuring that EU allocations are additional to national financing, and do not simply replace national measures (see, for instance, the discussion of EU economic and social cohesion in Chapter 15).

[19] So much so that in a speech to the European Parliament Jacques Delors, then president of the European Commission, offered a job and ECU 200,000 to anyone who could define subsidiarity in one page.

■ supporting competence, where the EU carries out actions to support, co-ordinate or supplement the actions of the member states.

Table 1.1   Division of competences between the EU and member states

Exclusive competence	Shared competence	Supporting competence
Customs union	Internal market	Protection and improvement of human health
Establishing the competition rules necessary for functioning of the internal market	Social policy, for the aspects defined in the Treaty	Industry
Monetary policy for euro countries	Economic, social and territorial cohesion	Culture
		Tourism
The conservation of marine biological resources under the Common Fisheries Policy	Agriculture and fisheries (excluding the conservation of marine biological resources)	Education, youth, sport, and vocational training
The Common Commercial Policy	Environment	Civil protection
	Consumer protection	Administrative co-operation
	Transport	
	Trans-European networks	
	Energy	
	The area of Freedom, Security and Justice	
	Common safety concerns in public health matters for aspects defined in the Treaty	

1.12   The EU in the world

The success of the EU as an integrated bloc has meant that it has emerged as one of the main partners in world trade and foreign direct investment (FDI), as shown in Figures 1.1–1.3, and Table 1.2. The steady increase in EU(27) exports and imports between 2003 and 2008 was reversed in 2009 when total merchandise trade fell by €581 billion to a total of €2,293 billion. If intra-EU trade is also taken into account the share of the EU in world trade is much higher. In 2009 intra-EU(27) merchandise trade amounted to €2,194 billion, a little over twice the value of the exports of the EU(27) to non-member countries.[20] The share of services in total EU(27) exports was 30.3 per cent in 2009, when the EU(27) had exports of 479 billion and a surplus of €64 billion in service transactions with the rest of the world.

---

[20] Despite the high share of intra-EU trade in total EU trade, Delgrado (2006) argues that intra-EU trade integration is less than might be expected in an integrated economic area. Unless otherwise stated, the statistics in this section are taken from Eurostat and the European Commission, DG Trade.

Figure 1.1 Share in world exports of merchandise trade excluding intra-EU trade, 2009

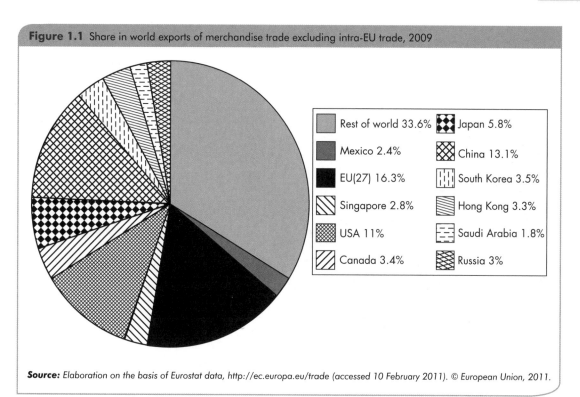

Rest of world 33.6% Japan 5.8%

Mexico 2.4% China 13.1%

EU(27) 16.3% South Korea 3.5%

Singapore 2.8% Hong Kong 3.3%

USA 11% Saudi Arabia 1.8%

Canada 3.4% Russia 3%

Source: *Elaboration on the basis of Eurostat data, http://ec.europa.eu/trade (accessed 10 February 2011). © European Union, 2011.*

Figure 1.2 Share in world imports of merchandise trade excluding intra-EU trade, 2009

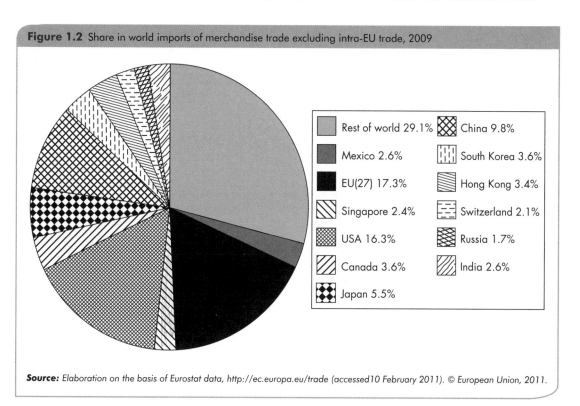

Rest of world 29.1% China 9.8%

Mexico 2.6% South Korea 3.6%

EU(27) 17.3% Hong Kong 3.4%

Singapore 2.4% Switzerland 2.1%

USA 16.3% Russia 1.7%

Canada 3.6% India 2.6%

Japan 5.5%

Source: *Elaboration on the basis of Eurostat data, http://ec.europa.eu/trade (accessed 10 February 2011). © European Union, 2011.*

Figure 1.3 Share in inward stocks of FDI from the world, 2009

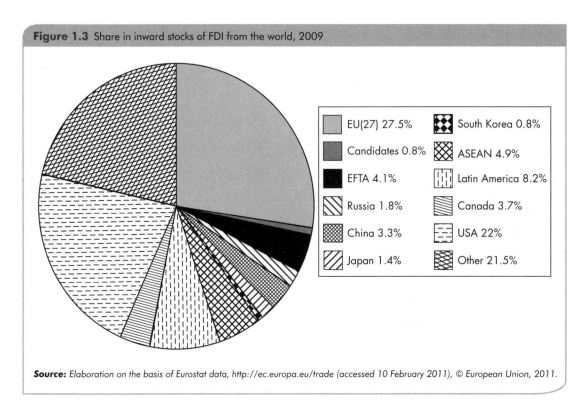

EU(27) 27.5%   South Korea 0.8%

Candidates 0.8%   ASEAN 4.9%

EFTA 4.1%   Latin America 8.2%

Russia 1.8%   Canada 3.7%

China 3.3%   USA 22%

Japan 1.4%   Other 21.5%

Source: Elaboration on the basis of Eurostat data, http://ec.europa.eu/trade (accessed 10 February 2011), © European Union, 2011.

In 2009 the EU(27) share in outward stocks of FDI in the world was 34.6 per cent, compared with 28.2 per cent for the USA, 6.4 for EFTA, 4.9 for Japan and 3.7 per cent for Canada. Figure 1.3 illustrates the main inward stocks of FDI in the world in 2007. Outflows of the EU(27) FDI to the rest of the world fell from €496 billion in 2007 to €274 billion in 2009, while inflows to the EU decreased from €400 billion in 2007 to €219 billion in 2009. [21]

Table 1.2 Trade balance (€ billion)

	2007	2008	2009
EU(27) with extra EU(27)	−192.8	−255.1	−102.9
Canada	4.2	6.3	−40.5
USA	−600.7	−588.2	−467.3
China excluding Hong Kong	246.5	259.2	188.5
Japan	49.0	−4.3	6.5

Source: Eurostat data, http://ec.europa.eu/trade (accessed 10 February 2011), © European Union, 2011.

---

[21] Eurostat foreign direct investment statistics http://epp.eurostat.ec.europa.eu/statistics_explained/index.php/Foreign_direct_ investment_statistics, accesed 10 February 2011 @ European Union 2011.

Table 1.3 presents comparative statistics for the economic weight and performance of the EU vis-à-vis other major international economic actors. Its weight in the world economy and the repercussions of EU policies for other countries imply a growing need for the EU to adopt a more active and responsible role for the international economy, a topic that is taken up in Chapters 18 and 19.

Table 1.3 Comparative economic indicators

	Population[a] (million) 2010	Area[a] (1000 sq km) 2010	Total GNI (US$ billion using current PPP) 2009	Inflation rate (consumer price index) 2009	Unemployment rate[b] (%) 2010	Growth (%) 2009
EU(27)	501	4,303	15,599[c]	1.0[a]	9.6[a]	−4.2[a]
Japan	93.2	364	4,269	−1.4	4.9	−5.2
USA	318	9,159	14,011	−0.4	9.4	−2.6
China	1,354	9,597	9,170	−0.7	4.2[d]	9.1
India	1,215	3,287	3,758	10.9	8.0[d]	7.7
Brazil	195	8,514	1,976	4.9	5.3[d]	−0.2
Russia	140	16,378	2,604	11.7	7.2[d]	−7.9

PPP purchasing power parity

[a]Eurostat, © European Union, 2011.

[b]Unemployed persons as percentage of the labour force.

[c]2007 for Malta and 2008 for Cyprus.

[d]Trading Economics statistics, http://www.tradingeconomics.com (accessed 10 February 2011). The data for China are for March 2010 and for India are for 2007.

Source: Unless otherwise stated the statistics are taken from World Bank, http://data.worldbank.org/indicator (accessed 10 February 2011) and elaborations on the basis of World Bank data.

Summary of key concepts

■ The term **European Economic Community** dates from the Treaty of Rome of 1958. The widespread use of **European Community** dates from a resolution of the European Parliament of 1975 when it was decided to drop the word 'economic'. With the Maastricht Treaty the European Community was reinforced and flanked by two other 'pillars': Justice and Home Affairs, and the Common Foreign and Security Policy. The three together formed the **European Union**. As a result of the Amsterdam Treaty, many aspects of Justice and Home Affairs were brought under the Community pillar, and the name of the third pillar was changed to reflect its residual competences: Police and Judicial Co-operation in Criminal Matters. The Lisbon Treaty abolished the pillar structure, and the European Union replaced the European Community as a legal personality.

■ There were six original members of the European Economic Community: Belgium, France, Germany, Italy, Luxembourg and the Netherlands. Denmark, Ireland and the UK joined in 1973, Greece in 1981, Spain and Portugal in 1986 and Austria, Finland and Sweden in 1995.

Ten countries joined the EU in 2004: Cyprus, the Czech Republic, Estonia, Hungary, Latvia, Lithuania, Malta, Poland, Slovakia and Slovenia. Bulgaria and Romania joined in 2007. Croatia, the Former Yugoslav Republic of Macedonia, Iceland, Montenegro and Turkey are candidate countries. Albania, Bosnia and Herzegovina, Kosovo and Serbia are potential candidate countries.

- Economic integration can be defined as the elimination of barriers to the movement of products and factors of production between a group of countries (**negative integration**) and the introduction of common policies (**positive integration**).

- The **stages of integration** are: a free trade area, a customs union, a common market, economic and monetary union, and political union.

- The **acquis communautaire** is the body of EU legislation, practices, principles and objectives accepted by the member states.

- **Subsidiarity** is the principle that decisions should be taken at the lowest level that permits effective action.

- The **principle of conferral** is a fundamental principle of EU law, according to which the EU is a union of member states, and all its competences are voluntarily conferred on it by its member states.

- The EU has become one of the major global actors in terms of trade and FDI.

Questions for study and review

1 Define 'integration' and indicate the different stages of integration.
2 What are the different approaches to integration?
3 What do we mean by the term *acquis communautaire*?
4 What do we mean by the term 'subsidiarity'? What policies do you think should be the responsibility of the EU?
5 Describe the economic weight of the EU in the world.

Online Learning **Centre**

When you have read this chapter, log on to the Online Learning Centre website at **www.mcgraw-hill.co.uk/textbooks/senior** to explore weblinks, chapter-by-chapter test questions, case studies and more online study tools.

Chapter 2

A Brief History of European Integration

Learning Objectives

By the end of this chapter you should be able to understand:

- ✓ The initial failure to create a supranational organization in Europe after the Second World War
- ✓ The purpose of setting up the European Coal and Steel Community
- ✓ The failure of early attempts to promote European co-operation on defence and to set up a common policy on agriculture
- ✓ Why the integration process gained a new impetus in the mid-1950s
- ✓ The principal objectives and policies set out in the Treaty of Rome
- ✓ The main elements of the European Economic Community (EEC) in the 1960s: trade and agriculture
- ✓ The 1969 Hague Summit: deepening, widening and completion of the integration process
- ✓ The years of Eurosclerosis in the 1970s
- ✓ Why the Single Market project was introduced, and its main features
- ✓ The Maastricht Treaty, economic and monetary union, and the economic crisis
- ✓ The ongoing enlargement process; the Mediterranean Programme and the European Neighbourhood Policy
- ✓ The Lisbon Treaty and beyond

2.1 Introduction

The main aim of this chapter is to provide an overview of the chief events leading to the creation of the EEC in 1958, and the most important developments in its subsequent history. Discussion of almost all of these later developments is taken up in more detail in the following chapters. The Appendix to this chapter provides a brief chronology of the process of European integration.

2.2   The origins of European integration

The idea of a united Europe dates back several centuries, but in the years following the Second World War it acquired a greater urgency.[1] The aim was to make another war in Europe materially impossible, and to co-operate in the post-war reconstruction process. At the same time, the creation of the Eastern bloc and the perceived Soviet threat left Western Europe feeling divided and vulnerable. After the war the USA and the USSR emerged as the two superpowers (an international scenario to last until the 1990s), and it became increasingly evident that only a united Europe would carry weight at an international level.

During the early years, most of the initiatives to carry forward the integration process came from France, usually backed by Germany and the Benelux countries. Despite widespread popular belief in the European ideal, the position of the other 'large' founder member of the Community, Italy, often appeared confused and contradictory, possibly reflecting the overriding concern with the internal political situation.

British ambivalence towards the integration process soon became apparent. Britain had emerged victorious from the war, participating in meetings such as Yalta to create a new world order. Great importance was attached to the 'special relationship' with the USA. In addition, much trade was still carried out with former members of the Empire rather than with continental Europe.

2.3   Background to the integration process: the 1940s

The first European organization to be created after the war was the **UNECE** (United Nations Economic Commission for Europe), which was set up as a regional organization of the UN in Geneva in 1947. Its initial aim was to carry out economic reconstruction and encourage co-operation among all the states of Europe: East, West and Central. Soon after creation of this organization, the East–West division of Europe became a reality and the USSR feared Western influence on its satellites. The **UNECE** was to prove the last pan-European organization for many years. It remained in operation as a useful research centre for East–West studies, and subsequently for analysis of the transition of countries in Central and Eastern Europe and the former Soviet Republics into market economies and functioning democracies.

The European integration process gained a new impetus in 1947 with the introduction of the **Marshall Plan**. A bad harvest in 1946 increased food prices, and the severe winter of 1947/48 led to a fuel crisis. The continental European countries faced an acute shortage of foreign reserves as the result of a combination of huge import requirements and limited exports. US General George Marshall proposed a programme to aid Europe. It was initially suggested that the programme would be administered through the **UNECE**, but this was opposed by the USSR, which feared an increase of Western influence on its satellites. The Marshall Plan involved US and Canadian aid to sixteen European countries. The aid was to be conditional on the European countries dismantling barriers to trade among themselves, and co-operating in the creation of a European organization to administer the aid programme.

In 1948 this led to the creation of the OEEC (Organisation for European Economic Co-operation). There was a difference of opinion between Britain and France as to whether this organization should be based on intergovernmental co-operation, or whether a supranational element should be injected, as favoured by the French (with US support). The French pushed for an international secretariat that could take initiatives on major issues, but in the end the British view prevailed. The OEEC led to the

---

[1] See Swann (2000), Milward (1984, 2000) and Craig and De Burca (2007) for more detailed accounts of the historical background. For glossaries of the various terms used in this chapter see the Europa Glossary of the EU at http://europa. eu/legislation_summaries/glossary/ (accessed 17 February 2011) or the website of Baldwin and Wyplosz (2006) at www. mcgraw-hill.co.uk/textbooks/baldwin (accessed 17 February 2011).

setting up of the European Payments Union in 1950, and was the forum in which the six founding members of the EEC began the discussions that led to the Treaty of Rome. After the winding up of Marshall aid, in 1961 this organisation was transformed and became the **OECD** (Organisation for Economic Co-operation and Development) (see Box 2.1).[2]

The economic division of Europe was formalized in 1949 with the creation of the **Comecon or CMEA** (Council for Mutual Economic Assistance).[3] In addition to the USSR and smaller Central and East European countries, Cuba, Mongolia and Vietnam were also CMEA members. The founding of the CMEA was largely a political response to the Marshall Plan, but the organization really only became active after the signing of the Treaty of Rome in 1957. Though the CMEA never became a supranational body like the Community, Soviet hegemony implied a certain degree of political integration. The CMEA was formally dissolved in September 1991.

In 1948 pro-European statesmen (including Churchill) rallied at a Congress of Europe in The Hague and called for progress towards economic and political union in Europe, if necessary by sacrificing some national sovereignty. It was decided to create the **Council of Europe**, but again attempts to create a supranational European organization failed, largely due to opposition from Britain and the Scandinavian countries, who were among the founder members. The French and Belgians were in favour of a European parliamentary assembly which could use majority voting, but the powers finally agreed for the first Consultative Assembly were so limited that its first president, the Belgian Paul-Henri Spaak, resigned.

Set up in Strasbourg in 1949, the Council of Europe is *not* an institution of the European Union. Though the Council of Europe disappointed the federalists, it provided the seat for various debates and initiatives in the European integration process, and continues to play an important role in the field of human rights, rule of law and democracy (see Boxes 2.2 and 2.3).

2.4 Integration by sector

The failure of federalist attempts to create a supranational European architecture in both the OEEC and Council of Europe brought about a change in tactics, with subsequent proposed initiatives in European integration adopting a more neo-functionalist approach. It was felt that less ambitious plans to co-operate in specific economic sectors might provide experience in working together, and could also induce spillover into increased political co-operation.

---

[2] Following the EEC/EFTA division, see below.

[3] For many years the term 'Comecon' was generally avoided in Central and Eastern Europe as it was considered reminiscent of the Cold War.

Box 2.2

The Council of Europe

Based in Strasbourg, the Council of Europe includes virtually all the countries of Europe. It deals with areas such as culture, education, the environment, control of the international drugs trade, and medical ethics. From 1989 it was active in promoting constitutional and institutional reforms to assist democratic consolidation in Central and Eastern Europe and certain former Soviet Republics.

In 1950 a European Convention on Human Rights was also drawn up, and in 1995 a Framework Convention for the Protection of National Minorities was also signed. The organs of the Council of Europe include a parliamentary assembly, a committee of foreign ministers and, probably the best known and most effective of its institutions, the Court of Human Rights. Previously separate, two of the organs of the Council of Europe, the European Commission of Human Rights and the Court of Human Rights, were merged in 1998. Since 1999 a Commissioner for Human Rights has been responsible for promoting awareness and respect for human rights in the member states of the Council of Europe.

In theory, membership of the Council of Europe is only for those countries able and willing to sign and implement its treaties, but in practice tensions may arise. It is frequently argued that the Council is in a stronger position to influence countries if they are members. At the time of their accession there was much controversy about countries such as Russia and Croatia, which were considered to have shortcomings with regard to freedom of expression and the rule of law. When Georgia joined in 1999 the government was given a list of needed reforms and deadlines for introducing them. Other countries, such as Belarus, have been excluded on the grounds that they are undemocratic and fail to respect human rights.

The Council of Europe can play an important role for countries outside the EU as membership may provide evidence that they belong to Europe, as well as giving such countries some say in a pan-European organization.

Box 2.3

The Organization for Security and Co-operation in Europe

There is a certain overlap of functions between the Council of Europe and the Organization for Security and Co-operation in Europe (OSCE). Created in 1975 during the era of détente, the aim of what was then known as the CSCE (Conference on Security and Co-operation in Europe) was to promote East–West dialogue. The 'final act' of the CSCE was signed in Helsinki and was primarily of interest to Western countries as a means of improving human rights in the Eastern bloc, while the Eastern partners were mainly concerned with economic and technological co-operation. The final act set out four Helsinki 'baskets': security and disarmament; economic and technological co-operation and protection of the environment; co-operation in humanitarian and other fields; and the commitments of the signatory states. Following the collapse of the Eastern bloc, this organization was transformed into the OSCE, and became focused on an ongoing process of ensuring that commitments were being implemented. The main function of the OSCE is to provide a forum for its members to discuss and co-operate on security issues, and to ensure the operation of democratic practices (in particular, free and fair elections). It is active in early warning, conflict prevention, crisis management and post-conflict rehabilitation. OSCE membership includes most European countries, the USA, Canada and various former Soviet Republics. In theory at least, the Council of Europe is responsible for codifying and upholding legal rules, whereas the obligations of the OSCE are only politically binding; its main function is to encourage improved practices in areas of tension.

2.5 The European Coal and Steel Community

The combination of US aid and the determination of the German people soon led to post-war recovery of the German economy. The question became how to allow Germany to regain her powerful position in what were then the strategic industries of iron, steel and coal production without endangering peace in Europe. At the time a large majority of all energy needs in Europe were met by coal. Moreover, it was realized that Allied control of coal and steel production in the Ruhr could not continue indefinitely.

The proposed solution was the Schuman Plan which was elaborated by Jean Monnet (then in charge of the French Commissariat du Plan, see Box 2.4), and put forward by the French foreign minister, Robert Schuman (Box 2.5). The Schuman Plan aimed at making war in Europe not only 'unthinkable, but materially impossible' through the creation of a common market for iron, steel and coal in Europe. For Germany this offered a passport to international respectability and an end to Allied occupation and checks on economic recovery (Swann, 2000). For France the plan provided a means of concluding French occupation of the Saarland, since handing the Saarland back to Germany would be more acceptable if Germany formed part of a common market in coal and steel. The plan was also attractive to the federalists, who were disappointed by the failure to transform the OEEC into a supranational organization.

Box 2.4

Jean Monnet (1888–1979)

Jean Monnet was a French economist and diplomat, at times called the 'Father of Europe'. As director of the post-war planning commission in France, he was the initiator of the Monnet Plan (1947–53) for the modernization and re-equipment of French industry. Monnet was instigator of the Schuman Plan in 1950, and first president of the European Coal and Steel Community (ECSC). In 1950 he also fostered the eventually unsuccessful plan to create a European Defence Community.

During the war, Monnet turned down an invitation to join de Gaulle's government-in-exile in London. In the summer of 1940 he persuaded Churchill to make an offer of Franco-British Union. He was convinced of the importance of US support for the war effort, and for several years was technically a senior British civil servant in Washington with his French passport personally endorsed by Churchill. In some French circles Monnet's vision, which led him to work so closely with the USA and Britain, was criticized. An interesting account of his life is provided in his memoirs (Monnet, 1978).

Box 2.5

Robert Schuman (1886–1963)

Although born in Luxembourg, Schuman's family came from Lorraine and he grew up in Metz while it was under German rule. A prominent statesman in post-war years, Schuman always emphasized the importance of Franco-German rapprochement.

Schuman entered politics when Lorraine was returned to France, becoming prime minister (1947–48) and foreign minister (1948–53) in the Fourth Republic. He was a member of the Mouvement Républicain Populaire (MRP), a centrist, Christian Democrat party.

The 9th of May, which is the day on which Schuman announced the plan for setting up the ECSC, is still celebrated as a holiday in EU institutions.

According to the Schuman Plan, production of steel and coal should be 'pooled' (the famous 'black pool') and placed under a supranational High Authority. The aim was to eliminate trade barriers and increase competition, but since in such highly regulated sectors many exceptions had to be allowed, the approach was essentially that of 'regulated competition'. The High Authority could levy taxes, influence investment and fix minimum prices and production quotas in times of 'imminent' and 'manifest' crisis.

Abhorring the transfer of sovereignty to an authority that was 'utterly undemocratic and responsible to nobody' (Attlee, speaking in the House of Commons[4]), the UK remained out of the initiative. France, Germany, Italy and the Benelux countries (which were to become the founder members of the EEC) went ahead and signed the Treaty of Paris, establishing the ECSC in 1951. The new Community was to lay the foundations for Franco-German post-war reconciliation, which was to prove the cornerstone and driving force in the integration process.

2.6   Attempts at co-operation in defence

Given the aim of rendering war in Europe impossible, and the fear of the perceived Soviet threat, it was to be expected that a common defence policy would be one of the main aims of the European integration process. As a first response to creation of the Eastern bloc, in 1948 France, the UK and the Benelux countries signed the Treaty of Brussels which provided for a system of mutual assistance in the event of attack. Western defence efforts acquired an Atlantic flavour from 1949 when these countries joined with the USA, Canada, Denmark, Italy, Norway, Portugal and Iceland to form **NATO** (North Atlantic Treaty Organization).

With the outbreak of the Korean War in 1950, the USA and the UK were in favour of German rearmament. France was against this idea and also opposed Germany becoming a member of NATO, instead proposing the creation of a European army with West German participation (the Pleven Plan). The UK was not opposed to such an initiative but was against being directly involved, partly because of the 'special relationship' with the USA and partly because the French proposal contained supranational elements.

Negotiations among the six future founding members of the EC went ahead with a view to creating a **European Defence Community** (EDC). The institutional structure of the Community was to be similar to that of the ECSC, with a Joint Defence Commission, a Council of Ministers, a Parliamentary Assembly and a Court of Justice. There was to be a combined army with a single uniform and flag, and its own budget. In order to ensure control of the European army, political integration was also to be strengthened, and in 1953 a draft proposal for the creation of a European Political Community was also presented. It was envisaged that after a transitional period, the institutions of the ECSC, the EDC and the European Political Community would be fused.

In 1952 the Treaty on the EDC was signed, but required ratification by the six participating states. In 1954 the French parliament refused to ratify the Treaty (though the other five countries involved had done so). There was reaction to the supranational element of the proposal, with the French Right objecting to the creation of an army under European control,[5] especially as the UK was not involved. At the same time the French Left feared German rearmament.

The solution to this impasse was the creation of the **Western European Union** (WEU) in 1955. This was a traditional intergovernmental organization whose founding members were the original European Communities (EC; 6) plus the UK. Its aim was to provide a European framework in which Germany could be rearmed and enter NATO, and in which the last vestiges of Allied occupation of Germany could be removed. The WEU remained relatively ineffective for almost thirty years before the question of an EU security initiative was revived (as described in the Online Learning Centre for

---

[4] Quoted in Swann (2000: 7).

[5] News that the Treaty had failed ratification led to a rendering of the 'Marseillaise' in the French parliament.

this book). In 2010 it was announced that the WEU would to be disbanded, following the new powers for foreign and security policy given to the EU by the Treaty of Lisbon (see Chapter 3).

2.7 Agriculture: towards the creation of the Common Agricultural Policy

For many years the Common Agricultural Policy (CAP) was considered the cornerstone of the integration process.[6] In the immediate post-war period there were several strong reasons for creating a common market for agricultural products:

- The initial deal is frequently said to be an exchange of interests between France who was seeking markets for her agricultural exports, and Germany who was anxious to reduce tariffs in order to ensure outlets for her industrial exports. However, Milward (2000) argues that agricultural exports were only a secondary, subordinate issue for both countries, and not a proportional counterbalance to manufacturing trade. Having decided on an industrial common market, France wanted an outlet for its agricultural surpluses. Germany had a tradition of heavy protection and substantial income support for the agricultural sector, and was also keen to transfer part of the burden of such policies to the Community level. Italy and the Netherlands also considered that a common agricultural market would provide opportunities for developing their typical forms of production (Mediterranean, and dairy products and vegetables respectively), though in the event the latter was more successful in realizing this objective.

- At the time, agriculture was extremely important economically, socially and politically. In 1958, agriculture accounted for 20 per cent of the labour force in the original EC(6) countries and generally incomes were lower than in non-agricultural sectors. In some countries and areas the farm vote was a strong force to be reckoned with.

- The farm policies in the original EC(6) countries were very different and had to be harmonized; otherwise, differences in agricultural price levels and support measures would cause distortions in intra-EC trade.

- The introduction of a common market for agriculture would encourage competition and specialization according to the principle of comparative advantage (see Chapter 4), thereby increasing the productivity of the sector. Insofar as this resulted in lower food prices, there might be less pressure for wage increases.

- The harmonization of agricultural prices was envisaged as the first step towards harmonization of wage levels, which was considered necessary for the creation of a common market in industrial products and services.

2.8 The proposed 'green pool'

In 1950 in response to a French initiative, the Special Committee of the Council of Europe agreed to consider the prospects for agricultural integration in Europe. The French presented a proposal, known as the Charpentier Plan, to create a 'green pool' in Europe similar to the 'black pool' of the ECSC. This would entail:

- common agricultural prices;
- the elimination of trade barriers between the member states;
- preference for the producers of the member states, that is, they could sell at lower prices on the domestic market than producers from third countries; and
- a High Authority with supranational powers.

---

[6] See Tracy (1989) for a more detailed account of the foundation of the CAP.

Although the UK and Denmark were strongly opposed to the supranational element of the Charpentier Plan, the Special Committee of the Council of Europe accepted the proposals, and it was agreed to prepare a draft treaty along the lines of the plan.

In 1951 the main elements of the proposal were presented formally in the Pfimlin Plan (taking the name of the French agricultural minister), and they were discussed at the Paris Conferences of 1952 and 1954, which enabled the positions of the various countries to become more precisely defined. However, during these years little progress towards an agreement on agricultural integration was made as France was distracted by the turbulent internal politics of the last days of the Fourth Republic.

2.9 Towards the Treaties of Rome

By 1955 the rift between the European countries that wanted to limit integration to intergovernmental co-operation and those that preferred the creation of a supranational authority could no longer be breached. The UK and the Scandinavian countries were in favour of the creation of a free trade area and co-operation on agricultural questions within the OEEC framework. In this context any supranational initiative could be blocked as each of the member states had the power of veto.

The six founding members of the EEC ('the Six') were not satisfied with this arrangement and in 1955 the Benelux countries presented a Memorandum. This called for the creation of a common market, and specific action in the areas of energy and transport. Though political union was recognized as an ultimate aim, the practical difficulties encountered in its implementation suggested that it was preferable to concentrate on more specific, concrete aims of economic integration.[7] It was considered that the experience gained in working together would then pave the way for political integration. The aim was to 'work for the establishment of a United Europe by the development of common institutions, the progressive fusion of national economies, the creation of a common market and the progressive harmonization of social policies' (1955 Memorandum).

The foreign ministers of the Six at the Messina Conference considered the ideas of the Memorandum, and it was agreed to set up an intergovernmental committee under the Belgian foreign minister, Paul-Henri Spaak, which would study the problems and prepare the treaties necessary for establishing a common market and energy pool. Initially the UK (as a member of the WEU and associate of the ECSC) participated in the activities of the Spaak Committee, but withdrew in 1955 because the UK remained in favour of simply strengthening the OEEC framework, and preferred a free trade arrangement to the creation of a customs union.

In Venice in 1956 the foreign ministers of the Six accepted the results of the Spaak Committee, and work began on the drafting of the two treaties establishing the European Economic Community and Euratom. These were signed in Rome in March 1957, and entered into force from January 1958.

Two external events help to explain the speed with which the Six worked towards agreeing the Rome Treaties: Suez and the Soviet invasion of Hungary. In 1956 as a reaction to Egyptian raids across the border, Israel invaded Egypt and was subsequently supported by an Anglo-French force. France and Britain opposed Nasser's nationalization of the Suez Canal in which they held shares. Fearing Soviet intervention, the USA exerted diplomatic and economic pressures, which led to the withdrawal of the Anglo-French troops. British and French relations with the USA became very strained, and it was again demonstrated that a weak and divided Europe would have no hope of standing up to the superpowers.

The same lesson emerged from the example of Hungary. In 1953 the Nagy government was permitted to introduce certain reforms such as the freeing of political prisoners, the relaxing of political and economic controls and the ending of collectivization. In less than two years Rakosi replaced Nagy, but in the face of wide-scale demonstrations, he was allowed to return to power in 1956. Nagy then declared Hungarian neutrality and the withdrawal from the Warsaw Pact, and released Cardinal Mindszenty, the

---

[7] See Swann (2000).

Primate of Hungary, from prison. In 1956, despite fierce resistance, Soviet troops occupied Hungary and Nagy was executed, and the West European countries were left feeling weak and vulnerable.

Faced with the decision of the Six to proceed with more ambitious forms of integration, in 1960 the European countries that then preferred intergovernmental co-operation decided to create EFTA (European Free Trade Association). The founder members of EFTA were the UK, Norway, Sweden, Denmark, Austria, Switzerland and Portugal. Subsequently Iceland (in 1970), Finland (in 1986) and Liechtenstein (in 1991) joined. As its name suggests, EFTA involved the creation of a free trade association for industrial products. Agricultural products were largely excluded from this arrangement.

2.10 The Treaties of Rome

The Treaties of Rome (signed in 1957 and entered into force in 1958) provide the legal basis for establishment of the EEC and the Euratom. The former is of greater concern here, with Euratom being created to co-ordinate the research programmes of member states for the peaceful use of nuclear energy. It was set up mainly in response to a French request, and subsequently shelved, again largely thanks to France. The Treaties are among the most fundamental elements of the *acquis communautaire*.

The Treaty of Rome establishing the EEC consists of 248 articles. Article 2 sets out the main objectives:

- Harmonious development;
- Continuous and balanced expansion;
- Increased stability;
- Ever more rapid growth in living standards;
- Closer links between the member states.

This short list has been the subject of considerable debate and controversy. The Treaty left open the fixing of priorities and the question of how possible conflicts between objectives were to be resolved. In particular, the list raises the fundamental economic question of how to reconcile equity ('harmonious development' and 'balanced expansion') with efficiency ('ever more rapid growth in living standards').

Subsequent treaties added modifications to the Treaty of Rome so that by the Lisbon Treaty (Article 3 TEU) the priorities read quite differently:[8]

> *... The Union's aim is to promote peace, its values and the well-being of it peoples.*
> *... It shall work for the sustainable development of Europe based on balanced economic growth and price stability, a highly competitive social market economy, aiming at full employment and social progress, and a high level of protection, and improvement of the quality of the environment. It shall promote scientific and technological advance. It shall combat social exclusion and discrimination, and shall promote social justice and protection, equality between women and men, solidarity between generations and protection of the rights of the child.*
> *It shall promote economic, social and territorial cohesion, and solidarity among Member States.*
> *It shall respect its rich cultural and linguistic diversity and shall ensure that Europe's cultural heritage is safeguarded and enhanced ...*

Article 3 of the Treaty of Rome listed the mechanisms by which the objectives were to be realized. A twelve-year transition period from 1958 until 1969[9] was envisaged for their implementation. The measures included:

---

[8] See Chapter 3 for a discussion of the Lisbon Treaty. Article 3 of the TEU sets out the objectives of the Union, while Articles 2 to 6 of the TFEU delimit the competences of the EU (see Chapter 1).

- the abolition of tariffs, and of quantitative and qualitative restrictions in intra-EC trade;
- the creation of a common external policy and, in particular, a common external tariff;
- the elimination of obstacles to the free movement of people, capital, goods and services;
- a common agricultural policy;
- a common transport policy;
- the introduction of means to ensure fair competition;
- the co-ordination of the economic policies of the member states to avoid balance of payments disequilibria;
- the creation of a European Social Fund to improve employment opportunities and raise living standards for workers;
- the creation of a European Investment Bank to help reduce regional disparities;
- special trade and development arrangements for colonies and former colonies.

Progress in implementing these measures has been very uneven. The elimination of tariffs on intra-EC trade and the introduction of the common external tariff were largely completed by mid-1968, eighteen months ahead of schedule.

However, despite many proposals, only limited steps were taken to remove non-tariff barriers and to free factor movements within the Community. As a result, these objectives had to be relaunched many years later in the programme to complete the Single Market from 1993. Linguistic and cultural differences partially account for the relatively limited increases in the movement of people, and similarly for the slow progress in the recognition of qualifications and in obtaining social security benefits in other member states. The Treaty called for liberalization of capital movements only insofar as this was necessary for the creation of a common market. The main instruments of the CAP were in operation from 1967. Already during the 1960s and 1970s some steps were taken in applying competition policy to limit the abuse of dominant position by private firms and against restrictive business practices.

According to Swann (2000), three main factors account for the inclusion of a common transport policy among the objectives of the Treaty of Rome:

1 Transport costs could act as a trade barrier, and measures to promote a cheap, efficient transport system in the Community could help to stimulate trade.

2 Transport has traditionally always been a heavily regulated sector and failure to harmonize policies could lead to distortions (as the experience of the ECSC showed).

3 The Treaty of Rome was a compromise, balancing the national interests of the founding countries, and the Netherlands in particular was anxious to include transport policy as part of the deal. Transport, especially through Rotterdam and along the Rhine, makes an important contribution to Dutch GDP.

Although envisaged as one of the first three common policies by the Treaty of Rome, embedded national interests meant that progress in introducing common measures on transport policy was slow. The Treaty was remarkably unencumbered with details concerning the implementation of a common policy. As late as 1985 there was a judgment of the European Court of Justice against the Council for failing to introduce a common transport policy, and calling for the situation to be remedied as soon as possible.[10]

Despite the mention of co-ordination of economic policies, the Treaty contains no specific commitment to macroeconomic co-ordination or to economic and monetary union. Various considerations (Tsoukalis, 1997) help to account for the reticence of the Treaty on this point:

[9] Divided into three four-year periods.

[10] See Chapter 6 for a more detailed discussion of EU transport policy.

- The importance of the dollar in the international monetary system at the time meant that there was little need or purpose to establish a regional monetary arrangement in Europe;
- Reasons of political feasibility (quite enough was already being taken on with the creation of the common market);
- Differences among the member states;
- In the golden age of Keynesian demand management (which entailed active intervention in an attempt to regulate economic activity), member states were reluctant to sacrifice autonomy of fiscal and monetary policies.

The European Social Fund (ESF) and European Investment Bank (EIB) envisaged by the Treaty were operational at an early stage. With the exception of the Italian Mezzogiorno, regional disparities among the original Six were relatively limited and the EIB was conceived essentially as an instrument to assist the Italian Mezzogiorno.

At the time of the Treaty, the prevailing view appears to have been that the transfers to and from the Community budget by the member states should roughly balance. Despite the references to 'harmonious' development and 'balanced expansion' in Article 2, the Treaty did not envisage extensive redistributional policies. Though various Community structural (social and regional) measures were introduced over the years, the spending involved was fairly limited, at least until 1988 when the Structural Funds were doubled (see Chapter 15).

The provision for special trade and aid arrangements with colonies and former colonies was a concession to France who wanted to maintain her links, but with the other EC members (and Germany in particular) helping to foot the bill. Trade preferences to these countries were extended throughout the Community, and aid was granted through the European Development Fund (EDF). From the 1960s many of these countries gained independence, and in 1963 (renewed in 1969) the Yaoundé agreements covering trade and aid arrangements were signed between the EC and former French colonies in Africa.

The entry of the UK into the Community in 1973 led to a reappraisal of development policy, resulting in the first Lomé Convention of 1975. Subsequent agreements followed in 1980, 1985 and 1990 (which was extended to cover a ten-year period) and the Cotonou Agreement of 2000. The Cotonou Agreement covered 79 ACP (African, Caribbean and Pacific) countries. From 2008 a process began of replacing the Cotonou Agreement with Economic Partnership Agreements (EPAs) with regional groupings of ACP countries, as these arrangements were more in line with WTO commitments (see Chapter 18).

2.11 The European Community in the 1960s

The twelve-year transitional period in which the provisions of the Treaty of Rome were to be implemented coincided with a particularly favourable international economic climate. Growth was rapid and employment in the EEC countries reached unprecedented levels, while inflation was rising but had not reached dangerous levels (see Tables 2.1–2.3 below). In general the economic performance of the Six outshone that of the USA and the UK.

It was in this climate that the tariffs and quantitative restrictions on intra-EC trade were dismantled and the common external tariff was introduced (by mid-1968).[11] Internal developments in EC commercial policy were linked to external events as the Six prepared common positions to negotiate as a single actor in the GATT (General Agreement on Tariffs and Trade) Kennedy Round over the 1964–67 period.[12] A precondition for agreeing tariff reductions for third countries was that the common external tariff should be in place. During the 1960s, trade, and in particular intra-EC trade, grew faster than output, and a 'virtuous circle' of trade liberalization and rapid growth seemed to be in operation. Growth eased the adjustment process rendering the reduction or elimination of trade barriers less painful.

---

[11] Important legal developments also occurred at this time, relating to the two leading cases of *Van Gend and Loos* (Case no. 26 of 1962) and *Costa v ENEL* (Case no. 6 of 1964). See Chapter 3.

The emergence of the EEC Six as a single actor and their successful economic performance encouraged the UK to apply for membership in 1961 and 1967, but on both occasions de Gaulle vetoed the application. The opposition of de Gaulle to any transfer of French sovereignty to the Community also meant that agreement on financing of the EC budget had to wait until 1970 (see Chapter 12), and an initiative to strengthen European political integration was blocked.

The 1960s also marked the birth of the CAP, which was then regarded by many as the greatest achievement in integration (see Chapter 13). In 1962, agreement was reached on the mechanisms for agricultural support, with the decision on the level of the common prices for agricultural products following in 1964 and being applied from 1967. The Mansholt Plan was presented in 1968 with radical proposals for restructuring EC agriculture in order to raise incomes and efficiency, but in the event only very limited measures to improve the structure of agriculture were implemented.

2.12   The 1969 Hague Summit

With the end of the transition period due in 1970, the search was on for new ways of relaunching the integration process. This gained new impetus in 1969 when Pompidou replaced de Gaulle. At the Hague Summit of 1969 a package was presented which was described by Pompidou as containing three main elements: completion, deepening and enlargement.

The completion of the integration process referred essentially to placing the financing of the CAP on a sounder footing. This entailed agreement on the own resources for the EC budget, and a slight increase in the budgetary powers of the European Parliament. The deepening process was to consist of gradual progress towards the creation of an economic and monetary union (EMU) by 1980, and the introduction of European Political Co-operation. The first EMU programme met with little success (also because of the difficult economic situation following the 1973 oil crisis), though in 1979 the EMS (European Monetary System) was introduced.

At the Hague Summit, it was agreed to study the best way of implementing European Political Co-operation (EPC), and a report was presented in 1970.[13] The basis for EPC was to be intergovernmental co-operation, and member states would attempt to work out common positions and agree on common actions. However, progress in developing common positions on foreign policy issues was slow before the 1990s.

With de Gaulle no longer on the political scene, the path to further enlargement of the Community was now open. This occurred in 1973 when the UK, Ireland and Denmark became members, while Norway (not for the last time) voted against membership in a referendum.

2.13   The Community in the 1970s: the years of Eurosclerosis

After the successes of the first twelve years, the Community entered a long period of stagnation when little progress was made in integration. Particularly after the 1973 oil crisis, the EC economy entered a phase of slower growth, higher unemployment, more rapid inflation and falling competitiveness (see Tables 2.1–2.3). The process of trade liberalization wavered, and non-tariff barriers were applied on trade both within the EC and with third countries in what became known as the 'new protectionism'.

---

[12] The GATT is described in Chapter 18.

[13] Though the membership was to be the same, the EPC was to be separate from EC institutions. There was to be no majority voting (qualified or otherwise), and member states were not obliged to agree.

Table 2.1 The economic growth of the EU(12), the USA and Japan (average percentage change in real GDP at constant prices)

	1960–69	1970–80	1980–90	1991–2000	2009	2010 forecast
Belgium	4.8	3.3	2.3	2.2	−2.8	2.0
France	5.5	3.3	2.2	1.9	−2.6	1.6
Germany[a]	4.5	2.7	2.1	1.5	−4.7	3.6
Italy	5.7	3.6	2.5	1.6	−5.0	1.1
Luxembourg	3.6	2.6	3.3	5.5	−3.7	3.2
Netherlands	4.4	2.9	1.9	2.9	−3.9	1.7
Denmark	4.8	2.2	1.8	2.4	−5.2	2.3
Ireland	4.3	4.7	3.0	7.3	−7.6	−0.2
UK	2.9	1.9	4.4	2.4	−4.9	1.4
Greece	7.6	4.7	1.6	2.4	−2.3	−4.2
Portugal	6.1	4.7	3.1	2.8	−2.5	1.3
Spain	7.7	3.5	3.0	2.7	−3.7	−0.2
USA	4.3	3.1	2.7	3.1	−2.6	2.9
Japan	10.4	4.4	4.2	1.5	−6.3	3.5

[a]West Germany up until 1989.

Source: OECD and own calculations on the basis of OECD for the decade averages, and Eurostat for and 2010, http://epp.eurostat. ec.europa.eu/tgm/table.do?tab=table&init=1&plugin=1&language=en&pcode=tsieb020 (accessed 11 February 2011), © European Union, 2011.

Table 2.2 Unemployment in the EU(12), the USA and Japan (average of annual rates, percentage of labour force)

	1960–67[b]	1974–1979[b]	1980–90	1991–2000	End Dec. 2010
Belgium	2.1	5.7	10.9	8.5	8.1
France	1.5	4.5	9.1	10.9	12.9[d]
Germany[a]	0.8	3.5	6.8	7.8	6.6
Italy	4.9	6.6	10.1	10.6	8.6
Luxembourg	0.0	0.6	2.5	2.5	4.9
Netherlands	0.7	4.9	9.6	5.1	4.3
Denmark	1.6	–	7.8	6.6	8.2
Ireland	4.9	7.6	14.4	11.1	13.8
UK	1.5	4.2	9.2	7.9	7.8[e]

Table 2.2   continued

	1960–67[b]	1974–1979[b]	1980–90	1991–2000	End Dec. 2010
Greece	5.2	1.9	6.8	9.9[c]	12.9[d]
Portugal	2.4	6.0	7.1	5.6	10.9
Spain	2.3	5.3	17.5	16.0	20.2
USA	5.0	6.7	6.9	5.6	9.4
Japan	1.3	1.9	2.5	3.3	4.9

[a]*West Germany up until 1989.*

[b]*This column is taken from Table 2.2 from* The New Economy Revisited, *2nd edn, by Loucas Tsoukalis. By permission of Oxford University Press.*

[c]*Commonly used definitions of unemployment rather than standardized rates.*

[d]*End Sept. 2010.*

[e]*End Oct. 2010.*

Source: *Unless otherwise stated, OECD and own calculations based on OECD data for the decade averages, and Eurostat, http:// epp.eurostat.ec.europa.eu/tgm/table.do?tab=table&language=en&pcode=teilm020&tableSelection=1&plugin=1 (accessed 11 February 2011), © European Union, 2011.*

Table 2.3   Inflation in the EU(12), the USA and Japan: consumer price index (average annual percentage change)

	1961–70	1974–79[b]	1980–90	1991–2000	2009	2010
Belgium	2.8	8.5	4.5	1.9	0.0	2.3
France	4.0	10.7	6.7	1.8	0.1	1.7
Germany[a]	2.5	4.7	2.8	2.3	0.2	1.2
Italy	4.0	16.1	10.4	3.8	0.8	1.6
Luxemboury	2.3	7.4	4.4	2.2	0.0	2.8
Netherlands	4.2	7.2	2.7	2.1	1.0	0.9p
Denmark	5.2	10.8	6.3	2.1	1.1	2.2
Ireland	4.8	15.0	8.3	2.6	−1.7	−1.6
UK	3.7	15.6	7.3	3.3	2.2	3.3
Greece	2.2	16.1	19.4	9.2	1.3	4.7
Portugal	3.7	23.7	16.7	4.7	4.0	2.7
Spain	5.8	18.3	9.7	3.9	−0.2	1.8
USA	2.5	8.5	5.4	2.8	−0.4	N/a
Japan	5.7	9.9	2.5	0.8	−1.4	N/a

p *provisional; N/a not available*

[a]*West Germany up until 1989.*

[b]*This column is taken from Table 2.3 from* The New Economy Revisited, *2nd edn, by Loucas Tsoukalis. By permission of Oxford University Press.*

Source: *Unless otherwise stated, OECD and own calculations based on OECD data for the decade averages, and Eurostat for 2009 and 2010, www.epp.eurostat.ec.europa.eu (accessed 3 August 2010), © European Union, 2011.*

Divergence in the economic policies and performance of the EC member states, and the more unstable international monetary situation meant that the first programme to introduce economic and monetary union had to be shelved. The main energies of the EC member states seemed concentrated on the seemingly endless squabbles about the level of agricultural price support and the EC budgetary mechanisms. As Tsoukalis (1997) notes, the energy expended on these debates would seem excessive given that the sums involved accounted for such a tiny fraction (then less than 1 per cent) of the Community's GDP.

These are often called 'the years of Eurosclerosis or Europessimism', but none the less a few successes must be noted (see the Appendix to this chapter): the 1973 enlargement; the creation (albeit on a small scale) of the European Regional Development Fund in 1975; the establishment of the European Monetary System; the introduction of direct elections to the Parliament in 1979, and the entry of Greece in 1981. The path was also prepared for Spanish and Portuguese accession in 1986.

2.14   The relaunching of integration: the Internal Market Programme

By the mid-1980s there was growing discontent in the Community about poor economic performance and loss of competitiveness, particularly when compared with rivals such as Japan and the USA. Some governments of the EC member states, such as those of Thatcher, Kohl and even Mitterand, were committed to deregulation as a means of stimulating output and trade.

Against a background of increasing frustration with the slow pace of integration, Jacques Delors became president of the Commission in 1985. The strategy chosen to revive the integration process was the completion of the internal market. The objective was to eliminate barriers at the frontiers between member states and promote the freedom of movement of labour, capital, goods and services. In 1985 France, Germany and the Benelux countries signed the Schengen Agreement, which aimed at the removal of checks on people at borders. Schengen was incorporated into the Amsterdam Treaty (signed in 1997 and entered into force in 1999), and its membership was gradually extended (see Chapter 6).

Freedom of movement of goods and services entailed eliminating the remaining non-tariff barriers on trade between the member states, one of the most important of which was differences in standards. A key element of the Community's strategy in tackling differences in standards was to rely as far as possible on the principle of mutual recognition. This was defined in the much cited *Cassis de Dijon* case of 1979 when the European Court of Justice established the general principle that all goods lawfully manufactured and marketed in one member state should also be accepted in other member countries. Certain exceptions were allowed if they were necessary to protect public health, the fairness of commercial transactions and the defence of the consumer.

The introduction of the Single or Internal Market Programme had the effect of launching a new phase in the integration process, spilling over into renewed efforts in institutional reform, reinforced EC social, regional and competition policies, and economic and monetary union. Reform of the Community decision-making process was necessary to ensure that all the legislation could be introduced in time to meet the January 1993 deadline for introduction of the Single Market. The programme was initially presented as an exercise in deregulation and received wholehearted support from the EC member states and business community. However, the weaker countries and regions of the Community feared that they might not be able to meet the increased competitive pressure implied by the Single Market, and that, as a result, regional disparities might worsen. To assuage these fears, in 1988 it was agreed to double the Community Structural Funds and to reform the way in which they operated (see Chapter 15). The Single Market Programme spurred a spate of mergers in the Community and led to a tightening of competition policy (see Chapter 16). Introduction of a single currency (see Chapters 9–11) could be regarded as a further step in completing the Single Market.

2.15 The Maastricht Treaty, economic and monetary union and the economic crisis

In addition to creating the European Union, the Maastricht Treaty (which entered into force in 1993) envisaged a strengthening of the Community. This would consist of economic and monetary union (EMU), greater economic and social cohesion, some institutional reform (including increased powers for the European Parliament, see Chapter 3), the creation of European citizenship (see Chapter 1) and the extension of EU competence to new areas.

The Treaty of Maastricht set out the three stages in the process of implementing EMU, fixing dates and describing the objectives to be reached in each stage. In addition, it presented criteria to be satisfied before member states could participate in EMU and allowed for certain countries to opt out. The third stage of EMU began on 1 January 1999 with eleven countries as full participants; Greece also joined subsequently, Denmark and the UK chose to opt out, and Sweden decided not to participate and remained out on technical grounds. Slovenia adopted the euro in 2007, Malta and Cyprus in 2008, Slovakia in 2009 and Estonia in 2011.

The objective of greater economic and social cohesion in the Treaty was translated into an increase in transfers through the Structural Funds to the poorer regions of the Community. The Treaty was also accompanied by a separate protocol known as 'the Social Chapter', which aimed at improving living and working conditions (see Chapter 7). Initially the Social Chapter was accepted by only eleven of the twelve member states and had to wait until 1997 when it was signed by the Blair government for the UK. The new areas of competence introduced by the Treaty of Maastricht refer to an increased role for the Community in education, culture, public health and the environment. In addition, there was to be the development of trans-European networks in transport and energy.

The international economic crisis from 2007 presented new challenges for the eurozone. As described in Chapter 11, the initial reaction of the European Central Bank (ECB) was to reduce interest rates and announce measures to shore up the banking system. Following the collapse of the Lehman Brothers bank in the USA in September 2008, the EU countries agreed a rescue plan to assist their financial sectors and introduce a co-ordinated fiscal stimulus.

In 2010, high levels of public deficit and debt in Greece led to fear of default. After months of delay, in May 2010 agreement was reached on an EU/IMF package of assistance for Greece. The EU also decided on a bail-out fund for eurozone countries of up to €750 billion, including a special-purpose European Financial Stability Facility (EFSF) of up to €440 billion. The ECB also decided to intervene in markets to buy government bonds. A fundamental debate on governance of the eurozone was launched, with proposals to improve surveillance and monitoring, tighten sanctions, and increase solidarity and co-ordination between member states.

In 2010, agreement was reached on an EU/IMF bail-out package for Ireland in the wake of collapse of the Irish property boom. The eurozone finance ministers also agreed on a permanent European Stability Mechanism (ESM) for dealing with debt crises in the eurozone to come into operation from 2013. In May 2011 a bail-out was agreed for portugal.

In September 2010 the Commission presented proposals for reform of EU economic governance. In March 2011, following various initiatives by Germany and France (see Chapter 11), EU leaders expressed support for the Commission's proposals, and agreed a 'grand bargain' known as the Euro-Plus Pact, which aimed at strengthening the mechanisms available for future bail-outs of eurozone countries in exchange for tighter monitoring and co-ordination of the economic policies of member states. In July 2011 a second bail-out was agreed for Greece.

2.16 EU enlargement

In part because they feared that with the Single Market Programme their industries would lose relative competitiveness, in 1990 the EFTA countries began formal negotiations of the creation of a European

Economic Area (EEA). This would enable the EFTA countries to participate in a unified market but imposed strong limits on their ability to participate in decision making. In the event, three of the EFTA countries (Austria, Sweden and Finland) opted for EU accession, joining in 1995 (see Table 2.4; Table 2.5 provides the comparable data for countries joining the EU in 2004 and 2007; and for the present and potential candidate countries, see Table 19.1 in Chapter 19). In a referendum, Norway again decided against EU membership, while the Swiss voted even against participation in the EEA. When the EEA came into operation in January 1994, the EFTA members were limited to Norway, Iceland and Liechtenstein.

Table 2.4 Selected economic indicators for Austria, Sweden and Finland (%)

	Growth 1991–2000	2009	2010	Unemployment 1991–2000	End Dec. 2010	Inflation 1991–2000	2009	2010
Austria	2.4	−3.9	2.0	5.2[a]	5.0	1.9	0.4	1.7p
Finland	2.0	−8.2	4.1f	12.5	8.1	2.1	1.6	1.7
Sweden	2.0	−5.3	4.8f	7.6	7.8	2.6	1.9	1.9

p provisional; f forecast

[a]Commonly used definitions of unemployment rather than standardized rates.

Source: Own elaborations based on OECD data for 1991–2000, and Eurostat for 2009 and 2010, © European Union, 2011.

Following the collapse of the Eastern bloc in 1989, the smaller Central and East European countries wanted tighter links and eventual membership of the EC. The Community responded first by offering trade and co-operation agreements to these countries, but was slow to offer them an accession strategy. The 1993 Copenhagen European Council set out the conditions that the applicant countries have to fulfil in order to join the EU.[14] Between 1994 and 1996 ten Central and Eastern European countries (CEECs) applied for EU membership. All these countries signed association agreements with the EU and all were participants in the EU pre-accession strategy to help prepare them for membership.

In July 1997 the Commission published the document *Agenda 2000*, which analysed the steps needed to prepare both the EU and accession countries for enlargement, and included 'opinions' on the readiness of each of the applicant countries to join the EU. At the December 1997 Luxembourg Summit it was decided to open accession negotiations with Cyprus and five CEECs: the Czech Republic, Estonia, Hungary, Poland, Romania and Slovenia. These negotiations began in 1998.

At the Helsinki Summit it was also decided to begin negotiations for accession with six further candidates: Bulgaria, Latvia, Lithuania, Malta, Romania and Slovakia, and to declare Turkey a candidate. Malta's application had lapsed in 1996 but was subsequently resumed in 1998. Negotiations with these six countries began in February 2000.

Ten new member states joined the EU in May 2004 in time to participate in the European Parliament elections of 2004, while Bulgaria and Romania joined in 2007 (see Table 2.5).

In 2005 the EU decided to begin negotiations for membership with Croatia and Turkey. The negotiations with Turkey are proving lengthy, with little progress being made (see Chapter 19). In 2005 the Former Yugoslav Republic of Macedonia was declared a candidate country. Following the economic crisis and collapse of its banks, Iceland applied for EU membership in 2009 and began accession negotiations in June 2010. Disagreements with the UK and the Netherlands over compensation for bank losses could hold up the accession process. In 2010 Montenegro was declared a candidate country, but a date for beginning accession negotiations was not set.

---

[14] The European Councils, also referred to here as summits, are attended by heads of state and/or of the government of the EU member states (see Chapter 3).

Table 2.5   Selected economic indicators for the member states that joined the EU in 2004 and 2007 (%)

	Growth 2009	2010	Unemployment End Dec. 2010	Inflation 2009	2010	GDP per capita in PPS[a] 2009
BG	−4.9	−0.1f	10.1	2.5	3.0	44[b]
CZ	−4.1	2.4f	7.7	0.6	1.2	82
EE	−13.9	2.4f	19.0[c]	0.2	2.7	64
CY	−1.7	0.5f	7.3	0.2	2.6	98
LT	−18.0	−0.4f	18.3[c]	3.3	−1.2	52
LI	−14.7	−0.4f	18.3[c]	4.2	1.2	55
HU	−6.7	1.1f	11.7	4.0	4.7	65
MA	−1.9	3.1f	6.2	1.8	2.0	81
PL	1.7	3.5f	10.0	4.0	2.7	61
RO	−7.1	−1.9f	7.3[c]	5.6	6.1	46
SL	−8.1	1.1f	7.8	0.9	2.1	88
SK	−4.8	4.1f	14.5	0.9	0.7	73
EU(27)	−4.2	1.8f	9.6	1.0	2.1	100

f forecast

[a]purchasing power standards EU(27) = 100.

[b]2008.

[c]end Sept. 2010.

Source: Eurostat, www.epp.eurostat.ec.europa.eu (accessed 3 August 2010), © European Union, 2011.

In 1999 the EU introduced the Stabilisation and Association process, which offered eligible West Balkan countries the possibility of signing Stabilisation and Association Agreements and eventual EU membership. The EU is considering the possibility of further enlargements to potential candidate countries in the Western Balkans: Albania, Bosnia and Herzegovina, Kosovo and Serbia.

2.17   From the Mediterranean Policy to the European Neighbourhood Policy

There was an attempt to counterbalance the eastward developments of the EU with a strengthening of the EU Mediterranean Policy. This was strongly favoured by the present southern members of the Union, partly as a means of stemming the growing flow of immigration across the Mediterranean, but also to increase security in the area. At the Barcelona Summit of 1995 it was agreed to set up the Euromed Programme to increase aid and create a free trade area in the Mediterranean region by 2010 (see Chapter 18). In 2008 the Barcelona process was relaunched in Paris as the Union for the Mediterranean. The unrest in North Africa and elsewhere in 2011 led to a surge in migration towards the EU and illustrated the underlying weakness of EU policies towards third countries in the Mediterranean area.

In 2004 the European Neighbourhood Policy (ENP) was set up to deal with relations between an enlarged EU and its eastern and southern neighbours. The aim was to prevent new dividing lines emerging between the EU and its neighbours, and to enhance security and narrow the prosperity gap on the new external borders of the EU. The ENP offered EU neighbours greater political, security, economic and cultural co-operation. The ENP is for countries with no immediate prospect of EU membership and covers Ukraine, Moldova and other ex-Soviet republics, and Southern Mediterranean countries, but not the Western Balkans (given the possibility of accession to the EU by these countries). To reinforce the ENP the policy was flanked by three regional initiatives: the Union for the Mediterranean (see above) and the Black Sea Synergy, both created in 2008, and an Eastern Partnership inaugurated in Prague in 2009.

The ENP had been launched with Russia specifically in mind, but was rejected by Russia as inadequate (see Chapter 18). The EU has a Partnership and Co-operation Agreement with Russia, and in 2003 agreed to reinforce co-operation by setting up four common spaces covering: economic relations and the environment; Freedom, Security and Justice; external security; and research and education, including cultural aspects. The EU is heavily dependent on Russia for energy imports, but at times, in particular after the 2004 enlargement, relations have been tense.

2.18 From the Luxembourg Process and the Lisbon Strategy to Europe 2020

In 1997 the Luxembourg Process, or European Employment Strategy (EES), was set up (see Chapter 7). This aimed at improving 'employability' and encouraging the adaptability of businesses and their employees.

Concerns with relatively low EU productivity led the Lisbon European Council of 2000 to launch a 'new strategic goal' aimed at economic, social and environmental renewal for the following ten years. The objective was to create a knowledge-based economy focusing on better use of information, science, and research and development, and more flexible labour markets (see Chapter 7).

Despite an attempt at its revision in 2005, the Lisbon Strategy led to a great deal of rhetoric and rather less concrete change. With the economic crisis the situation worsened, with high levels of unemployment, and sluggish growth (see also Tables 2.1–2.5 above) in some countries.

To meet these difficulties, in 2010 the EU launched the Europe 2020 Strategy, which entailed more co-ordination of economic policies, the introduction of key targets, and improved monitoring in order to promote smart (knowledge-based), sustainable (environmentally friendly) and inclusive (increasing employment and reducing poverty) growth. It can only be hoped that Europe 2020 proves more effective than its predecessor.

Environmental concerns acquired a growing importance in EU policy and were a central element in both the Lisbon Strategy and Europe 2020. The EU signed the Kyoto Protocol to limit emissions of greenhouse gases between 2008 and 2012, but was less successful in helping to broker a follow-up agreement (see Chapter 14). The EU adopted the 20-20-20 package on energy and climate change, which sets binding targets of 20 per cent of EU energy requirements being met by renewable sources, a reduction in energy consumption by 20 per cent, and a 20 per cent cut in greenhouse gas emissions; all by 2020.

2.19 From the Amsterdam to the Lisbon Treaty

The prospect of enlargement gave a new urgency to the question of institutional reform of the EU as it was necessary to ensure that the decision-making process could function with a growing number of members. The Treaty of Amsterdam (which came into force in 1999) and the Nice Treaty (which came into force in 2003) were intended to resolve these questions but fell well short of expectations. For that reason, in 2001 EU leaders agreed to set up a Constitutional Convention aimed at drawing up a Constitutional Treaty (see Chapter 3), but this was rejected in referenda in France and the Netherlands in 2005, and a 'period of reflection' on the future of Europe was launched. In 2007 the Lisbon European Council signed what became known as the Lisbon Treaty, but this was rejected in a first Irish referendum of 2008. Following a second Irish referendum of October 2009, the Lisbon Treaty came into force on 1 December 2009. Chapter 3 sets out the main features of the Lisbon Treaty and indicates how it has altered EU decision-making institutions.

Summary of key concepts

- After the unsuccessful efforts to set up a supranational organization in Europe, there was a change in tactics. In line with the neo-functionalist approach, there were various attempts at integration by sector.

- The **European Coal and Steel Community** (or 'black pool') was set up in 1951 with the aim of making war in Europe 'materially impossible'.

- Attempts to set up a **European Defence Community and a 'green pool' for agriculture** failed, largely because of France.

- Article 2 of the **Treaty of Rome** set out the main objectives of the EEC, while Article 3 set out the mechanisms by which these were to be realized. Progress in implementing the measures was very uneven, but a Common Commercial Policy and the Common Agricultural Policy were soon operating.

- The **1969 Hague Summit** called for widening (enlargement), deepening (economic and monetary union) and completion (a settlement to the budgetary question) of the Community.

- The 1970s and early 1980s were the years of **Eurosclerosis** or **Europessimism**, when much of the energy of the Community was spent on quarrels over the budget and agricultural spending.

- When Jacques Delors became president of the Commission in 1985, his strategy to relaunch the integration process was the completion of the **Single Market**.

- In addition to creating the European Union, the Maastricht Treaty set out the steps for establishing **economic and monetary union**. The economic crisis created tensions for the eurozone and, in particular, for **Greece, Ireland and Portugal**.

- The EFTA countries began to negotiate the creation of an **EEA** which would enable them to participate in the Single Market but which limited their ability to participate in decision making. In the event, **three of the EFTA countries (Austria, Sweden and Finland) opted for EU accession in 1995**. In a referendum, Norway again decided against EU membership, while the Swiss even voted against participation in the EEA.

- In **2004, ten new countries joined the EU, and Bulgaria and Romania joined in 2007**.

- In October 2005 the EU decided to begin negotiations for membership with **Croatia and Turkey**, but the negotiations with Turkey are proving lengthy. The **Former Yugoslav Republic of Macedonia** was declared a candidate country in 2005, as were Iceland and Montenegro in 2010.

- At the Barcelona Summit of 1995 it was agreed to set up the **Euromed Programme** to increase aid and create a free trade area in the Mediterranean region and this was replaced by the **Union for the Mediterranean** in 2008. In 2004 the **European Neighbourhood Policy** was established to provide closer co-operation with EU neighbours that have no prospect of EU accession.

- In 1997 the Luxembourg Process, or **European Employment Strategy** (EES), was launched.
- In March 2000 the **Lisbon Strategy** was introduced to create a knowledge-based economy in ten years. It was replaced in 2010 by the **Europe 2020** programme to promote smart, sustainable and inclusive growth.
- The **20-20-20** plan sets binding targets of 20 per cent of EU energy requirements being met by renewable sources, a reduction in energy consumption by 20 per cent, and a 20 per cent cut in greenhouse gas emissions, all by 2020.
- The Treaties of Amsterdam and Nice, the proposed Constitutional Treaty, and the Lisbon Treaty were all intended to introduce the necessary **institutional changes** for an enlarged EU.
- The **Lisbon Treaty** came into force on 1 December 2009.

Questions for study and review

1 How far do the federalist and neo-functionalist approaches to integration help to explain the initiatives of the 1940s and 1950s (see also Chapter 1)?
2 Describe the main functions of the OECD.
3 What are the main differences between the Council of Europe and the OSCE?
4 Describe the main objectives of the Treaty of Rome, and the mechanisms by which these objectives were to be realized.
5 How successful was the Community in implementing the policies envisaged by Article 3 of the Treaty of Rome?
6 What strategy was used to overcome the years of Europessimism or Eurosclerosis?
7 What have been the main European integration initiatives since the 1990s?
8 Write a brief essay about the economic history of the EU.

Online Learning **Centre**

When you have read this chapter, log on to the Online Learning Centre website at **www.mcgraw-hill.co.uk/textbooks/senior** to explore weblinks, chapter-by-chapter test questions, case studies and more online study tools.

pter 2 Appendix

A chronology of European integration

1950

In a speech inspired by Jean Monnet, Robert Schuman proposes the pooling of coal and steel resources between France and Germany, and any other European country that wishes to join them.

1951

The Six (France, Germany, Italy and the Benelux countries) sign the Paris Treaty establishing the European Coal and Steel Community.

1952

The Treaty establishing the European Defence Community (EDC) is signed in Paris.

1954

The French parliament rejects the EDC Treaty.

1955

The Western European Union (WEU) is created.
At Messina the foreign ministers of the Six decide to launch a new integration initiative aimed at the creation of a common market, and common policies for agriculture, transport and the civilian use of nuclear energy.

1958

The Treaties of Rome enter into force, and the EEC and Euratom are created.

1960

The European Free Trade Association (EFTA) is set up.

1962

Key decisions on the Common Agricultural Policy (CAP) are taken. The decision on common prices will not be reached until 1964 and will come into operation in 1967.

1963

De Gaulle vetoes UK application to join the EC. A second veto follows in 1967.

1966

The Luxembourg compromise enters into force, with France resuming its seat in the Council in return for use of the unanimity rule when any country deems an issue to be of 'vital national interest'.

1967

The Treaty merging the EEC, the European Coal and Steel Community (ECSC) and Euratom enter into force.

1968

Remaining customs duties in intra-EC trade in manufactured goods are removed eighteen months ahead of schedule, and the Common External Tariff is introduced.

1969

The Hague Summit agrees on proposals to deepen (EMU by 1980), widen (allow Denmark, Ireland and the UK to join) and complete (by introducing own resources) the Community.

1973

Denmark, Ireland and the UK join the Community.

1975

The European Regional Development Fund is established.
The Treaty of Brussels, giving the European Parliament wider budgetary powers and establishing the Court of Auditors, is signed and enters into force in 1977.
The first Lomé Convention was signed between the Community and developing ACP (African, Caribbean and Pacific) countries. Later Lomé conventions entered into force in 1980, 1985 and 1990 and from 2000 there was the Cotonou Agreement. This is in the process of being replaced by EPAs from 2008.

1979

European Monetary System (EMS) starts to operate.
The first direct elections to the European Parliament are held.

1981

Greece joins the EC.

1985

Jacques Delors is appointed president of the Commission and announces the Single Market Programme.
France, Germany and the Benelux countries sign the Schengen Agreement, committing themselves to the gradual removal of checks on people at borders. The Amsterdam Treaty that came into force in 1999 incorporated the Schengen Agreement, which was extended to other EU countries except the UK and Ireland, while Denmark has a partial opt-out, reserving its position on all questions except visas.

1986

Spain and Portugal become members of the Community.

1987

The Single European Act enters into force.
Turkey applies to join the EU.

1988

The financial perspective covering EC expenditure and resources for the 1988–92 period is agreed and includes a reform of the Structural Funds.

1989

June: Elections to the European Parliament.
November: The fall of the Berlin Wall.

1990

October: German unification.

1991

October. Agreement is reached on the terms of a European Economic Area (EEA) treaty.
December: The Maastricht European Council reaches agreement on the Treaty on European Union.

1992

May: The MacSharry Reform of the CAP is agreed.
December: The Edinburgh European Council decides the financial perspective for 1993–99 ('Delors 2' or the bill for Maastricht), and on further reform of the Structural Funds with the introduction of the Cohesion Fund.

1993

January: Introduction of the Single Market.
November: The Maastricht Treaty enters into force.

1994

April: The GATT Uruguay Round is signed at Marrakech.
June: Elections to the European Parliament.

1995

January: Austria, Finland and Sweden join the EU. Norway remains out after a referendum that rejected EU membership.
January: A new European Commission with Jacques Santer as president.
February: The Barcelona European Summit decides to create Euromed, a free trade area involving Mediterranean countries, by 2010.

1997

July: Agenda 2000.
October: Amsterdam Treaty is signed.
November: The Luxembourg Process, or European Employment Strategy (EES), is launched.
December: The Luxembourg European Council decides to open enlargement negotiations with the Czech Republic, Estonia, Hungary, Poland, Slovenia and Cyprus.

1998

March: Accession negotiations start with five countries of Central and Eastern Europe and Cyprus.
May: The Brussels Summit decides to set up the European Central Bank and determines which member states are ready to enter the third stage of EMU.

1999

January: Beginning of third stage of EMU.
March: Berlin Agreement on Agenda 2000 (including financial perspective for the period 2000–06).
May: The Amsterdam Treaty enters into force.
June: Direct elections to the European Parliament.
September: New European Commission with Romano Prodi as president.
October: The Tampere European Council decides to make the EU an area of Freedom, Security and Justice.
December: The Helsinki European Council takes the decision to open accession negotiations with Malta and the other five CEECs that have applied for membership and to treat Turkey as a candidate.
December: Agreement to create an EU rapid-reaction force to assist peacekeeping.

2000

February: Accession negotiations begin with Bulgaria, Latvia, Lithuania, Malta, Romania and Slovakia.

March: The Lisbon European Council sets the creation of a 'knowledge-based economy' as a priority for the EU.

December: The Nice European Council reaches agreement on the text of a new treaty.

2001

June: The Gothenberg European Council reaffirms the objective to complete negotiations with a first wave of candidate countries so they can join the EU in time for the European Parliament elections of 2004.

June: Ratification of the Nice Treaty is rejected by the Irish in a first referendum, but passes in a second referendum in October.

December: The Laeken European Council decides to set up the European Convention to work on drafting a Constitutional Treaty.

2002

January: Euro notes and coins come into circulation. Coins and notes in national currencies are withdrawn in the euro countries.

December: Copenhagen European Council confirms the deadline of 2004 for accession of ten applicant countries and indicates 2007 as a possible date for Bulgarian and Romanian accession. A decision on Turkey will be taken in December 2004.

2003

March: As part of the Common Foreign and Security Policy the EU takes part in peacekeeping missions in the Balkans replacing NATO, first in the Former Yugoslav Republic of Macedonia, and then in Bosnia and Herzegovina.

March: The European Commission launches the European Neighbourhood Policy (ENP) to deal with relations between an enlarged EU and its eastern and southern neighbours.

July: The European Convention completes its work on the draft Constitutional Treaty.

October: The Intergovernmental Conference to draw up the Constitutional Treaty begins.

December: The Brussels European Council fails to reach agreement on the Constitutional Treaty.

2004

May: Ten new member states join the EU.

June: Elections to the European Parliament.

June: The European Council agrees on the Constitutional Treaty.

November: A new European Commission takes office with Barroso as its president.

2005

May: The Constitutional Treaty is rejected in a referendum in France.

June: The Constitutional Treaty is rejected in a referendum in the Netherlands. Following the referenda a period of reflection on the future of Europe is launched.

October: Accession negotiations begin with Croatia and Turkey.

December 2005: EU leaders agree on the financial perspective setting out EU expenditure and revenue for the 2007–13 period.

December: The Former Yugoslav Republic of Macedonia is declared a candidate country.

2006

May: An Interinstitutional Agreement between the European Parliament, the Council and the Commission formalizes the financial perspective setting out EU expenditure and revenue for the 2007–13 period.

2007

January: Bulgaria and Romania join the EU.
January: Slovenia adopts the euro.
June: Under the German presidency the EU agrees to work towards a new treaty.
October: The European Council agrees on the text of the Lisbon Treaty.
December: EU leaders sign the Lisbon Treaty.
December: Schengen is extended to all the countries that joined the EU in 2004 except Cyprus.

2008

January: Cyprus and Malta adopt the euro.
February: The Black Sea Synergy is inaugurated in Kiev.
June: The Lisbon Treaty is rejected in a first referendum in Ireland.
July: Union for the Mediterranean is launched in Paris.
August: ECB injects €95 billion into banking system.
October: EU countries agree on a co-ordinated rescue package for their financial sectors.

2009

January: Slovakia adopts the euro.
May: Inauguration of the Eastern Partnership in Prague.
May: Agreement on EU/IMF package of up to €110 billion to help Greece.
June: European Parliament elections.
July: Iceland requests EU membership.
September: Barroso confirmed for a second term as Commission president.
October: Ireland votes in favour of the Lisbon Treaty in a second referendum.
December: The Lisbon Treaty comes into force.

2010

March: Europe 2020 strategy to create growth and jobs launched.
May: EU/IMF bail-out for Greece.
May: Agreement reached on a bail-out fund for eurozone countries of up to €750 billion to meet the sovereign debt crisis.
June: Iceland becomes a candidate country.
November: EU/IMF bail-out for Ireland.
December: Montenegro becomes a candidate country.
December: Germany and France delay the extension of Schengen to Bulgaria and Romania on the grounds of need to intensify the fight against corruption and organized crime.

2011

January: Estonia adopts the euro.
February: Germany and France propose Competitiveness Pact.
March: European Council agrees Euro-Plus Pact.
May: EU/IMF bail-out is agreed for Portugal.
July: A second bail-out is agreed for Greece.

Chapter 3

The Decision-Making Institutions of the European Union

Learning Objectives

By the end of this chapter you should be able to understand:

- ✓ The most important changes introduced by the Lisbon Treaty
- ✓ What are the main, decision-making institutions of the EU
- ✓ The structure and functions of the European Commission
- ✓ The role of the Council and the European Council
- ✓ The system of voting in the Council
- ✓ The organization and role of the European Parliament
- ✓ The role of the Court of Justice
- ✓ The main features of the Court of Auditors
- ✓ The decision-making procedures of the EU
- ✓ What we mean by 'differentiated integration' and enhanced co-operation

3.1 Introduction

One of the main difficulties of the EU is that of accommodating its institutional structure to a growing membership, at the same time ensuring that decision making respects democratic principles and is 'as close to the citizens as possible'. An increasing membership adds to the difficulty of ensuring 'efficiency', or what is usually defined in the EU context as ability to take decisions. Respect for democratic principles generally entails legitimacy of the decision-making process, but there has been growing criticism of EU institutions as not being answerable to the preferences of its citizens. The European initiative has been driven mainly by political elites, and opinion polls and referenda often reveal a disturbing lack of confidence in the EU on the part of the public. As will be shown in this chapter, the EU is accused of having a 'democratic deficit' in that the practices and operation of its decision-making institutions are said to fall short of democratic principles, and in recent years there have been various attempts to meet this criticism through reform of EU decision making.

Difficulties arise in analysing EU decision making because the EU is neither a country nor a 'traditional' international organization. The institutions of the EU appear messy and complex, and are very different from those of a country such as the USA, which are based on the distinction between legislature, executive and judiciary. EU institutions have been evolving over time and reflect successive compromises to balance various (and varying) interests.[1]

In this chapter, recent steps in the process of reform of EU decision-making institutions, and in particular the changes implied by the Lisbon Treaty, are described. Then there follows an introduction to EU decision-making institutions, each of which is subsequently analysed in more detail. The issue of 'differentiated integration' or 'enhanced co-operation', in order to allow those member states which are willing and able to proceed more rapidly with integration to do so, is then addressed, before evaluating the process of institutional change in the final section.

3.2 Towards the Lisbon Treaty

Following the unsuccessful attempts in the Amsterdam and Nice treaties to prepare EU institutions for enlargement, in 2001 an EU summit at Laeken in Belgium agreed on the creation of a Constitutional Convention to draw up a Constitutional Treaty aimed at making EU decision making more democratic, transparent and efficient.[2] The draft Constitutional Treaty was signed in Rome in 2004, but before coming into operation had to be ratified by all the member states, either by a vote in the national parliament or by a referendum. In May 2005 France rejected the Constitutional Treaty in a referendum, and this was followed by a negative outcome in a Dutch referendum of 1 June 2005. A 'period of reflection' on the future of Europe was subsequently launched.[3]

Meeting in Berlin in March 2007 at the celebrations of the fiftieth anniversary of the Treaty of Rome, EU leaders agreed to the Berlin Declaration, which aimed at working towards a new treaty for the EU before the elections to the European Parliament in 2009. In June 2007, under the German presidency (thanks also to the efforts of Angela Merkel), the EU leaders agreed on the outline of a draft Reform Treaty to replace the Constitutional Treaty. An Intergovernmental Conference (IGC) began work in July. Intergovernmental conferences are necessary for revisions of the treaties (in contrast, the Constitutional Treaty would have replaced earlier treaties), and have been frequent since the mid-1980s. Intergovernmental conferences entail regular meetings between national representatives at various levels to prepare the drafts of treaty changes, or new treaties.

---

[1] According to Article 207 TFEU (ex-Article 133 TEC), the European Commission negotiates trade agreements on behalf of the member states, in consultation with a special committee known formerly as the 133 Committee and now the 207 Committee. The 207 Committee is made up of representatives of all the member states, and the European Commission. The 207 Committee meets on a weekly basis to discuss all trade policy issues affecting the EU, from WTO negotiations, to trade problems with specific products, or trade implications of other EU policies. Since the Lisbon Treaty the Council acts by qualified majority voting on trade agreements, but agreements involving services or intellectual property rights require a unanimous vote in the Council. Major treaty ratifications covering more than trade need assent by the European Parliament.

[2] The EU Convention was composed of representatives of the governments of member states and of the then candidate countries, the European Parliament, Commission and Council, and of national parliaments. Giscard d'Estaing was chosen as president of the Convention, with two vice-presidents, Giuliano Amato and Jean-Luc Dehaene (former prime ministers of Italy and Belgium, respectively). Both the name and the rhetoric deliberately echoed the 1787 Philadelphia Constitutional Convention, whose role had been to mould a federation out of the thirteen original US states.

[3] During this time the Amato Group, or Action Committee for Democracy (ACED), backed by the Barroso Commission, worked unofficially on a new draft treaty.

The European Council (composed of heads of state and/or of government, as described below) accepted the text of this Reform Treaty in a summit in Lisbon in October 2007.[4] What then became known as the Lisbon Treaty was signed by the European Council at a special meeting in Lisbon in December 2007.[5] Before coming into force the Treaty had to be ratified by all the member states, and the aim was to complete this process so the Treaty could come into operation by January 2009 before the European Parliament elections in June 2009. By its constitution as interpreted by its Supreme Court (the 1987 Crotty judgment), Ireland had to hold a referendum, but all other member states decided on ratification by their national parliaments. The Irish rejected the Lisbon Treaty in a first referendum in June 2008, but then accepted it in a second referendum of October 2009. The Treaty came into force on 1 December 2009. Box 3.1 sets out the main changes introduced by the Treaty, and these are discussed in more detail below in the context of the individual EU institutions.

Box 3.1

Main changes introduced by the Lisbon Treaty

- A single legal personality for the EU replacing the pillar structure.
- A European Council president holding office for two and a half years renewable once. The first such president from 2009 was the Belgian Herman Van Rompuy.
- A new High Representative of the Union for Foreign Affairs and Security Policy. Due to British reservations, the term 'EU Foreign Minister' was dropped. The first High Representative from 2009 was the British Baroness Catherine Ashton.
- Direct election of the president of the Commission by the European Parliament.
- A 'double-majority' voting rule is to be introduced in the Council, with 55 per cent of member states and 65 per cent of the population necessary to pass a measure by qualified majority vote. A blocking minority requires a minimum of four states. To meet Polish requests, the new system will apply from 2014, with a transitional period until 2017 during which time voting weights of the Nice Treaty can be applied if a proposal is of political sensitivity for a member state. From 2014, additional provisions will also allow a minority of member states to delay key decisions taken in the Council by qualified majority voting for 'a reasonable time', and this is known as the Ioannina Clause.
- Extending qualified majority voting to over forty more policy areas.
- The number of members of the European Parliament is to be fixed at a maximum of 751, with a minimum of 6, and a maximum of 96 per country. The 750-plus-one formula (with the extra seat requested by Italy) assumes that the president of the European Parliament will not vote.
- Strengthening the national parliaments by giving them the right to raise objections to proposed EU legislation; reinforcing the principle of subsidiarity; and increasing their role in responding to new applications for EU membership.
- Reference to new challenges such as climate change and energy solidarity.

---

[4] Several concessions were necessary to reach agreement, including an extra member of the European Parliament for Italy, and stronger blocking powers for minority groups of states (see Box 3.1). The possibility of increasing the number of advocates general (see the discussion of the Court of Justice below) was granted as a concession to Poland following a highly controversial intervention in which the prime minister, Jaroslaw Kaczynski, argued that Poland should have increased representation as it would have had a substantially larger population had it not been for the Second World War.

[5] The UK prime minister, Gordon Brown, failed to take part in the main ceremony and signed the Treaty later on his own, maintaining that he had a prior domestic political engagement.

- An attempt to list the competences of the EU.
- The European Security and Defence Policy (see the Online Learning Centre of this book) is renamed the Common Security and Defence Policy (CSDP), and is to be responsible for tasks relating to peacekeeping, conflict prevention and international security. The CSDP would involve the progressive framing of a common Union defence policy subject to unanimous agreement of the European Council, and approval by all the member states through their usual constitutional procedures. Such changes were subject to the proviso that they 'shall not prejudice the specific character of the security and defence policy of certain Member States and shall respect the obligations of certain Member States, which see their common defence realised in the North Atlantic Treaty Organisation (NATO)' (Article 42 TEU). The Treaty also allows for 'permanent structured co-operation' among member states wanting a higher level of commitment.
- A 'solidarity clause' envisages joint action if a member state is 'the object of a terrorist attack or the victim of a natural or man-made disaster' (Article 222 TFEU).
- The possibility of withdrawal of a member state from the EU (Article 50 TEU).*

*The only withdrawal to date has been that of Greenland, which left the Community with effect from February 1985. Greenland remains associated with the EU and has an agreement covering fisheries. With the Lisbon Treaty, change in the status of an overseas territory of France, Denmark or the Netherlands no longer requires a Treaty revision. This provision was requested by the Netherlands, which is reviewing the status of Netherlands Antilles and Aruba.

The UK had promised a referendum on the Constitutional Treaty. Both Tony Blair and Gordon Brown maintained that a referendum on the new Treaty was not necessary as certain 'red lines' had not been crossed since the UK is to maintain its veto over foreign policy, common law (so the Charter of Fundamental Human Rights would be without legal effect in the UK – see below), and social security and tax laws.[6]

Many observers (including the European Scrutiny Committee of the House of Commons) argued that the Lisbon Treaty was substantially the same as the Constitutional Treaty, a position denied by the then British foreign affairs minister, David Miliband.

Unlike the Constitutional Treaty, the Lisbon Treaty dropped reference to certain symbols of the EU such as the flag and anthem.[7] The 'constitutional' label was abandoned, and the Lisbon Treaty returned to the traditional method of treaty change through amendment, rather than replacing existing treaties as the Constitutional Treaty would have done. The Treaty Establishing the European Communities (TEC) was renamed the Treaty on the Functioning of the European Union (TFEU) and its articles were renumbered. However, it was not merged with the Treaty on European Union (TEU), as the Constitutional Treaty had proposed.

Unlike in the Constitutional Treaty, the full text of the Charter of Fundamental Human Rights has not been integrated into the Lisbon Treaty, but is indicated by a short cross-reference with the same legal value (Article 6 TEU). The Charter sets out political, social and economic rights on citizens and aims at ensuring that EU legislation does not contradict the European Convention on Human Rights of the Council of Europe (see Chapter 2), which has been ratified by all EU member states. According to Protocol No. 30 attached to the Lisbon Treaty, the Charter is only legally binding in the UK and Poland to the extent that it confirms rights or principles already recognized in those countries (that is

---

[6] Critics maintained that the UK veto on foreign policy was undermined by the strengthening of EU competence in this area implied by the Treaty (see Box 3.1).

[7] Sixteen member states declared their allegiance to these symbols, but the declaration annexed to the Lisbon Treaty is not legally binding.

to say, these countries received an opt-out). The Czech Republic received an assurance that the terms do not apply retroactively.[8]

As explained in Chapter 1, the three-pillar structure of the EU has been replaced, with increased competence of the EU over Common Foreign and Security Policy (CFSP), and Police and Judicial Co-operation in Criminal Matters (PJCCM). In general, the Treaty allows member states to opt out of EU policies in the areas of police and criminal law. The UK is not obliged to co-operate on PJCCM and will maintain its veto on foreign policy and defence issues. The reference to 'free and undistorted competition' in the treaties was removed at the request of France.[9]

3.3   The decision-making institutions of the EU

The main decision-making institutions of the EU are:[10]

- The European Commission;
- The Council;
- The European Council;
- The European Parliament (EP);
- The European Economic and Social Committee (EESC);
- The Committee of the Regions;
- The European Court of Justice (ECJ);
- The Court of Auditors.

In general, the European Commission proposes new legislation, while the Council and Parliament pass the laws (and these three together are sometimes known as the 'institutional triangle' producing the policies and laws that apply throughout the EU). The following sections explain the roles of the various institutions.

3.4   The European Commission

With the Lisbon Treaty the term 'European Commission' or simply 'Commission' (already widely used) replaced the more cumbersome 'Commission of the European Communities'. In a strict sense the 'European Commission' is made up of the one commissioner (described below) from each of the member states, but more generally the term 'Commission' is used to refer to all the officials (*fonctionnaires*) working for the institution (see Box 3.2). The language staff takes up roughly 15 per cent of this full-time, permanent bureaucracy. The working languages are usually English, French and German.

---

[8] According to Protocol No. 30, Article 1 of the Treaty, 'The Charter does not extend the ability of the Court of Justice of the European Union, or any court or tribunal of Poland or of the United Kingdom, to find that laws, regulations or administrative provisions, practices or actions of Poland or the United Kingdom are inconsistent with the fundamental rights, freedoms and principles that it reaffirms . . .'. The Czech concession was in response to a request of President Vaclav Klaus. It was aimed at ensuring that ethnic Germans and Hungarians required to leave Czechoslovakia after the Second World War under the Benes decrees could not use the Charter to reclaim their property.

[9] Article 3 of the EC Treaty refers to 'a system ensuring that competition in the internal market is not distorted'. French president Nicolas Sarkozy argued that competition was not an end in itself.

[10] This list does not include the other institutions of the EU, and, for example, the financial institutions such as the ECB (European Central Bank), the ESCB (European System of Central Banks) etc. that are discussed in Chapter 11.

Box 3.2

The Berlaymont

Much of the Commission is housed in the famous Berlaymont Building in Brussels. It is extremely easy to get lost in the curved corridors of a building shaped like a cross and thirteen floors high. Considered the symbol of the Commission, and appearing on the news nearly every time Brussels is mentioned, the Berlaymont was riddled with asbestos, and was evacuated for ten years while the asbestos was removed. During that time white protective sheeting shrouded the building, provoking the inevitable comment that it looked like a work by the Bulgarian-born artist Christo.

The commissioners at the head of the Commission are responsible for one or more areas of policy and are required to act independently of national interests. Many come from prominent political careers in their own countries. A president heads the Commission and can play an important role in influencing the image of the Commission and determining the pace of integration. For instance, the personal role of Commission president Jacques Delors (from 1985 to 1995) was fundamental for the development of the Single Market project and economic and monetary union. The Portuguese José Manuel Barroso was president of the Commission from 2004 to 2009, and again from 2009. The commissioners generally try to take decisions by consensus on a 'collegial basis', and a small cabinet backs each. One or more vice-presidents assist the president. Created by the Lisbon Treaty, the High Representative for Foreign Affairs and Security Policy (Baroness Catherine Ashton since 2009) is automatically a vice-president of the Commission.

France, Germany, Italy, Spain and the UK had two commissioners prior to the 2004 enlargement, but then gave up their second commissioner. Both the Nice Treaty and the Lisbon Treaty envisaged reductions in the number of commissioners to less than the number of member states.[11] However, the Lisbon Treaty also allows for a unanimous decision of the European Council to change the number of commissioners. To reassure the Irish that the interests of smaller member states would be adequately taken into account, and increase the chances of a yes vote in the second Irish referendum on the Lisbon Treaty, the European Council agreed to continue with one commissioner per member state after December 2009 when the Treaty entered into force.

The earlier versions of the Nice and Lisbon treaties reflect the view that a smaller Commission would be less cumbersome and more efficient, and would be freer from national ties. As commissioners are required by the treaties to be independent of national interests, insisting that each country has their commissioner is in a sense contradictory. However, the full participation of each member state in the Commission is felt to increase its public acceptability and to ensure that the concerns of each member state are taken into account. Moreover, the Commission often relies on support from the member states to push forward its initiatives, and if a member state lacks a commissioner this support may be less forthcoming. Media visibility is also likely to be lower in a country without a commissioner (Tracy, 2009).

The commissioners are chosen for a five-year period. The Lisbon Treaty entails election of the new president by the European Parliament based on nominations by the European Council,[12] and taking into account the election results of the European Parliament. This is likely to lead to increased politicization, and a tighter link between the president and the ideological majority in the EP.[13]

---

[11] According to the Protocol on Enlargement annexed to the Nice Treaty, when the EU reaches 27 members the number of commissioners 'shall be less than the number of member states and will be agreed by the Council acting unanimously'. A future rotation system based on 'the principle of equality' would have to be agreed. The Lisbon Treaty envisaged a smaller Commission from 2014, with commissioners being sent from only two-thirds of the member states on the basis of equal rotation.

[12] Since the Nice Treaty the European Council proposes the president of the Commission by a qualified majority rather than the earlier requirement of 'common accord'.

[13] Already in 2004 the political affiliation of Barroso corresponded to that of the European Parliament.

The commissioners are proposed by their national governments. The Council, by common accord with the president-elect, adopts the list of persons. Once chosen, the commissioners are subject to a vote of approval by the European Parliament.[14] Until 2003 the 'collegial' nature of the Commission (which implies collective responsibility) meant that the European Parliament could only dismiss it as a whole. There were calls for dismissal of the Commission in 1997 over the treatment of BSE ('mad cow disease') and again over the 1999 scandal (see Box 3.3). Since the Nice Treaty (confirmed in the Lisbon Treaty as Article 17 TEU) the Commission president can require an individual member of the Commission to resign.

Box 3.3

The 1999 scandal

The events of 1999 constitute one of the most profound institutional crises in the history of the EU, and a milestone in the shift in the balance of power between the Commission and the European Parliament. The starting point was the reluctance of the European Parliament to approve the accounts relating to the 1996 budget, accusing the Commission of mismanagement, cronyism and fraud. In January 1999 a motion of censure against the Commission was tabled, but in the event the European Parliament voted in favour of a compromise measure consisting of an independent inquiry into allegations against the Commission. The results of this inquiry were published in March 1999, and accused the Commission on a number of counts. Irregularities were found in programmes relating to humanitarian aid (with the discovery of fictitious contracts supposedly granting aid to Rwanda and former Yugoslavia), tourism, and educational and training programmes. There was said to be evidence of nepotism, and of bending staff rules to appoint acquaintances, in particular in the case of Edith Cresson, the commissioner responsible for health and educational programmes. The most famous attack was against the appointment of a 70-year-old dentist from her home town as a 'scientific adviser', on a salary said to be $4,500 a month, with his son also receiving a consultancy contract.* The Security Office, which was directly responsible to the president, was accused of operating as a regulation-free zone granting 'small favours' to colleagues such as the cancellation of parking fines, practising dubious recruitment practices (so that it appeared like a private club for retired Belgian policemen) and permitting irregularities such as the disappearance of office furniture and equipment. The president of the Commission, Jacques Santer, was said to have lost control of the institution he was supposedly running, allowing a 'culture of complacency' to arise. The immediate reaction was a press release in which Santer announced that he was 'whiter than white' and protested that it was misleading and distorting to judge the output of the Commission on the basis of a few cases of fraud. A code of conduct was drawn up for those working in the Commission, but the damage was done and in March 1999 the Santer Commission resigned.

*The Economist, 6 March 1999.

When a new Commission comes into office, a complex and controversial process of deciding the allocation of portfolios begins. Each commissioner is responsible for one or more portfolios, or policy areas, and balancing the relative importance of the portfolio(s) given to each commissioner is a delicate process.

The commissioner also takes charge of at least one of the Directorates-General (DGs) into which the Commission is divided. Each DG covers a main policy area such as external relations or agriculture. In addition some of the Commission staff work for services such as the Legal Service. The system of vertical hierarchies means that at times there is insufficient co-ordination between the various DGs. Following the 1999 scandal (see Box 3.3), various reforms in the organization of the Commission were

---

[14] Leading, notably, to the call on Italy to retract the candidacy of Rocco Buttiglione in 2004 allegedly because he maintained that homosexuality was a sin but not a crime. In 2009 the initial commissioner proposed by Bulgaria, Rumiana Jeleva, decided to step down allegedly over possible conflict of interest of her husband's business activities.

introduced. Among the many changes was the substitution of names for numbers of the various DGs, so that, for example, what was DGVI is now called the Directorate-General for Agriculture and Rural Development.

3.4.1 The functions of the European Commission

In the literature, the phrase 'The Commission proposes and disposes' is frequently used to describe its functions, but a more complete list would include the following:

- The Commission has to 'promote the general interest of the Union and take appropriate initiatives to that end' (Article 17 TEU), and is involved at each stage in the EU legislative process. Commission proposals are not drawn out of thin air but are generally the result of a lengthy process of consultation involving interest groups, national civil servants, politicians and so on. Over the years the European Council and the European Parliament have played an increasing role in proposing policy initiatives.[15] Since the Lisbon Treaty a million citizens may sign a petition inviting the Commission to submit a proposal on any area of EU competence. This is only about 0.2 per cent of the EU population, and it is not yet clear how the citizens' initiative will operate in practice.

- The Commission 'disposes' or has to 'exercise co-ordinating, executive and management functions' (Article 17 TFEU). This 'management' role of the Commission is important in the day-to-day running of policies such as the Common Agricultural Policy and Common Commercial Policy.

- The Commission has certain autonomous powers in areas such as competition policy, and negotiates for the EU on some policy issues including foreign trade. It represents the EU in international organizations such as the Organisation for Economic Co-operation and Development (OECD), the United Nations and the World Trade Organization (WTO).

- The Commission prepares the annual preliminary EU draft budget and is responsible for executing the budget, and submitting accounts at the end of each financial year. Most actual spending is done by national and local authorities, but is subject to the supervision of the Commission and Court of Auditors (see below).

- The Commission acts as guardian (or 'watchdog') of the treaties, ensuring that their provisions are applied. If a firm, institution or member state is found to be acting contrary to the treaties, the Commission may make a recommendation or issue a reasoned opinion (see Box 3.4), impose a fine, or even refer the matter to the Court of Justice.

- The Commission may publish formal presentations (White and Green Papers) on specific policy areas in order to make the position of the Commission known and obtain reactions before the start of the legislative procedure. Green Papers present broader, initial ideas of the Commission, while White Papers set out more detailed guidelines for policy proposals.

With the ending of the pillar structure of the EU, the Lisbon Treaty entailed an extension of Commission powers (including those of initiative) over matters related to the former third pillar (Police and Judicial Co-operation in Criminal Matters), but refrained from giving the Commission a substantial increase in competences on the Common Foreign and Security Policy.

The fact that the Commission is not elected (but rather is composed of technocrats) and is not directly answerable to the public is one aspect of the problem of the 'democratic deficit'.[16] The Commission derives its legitimacy from its independence from national interests and its expertise on EU matters, but its lack of accountability and transparency is frequently called into question.

---

[15] The Maastricht Treaty introduced the 'request clause', which permits the Parliament to 'request' the Commission to submit any proposal where the EP decides by absolute majority that new legislation is needed (now Article 225 TFEU).

[16] This type of complaint was raised as early as the 1960s in particular by de Gaulle (Bainbridge, 2002: 197).

Box 3.4

EU legislative instruments

A **regulation** is 'binding in its entirety and directly applicable' in all member states (Article 288, TFEU).

A **directive** fixes an objective, which is binding, but leaves the choice of method to achieve that aim to the member states. Unlike a regulation, a directive therefore has to be transposed into national legislation before entering into force. In practice the distinction between regulations and directives is less clear-cut as regulations generally also require some transposition into national legislation, while directives are rarely a simple statement of objectives.

Decisions deal with specific problems and are binding on those to whom they are addressed, which may include member states, companies or individuals.

In contrast, **recommendations** and **opinions** have no binding force.

The proposal of the draft Constitutional Treaty that regulations should be called 'European laws' and directives should be called 'European framework laws' was dropped in the Lisbon Treaty.

In the shifting balance of power between EU institutions, the Commission has been losing power. Successive reforms of EU institutions have strengthened the European Parliament, while the European Council has increasingly gained responsibility for setting priorities and establishing the policy agenda. This tendency is likely to be reinforced by the creation of a longer-term president of the European Council (see below), who could act as a rival to the Commission president.

3.5 The Council

What is sometimes called the Council of the European Union or 'Council of Ministers' is referred to simply as 'Council' in the TEU and TFEU. The Council was initially the principal decision-making institution of the EU alongside the Commission, but with successive treaties it has increasingly carried out legislative and budgetary powers jointly with the European Parliament. It is the only EU institution that directly represents the member states, and in the past was occasionally referred to as the 'brake on European integration', reflecting the (rather simplistic) view that Commission proposals presenting the EU position were checked by national interests in the Council.

The Council is composed of representatives of each of the member states at the ministerial level and is attended by European Commissioners responsible for the policy area(s) concerned. The composition of the Council varies according to the question considered, so there is a Foreign Affairs Council; a Council of Economic and Finance Ministers ('Ecofin'); a Justice and Home Affairs Council; a Council of Agriculture and Fisheries Ministers; a Council of Transport, Telecommunications and Energy Ministers, and so on. In 1998 there were 23 Councils of this type, but by 2010 the number had fallen to 10. With so many specialized Councils, consistency and unity of operation may be difficult to achieve so there is a General Affairs Council to ensure the consistency of the work of different Councils and to follow up meetings of the European Council.

The main functions of the Council are:[17]

- to pass European laws – jointly with the European Parliament in many policy areas;
- to co-ordinate the broad economic policies of the member states;

---

[17] This list is take from www.europa.eu/institutions/inst/council/index_en.htm (accessed 14 May 2010).

- to conclude international agreements between the EU and other countries or international organizations;
- to approve the budget of the EU, jointly with the European Parliament;
- to develop the Common Foreign and Security Policy of the EU, based on guidelines set by the European Council;
- to co-ordinate co-operation between the national courts and police forces in criminal matters.

The legislative instruments of the EU are set out in Box 3.4.

The Council is assisted in its work by the Committee of Permanent Representatives (**Coreper**), which is composed of ambassadors of the delegations of the member states in Brussels. The Coreper helps to prepare Council meetings, and may take decisions on issues that are not controversial. On agricultural questions the Special Committee for Agriculture carries out this role. It is estimated that some 90 per cent of all Council decisions are taken by Coreper and the Special Committee on Agriculture, or in working groups of national officials before the Council of Ministers even meets, though the 10 per cent that remains almost invariably concerns the more controversial questions. The Council generally meets in Brussels, where there is a Council secretariat served by a staff. The secretariat travels to Luxembourg when the Council works there, and is widely credited with having some policy influence.

3.6   The European Council

The heads of state and of government together with the president of the Commission make up the **European Council**.[18] Though the summits of heads of state date from 1961, the European Council only received formal recognition as a Community body in the Single European Act 1987 and officially gained the status of an EU institution separate from the Council with the Lisbon Treaty. The Single European Act 1987 required summits of the European Council 'at least twice a year', but the Lisbon Treaty amended this to twice every six months.

The European Council plays an important role in providing overall political direction to the Union, defining priorities, goals and strategies, setting broad economic guidelines, and in resolving problems that have proved intractable at the Council level.[19] In general the European Council takes decisions on the basis of consensus, and implementation of the measures is left to the other EU institutions.

The Lisbon Treaty introduced a **president of the European Council** who holds office for two and a half years, renewable for a following term. The president (Herman Van Rompuy since 2009) is elected by a qualified majority of members of the European Council and, unlike the president of the Commission, is not subject to approval by the European Parliament. By the same procedure the European Council can require the resignation of its president in cases of impediment or serious misconduct. The president is responsible for co-ordinating the work of the European Council, hosting its meetings, and reporting its activities to the European Parliament, but also plays a role in external representation of the EU.

Alongside the new **presidency** of the European Council, the Lisbon Treaty entails continuation of the system of rotating presidencies of the Council. With the exception of the Foreign Affairs Council (which since the Lisbon Treaty is chaired by the High Representative for Foreign Affairs and Security Policy, Catherine Ashton), the presidency of the various other Councils rotates among the EU member states in six-month terms. Up until 1998 the sequence followed the alphabetical order of the names of member states in their own languages, but subsequently this was changed to ensure a better balance between countries (see Box 3.5).

---

[18] The term 'heads of state and of government' is used because France reserves the right to send both.

[19] The Lisbon Treaty establishes that the European Council should 'provide the Union with the necessary impetus for its development and shall define the general political directions and priorities thereof' (Article 15 TEU). In addition, it should formulate a draft on the 'broad guidelines of the economic policies of the member states and of the Union' (Article 121 TFEU).

Box 3.5

The order of the presidency

	January–June	July–December
2007	Germany	Portugal
2008	Slovenia	France
2009	Czech Republic	Sweden
2010	Spain	Belgium
2011	Hungary	Poland
2012	Denmark	Cyprus
2013	Ireland	Lithuania
2014	Greece	Italy
2015	Latvia	Luxembourg
2016	The Netherlands	Slovakia
2017	Malta	UK
2018	Estonia	Bulgaria
2019	Austria	Romania
2020	Finland	

The presidency may allow a particular member state to press for policy decisions and initiatives in which it is particularly interested. The country holding the presidency has the power to set the agenda; draft compromises; play the role of honest broker in negotiations; and attempt to ensure the continuity and consistency of policy making. Holding the presidency is often a matter of national pride and may be used to increase awareness of the EU in that country.[20]

The interval between successive presidencies may lead to a lack of experience, and encourage countries to exploit the presidency for domestic interests. In order to provide continuity, and to assist smaller countries holding the presidency, in the 1980s the **Troika** was introduced and entailed that countries immediately preceding and following flank the current holder of the presidency. The Lisbon Treaty confirmed this system of trio or **triple presidency**.

The High Representative for Foreign Affairs and Security Policy created by the Lisbon Treaty replaces the High Representative for the Common Foreign and Security Policy ('Mr CFSP' or Javier Solana from 1999 until 2009), and is president of the Foreign Affairs Council and vice-president of the Commission. The Lisbon Treaty also envisaged a European External Action Service (EEAS) to back the High Representative and work in co-operation with the diplomatic services of the member states (though the Treaty was surprisingly short on details about its organization). The EEAS consists of officials seconded from the Council, Commission and national diplomatic services, but practical difficulties plagued the early process of its creation.

---

[20] A diplomatic incident occurred at the beginning of Czech presidency in 2009 when a sculpture called 'Entropy' by the Czech artist David Černý was placed in front of the Council building. The apparent aim was to demolish national stereotypes, but the statue caused outrage as not all countries were pleased with how they were depicted. See the BBC coverage of the statue at http://news.bbc.co.uk/2/hi/7827738.stm (accessed 22 February 2011).

The establishment of a longer-term European Council presidency is aimed at providing continuity and answering the famous question supposedly of Kissinger of 'Who should I call if I want to phone Europe?'.[21] However, at times the solution seems to cause rivalries and overlapping responsibilities, for instance between the European Council president, Commission president, the High Representative, and government of the country holding the rotating presidency of other Council formations.

3.7 Voting rules in the Council of Ministers

The Council of Ministers may take decisions by **unanimity, simple majority or qualified majority voting** (QMV). According to the treaties, unless otherwise specified, simple majority will be the rule, but almost invariably the treaties specify that QMV or unanimity voting should be used.[22]

Qualified majority voting is the most widely used system of voting in the Council, and even before the Lisbon Treaty could be used for about 80 per cent of Council decisions. In practice, however, the voting norm is that attempts are generally made to reach consensus (Hayes-Renshaw et al., 2005). Until 2014 the voting rules of the Nice Treaty apply, and these entail that each of the ministers in the Council is allocated a certain number of votes reflecting (very roughly) the population of the country of origin. With each enlargement of the EU, adjustments are necessary in the allocation of votes and the number of votes necessary to block a proposal. Table 3.1 illustrates the weights of each of the EU(27) as allocated by the Nice Treaty.

Between 2007 and 2014, the QMV rule for passing a measure in the EU(27) requires:

- 255 out of a total of 345 votes, or 73.9 per cent of the votes;
- a majority of member states (a two-thirds majority in some cases); and
- a member of the Council may request verification that the qualified majority represents at least 62 per cent of the EU population, and if that condition is not met the decision will not be adopted.

Given the complexity of the solution agreed at Nice, the Lisbon Treaty entails a simpler system based on a 'double majority', so that 55 per cent of member states representing at least 65 per cent of the EU population will be required to pass a measure from 1 November 2014.[23] A blocking minority would require at least four member states. Between 2014 and 31 March 2017 new voting rules will apply, but the Nice voting weights can be applied if a proposal is of political sensitivity for a member state. In response to Polish request, from 2014 a new version of the Ioannina Compromise applies, allowing small minorities of EU member states more scope to call for deferral and re-examination of EU decisions.[24]

The requirement in the Nice and Lisbon treaties that a certain percentage of member states should back a measure was introduced to favour the interests of smaller member states, while the population

---

[21] According to Gideon Rachman, writing in the *Financial Times* of 24 September 2009, Kissinger denied that he made the statement. Kissinger was more in favour of divide and rule and was not happy with the Danish president of the Council he was dealing with at the time who was attempting to represent the whole EU.

[22] For a theoretical analysis of different voting rules using the New Political Economy approach (explained in Chapter 4) see Buchanan and Tullock (1962). For an application of this type of approach to EU decision-making in the case of the Common Agricultural Policy see Senior Nello (1997).

[23] When the Council is not acting on a proposal of the Commission or the High Representative for Foreign Affairs and Security Policy the necessary majority of member states increases to 72 per cent, representing 65 per cent of the EU population (TFEU Article 238). Strangely, there are no formal legal specifications on how to report population statistics.

[24] The Ioannina Compromise was introduced in 1994 with the enlargement of the EU to 15 states. In the Lisbon version of the compromise set out in a Declaration annexed to the Treaty, member states representing three-quarters of either the population or number of states necessary to form a blocking minority can request the Council to continue its work to find an agreement with broader support. The deferral of the decision must take place 'within a reasonable time without prejudicing obligatory limits laid down by Union law'. EU laws generally require a Council agreement within three months of a Commission proposal or Parliament opinion. Initially the Polish government argued that they had been promised a deferral period of up to two years, but in the Declaration no time limit is mentioned.

requirement reflects the interests of larger countries. The aim of introducing these voting rules is to increase legitimacy in an attempt to reconcile two views of the EU. The EU can be regarded either as a union of states or as a union of people. In the case of a union of states, equality of power (or the ability to influence decisions) would require each state to have equal voting power. For a union of people, each citizen should have the same voting power. The hybrid nature of the EU requires some compromise between the two. Traditionally this was achieved through over-weighting the votes of the smaller member states in QMV. The Treaty of Nice increased the weight of larger countries in QMV, implying a shift of the compromise away from the union-of-states concept.[25] This is to some extent corrected by the requirement that at least 50 per cent of member states support a measure. The introduction of these rules renders this dual nature of the EU more explicit.

One of the aims of the Nice and Lisbon treaties was to increase the efficiency of EU decision making, or the ability to pass legislation. This can be defined as 'passage probability', or the chances of reaching a majority on an issue given a particular voting rule. Baldwin and Wyplosz (2009) found that, compared with applying the status quo in an EU of either 15 or 27, the Nice Treaty actually reduced the passage probability of QMV in the Council.[26] However, at least in the early years after

Table 3.1 Weights in the Council of Ministers according to the Nice Treaty

EU(15)	Population (millions) Jan. 2010	Vote in the Council after Nice	New member states	Population (millions) End 2009	Vote in the Council after Nice
Germany	81.8	29	Poland	38.2	27
France	64.7	29	Romania	21.5	14
UK	62.0	29	Czech Rep.	10.5	12
Italy	60.3	29	Hungary	10.0	12
Spain	46.0	27	Bulgaria	7.6	10
Netherlands	16.6	13	Slovakia	5.4	7
Greece	11.3	12	Lithuania	3.3	7
Portugal	10.6	12	Latvia	2.3	4
Belgium	10.8	12	Slovenia	2.0	4
Sweden	9.3	10	Estonia	1.3	4
Austria	8.4	10	Cyprus	0.8	4
Denmark	5.5	7	Malta	0.4	3
Finland	5.4	7			
Ireland	4.5	7			
Luxembourg	0.5	4			

Source: *Eurostat (for the population data), http://epp.eurostat.ec.europa.eu/tgm/table.do?tab=table&plugin=1&language=en&pcode=tps0000 1 (accessed 11 February 2011),© European Union, 2011 and Protocol on the enlargement of the European Union, annexed to the Nice Treaty.*

---

[25] See Laruelle and Widgren (1998), and Baldwin and Wyplosz (2009) for more detailed analyses of this issue.

[26] 'Passage probability' is defined as the number of all possible winning coalitions divided by the number of all possible coalitions.

the 2004 and 2007 enlargements, the feared paralysis of decision making failed to occur and EU institutions seemed to demonstrate a certain resilience and capacity to adapt.

The Lisbon Treaty (Article 16 TEU) requires the Council to meet in public when it deliberates and votes on EU legislation, and this could increase the difficulty of deciding on legislation. Ministers may be reluctant to make major concessions if this is rendered public, and, in the past, compromises were often possible only because attendance at Council sessions was restricted, for instance, just to ministers (Tracy, 2009).

The debates about the relative weights of countries have been heated and acrimonious in successive attempts to reform the treaties. This is because weights in the Council are generally assumed to reflect the power of a member state to influence the outcome of the decision-making process. Various empirical studies have been carried out to test this hypothesis. Baldwin (2007) and Kandogan (2005a) find a close correlation between the number of votes of the poorer member states and spending on what is now called economic and social cohesion.[27] Kandogan (2000) also finds a similar result for the link between the number of member states with a strong interest in agriculture and agricultural spending. On the basis of the experience of successive enlargements Kandogan (2000, 2005a) concludes that the allocation of voting power in the Council is more important than the initial budgetary deal for the new member state, as voting power will determine successive budgetary outcomes.

3.7.1 How voting rules in the Council have evolved over time

During the early years of the Community (1958–65) unanimity voting was generally used. In 1965 the Commission (under the aegis of its president, Walter Hallstein) put forward proposals for the financing of the Common Agricultural Policy (CAP), the introduction of own resources for the Community budget and increased powers for the European Parliament, which were also aimed at ensuring democratic control of Community spending. At the same time, the third phase of the transitional period for introducing the Community was due to begin in 1966, and the Commission called for implementation of the Treaty of Rome with respect to the use of the qualified majority vote.

The French president, de Gaulle,[28] fiercely contested these proposals, and instructed his ministers to boycott meetings of the Council of Ministers. The non-participation of France in Council meetings became known as the 'Empty Chair' crisis, and had the effect of paralysing EC decision making for six months. The crisis coincided with presidential elections in France, and following the failure of de Gaulle to win outright in the first ballot of December 1965, he let it be known that a more conciliatory tone would be adopted towards the Community. As an important agricultural producer, France was also concerned to ensure adequate financing for the CAP, which then absorbed about 90 per cent of EC spending.

Following de Gaulle's success in the second ballot, negotiations with the Community were resumed, leading to the Luxembourg compromise in early 1966. This entailed that whenever any member state declared that a measure affected a 'vital national interest', the Council would endeavour to reach solutions within a reasonable time that could be adopted by unanimity. Though in practice during the following years the Luxembourg compromise was seldom invoked, unanimity became the rule, and majority voting was rarely used, except occasionally on details of agricultural policy or budgetary matters.

It was only with the 1987 Single European Act that this situation changed, with the number of areas subject to the QMV rule being substantially extended. The Act specified that all measures relating to completion of the Single Market were to be decided on the basis of QMV, which was probably the only way of ensuring that the 1993 deadline could be reached. The Maastricht and Amsterdam treaties brought limited extensions of the areas where QMV was to be used, but unanimity continued to be used in many areas.

The fact that so many areas remained under the unanimity-voting rule (with any member state able to threaten use of a veto) raised a spectre of even greater risk of deadlock and the breakdown of

---

[27] See Chapter 15 for a discussion of EU policies on economic and social cohesion.

[28] According to de Gaulle, the provisions for QMV in the Treaty of Rome had been negotiated during the Fourth Republic when France was politically weak, and he was in favour of 'taking our destiny back into our own hands' as it was unacceptable that 'a foreign majority can constrain recalcitrant nations' (quoted in Bainbridge, 2002: 360).

decision making in an enlarged EU. To meet this problem the Nice Summit agreed that QMV would be extended to 29 of the 70 Treaty Articles that were still subject to unanimity. However, national sensibilities meant that the right of veto in the Council was maintained in many crucial areas.[29]

The Lisbon Treaty entailed a further extension of QMV in areas such as energy, asylum and immigration, so that unanimity is limited to relatively few areas such as those relating to constitutional issues, taxation, social security, treaty revision, defence, foreign policy, and operational police co-operation.

3.8 The European Parliament

Initially, the European Parliament (EP) was primarily a consultative body, but with each successive treaty, its legislative powers have increased. Since the Lisbon Treaty, the Council and European Parliament decide jointly on most legislation (see the description of legislative procedures below).

The EP is elected every five years, and, since 1979, a system of direct election has been used. The EP is the only directly elected EU institution, but the elections tend to be fought mainly on national issues. The elections often seem to be a vote of confidence about the incumbent national government. As Figure 3.1 indicates, the low turnout (43 per cent on average in 2009) illustrates

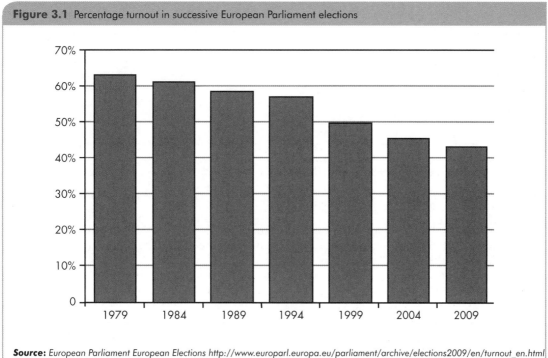

Figure 3.1 Percentage turnout in successive European Parliament elections

Source: *European Parliament European Elections http://www.europarl.europa.eu/parliament/archive/elections2009/en/turnout_en.html accessed 22 April 2010, @ European Union 2011.*

---

[29] For instance, the UK managed to ensure that unanimity remained for tax questions and social security. Spain insisted on keeping unanimity for decisions relating to the Cohesion Fund, while Germany demanded it for movement of professionals. France was able to block an extension of QMV for trade in audiovisual services, culture, education, health and social services. Denmark and Greece obtained exceptions from the QMV for maritime transport.

how the EP has failed to secure a hold over public opinion. In particular, turnout has been low in many of the new CEEC member states.[30]

Table 3.2 Representation in the 2009–2014 European Parliament

EU(15)w	Population (millions) Jan. 2010	Allocation of seats in the 2009–14 EP	Inhabitants per MEP ('000) in the 2009–14 EP	New member states	Population (millions) end 2009	Allocation of seats in the 2009–14 EP	Inhabitants per MEP ('000) in the 2009–14 EP
Germany	81.8	99	828	Poland	38.2	50	762
France	64.7	72	893	Romania	21.5	33	651
UK	62.0	72	856	CzechRep.	10.5	22	477
Italy	60.3	72	833	Hungary	10.0	22	455
Spain	46.0	50	916	Bulgaria	7.6	17	447
Netherlands	16.6	25	660	Slovakia	5.4	13	415
Greece	11.3	22	514	Lithuania	3.3	12	275
Portugal	10.6	22	482	Latvia	2.3	8	288
Belgium	10.8	22	491	Slovenia	2.0	7	286
Sweden	9.3	18	500	Estonia	1.3	6	217
Austria	8.4	17	494	Cyprus	0.8	6	133
Denmark	5.5	13	423	Malta	0.4	5	80
Finland	5.4	13	408				
Ireland	4.5	12	367				
Luxembourg	0.5	6	83				

Source: *Protocol on the enlargement of the European Union, annexed to the Nice Treaty, and population data, from Eurostat, http://epp. eurostat.ec.europa.eu/tgm/table.do?tab=table&plugin=1&language=en&pcode=tps00001 (accessed 11 February 2011), © European Union, 2011.*

The Amsterdam Treaty set a ceiling of 700 on the future size of the EP, but this was exceeded with abandon. Following the accession of Bulgaria and Romania the EP had 785 members in 2007, down to 736 after the June 2009 elections (see also Table 3.2). The Lisbon Treaty set a limit of 751 members, with a minimum of 6, and a maximum of 96 per country. The 750-plus-one formula assumes that the president of the European Parliament will not vote.[31] The seats are apportioned

---

[30] The turnout in the new CEEC member states was: Slovakia (17 per cent in 2004 and 20 per cent in 2009), Poland (21 per cent in 2004 and 25 per cent in 2009); Lithuania (falling from 48 per cent in 2004 to 21 per cent in 2009); Estonia (rising from 26 per cent in 2004 to 44 per cent in 2009); the Czech Republic and Slovenia (both with 28 per cent in 2004 and 2009); Hungary (38 per cent in 2004 and 36 per cent in 2009); Latvia (41 per cent in 2004 and 54 per cent in 2009); Romania (28 per cent in 2009); and Bulgaria (39 per cent in 2009). In the 2009 elections the highest turnout was in Belgium and Luxembourg, both with over 90 per cent, while the lowest turnout in the EU(15) was in the UK (35 per cent), the Netherlands and Portugal (37 per cent), France (41 per cent) and Germany (43 per cent). Data from www. ukpolitical.info/european-parliament-election-turnout.htm (accessed 22 April 2010).

[31] Under the Lisbon Treaty the composition of the EP is to be decided by the European Council acting by unanimity on the basis of an initiative by Parliament and after obtaining its consent (Article 14 TEU). The composition of the EP will require further changes to take account of demographic changes and/or future enlargements of the EU.

roughly according to the populations of the member states (though again there is a bias to ensure adequate representation of the smaller member states). The EP elects its president from among its members.

The MEPs are organized into large groupings that reflect political leaning rather than nationality. After the 2009 elections these were: the European People's Party (Christian Democrats) with 265 MEPs,[32] the Progressive Alliance of Socialists and Democrats in the European Parliament (184 MEPs), the Group of the Alliance of Liberals and Democrats for Europe (84 MEPS), the Greens/European Free Alliance (55 MEPs), the European Conservatives and Reformists (55 MEPs); the Confederal Group of the European United Left–Nordic Green Left (35 MEPs); Europe of Freedom and Democracy Group (32 MEPs) and non-attached (26 MEPs). Many MEPs were initially national politicians, or in the media and sport (see also Box 3.6). Since the Lisbon Treaty MEPs have been voting more frequently along party lines.

Box 3.6

Proposed reforms of the European Parliament

During the debate on the European Convention, one of the proposed reforms of the EP entailed setting up a second chamber drawn from representatives of national parliaments. Elections to the EP have been contested largely on the basis of national issues in the various member states, and the Italian experience suggests a further drawback of the proposed reform. Many of the Italian members of the EP are also national politicians. In March 1999 a survey carried out by the French *Journal du Dimanche* found that, on average, Italian MEPs had been absent from 41.6 per cent of the plenary sessions of the EP, followed by the Danes (35.7 per cent) and the French (30 per cent). An article in the Italian newspaper *La Repubblica* of 8 March 1999 confirmed that party secretaries who were also MEPs rarely attended the EP. For instance, the head of the Northern League, Umberto Bossi, attended only 6 per cent of the sessions, and Gianfranco Fini of the National Alliance attended 11 per cent.

The Italian MEPs were also the most highly paid in the EU (at about €11,000 a month compared with a salary of €800 for MEPs from the Baltic States in 2005). In 2002 a coalition including Italians, Spanish and Germans blocked efforts to introduce the same salary for all MEPs. The salary of German MEPs would have increased to the average, but the German government was against such a measure at a time of fiscal austerity.

There was also a decade-long debate in the EP about whether to introduce a system to ensure that receipts backed expenses. MEPs were entitled to club class travel, but many flew economy and pocketed the difference as they were only required to produce a boarding card to claim expenses.

In 2005 agreement was finally reached to introduce a common salary, but only from the EP elected in 2009. The new system involved an annual salary of €92,000, a non-contributory pension fund, an annual allowance of €50,424 to run a constituency office, attendance allowances of €298 a day and travel expenses.* In March 2009 almost 70 per cent of MEPs voted to keep future expenses secret, though some British, Dutch and Scandinavian parties have committed their MEPs to publishing accounts.

*The Economist, 30 May 2009.

---

[33] In a rather controversial move in 2009 the UK Conservative Party left the European People's Party.

The party relationships of members of these broad groups tend to be loose, but advantages such as increased possibility of obtaining places on committees or other official positions can be derived from membership. Most of the detailed work takes place in committees dealing with different policy areas.

Box 3.7

The problem of languages in the EU

In 2005 the Directorate-General for Translation translated 1,324,231 pages, while the Directorate-General for Interpretation provided interpreters for more that 11,000 meetings. For many years, French was the dominant language of the Community, but English and German are more widely spoken in the countries that joined the EU in recent enlargements. According to the *Financial Times* (28 November 2003), an analysis of candidates from the new member states for Commission posts found that 83 per cent spoke English, 34 per cent German and 24 per cent French.

One of the proposals to meet the problem of languages was to charge member states for using their native language. The proposal would not apply to ministerial meetings where full interpreting services would be provided, but it was suggested for working groups. In 2004 the commissioner then responsible for administrative reform, Neil Kinnock, also called for Commission reports to be shorter, and not exceed fifteen pages.

On one occasion (24 March 2006), Ernest-Antoine Seillière, the head of the employers' association BusinessEurope, spoke to EU leaders at a Brussels summit in English. The French president, Jacques Chirac, walked out in protest.

In 2011 there was a proposal to allow Britons to take an 'English-only' entrance exam to work in Brussels.* Usually candidates have to take the exam in a foreign language and demonstrate knowledge of a third EU language. However, in recent years there has been a shortage of British applications, and language seemed the reason. In 2010, Britain accounted for 1.5 per cent of graduate applications for the EU institutions compared with over 12 per cent of the EU population and 5 per cent of those already working for the EU.

*Financial Times, 21 February 2011.

The EP makes use of the 23 official languages (see also Box 3.7) of the EU(27), which does not always make for lively debate.

The official seat of the EP is Strasbourg, but its committee meetings and sometimes also plenary sessions take place in Brussels. Luxembourg is home to the general secretariat of the EP; hence the famous 2,500 trunks in the corridors to accommodate the various moves of personnel. It is estimated that the move costs about €180 million a year.[33]

3.8.1   The functions of the European Parliament

Since the Lisbon Treaty the EP exercises legislative and budgetary functions jointly with the Council, and plays a role in democratic supervision and political control of other EU institutions, and in particular the Commission.

With regard to **legislation**, traditionally the role of the EP was to be consulted during the legislative process (see the description of the legislative procedures below). The Maastricht Treaty introduced the co-decision procedure (see below), which places the Council and Parliament on equal footing. With the Lisbon Treaty use of the co-decision procedure was extended (for instance to areas such as Freedom, Security and Justice, agriculture, and the Common Commercial Policy), and it became the 'ordinary legislative procedure'. However, an 'emergency brake' allows a member state that considers proposed

---

[33] *Financial Times*, 12 April 2011.

legislation to affect fundamental aspects of its legal system to refer the matter to the Council and so suspend the co-decision procedure. According to CEPS et al. (2007), the increase in the use of co-decision might require reform of EP procedures to ensure efficiency, in particular, in committees.

The Parliament examines the annual work programme of the Commission in order to consider what new legislation is appropriate and ask the Commission to put forward proposals. The Commission is also required to inform the EP on a regular basis of its committee proceedings.

The Lisbon Treaty gave the EP **budgetary powers** over all types of spending.[34] However, the final word on multi-annual financial frameworks (which set out expenditure and payment ceilings for a number of years, see Chapter 12) rests with the Council, though subject to consent of the EP (Article 312 TFEU). The EP's committee on budgetary expenditure is responsible for monitoring expenditure. Parliament makes an annual assessment of the management of the budget before approving the accounts and granting 'discharge' to the Commission on the basis of the Annual Report of the Court of Auditors.

Parliamentary assent (see below) is necessary before important agreements can be concluded, such as those with third countries or international organizations, and, in particular, its assent is necessary for treaties of accession or association. The EP has no power to amend decisions under this procedure, but it can comment on them.

The EP has **supervisory powers** over the work of the Commission. Since the Lisbon Treaty the EP elects the new Commission president on a proposal of the European Council. The new Commissioners are subject as a body to a vote of consent by the EP. It can vote on a motion of censure requiring the whole Commission to resign. Parliament regularly examines reports sent by the Commission (such as the Annual General Report) and can question the Commission. The Parliament also monitors the work of the Council.

The Maastricht Treaty gave the EP the power to investigate alleged contraventions of Community law and to appoint an **ombudsman**[35] to receive complaints from any EU citizen about suspected maladministration on the part of any EU institution. The ombudsman may take the initiative in making investigations. The results of any inquiry are sent to the EP and to the institution concerned, but the ombudsman has no right of sanction. The first ombudsman, elected for the 1995–2000 period, and again from 2000, was a Finn, Jacob Magnus Soderman, who had previously acted as parliamentary ombudsman in Finland. The Greek P. Nikoforos Diamandouros was elected ombudsman in April 2003 and continued in the 2009 Parliament.

The EP is an important **forum for discussion**. The Parliament sets its own agenda for discussions, invites outside speakers and can send out delegations and fact-finding missions.

3.9   The role of national parliaments

During the debate leading to the Lisbon Treaty, the prime minister of the Netherlands, Jan Peter Balkenende, insisted on an increased contribution of national parliaments to the functioning of the EU as a 'red line' issue.

With the Lisbon Treaty (Article 12 TEU), national parliaments have been given a greater role with regard to:

- being informed by EU institutions;
- monitoring the proper application of the subsidiarity principle. In most cases national parliaments would have eight weeks to study draft legislative acts of the Commission to decide whether to send a reasoned opinion stating why the national parliament considers the proposal to be incompatible with subsidiarity (Protocol 1 to the Lisbon Treaty);

---

[34] Previously the EP could only accept or reject the whole budget and did not have powers to amend 'compulsory' expenditure, the main component of which was agriculture (see Chapter 12).

[35] The ombudsman is an institution of Scandinavian origin, and the first ombudsman was appointed in Sweden in 1809.

- participating in the mechanisms to evaluate implementation of policies relating to freedom, security and justice;
- revision of the EU treaties;
- responding to new applications for EU membership;
- co-operation between national parliaments and with the EP (Protocol No. 1 to the Lisbon Treaty).

Despite the additional complication of the proposed new measures, the reform may have the advantage of developing networks, tightening the links between the EU and national levels, and stimulating debate and awareness of EU issues.

3.10   The European Economic and Social Committee

The European Economic and Social Committee (EESC, also known as Ecosoc) has its origins in the French notion of including the 'social partners' (and, in particular, trade unions and employers) in social dialogue. This entails consulting them on proposed legislation. In practice, the representatives from each member state in the EESC are drawn from three categories: trade unions, employers and 'other interests'. The EESC represents the various economic and social components of the EU, including producers, workers, consumers and 'other parties representative of civil society, notably in socio-economic, civic, professional and cultural areas' (Article 300 TFEU). Based in Brussels, following the 2007 enlargement the EESC had 344 members,[36] and the Lisbon Treaty limited this to a maximum of 350.

The Treaty of Rome and successive treaties envisage the EESC being consulted during the legislative process, but there is no obligation to take its opinions into account. The EESC can also prepare opinions on its own initiative (Article 304 TFEU). Though its influence on the legislative process is less than that foreseen at the time of the Treaty of Rome, the expertise of the EESC can prove a useful source of information and is valued in many circles, including the EP and Commission.

The aim of the EESC is to bolster the role of civil society and encourage it to become more involved in EU decision making as a growing alternative to the party political participation of electorates. The EESC has emerged as an important institutional forum for social partners to engage in key discussions of different aspects of integration. Many items raised by the social partners in the EESC have found their way into the proposals of the European Commission.

3.11   The Committee of the Regions

The Maastricht Treaty created the Committee of the Regions, which shares its secretariat with the EESC. The Committee consists of regional and local representatives appointed for five-year terms, whose function is to advise the European Parliament, Council and Commission on regional problems and policies, and on issues involving cross-border co-operation. The Committee of the Regions has the same number of representatives per member state as the EESC and is also limited by the Lisbon Treaty to a maximum of 350. It must be consulted on matters affecting regional interests; it can also issue opinions on its own initiative but suffers from a relatively low profile.[37]

---

[36] The four largest EU member states each have 24 members; Spain and Poland have 21; Romania has 15; Belgium, Bulgaria, Greece, the Netherlands, Austria, Portugal, Sweden, Hungary and the Czech Republic have 12; Denmark, Ireland, Finland, Lithuania and Slovakia have 9; Latvia, Slovenia and Estonia have 7; Luxembourg and Cyprus have 6, and Malta has 5.

[37] In 2003 the Committee of the Regions was involved in a financial scandal when the Court of Justice forced its most senior civil servant to resign over severe irregularities. The Committee of the Regions was accused of travel expense fraud, and falsification of records to claim expenses by, for example, arranging 'fake' meetings on the eve of official meetings (*Financial Times*, 14 April 2003 and 19 September 2003).

3.12 The Court of Justice

The Lisbon Treaty gave the EU legal personality and abolished the pillar structure, and as a result what was previously known as the Court of Justice of the European Communities became known as the Court of Justice of the European Union with some corresponding changes in its jurisdiction. The European Court of Justice (ECJ) acquired general jurisdiction to give rulings in the area of Freedom, Security and Justice, though not, in most cases, over the Common Foreign and Security Policy, which remains subject to special rules and procedures.[38] Apart from in the UK and Poland, which have derogations, the Court can also adjudicate on matters relating to the Charter of Fundamental Rights.

The Court of Justice of the European Union comprises the ECJ, the General Court and the Civil Service Tribunal. The Court of Justice is composed of one judge from each member state, assisted by eight advocates-general, though the number of advocates-general can be increased by the Council acting unanimously (Article 252 TFEU).[39] All appointments are for six-year renewable terms, and the judges choose a president every three years. Judges are appointed by common accord of the governments of the member states, and, since the Lisbon Treaty, a panel gives an opinion on their suitability to carry out their duties. For the sake of efficiency the Court rarely sits with all 27 judges, but rather as a 'Grand Chamber' of 13, or smaller chambers of 3 or 5 judges.[40]

Before the Lisbon Treaty the General Court was called the Court of First Instance and was set up in 1988. It is also composed of one judge from each member state appointed for renewable terms of six years. The General Court has powers to hear direct actions brought by individuals, companies and certain organizations, and actions brought by the member states against the Commission. It has an appeal function in certain areas, and has particular expertise in competition policy. The European Civil Service Tribunal adjudicates in cases between the EU and its civil service.

The ECJ is responsible for interpreting EU law and adjudicating on disputes arising from the interpretation of the treaties and the legislation based upon them. If national law and EU law conflict, the latter takes precedence: in other words national courts must apply EU law rather than a national rule even against their own governments in a situation which falls within the scope of the treaties. The ECJ is the highest court to which disputes on EU law can be taken, and national courts must abide by its judgments. Since the Maastricht Treaty the Court can impose fines on recalcitrant countries.[41] The Court cannot initiate cases, but makes judgments on cases referred to it by EU institutions, national governments and courts, corporate bodies and individuals. The Court can only act within the powers given by the treaties.

Despite being handicapped by a relatively small staff, the Court has played a 'discrete but substantial role in furthering the objectives laid down in the Treaties' (Bainbridge, 2002). Some of its rulings have established important principles, in particular in fields such as competition policy and equal pay.[42] The ruling in the famous 1979 *Cassis de Dijon* case formed the basis for mutual recognition of each other's standards by EU member states. This role of the Court in carrying forward the integration process has frequently been criticized, and certain member states have accused the Court of being the unguarded back door through which national sovereignty is being carried away.

---

[38] According to the treaties, the Court does have certain powers, such as those to monitor the delimitation of the competences of the EU and the CFSP.

[39] Poland wanted the number to increase under the Lisbon Treaty, with a system of rotation for the smaller countries.

[40] EU Glossary, http://europa.eu/legislation_summaries/glossary/eu_court_justice_en.htm (accessed 31 August 2011).

[41] Fines have been imposed on Italy, for example, for non-application of the milk quotas (see Chapter 13).

[42] This was also the case for the two leading cases of *Van Gend and Loos* (Case no. 26 of 1962) and *Costa v. ENEL* (Case no. 6 of 1964). In these cases the Court of Justice expounded its doctrine concerning the 'direct effect' of certain provisions of the Treaty of Rome. This entails that where provisions of the Treaty impose on the member states clear and unconditional obligations, and the implementation or effectiveness of the provisions is not dependent on any further action of state, Community law not only imposes obligations on individuals, but also confers rights on them, which are enforceable in the courts of the member states.

It has also been claimed that the Court is not sufficiently transparent and is too slow in its procedures, though this is less the case than in certain member states. The delays are largely due to the overload of work; indeed, the aim of setting up the Court of First Instance (subsequently renamed General Court) was to reduce the burden on the Court of Justice by delegating more work to lower levels.

3.13   The Court of Auditors

The collection and spending of EU funds is subject to external control by the Court of Auditors in Luxembourg. The Court's authority extends to all institutions (including those in third countries) receiving or handling EU funds. Created by the Treaty of Brussels of 1975, the Court started operating in 1977 and has one member from each member state elected for a renewable six-year term.

The Court is responsible for ensuring that all expenditure corresponds to the legal provisions, that correct accounting practices have been used, and financial objectives have been met. In practice, it has mainly been concerned with checking on fraud and the proper use of funds. The findings of the Court are published in an annual report, and other reports on specific topics may also be produced. Initially the Court could simply bring irregularities to the notice of the authorities responsible for the institution concerned (and its findings were frequently ignored), but since the Treaty of Maastricht it can refer cases to the ECJ.

For fifteen successive years up to 2010 the Court refused to sign off EU accounts, maintaining that they could not verify a large share of the funds. In its 2006 report the Court found accounting errors in two-thirds of the EU budget, while the 2008 report stated that accounting errors in expenditure on economic and social cohesion cost over 5 per cent of EU spending in this policy area.[43]

3.14   The decision-making procedures of the EU

Until the Single European Act of 1987, the legislative procedure was based on what is known as the **consultation procedure**. As shown in Figure 3.2, this essentially consisted of a Commission proposal being passed to the European Parliament and European Economic and Social Committee, and, since the Maastricht Treaty, to the Committee of the Regions for 'consultation'. The significant feature of this procedure was that there was only one reading by the EP. The Council would take the final decision, using the appropriate voting rule. It is important to note that neither the Commission nor the Council was bound to accept eventual amendments proposed by the EP.

The Single European Act 1987 introduced the **co-operation procedure** as a means of strengthening the role of the EP in the legislative process. The procedure allowed the EP to amend legislation. This required two readings by the EP. This procedure is no longer used, and the Treaty of Amsterdam transferred most of the areas formerly dealt with under this procedure to the co-decision procedure.

The Maastricht Treaty introduced the **co-decision procedure**, and successive treaties all entailed an extension of its use. The Lisbon Treaty envisaged near-generalization of the co-decision procedure, extending it to about forty other fields, and it became known as the ordinary legislative procedure (Article 294 TFEU). The aim of wider use of the co-decision procedure was to reinforce the power of the EP so it shares legislative power jointly with the Council. A consequence was a shift in the balance of power away from the Commission. The main innovations of this procedure were:

- to allow the EP to veto legislation in certain cases;
- to add the possibility of a third reading of legislative proposals for the EP; and
- the creation of a Conciliation Committee to help the Parliament and Council to reach agreement.

---

[43] According to Civitas, EU Facts, http://www.civitas.org.uk/eufacts/FSINST/IN6.htm (accessed 18 May 2010).

Figure 3.2 The decision-making procedures of the EU

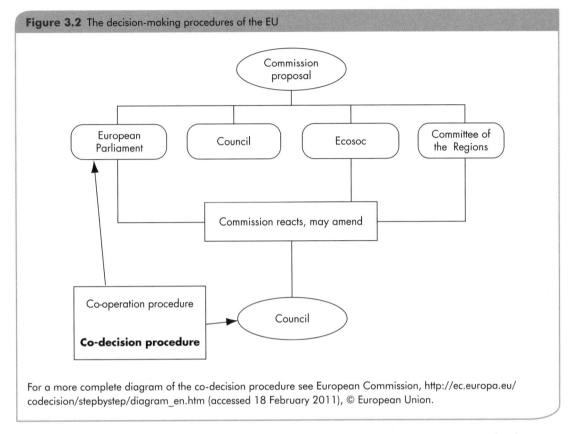

For a more complete diagram of the co-decision procedure see European Commission, http://ec.europa.eu/codecision/stepbystep/diagram_en.htm (accessed 18 February 2011), © European Union.

The **assent procedure** entails the Council having to obtain the assent of the EP on certain decisions. As mentioned above, it applies to important international agreements, including decisions on new countries joining the EU. According to this procedure, the EP can give or withhold its assent to a legislative proposal, but it does not have the power to amend it.

3.15 'Flexibility' or 'enhanced co-operation'

The number of policy areas dealt with by the EU is growing, and so too is its membership. There is increasing concern about the efficiency of EU decision making and the need to ensure that progress in integration is not limited to the pace of the slowest. The widening membership of the EU is bringing growing diversity, and with it the idea that more 'flexibility' or 'differentiated integration' will be necessary. Flexibility or differentiated integration allows those countries that are willing and/or able to do so to proceed faster in some areas of integration.

One mechanism of flexibility is 'enhanced co-operation', by which the Council authorizes a group of member states to move ahead while remaining within the EU framework. The Amsterdam Treaty first introduced 'enhanced co-operation' (where it was called 'close co-operation') and stipulated various conditions for its use, but it was soon evident that these were too restrictive to realize in practice.[44]

---

[44] The Amsterdam Treaty required close (or enhanced) co-operation to: respect the treaties and objectives of the EU; involve a majority of member states; not affect the rights and obligations of states not participating; allow any other member state to join at a later stage; be introduced as a last resort; not impede the operation of the *acquis*; and be open to veto by any single country that feels that vital interests are being threatened.

Subsequent treaties aimed at rendering use of enhanced co-operation easier,[45] and the Lisbon Treaty (Article 20 TEU and Articles 326 to 334 TFEU) requires enhanced co-operation to:

- further the objectives of the EU, protect its interests and reinforce the integration process;
- respect the 'competences, rights, and obligations' of non-participating member states;
- be open to all member states at any time;
- be adopted as a last resort;
- be authorized initially by a unanimous vote of the Council;
- involve at least nine member states, and promote membership to as many member states as possible;
- set out the conditions for joining the initiative; and
- be open to the participation of all members of the Council in its deliberations, though only the participants in enhanced co-operation can vote.

The Lisbon Treaty (Article 333 TFEU) also envisages a passerelle system whereby participating member states can amend the procedures they use for implementing enhanced co-operation (for example by switching from unanimity to qualified majority voting).[46]

Following the Amsterdam Treaty, enhanced co-operation was not used, though it was considered on a number of occasions, as, for example, for minimum taxation of energy products, a statute for EU companies, an EU arrest warrant and a common consolidated basis for taxation of company profits (CEPS et al., 2007). An early example of its use under the Lisbon Treaty was over divorce laws in June 2010.[47]

The limited use of enhanced co-operation to date is partly because alternative mechanisms have been developed such as intergovernmental co-operation outside the EU (as in the former CFSP and JPCCM pillars), and partly because the treaties envisage other forms of flexibility, such as transitional periods, which often seem more appropriate and simpler to implement than the enhanced co-operation.

Transitional periods may be used before countries are able to sign up fully for certain policies. This is sometimes referred to as a 'multi-speed' Europe, though the precise definition of this term varies in the literature. A multi-speed EU generally assumes that all member states will arrive at the same destination but require different speeds to do so. It implies that the goal for all member states would be that of membership in all aspects of the Union, but that member states (or the EU as a whole) may need more time to prepare for such membership. For instance, there was a delay before Greece could adopt the euro. In the case of the new Central and East European member states, long transitional periods were also applied in areas such as labour movement, the CAP, land ownership and environmental regulations.

In contrast, in what is often referred to as a variable geometry EU, or Europe *à la carte*, all the member states can pick and choose whether to participate in different policies on the basis of preference rather than ability. In contrast to a multi-speed EU, it is not assumed that all member states will arrive at the same destination. Member states can choose voluntarily to remain outside certain policies or co-operation frameworks. There are various precedents for this, such as the UK opt-out of the Social Charter in 1989 and Social Chapter in 1993 (see Chapter 7); the UK and Danish opt-outs of full participation in the third stage of EMU, and the UK, Irish and partial Danish opt-outs of Schengen (see Chapter 6). However, here there is a risk that a 'hard core' of member states, having all signed up

---

[45] The Nice Treaty removed the simple right of any member state to veto the process. According to the Amsterdam Treaty, enhanced co-operation required a majority of states, but this was modified to participation by eight member states in the Nice Treaty (at the time the 'critical mass' of eight corresponded to a majority of member states).

[46] The 'passerelle' or bridging clause would not apply to decisions with defence or military implications. The EP has to be consulted and a unanimous decision by Council is required to use this mechanism.

[47] Fourteen member states decided to apply harmonized rules when international couples choose the legal code under which they divorce or begin legal separation. The countries are: Belgium, Bulgaria, Germany, France, Spain, Italy, Hungary, Latvia, Luxembourg, Malta, Austria, Portugal, Romania and Slovenia.

for the same policies, would decide to proceed with even deeper integration, and other member states would find that their options of eventually joining the hard core are excluded.

Traditionally, the notion of a core group of EU countries proceeding more rapidly with integration generally rotated around the concept of the Franco-German relationship (often backed by the Benelux countries) as being the driving force of integration. Although the Franco-German alliance had long provided the momentum for many of the initiatives in European integration, there was a growing feeling that it might prove inadequate to propel the process in an enlarged EU. The misgivings were reinforced because at times co-operation between the two countries seemed geared to furthering national rather than EU interests, as in the October 2002 agreement on the CAP (see Chapter 13), or the 2004 controversy over the Stability and Growth Pact (see Chapter 11).

If the EU fails to permit sufficient possibilities for differentiated integration within its structures, there is a risk of flexibility by default with initiatives taking place outside the EU. The problem becomes one of finding a middle road, with some variable geometry to allow flexibility within EU structures, while at the same time avoiding excessive variable geometry that might undermine the cohesion and common core of the EU.

3.16 Evaluation

For many years the energies of the EU were absorbed by the question of institutional reform. The Amsterdam Treaty was patently inadequate to meet the challenges of enlargement. Though the Nice Treaty resolved some of the 'Amsterdam leftovers', and announced in an annexed Declaration on the Future of Europe that the EU had 'completed the institutional changes necessary for the accession of new member states', that same Declaration launched a new round of debate on reform. The prolonged discussion in the Constitutional Convention and over the Constitutional Treaty led eventually to agreement on the Lisbon Treaty. The final compromise on that Treaty permitted EU member states to sell the deal to their domestic public. For instance, the UK maintained that certain 'red lines' were not crossed as its veto was kept in various policy areas. The Dutch 'red line' was respected by increasing the role of national parliaments, while Poland obtained concessions over the application of the new voting rules in the Council.

How far do the changes introduced by the Lisbon Treaty render EU decision making more democratic, transparent and efficient?

The Constitutional Treaty had aimed at simplifying and clarifying the legal basis of the EU by replacing earlier treaties. This objective was certainly not achieved by the Lisbon Treaty, which returns to the traditional method of treaty revision and maintains two treaties and numerous protocols.

A longer-term European Council president could contribute to continuity and a higher profile for the EU, but there may also be overlapping of responsibility and rivalry with other figures such as the Commission president or High Representative for Foreign Affairs and Security Policy.

The new voting rules in the Council will eventually be more straightforward, but in practice the tradition of trying to reach consensus seems likely to continue, and the spectre of deadlock in an enlarged EU has not been completely removed. However, the process by which consensus is reached may also lead to greater understanding, co-operation and convergence of views. Moravcsik (1998) maintains that the EU has made executives more accountable to their citizens as the actions of government ministers are no longer scrutinized just at home but also at the EU level, and governments have to account not just for their domestic record but also for what they have achieved in Brussels.

Election of a Commission president by the EP on the basis of a nomination by the European Council taking into account the composition of the Parliament is likely to politicize the role. Already with Barroso in 2004 the tighter link with the majority in the EP became apparent, though subsequently he seemed concerned to establish his impartiality.

The increase in its legislative and budgetary powers would add to the legitimacy of the EP, but aspects of its gravy train image still need to be tackled. The more active role of national parliaments would be an additional complication, but seems likely to add to awareness and links between the EU and national levels.

However, even with the Lisbon Treaty the problem of the 'democratic deficit' of the EU has not been resolved. Commissioners are not elected, and are said to be technocrats wielding more power than is justified by their limited democratic mandate. The system is said to be executive dominated, and though control by the EP or national parliaments has increased, its effectiveness remains limited. Elections to the EP are fought mainly over national issues. The supremacy by which EU law overrides national law has been challenged, and the Court of Justice has been accused of acquiring powers for itself and EU law not formally given by any treaty.

The EU is attacked as being too distant from its citizens, while its decision-making process is difficult for them to understand. On various occasions when EU decision makers have appealed to their citizens for approval (such as on the Constitutional Treaty in France and the Netherlands, or the Nice and Lisbon treaties in Ireland), the outcome has not been what they expected. European integration has been confirmed as a process carried forward by elites.

Despite successive treaty reforms the EU decision-making process is still far from being transparent and accessible. Though the debate about the future architecture of the EU seems set to continue, after so many years discussing institutional change there is a certain reform fatigue. Few member states would be willing to embark on another phase of treaty change in the near future. However, some institutional modifications are possible without treaty change. Many aspects of the Lisbon Treaty have yet to be implemented, and others have still to be spelt out. It seems likely that the process of evolution of EU decision making will continue, though at a slower pace than in recent years.

Summary of key concepts

- Following the rejection of the Constitutional Treaty in referenda in France and the Netherlands, in 2007 EU leaders agreed on the **Lisbon Treaty**. This aims at rendering EU decision making more efficient and legitimate through changes such as an elected Commission president, simpler voting rules in the Council, a longer-term European Council president, increased legislative and budgetary powers for the EP, a High Representative for Foreign Affairs and Security Policy, and more involvement of national parliaments.

- The **main decision-making institutions** of the EU are: the European Commission, the Council, the European Council, the European Parliament, the European Economic and Social Committee, the Committee of the Regions, the Court of Justice and the Court of Auditors.

- The functions of the **Commission** are: to present legislative proposals; to implement decisions; to exercise certain autonomous powers in areas such as competition policy and trade negotiations; to prepare the annual preliminary draft budget for the EU; to act as guardian (or 'watchdog') of the treaties; and to present White and Green Papers on specific policy areas.

- The **Council** takes final decisions on legislation jointly with the European Parliament. The composition of the Council varies according to the policy area considered.

- The heads of state and of government together with the president of the Commission make up the **European Council**. The European Council plays an important role in providing overall political direction to the Union and in resolving problems that have proved intractable at a lower level.

- The Lisbon Treaty introduced a **European Council president** holding office for two and a half years, renewable once, and a **High Representative for Foreign Affairs and Security Policy** who heads the Foreign Affairs Council.

- The **presidency** of the other Councils rotates among the EU member states in six-month terms. The country holding the presidency has the power to set the agenda and further policy objectives in which it has a particular interest.

- The Council of Ministers may take decisions by **unanimity, simple majority or qualified majority voting.** Successive treaties have increased the number of policy areas subject to QMV. In practice there are usually attempts to reach consensus.

- The **European Parliament** was traditionally a consultative body, but over the years its powers have increased and it now legislates jointly with the Council. Since 1979 a system of direct election every five years has been used. The functions of the Parliament are: to be consulted during the legislative process and to use the power of amendment, and of veto in certain circumstances; to exercise budgetary powers; to grant assent to important agreements with third countries or international organizations; to exercise supervisory powers over the work of the Commission; to investigate alleged contraventions of EU law and to appoint an ombudsman; and to act as a forum for discussion.

- The **European Economic and Social Committee** and the **Committee of the Regions** are consulted during the legislative process.

- The **European Court of Justice** is responsible for interpreting EU law and adjudicating on disputes arising from the interpretation of the treaties and the legislation based upon them.

- The expenditure of all the EU institutions is subject to control by the Commission and European Parliament, and since 1977 to external control by the **Court of Auditors.**

- The **decision-making procedures** of the EU are the consultation procedure, the co-operation procedure, the co-decision procedure and the assent procedure. With the Lisbon Treaty the co-decision procedure became the ordinary legislative procedure.

- The question of allowing **flexibility or differentiated integration** is rendered more urgent as the increasing membership of the EU is bringing growing diversity. The Lisbon Treaty allows for **enhanced co-operation.**

Questions for study and review

1 Describe the organization and functioning of the European Commission. What are the main criticisms levelled against the Commission?
2 Why was it necessary to reform the system of voting in the Council of Ministers? What system of voting do you consider appropriate for the EU?
3 Explain the qualified majority system of the Council.
4 What are the advantages and disadvantages of having a longer-term European Council president?
5 Describe the European Parliament and indicate its main functions. What reforms are necessary to increase the democratic accountability of the European Parliament?
6 Explain the co-decision procedure. How has the role of the European Parliament in EU decision making changed over time?
7 How would you resolve the problem of languages in the EU?
8 Describe and criticize the reforms entailed by the Lisbon Treaty.
9 What are the dilemmas posed by flexibility or differentiated integration?
10 What measures could be taken to tackle the democratic deficit?
11 How do you envisage the future architecture of Europe?

Online
Learning **Centre**

When you have read this chapter, log on to the Online Learning Centre website at **www.mcgraw-hill.co.uk/textbooks/senior** to explore weblinks, chapter-by-chapter test questions, case studies and more online study tools.

Chapter **4**

The Theory of Trade and the EU

Learning Objectives

By the end of this chapter you should be able to understand:

- ✅ The main traditional arguments in favour of free trade (absolute advantage and comparative advantage)
- ✅ What we mean by the Heckscher–Ohlin theorem and the Heckscher–Ohlin–Samuelson theorem
- ✅ The implication of 'new' trade theories (intra-industry trade and product differentiation, static economies of scale, and the learning process)
- ✅ The effect of introducing a tariff in a small nation
- ✅ The effect of introducing a tariff in a large nation
- ✅ The impact of introduction of a tariff on the partner country
- ✅ What are the most frequently used non-tariff barriers to trade, and how they are applied by the EU
- ✅ The main arguments given in favour of protection
- ✅ What we mean by the political economy of protectionism

4.1 Introduction

The aim of this chapter is to introduce the different concepts used in the theory of trade, which will be used in the following chapter to explain integration. Integration is generally advocated for motives that are a mixture of politics and economics, and can perhaps be summarized as the desire to spread 'peace and prosperity', though other aims have also always played a role. The idea of using integration to avoid further wars in Europe ('peace') emerged clearly in the process of constructing the European Community in the years after the Second World War (see Chapter 2). Prosperity is generally associated with the benefits to be obtained by removing barriers to trade, and by permitting freedom of movement of goods, services, labour and capital.

In order to explain how integration is expected to lead to prosperity, it is first necessary to indicate the main arguments in favour of free trade. After a review of the classical concepts of absolute and comparative advantage, there is a brief discussion of the Heckscher–Ohlin–Samuelson framework. The second half of the chapter deals with protectionism, and, in particular, a description of the most commonly adopted obstacles to trade and the main arguments used to justify their introduction.

Then follows a brief review of some political economy explanations of the prevalence of protectionist measures. Those who are already familiar with international economics can skip this chapter and move straight to the analysis of integration in Chapter 5.

4.2   The main arguments in favour of free trade

Many of our arguments in favour of free trade still owe much to the work of the classical economists Adam Smith and David Ricardo.[1] These writers illustrated that trade between two countries could be mutually beneficial (a 'win–win' game, to use more recent terminology) thanks to the specialization of production. These theories were based on restrictive assumptions, and, when relaxed (as the section on globalization in Chapter 7 discusses), a wide literature suggests that while trade liberalization leads to overall gains, there may be winners and losers in the process. The evolution of the new trade theory essentially involves relaxing various of the assumptions.

4.3   Absolute advantage

Adam Smith illustrated the principle of absolute advantage, arguing that 'what is prudent in the conduct of every private family can scarce be folly in that of a great kingdom. A family will not make at home what it costs less to buy from outside. A taylor [sic] will not make his own shoes, but will buy them from a shoemaker.'

With two nations, if one country is more efficient in the production of one good, and less efficient in the production of another, then each country should specialize in the production of the good for which it has an absolute advantage. Part of the output of that country can be exchanged for the good for which it has an absolute disadvantage. In this way resources will be used in the most efficient way possible. For instance, according to this principle, in trade between the two countries, Ecuador should specialize in the export of bananas and Argentina in that of beef.

4.4   Comparative advantage

In practice, Smith's concept of absolute advantage explains only a small share of international trade. From this point of view, the concept of comparative advantage developed by David Ricardo is much more useful. According to the principle of comparative advantage, even when one country is less efficient in the production of both goods there is a basis for mutually beneficial trade. An example frequently given in the textbooks is that of Justice Holmes of the US Supreme Court. Justice Holmes was, apparently, a very speedy typist, and could type twice as fast as his secretary. She could earn $10 an hour with the amount she typed, but he could earn $20. However, he would receive $100 an hour from his legal activity, so it was in his interest to concentrate on that. With every hour he spent typing he would earn $20 but would forgo $100, so the net loss would be $80.

According to the principle of comparative advantage, even if one country has an absolute disadvantage in the production of both goods, it should specialize in the production and export of the good where its absolute disadvantage is smaller and import the product where its absolute disadvantage is greater. The country with an absolute advantage in the production in both goods should specialize in the production and export of the product where its absolute advantage is greater, and import the good for which its absolute advantage is smaller. Thus, for example, if the USA has an absolute advantage in the production of grain and clothing compared with the EU, but its absolute

---

[1] Smith's *Wealth of Nations* was published in 1776, while Ricardo's *Principles of Political Economy and Taxation* was published in 1817. See also the contribution of economists such as Petty, Law or Quesnay.

advantage is greater for grain, it should specialize in grain production, and export grain in exchange for clothing.

Comparative advantage still remains an important element of the toolkit in explaining the advantages of free trade, so it is useful to provide an example of how this principle works in practice. Ricardo based his approach on the labour theory of value, by which the price of a product is said to depend exclusively on the amount of labour used in its production. This theory requires:

- either that labour is the only factor used in making products, or that the ratio between labour and other factors such as land or capital is constant; and
- that labour is homogeneous and there are no differences in skills between people.

Clearly, these are extremely restrictive assumptions, and have been eliminated in most later evolutions of the theory.[2]

To illustrate the principle of comparative advantage it is useful to take a simple example with only two partners involved in trade, the EU and the USA, and two products, wheat and wine. It is assumed that with one hour of work a US labourer can produce 6 units (tonnes) of wheat, or 4 units (litres) of wine. With one hour of work an EU labourer can produce 1 unit of wheat or 2 units of wine (quality differences are ignored in this highly simplified model). The USA has an absolute advantage in the production of both goods, but its advantage is greater in the production of wheat. Similarly, the EU has a disadvantage in the production of both goods, but the disadvantage is less in the production of wine (see Table 4.1). In the USA, 6 units of wheat can be exchanged for 4 units of wine. If, in international trade, more than 4 units of wine can be obtained for 6 units of wheat, it is to the advantage of the USA. In the EU, 2 units of wine can be exchanged for 1 unit of wheat. If more wheat could be obtained, it would be to the advantage of the EU.

Table 4.1 Comparative advantage

	USA	EU
Wheat (tonnes produced in 1 labour-hour)	6	1
Wine (litres produced in 1 labour-hour)	4	2

Assume that with the opening of trade between the EU and USA it is possible to exchange 6 units of wine for 6 units of wheat. The EU will gain, because before the opening of trade 12 units of wine had to be given for 6 units of wheat and now only 6, so there is a saving of three labour-hours. The USA will also gain, as, before, 6 units of wheat could only be exchanged for 4 units of wine, but now it can obtain 6 units of wine, so there is a saving of 2 units of wine (30 minutes of labour).[3] If the EU is less efficient than the USA in the production of both goods, how can it export to the USA? The answer is that wages are lower in the EU, so that when the prices of the two products are expressed in the same currency, wine will be cheaper in the EU, and grain will cost less in the USA.

If the wage in the USA is $6 an hour, 1 unit of grain will cost $1 and 1 unit of wine will cost $1.50. If the wage in the EU is €2 per hour, then the price of a litre of wine is €1, and that of a tonne of grain is €2. With an exchange rate of $1 = €1, the prices in the EU will be $1 for a unit of wine, and $2 for a unit of grain. Traders will have an incentive to buy wine in the EU and trade it for grain in the USA. With an exchange rate of $0.5 per euro, the EU price would be $1 for grain and $0.5 for wine. There would be very strong pressure to sell EU wine in the USA, but no incentive to sell US grain in the EU. The value of the dollar against the euro would have to fall.

---

[2] See, for example, Salvatore (2010) or Krugman and Obstfeld (2011) for a discussion of this point.

[3] The only exception is the unlikely case in which the absolute disadvantage that one country has with respect to the other is the same for the two products. This would occur in the above example if the EU could produce 3 units of grain with one labour-hour.

With an exchange rate of $2 = €1, then the EU price would be $4 for grain, and $2 for wine. There would be very strong pressure to buy grain in the USA, but it would be impossible to sell EU wine to the USA, and so the euro rate against the dollar would have to fall.

4.5   The Heckscher–Ohlin theorem

Classical economists such as Ricardo explain the advantages of international trade on the basis of specialization according to comparative advantage, but fail to analyse in any detail what determines the comparative advantage of a country. Later developments in trade theory, and in particular, the Heckscher–Ohlin theorem, try to explain the pattern of comparative advantage between countries. In other words, why does a country have a comparative advantage in the production of a particular good? According to this approach, trade can be explained by the pattern of endowment of countries with different factors of production.

For purposes of simplification, the Heckscher–Ohlin theorem can be presented using a highly simplified case of two countries (1 and 2), two products (X and Y) and two factors (labour L and capital C). A country is said to have an abundance of a certain factor if the ratio of the total amount of one factor, say labour to capital, is higher than in the other country, and if the cost of labour relative to capital is less than in the other country.[4] If the production of one of the goods, say X, requires more labour relative to capital than the other good, then product X is said to be labour intensive. According to the Heckscher–Ohlin theorem, a country will export the commodity whose production is intensive of the factor in which the country is relatively abundant. For example, if China has an abundance of cheap labour, and the production of clothing is labour intensive, China will tend to export clothing. In contrast, if the USA has a factor abundance of capital (or skilled labour), and computers are intensive of capital (or skilled labour), China will specialize in textiles and import computers, while the USA will specialize in computers and import textiles.

This explanation works rather well in accounting for trade between countries with different endowments of factors of production such as land, labour or capital. For example, it may explain certain trade flows between developing and industrialized countries. However, it works less well for trade between similar countries, such as most of those of Western Europe.

Figure 4.1 can be used to illustrate the Heckscher–Ohlin theorem. Country 1 is assumed abundant in labour, while country 2 has an abundance of capital. Product X is assumed intensive of labour, while product Y is intensive of capital. In Figure 4.1, quantities of product X are indicated on the horizontal axis and quantities of product Y on the vertical axis.

The model is based on various simplifying assumptions.[5] The two countries are assumed to have the same technology and to be operating under conditions of perfect competition. They are also assumed to produce some of both goods X and Y, and production of both goods takes place with constant returns to scale. This implies that if the amount of inputs is increased in the production of a good, the amount of the good produced will increase by a proportional amount. The preferences of consumers are assumed to be identical in the two countries. All resources are used in each country (there is no unemployment in the factors of production). It is assumed that there is perfect mobility of factors of production within a country, but no mobility between countries. There are no transport costs or barriers to trade, such as tariffs. The exports and imports between the two countries are assumed to balance.

The production possibility frontier (PPF) shows the alternative combinations of the two products that a country can produce by fully utilizing its resources and making use of the best technology available. Each country must be on the production possibility curve to be in equilibrium, since points below the curve are inefficient, while points above cannot be reached. The slope of the production possibility curve in absolute terms indicates the opportunity cost of X, or the amount of Y which has to be given up to release enough resources to produce one additional unit of X. Under conditions of

---

[4] In case of conflict between the two criteria, the second is decisive.

[5] See Salvatore (2010) for a discussion of these assumptions and what happens when they are relaxed.

Figure 4.1 The Heckscher–Ohlin theorem

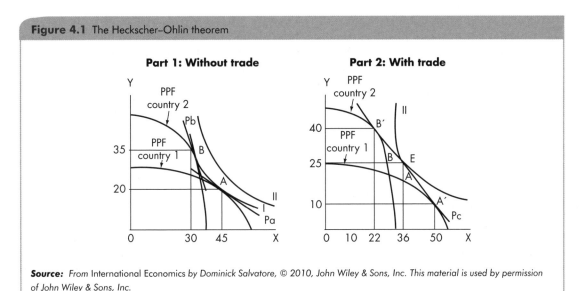

Source: From International Economics by Dominick Salvatore, © 2010, John Wiley & Sons, Inc. This material is used by permission of John Wiley & Sons, Inc.

perfect competition each country will produce a combination of the two goods such that opportunity cost is equal to the ratio of the prices of X and Y (Px/Py).

As shown in the diagram, the PPF for country 1 is flatter and wider than that for country 2. This is because country 1 has an abundance of labour, and product X is intensive of labour, so country 1 can produce a greater quantity of X than country 2.

The curves I and II are community indifference curves which show the various combinations of the two products that yield the same level of satisfaction or utility to a country.[6] Higher indifference curves indicate higher levels of satisfaction. For simplicity, in the example here, preferences of consumers in the two countries are assumed identical so the same collective indifference curves can be used for each.

The marginal rate of substitution (MRS) is the amount of good Y that the country has to give up in order to consume an additional unit of X while remaining on the same indifference curve. The MRS is given by the slope of an indifference curve in absolute terms at the point of consumption of the two goods. Moving down along the indifference curves shown in Figure 4.1, the MRS will decrease because of diminishing marginal utility. This implies that, after a certain point, increasing quantities of a good consumed yield smaller and smaller increases in utility.

In the absence of trade the equilibrium of each country is at the point where its production possibility curve is tangent to the highest collective indifference curve possible. This occurs at A for country 1 and at B for country 2. Country 1 will produce and consume 45 X and 20 Y, while country 2 will produce and consume 30 X and 35 Y. The tangent of the PPF and highest indifference curve at point A indicates the relative price – Px/Py of the two goods, or Pa, in country 1. Similarly, the relative price of the two goods in country 2 is Pb. In country 1 the relative price of X is lower (Pa is less than Pb in absolute terms) than in country 2 and country 1 has a comparative advantage in the production of X, while country 2 has a comparative advantage in the production of Y.

With trade (see part 2 of Figure 4.1) it will be to the benefit of country 1 to export good X to country 2 in exchange for good Y. Country 1 will therefore specialize in the production of X, moving down its production possibility curve to the right. As it does so, the increasing slope of the production possibility curve implies that the opportunity cost of X will rise, and the price of X relative to Y will increase.

---

[6] A discussion of the well-known problems with collective indifference curves is beyond the scope of the analysis here.

Without trade, the price of Y relative to X in country 2 is lower than in country 1. With trade, country 2 has an advantage in specializing in the production of Y, moving up along its production curve and selling Y to country 1 in exchange for X. In this case the price of X relative to Y will fall (or, in other words, the price of Y relative to X will rise) in country 2.

This process of specialization will continue until the relative price Px/Py is the same in both countries. This occurs when production of the two goods reaches A' in country 1 and B' in country 2. At this point, country 1 produces 50 X and 10 Y. Country 2 produces 22 X and 40 Y. At the relative price Pc country 1 will export 14 X in exchange for 15 Y from country 2. In this way both countries reach equilibrium at E in part 2 of the diagram, where they consume 36 X and 25 Y. Both countries benefit from trade since they can reach the higher indifference curve II.

4.6   The Heckscher–Ohlin–Samuelson theorem

According to the Heckscher–Ohlin–Samuelson theorem, the liberalization of trade will bring about the equalization of relative and absolute returns to the factors of production between countries or regions. This theorem is a corollary of the Heckscher–Ohlin theorem explained above and is based on the same restrictive assumptions.

Returning to the model used above, as country 1 (China) specializes in the production of X (which is labour intensive) and reduces the production of Y (which is capital intensive), the demand for labour relative to capital will rise. This will cause the price of labour (w, or wages) relative to that of capital (r, or the interest rate) to rise. Country 1 is labour abundant, so initially the price of labour relative to capital is lower than in country 2, but with trade the relative price for labour will rise in country 1. The opposite will occur in country 2 (the USA). As country 2 specializes in the production of Y the demand for capital relative to labour will rise and so too will r relative to w. Trade will continue until the relative prices of the two factors are the same in the two countries.

Figure 4.2 can be used to illustrate this process. The vertical axis indicates the price of product X relative to product Y (Px/Py). The horizontal axis shows the price of labour relative to the price of

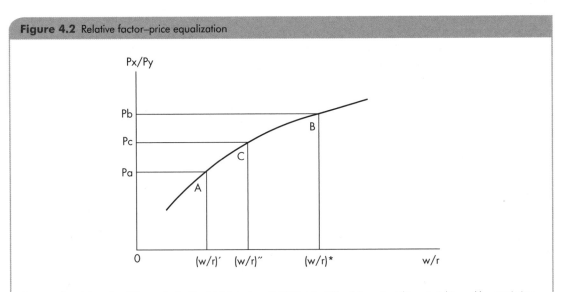

Figure 4.2 Relative factor–price equalization

Source: From International Economics by Dominick Salvatore, © 2010, John Wiley & Sons, Inc. This material is used by permission of John Wiley & Sons, Inc.

capital (w/r). It is assumed that there is perfect competition, and that both countries use the same technology, so each value of Px/Py is associated with one and only one value of w/r.

Before trade, country 1 is at point A, with w/r = (w/r)' and Px/Py = Pa. Country 2 is at B with Px/Py = Pb and w/r = (w/r)".With trade, country 1 specializes in the production of X, causing Px/Py and w/r to rise. Country 2 specializes in Y, causing Px/Py (which is the inverse of Py/Px) to fall, so causing a reduction in w/r. The process will contine until both countries are at C, where Px/Py = Pc and w/r = (w/r)*.

So far what has been demonstrated is how trade leads to equalization of the relative price for the two factors in the two countries. Given the assumptions of the model (perfect competition in the product and factor markets, constant returns to scale and that both countries use the same technology), trade will also lead to the equalization of absolute factor prices. In other words, the real wage and the real rate of interest will be the same in the two countries.

Trade can therefore be said to act as a substitute for the international mobility of factors. With perfect mobility, labour would move from where wages are lower to where they are higher until wages are the same in both countries. Similarly, capital would move from where interest rates are lower to where they are higher until interest rates are the same in both countries. There is, however, a difference between trade and factor mobility. Trade acts on the demand for factors of production, whereas factor mobility acts on their supply.

4.7 New trade theories

Given the very restrictive assumption of the traditional framework, there is now a rapidly expanding literature on the 'new trade theory', which tries to go beyond the efficiency gains from reallocating resources according to comparative advantage. These theories are more eclectic than the elegant traditional framework and incorporate a wide variety of elements. For instance, though the discussion here cannot be exhaustive, different strands of this literature attempt to accommodate aspects such as:

- imperfect competition and product differentiation (see below);
- political economy arguments (see the discussions at the end of this chapter and in Chapter 5);
- new growth theory (see Chapter 5);
- the New Economic Geography (see Chapter 15); and
- open-economy macroeconomics (see Chapter 11).

4.8 Intra-industry trade and product differentiation

A large percentage (70–80 per cent in many cases) of trade between EU countries consists of exports and imports of the same product or group of products. For instance Italy exports Fiat, and imports BMW from Germany and Renault from France. This is known as **intra-industry trade** and arises when products are substitutes for each other but are slightly different (see Box 4.1 and Grimwade (2000) for a more detailed discussion of this topic). This kind of **product differentiation** means that a firm or plant can specialize in a few varieties of the product, making use of longer production runs, more specialized machinery and labour, and so on. Other varieties of the product can be imported. As a result, consumers may have a wider range of products available at lower prices. The products are differentiated but similar and therefore substitutes.[7]

---

[7] Models of monopolistic competition are frequently used to analyse this type of market.

Box 4.1

The Grubel–Lloyd index

One of the most widely used measures of intra-industry trade is the Grubel–Lloyd index:

$$T = 1 - \frac{|X - M|}{(X + M)}$$

where X and M represent respectively the exports and imports of a particular commodity group i. The straight-line parentheses indicate that the value is in absolute terms. T may take values between 0 and 1. If T is zero there is no intra-industry trade, and the countries are specialized in different product categories indicating inter-industry trade. If T is 1 all trade is intra-industry, and the countries are specialized in the same product categories.

The index is frequently calculated using the Standard International Trade Classification (SITC). This breaks trade down by product category, and the number of digits indicates the level of disaggregation (00, 001, 0015, etc.). One of the difficulties in using the Grubel–Lloyd index is that the results may reflect the level of disaggregation of the statistics used.

A further shortcoming of the index is that products within the same classification group may be very different in terms of quality. Distinction is therefore sometimes made between vertical intra-industry trade (reflecting quality differences) and horizontal intra-industry trade in products of similar quality.

4.9   Static economies of scale

Static economies of scale occur when an increase in the use of inputs results in a more than proportional increase in output. In other words, the unit costs of production fall as the scale of production rises. This may arise, for example, from the use of more specialized machinery, or from the division of labour with workers specializing in the tasks they perform. A classic example is the assembly-line production introduced by Henry Ford.

Figure 4.3 can be used to illustrate how mutually beneficial trade between countries can arise from economies of scale.[8] The same highly simplified model is based on two countries, 1 and 2, and two products, X and Y, and two factors of production are used. In Figure 4.3, quantities of product X are indicated on the horizontal axis and quantities of product Y on the vertical axis. The two countries are assumed to be identical in all respects so the same PPF B′B in Figure 4.3 can be used for both of them. In the case of economies of scale, the production possibility curve is convex to the origin. The two countries are assumed identical, so the same indifference curves can be used for both.

The equilibrium position before trade, A, will therefore be identical for both countries. At A, each country is at the point where the production possibility curve is tangent to the highest collective indifference curve possible. At A, both countries can produce and consume 40 units of X and 40 units of Y. The equilibrium point before trade, A, is not stable since if, for any reason, one of the countries, say country 1, increased its production of X, the price of X relative to Y would fall, and the country would move along its **production curve** until it became fully specialized in the production of X (producing only X and no Y) at point B. In the same way, if for some reason country 2 increased its production of Y, it would continue moving up and left along its PPF until it became fully specialized in

---

[8] The analysis here is based on Salvatore (2010).

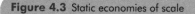

Figure 4.3 Static economies of scale

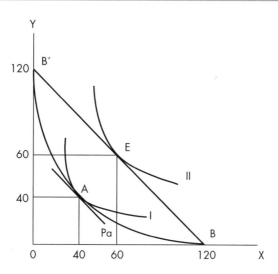

Source: From International Economics by Dominick Salvatore, © 2010, John Wiley & Sons, Inc. This material is used by permission of John Wiley & Sons, Inc.

the production of Y at B′. As the two countries are assumed identical, it is purely a matter of accident which country specializes in the production of which good.

At the equilibrium point B, country 1 produces 120 units of X, while at B′ country 2 produces 120 units of Y. With trade, country 1 could exchange 60 units of X for 60 units of Y and move to the new equilibrium point E that is on the higher collective indifference curve II. Similarly, country 2 could sell 60 Y for 60 X and also move to E. As a result of specialization based on economies of scale and trade, both countries gain 20 X and 20 Y compared with the equilibrium point A. This is a highly simplified model, and in practice the two countries do not have to be identical to draw mutual benefit from trade based on economies of scale.

4.10 The learning process

Dynamic economies of scale are associated with the learning process. This process entails that a firm will have a unit cost advantage because of the experience it acquires through cumulative production of goods and services. The fall in cost may be due to technological improvements, better organizational structures and/or better performance of workers. For example, the experience gained by McDonald's in producing hamburgers (how many billion sold?) enables it to compete against new firms attempting to enter the market and facing much higher initial costs. In contrast to static economies of scale, these dynamic economies of scale are independent of the degree of capacity utilization of the firm and accrue as a function of cumulative output. The firm that first moves down the 'learning' curve of a strategic industry will gain a cost advantage over its competitors. The existence of these experience economies may render it difficult for new entrants to enter the market. According to strategic trade theory (see below), there may be a case for subsidizing or protecting strategic industries to help

domestic firms move down the learning curve first. Economic policy should also ensure that markets are on an adequate scale to allow such learning effects to be exploited. Figure 4.4 illustrates a learning or experience curve, where Cn is the cost of the nth unit produced.[9]

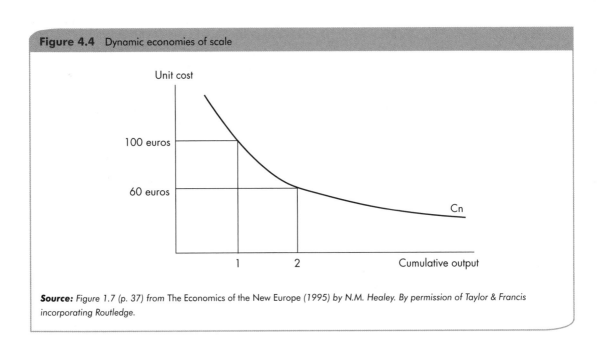

Figure 4.4 Dynamic economies of scale

Source: Figure 1.7 (p. 37) from The Economics of the New Europe (1995) by N.M. Healey. By permission of Taylor & Francis incorporating Routledge.

4.11 Tariffs

In most economic textbooks the discussion of the theory of trade policies begins with an analysis of tariffs.[10] This is because at least up until the First World War it was widely accepted that if trade barriers were introduced for protectionist purposes they should be confined to tariffs (see Box 4.2). In the GATT/WTO context (see Chapter 18), tariffs are considered the 'lesser evil' compared with other trade barriers because they are more transparent. The GATT/WTO favours the conversion of other non-tariff barriers (NTBs) into tariffs.

An import tariff is a tax or duty levied on a product when it is imported into a country. Tariffs can be ad valorem, specific or compound. An ad valorem tariff entails a percentage increase in the price of the imported product. If, for example, p is the price of the good before the tariff, when a tariff rate t is applied the price will become $(1 + t)p$. A 10 per cent tariff on a bicycle worth €100 would increase the price of the bicycle in the importing country to €110. Ad valorem tariffs are the type most frequently used by the EU. A specific tariff is a fixed lump sum levied on an import. For instance, a specific tariff of €5 would increase the price of the bicycle to €105. The USA uses both ad valorem and specific tariffs. A compound tariff combines an ad valorem and a specific tariff. With a 10 per cent ad valorem tariff and a specific tariff of €5, the price of the imported bicycle would rise to €115.

---

[9] This example is taken from Healey (1995).

[10] The discussion here is restricted to tariffs on imports. With the food shortages and high agricultural prices in 2008 many developing countries also used tariffs on exports. See Chapter 13 for a similar type of analysis of the economic effects of export subsidies.

Tariff levels

As explained in Chapter 2, the Treaty of Rome envisaged the elimination of tariffs on trade between member states, and the EU met this objective six months ahead of schedule in 1968. The EU continues to apply tariffs (the common external tariff) on trade with third countries, but over time the level of these tariffs has shrunk as a consequence of the various GATT rounds (see Chapter 18 and the Online Learning Centre of this book).

Though difficult to measure in practice, the average level of world tariffs effectively applied has fallen substantially from roughly 40 per cent in 1948 to a simple unweighted mean for all products of 7 per cent in 2008 according to the World Bank.[11] Problems arise in calculating average tariff rates, for a number of reasons: actual tariffs are often lower than the rates 'bound' by GATT agreements; in order to calculate averages, account has to be taken of weights of the good in trade; in practice there are likely to be exceptions to non-discrimination (that is, to most favoured nation treatment; see Chapter 18); if tariffs are too high they are prohibitive and no trade will take place, and tariffs change over time.

4.12 The economic effects of introducing a tariff in a 'small nation'

In order to analyse the economic effects of a tariff on imports, it is useful to make certain simplifying assumptions. The analysis here is partial equilibrium in that it only considers the market of the good on which the tariff is levied, ignoring the implications for other economic sectors or for factor markets. It is assumed that there are no stocks of the product, and transport costs or possible externalities are not taken into account.

For simplicity, the discussion here relates to an ad valorem tariff so, if p is the price of the good before the tariff, when a tariff rate t is applied, the price will become $(1 + t)p$. Initially it is assumed that the country is a 'small nation', so that any changes in its supply or demand for that product will have no impact on the international terms of trade or world price level for that product.

The demand and supply curves (assumed linear for simplicity) of a country for the traded good in question are shown in Figure 4.5. Prior to the introduction of the tariff, the domestic price of the product in the country is assumed equal to the world price Pw. At this price the country will produce Qs and demand Qd of the product. The country will therefore import Qd – Qs (equivalent to the excess demand) of the product.

With the introduction of the tariff t the domestic price for the product will rise to $(1 + t)Pw$, or Pd in the diagram. Assuming a small nation, the world price will remain unchanged at Pw. The new higher internal price will be Pd. The introduction of the tariff will entail the following effects on demand, supply and foreign trade:

- The quantity demanded will decline from Qd to Q'd;
- The quantity supplied will increase from Qs to Q's;
- The quantity imported will fall from (Qd – Qs) to (Q'd – Q's).

The tariff will also have the following 'financial' effects:

[11] Trading Economics, http://www.tradingeconomics.com/world/tariff-rate-applied-simple-mean-all-products-percent-wb-data.html (accessed 3 March 2011).

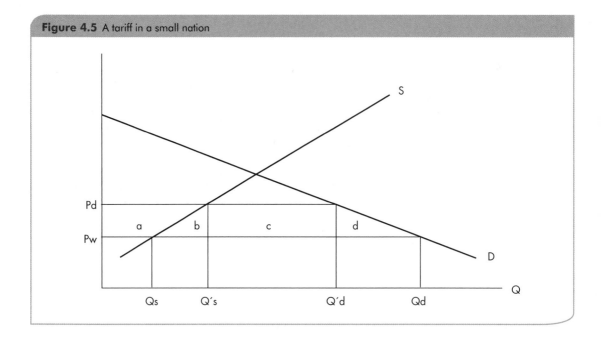

Figure 4.5 A tariff in a small nation

- Consumer expenditure on the product will change from QdPw before introduction of the tariff to Q'dPd with the tariff;
- Producer revenue will increase from QsPw before the tariff to Q'sPd after the tariff is introduced;
- The trade balance (or, in this case, the amount spent on imports) will improve from (Qs – Qd)Pw to (Q's – Q'd)Pw.

Introduction of the tariff will redistribute welfare between the three main groups in society: taxpayers, consumers and producers. In order to assess these effects, it is first necessary to introduce two concepts: consumer and producer surplus.

Consumer rent or **surplus** is defined as the difference between the price a consumer is prepared to pay for a certain quantity of a product and the price that is effectively paid for that quantity. This concept may be applied to an individual consumer or to the overall demand curve in a particular market. As shown in Figure 4.6, with a demand curve D and price 0A, consumer surplus is indicated by the triangle ABC.

Producer rent is the difference between the total revenue and total cost of the producer and can be considered as the profits of the producer. Ignoring fixed costs, the total cost of producing a certain quantity is given by the area under the marginal cost curve (which coincides with the supply curve). As mentioned above, producer revenue is given by the price received by the producer multiplied by the quantity produced. In Figure 4.7, with a supply curve S and price 0F, producer revenue is equal to 0FGQ and total cost is 0HGQ, so that producer rent is indicated by the triangle HFG.

The introduction of the tariff will alter consumer and producer surplus and the income of taxpayers. The tariff entails an increase in the price received by producers so, as Figure 4.5 above shows, there is an increase in producer surplus equivalent to area a. The consumers also have to pay a higher price for the product, so there will be a reduction in consumer surplus equivalent to area a + b + c + d. There is an increase in government revenue of area c.

The tariff is a source of revenue for the government budget.[12] The total revenue for the budget will be equal to the unit value of the tariff (Pd – Pw) multiplied by the quantity imported after

---

[12] See the discussion on the sources of revenue of the EU budget in Chapter 12.

Figure 4.6 Consumer surplus

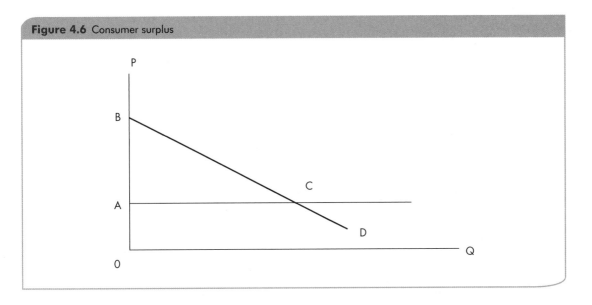

introduction of the tariff (Q'd – Qs). In Figure 4.5 this corresponds to the area of the rectangle c, or (Pd – Pw) × (Q'd – Q's). If this revenue is used in a socially useful way, it represents a welfare benefit to the country. This benefit could be considered an increase in the income of taxpayers in that, *ceteris paribus*, in the absence of the tariff the government would have to impose higher taxes to obtain the same amount of revenue. It is, however, possible that the revenue from the tariff is not used in

Figure 4.7 Producer surplus

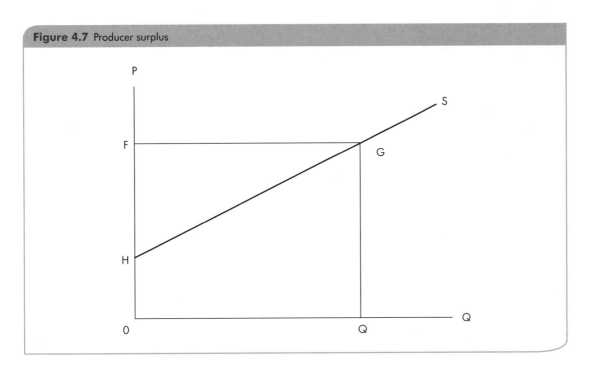

a socially useful way. For instance, a share of the revenue may be used to cover the administrative costs of levying the duty, and government funds spent in this way represent a net welfare loss to the community.

In order to calculate the overall net welfare effect of the tariff, it is necessary to assume that value of each euro lost by any individual is the same as that of any euro gained, regardless of who undergoes the loss or gain. With this assumption it can be seen that only part of the loss in consumer surplus is compensated by the gain in producer rent and the increase in government revenue. The net welfare cost of the tariff is indicated by the two triangles b and d in Figure 4.5.

Triangle b represents the net economic cost on the production side. It reflects the worsening in the allocation of resources as a result of introduction of the tariff. Triangle d represents the net welfare cost on the consumption side, because the tariff raises the price of the good relative to other products, causing a distortion in consumption. A numerical example of the effects of introducing a tariff in a small nation is included in Appendix 1.

4.13   The effect of introducing a production subsidy

Subsidies on domestic production may also distort competition and act as a barrier to trade. The difference between a tariff and a producer subsidy can be seen from Figure 4.8. The main difference between a tariff and a producer subsidy is that the introduction of producer subsidies leaves the domestic price unchanged for consumers. As Figure 4.8 shows, with the producer subsidy the domestic price to producers rises to Pd, while the price paid by consumers remains Pw. Producer surplus rises by area a, the cost of the surplus to budget contributors is area a + b (that is, the unit cost of the subsidy, Pd – Pw times the new quantity of output Q's). The net welfare loss is triangle b.

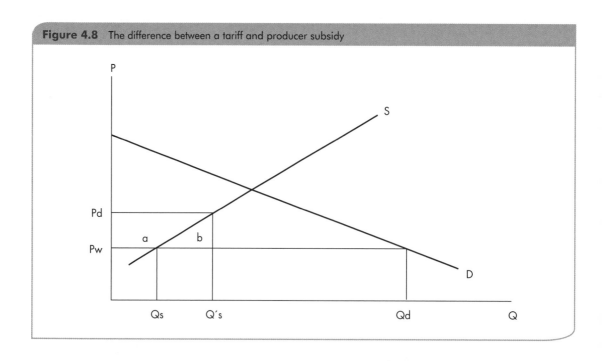

Figure 4.8   The difference between a tariff and producer subsidy

4.14 The effect of introducing a tariff in a 'large nation'

In Figure 4.5 it was assumed that introducing a tariff would leave the world price for the product unchanged. However, it is possible that the introduction of a tariff will lower the world price for a product. The tariff raises the domestic price for that product, increasing production and reducing consumption. The country will therefore import less after the tariff is introduced, reducing the demand for that product on world markets. The *ceteris paribus* clause implies that supply on world markets remains unchanged. If that country accounts for a large share of world trade, the reduction in net imports for the product, with supply on world markets unchanged, will reduce the price on world markets. The assumption that the country is a 'large nation' implies that the introduction (or removal) of a policy such as a tariff will affect the price for that product on world markets or, in other words, that country's terms of trade.

If, as in the case being considered here, the country is a net importer, the reduction in world price will constitute a net welfare gain for that country. In other words there will be a transfer from exporters in the rest of the world to that country. This situation is shown in Figure 4.9. In the diagram, the introduction of a tariff leads to a reduction in the world price level to P'w. As a result, the internal price after introduction of the tariff will be P'd, or $(1 + t)$P'w, which is less than $(1 + t)$Pw.

In this case the reduction in consumer surplus is indicated by area $f + g + h + k$; the increase in producer rent is area f. The increase in government revenue is area h, which represents a transfer from internal consumers (because of the higher domestic price now paid) and area m, which consists of a transfer from producers in the rest of the world (because of the lower world price which they now receive).

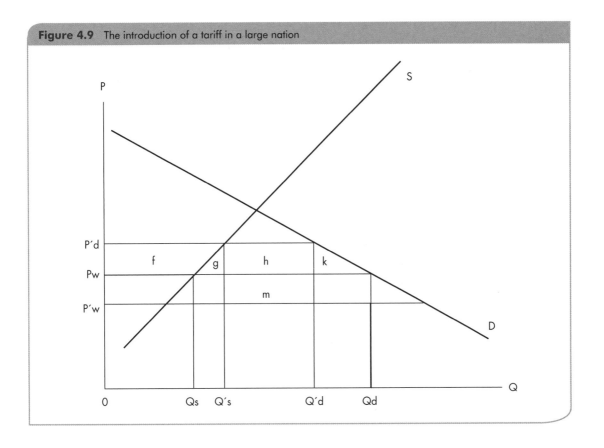

Figure 4.9 The introduction of a tariff in a large nation

The net welfare effect for the country introducing the tariff now consists of: the net welfare cost on the consumption side, triangle k; the net welfare cost on the production side, triangle g, and a net welfare gain, rectangle m, which represents transfers from the rest of the world.

It is possible that the net welfare gain represented by rectangle m outweighs the net welfare loss represented by the two triangles g and k. In this case the introduction of a tariff entails an increase in net welfare for the country. This has encouraged countries to seek the so-called optimal tariff, which leads to the maximum increase in net welfare possible for the country imposing a tariff (see below). A numerical example of the effects of introducing a tariff in a large nation is included in Appendix 2.

4.15 The effects of introducing a tariff on the exporting country

It is useful to show the effects of introducing a tariff by the home country on an exporting country.[13] For simplicity it is assumed that there is only one foreign country (called 'foreign'). The two countries are assumed to be small nations and have increasing production costs.[14] Figure 4.10a illustrates the demand and supply curves in the home country, and Figure 4.10b illustrates MDh, or the home import demand for X. At price P′ home supply equals home demand and there is no import demand for X. At price P″ home demand exceeds home supply of X by HJ, and this is equal to import demand 0M.

Figure 4.11a illustrates the supply and demand curves for X of the foreign country that are used to derive the export supply of X by the foreign country XSf in part (b) of the figure. At price P′ demand and supply are in equilibrium on the foreign market, and foreign export supply is zero. At price P″ foreign supply exceeds foreign demand by amount FG of product X, and foreign export supply 0H

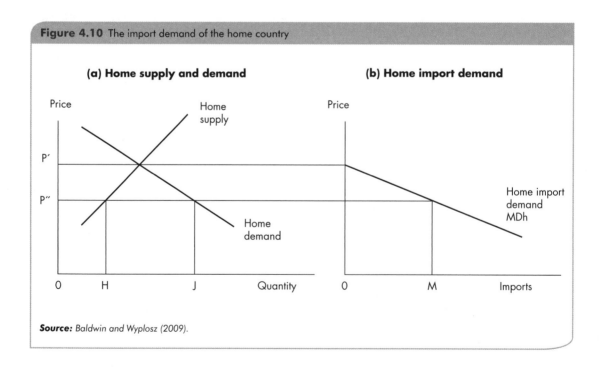

Figure 4.10 The import demand of the home country

(a) Home supply and demand

(b) Home import demand

Source: Baldwin and Wyplosz (2009).

---

[13] The discussion here follows Baldwin and Wyplosz (2009).

[14] The analysis is extended to the case of a large nation in Chapter 5.

Figure 4.11 The import supply of the home country, or the export supply of the foreign country

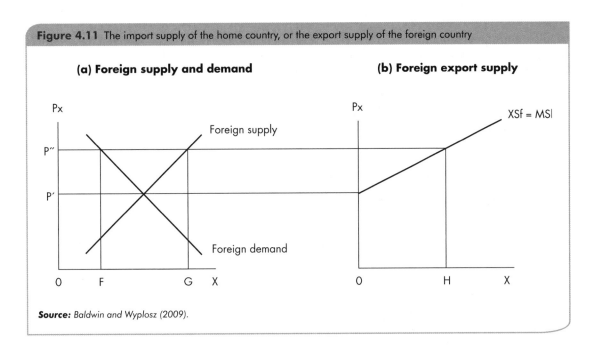

Source: Baldwin and Wyplosz (2009).

is equal to FG. In the simple two-country model, foreign export supply XSf is equal to home import supply, so can be labelled MSh.

The left-hand part of Figure 4.12 shows the export supply of X by the foreign country, while the right-hand part combines the import demand and import supply for X in the home country and

Figure 4.12 The effect of a tariff on the home and foreign countries

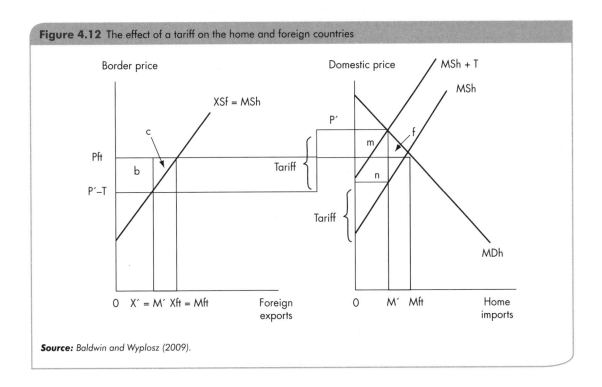

Source: Baldwin and Wyplosz (2009).

shows the effect of the tariff T on home imports and foreign exports. The tariff raises the price faced by home consumers and producers from Pft to P′. The border price or the price received by foreigners falls to P′ – T. The volume of imports falls from Mft (or Xft exports where ft stands for free trade) to M′ (which is equal to X′).

The welfare loss from the tariff to the foreign country is rectangle b (because of the lower price received) and triangle c (because of loss of sales). The home country receives a welfare gain from tariff revenue equal to the unit value of the tariff (t) times the volume of imports M′, indicated by rectangles m and n. The loss in private surplus (that is, the sum of changes in consumer and producer surplus) is equal to areas f and m. The overall impact on welfare for the home country is therefore area n minus area f. In terms of the analysis of the effects of a tariff above, triangle f is equal to the sum of triangles b and d in Figure 4.5.

4.16 Non-tariff barriers and the 'new protectionism'

Despite the success of the GATT in reducing tariffs, from the 1970s international trade became increasingly subject to NTBs, in what is referred to as the 'new protectionism'. In particular, the Uruguay Round attempted to extend the jurisdiction of GATT regulations to cover these NTBs. The following list includes some of the main NTBs, but does not pretend to be exhaustive:[15]

- quotas on imports;
- voluntary export restraint agreements;
- cartels;
- anti-dumping duties;
- export subsidies;
- differences in standards and technical specifications, and administrative measures;
- discrimination in public procurement.

A **quota on imports** is a quantitative restriction imposed by the state on imports of a particular product. The quota may entail a limit on all imports of a particular product (or group of products) or it may relate to imports of a product from a particular country or group of countries. In general, a system of import quotas is implemented through the granting of import licences. In principle the GATT/WTO forbids quotas on imports, but in practice various exceptions have been allowed (see Box 4.3).

Box 4.3

EU quotas

The EU applies seasonal quotas to the imports of some agricultural products. Quotas on the imports of certain textiles and clothing were applied under the Multifibre Agreement, though these had to be phased out by January 2005 in line with the GATT Uruguay Round Agreement (see Chapter 18 and the Online Learning Centre of this book), though in some cases they were replaced with anti-dumping measures. Another exception permitted by the GATT was on imports from non-market economies, so the Community applied quotas on the imports of certain goods (such as footwear, glass products, some agricultural goods and so on) from the former centrally planned countries of Central and Eastern Europe. These were eliminated as part of the trade concessions granted from 1989 on.*

* See Senior Nello (1991) for a description of how these quotas operated, and their elimination.

---

[15] For reasons of space a formal analysis of these various measures based on the use of diagrams is not included here. For studies of this type see, for example, Salvatore (2010) or Krugman and Obstfeld (2011).

The economic effects of a quota on imports can be analysed using Figure 4.13. In the absence of the quota on imports it is assumed that a particular country imports quantity Qd – Qs at world price P_w. If the state introduces a quota limiting the quantity of imports to Q'd – Q's, the domestic price will rise to Pd because there is excess domestic demand for the product. Assuming perfect competition, the effect of the quota on the domestic price, quantity produced, quantity demanded and level of imports will therefore be the same as that of a tariff that increases the domestic price level from Pw to Pd (see Figure 4.5)

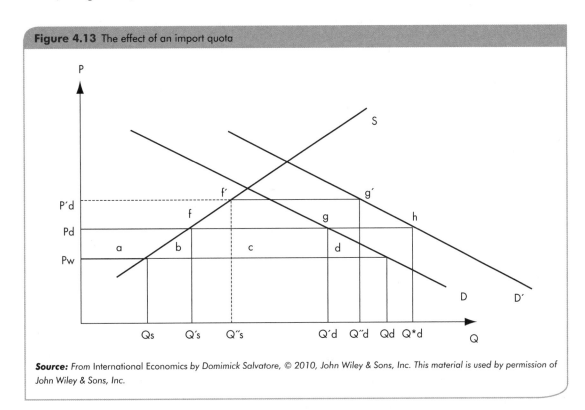

Figure 4.13 The effect of an import quota

Source: From International Economics by Domimick Salvatore, © 2010, John Wiley & Sons, Inc. This material is used by permission of John Wiley & Sons, Inc.

If the assumption of perfect competition is relaxed, there is a possibility that the introduction of an import quota converts a potential monopoly into an actual monopoly. The quota will have the effect of protecting the domestic firm(s) from foreign competition. In the case of a tariff, domestic producers cannot raise prices above Pw without losing their market share because domestic consumers will prefer to buy imports.

One of the main differences between a quota on imports and a tariff relates to government revenue. In the case of a tariff, which raises the domestic price to Pd, the state benefits from the customs duties indicated by rectangle c in Figure 4.13 (see also Figure 4.5 above). For a quota, those holding import licences can generally appropriate the benefits indicated by rectangle c.

It is also possible that the state can acquire part of the revenue from the quota by organizing an auction of the import licences. With perfect competition and an efficient auction, the revenue to the state from an import quota Qd – Qs and a tariff Pd – Pw would be the same. However, while such a result is in theory possible, in practice it is unlikely to occur.

In the case of a shift of the demand curve from D to D', the quota limiting imports to amount Q'd – Q's (or g – f) would cause an increase of the domestic price to P'd, with imports of Q"d – Q"s (equal to g' – f' or Q'd – Q's). In contrast, with a shift of the demand curve from D to D' and a tariff that increases domestic prices from Pw to Pd the amount of imports would increase to h – f (or Q*d – Q's), while the domestic price would remain Pd.

The question that inevitably arises is why a government should introduce a quota rather than a tariff when it stands to lose a source of revenue. The reply probably lies in the fact that the quota on imports offers a better guarantee that the quantity of imports will be limited. Though in theory the same restriction on imports could be achieved through a tariff, this requires knowledge of the position and slope of the demand and supply curves for the product. In practice such knowledge is rarely forthcoming, and moreover the demand and supply curves are subject to frequent shifts.

Voluntary export restraint agreements (VERs) entail an export restriction which in formal terms was imposed unilaterally by the exporting country, but in practice was usually introduced in response to pressure from the government or industry in the importing country (see Box 4.4).[16] VERs were essentially bilaterally negotiated agreements. The export restraint involved could operate through quotas and/or minimum export prices. Although these arrangements appear to be an improvement on the autonomous setting of policy, it must be questioned how far they were in fact 'voluntary'. Often the exporter had to accept the demands made by the importing country or risk the unilateral imposition of a tariff, quota or anti-dumping measures against its products. The GATT Uruguay Round Agreement required VERs to be phased out by 1999.[17]

Box 4.4

Voluntary export restraint agreements

VERs were used by the EU and USA to limit exports of steel, electronic products, cars and other products, in particular from Japan, Central and Eastern Europe and Korea. Following the 1973 oil crisis there was a sharp drop in the demand for steel, and the Community threatened its major suppliers with anti-dumping measures unless they signed VERs. The Community applied VERs on steel, textiles and some agricultural products from most of the smaller Central and Eastern European countries during the 1970s and 1980s.

VERs were probably less effective than quotas in limiting the quantity of imports, as exporters were generally reluctant to cut their market share. VERs also tended to lead to a continual upgrading of products since the limit on quantity encouraged exporters to supply products of higher quality and price. As the VER usually applied to the main supplier, at times there was a tendency to switch to other exporters, or even for the main supplier to redirect exports through other countries.

An international **cartel** is an agreement between suppliers in different countries to restrict production and exports in order to increase their prices and profits. Perhaps the most famous example of a cartel is that of OPEC (Organization of the Petroleum Exporting Countries; see Box 4.5). The

---

[16] Orderly marketing arrangements (OMAs) were a sub-category of VERs involving government-to-government arrangements.VERs also included agreements with the direct participation of industry.

[17] Figure 4.5, which was used to illustrate the effects of a tariff, can also be applied to the case of a voluntary export restriction. The example again is of an importing country, which is assumed to be a small nation. Prior to introduction of the VER, at the world price level of Pw, imports amount to Qd – Qs. With the VER the quantity imported is reduced to Q'd – Q's, and the price in the importing country rises to Pd. In the case both of a tariff and of a quota, rectangle c represents a benefit for the importing country (for the state in the case of a tariff and for the holders of import licences for a quota). In contrast, in the case of a VER, rectangle c represents a benefit for the exporting country. This is one of the reasons why an exporting country generally, preferred a VER to a tariff or quota.

A further difference between VERs and quotas arises in that the application of the VER may cause producers in the exporting country to form a cartel This may occur if, for example, the government leaves responsibility for the allocation of export quotas to the sector in question. The formation of a monopoly cartel may lead to producers in the exporting country exporting less at a higher price than the quantitative restriction fixed by the VER. Under such circumstances the VER offers a higher level of protection for the importing country (a smaller quantity of imports at higher prices) than an import quota applying the same quantitative limit as the VER.

USA prohibits cartels between national producers but, as explained in Chapter 16, in the EU they are simply heavily regulated.[18]

Box 4.5

OPEC

The Organization of the Petroleum Exporting Countries (OPEC) is probably the most famous example of an international cartel. OPEC was founded in Iraq in 1960, and meets regularly to discuss prices and, since 1982, to set crude oil production quotas. Original OPEC members were Iran, Iraq, Kuwait, Saudi Arabia and Venezuela. Subsequently, the organization expanded to include Qatar (1961), Indonesia (1962), Libya (1962), the United Arab Emirates (1967) Algeria (1969) and Nigeria (1971). Ecuador and Gabon were members of OPEC, but Ecuador withdrew in 1992, and Gabon left in 1995. Although Iraq remains a member of OPEC, Iraqi production has not been a part of any OPEC quota agreements since March 1998.

Dumping consists essentially in the practice of international price discrimination, when the price charged by an exporter to a foreign market is lower than the domestic price for that product. Distinction is frequently made between sporadic, predatory and persistent dumping.

As the name suggests, sporadic dumping occurs occasionally when, because of a change in the pattern of demand or an error in production plans, a firm finds itself with an unsold surplus. Rather than risking disruption of the domestic market, the firm will sell this surplus at a low price abroad. In this case below-cost sales may occur. Predatory dumping is aimed at eliminating competing firms from international markets. The firm will charge low prices in order to drive its competitor(s) out of the market. Even though this may entail setting prices below costs for a time, the firm will be able to raise prices again once the competitor has been eliminated. Persistent dumping is practised by a producer with monopoly power who attempts to use price discrimination between different markets in order to maximize profits. This price discrimination is possible only if the markets are separate, for instance as a result of incomplete information, transport costs, trade barriers and so on. In other words, re-trading between the individual markets is impossible.

If dumping is found to cause injury or threat of injury to domestic producers, the WTO regulations permit a country to impose an **anti-dumping duty** (see Box 4.6). A frequent complaint is that countries may use anti-dumping duties as an instrument of protectionism.

Export subsidies may involve giving direct payments, tax breaks or low interest loans to exporters, subsidized loans to foreign purchasers, and assistance in export promotion (through advertising, trade fairs, meetings and so on). Though export subsidies are subject to a general ban by the WTO, in practice there are many exceptions to this rule. These include the agricultural export subsidies for which the EU is highly criticized by its trading partners (see Chapter 13). The WTO permits the granting of credits to clients by exporting firms and government-backed guarantees for certain risks to foreign direct investment, though the Organisation for Economic Co-operation and Development (OECD) tries to ensure that these are not used to promote domestic firms in an unfair way.[19] Countries sometimes use tax breaks to promote exports, but the WTO ruled against the system of Foreign Sales Corporations used by the USA (see the Online Learning Centre of this book).

Technical restrictions and standards and other administrative regulations may act as barriers to trade. These include safety regulations (for instance for electrical equipment), health regulations (in

---

[18] Chapter 16 also contains a formal analysis of the effects of a cartel.

[19] Export credit subsidies and foreign investment guarantees are generally granted by special government-backed agencies. In France, for example, there is the Banque Française pour le Commerce Extérieur, and in Britain, the Export Credit Guarantee Department. In certain other countries the loan is granted by commercial banks, but interest rate payments are subsidized by a transfer from the government to the bank.

Box 4.6

EU anti-dumping

EU anti-dumping legislation is a sphere where authority is very much in the hands of the EU rather than its member states. The legislation draws heavily on the GATT/WTO Articles relating to dumping. According to EU legislation, dumping is said to occur when the price of an export to the EU is lower than its 'normal value'. The Commission acting on its own initiative never opens EU anti-dumping procedures; it is always at the request of one or more producer who represents the 'EU industry'. If dumping is found to cause injury or threat of injury, and the 'interest of the EU' so requires, the Commission may impose an anti-dumping duty, though in most cases it simply insists on a price undertaking from the exporting country involved.

In addition to anti-dumping measures, the EU trade defence instruments include anti-subsidy measures and safeguards. Anti-subsidy rules cover subsidies by governments or public bodies, whereas safeguards are intended for situations in which EU industry is affected by an unforeseen, sharp and sudden increase on imports.

At the end of February 2011 the EU had 135 anti-dumping measures and 8 anti-subsidy measures in force. There were undertakings in force with 8 countries covering 12 products and 58 investigations were ongoing. The sector most involved was chemicals and allied products. In 2010 the EU opened 18 new trade defence investigations, of which 10 were against China, 3 against India, and one each against Bosnia and Herzegovina, Indonesia, Malaysia, Thailand and the USA.*

* European Commission (2009a) and http://trade.ec.europa.eu/tdi (accessed 3 March 2011) for the more recent statistics.

particular for food products) and labelling requirements. **Differences in standards and technical barriers** probably represent the main barrier in trade between developed countries. Firms also frequently complain about **customs formalities**, which may cause delays, additional costs, and even block trade. Differences in tax systems may also have to be offset at the border. The Single Market project aimed at removing these barriers between EC member states (see Chapter 6), and there have been attempts to reduce their impact on trade with third countries (see Box 4.7).

Lack of transparency in **government procurement** may also act as a barrier to trade since local, regional and national authorities tend to buy from firms of their own country (see Chapter 6).

Box 4.7

Standards, technical restrictions and other administrative regulations in EU–US trade

A major objective of the Single Market Programme is to prevent differences in standards, technical restrictions and other administrative regulations from acting as barriers to intra-EU trade, but the problem also arises in trade between the EU and other countries such as the USA. Publications such as the US *Trade Review* or the European Commission's report *United States Barriers to Trade and Investment* describe many of these barriers. For example, the report for 2008 (European Commission, 2009b) complains of excessive invoicing requirements on exports to the USA and failure to recognize that the EU is a customs union (with consequent non-acceptance of EU certificates of origin by US customs authorities). It points to regulatory and technical barriers, such as those caused by the pharmaceutical approval system, and the labelling requirements for products such as cars and textiles. The USA is accused of relatively low implementation of standards set by international standardization bodies. Fears are expressed that some of the national security measures (such as those relating to international maritime container trade or 'bioterrorism' measures for food and feed products) could have a negative impact on trade flows.

4.17 The main arguments presented in favour of protection

Protectionism may be advocated for **non-economic reasons**, such as for defence, national pride or to further foreign policy objectives. For instance, the need to ensure sufficiency of supply in times of war has frequently been advanced to justify protection in sectors such as agriculture, shipbuilding, energy, steel production and so on. However, such explanations seem incomplete as an account of the behaviour of Western industrialized countries and are difficult to apply to some of the sectors most affected by protectionism.

The **infant industry** case is probably the oldest and best-known argument advanced in favour of protection. When an industry is first set up it may need time to acquire experience or competence (in terms of managerial resources, networks of suppliers, financial capabilities and so on), or to reach a sufficient size to benefit from economies of scale. A new industry will therefore not be able to compete with a foreign industry that is already well established. According to this argument, the new industry should therefore be protected, for instance by a tariff, until it is large enough to compete with foreign firms.

However, for this argument to be valid the industry must eventually succeed in becoming competitive with foreign industry at the free trade world price; moreover the eventual benefit from the industry must exceed the cost of protection. Protection initially increases the price that consumers have to pay, and for this to be justified it must be offset by the lower costs and prices that consumers will pay when the industry is established. Even if these two conditions are satisfied, it would be preferable to use a production subsidy rather than a tariff since subsidies are more transparent, less distorting and also tend to be easier to remove.

The practical implementation of protection of infant industries also encounters difficulties. For instance, how is the decision concerning which industries to be protected taken? And is there a risk of this selection process becoming politicized? When is the industry to be weaned, and is there likely to be pressure to prevent the protection ending? Even where protection helps an industry to become established, could this have occurred even without the protection? Clearly a general answer cannot be given to such questions and the outcome will depend on the particular case in question.

Another argument in favour of protectionism that has a long history is that of the **optimal tariff**. John Stuart Mill noted that if Britain introduced a tariff on a good widely used, consumption would decline causing the world price to fall. As a result, foreign producers would bear part of the cost of the tariff. This argument only applies in the case of a large nation that is able to influence the level of world prices.[20] The risk of introducing a tariff for this reason is that of retaliation on the part of other countries.

The **senescent industry** argument is frequently used, and maintains that protectionist measures may be necessary to avoid unemployment. However, the probable impact of such measures is simply to delay adjustment, and it is likely that the jobs saved in the declining sectors will be less numerous and will have less favourable prospects than those lost or forgone in non-subsidized sectors.

4.18 Second best

The traditional theory advocating free trade according to the principle of comparative advantage is based on some extremely restrictive assumptions, and in particular that there is perfect competition in factor and product markets at both national and international levels. This assumption is violated at a national level by cases of monopoly, oligopoly and imperfect competition, while at an international level the assumption appears even more heroic.

---

[20] For the country to benefit from introduction of the optimal tariff, it is also necessary that the transfer from the rest of the world following introduction of a tariff exceeds the net welfare loss to domestic producers and consumers.

If the conditions of perfect competition are not verified, then we are in a situation of **second best**. Second best implies that if the conditions of perfect competition are violated in some part of the economy, it need not be optimal for the rest of the economy to attain a perfectly competitive equilibrium. In other words, it is not possible to know whether the introduction of an additional distortion will increase (while still remaining in a suboptimal situation) or reduce total welfare. The situation may actually be improved by violating further conditions of perfect competition. In the context of the debate on protectionism this implies that it is impossible to say a priori whether a move towards free trade will improve the situation, or whether the introduction of a protectionist measure will worsen it. Under such conditions it is necessary to examine the specific case in question to decide on the most appropriate policy.

Meade (1962) provided a useful analogy for understanding the concept of second best. Let us consider a person trying to reach the highest possible peak in a group of mountains. Going towards the highest peak, the mountaineer will at times have to climb smaller mountains and descend the other side: the path to the highest peak is not always upwards. Assume, for example, in Figure 4.14 the mountaineer has reached B, but discovers that there is a deep gorge at D over which it is impossible to cross. If the climber wants to reach the highest peak possible under the circumstances, he should not remain at B, nor move to D in order to try and reach V, but should return to A.

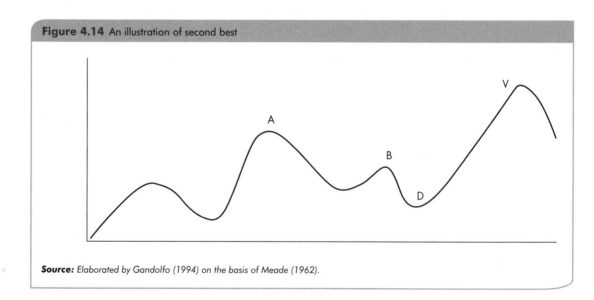

Figure 4.14 An illustration of second best

Source: *Elaborated by Gandolfo (1994) on the basis of Meade (1962).*

4.19 More recent arguments in favour of protection: strategic trade theory

Given the shortcomings of the traditional theory, there have been numerous attempts to develop new approaches to the study of international trade, which no longer rely on the assumption of perfect competition. The differences among authors are such that it is difficult to present a synthesis of this type of approach. What emerges from the literature, however, is an emphasis on dynamic phenomena that may influence the productive conditions of a firm. In this world, technology, and both static and dynamic economies of scale, may play a crucial role. These phenomena may enable a firm to gain a competitive advantage regardless of the initial endowments of factors of production in that country. This implies that comparative advantage may in some sense be created and may be of a temporary nature.

The idea that competitive advantage can be created underlies **strategic trade theory**, which advocates an active government trade policy and protectionism. According to this approach, a government may create a competitive advantage for its firms in high-technology industries through temporary protection, subsidies and tax breaks. Strategies to promote investment in infrastructure, people and research and development may also play an important role. Unfortunately, this approach shares many of the shortcomings of the infant industry argument: choosing which sectors will be future winners is as difficult as betting on horses, and too much government intervention may invite similar measures by major competitors.

4.20 The political economy of protectionism

The effect of trade protection for a particular product, say steel, is to raise domestic steel prices. Steel producers in that country will benefit, while consumers will have to pay higher prices. However, the benefits to the producers can be very high, while the cost to consumers is spread. The expected benefits to producers from protection may be sufficient to induce them to take on the costs of lobbying governments to introduce protectionist measures. The costs of lobbying may include the time, effort and expense needed to obtain information, organize a pressure group, signal preferences and carry out

Box 4.8

The political economy of protectionism

The work by Olson (1965) provides a key in identifying the elements of success in pressure group activities. Olson explains the decision to join and participate in the activities of a pressure group in terms of expected benefits and costs. In the case of lobbying, the benefits relate to the probability of obtaining a favourable policy outcome, and the size of the per capita transfer to the beneficiary group.

The costs of pressure group activities include the costs of signalling preferences, organization and administration of the group and lobbying. According to Olson, the costs of organization and co-ordination may be higher, and the group may be rendered less effective with numerous members, each of whom feels that, whether they participate in the activities of the group or not, will not be noticed.[*] In other words there is a tendency for the members to 'free ride'. Olson argues that one way of overcoming free-riding is by offering selective incentives to ensure membership or participation in the activities of a group. Alternatively, Olson maintains that the problem of free-riding can be avoided in the case of what he calls a 'privileged group'. This involves one or more members of the group whose size or interest in having the goal of collective action is sufficient to induce them to take on the task of obtaining the common goal.

Downs (1957) provides an explanation of how, in a 'democratic system', a policy can serve the interests of a special group rather than those of the public as a whole. According to Downs, politicians are assumed to maximize their chances of re-election by competing for votes. They will adopt or reject a proposal on the basis of how many votes are expected to support or oppose it. However, voters will only reveal their preference if there is some advantage in doing so, such as action by the politician in favour of the voter. Information and signalling costs are involved in forming and expressing a preference. The rational voter will only undertake these costs if there is some incentive to do so. The fundamental theoretical insight of Downs is to illustrate why taxpayers and consumers may be 'rationally ignorant'.

[*]Olson refers to this type of group as a 'latent' group.

lobbying activities (see Box 4.8). The cost to consumers of the higher steel prices may be insufficiently high to induce them to organize any kind of protest. The government may have an incentive to give in to the requests of the steel lobby, knowing that consumers will be unlikely to organize any kind of effective resistance.

This type of political economy argument is very powerful in explaining the pervasiveness of protectionist measures. In the EU and USA, aside from steel, protection tends to be high in agriculture, textiles and clothing, and the automobile industry.

Summary of key concepts

- Many of our arguments in favour of free trade still owe much to the pioneering work of the classical economists **Adam Smith** and **David Ricardo** who illustrated that trade between two countries could be mutually beneficial thanks to the specialization of their production.

- The **Heckscher–Ohlin theorem** explains patterns of trade in terms of the endowments of factors of production of countries. For example, a country which has an abundance of cheap labour will specialize in the production of labour-intensive goods.

- According to the **Heckscher–Ohlin–Samuelson** theorem, under certain very restrictive assumptions, the liberalization of trade will bring about the equalization of relative and absolute returns to the factors of production between countries.

- **New trade theories** take into account aspects such as: imperfect competition, political economy arguments, new growth theory, the new economic geography, and open economy macroeconomics.

- Much trade between EU countries consists of **intra-industry trade**. This arises from product differentiation and means that each country (or producer) can specialize in a few varieties of the product and exploit economies of scale.

- **Static economies of scale** occur when the unit costs of production fall as the scale of production rises. Dynamic economies of scale are associated with the **learning process**.

- An import **tariff** is a tax or duty levied on a product when it is imported into a country. Tariffs can be ad valorem, specific or compound.

- Among the main **non-tariff barriers** are: quotas, voluntary export restraints (VERs), cartels, anti-dumping measures, trade facilitation measures (including customs procedures, measures to promote exports and so on), differences in standards and technical specifications, and lack of transparency in government procurement.

- The **effect of trade protection** for a particular product is to raise domestic prices. Producers in that country will benefit, while consumers will have to pay higher prices. However, the benefits to the producers can be very high, while the cost to consumers is diffused. Producers may have an incentive to lobby government to introduce protection in their favour, while consumers may feel that it is not worth their while to object.

Questions for study and review

1 What are the main arguments in favour of free trade?
2 Describe the main obstacles to trade and their use by the EU (see also Chapters 13 and 18)?
3 Explain how non-tariff barriers have a negative effect on trade.
4 Illustrate how political economy reasons may help to explain the high levels of protection in sectors such as agriculture, steel or textiles.
5 Exercise on the effects of a tariff in a small nation (see Appendix 1 for an example of how to carry out the exercise). The quantity of a commodity supplied in a country is 24 tonnes, the quantity demanded (Qd) is 60 tonnes, and the world price (Pw) is €6/tonne. A tariff is introduced which raises the domestic price (Pd) to €7/tonne. The elasticity of demand is –0.3 and the elasticity of supply is 0.5. Calculate the effects of the tariff on: producer revenue, consumer expenditure, the trade balance and total welfare.[21]
6 Exercise on the effects of introducing a tariff in a large nation (see Appendix 2 for an example of how to carry out the exercise). It is assumed initially that in conditions of free trade the quantity supplied (Qs) by a country is 200 tonnes, the quantity demanded (Qd) is 400 tonnes, and the world price (Pw) is €4/tonne. A tariff is introduced which raises the domestic price (Pd) to €5/tonne and as a result the world price P′w falls to €3.5/tonne. The elasticity of demand is –0.5 and the elasticity of supply is 0.4. Calculate the effects of the tariff on: producer revenue, consumer expenditure, the trade balance and total welfare.

Online
Learning **Centre**

When you have read this chapter, log on to the Online Learning Centre website at *www.mcgraw-hill.co.uk/textbooks/senior* to explore weblinks, chapter-by-chapter test questions, case studies and more online study tools.

---

[21] As a tip, calculate the total welfare effects using both approaches to ensure that they coincide. The country is a small nation, and for simplicity the demand and supply functions are assumed to be linear. It is also assumed that there are no stocks of the product or externalities. The approach used is partial equilibrium.

Chapter 4 Appendices

Appendix 1: A numerical example of the effect of introducing a tariff in a small nation

A simple numerical example can be used to calculate the effects of introducing a tariff.[22] It is assumed initially that the quantity supplied (Qs) by the country is 8 tonnes, the quantity demanded (Qd) is 30 tonnes, and the world price (Pw) is €2/tonne. A tariff is introduced which raises the domestic price (Pd) to €3/tonne (see Figure A4.1).

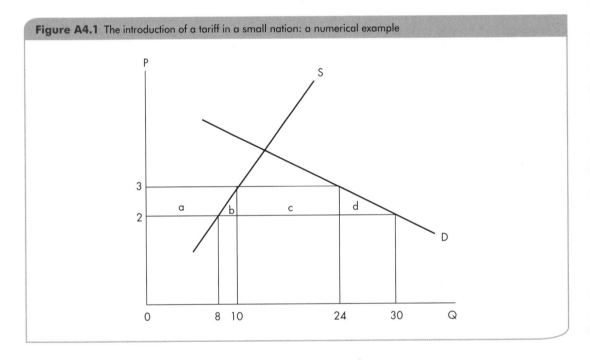

Figure A4.1 The introduction of a tariff in a small nation: a numerical example

The elasticity of supply (Es) with respect to price can be defined as the ratio of the proportional change in the quantity supplied to the proportional change in price that brought it about. In symbols we have:

$$Es = \frac{\frac{\Delta Qs}{Qs}}{\frac{\Delta P}{P}}$$

---

[22] The exercises presented here are a slightly different version of these developed by Professor Secondo Tarditi in 1992 in an unpublished manuscript 'Esercitazioni' at the faculty of Economics 'Richard Goodwin' of the University of Siena.

Which can be rewritten as:

$$\frac{\Delta Qs}{Qs} = Es\,\frac{\Delta P}{P}$$

Assuming an elasticity of supply of 0.5 we can now calculate the new quantity supplied (Q's) after introduction of the tariff.

$$\Delta Qs = QsEs\ \frac{(\Delta P)}{P} = 8\,\frac{(0.5 \times 1)}{2} = 2$$

$$Q's = Qs + \Delta Qs = 8 + 2 = 10$$

In the same way the new quantity demanded (Q'd) can be calculated. The elasticity of demand with respect to price (Ed) can be defined as the ratio of the proportional change in the quantity demanded to the proportional change in price that brought it about. In symbols we have:

$$Ed = \frac{\dfrac{\Delta Qd}{Qd}}{\dfrac{\Delta P}{P}}$$

Which can be rewritten as:

$$\frac{\Delta Qd}{Qd} = Ed\,\frac{\Delta P}{P}$$

Assuming a price elasticity of demand of –0.4 (in general the price elasticity of demand is negative since in most cases an increase in price provokes a reduction in the quantity demanded), the new quantity demanded can be calculated:

$$\Delta Qd = Qd\left(Ed\,\frac{\Delta P}{P}\right) = 30\,\frac{(-0.4 \times 1)}{2} = -6$$

$$Q'd = Qd + \Delta Qd = 30 - 6 = 24$$

Before introduction of the tariff, producer revenue is:

$$Q's\ (Pw) = 8 \times 2 = 16$$

With the tariff it becomes:

$$Q's\ (Pd) = 10 \times 3 = 30$$

Before the introduction of the tariff, consumer expenditure is:

$$Qd\ (Pw) = 30 \times 2 = 60$$

After the introduction of the tariff it becomes:

$$Q'd\ (Pd) = 24 \times 3 = 72$$

Before the introduction of the tariff, the trade balance is:

$$(Qs - Qd)\ Pw = (8 - 30)\ 2 = -44$$

With the tariff it becomes:

$$(Q's - Q'd)\ Pw = (10 - 24)2 = -28$$

(Note: The world price is used to calculate the trade balance, but the domestic price is used to calculate producer revenue and consumer expenditure.)

The loss in consumer surplus is given by:

$$-0.5 \, (Pd - Pw) \, (Qd + Q'd) = -27$$

The increase in producer surplus is given by:

$$0.5 \, (Pd - Pw) \, (Qs + Q's) = 9$$

The impact on the government budget (or the income of taxpayers) is:

$$(Pd - Pw) \, (Q'd + Q's) = 14$$

The total effect of introducing the tariff on welfare is given by: loss in consumer surplus plus increase in producer surplus plus increase in government revenue:

$$-27 + 9 + 14 = -4$$

Alternatively, the effect of introducing the tariff on total welfare can be calculated using the net welfare effects. Triangle d in Figure A4.1 is the net loss of welfare on the consumer side:

$$- 0.5 \, (Pd - Pw) \, (Qd - Q'd) = - 0.5 \, (3 - 2) \, (30 - 24)$$

$$= - 3$$

Triangle b is the net loss of welfare on the production side (reflecting the worsening in the allocation of resources):

$$- 0.5 \, (Pd - Pw) \, (Q's - Qs) = - 0.5 \, (3 - 2) \, (10 - 8)$$

$$= -1$$

The total effect on welfare is the sum of the two net effects −4.

Clearly the result must be the same as the total welfare effect calculated using the alternative method above.

Appendix 2: A numerical example of the effects of introducing a tariff in a large nation

Before the tariff is introduced it is assumed that:

Pw = €40/tonne

Qd = 1,400 tonnes

Qs = 800 tonnes

Ed = −0.5

Es = 0.6

Assume that a tariff of €20/tonne is then introduced causing the world price to fall to €37/tonne. The new domestic price will be €57/tonne (see Figure A4.2).

Recalling the formula for the elasticity of supply with respect to price (Es), it is possible to calculate the new quantity supplied (Q's) after introduction of the tariff:

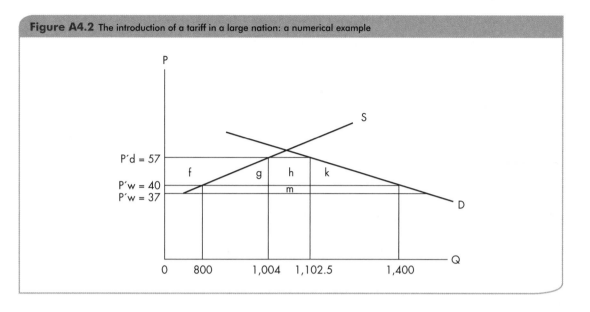

Figure A4.2 The introduction of a tariff in a large nation: a numerical example

$$Es = \frac{\frac{\Delta Qs}{Qs}}{\frac{\Delta P}{P}}$$

Which can be rewritten as:

$$\frac{\Delta Qs}{Qs} = Es\frac{\Delta P}{P}$$

$$\Delta Qs = \frac{Qs\ Es(\Delta P)}{P} = \frac{800(0.6 \times 17)}{40} = 204$$

$$Q's = Qs + \Delta Qs = 800 + 204 = 1{,}004$$

Similarly, the formula for elasticity of demand (Ed) can be used to calculate the new quantity demanded (Q'd):

$$Ed = \frac{\frac{\Delta Qd}{Qd}}{\frac{\Delta P}{P}}$$

Which can be rewritten as:

$$\frac{\Delta Qd}{Qd} = Ed\frac{\Delta P}{P}$$

$$\Delta Q = Qd\left(Ed\frac{\Delta P}{P}\right) = 1{,}400\left(-0.5 \times \frac{17}{40}\right) = -297.5$$

$$Q'd = Qd + \Delta Qd = 1{,}400 - 297.5 = 1{,}102.5$$

Foreign trade without the tariff (that is, net imports) is given by:

$$Qs - Qd = 800 - 1{,}400 = -600$$

With the tariff it becomes:

$$Q's - Q'd = 1{,}004 - 1{,}102.5 = -98.5$$

Before introduction of the tariff producer revenue is:

$$Qs\ (Pw) = 800 \times 40 = 32{,}000$$

With the tariff it becomes:

$$Q's(Pd) = 1{,}004 \times 57 = 57{,}228$$

Before the introduction of the tariff consumer expenditure is:

$$Qd\ (Pw) = 1{,}400 \times 40 = 56{,}000$$

After the introduction of the tariff it becomes:

$$Q'd\ (Pd) = 62{,}842.5$$

Before the introduction of the tariff the trade balance is:

$$(Qs - Qd)\ Pw = -24{,}000$$

With the tariff it becomes:

$$(Q's - Q'd)\ P'w = -36{,}445$$

(Note: The world price is used to calculate the trade balance, but the domestic price is used to calculate producer revenue and consumer expenditure.)

The loss in consumer surplus is given by:

$$-0.5\ (Pd - Pw)\ (Qd + Q'd) = -21{,}271.25$$

The increase in producer surplus is given by:

$$0.5\ (Pd - Pw)\ (Qs + Q's) = 15{,}334$$

The impact on the government budget (or the income of taxpayers) is:

$$(Pd - P'w)(Q'd - Q's) = 1{,}970$$

The total effect of introducing the tariff on welfare is given by: loss in consumer surplus plus increase in producer surplus plus increase in government revenue:

$$-21{,}271.25 + 15{,}334 + 1{,}970 = -3{,}967.25$$

Alternatively, the effect of introducing the tariff on total welfare can be calculated using the net welfare effects. Triangle k in Figure A4.2 is the net loss of welfare on the consumer side:

$$-0.5\ (Pd - Pw)\ (Qd - Q'd) = -0.5\ (57 - 40)\ (1{,}400 - 1{,}102.5) = -2{,}528.75$$

Triangle g is the net loss of welfare on the production side (reflecting the worsening in the allocation of resources):

$$-0.5\ (Pd - Pw)\ (Q's - Qs) = -0.5\ (57 - 40)\ (1{,}004 - 800) = -1{,}734$$

Rectangle m represents the transfers from producers in the rest of the world to consumers in that country (a reduction in world prices is a welfare gain for an importing country):

$$(Pw - P'w)(Q'd - Q's) = 295.5$$

The total effect on welfare is the sum of the three net effects:

$$-2{,}528.75 - 1{,}734 + 295.5 = -3{,}967.25$$

Clearly the result must be the same as the total welfare effect calculated using the alternative method above.

Chapter 5

The Economics of Integration

Learning Objectives

By the end of this chapter you should be able to understand:

- ✔ The concepts of trade creation and trade diversion
- ✔ The effects of forming a customs union on the home and partner countries
- ✔ The different effects of non-discriminatory liberalization of trade and preferential trade arrangements
- ✔ The conditions under which a customs union is likely to increase welfare
- ✔ The reasons that countries may prefer preferential trade arrangements to non-discriminatory trade liberalization
- ✔ What we mean by the dynamic effects of integration
- ✔ The link between growth and integration
- ✔ Why there may be a tension between regional trade blocs and multilateral trade liberalization

5.1 Introduction

The early economic analysis of integration relies heavily on what is known as 'customs union theory'. One of the questions to arise was why preferential arrangements should be preferred to unilateral trade liberalization. Traditionally, 'customs union theory' attempted to address this question and assess the effects of customs unions using instruments based on the concepts of welfare economics. More recent analysis has taken into account the dynamic effects of integration and phenomena such as economies of scale, increased competition and better opportunities for more rapid technology transfer. According to empirical studies, these dynamic effects of integration seem far more important than the static welfare effects.

5.2 The costs and benefits of integration

The early literature on integration used customs union theory to analyse the so-called **static effects** of integration on welfare, making use of the distinction made by Viner (1953) between trade creation

and trade diversion.[1] **Trade creation** arises when domestic production is replaced by cheaper imports from a partner country. **Trade diversion** involves low-cost imports from suppliers in third countries being replaced by more expensive imports from a partner country. It was generally assumed that integration would lead to a welfare gain because the positive effect of trade creation would exceed the possible negative effects of trade diversion.[2]

Viner considered the costs and benefits of forming a customs union only from the point of view of production, and assumed that products were always consumed in the same proportion. Lipsey (1957) pointed out that the customs union is also likely to have an effect on the consumption side. It is also ambiguous as to whether the terms 'trade creation' and 'trade diversion' refer to trade flows or welfare effects, but Pelkmans and Gremmen (1983) have illustrated that changes in trade flows can be a misleading indicator of welfare changes.

5.3 Trade creation

The 'static' effect of a customs union can be illustrated with the help of a diagram similar to that of Figure 4.4 in Chapter 4. Figure 5.1 shows the domestic demand (Dx) and supply (Sx) curves for product X of a country that imports that product, say Belgium. Assume that the free trade price of a commodity is Px = €1 in country 1 (say Germany), and Pw = €2 in country 2 (or the rest of the world). For simplicity, Belgium is assumed to be a 'small nation' in the sense that its economy is too small to affect the prices

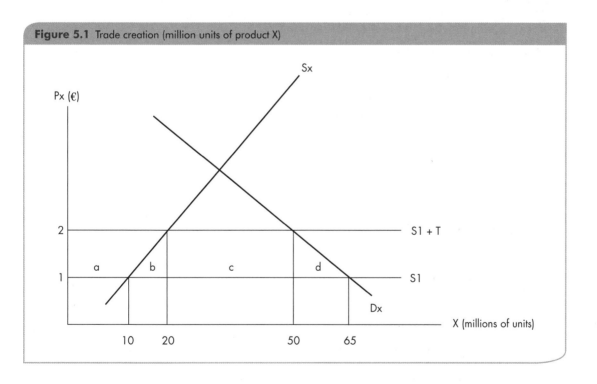

Figure 5.1 Trade creation (million units of product X)

---

[1] In the subsequent literature there was further refinement of the different effects of integration. For example, external trade creation was said to arise when the faster growth of the integration unit led to higher imports from the rest of the world. Trade suppression may arise when creation of the customs union leads to production in one of the partners stopping and production shifting to the other partner, which had previously imported from the rest of the world.

[2] The rules of the GATT/WTO were aimed at ensuring that this is the case (see Chapter 18).

in Germany or the rest of the world. Assume initially that Belgium imposes a non-discriminatory ad valorem tariff of 100 per cent on imports from all sources. S1 represents the perfectly elastic supply curve of Germany with free trade, and S1 +T is the tariff-inclusive German supply curve. Belgium will import commodity X from Germany at a price of Pd = €2, reflecting the effect of the tariff. It will not import from the rest of the world, since after the tariff the price in Belgium would be €4.

If Belgium now forms a customs union with country 1 (Germany), the tariffs will be removed on German imports but not on those from the rest of the world. Belgium can now import at Px = €1 from Germany, and at this price Belgium will produce 10 million units of X, consume 65 million units, and import 55 million units.

The increase in consumer surplus as a result of creation of the customs union is area a + b + c + d. The loss in producer surplus is indicated by area a. Belgium loses its tariff revenue on imports from Germany (rectangle c). The net positive impact on welfare as a result of the customs union therefore comprises triangles b and d. Triangle b represents the welfare gain on the production side as a result of improved allocation of resources with the shift in the production of 10 million X from less efficient domestic producers to lower cost producers in the partner country Germany. Triangle d represents the welfare gain on the consumption side from creation of the customs union. With the lower prices in the customs union, Belgian consumption will increase by 15 million units. Together, triangles b and d illustrate the net increase in welfare as a result of establishing the customs union.

A strict application of Viner's term 'trade creation' would refer simply to the production side and the effect of replacement of the more expensive domestic production of 10 million X by imports from the partner country, Germany. Many economists use the term 'trade creation' to cover the total net increases in welfare on both the production and the consumption sides, that is, triangles b and d in the diagram. It is probably more precise to refer to triangle b as the trade creation effect, and triangle d as the consumption effect of forming a customs union.

5.4 Trade diversion

Figure 5.2 illustrates the case of trade diversion.[3] Again Dx and Sx are domestic demand and supply of commodity X in the country in question (Belgium). S2 and S3 are the free trade, perfectly elastic supply curves of commodity X in country 2 (say the USA) and country 3 (say France) respectively. With a 100 per cent non-discriminatory tariff, the home country (Belgium) will import from country 2 (the USA) at a price of €2. At this price Belgium will produce 35 million units and consume 60 million, so 25 million units are imported from country 2 (the USA). There will be no imports from France as the price inclusive of tariff is €3.

Assume that Belgium now forms a customs union with country 3 (France) but not with country 2 (the USA). As a result, tariffs are removed on imports from France, but the 100 per cent tariff remains on imports from the USA. After formation of the customs union Belgium will import from France at price €1.50. At this new price Belgium will produce 30 million units, and consume 70 million, importing 40 million units from country 3 (France).

With the customs union the imports of Belgium have been diverted from more efficient producers in country 2 (the USA) to less efficient producers in country 3 (France), so there is a worsening in the allocation of resources. Five million units of X (35 – 30 million) are now imported from the partner country, France, rather than being produced at home in Belgium, while 25 million units (60 – 35 million) that were previously imported from the USA are now imported from France.

Belgium will no longer receive tariff revenue. The welfare loss from trade diversion is indicated by the area of rectangle f. The 25 million units that were previously imported from more efficient country 2 (the USA) whose free trade price is €1 per unit are now imported from country 3 (France) with a free trade price of €1.50. In this case the welfare loss will be €12.5 million.

---

[3] This type of analysis was first used by Kindleberger (1973).

Figure 5.2 Trade diversion (million units of product X)

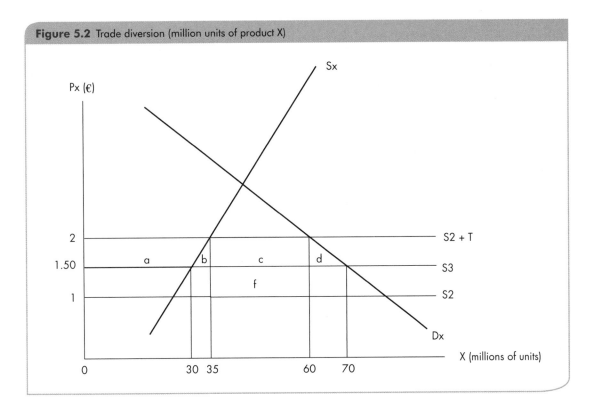

Triangles b and d reflect the welfare gain from the customs union as more expensive production in Belgium is now replaced with cheaper imports from France. The welfare gain on the production side due to trade creation (triangle b) is equal to €1.25 million, while that on the consumption side (triangle d) is €2.5 million.

The total impact on welfare as a result of formation of the customs union is given by the sum of the areas of the two triangles (b and d), representing a welfare gain due to the trade creation and consumption effects, minus the area of the rectangle (f) representing welfare loss due to trade diversion. In this case the total effect on welfare is equal to –8.75 million euros (2.5 million + 1.25 million – 12.5 million), so creation of the customs union causes a net welfare loss.

If the sum of the areas of the two triangles representing welfare gain is greater than the area of the rectangle representing the welfare loss due to trade diversion, formation of the customs union will cause a net welfare gain for the home country. The idea that a customs union is either 'trade creating' or 'trade distorting' is misleading; Figure 5.2 illustrates that a customs union may give rise to both effects.

5.5 The effect of a customs union on the partner country

The analysis can be extended to consider the effect of forming a customs union on the partner country. Figure 5.3a illustrates the demand and supply curves for product X in the partner country, while Figure 5.3b illustrates the demand and supply curves for the home country. The two countries are assumed to be small and have increasing production costs. The costs of production are assumed to be higher in the home country, and for simplicity it is assumed that at the initial level of protection the partner country is just self-sufficient at the perfectly elastic world price Pw.[4] The partner country therefore does not need to protect its industry from world competition. Before creation of the customs union, the home country applies a tariff that raises its domestic price to Ph. With the creation of the customs union trade is liberalized between the home and partner country, and they introduce a common external tariff in trade with the rest of the world. The price including the common external tariff is indicated by Pcu in Figure 5.3.

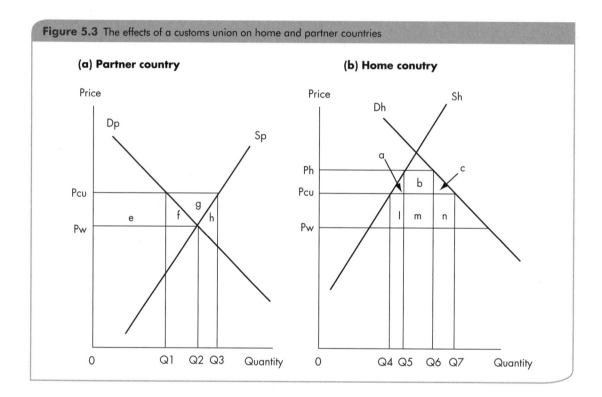

Figure 5.3 The effects of a customs union on home and partner countries

(a) Partner country

(b) Home conutry

In the home country the reduction in the apparent price of imports will lead to a welfare gain of a on the production side due to trade creation, a welfare gain on the consumption side of c, and a welfare loss of m due to the diversion of imports from the rest of the world.

In the partner country prices will rise because of increased protection. Equilibrium occurs in the customs union when the combined supply of the two countries equals their combined demand (and Q1Q3 = Q4Q7). The increase in price from Pw to Pcu in the partner country causes an increase in producer surplus of e + f + g and a reduction in consumer surplus of e + f. The partner country is able to increase its exports to the home country to Q1Q3 and obtain a net welfare gain of area g.

In the example the net welfare benefit of the partner country rises. This is sometimes called 'trade creation'. However, more accurately this is an income transfer from the home country to the partner country. The home could have imported quantity Q4Q7 from the rest of the world, rather than from the partner country at Pcu. In this way the home country would have received revenue of l + m + n from the common external tariff. Instead, this passed to the partner country with areas f + g representing profit, while area h is the additional cost of production compared with the lower world price Pw.

---

[4] The simplifying assumption of initial self-sufficiency of the partner country is taken from Robson (1984).

In this example there is a net welfare loss for the home country (rectangle m is greater than the sum of triangles a and c), and a net welfare gain for the partner country of triangle g. There will be a net welfare loss for the rest of the world, whose exports are replaced by exports from the partner country.

5.6 The difference between non-discriminatory tariffs and preferential arrangements

The analysis based on import demand and supply curves shown in Chapter 4 is also useful to illustrate the difference between non-discriminatory tariffs and preferential arrangements.[5] Non-discriminatory tariffs could be, for example, those extended to all WTO members on the basis of the most favoured nation clause (MFN), as explained in Chapter 18.

Figure 5.4 illustrates the effect of the home country introducing an MFN tariff on the partner country and the rest of the world. XSrow indicates the export supply of the rest of the world, and XSp shows the export supply of the partner country. Prior to introducing the tariff, at the free trade world price Pft the home country will import a total of M of product X of which Xp comes from the partner country and Xr comes from the rest of the world. MSh shows the import supply of the home country in a situation of free trade. With the tariff the import supply curve in the home country becomes MSh + tariff, and the domestic price in the home country rises to P′. The border price (that is, the price received by exporters) falls to P′ − T in both the partner country and the rest of the world. As a result, home imports fall to M′, of which X′p comes from the partner country and X′r from the rest of the world. The home country receives a welfare gain of b and a welfare loss of c, while the partner receives a welfare loss of f and the rest of the world suffers a welfare loss of e (see Chapter 4 for an explanation of these effects).

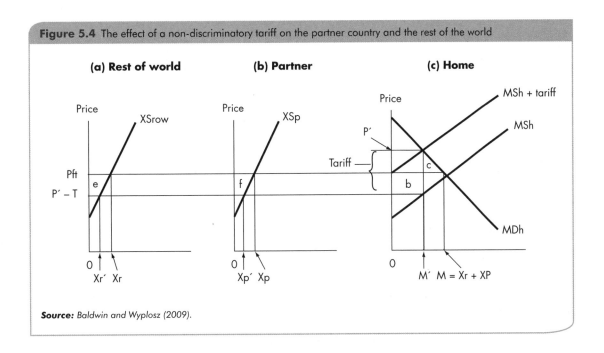

Figure 5.4 The effect of a non-discriminatory tariff on the partner country and the rest of the world

Source: Baldwin and Wyplosz (2009).

---

[5] The analysis in this section follows Baldwin and Wyplosz (2009).

A customs union involves all members eliminating trade barriers with their partners and introducing a common external tariff towards the rest of the world. In the interests of simplification, before analysing the effect of a customs union on the partner country, it is useful to consider the effect of just one country introducing a unilateral preferential trade arrangement.

In Figure 5.5 MSmfn shows the supply of imports of product X in the home country with a non-discriminatory (or MFN) tariff, and MSh shows the import supply in a situation of free trade. MSpta shows the import supply in the home country with a preferential trade arrangement. As the trade liberalization is preferential, MSpta is assumed to be lower than MSmfn. In this simple model with two exporters, a partner and the rest of the world, preferential trade liberalization applies only to the partner, and MSpta can be assumed to lie halfway between MSh and MSmfn. However, the rest of the world cannot supply the home market at a price less than Pa, which represents their zero export supply price (P′) plus the tariff T. Up to Pa only firms from the partner country will supply imports. The import supply curve MSpta with a preferential trade arrangement therefore takes the form shown in Figure 5.5.

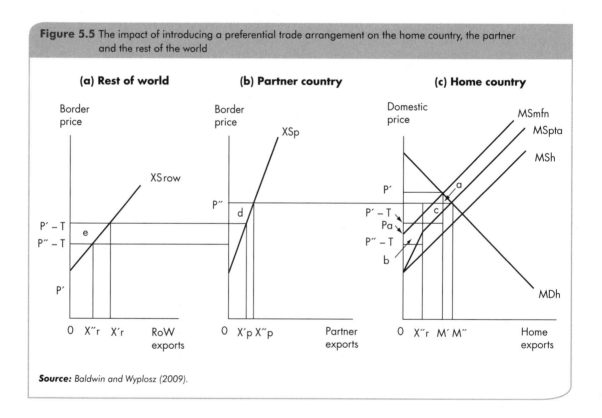

Figure 5.5 The impact of introducing a preferential trade arrangement on the home country, the partner and the rest of the world

Source: Baldwin and Wyplosz (2009).

With a non-discriminatory tariff, the import supply curve MSmfn and the import demand curve in the home country intersect at price P′. The border price received by exporters in both the rest of the world and the future partner country is P′ – T.

With the preferential trade arrangement the new domestic price becomes P″, and this is also the border price in the partner country joining the preferential arrangement. The border price in the partner country therefore rises from P′ – T to P″ as a result of creating the preferential trade arrangement. In contrast, following the introduction of the preferential trade arrangement, the border price in the rest of the world falls from P′ – T to P″ – T. The exports from the partner country rise from X′p to X″p, while those of the rest of the world fall from X′r to X″r.

The welfare effects of introducing the preferential trade arrangement can also be shown in the diagram. The partner country gains area d because it can sell a larger quantity at a higher price. The rest of the world has a welfare loss of e since it sells a smaller quantity at a lower price.

Following the introduction of the preferential trade arrangement home imports increase from M' to M", with X"r of the latter coming from the rest of the world and M" – X"r coming from the partner country. The increase in total imports from M' to M" leads to a welfare gain due to the increased volume of imports equal to area a, and the lower price of imports from the rest of the world leads to a welfare gain equal to rectangle b (the price difference (P' – T) – (P" – T) times the imports from the rest of the world X"r). The higher price of imports from the partner implies a welfare loss equal to the area of the rectangle c or the price difference P" – (P' – T) multiplied by the quantity of imports (M' – X"r). The effect of the price difference does not apply on the extra amount of imports M" – M' as initially the home country did not import this quantity. The total net welfare effect on the home country as a result of formation of the preferential trade agreement is a + b – c.

In the case of a customs union, the partner country will also eliminate tariffs on its imports from the home country but not on those from the rest of the world. For simplicity, to illustrate the case of a customs union it can be assumed that the home country imports good X from the partner country and exports good Y to the partner country. The rest of the world exports product X to the home country, and product Y to the partner country. The home, the partner and the rest of the world are also assumed symmetric in all aspects, including the tariffs initially applied on imports.

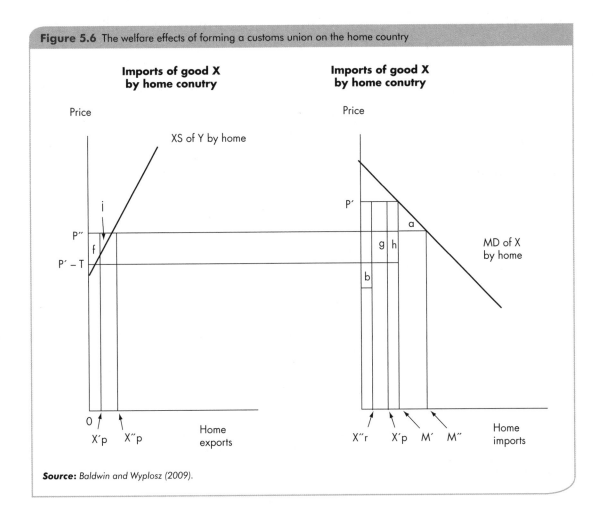

Figure 5.6 The welfare effects of forming a customs union on the home country

Source: Baldwin and Wyplosz (2009).

Figure 5.5 can also be used to analyse the effect of the partner eliminating the barrier on imports of Y from the home country. This simply requires inverting the partner and home countries as parts (b) and (c) of Figure 5.5 (which is possible due to the symmetry assumption). The partner country then becomes the importing country (of Y), and the home country is an exporter (of Y).

The total welfare effects of forming a customs union for the home country are shown in Figure 5.6. To explain the welfare effects more precisely, area c of Figure 5.5 is divided into areas g and h, and area d is broken down into f and j. On the import market for product X the home country gains areas a and b and loses areas g and h (g + h is equal to area c in Figure 5.5), while on its export market for product Y it gains areas f and j (area d in Figure 5.5). The welfare loss of areas h and g to the home country is the result of paying the higher price after the tariff cut on imports from the partner. Part of this loss, area h simply represents a transfer to the partner country which receives higher prices for its exports. Area h is equal to area f. The home country's loss of area h on its imports of product X will be offset by a gain of area f for the partner country's exports of X. Similarly for product Y (because of the assumption of symmetry), the loss of area h on the partner country's imports of Y will be equal to the home country's gain of f on its exports of Y.

In contrast, area g represents trade diversion because of switching from cheaper exports from the rest of the world to exports from the higher-cost partner country. The size of this welfare loss is given by the quantity of supply switching X'p – X"r multiplied by the price difference P" – (P' – T). Given that h = f, the total net welfare effect on the home country from formation of the customs union is a + b + j – g.

 5.7   # The conditions under which a customs union is likely to increase welfare

From the analysis here it emerges that the net effect of forming a customs union on the welfare of the home country may be positive, negative or zero. This is known as 'Viner's ambiguity'. *Ex ante* general predictions of the welfare effects of introducing customs unions cannot be given as they will depend on the case in question. The analysis of the introduction of a customs union is a case of second best in which a shift from one suboptimal situation to another does not permit generalizations about the overall effect on welfare.

However, even from this simplified analysis, certain principles about the effect of introducing a customs union on welfare can be deduced and, in general, the benefits are likely to be higher:

- the higher the original level of the tariff before forming the customs union;[6]
- the lower the common external tariff towards the rest of the world;[7]
- the higher the number of countries joining a customs union, and the greater their size. Under these circumstances there is more likelihood of low cost producers within the customs union;
- the smaller the differences in costs of production between the members of the customs union and third countries;[8]
- the closer the countries are geographically, as transport costs will be lower;
- the more competitive (producing the same goods), rather than complementary (producing a different range of goods), the economies of the member states are. In this way there will be more opportunities for specialization;
- the greater the trade flows and economic relations between the countries before forming the customs union.

---

[6] This can be seen by using Figure 5.2 or 5.5 to consider the effect of a higher initial tariff.

[7] To verify, consider the effect of applying a lower common external tariff in Figure 5.3 or 5.5. Kemp and Wan (1976) demonstrated that the external tariff of a customs union can be set so as to bring trade diversion down to zero, so that creation of the customs union would increase world welfare. However, this result requires that countries bargain to achieve these optimal external tariffs and this is generally not the case in practice.

[8] Again Figures 5.2 or 5.3 can be used to see this effect.

5.8 Terms of trade effects

The traditional static analysis assesses the overall impact of a customs union by comparing the situation before and after creation of the customs union. However, Cooper and Massell (1965) challenged this approach, arguing that the comparison should be made between discriminatory reduction of tariffs, as in the case of a customs union, and a non-discriminatory elimination of tariffs.[9] They argue that a non-discriminatory removal of tariffs would not involve trade diversion and would be superior. The question then becomes: why do countries create customs unions (or preferential trade liberalization) rather than use non-discriminatory trade arrangements?

One reason given is the possible terms-of-trade loss from unilateral trade liberalization, and the possible terms-of-trade gain that may arise for the customs union as a whole as a result of discrimination against the rest of the world.[10] The single member states may be too small to affect their external terms of trade individually, but together they are able to affect the terms of trade with third countries. Given the weight of the EU in world trade, this argument could be quite important. However, some countries in the rest of the world are also large nations (such as the USA or Japan) so, as indicated in Chapter 4 in the context of the optimal tariff argument, the customs union could risk retaliatory measures from other countries.

5.9 The dynamic effects of integration

Over time, attempts to assess the effects of integration and explain why countries opt for preferential trade arrangements rather than multilateral liberalization, has entailed a shift in emphasis towards the so-called dynamic effects of integration. These have evolved in parallel with the development of new trade theories described in Chapter 4. Among the most comprehensive studies of these dynamic effects were those carried out in the context of the Single Market Programme (see Chapter 6). Studies such as the Cecchini Report (Cecchini, 1988) and that of Emerson et al. (1989) argued that the benefits from these dynamic effects could be as much as five or six times as large as the static effects of integration. As indicated below, the extent to which the various dynamic effects of integration have actually come to fruition in the EU is taken up in later chapters. The dynamic effects of integration include:

- **Increased competition.** By bringing down the barriers integration should lead to reductions in costs and prices and encourage the restructuring of industry (see Figure 6.1 in Chapter 6).
- **Economies of scale.** With integration, firms operate in a larger market and have more opportunities for exploiting economies of scale (see Chapter 4). The issue then becomes whether there is more scope for exploiting economies of scale at the EU level rather than the national or international level (see Chapter 6).
- **Technology and knowledge transfers.** It is frequently argued that economic integration also contributes to technological progress. However, this is increasingly a global rather than a regional phenomenon: as explained in Chapter 15, location counts.
- **Political economy arguments.** Sectoral interests may explain why a country prefers a regional trade bloc to multilateralism (see below), and it may be easier to deal with the adverse effects of lobbying in a larger integration unit.
- **Increased bargaining power at an international level.** By presenting a more united front, a regional bloc such as the EU would be able to carry more weight vis-à-vis its main trading partners.
- **More rapid growth.** The link between growth and integration is taken up in more detail in the next section.

---

[9] The approach used in Figures 5.5 and 5.6 provides a toolkit for carrying out this type of comparison.

[10] See the discussion of Figure 4.7 for an explanation of the terms-of-trade effect.

5.10   Growth and integration

According to orthodox neo-classical growth theory (based on the pioneering work of the Nobel laureate Robert Solow (1956), the key determinant of growth is capital accumulation. As more capital is added to a fixed amount of labour, output per worker increases, but by a progressively smaller amount for each additional unit of capital because of diminishing returns. The basic assumption of the Solow model is that since people save and invest a certain percentage of their income each year, the inflow of investment is a fixed fraction of output per worker. If y is output per worker, the curve sy in Figure 5.7 shows investment per worker (which is equal to savings per worker). The shape of the sy curve reflects diminishing returns.

The ratio of capital to labour in an economy will depend on investment, but also on depreciation, since old capital has to be replaced and repaired. A constant fraction of stock capital n is assumed to depreciate each year. The straight line n(k/l) shows the depreciation per worker that increases in proportion with the amount of capital per worker. At E investment is sufficient to keep capital per person constant. At E the inflow of investment just equals depreciation. At this point the capital/labour ratio reaches its equilibrium k/l*, or steady state. Below E, investment exceeds depreciation and capital per worker will rise. Above E, depreciation exceeds investment so capital per worker will fall. Accumulation of capital cannot be an ongoing source of long-run growth.

In order to explain ongoing rates of growth other elements have to be introduced into the Solow model. If, for instance, technological progress is introduced, this will lead to increased output per worker, thus raising investment and the capital/labour ratio. Technological progress causes the sy curve to rotate upwards each year. Figure 5.7 shows the effect of one such rotation in which the sy curve is translated to s'y, and the new capital/labour ratio becomes k/l'.

Endogenous growth theory as developed by Romer (1986) provides other explanations of long-term growth. Continual growth of output per person in the long run requires ceaseless accumulation of factors of production. In order to endogenize growth, it is necessary to endogenize investment. The decision

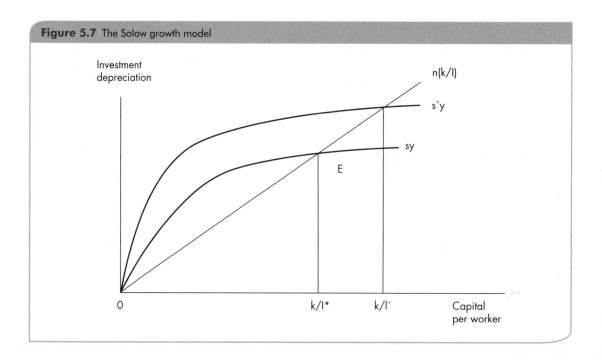

Figure 5.7 The Solow growth model

to accumulate factors of production will depend on the costs and benefits of investment. Continual accumulation therefore requires that the return on investment does not fall as capital stock rises.

Various accounts of how this may occur have been advanced. Much of the literature relies on the concept of productivity-boosting knowledge capital. For example, a firm may invest in knowledge to increase its advantage vis-à-vis other firms. The additional profits from exploiting this knowledge represent the return on investment in knowledge capital for the firm. However, the investment will have a spillover effect in increasing the stock of knowledge in the economy. It is assumed that this spillover will increase the productivity of resources used in innovating.

The model developed by Lucas (1988) focuses on the role played by human capital in contributing to growth.[11] Individuals will invest in skills because they expect that there will be adequate capital for their higher skills to be reflected in higher salaries. Firms invest in capital as they anticipate that there will be sufficient skilled workers for the firm to earn a profit. There is a positive spillover as those investing in human capital do not consider the output-boosting effect that their investment will have.

The elimination of barriers implied by integration may facilitate international flows of knowledge. This could reduce the cost of innovation, thereby increasing the private return on research and development (R&D) and encouraging more resources to be drawn into innovation. At the same time, the creation of a larger market could increase the profitability of innovation.

According to this approach, integration could also have a positive effect on financial markets, thereby leading to higher levels of investment and long-term growth. In particular, greater competition might encourage more efficiency in financial markets, enabling a reduction in the spread between the return earned by savers and the costs of funds to investors (Baldwin, 1994).

A lesson from approaches based on the new growth theory is that public intervention can contribute to growth by encouraging R&D and rendering the appropriation of new technology easier. The message for the EU is therefore that in order to foster growth, measures to promote R&D, improvements in human capital and more efficient financial markets are necessary.

As Deardorff and Stern (2002) maintain, empirical estimates of the impact of European integration on growth run into problems since it is problems to isolate integration from other variables influencing growth. None the less, Baldwin (1989) and Italianer (1994) found substantial growth effects from the Single Market Programme (see Chapter 6). Crafts and Toniolo (1996) provide an extensive analysis of growth in the Europe since 1945.

5.11 Political economy arguments to explain why countries may prefer regional trade blocs to multilateral liberalization

Johnson (1965) introduces political economy arguments to maintain that countries with a strong preference for industrial production that are (or feel themselves to be) at a comparative disadvantage vis-à-vis the rest of the world may favour the creation of a customs union or preferential trade arrangements.[12] According to this view, governments use tariffs to achieve certain non-economic objectives. Countries are assumed to have a preference for industrial production, so consumers are prepared to expand industrial production beyond what would occur in a free trade scenario. Governments are assumed to respond rationally to the demands of the electorate and will use protection to expand industrial production. Tariffs are the usual instrument used, since most types of export subsidy are ruled out by the WTO, and domestic political considerations lead to a preference for tariffs rather than production subsidies because of the burden posed by the latter on domestic taxpayers.

El-Agraa (2007) modifies Johnson's model by considering industrial production not as a single aggregate but as a variety of products for which countries have varying degrees of comparative advantage. In this way countries can be both exporters and importers of industrial products.

---

[11] This could be regarded as a special case of the knowledge capital argument.

[12] The argument is easily extended to countries having a preference for agricultural production.

Considering a simplified case with only two countries, one will be a net exporter and the other a net importer of any industrial product. For each country the prospective gain from tariff reduction lies in the expansion of industrial production. With non-discriminatory trade liberalization the reduction of the home country's tariff is considered a source of loss that must be compensated by tariff reductions on the part of the other country.

With a customs union, trade creation is not considered as a means of replacing higher cost production with cheaper imports but is regarded as the price to be paid for expanding export markets. Trade diversion offers a chance for increasing production within the customs union by replacing imports from the rest of the world with imports from the partner. As a result, trade diversion is preferable to trade creation for the home country since no sacrifice of domestic production is necessary. Stress is also placed on the gains to domestic industry from economies of scale, increased competition and the growth potential of a larger market area as a result of establishing the customs union. Preferential trade liberalization gives rise to chances for expanding industrial production to an extent not possible through non-discriminatory liberalization.

The choice for a country then becomes whether to form or join a customs union. According to Johnson's model as refined by the El-Agraa assumption, a country will join a customs union only if it considers that its comparative advantage in some forms of industrial production is strong enough for its industrial production to increase (or for any loss in industrial production to be compensated by greater efficiency). Other member states will allow the country to join only if they think that there is no threat of the new member increasing its industrial production at the expense of their own. As a result, customs unions are likely to be negotiated between countries with a similar preference for industrial production and a similar degree of comparative advantage in industrial production (or, in other words, a similar level of economic development).

As Johnson argues, this approach helps to explain why the Treaty of Rome attempted to ensure that each of the member states maintained a 'fair share of production', even if this required additional mechanisms such as the measures to promote growth in Southern Italy.

Grossman and Helpman (1995) developed the political economy argument, explaining policy formation as the outcome of lobbying and competition among industries. In this framework free trade negotiations become a process of providing a sufficient balance between the interest groups of a country.

Baldwin (2006a) makes use of new trade theories to introduce also the 'juggernaut' approach to trade liberalization. New trade theories allow for differences in firm size and efficiency to explain why the largest and most efficient firms export, while small and medium firms tend to sell domestically. Large firms want access to foreign markets to expand exports, but the price to pay is a lowering of tariffs and expansion of imports. This will add to the competitive pressures on small and medium firms that sell locally. Some of the smaller firms may be forced out of the market, but larger firms can compensate increased competition at home with expanded foreign markets. Introducing political economy arguments, the larger exporting firms may be more effective at lobbying governments, also because they are less numerous, so have lower costs of organizing interest group activities (and overcoming the problem of free-riding indicated by Olson (1965), see also Chapter 4).

5.12   Empirical research on the effects of integration

Many of the early empirical studies of the formation and successive enlargements of the EC were based on customs union theory. This type of approach generally involves an attempt to measure the effects of passing from free trade to a customs union. Over time, customs union theory became somewhat anachronistic, as in later enlargements most countries joining the EU already had a free trade area or customs union with the Community. For instance, thanks to the Europe Agreements the new Central and East European member states had a free trade area for manufactures and passed to a single market (with some derogations) with enlargement. Turkey already has a customs union with the EU, though agricultural goods are largely excluded.

Early empirical research based on the customs union approach (that is, attempting to measure trade creation and trade diversion) found the effects of integration surprisingly small. Though there

are considerable variations in the results, in general the gains from creation of the Community were found to be in the order of 1–2 per cent of GDP (Lipsey, 1960; Harrop, 2000). This was partly because trade was generally a rather small share of GDP, and most of the studies concentrated on tariff reductions, but tariffs were already relatively low. The reward seemed remarkably small for all the effort of creating the Community, so led to questioning of the approach, and the emergence of the view that integration probably also involved dynamic effects (see above).

The aim here is not to present a comprehensive overview of the research on integration effects, but to give an indication of some of the approaches used which may be useful. For surveys of this literature see, for example, Pomfret (1986) or Baldwin and Venables (1995).

A first distinction can be made between *ex ante* and *ex post* analyses of the effects of integration. An **ex ante** analysis attempts to estimate the future effects of setting up an integration bloc, or enlargement to new members. In this case, information is available concerning the present, pre-integration situation, but predictions have to be made about the likely impact of beginning or extending the integration process.

Ex post analyses of the effects of integration take place after the process has been in operation for some time. In this case, data are available on what has occurred with integration, but the difficulty lies in attempting to assess what would have happened in its absence. In other words, it is necessary to assess likely developments in economic variables such as trade, production and consumption if there had been no integration. This entails constructing an **anti-monde** or fictitious world in which the integration bloc is absent or the country in question remains outside it. The *anti-monde* is then compared with actual developments in order to assess the integration effect. As the approach is based on an unknowable *anti-monde* that cannot be tested against experience, ultimately the evaluation of estimates based on this type of approach is largely a matter of judgement about the plausibility of the simplifying assumptions made about the *anti-monde*.

Most of the early studies concentrated on the trade effects of integration, attempting to impute hypothetical trade flows from existing trade flows by various methods such as:

- extrapolating developments existing prior to the creation or extension of the integration process;
- comparing developments in the integration bloc with what was happening in third-party countries.

Surveys of empirical estimates of the trade effects of the EC using extrapolation are provided in Mayes (1978), Winters (1987) or Srinivasan et al. (1993). The surveys suggest that there was evidence for trade creation in the 1970s and 1980s, and though trade diversion was estimated to be much lower scale, it appeared to be substantial in the agricultural sector. Among the best-known studies of this type for the EEC are those by Balassa (1967, 1974, 1975), Truman (1969) and Sellekaerts (1973). A more recent application of this type of approach was carried out by Bojnec and Ferto (2007) to assess the impact of the 2004 and 2007 enlargements on food and agricultural trade, and they found evidence of trade creation.

Balassa (1967, 1974) proposed a method that uses the *ex post* income elasticity for imports, and assumes that this would have remained constant in the absence of integration. The *ex post* income elasticity of demand is defined as the ratio of the average annual rate of change in imports to that of GDP, both expressed in constant prices. The method consists of comparing the elasticities for intra-EC trade and extra-EC trade for periods before and after integration. Under *ceteris paribus* conditions, a decline in the income elasticity of demand for extra-EC imports indicates trade diversion. Alternatively, according to Balassa, a rise in this elasticity for intra-EC imports indicates gross trade creation, while an increase in these elasticities from all sources indicates overall trade creation. Balassa compared the pre-integration period (1953–59) with two post-integration periods (1959–65 and 1965–70) and found evidence for overall trade creation, though there appeared to have been trade diversion for foodstuffs.

There are, however, certain drawbacks to the approach and, in particular, that of defining the *anti-monde* and assuming that all, and only, integration effects are picked up in changes in the income elasticity of demand for imports. Moreover, the results of the approach depend on the choice of base period, and supply-side effects are ignored.

Kreinen (1972) carried out a comparison of EEC performance with that of third countries such as the USA, the UK and other industrial countries outside Europe. Clearly, the results depend heavily on the country chosen as a control group to 'normalize' trade shares. Kreinen's results suggest that trade creation was far more substantial than trade diversion.

In the more recent literature on empirical assessments of the effects of integration, two approaches that figure prominently are gravity models and computable general equilibrium models (see Burfisher et al. (2004) for a review of this literature).

The **gravity model** approach involves attempting to predict the level of bilateral trade flows on the basis of variables such as GNP, population, geographical distance and preferential trading arrangements. Gravity models are often relatively successful in predicting trade flows between countries but have been criticized for lacking theoretical underpinnings. The estimated coefficients of the model may reflect unrelated developments occurring at the same time rather than integration effects. Gravity models were developed by Tinbergen (1952), and have been applied to the EC by Verdoorn and Schwartz (1972), Aitken (1973) and, more recently, Frankel (1997), Soloaga and Winters (1999) and Kandogan (2005b). Other studies (Frankel and Rose, 2000; Rose, 2000, 2002; Baldwin, 2005) have used gravity models to show how introducing a common currency appears to have encouraged trade growth (see Chapter 9).

Following the collapse of communism in Central and Eastern Europe in 1989, various authors used gravity models to assess the 'normal' level of trade with the EC, that is, what trade would have been had communism never been introduced in those countries. Among the most well-known studies of this type are those of Wang and Winters (1991), Hamilton and Winters (1992), Baldwin (1994), Faini and Portes (1995) and the Transition Reports of the European Bank for Reconstruction and Development (various years).[13]

Wilhelmsson (2006) used a gravity model to assess the impact of the 2004 enlargement on trade between the EU(15) and the new Central and Eastern European member states, and found evidence for significant trade creation and limited trade diversion. Gravity models were also used to analyse foreign direct investment (FDI) in the new member states (see, for example, Bevan and Estrin, 2004; Demekas et al., 2007; Bellak et al., 2008).

Computable general equilibrium (CGE) models attempt to take into account the repercussions of trade liberalization on the whole of the domestic economy and on trading partners. The aim of a CGE model is to specify the conditions for equilibrium in all markets and countries. As described in Chapter 6, models of this type were used to assess the impact of the Single Market Programme and, as shown in Chapter 15, the evolution of regional disparities in the EU. In a review of the CGE literature, Robinson and Thierfelder (2002) find that, according to most studies, integration increases the welfare of participants, trade creation tends to be larger on aggregate than trade diversion, and welfare effects are generally larger if features of new trade theory are considered and if there is an enlargement of membership.

European Commission (2009e) provides a survey of *ex ante* studies, including those based on the CGE approach, to assess the costs and benefits of the 2004 and 2007 enlargements. A common conclusion of these studies was that enlargement would lead to large net benefits for the EU as a whole, in particular for the new member states. Among the benefits from enlargement that emerge from these studies are intensified trade and FDI, lower risk premiums, macroeconomic stability, an improved framework for economic governance, and structural reforms induced by the prospect of EU membership.

Schiff and Winters (2003) have criticized the use of CGE models to analyse the impact of integration as they are generally based on the assumption that products are differentiated by country of origin, so all countries appear to have some market power. As a result, it is argued that these models tend to overestimate the terms of trade effects of integration.

---

[13] For a discussion of the application of gravity models to the Central and Eastern European countries (CEECs) see Senior Nello (2002).

5.13 Regionalism versus multilateralism

One of the more recent developments in the theory and practice of integration has been the emergence of a new wave of regionalism in the sense of a proliferation of regional trade blocs (see also Chapter 18), which has been accompanied by a revived debate in the literature on the virtues or otherwise of regional co-operation.

The explosion of regional blocs since the 1990s follows the first wave of regional trade agreements mainly between developed countries in the 1950s and 1960s.[14] A total of 474 regional trade agreements in force were notified to the WTO by 31 July 2010.[15] About half the value of international trade is covered by such agreements (Josling, 2007). With the collapse of the Doha Round negotiations, this process is likely to continue. What is more, in 2006 the EU ended its moratorium on negotiating new free trade agreements.

Ethier (1998a, b) has identified some main features of this new proliferation of regional trade agreements (RTAs):[16]

- Recent RTAs typically involve at least one developing country linking to more developed countries;
- Membership generally follows a significant unilateral liberalization – for instance, by the Central and East European countries in the case of the EU, and by Mexico for the North American Free Trade Agreement (NAFTA);
- RTAs are rarely restricted to trade aspects;
- Developing countries tend to make bigger concessions in RTAs, often because the tariffs of developed countries are already low.

According to Ethier (1998a, b), regionalism is the means by which new countries enter the multilateral system and attempt to attract foreign direct investment.

Parallel to this growth in the number of regional trade blocs, a theoretical toolkit on regional co-operation has emerged since the 1990s. This approach places the issue of regional integration in the wider context of multilateral, worldwide trade liberalization. The literature attempts to address the question of whether regional co-operation acts as a stumbling block to or a building block for multilateral trade liberalization (Bhagwati et al., 1998) and to identify the conditions for successful regional initiatives. Bhagwati and Panagariya (1996) define building blocks as RTAs that either further multilateral negotiations, or continue adding new members until the bloc converges on global free trade. In contrast, stumbling blocks are defined as giving rise to trade diversion and protectionism, and as being closed to expansion.

Bhagwati (1993) introduced the concept of a dynamic time path: the question is not simply whether the RTA was beneficial or not in itself, but whether its dynamic effect was to accelerate or to slow the ongoing process of reducing trade barriers worldwide.

As the traditional Heckscher–Ohlin–Samuelson framework, along with static customs union theory centred on the notions of trade creation, trade diversion and terms-of-trade effects, was inadequate to analyse the new RTAs, the literature increasingly made use of the new trade theories described in Chapter 4 (see, for example, Krugman, 1991a; Frankel, 1997).

An important contribution to the regionalism versus multilateralism debate is that of Baldwin (1993), who introduced the domino effect in favour of the argument that regional integration

---

[14] See Baldwin (2006a) for a description of this first wave of regionalism.

[15] For a database on RTAs see the website of the WTO at http://www.wto.org/english/tratop_e/region_e/region_e.htm (accessed 7 March 2010).

[16] The term here is in a wide sense to cover arrangements at the various stages of integration described in Chapter 1.

promotes worldwide trade liberalization. According to this model, the preferential lowering of some trade barriers causes new pressures for outsiders to join, and as the trade bloc grows, the pressures to join become bigger. Outsiders want to become insiders, increasing the incentives to add members to the integration bloc. This enlarges the market, causing other countries to be pulled in as well.

Not all the literature is so confident of the proliferation of regionalism promoting multilateral trade liberalization. Regional trade blocs may follow a hub-and-spoke pattern, being organized around one or more large country, and this may place the smaller member states at a disadvantage with regard to bargaining power.

Bhagwati et al. (1998) refer to the 'spaghetti bowl' phenomenon caused by the overlapping of complex systems of trade concessions. This may help to explain why the EU has often preferred free trade associations to customs unions with the applicant countries (with the notable exception of Turkey, where the motives were political as much as economic). Bhagwati and Panagariya (1996) also express fears that RTAs may be trade distorting, though, as illustrated above, this is an empirical question, depending on the case in question.

Krugman (1993a) developed a model to show how world welfare varies with the number of RTAs, finding that world welfare is maximized when there is worldwide free trade (in effect one trading bloc), but minimized when the number of RTAs is relatively low.

Winters (1996) argues that sector-specific lobbies may be a danger with regionalism as they may prevent blocs moving towards global free trade: with lobbies trade diversion may be good politics even if it is bad economics. Regionalism may affect the way countries interact and respond to shocks in the world economy. Though Winters maintains that the jury is still out on whether regionalism promotes multilateralism, he argues that regionalism may increase the risks of a catastrophe in the world trading system.

The new regionalism approach may also help to identify the characteristics that are likely to lead to success (or failure) of a regional bloc. A study by the World Bank (2000) argues that a strong liberalizing arrangement with the right partner (preferably rich, large and open) may lead to a virtuous circle of increased credibility, investment, growth and political stability. This may help to explain the interest of Mexico in NAFTA and of the successive waves of applicant countries in joining the EU.

Regionalism is here to stay, and dealing with it could provide a means for the WTO to reinvent its role. The WTO could provide research and information of the likely consequences of the proliferation of bilateral and regional deals, and create a negotiating forum for the co-ordination and harmonization of rules of origin. In 1996 the WTO created the Regional Trade Agreements Committee to monitor whether such agreements are consistent with WTO obligations, and in 2006 a Transparency Mechanism for RTAs was established. In order to correct a possible increase in power asymmetry in a hub-and-spoke system of regional blocs, the WTO could also provide a forum for the smaller or economically weaker spoke countries to co-ordinate their positions and increase their bargaining power.

Summary of key concepts

- Viner (1953) introduced the concepts of **trade creation and trade diversion** on which customs union theory is based. Trade creation arises when domestic production is replaced by cheaper imports from a partner country. Trade diversion results from low-cost imports from suppliers in third countries being replaced by more expensive imports from a partner country. Usually these concepts are taken to refer to welfare effects rather than trade flows. The welfare effects of forming a customs union on the consumption side also have to be taken into account.

- The net effect of forming a customs union on the welfare of the home country may be positive, negative or zero. This is known as **Viner's ambiguity**.

- The **benefits of forming a customs union** are likely to be higher: (1) the higher the original level of the tariff before forming the customs union; (2) the lower the common

external tariff towards the rest of the world; (3) the higher the number of countries joining a customs union and the greater their size; (4) the smaller the differences in costs of production between the members of the customs union and third countries; (5) the closer the countries are geographically; and (6) the more competitive (producing the same goods), rather than complementary (producing a different range of goods), the economies of the member states are.

■ In order to explain **why a country should prefer a customs union to non-discriminatory trade liberalization** the early literature advanced arguments such as terms-of-trade effects and economies of scale. Johnson argued that the political economy argument – that governments may have a preference for industrial production – can be used to explain why they favour preferential trade arrangements.

■ **Early empirical research** based on the customs union approach found the effects of integration surprisingly small.

■ The **dynamic effects of integration** are: economies of scale, increased competition, specialization, increased bargaining power at an international level, and technological progress. These effects are generally considered to be greater than the traditional static integration effects.

■ Integration may contribute to long-term **growth** by encouraging R&D, technology diffusion, improved human capital and more efficient financial markets. In practice, empirical studies may encounter difficulties in isolating integration from the other variables having an impact on growth.

■ There has been much recent debate as to whether **regional co-operation** helps or hinders multilateral trade liberalization.

Questions for study and review

1 Describe the static and dynamic effects of integration.
2 Compare the effects of non-discriminatory trade liberalization with a preferential trade arrangement or customs union.
3 What explanations have been given of why countries may prefer preferential trade agreements to non-discrimination?
4 Under what conditions is a customs union likely to lead to an increase in welfare?
5 Indicate some of the results of empirical studies to assess the effect of integration.
6 Provide examples of how regional integration can promote multilateral trade liberalization.
7 Exercise on trade creation. Use the example of trade creation in the text to calculate the effects of formation of a customs union on: producer revenue, consumer expenditure, the trade balance and total welfare in Belgium (see also the Appendices to Chapter 4 for examples of how to calculate these effects).
8 Exercise on trade diversion. Assume that the free trade price of commodity X is equivalent to €2 in the USA, and €3 in Luxembourg. Initially Belgium applies a 100 per cent tariff on all imports, and produces 60 million units of X and consumes 80 million units. Belgium then forms a customs union with Luxembourg, but maintains the 100 per cent tariff with the USA. After formation of the customs union Belgium produces 50 million units of X, consumes 100 million X and imports 50 million X. Calculate the net impact on welfare as a result of formation of the customs union.

Online
Learning **Centre**

When you have read this chapter, log on to the Online Learning Centre website at ***www.mcgraw-hill.co.uk/textbooks/senior*** to explore weblinks, chapter-by-chapter test questions, case studies and more online study tools.

Chapter 6

The Single Market

Learning Objectives

By the end of this chapter you should be able to understand:

- ✓ How much specialization of industry there is in the EU
- ✓ The main forms of non-tariff barrier still applied in the EU
- ✓ What advantages were expected from the Single Market Programme
- ✓ What were the main steps in introducing the Single European Market (SEM)
- ✓ How important the Single European Act (SEA) was in the integration process
- ✓ The difficulties encountered in the liberalization of services in the EU, in particular, in areas such as financial markets and transport
- ✓ What were the estimated effects of the Single Market on the European economy
- ✓ The main elements of the Monti Report and the Commission's 2010 proposals to complete the Single Market

6.1 Introduction

This chapter begins with a historical account of the introduction of the Single Market Programme. Following a brief discussion of the problems of implementation, each of the main aspects of the Programme is then discussed in turn: frontier controls, differences in national rules and regulations, fiscal harmonization, public procurement and services. The final part of the chapter deals with attempts to assess the achievements of the Single Market Programme, and discusses recent initiatives aimed at its 'completion'.

The chapter is closely linked to the following chapter on more recent strategies to increase EU competitiveness, and Chapter 16 on competition policy, which can in a sense be considered as 'policing the Single Market'.

As will be explained in the chapter, there have been many attempts to 'complete' the Single Market Programme, but the latest, and one of the most important, was that launched in 2010 by former Commissioner for Competition Policy Mario Monti (Monti, 2010). Many of the suggestions of the Monti Report will be mentioned here in dealing with various aspects of policy, as they were instrumental in shaping the European Commission document of October 2010 *Towards a Single Market*

Act For a highly competitive social market economy. This sets out a work programme of fifty proposals to improve the operation of the internal market.

6.2 Background to the Single Market Programme

Following the 1979 increase in oil prices, the European economy experienced a prolonged recession with stagnating output, rising unemployment and declining world export shares. During these years the terms 'Eurosclerosis' and 'Europessimism' were coined to describe the flagging process of integration. The main energies of the Community appeared absorbed by budgetary squabbles and the annual marathons to fix agricultural prices.

The EC member states were becoming increasingly concerned about the growing lag between their economic performance and that of countries such as Japan and the USA, especially in high technology sectors.[1] The Community was losing its world market share not only in industries such as automobiles and industrial machinery but also in rapidly growing sectors such as information technology and electronics. Moreover, EC markets were increasingly being penetrated in these sectors by foreign firms.

In searching for the explanation for this lack of competitiveness, European industrialists and policy makers laid the blame on the fragmentation of the EC market. The EC business lobby soon began to press for EC initiatives to overcome this disadvantage, and the initial response of the Community was to introduce a series of measures to promote co-operation in research and development among European firms.

Theoretical studies, such as that of Krugman (1991b), also provided evidence of the fragmentation of the EC market. Krugman argued that the four large countries of the EC were comparable in size and population to the four great regions of the USA: the North-East (New England and the mid-Atlantic), the Midwest (the north-central and western north-central states), the West and the South. Examining industrial specialization as measured by share of manufacturing employment, Krugman found that the level of specialization in the USA was higher than in the EC, even though the distances were greater. The Midwest could be compared to Germany in that both were centres of heavy, traditional industry, while the South was similar to Italy with light, labour-intensive industry. However, while there was almost no textile production in the Midwest, Germany still accounted for a substantial share. As shown in Table 6.1, Italy had a far higher share of machinery and auto production than the American South. Krugman attributed the lower level of specialization in the EU to the continued existence of non-tariff barriers.[2]

Table 6.1   Industrial specialization (share of manufacturing employment) in Germany, Italy and the USA (%)

	Germany	Italy	Midwest	South
Textiles	3.7	9.1	0.3	11.7
Apparel	2.6	5.6	2.4	10.6
Machinery	15.8	12.9	15.0	7.1
Transport equipment	13.2	10.4	12.8	5.9
Automobiles	38.4	17.6	66.3	25.4

Source: Krugman (1991b).

---

[1] Where possible, in this chapter the terms 'EC' or 'Community' have been used when reference is prior to implementation of the Maastricht Treaty, and the term 'EU' is used subsequently.

[2] In the literature various indices to measure specialization have been developed. For an overview of these indices see Coombes and Overman (2004).

In 1985, when Jacques Delors became president of the Commission, the Single (or Internal) Market Programme was announced as a strategy to raise EC competitiveness.[3] The idea was to return to and complete the original objectives set out in the Treaty of Rome. The removal of tariffs on intra-EC trade was considered a major factor contributing to the quadrupling of that trade in the first decade of the Community, with intra-EC trade growing twice as fast as world trade over that period. If the Community could now eliminate non-tariff barriers between its members, the earlier success of the Community could perhaps be repeated.

The main non-tariff barriers identified were:

- frontier controls;
- differences in technical specifications and standards;
- restrictions on competition for public purchases;
- restrictions on providing certain services (in particular financial and transport services) in other EC countries;
- differences in national tax systems.

The Commission divided these barriers into three somewhat arbitrary categories: physical barriers, fiscal barriers and technical barriers (all the rest). The third category lumps together measures such as differences in technical specifications and public procurement procedures with institutional restrictions on the free movement of people and capital, etc.

The choice of completion of the Single Market to relaunch the integration effort represented a major strategic decision on the part of Delors and the Commission. Following the Hague Summit of 1969, economic and monetary union was the main integration objective of the 1970s. The difficulties encountered and limited success realized help to explain the search for an alternative.

6.3 Expected advantages of the Single European Market

In the late 1980s the EC Commission sponsored what was probably the most extensive single assessment of the likely effects of an economic policy ever carried out. The results were published in sixteen volumes and are known as the Cecchini Report, or 'Costs of non-Europe'.[4] As will be shown below, many of the results of the study have been subject to heavy criticism, but the description of the various approaches used in the analysis is interesting both as a guide to many of the prevailing theories on integration at the time and as an insight into the views of the Commission.

Traditionally, assessments of the impact of economic integration tended to be based on the 'static' concepts of trade creation and trade diversion (see Chapter 5). However, empirical studies of integration effects increasingly pointed to the gap between the traditional theory and real issues, and stressed the need to take dynamic effects such as increased competition, growth and the scope for exploiting economies of scale into account.[5] As will be shown below, dynamic effects figure strongly in the analysis of expected benefits of the Single Market.

Studies such as the Cecchini Report emphasize the impact that the Single Market was likely to have in reducing prices and costs. Prior to the 1993 Programme, large price differences existed between EC states,[6] and these were taken as an indication of the degree of market fragmentation.

---

[3] The term 'Internal Market' is generally adopted by the Commission and is used in the Lisbon Treaty. As Monti (2010) maintains, 'internal' may create confusion with the national domestic market, or carry overtones of 'fortress Europe' for observers from third countries, while 'single' implies a sense of commitment or actions to be taken.

[4] Cecchini (1988).

[5] See Chapters 4 and 5.

[6] According to Emerson et al. (1989), the average variation from EC mean price without indirect taxes in 1985 across countries was 15 per cent for consumer goods and 12 per cent for capital products (taking the EC(9) members prior to 1981 as 100). In the service sectors these variations were even greater, amounting to 28 per cent for road and rail transport, 29 per cent for financial services, 50 per cent for telephone and telegram services and 42 per cent for electrical repairs.

Figure 6.1 provides a useful shorthand illustration of the expected effect of the SEM on costs and prices. The elimination of barriers would enable firms from other EC member states to sell at lower prices in a particular EC country, say Italy. The increased competition from other EC firms selling at lower prices on the Italian market would first induce Italian firms to reduce excess profits and wages and eliminate inefficiencies within the firms. Subsequently, the increased demand resulting from lower prices would encourage restructuring and attempts to exploit economies of scale, both through mergers and through new investment.

Figure 6.1 The effects of eliminating cost-increasing trade barriers

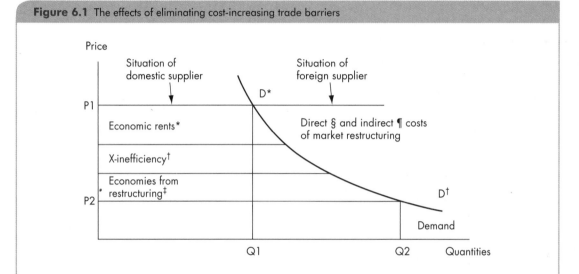

* *Economic rents consist of the margin of excess profit or wage rates that result from market protection.*

† *X-inefficiency consists of, for example, the costs of overstaffing, excess overhead costs and excess inventories (i.e. inefficiencies not related to the production technology of the firm's investments). Because the firm is not operating in a competitive environment, there is inadequate pressure to cut these costs.*

‡ *Economies from restructuring include, for example, greater economies of scale, or the benefits obtained when inefficient production capacity is eliminated and new investments are made.*

§ *Direct costs include delays at the frontier and the cost of differing technical regulations, which would immediately fall if market barriers were eliminated.*

¶ *Indirect costs are those that would fall as foreign suppliers adjust to the more competitive situation with more efficient production and marketing.*

Source: *Figure 2.2 (p. 26) from The Economics of 1992 (1989) by Michael Emerson et al. By permission of Oxford University Press.*

It was argued that these processes would free resources for alternative productive uses, so raising the levels of investment and consumption sustainable in the Community. The rationalization of production and distribution would increase productivity, thereby reducing prices and costs.

In the case of public procurement, the cost savings would release resources enabling governments either to cut taxes or to carry out other growth-inducing activities. The liberalization of financial services was of particular importance to the Programme since the reduced cost of credit would stimulate increased consumer demand and investment. It was estimated that these benefits would be apparent after a period of 5–6 years (see the section on the achievements of the Single Market Programme below).

6.4 The timetable for the introduction of the Single European Market

In March 1985 the new president of the Commission, Jacques Delors, presented his programme for the Single Market to the European Parliament. Later that year the Cockfield White Paper *Completing the Internal Market* was presented at the European Council in Milan (European Commission, 1985). This called for the elimination of barriers between EC countries by the end of 1992 and set out 282 measures necessary to achieve this aim.

Many of these measures had been around as draft proposals for many years, and although the completion of the Single Market was not a new idea, it now acquired a new impetus. The way in which the Programme was presented represents a major marketing success: the timetable set out deadlines that represented precise targets, and focused the attention of politicians and business. The Commission, and in particular Delors, was largely responsible for introducing what was to become a self-fulfilling prophecy. The personal style of Lord Cockfield, Commissioner for the Internal Market, who emphasized the technical and low-key nature of the Programme, also contributed to its success.

The emphasis on deregulation meant that the Programme coincided with the economic doctrine being advocated at the time by politicians such as Thatcher and Reagan. Initially the Programme seemed to be concerned with rules, not money, so did not appear a threat to national governments. However, it was soon to emerge that the Programme would have to be flanked by redistributive measures to compensate the weakest regions and sections of the population.

The Milan Summit also had to decide on the intergovernmental conferences to prepare the necessary revision to the existing treaties. Initially the UK, Denmark and Greece were opposed to the proposed institutional reforms that would increase the use of majority voting in the Council, strengthen the European Parliament and extend the use of European Political Co-operation. The decision of the Italian presidency to go ahead on a majority vote was unexpected and without precedent (Tsoukalis, 1997).

The three governments that had initially opposed institutional reform soon overcame their misgivings. In part this reflected a fear of being excluded and not being able to influence the decision-making process. However, in the case of the UK in particular, institutional reform was seen as the necessary price to pay for the Single Market, which was an objective strongly favoured by national politicians and the business community.

6.5 The Single European Act

The Single European Act (SEA) sets out the formal procedure necessary to implement the 1993 Programme. It also modified the EC decision-making process and called for a revived integration effort in other fields such as technology and in monetary, social, regional and external policies. The SEA defined the Single European Market as 'an area without internal frontiers in which the free movement of goods, persons, services and capital is ensured'.

The SEA represented the first major revision to the treaties, but at the time its importance was underestimated. With the benefit of hindsight it can be argued that the SEA launched a new phase in the integration process, spilling over into renewed efforts in political union, institutional reform, economic and monetary union, and reinforced EC social, regional and competition policies. The way in which the Single Market Programme pushed the integration process forward in other areas lends itself well to interpretation according to the neo-functionalist approach (see Chapter 1).

With regard to institutional reform, qualified majority voting was to be used in the Council for the harmonization of national rules and regulations.[7] Unanimity voting was still to be used in the Council for

---

[7] This voting rule was also extended to the liberalization of capital movements and of sea and air transport. The quid pro quo for wider use of majority voting was a safeguard clause that would allow member states to continue to apply national provisions after the introduction of new EC rules in certain circumstances. This was to ensure that standards for the protection of the environment or working conditions would not deteriorate.

questions relating to fiscal policy, the free movement of persons, and the rights and interests of employees. This was because these were sensitive issues on which the EC member states held divergent views.

The SEA stipulates that any institutional change in economic and monetary policy would require a new revision of the treaties, a prospect that seemed unlikely at the time (see Chapter 10). However, the SEA contains formal recognition of the European Monetary System (EMS) and the role of the European Currency Unit (ECU). As discussed in Chapter 9, economic and monetary union (EMU) is linked to completion of the internal market, as exchange rate uncertainty between currencies can be regarded as another obstacle to trade. The introduction of a single monetary unit would confirm the reality of the Single Market, but this in turn would push the integration process further. Democratic control of the new European Central Bank would require further steps in the direction of political union.

Title V of the SEA deals with 'economic and social cohesion' to ensure harmonious development and the reduction of regional disparities. The weaker regions, and in particular the periphery of the Community, feared that they would not be able to withstand the increased competition implied by the Single Market and that there would be a worsening of regional and sectoral imbalances. In response to their requests, Article 130d SEA calls for effective co-ordination and rationalization of the Structural Funds (see Chapter 15).

Certain derogations and special provisions were permitted in order to take account of the heterogeneity and different levels of development of EC member states, but the outcome was far from permitting a multi-speed Europe.

The SEA also called for increased Community responsibility for social policy, in particular on questions relating to the health and safety of workers. In 1988 the idea of a 'Social Europe' was launched, which entailed identifying the regions and industries most likely to be negatively affected by the 1993 Programme and offering some measures of compensation. It was also argued that social policy measures were necessary in order to ensure a 'level playing field' and prevent the internal market being undermined by the phenomenon of 'social dumping'. Social dumping refers to fear that employment will be lost in member states where better social standards are reflected in higher labour costs. There may be downward pressure on wages, social security conditions and minimum health and safety regulations in those countries in order to prevent loss of market share. This phenomenon is attributed to 'unfair competition' from countries (for example, China) in which labour laws are less restrictive. A major aim of both the 1989 Social Charter and the Social Chapter of the Maastricht Treaty was to prevent this type of 'social dumping' (see Chapter 7).

One of the immediate effects of announcement of the Single Market Programme was to induce a rapid increase in the number of cross-border mergers of EC firms, which rose from 200 in 1985 to some 2,000 in 1989 (Tsoukalis, 1997). This led to a tightening of EC competition policy and, in particular, the introduction of *ex ante* Community authority over mergers from 1989 (see Chapter 16).

6.6　Implementation of the Single Market Programme

At the EC level, rapid progress was made in passing the necessary measures for the Single Market Programme and, according to the Commission, 95 per cent of the legislative programme set out in 1985 was complete by 31 December 1992.[8] The transposition of EC measures into national legislation was to prove a slightly more lengthy process, but the real difficulties arose in implementation of the measures and the granting of temporary derogations.

Subsequently, the European Commission attempted to tighten up on enforcement and implementation procedures. The 1997 Amsterdam European Council endorsed an Action Plan that entails the Commission drawing up a Single Market Scoreboard every six months (see Box 6.1). The Scoreboards indicate whether member states meet the objectives of:

- an average deficit of transposition into national law of less than 1.5 per cent (reduced to 1 per cent in 2007);

---

[8] The main exceptions related to company legislation, fiscal harmonization and intellectual property rights.

- zero tolerance for legislation not transposed after two years or more;
- reducing the number of cases of infringement.

Box 6.1

The Single Market Scoreboard

According to the Single Market Scoreboard, in May 2010 the transposition deficit (that is, the percentage of internal market legislation not yet introduced into national legislation by member states) was 0.9 per cent for the EU(27). The countries with the highest transposition deficits were Greece, Portugal, Poland, Luxembourg, the Czech Republic, Cyprus, France, Italy and Austria, all of which were above the 1 per cent target.

According to the Scoreboard, the countries with the highest number of long outstanding directives (legislation not transposed after two years or more) in May 2010 were Greece (five directives), Ireland, Luxembourg, and Austria (with four each), Portugal (two) and France, Poland, Sweden and the UK (all with one). The member state with the longest transposition delay was Ireland, which had not transposed a directive of 2003 (2003/35/EC) relating to certain environmental programmes. Adding the number of directives not correctly transposed into national legislation to those not transposed, the countries with the worst record are Greece, Poland, Portugal, Italy and the Czech Republic.

Belgium, Greece, Italy, Spain, France, Germany, Portugal and the UK (in that order) were the countries with most pending cases of infringement in May 2010. The sectors with the highest number of infringement cases are taxation and customs, and environmental measures.

Since 1987 there have been 'package meetings' of experts from the member states and the Commission to discuss a 'package' of cases under examination by the Commission for violation of Community law with the aim of solving cases without the need for further legal action.

In 2002 the redress system for implementation of internal market rules (SOLVIT) was introduced by the EU member states (plus Norway, Iceland and Liechtenstein) in order to improve implementation of internal market rules (see Box 6.2). Previously, victims of failure to apply rules (such as non-recognition of a valid diploma or denial of market access for a product) had to appeal to national courts or to the Commission. Under the new system victims can refer the case by internet or telephone to the SOLVIT office in their own member states, and the office will raise the case with the country in which the misapplication has occurred. In 2010 SOLVIT handled about 3,800 cases of which 1,363 fell within its competence, and 90 per cent of those cases were resolved.

In 2007 the Internal Market Information system (IMI) was set up to allow exchanges of information between member states, using a pilot study on recognition of professional qualifications.

Box 6.2

Examples of SOLVIT cases

A Portuguese breakdown vehicle was transporting a damaged Portuguese car from Belgium to Portugal and was fined €600 by the Spanish police because the breakdown vehicle was not fitted with tachograph equipment. The Portuguese SOLVIT office pointed out that breakdown vehicles were not required to have this equipment by EU regulations, and the fine was refunded.

Portuguese citizens living in France had difficulties proving their French address when making payments or when stopped by the police. Mrs de Freitas, a Portuguese citizen living in France, obtained the help of SOLVIT in convincing the French authorities to issue residence permits to Portuguese citizens living in France.

Source: *Internal Market Scoreboard 2003 and SOLVIT home page, http://ec.europa.eu/SOLVIT/site/index_en.htm (accessed 10 November 2010), © European Union, 2011.*

The European Commission maintains that differences in the price of a single model of new car between member states may reflect fragmentation of markets and lack of competition and so serve as evidence that the internal market is not working in this sector (see Box 6.3). These reports suggest that over time there has been price convergence overall among the EU member states.

Box 6.3

Car prices in the EU

Since 1992 the European Commission has carried out a survey of price differences of new cars net of taxes between the member states. In 2009, car prices fell in real terms by 0.6 per cent, and price differences between member states also shrank, with the average standard deviation going down from 9.8 per cent to 8.5 per cent. This is in contrast to 2008 when price differences increased because of currency turbulence and differing reactions to the economic crisis such as incentives to renew national fleets. Price differences for passenger cars seemed to be smaller than for other consumer goods such as food, where the dispersion index for sixteen products was 34.4 per cent in 2009. The cheapest countries in the EU for cars in 2009 were the UK, Sweden and Denmark, and in the eurozone they were Malta, Greece and Finland. The most expensive countries were Germany, Luxembourg and France. Large cars tended to have less price dispersion, and, at the manufacturer level, price dispersion was lowest for BMW and Mercedes in 2009.*

*European Commission Car Price Report of 2010, © European Union, 2011. http://ec.europa.eu/competition/sectors/motor_ vehicles/prices/2010_07_a.pdf (accessed 2 November 2010).

 6.7 ## The main elements of the Single Market Programme: the Schengen Agreement and other aspects of the removal of frontier controls

A key aim of the removal of frontier controls is to facilitate free movement of people within the EU. In 1985 Benelux, Germany and France formed the Schengen Group with the aim of eliminating border controls between each other as rapidly as possible.[9] Subsequently other countries joined the group, though the UK and Ireland opted out (but they participate in police and judicial co-operation). Denmark has signed the Schengen Agreement, but has a partial opt-out, and can choose whether to apply new measures on all questions except visas. In December 2007 Schengen was extended to the all the countries joining the EU in 2004 except Cyprus. Non-EU members of Schengen are Iceland, Norway and Switzerland. A protocol on the participation of Liechtenstein was signed in 2008.

In December 2010 France and Germany blocked the accession of Romania and Bulgaria to Schengen. The two countries had been updating their border security, computer systems and airport infrastructure. However, the question was linked to their slow progress with regard to the Co-operation and Verification Mechanism designed to improve the performance of the judiciary and assist in the fight against corruption and (in the case of Bulgaria) organized crime.[10]

Schengen implies the removal of all controls on people (whether they are citizens of the EU or of third countries) when they cross frontiers between member states, though a safeguard clause allows a country to reinstate controls in the event of a serious threat to public policy, public health or public security. In 2011 Schengen seemed at risk. Faced with extraordinary flows of immigrants (see Chapter 8) Italy issued Tunisian migrants with documents allowing them to travel in the EU, and France stopped them at its border. Denmark reinstated guards and spot checks along its frontier.

---

[9] The name Schengen derives from the town near the Luxembourg, French and German borders.

[10] See Chapter 19.

[11] 1997 for Italy, Austria and Greece.

In 1990 the Schengen countries agreed a Convention on Application of the Agreement, which entered into force in 1995,[11] and was incorporated into a protocol to the Amsterdam Treaty in 1999. In addition to a mechanism for settling disputes, this set out a series of provisions on issues such as extradition, drugs, firearms, asylum, visas, the transmission of personal data, and co-operation between national police forces, including the establishment of Europol.[12] The Schengen Information System (SIS) was set up and consists of a computer network for the exchange of information between national police forces (also adopted by the UK and Ireland). This acts as a joint automated search system and involves creating and maintaining data files on persons and certain objects (firearms, stolen or lost vehicles, banknotes, official documents and so on). Some aspects of Schengen have been challenged on grounds of privacy and accountability. For instance, it has been claimed that the SIS may run counter to national legislation on data protection and could therefore infringe civil liberties.

Box 6.4

Football integration

One of the effects of the Single Market was to encourage integration of soccer. Football integration has paralleled the overall integration process. In 1956 the first European Cup was played and, as in the case of the EEC, initially the UK failed to participate.* With the Single Market objective of free movement of labour it was no longer legal for EU teams to limit the number of citizens they had from other EU states. At about the same time the European Court decided that footballers were free to move anywhere after the end of their contract without their club demanding a transfer fee. Wages and transfers increased, and the Champions League emerged.

The Treaty of Rome was signed in 1957 and entered into force in 1958, which was also the debut of Manchester United as the first English club to enter the European Cup. To celebrate, 50 years after signing the Treaty in 2007, Commission President Barroso decided to hold a match between Manchester United and the EU.† The EU team was coached by Marcello Lippi and included players such as David Beckham, Steven Gerrard, Gianluca Zambrotta, Carles Puyol, Grégory Coupet and the Brazilian Ronaldinho (who had applied for Spanish citizenship). The EU strip was not blue with yellow stars, but white with blue trim.

*The Economist, 31 May 2003.

† Financial Times, 2 March 2007.

Other aspects of the elimination of border controls required by the internal market include the abolition of customs formalities, veterinary and road safety checks at frontiers. In addition, quantitative restrictions could no longer be applied at the national level by EC member states and had to be replaced by EC measures.[13] The Cecchini Report estimated that industry would save €8 billion a year, and government would save €1 billion per year if frontier controls were removed.

In addition to these measures of negative integration, positive integration (see Chapter 1) or the introduction of common policies was used to facilitate the right to work in other member states (see Box 6.4) and to develop exchange programmes, including EU programmes such as:

- ERASMUS (university exchanges);
- Leonardo da Vinci (training and vocational education);

---

[12] See the Online Learning Centre of this book for a description of Europol. The Schengen Agreement also envisages cross-border surveillance and cross-border pursuit of suspects by police officers.

[13] This had important implications for the quotas on textile products permitted by the Multifibre Agreement (MFA), and entailed abolition of the monetary compensatory amounts of the Common Agricultural Policy (a system of taxes and subsidies levied at the border to cushion the impact of exchange rate changes on the system of price support). The Single Market Programme and the transition of Central and Eastern Europe from 1989 also account for the elimination of the different quotas applied by the member states on imports from the former CEEC 'non-market economies'.

- Comenius (for schools in order to help increase understanding of the range of European cultures and languages); and
- Grundtvig (for adult education).

Created in 1987, the ERASMUS programme allows about 200,000 students to study and work abroad each year.[14] The programme also extends to the three countries of the European Economic Area (Iceland, Liechtenstein and Norway), and Turkey.

There has also been a renewed effort to encourage recognition of university diplomas and other professional qualifications in respective member states. In 2010 the Bologna Process relaunched the aim of creating a European Higher Education Area in which students from 46 participating countries can choose from a wide range of courses, and benefit from smooth recognition procedures.

Though legislation permitting the residence of EU workers and their families in other member states had existed for some time, measures to promote easier residence for other categories, such as pensioners and students, were also passed. The European Employment Services (EURES) network was established to provide information on job opportunities in EU states.

6.8   Differences in national rules and regulations

According to Mattera (1988), at the time when the Single Market Programme was launched, differences in standards and technical barriers accounted for some 80 per cent of the remaining barriers to intra-EC trade. Though the words are sometimes used interchangeably, technical regulations refer to legally binding rules relating to the health and safety of consumers, while 'standards' are voluntary and aim to provide adequate information and ensure the quality of a product.

Barriers, supposedly on 'health' grounds, were levied, for example, on chocolate and French mineral water by Germany, and by Italy on imports of pasta not using durum wheat. In some cases differences in technical regulations prevented cross-border trade, while in others it added to the costs of firms that had to modify their products to meet the requirements of other EC countries.

Article 30 of the Treaty of Rome prohibits quantitative restrictions on intra-EC trade and 'all measures having an equivalent effect'. In the 1974 *Dassonville* ruling of the European Court of Justice, it was argued that 'measures having an equivalent effect' included 'all trading rules enacted by member states which are capable of hindering directly or indirectly, actually or potentially intra-EC trade'.

One way of eliminating these barriers to trade between member states is by harmonizing the national standards and technical regulations of member states. This 'old approach' has proved slow and inefficient as the detailed, technical legislation involved is complex and costly. It also runs the risk of excessive uniformity and bureaucratic interference. The topic is one on which feelings run high, with complaints that 'Eurocrats' are concerned with 'measuring the size of sausages', 'shape of cucumbers', or determined to bring about the demise of rare breeds and crops. Against this, however, excessive deregulation runs the risk of inadequate protection for consumers.

The solution reached by the Community was to rely as far as possible on the principle of mutual recognition, which was defined in the much-cited Cassis De Dijon case of 1979. In this case the European Court of Justice ruled against a German prohibition of imports of a French liqueur on the grounds that it did not conform to German rules and regulations, and established the general principle that all goods lawfully manufactured and marketed in one member state should be accepted also in other member countries. At the same time, the Court recognized the need for some exceptions relating to public health, the fairness of commercial transactions and the defence of the consumer.[15] The mutual recognition principle has also been extended to some dealings with third countries, including the USA (see also Chapter 17).

---

[14] European Commission, http://ec.europa.eu/education/lifelong-learning-programme/doc80_en.htm (accessed 2 November 2010).

[15] According to European Commission (2007a), the mutual recognition principle covered about 20 per cent of EU industrial production and 26 per cent of intra-EU manufacturing trade.

While mutual recognition may work for relatively simple products, this is far less the case for more complex goods (Pelkmans, 2007). When a product was denied access to a country there was no clear procedure for a company to challenge a negative decision so the company was forced to modify the product or abandon that market. Regulation 764/2008 (which came into operation in May 2009) attempted to address these shortcomings by increasing the information available and improving procedures.

To speed up the process of harmonization, in 1985 a 'new approach' was developed. Wherever harmonization of rules at the EU level was deemed necessary, it was decided that this should be limited to essential objectives and requirements. Directives cover large groups of products and hazards, and specify the essential safety, or other requirements the product must meet. The manufacturers are free to choose between applying either the appropriate EU standard or any other technical specifications that meet these essential requirements. The new approach entailed the setting up of conformity assessment procedures and the CE marking (though this does not apply on certain categories of goods such as food and beverages, and health and beauty products). The CE marking implies that the manufacturer declares responsibility that the product satisfies the essential requirements of the relevant directives, and is in line with the conformity assessment so can circulate freely in the EU. Compliance is voluntary and manufacturers may choose not to observe EU standards, but the onus is on them to prove that their product is safe.

In 2008 a New Legislative Framework was adopted to modernize the 'new approach' by introducing better rules on market surveillance; improving conformity assessments; and clarifying the meaning of the CE trade mark (as in some sectors consumers felt they were not effectively protected). It has been estimated that the trading volume of products covered by the new approach exceeds some €1,500 billion a year.[16]

The task of defining technical specifications is left to private standardization bodies. At EU level the standardization bodies are: the CEN (Comité Européen de Normalisation), CENELEC (Comité Européen de Normalisation Electrotechnique) and ETSI (European Telecommunications Standards Institute). The membership of these organizations consists of national standardization bodies.

For over a decade there have been attempts to introduce an EU patent. A US patent costs about €1,850, but a European patent validated in thirteen countries would cost about ten times as much, with translations alone costing about €14,000.[17] The member states disagree over translation rules, with Spain and Italy objecting to the proposal to limit translation to English, French and German. In November 2010 a group of countries suggested using enhanced co-operation (see Chapter 3) to proceed with the proposal.

The EU and, in particular, the DG for Consumer Affairs of the Commission are also active in the field of protecting consumer rights, and their initiatives can be divided into four main categories:

- Actions for the protection of consumer health and safety. These include rules on the testing and registration of pharmaceutical, medical and cosmetic products, measures to ensure the safety of toys, health controls, labelling for food and agricultural products and so on;

- Protection of the economic interests of consumers by, for instance, measures against unfair contracts and misleading advertising;

- Actions to ensure that consumers have comparative information, through rules on packaging and labelling, and support for consumer organizations;

- Measures to ensure the right of consumers to redress, with simple clear procedures.

The Commission has set out a Consumer Policy Strategy and Programme for the 2007–13 period which is focused on three main objectives: empowering EU consumers; enhancing their welfare in terms of price, choice, quality, diversity, affordability and safety; and protecting consumers

---

[16] http://ec.europa.eu/enterprise/policies/single-market-goods/regulatory-policies-common-rules-for-products/new-legislative-framework/ (accessed 2 November 2010).

[17] Europa Press Release, 1 July 2010, http://europa.eu/rapid/pressReleasesAction.do?reference=IP/10/870 (accessed 10 November 2010).

tively from the serious risks and threats that they cannot tackle as individuals (European Commission, 2007b).

6.9 Fiscal harmonization

Differences in national tax systems represent a barrier to completion of the internal market in two ways. In the first place, tax differences may cause price distortions and so undermine the competitive process. Secondly, differences in national taxation have to be adjusted at the border, thereby necessitating controls at the frontier. Moreover, operating with different tax systems adds to the cost and complexity of doing business in other EU countries. The question of taxation is also central to the debate on exit strategies from the economic crisis (see Chapter 11) and reform of financing of the EU budget (see Chapter 12).

The EU has made slow progress in introducing fiscal harmonization, partly because this is one of the areas where unanimity voting is required in the Council. The power to tax is central to the sovereignty of a country, and differences in tax systems frequently reflect underlying differences in culture and tradition.

Article 99 of the Treaty of Rome called for harmonization of indirect taxes, but the Treaty is rather vague on what is meant by harmonization (Ardy and El-Agraa, 2007). Article 100, for example, states only that 'laws should be approximated'.[18] Although the Single European Act called for 'harmonization of legislation concerning turnover taxes, excise duties and other forms of indirect tax' (Article 17), to date the approach adopted has been that of approximation rather than harmonization of taxes.

The emphasis on indirect taxation reflects the assumption that goods and capital are more mobile than labour, and so more sensitive to differences in national tax systems. It probably also reflects political feasibility, as agreement of the member states on issues relating to direct taxes seems even more difficult to reach.

At the time of the Treaty of Rome the system of indirect taxation adopted by the member states varied considerably, and one of the main achievements of the Community was to introduce a common system of turnover tax from 1967, based on the French VAT (value added tax).[19] This was considered necessary as a percentage of VAT returns constitutes one of the own resources of the EU budget (see Chapter 12).

In 2007 VAT-type taxes accounted for 17.3 per cent of the total tax revenue of the member states.[20] Since 2007 the system has been regulated by the VAT Directive.[21] This provides general indications on what are to be considered as taxable transactions and persons, rates of VAT, possible deductions and so on. It also exempts certain goods and services from VAT, such as medical care, social security work, school and university education, insurance and the granting of credit.

However, application differs greatly from country to country. Differences relate to tax coverage (which products are liable to tax), the number of VAT rates and their levels. As shown in Table 6.2, Denmark applied only one VAT rate in 1991/92, while Ireland applied six. The standard rate applied varied from 15 per cent in Spain, West Germany and Luxembourg, to 25 per cent in Denmark. Differences also arose as to which products were subject to reduced rates either to compensate for the

---

[18] Harmonization entails introducing common legislation, while approximation involves bringing national laws more in line with each other.

[19] With the exception of France, the other original EC members applied a cascade system. This was a multi-stage tax levied on the gross value of output at each stage of the production process. At each stage the tax was levied on selling price, and this price might reflect tax paid at an earlier stage. The system was therefore cumulative and provided an incentive to vertical integration. In contrast, VAT is neutral towards vertical integration and has the advantage that it is self-policing since the purchasing firm has an interest in obtaining an invoice from suppliers showing that taxes on inputs have been paid. VAT is paid at each stage in the productive process (including marketing) on the value added at that stage.

[20] Eurostat, *Tax Revenue in the European Union*, http://epp.eurostat.ec.europa.eu/cache/ITY_OFFPUB/KS-SF-09-043/EN/KS-SF-09-043-EN.PDF (accessed 3 November 2010).

[21] Council Directive 77/388/EC known as the Sixth VAT Directive regulated the system for many years, but was amended on several occasions, and replaced from 2007 by Directive 2006/112/EC or the VAT Directive. See http://europa.eu/legislation_summaries/taxation/l31057_en.htm (accessed 14 April 2011), for a summary of the main elements of the VAT Directive.

Table 6.2 VAT rates in the member states in 1991/92 and July 2010 (%)

Country	Standard 1991/92	Reduced 1991/92	Increased 1991/92	Standard 1 July 2010	Reduced 1 July 2010	Country	Standard 1 July 2010	Reduced 1 July 2010
Belgium	19.5	1, 6 and 12	—	21	6/12	Austria	20	10
Denmark	25	—	—	25	—	Finland	23	9/13
Germany	15	7	—	19	7	Sweden	25	6/12
Spain	15	6	28	18	4/7	Bulgaria	20	7
France	18.6	2.1 and 5.5	—	19.6	5.5	Czech Republic	20	10
Greece	18	4 and 8	—	23	11	Estonia	20	9
Italy	19	4, 9 and 12	38	20	10	Cyprus	15	5/8
Ireland	21	0, 2.7, 10.0, 12.5, and 16	—	21	13.5	Latvia	21	10
Luxembourg	15	3 and 6	—	15	6/12	Lithuania	21	5/9
Netherlands	18.5	6	—	19	6	Hungary	25	5/18
Portugal	16	5	—	21	6/13	Malta	18	5
UK	17.5	0	—	17.5	5	Poland	22	7
						Romania	24	5/9
						Slovenia	20	8.5
						Slovakia	19	6/10

Source: http://ec.europa.eu/taxation_customs/resources/documents/taxation/vat/how_vat_works/rates/vat_rates_en.pdf (accessed 2 November 2010), © European Union, 2011, and (for the 1991/92 rates) OECD Country Reports and Rates of Value Added Tax, www.oecd.org/dataoecd/12/13/34674429.xls (accessed 2 November 2010).

regressive nature of VAT, or for merit goods, such as books and cultural services. For example, the UK applied zero rating to foodstuffs, gas and electricity.

The 1985 White Paper called for the reduction or elimination of fiscal barriers, and in 1987 the Commission produced detailed proposals on how to reach this objective for VAT. The negotiations were heated and prolonged. Higher rate countries such as Ireland and Denmark feared the loss of VAT revenue. Low rate countries such as Germany feared that increased VAT could add to inflationary pressures. The UK and Ireland wanted to maintain zero rating on 'social necessities' such as foodstuffs to offset the regressive nature of VAT.

The compromise eventually reached entailed a standard minimum rate of VAT of 15 per cent and a list of products (food, pharmaceuticals, energy, water, hotels, passenger transport and so on) on which a reduced rate of 5 per cent could be applied. Subsequently a band of 15–25 per cent was introduced for the standard rate. Existing zero rates could be continued but not extended.

As can be seen from Table 6.2, over time convergence has been minimal.[22] In 2011 the European Commission is to publish a new VAT strategy on the basis of a Green Paper carrying out a fundamental review of the VAT system.[23]

Traditionally, VAT in the EU was applied according to the principle of destination, in other words it was paid in the country of consumption. If a product were traded between two member states, the tax would be paid in the importing country, and VAT paid in the exporting country would be refunded. This may be complex and costly for firms due to lack of knowledge about the legislation and language of the country to which they are exporting. The Commission proposed that with the introduction of the Single Market, the destination system should be replaced by a system based on the principle of origin (also known as the 'common market' principle), but little progress has been made in this direction, and reform of the system remains a long-term goal.

Excise duty accounts for over 10 per cent of the total tax revenue of the member states.[24] There are considerable differences in the level and coverage of excise duties (on petrol, alcohol and cigarettes) in the various EU countries (see Box 6.5). These reflect differences in social customs, public health considerations and the revenue requirements of governments of the member states. In some cases decisions are also influenced by the existence of state monopolies (for example tobacco for many years in Italy).

Little progress has been made in reducing differences in national systems of excise duties in the EU. The member states have adopted common lists of products on which excise duties apply, and these are divided into alcoholic, tobacco and petroleum products. The 1993 Programme simply entailed minimum rates of duty for alcohol, tobacco, cigarettes and mineral oil, and an imprecise commitment to harmonization in the medium term. In the meantime goods could circulate an interconnected circuit of customs deposits and were subject to duty only when and where they left that circuit. Products subject to excise duty can be taken from one country to another for 'personal consumption' (see Box 6.5).

Duty free sales have no place in an internal market, but their abolition entailed a serious loss of revenue for airports and ferry companies. It was eventually decided to allow sales of duty free goods on intra-EU trips to continue until 1999 when, despite protests by certain member states (the UK, France and Germany), they were abolished.

Though the Commission has presented various proposals, little progress has been made in harmonizing direct taxes, also because a unanimity vote is required. Top personal income taxes range from a minimum of 10 per cent in Bulgaria to a maximum of 56.4 per cent in Sweden in 2010, with the new member states in general having lower top rates.[25]

The fear of 'tax competition' came to the fore from the mid-1990s. It was argued that with the removal of barriers, capital, in particular, would become more mobile, and governments would be tempted to lower taxes to attract firms and investment. Almost all member states have decreased their taxes on corporate income over the past two decades, and in the EU(27) they fell from 35.3 per cent in 1995 to 23.2 per cent on average in 2010.[26] There has been a shift in the burden to taxation to labour (which was less mobile) through personal income taxes and social contributions.

---

[22] This is despite the fact that in a 2004 survey (European Commission, 2006a) 86.1 per cent of large businesses quoted cross-border payment or refund of VAT as a major difficulty, and 53.5 per cent of large firms have not requested refunding at some point because of complexity of procedures.

[23] This is one of the fifty proposals presented in European Commission (2010a) described below.

[24] This statistic is taken from http://www.europedia.moussis.eu/books/Book_2/5/14/02/03/index.tkl?all=1&pos=176 (accessed 3 November 2010).

[25] European Commission (2010b).

[26] European Commission (2010b).

Box 6.5

Excise duties in the Single European Market

According to Commons (2002), the duty on a pint of beer was 30 pence in the UK, 5 pence in France, 3 pence in Germany and 7 pence in the Netherlands. Duty on a 70 cl bottle of spirits was £5.48 in the UK, £2.51 in France and £1.19 in Spain. Duty on a 75 cl bottle of wine was £1.16 in the UK, 2 pence in France and zero in Spain. Total excise duty on a packet of cigarettes was £2.80 in the UK, £1.22 in France, £1.00 in the Netherlands and 99 pence in Belgium.

The differences had narrowed little by January 2011. Excise duty on a litre of still wine varied from the equivalent of €2.8 in Finland, €2.6 in Ireland (or €3.8 on wine of more than 15 per cent volume), €2.6 in the UK, €2.1 in Sweden, to 0.03 in France, and zero in a number of EU member states such as Italy Spain or Austria.*

Under the Single Market, initially there were fixed amounts of the quantities of products subject to excise duty that could be taken from one country to another for 'personal consumption' but this was subsequently increased to an 'unlimited quantity' of goods for personal use of the traveller. Differences in excise duties between the member states were sufficient to stimulate a lively trade exploiting these personal allowances, exerting pressure for market-induced harmonization and creating significant losses of revenue for some of the member states (notably the UK). The UK fixed indicative levels of amounts for 'personal use' (10 litres of spirits, 90 litres of wine, 110 litres of beer, 200 cigars, 800 cigarettes and so on) and in 2000/01 seized some 10,000 vehicles engaged in this trade. The European Commission took the UK to the Court of Justice for this policy, but the matter was settled out of court in 2006, with Britain introducing less severe sanctions for offenders.

Sweden and Finland were initially allowed to maintain state monopolies on retailing alcohol and, together with Denmark, until 2004 they also maintained tighter limits on how much alcohol travellers could bring back from other EU states. In 2007 the European Court of Justice ruled that the Swedish alcohol monopoly was not compatible with EU law as it was against the principle of movement of free goods. The monopoly continued, but in 2011 'yard sales' of producers selling alcohol beverages on their own premises were permitted.

*European Commission, http://ec.europa.eu/taxation_customs/resources/documents/taxation/excise_duties/alcoholic_beverages/rates/excise_duties-part_i_alcohol_en.pdf (accessed 3 March 2011).

Taxes on corporate income were particularly low in Ireland and the new member states.[27] As explained in Chapter 11, with the 2010 bail-out there was pressure, in particular from France and Germany, on Ireland to raise its tax rate. Since 2001 the European Commission has been presenting proposals to improve co-ordination of national tax policies in the EU. In 2011 the European Council agreed to develop a common consolidated corporate tax base (CCCTB).[28]

In 2003, after a long debate, agreement was reached among the member states to start exchanging information from 2005 on non-residents' savings so that each country could tax its citizens on such

---

[27] The Irish rate was 12.5 per cent in 2010 compared with 33.3 per cent in France and 30.2 per cent in Germany (*Financial Times*, 25 November 2010).

[28] See Chapter 11. This was one of the 50 proposals presented in European Commission (2010a). See Document COM(2001)582 for the 2001 proposal.

savings.[29] Germany and the Scandinavian countries were in favour of this measure, claiming that they forgo a large share of tax revenue because their wealthier citizens transfer savings to non-resident accounts. The UK and Luxembourg were thought to be the prime beneficiaries of such flows, and the UK was strongly opposed to the measure fearing it would encourage investors to place their holdings outside the EU. Austria, Belgium and Luxembourg obtained a transitional period during which they were exempt from exchanging information, but had to levy a withholding tax instead. In 2004 similar measures were extended to non-EU tax havens such as Switzerland and Liechtenstein.

6.10 The liberalization of public procurement

Public orders accounted for about €2,155 billion or 17–18 per cent of EU GDP in 2008.[30] According to the Cecchini Report (1988), only one public procurement contract out of fifty was granted to a firm from another country, and governments were overspending by the equivalent of €22 billion, often paying 25 per cent more than their private counterparts.[31] Only part of public purchases (public procurement) is subject to tender or formal contract (about €389 billion in 2008).

Measures relating to public procurement have been introduced in the sectors of telecommunications, water, energy and transport; to assist small and medium enterprises in competing for public procurement; and to provide legal remedies to firms that feel they have been unfairly excluded from contracts. However, in practice, public procurement has proved one of the most difficult markets to open. According to Monti (2010), cross-border procurement accounts for only about 2 per cent of the total number of bids, and some sectors such as defence are subject to special rules. In 2010 an assessment of EU public procurement legislation was carried out based on wide-ranging consultations to enable the Commission to make legislative proposals in 2012 at the latest. The reform would aim at simplifying and updating EU rules to render the awarding of contracts more flexible and transparent, and to enable public contracts to provide more support to other policy goals such as the environment, innovation, employment and social inclusion (European Commission, 2010a).

6.11 Liberalization of the service industries

Just as is the case with goods, the advantages of liberalizing services are said to be based on the improved allocation of resources with international specialization and the opportunities for exploiting economies of scale.

However, traditionally countries tend to apply restrictions on trade in services. These are said to be necessary, for example, to protect consumers and to ensure safety and minimum standards (medical services) and financial solidarity (the banking system). Alternatively, restrictions are said to be justified to protect national industries,[32] for instance for strategic or prestige reasons (air transport), to control key technologies (information science or telecommunications), for regional, social or environmental reasons (rail transport) or for cultural reasons (audiovisual services).

---

[29] Italy threatened to veto the agreement until the question of the fines on Italian milk farmers not respecting their quotas was resolved (see Chapter 13).

[30] The data for 2008 are from Monti (2010).

[31] European Commission (2003a).

[32] See also Chapter 17.

Restrictions on free trade in services may take various forms:

- authorization procedures;
- quantitative restrictions;
- reserving a certain share of the market for home producers;
- government procurement;
- requirements with regard to labour qualifications;
- technical requirements and standards;
- exchange controls;
- subsidies.

The Treaty of Rome defined services as 'all those activities normally provided for remuneration insofar as they are not governed by the provisions relating to the freedom of movement of goods, capital and persons' (Article 50). The Treaty called for two types of freedom in this context:

- To provide services: any company of a member state can provide services in other member states without having to set up an office there (Article 49);
- To set up an establishment (Article 43): companies (or persons) from one member state may set up an establishment in another member state on the same conditions as nationals of the other member state (the principle of national treatment).

The Lisbon Treaty includes a Protocol (No. 26) on services of general interest, which calls for respect for the role and discretion of national, regional and local authorities, and differences in the needs and preferences of users. Services of general interest range from the so-called network services (such as energy, telecommunications and transport) to education, waste management, health and social services. The Protocol stresses the joint responsibility of the EU and member states, and establishes the legal basis for EU action.

Progress in liberalizing the EU service sector in the Community has been slow. Services account for 70 per cent of economic activity in the EU, but only 20 per cent of intra-EU cross-border trade (Monti, 2010).

6.11.1 The Services Directive

In 2004 the Commissioner for the Internal Market, Frits Bolkestein, proposed a directive to create an effective Single Market for services by removing a large number of barriers that prevent or discourage cross-border trade. *Inter alia* the initial proposed directive envisaged applying the country of origin principle, which would mean that if a service operator were operating legally in one member state (that is, following home-state legislation), it could offer its services freely in others. There were widespread protests that the directive would lead to unfair competition (the 'Polish plumber' was considered the personification of the fear that there would be a huge influx of low-paid workers from Central and Eastern Europe,[33] and in some circles there was reference to the 'Frankenstein' Directive).

In April 2006 the Commission presented a revised proposal, which was adopted by the European Parliament and the Council of Ministers in December 2006, and had to be transposed into national legislation by 2009.[34] According to Monti (2010), the directive entails a thorough review of the regulatory framework at national, regional and local levels, so efforts by the Commission to ensure full and rapid implementation of the directive were necessary.

---

[33] See http://en.wikipedia.org/wiki/Polish_plumber for a picture of the original poster of the Polish plumber.

[34] It was adopted as Directive 2006/123/EC.

Under the new directive it should be easier for businesses to establish anywhere in the EU and to provide services across borders, but the country of origin principle has been removed. Businesses should be able to complete all formalities online with a single point of contact. However, member states are able to apply restrictions that are non-discriminatory, necessary and proportionate if this is necessary to protect public safety, social security, health and the environment. Member states are obliged to remove unnecessary obstacles (such as the need to open a national office or register with the local authorities).

Service providers are to be supervised by 'mutual evaluation', that is, under enhanced provisions for co-operation between national authorities, backed up by an electronic information system allowing authorities to exchange information. There is to be limited harmonization of rules including rights for recipients of services (consumers and other businesses), and information requirements. In 2011 the European Commission will indicate specific measures to improve the working of 'mutual evaluation'.[35] The Service Directive covers:

- business services such as management consultancy, advertising, certification and testing, facilities management including office maintenance, and the services of commercial agents;
- services provided to businesses and consumers such as estate agents and letting services, construction architects, distributive trades and the organization of trade fairs;
- consumer services, such as tourism, amusement parks, plumbers and electricians.

Financial services, telecommunications, transport services, broadcasting and recognition of professional qualifications were already covered by specific legislation so were excluded from the directive.

In line with the European Parliament's amendments, the revised proposal does not affect labour law (such as collective agreements and domestic legislation on working hours and minimum wages), posted workers (for which there is separate legislation, see below), health care, social services relating to social housing, childcare, support of families and persons in need, activities related to the exercise of official authority, temporary work agencies, private security services, gambling and audiovisual services.

According to the Netherlands Bureau for Economic Policy Analysis (2007), EU-wide economic gains from the Service Directive could amount to €60–€140 billion, or on conservative estimates an increase in growth by 0.6–1.5 per cent of GDP.

6.11.2 The posting of workers

The posting of workers also proved controversial in the EU. Posted workers are employed by a firm, and work for a time in a member state other than the country in which work is normally carried out. A directive of 1996 requires firms to guarantee a central core of mandatory protective legislation (for example covering certain conditions of work and employment) in the country where the work is carried out. None the less, in the host country there may be fears that local firms cannot match the competition of posted workers subject to less restrictive regulations in their home country, with the risk of pressure to relax legislation and instigate a 'race to the bottom'.

To meet these fears, transitional measures were introduced after the 2004 and 2007 enlargements. In order to avoid disruption in certain vulnerable sectors member states can limit the temporary movement of workers providing services provided they respect the general transitional arrangements to free movement of labour (see Chapter 8).

In an attempt to meet dissatisfaction with the working of the directive, in 2006 the Commission published *Guidance on the Posting of Workers in the Framework of the Provision of Services*.[36] Businesses providing services should encounter less bureaucracy, quicker procedures and fewer obstacles (such as

---

[35] This was one of the fifty proposals presented in European Commission (2010a).

[36] European Commission (2006b).

no obligation to have a permanent representative or to obtain prior authorization in the host country, though some service companies may have to obtain a general authorization). Member states must make it clear what they require of companies when they post workers, and can ask for a declaration on the posting of workers prior to the beginning of work. Companies must have better information regarding wages and working conditions. Service providers must keep social documents such as those relating to health and safety at work. The Commission is to help the exchange of information and administrative co-operation between member states.

6.12 The liberalization of individual service industries

The liberalization of services is rendered complicated by the fact that the various service industries have very different characteristics. For instance, services can be provided across the border (internet services), by the customer moving to the producer (such as in tourism), or by the producer moving to the customer (for instance in the construction trade). Given this diversity, most of the discussion here is limited to financial services, transport, telecommunications, and postal services (see Box 6.6).[37] Energy is dealt with in Chapter 14. Water is not discussed here, but was singled out by the European Commission as an area where EU initiatives could prove beneficial.[38]

Box 6.6

Postal services

After a year-long deadlock with heated opposition being expressed by countries such as France and Luxembourg, in 2007 agreement was reached on liberalizing the EU postal market from 2011 (compared with 2009 in the initial Commission proposal). This implies that national operators will no longer have a monopoly on mail below a certain weight (50 g) known as the 'reserved area', though it seems likely that many incumbents will retain this business.

6.12.1 Financial services

The Cecchini Report (1988) expected roughly one-third of the gains from completion of the internal market to come from liberalization of financial services. The 1985 White Paper identified the main barriers in this sector as controls on capital movements and different regulatory frameworks for banks and other financial institutions. Liberalization was to be based on mutual recognition of different national systems, with harmonization being limited to essential legislation such as the taxation of savings and incomes from investment.

Freedom of movement of capital is generally advocated because it improves efficiency by increasing the supply of capital (additional savings will be mobilized if the prospects for investing them are better) and by enabling entrepreneurs in need of capital to raise greater amounts more tailored to their needs (see also the discussion of Figure 8.1 in Chapter 8).

The Treaty of Rome was very cautious about liberalization of capital movements, which was required only 'to the extent necessary to ensure proper functioning of the Common Market'. In part this reflected a fear of potential instability in capital markets, but capital controls were also considered

---

[37] See *Single Market News* (various issues) for case studies in these and other sectors, online at http://ec.europa.eu/internal_market/smn/index_en.htm (accessed 4 November 2010).

[38] European Commission (2003b).

a means of maintaining autonomy of monetary policy and of securing some exchange rate stability.[39] The Treaty allowed restrictions on capital movements in circumstances where movements of capital would cause disturbances in the capital market, or for balance of payments reasons.

In essence the Treaty of Rome was a framework agreement to be padded out by later legislation. Directives in 1960 and 1962 distinguished various types of transaction according to the degree of liberalization of capital movements,[40] but until the mid-1980s there were few Community initiatives. Some of the member states, such as Germany, the UK, the Netherlands and Belgium, proceeded with liberalization in transactions with countries outside the Community. However, France, Italy and the three new Mediterranean member states continued to make use of capital restrictions.

By the 1980s there was growing worldwide support for deregulation and liberalization of capital movements. Increasingly, capital controls were felt to be ineffective on a number of grounds, in particular because of:

- technological innovations, such as the use of computers and telecommunications, increased the ease and speed of capital movements, rendering it simpler to evade controls;

- unregulated offshore financial centres provided a means of avoiding restrictions;

- innovations in financial instruments, and the emergence of new and larger actors (such as financial conglomerates), rendered the task of regulation more complex.

Following a first modest step in 1986, in 1988 a directive called for complete elimination of controls on capital movements both between EC member states and with third countries. This was achieved from July 1990, with the later deadlines of 1992 for Ireland and Spain, and 1996 for Greece and Portugal, though Portugal liberalized all capital controls in 1992.[41]

With regard to the **banking system**, the main obstacles to establishing banks in other member states included authorization procedures, capital endowment requirements and restrictions on foreign acquisitions. In 1988 the average market share of foreign banks in member states was only 1 per cent.[42] According to the White Paper, liberalization was to proceed through mutual recognition and harmonization of essential legislation and also on the basis of control by the home country.

In 1989 three directives were passed which formed the basis for liberalization of the banking sector and a model for liberalization of other financial services. Of particular importance was the Second Banking Directive,[43] which established a single banking licence. Any bank that has received authorization by the appropriate authority in any EU state can provide services over the border and

---

[39] A theoretical justification for this kind of position is provided by the Mundell–Fleming model presented in the Appendix to Chapter 9. According to the model, autonomous monetary policy is incompatible with fixed exchange rates and free capital movements.

[40] Three categories were introduced for capital movements:
- *Fully free.* This included foreign direct investment, the purchase of real estate, short-term export credits, personal transactions such as the repatriation of earnings and former investments, and the purchase of quoted stocks in another member state.
- *Partly free.* These were: the issue of shares on the stock market of another member state, the purchase of non-quoted shares or shares in an investment fund by non-residents of that country and long-term trade credits.
- *No obligation to liberalize.* This category included short-term treasury bonds and other capital stocks, and the opening of bank accounts by non-residents of that country.

[41] A safeguard clause permitted the reintroduction of certain controls when the monetary or exchange rate policy of a member state was threatened. However, such controls could only be applied on capital movements liberalized under the 1988 directive, were limited to a maximum of six months and required approval of the Commission.

[42] European Commission (2003a).

[43] The other directives established principles and definitions regarding bank capital and the establishment of a minimum solvency ratio of 8 per cent.

can open branches in any other EU state without the need for further authorization. The home country has main responsibility for control of the bank's activities, while the host country shares responsibility for supervision of the liquidity of branches in its own territory, as well as for measures related to the implementation of national monetary policy. Similar systems of single licences were subsequently introduced for insurance and investment services.

The division of responsibility for supervision between the home and host countries was blurred from the outset and reflects reluctance on the part of the member states to give up their authority. The immediate response of the banking system to the liberalization process was to embark on a spate of mergers and co-operation agreements.

However, regulatory and other barriers continued to prevent the emergence of pan-European provision of services, and there was limited consolidation of the financial services industry (Monti, 1996). To remedy this situation, in 1999 a **Financial Services Action Plan** (FSAP) was launched. The Commission argued that EU financial markets had difficulty competing on an international scale and that an integrated EU capital market was important to ensure sustainable investment-driven growth and employment. The legislation for the FSAP at the EU level was largely in place by 2005. Its aim was to: create a single wholesale financial market to allow firms to raise capital on an EU-wide basis; complete a single EU retail market (relating to bank accounts, loans, insurance, mortgages, investment and insurance provided to individual consumers); ensure state-of-the-art prudential rules and supervision; and eliminate tax obstacles to financial market integration. Measures introduced include the directives on: taxation of savings income (see above in the section on fiscal harmonization), insider dealing and market manipulation, pension funds, and market abuse (see Chapter 16).

There was much debate in the context of the FSAP as to whether regulation of the EU securities market should be carried out on the basis of co-operation and mutual recognition among the national authorities of the member states (as favoured by many in the City of London), or whether there should be a single central regulator. These issues were dealt with in a report of a Committee of Wise Men chaired by Alexandre Lamfalussy (a former Belgian banker) in 2001. In what became known as the 'Lamfalussy procedure' it was decided that the EU should be responsible for passing broad framework laws, while committees of experts work out the technical details. The procedure involved four levels:

- Level 1 dealt with high-level framework legislation proposed by the Commission and voted on by the European Parliament and Council of Ministers;
- Level 2 comprised committees to advise on technical details and how measures should be implemented;
- Level 3 entailed representatives of national security agencies working through a series of committees to assist the Commission as it prepares level 2 legislation. Three committees were set up: the Committee for European Banking Supervisors, the Committee of European Insurance and Occupational Pensions, and the Committee of European Securities Regulators;
- Level 4 dealt with compliance and enforcement of legislation.

The aim of the procedure was to permit flexibility and effective regulation of a fast-changing sector and ensure adequate consultation of market professionals. One of the difficulties was that the framework leaves the member states to fill in the details of very complex legislation. In 2007 the Commission called for measures to enhance supervisory convergence and co-operation, in particular at level 3, where the committees had only advisory powers and could only issue non-binding guidelines and recommendations.

The tension between introducing common rules, while limiting interference and allowing sufficient flexibility to meet differing national situations was also evident in the long and confused process of introducing the MIFID, or Markets in Financial Instruments Directive. The directive, which entered into force in November 2007 covered wholesale and retail trading in securities, including shares, bonds and derivatives. According to the 'single passport', financial firms with the approval of their home authorities could operate throughout the EU. However, this also required harmonization of investor protection rules in areas such as investment advice and the handling of orders. The directive set out principles rather than detailed prescriptions because this was the only way agreement could be reached between member states. The member states encountered difficulties in transposing the legislation, while business and regulators were unsure how the new system would operate in practice. To meet these shortcomings, in September 2010 the Commission proposed revising the MIFID.

The weakness of financial regulation and supervision in the EU became evident with the economic crisis (see Chapter 11). Many technical rules were decided at the level of member state and there were differences between countries. Even where rules were harmonized, application varied. Also, supervision remained mainly at the national level and was uncoordinated and uneven. If national supervisors could not agree, there was no mechanism to resolve issues. This fragmentation imposed extra costs for financial institutions and increased the risk of their failure.

To remedy these difficulties an ad hoc high-level expert group on financial supervision was set up in October 2008 under former IMF managing director Jacques de Larosière. The report by the group was presented in 2009, and sets out a series of proposals for a new regulatory agenda, stronger co-ordinated supervision and effective crisis management procedures. The group called for convergence between member states on technical rules, and a mechanism for ensuring agreement and co-ordination between national supervisors. It also recommended the creation of an effective mechanism to ensure consistent application of rules, and co-ordinated decision making in some areas in emergency situations.

The recommendations of the de Larosière report formed the basis of Commission proposals of September 2009 (see Box 6.7) for a new supervisory framework for financial regulation. The package was agreed in September 2010. The framework entails the creation of a European Systemic Risk Board (ESRB) to oversee the stability of the financial system as a whole. There are three new European Supervisory Authorities (ESAs) for the financial services sector: a European Banking Authority, a European Insurance and Pensions Authority, and a European Securities and Markets Authority. The new authorities are composed of national supervisors with increased powers to detect risks across the financial system. The delay in agreeing the package was due, on the one hand, to fears (expressed mainly by the UK) that the measures would impinge on national sovereignty and, on the other, that the changes would be largely decorative. It was also claimed that the new rules could politicize the issues by requiring countries to seek compromises at the EU level.

A series of changes to financial regulation in the EU was also set in motion (see Box 6.7). In April 2009 tighter rules were agreed for credit rating agencies as these were blamed for failing to detect the true value of subprime-mortgage-backed securities (see Chapter 11), and in December 2010 agreement was reached on a reform of their regulation. After lengthy negotiations, insurance regulation was reformed in 2009, and new procedures to increase co-ordination of cross-border supervision were introduced. After two years of heated debate, in October 2010 agreement was reached on legislation establishing regulatory and supervisory standards for hedge funds, private equity and other alternative investment funds. The new rules will entail capital and disclosure requirements for fund managers across the EU. In 2009 new Capital Requirement Directives were agreed, and the Commission presented proposals to impose fines and higher capital requirements for banks with risky bonus policies for traders and top managers. The aim was to avoid the full burden of funding bail-outs falling on taxpayers in future bank failures, but some member states such as the UK and Germany had already introduced national bank levy plans. In 2009 the Commission also presented proposals to increase the transparency and ensure the financial stability of derivatives.

Box 6.7

Reform of EU financial supervision

October 2008	Commission proposal to review Capital Requirement Directives.
	De Larosière task force appointed to report on EU financial supervision.
November 2008	Commission proposes tighter rules on credit rating agencies.
	G20 Summit agrees on plan to reform global financial markets.
February 2009	De Larosière group presents report.
April 2009	G20 Summit in London.
	EU agrees tighter rules for credit rating agencies.
	EP agrees Solvency II involving new rules for insurance firms.
	Commission proposal to review capital requirements for banks to take into account risks related to re-securitization, trade books and managers' remunerations.
	Commission proposal on hedge funds, private equity and other alternative investment funds.
May 2009	EU adopts review of Capital Requirement Directives.
July 2009	Commission presents proposals to strengthen safety of derivatives.
	Commission proposals to impose fines and higher capital requirements for banks with risky bonus policies for traders and top managers.
September 2009	Commission presents proposed detailed legislative package for financial supervision.
May 2010	Commission presents proposals for more oversight of credit rating agencies.
September 2010	EU agrees new financial supervision package.
	Commission presents proposals to drive derivatives onto exchange, and subsequently announces a review of the MIFID framework (see text) and a communication on a crisis management framework.
October 2010	Agreement of reform on hedge fund rules.
December 2010	Agreement on regulation of credit rating agencies
January 2011	The new EU financial supervisory authorities (see text) come into operation.

Source: Adapted from EurActiv, 'Financial regulation: the EU's agenda', http://www.euractiv.com/en/financial-services/financial-regulation-eus-agenda-linksdossier-188497 (accessed 9 November 2010).

6.12.2 Transport

Transport plays an essential role in the EU economy, and accounted for about €500 billion in gross value added or 4.6 per cent of total EU gross value added and 4.4 per cent of employment in 2008.[44] The transport system was responsible for about 32 per cent of EU energy consumption in 2008, and caused about 19.5 per cent of all EU carbon dioxide emissions in 2007.

---

[44] The statistics in this paragraph are taken from European Commission (2010c).

Articles 3 and 74 to 84 of the Treaty of Rome (now Articles 90 to 100 TFEU) envisaged the creation of a common transport policy.[45] The common transport policy was to be based on non-discrimination, different regimes for different modes of transport, and the right of establishment but not freedom to provide services (access to other EC markets was dependent on EC provisions). This rather contradictory list already showed the difficulty in reaching common positions. The Treaty of Rome lacked details about how the common transport policy was to operate, and the actual design of the common policy was left to the Council.

Progress in introducing common transport measures proved slow and controversial because of different attitudes about the form that intervention in transport should take, and conflicts of interest among the member states.

In 1961 the Commission presented its proposals for the general principles of the common transport policy in a document known as the Schaus Memorandum after the first commissioner responsible for transport. The emphasis of the Commission's proposals was on deregulation, and this was bound to create controversy given the highly regulated nature of transport policy in the member states at that time.

Though the Economic and Social Committee (EESC, see Chapter 3) and the European Parliament accepted the principles of the Commission's recommendations, the Council took little action to implement the proposals. In 1962 the Commission presented an Action Programme still based on competition and liberalization, and again the proposals were opposed by the member states. It was argued that 'excessive' competition would cause safety standards to be undermined, lead to bankruptcies and render railways incapable of competing with road haulage (Swann, 2000).

Following the first enlargement of the Community in 1973, the Commission changed strategy and called for harmonization of national policies as a first step in introducing a common policy. A revised version of the Action Plan was presented in 1973. After a substantial delay, the Council called on the Commission to define its priorities. Over the next few years the Commission presented various proposals, but the Council failed to agree on the necessary steps for their implementation. Eventually, in 1982 the European Parliament decided to take the Council to the Court of Justice for failing to respect its obligation to introduce the common transport policy set out in the Treaty of Rome.

Since 1985, progress in introducing common transport measures has been more rapid for a number of reasons:

- Transport was an integral part of the 1993 Programme;
- In 1985 the European Court ruled that the Council should adopt measures to liberalize transport 'within a reasonable time';
- There was an international trend towards the liberalization of transport that was particularly evident in the USA during the Reagan years;
- In 1986 in the *Nouvelles Frontières* case the European Court of Justice ruled in favour of a French firm that had been charging prices below those fixed by the French authorities. This ruling gave leeway to the Commission to overrule national agreements.

In 1992 the Commission published a White Paper, *The Future Development of the Common Transport Policy*, aimed at liberalizing transport markets. With the exception of the rail sector, considerable progress was made in the following decade in realizing the basic aim of the White Paper to open up the transport market.

The Maastricht Treaty reinforced the legal, decision-making and financial bases of the common transport policy, and laid the basis for TENs, or trans-European networks, to improve transport, energy and telecommunications infrastructure with the help of EU financing.

---

[45] Article 91 TFEU sets out the main features of the common transport policy, which include common rules applicable to the internal transport of member states, the conditions for non-residents to operate in a member state, and measures to improve safety. According to Article 100 TFEU, the common transport policy applies to rail, road and inland waterways, but the Treaty envisages the Council extending its provisions to sea and air transport.

However, difficulties arose because the modal split between different forms of transport was increasingly biased towards road and air transport (see also Box 6.8), inducing additional problems of congestion and pollution. Infrastructure (for example, for rail freight transport) remained inadequate, and attempts to improve the situation through programmes such as the TENs suffered from inadequate financing, bureaucratic delays and complexities of co-ordination. New and different traffic patterns as a result of EU enlargement exacerbated the problems.

Box 6.8

Ryanair subsidies

Ryanair became the EU's leading low-cost airline by cutting out the frills, using one type of aircraft, flying its aircraft more frequently and concentrating on smaller regional airports to cut costs and shorten turnaround times. In February 2004 the European Commission ruled against airport subsidies granted by Charleroi (the airport used for Brussels) to Ryanair. The owner of Charleroi, the Walloon regional government, had given a 50 per cent reduction in landing fees to Ryanair, and contributed in money or kind to Ryanair's local hotel, office, training and marketing costs. According to the EU Commission, such assistance was discriminatory and ran counter to EU legislation on state aids.

In 2007 a Commission ruling blocked a Ryanair takeover bid for Irish flag-carrying airline Aer Lingus. The head of RyanAir, Michael O'Leary, not known for his understatement, referred to the chief antitrust regulator of the EU as an 'evil empire' among various other expletives reported in the popular press..

In 1998 the Cardiff European Council called for strategies with regard to sustainable development, also in transport, and this objective was also taken up in the Amsterdam Treaty and the Gothenburg European Council of 2001.

In 2001 the European Commission published a White Paper, *European Transport Policy for 2010: Time to Decide,* setting out sixty measures to be introduced, an Action Programme extending until 2010, and a monitoring process (European Commission, 2001). In 2006 a mid-term review of the Programme (European Commission, 2006d) assessed progress and reorganized the objectives into four main pillars:

1 **Mobility of people and businesses throughout the Union.** Measures would include: common rules for professional qualifications and working conditions in road transport; liberalization of international rail passenger transport; creation of a single European sky; an increase in airport capacity and measures to tackle the environmental consequences of air travel; and the creation of an internal shipping space and greater port capacity for maritime transport.

2 **Environmental protection, the security of energy supply, promoting minimum labour standards, and protecting passengers and citizens,** including the promotion of improvements with regard to passenger rights, safety, security and urban transport.

3 **Innovation to make the sector more efficient and more sustainable.** This would involve measures to improve energy efficiency, also by promoting new technologies, and increased investment in infrastructure, *inter alia* through the encouragement of co-financing with private sponsors. Galileo, Europe's satellite radio navigation system, would be used to improve measures of communication, navigation and automation.

4 **Action on the world stage so other countries help to share the objectives,** also in taking account of environmental protection or safety considerations.

In 2011 the European Commission is to adopt a White Paper on transport policy, which is intended to remove the remaining obstacles between different means of transport, and between national systems of transport (European Commission, 2010a).

6.12.3 Telecommunications

The telecommunications and information sectors were traditionally characterized by national monopolies in the provision of equipment and services. It was considered that with more than one supplier costly networks would be duplicated, leading to an overall loss in welfare. The Cecchini Report (1988) found price differences in telephone and telegraph services of as much as 50 per cent among member states prior to the introduction of the Single Market.

With the rapid technological progress in the information and telecommunications industry, the argument in favour of natural monopolies was undermined. There was strong pressure to liberalize both from corporate users of telecommunication services, and at the international level (see also Chapter 16).

A 1988 directive was aimed at the ending of national monopolies on equipment, and a further directive of 1990 called for liberalization of the provision of services (except basic telephone services). New Regulatory Agencies (NRAs), which were to be independent from both government and operators, were set up in all the member states to implement EU regulations.

In 2002 the EU adopted a new regulatory framework covering electronic communications networks and services (including all types of fixed and wireless telecoms, data transmission and broadcasting), and allowing telecoms operators and service providers to set up and offer their services throughout the EU.

The EU has launched programmes such as RACE (Research in Advanced Communications for Europe) and ESPRIT (European Strategic Programme for Research and Development in Information Technologies) and BRITE/EURAM (Basic Research in Industrial Technologies for Europe/European Research in Advanced Materials) to help EU firms develop new technologies.

Despite the attempts to create a single market, its implementation by national regulators meant that the market was fragmented and there were few pan-European operators. Instead, operators had to package their services in different ways to satisfy the varying regulatory requirements of the member states. In 2007 the EU presented proposals for an overhaul of telecommunications, a key sector in efforts to render the EU economy more competitive. Agreement was reached on a new regulatory framework in 2009 and this has to be transposed into national laws by May 2011. A new pan-European regulator, the Body of European Regulators of Electronic Communications (BEREC) has been set up to replace the previous loose co-ordination between national authorities. The aim is to open the telecoms market to competition, ensure regulatory consistency and strengthen the rights of consumers. National telecoms watchdogs would be allowed to split the service and network businesses of large operators as a last resort measure in order to allow access to rivals. The Commission would have powers of intervention if national telecoms authorities failed to address problems.

Agreement was also reached on a regulation to limit the costs of roaming (making and receiving mobile phone calls) charges from 2007. Revised rules were agreed in 2009 to cut roaming charges for voice calls and introduce new caps on SMS tariffs. The Commission has to report on the functioning of the new rules, and if necessary propose new legislation.

6.13   Assessments of the Single Market Programme

As stated above, at the time the Single Market Programme was launched the most extensive analysis of its likely effects was the **Cecchini Report**, which was based on the following methods of evaluation:

- **Opinion surveys of business.** These relied on questionnaires about the costs of given barriers and likely responses to their removal;

- **Industry case studies** of the cost structure of enterprises and the likely market barriers they face, including attempts to estimate the possible impact of restructuring the industry branch in response to increased competitive pressures;
- **Micro- and macroeconomic analyses** of the expected effects.[46]

The most discussed and controversial estimates were those based on a macroeconomic approach, which suggested that in the case of passive macroeconomic policies, the overall impact (after an estimated 5–6 years) of the Single Market Programme could be a 4.5 per cent increase in GDP, a 6 per cent reduction in the price level and the creation of about 2 million jobs. With a more active macroeconomic policy (reflecting the improved economic performance), there would be a 7 per cent increase in GDP, a 4.5 per cent reduction in inflation and the creation of 5 million jobs.[47]

With the benefit of hindsight, various criticisms of the Cecchini predictions of the internal market effects can be made. The analysis of the economic consequences of the Internal Market Programme shares the difficulty of all empirical analysis of integration in that it is almost impossible to separate the integration effect from overall economic developments.

In the report the estimates of direct benefits from reduced controls at the border were relatively small, while the estimates of secondary dynamic effects (economies of scale, restructuring, increased competition – see Chapter 5) were large. It is difficult to produce more than 'guestimates' or 'speculative ranges' concerning the size of such dynamic effects. In fact, the more important the effects are said to be, the more vague and less precise the Commission's analysis appeared.

Too much emphasis was placed on economies of scale in the Cecchini analysis. It had to be shown that they are possible only in a European rather than a national market and that they promote efficiency. Too little account was taken of the costs of adjustment or of the impact on regional disparities. The approach tended to emphasize the supply rather than the demand side, and the results were very sensitive to changes in the economic environment.

One of the criticisms of the Cecchini study that attracted much attention at the time was that of Baldwin (1989), who argued that the expected gains from the Single Market Programme might be far larger than those estimated in the Cecchini Report. The Cecchini study attempted to estimate how the Single Market Programme would increase the level of output rather than the rate of growth. In other words, according to Baldwin, the Cecchini Report was considering a one-off rather than a continuing effect.

An extensive review of the Single Market carried out by the European Commission in 2007 suggested that between 1992 and 2006 the estimated gains of the internal market amounted to 2.15 per cent of

---

[46] Various approaches were used, including:

- *A static, partial equilibrium approach*, which uses information obtained from the industry studies and other surveys to assess the net welfare effects on producers, consumers and government spending. The analysis is 'partial' equilibrium in the sense that each barrier and each economic sector is considered one at a time and the results are then aggregated. The approach ignores the extent to which barriers overlap and markets are interconnected. In other words, no account is taken of the consequences of changes in factor prices or in the relative prices of products as a result of reducing the barriers.

- *A general equilibrium microeconomics approach* which attempts to take into account the interactions between different sectors.

- *The use of macroeconomic models* in an attempt to show the evolution of costs, prices, income and other macroeconomic variables (including policy) as a result of introduction of the Single Market. The emphasis here is on what happens during the adjustment period, considering questions such as how quickly workers made redundant by the restructuring process can find work elsewhere.

- *Estimates of dynamic effects* were carried out, attempting to estimate how market conditions affect the rate of technological progress, innovations and the strategic reactions of business (through the learning process and so on).

[47] The results of the general equilibrium microeconomic approach suggest possible gains of 2.5 per cent of GDP (or ECU 70 billion) for a narrow conception of the gains from removing barriers, to a range of 4.5–6.5 per cent (ECU 125–190 billion) for a more competitive, integrated market.

GDP and 2.75 million extra jobs.[48] A later study by the Commission in 2010 updated this to 2.75 million additional jobs and growth of 1.85 per cent for the period 1992–2009, and suggested that completion of the Single Market could potentially produce growth of 4 per cent of GDP over the following ten years. [49]

6.14 The impact of the Single Market Programme on third countries

Emerson et al. (1989) estimated that the completion of the internal market would increase the competitiveness of EC industry, leading to a decline in imports from the rest of the world by as much as 10 per cent.[50] Fear of loss of relative competitiveness was a major factor in causing the European Free Trade Association (EFTA) countries to negotiate the European Economic Area, and this in turn led to EU accession by Austria, Sweden and Finland.

Countries such as Japan and the USA feared the prospect of a 'Fortress Europe' and attempted to ensure a foothold within the fortress through increased foreign direct investment. The rapid increase in Japanese firms operating in the Community led to a tightening of 'screwdriver' legislation in 1987 aimed at ensuring a minimum EC share of components in goods produced in the Community.

At the time, the Commission argued that this possible negative effect of increased EC competitiveness in reducing imports from the rest of the world would be offset insofar as higher GDP would lead to increased demand for imports.[51] Dealing with EU or mutually recognized standards, and EU rather than national quotas, also simplifies procedures for producers in third countries. It is difficult to isolate internal market effects from other developments, but, for instance, European Commission (1997a) maintained that the additional growth due to the Single Market was reflected in greater confidence at a world level, rendering the EU more willing to improve access to its markets.

6.15 'Completing' the Single Market: from the 10-point plan of 2003 to the initiative of 2007 to create a Single Market for the twenty-first century

In May 2003 the European Commission published a 10-point plan to improve the working of the internal market.[52] The priorities of the plan were to improve the implementation and enforcement of internal market legislation, encourage the free movement of services, remove the remaining barriers to trade in goods and create a free market for public procurement. In order to improve the conditions for business, the Commission aimed at fostering innovation and entrepreneurship, building in particular on the European Charter for Small Enterprises endorsed by the Feira Council of 2000.

---

[48] European Commission (2007a). The study also found that intra-EU trade rose by an estimated 30 per cent between 1995 and 2005, while cross-border investments increased, with the share of total foreign direct investment flows in the former EU(15) originating in other EU(15) countries rising from 53 per cent in 1995 to 78 per cent in 2005. As a result of more open public procurement rules it was estimated that there were savings to governments of 10–30 per cent. However, another report in the same year, European Commission (2007c), suggested that the effect of the Single Market was slowing down.

[49] European Commission (2010a).

[50] Emerson et al. (1989:182) also estimate the possible percentage changes in extra-EC imports for various sectors. These range from 0 for agriculture, –5.8 for textiles and clothing to –30.9 for communications, and –61.3 for credit and insurance.

[51] It has also been argued that the Single Market Programme could lead to changes in trade distribution, or the substitution of one third-country supplier for another. This may occur, for instance, because of the removal of national restrictions involving preferences for a particular third country, or group of countries, or because some countries are better able to adjust to the new situation than others.

[52] European Commission (2003b). The ten points of the plan were: enforcing the rules; integrating service markets; improving the free movement of goods; meeting the demographic challenge; improving essential services; improving conditions for business; simplifying the regulatory environment; reducing tax obstacles; introducing more open public procurement markets; and providing better information.

In 2006 an extensive public consultation on the Single European Market was carried out,[53] and on the basis of its results, the European Commission indicated various benefits of the internal market for EU citizens such as: opportunities to study abroad; easier travel in the EU; an improvement in the range and quality of products available; increased possibility of working or retiring in another member state; lower prices; and better protection of consumer rights. Various benefits for businesses were also indicated: greater possibility of economies of scale; improved networks for transport, telecommunications and electricity; easier cross-border trade; lower costs of setting up a new business; the advantages of EU standards and labels; new sources of financing, contracts and funding; and improved cross-border co-operation and technology transfer.

Despite the broad agreement emerging from the 2006 consultation that the Single Market has brought benefits, some (consumer organizations and small and medium enterprises (SMEs)) questioned how far the benefits have gone to consumers and small businesses. The survey suggested that gaps needed to be addressed in services (including retail financial services, insurance and transport), energy, taxation, free movement of workers, and intellectual property. It was also felt that there were problems with implementation and enforcement, and some of those responding called for the development of the 'social dimension' of the Single Market (see Chapter 7).

In 2007 the Commission carried out a review of initiatives of the previous twenty years related to the Single Market, assessing its achievements, and indicating ways in which it could be adapted better to meet the needs of the twenty-first century.[54]

6.16   The Monti Report of 2010

Requested by the president of the Commission Barroso, the Monti Report (2010) sets out the challenges for the Single Market. Political and social support for market integration have been eroded by 'integration fatigue' or decreased appetite for more Europe, and by 'market fatigue', or less confidence in the market as a result of the economic crisis. At the same time the welding together of EU markets is incomplete and the Single Market Programme is regarded as yesterday's business, with attention in recent years being deflected to enlargement, economic and monetary union and reform of EU institutions. The report stresses the importance of the Single Market for macroeconomic performance, increasing EU competitiveness through the Europe 2020 programme (see the next chapter), and for the solidity of the euro and monetary union. The emphasis the report places on the need to legitimize the Single Market appears appropriate after the lengthy and heated confrontation that accompanied the introduction of measures such as the Services Directive or new regulatory framework for telecoms.

A first set of recommendations in the report is concerned with building a stronger Single Market, and refers to the 'missing links', 'bottlenecks' and 'new frontier' of the Single Market project. 'Missing links' arise because in some cases the Single Market exists on paper, but multiple barriers and regulatory obstacles fragment the EU. 'Bottlenecks' occur because physical or legal infrastructure is lacking, or because dialogue between administrative systems frustrates the potential for greater economic gains. The 'new frontier' relates to missing sectors (such as e-commerce) that did not exist when the Single Market was created. To overcome these shortcomings the Report proposes measures to cater more for: the needs of citizens, consumers and SMEs; the digital market; green growth; the goods and services markets; workers; capital and financial services and physical infrastructure.

A second series of recommendations is aimed at building consensus for the Single Market. The Report points to the need to remove sources of friction between market integration at the EU level and social

[53] European Commission (2006c). The consultation received 1,514 replies from the public sector, individual businesses, citizens, academia and so on, though there were relatively few replies from the new member states and from regional and local authorities. See also Special Eurobarometer 254, and Flash Eurobarometer 180 and 190 of 2006.

[54] European Commission (2007c). The study indicated a number of priorities, including: more attention to the needs of citizens, consumers and SMEs; further integration of the EU economy; development of a knowledge society; improved regulation; a more sustainable EU; a market more responsive to the global context; and improved monitoring and better communication.

protection at the national level in order to create a 'highly competitive social market economy' (p. 65). In some cases this implies adjusting existing SEM rules to take account of social and local contexts; in others more co-ordination between national authorities is called for. The recommendations relate to: economic freedoms and workers' rights; social services and the Single Market; public procurement; taxation; competitiveness and cohesion; industrial policy and the external dimension of the Single Market.

A third set of proposals refers to delivering a strong Single Market, and deals with the issue of identifying appropriate modes of regulation and policy-making methods for the Single Market. The Report points out that a large part of the *acquis* refers to the Single Market and warns that regulation is appropriate only in certain circumstances (see also Pelkmans, 2010). Although directives can be adjusted better to local situations, the delays and risk of non-implementation leads the Report to prefer the 'clarity, predictability and effectiveness' (p. 93) of regulations where possible. In regulating new sectors from scratch, harmonization of regulations may be appropriate, but in other instances an EU framework alternative to, but not replacing, national rules might be more suitable. Wider use of impact assessment, in particular of the social dimension, is advocated as well as more involvement in the policy-making process of all organizations of interests. Rather than *ex ante* analysis of individual policy interventions, the report advocates *ex post* assessment of what actually works in a given area. Strengthening enforcement of Single Market legislation is recommended and it is suggested that in the longer term the Commission's powers under infringement procedures could be aligned with those it has under competition policy.

The final chapter of the Report calls for a package deal, with a comprehensive and consensual initiative to relaunch the Single Market and a strong role for the Commission and the president of the European Council in the process.

The Monti Report is impressive, less as a list of recommendations (though many of these are to be welcomed), than as an attempt to illustrate the importance and central role of the Single Market in the integration process. It represents a cry to address the problem of legitimacy of the internal market and the need to reconcile the project with social protection measures at the national level.

6.17 Towards a Single Market Act

In October 2010 the Commission presented the document *Towards a Single Market Act* which sets out fifty proposals to improve the working of the Single Market (European Commission, 2010a). Many of these proposals have been indicated above in the context of individual policies and they include measures to promote: creativity, a sustainable economy, assistance for SMEs and a business-friendly environment, innovation, taxation, infrastructure, solidarity, employment, a social market economy, protection of consumers and good governance. At the same time, an EU Citizens' Report 2010 was published aiming at dismantling obstacles that citizens encounter in their activities such as travelling, studying, retiring, buying and inheriting property, voting in another member state and so on.[55] The objective of introducing the Single Market Act at the end of 2012 was to commemorate twenty years of the Single Market. The marketing style is undoubtedly an attempt to replicate the style of the 1985 Cockfield White Paper, but whether such impetus can be repeated in a very changed economic environment remains to be seen.

6.18 Evaluation

The Single Market Programme was an important stimulus to restructuring of the EU economy, and in its absence there would probably have been slower growth and less job creation in Europe. The programme has also been important for its spillover into other areas of integration, including EMU, institutional reform, the 1995 enlargement, regional and social measures, and competition policy.

---

[55] European Commission (2010d). See also *EP Report on Delivering the Single Market to Consumers and Citizens*, A7-0132/2010 (rapporteur Louis Grech) of 3 May 2010 by the Internal and Consumer Protection Committee, http://www.europarl. europa.eu/sides/getDoc.do?pubRef=-//EP//NONSGML+REPORT+A7-2010-0132+0+DOC+PDF+V0//EN (accessed 5 November 2010).

However, following the economic success of the Community until the mid-1970s, the Single Market Programme failed to stem the growing gap in GDP and productivity compared with the USA (see also the next chapter). Various explanations for this shortcoming have been advanced:

- The Single Market Programme is incomplete, in particular in areas such as services, public procurement and taxes;
- The Single Market Programme was mainly restricted to product and capital markets, excluding liberalization of labour markets, which remained largely the prerogative of member states. Analyses, for example by Sapir et al. (2004), maintained that without greater labour market reform, liberalization of product markets would prove inadequate to trigger the reallocation of resources necessary to promote more rapid growth;
- The diagnosis at the time of the Single Market Programme, that the poor economic performance of the Community was due to fragmentation of markets and inability to exploit economies of scale, seemed increasingly dated in an environment characterized by the need to meet the challenges of globalization, knowledge-based economies and information and communication technologies (ICT).

The Monti Report and Commission initiative of 2010 were aimed at addressing these shortcomings of the Single Market Programme. At the same time, as explained in Chapter 7, the Lisbon Strategy of 2000 and the Europe 2020 programme attempted to launch economic, social and environmental renewal of the EU. As explained in Chapter 7, Europe 2020 seems likely to share some of the earlier weaknesses of the Lisbon Strategy, but is intended to flank the ongoing task of 'completion' of the Single European Market.

Summary of key concepts

- During the 1970s and early 1980s the EC member states were becoming increasingly concerned about the growing lag between their economic performance and that of countries such as Japan and the USA, especially in high-technology sectors. The explanation given was the **fragmentation of the EC market**.
- Krugman (1991b) found that the level of specialization in the USA was higher than in the EC, even though the distances were greater.
- In 1985 Jacques Delors launched the Single Market Programme as a strategy to raise EC competitiveness.
- The **main non-tariff barriers** that the Single Market Programme aimed at removing were: frontier controls; differences in technical specifications and standards; differences in national tax systems; and restrictions on competition for public purchases and on providing certain services (in particular, financial and transport services) in other EC countries.
- The **Cockfield White Paper** *Completing the Internal Market* (1985), called for the elimination of barriers between EC countries by the end of 1992 and set out 282 measures necessary to achieve this aim.
- The **Single European Act 1987** set out the formal steps necessary to introduce the Single European Market.
- In practice, **incomplete implementation** of the measures and the granting of temporary derogations have undermined the effectiveness of the Single Market.
- One of the main aims of removing **frontier controls** is to permit the free movement of people.
- **Standards and technical restrictions** may act as barriers to trade but may be needed to protect consumer interests.
- The EU has made slow progress in bringing the national **tax systems** of the member states in line with each other.

■ Little progress has been made in opening up **public procurement** to foreign firms.

■ In 2006 agreement was reached on a revised version of the **Services Directive** to create an effective Single Market for services.

■ With the Single Market Programme the movement of capital between member states was liberalized. With regard to **financial services**, any bank that has received authorization by the appropriate authority in any EU state can provide services over the border and can open branches in any other EU state without the need for further authorization. With the economic crisis the EU began to reform the regulatory and supervisory framework to reduce fragmentation and increase transparency of financial markets.

■ Difficulties in interpreting the Treaty of Rome, and different interests of the member states, meant that progress in introducing a common **transport** policy was slow. The Single Market Programme and the deregulation prevalent from the mid-1980s lent a new emphasis to introducing common transport measures.

■ The White Paper published by the Commission in 2001 set out the main objectives of EU transport policy until 2010: mobility of people and businesses; environmental measures and protection; innovation; and action on the world stage.

■ The Single Market Programme ended national monopolies of telecommunications and information services, and entails liberalization of postal services by 2011.

■ The **Cecchini Report** (1988) suggested that if macroeconomic policies remained unchanged, the overall impact (after an estimated 5–6 years) of the Single Market Programme could be a 4.5 per cent increase in GDP and a 6 per cent reduction in price levels. A 2010 Commission study estimated the increase in GDP at about 1.85 per cent for the period 1992–2009, and the creation of jobs at 2.75 million compared with the situation without the 1993 Programme.

■ In 2010 the **Monti Report** and the Commission initiative to launch a **Single Market Act** represent a renewed effort at 'completing' the Single Market.

■ Possibly the most **lasting effects** of the Single Market Programme are the kick-start it gave to the deregulation process and the spillover effect into other areas of integration such as institutional reform, the restructuring of EU firms through mergers and acquisitions, EMU, and social and regional measures.

Questions for study and review

1 Describe the main barriers causing fragmentation of the European market.
2 What were the expected advantages of the Single Market Programme?
3 Indicate the main steps in introducing the Single Market Programme.
4 What was the significance of the Single European Act in the integration process?
5 Describe, with examples, the areas where implementation of the Single Market Programme has been particularly slow.
6 What measures are necessary to introduce a Single European Market for financial services?
7 Why was it so difficult to introduce a common transport policy?
8 What developments from the mid-1980s led to acceleration in introducing common transport measures?
9 What measures do you consider necessary for the improvement of the EU transport system, and how far is the EU introducing such measures?
10 In practice, the effects of the Single Market Programme were different from those initially predicted. Explain why you think that this was the case.

11 Why is it probable that the Single Market will never be achieved?
12 Do you consider the Monti Report of 2010 contributes to the debate on the future of Europe?
13 How far are the efforts to launch a Single Market Act likely to be successful?

Research tasks

1 Choose a specific EU industry. Examine: the role of the Commission in promoting the achievement of the Single Market in that industry; the expected benefits that would come from the Single Market in the sector considered; and the potential obstacles (short-term and long-term) remaining to completing the Single Market in that industry.
2 Analyse the activities of the SOLVIT office in your country, using case studies.
3 Assess the main changes in regulation and supervision of financial markets introduced in response to the economic crisis from 2007.

Online
Learning **Centre**

When you have read this chapter, log on to the Online Learning Centre website at *www.mcgraw-hill.co.uk/textbooks/senior* to explore weblinks, chapter-by-chapter test questions, case studies and more online study tools.

Chapter 7

From the Lisbon Agenda to Europe 2020

Learning Objectives

By the end of this chapter you should be able to understand:

- ✓ What we mean by competitiveness
- ✓ The link between the economic crisis and competitiveness
- ✓ Some of the possible effects of globalization on EU countries
- ✓ What we mean by the Lisbon Agenda
- ✓ The criticisms made of the Lisbon Agenda
- ✓ The main elements of the Europe 2020 programme
- ✓ How effective the EU has been in promoting a knowledge-based society
- ✓ The link between EU social policy and the Europe 2020 programme
- ✓ The main elements of EU social policy
- ✓ What the EU is doing to increase employment
- ✓ The main aspects of the European Employment Strategy
- ✓ What the EU is doing to combat poverty
- ✓ How effective EU social and employment policy has been
- ✓ The outlook for the Europe 2020 strategy

7.1 Introduction

Years after the 1993 deadline for completing the Internal Market Programme, the EU continued to lag behind the USA in terms of competitiveness and productivity. Though it can be argued that the Single Market project is still not complete, the assumption that all the shortcomings of the European economy could be attributed to market fragmentation became increasingly questionable. Subsequently, low EU

productivity has been explained more frequently in terms of labour market rigidities, inadequate investment in education and training, and a technology gap, in particular with regard to information science.

In addition to the gap compared with US economic performance, there was also growing concern regarding the challenge posed by emerging countries such as the BRICs (Brazil, Russia, India and China), and by China in particular.

Raising competitiveness is also advocated to preserve the European model (combining economic, social and environmental objectives) in the face of demographic ageing; to reduce income disparities; or because slow growth makes the process of reform more difficult and may render the political influence of the EU negligible (Alesina and Giavazzi, 2006). As will be described in the first part of this chapter, the need to cope with the economic crisis and the strains of the eurozone also lent a new urgency to the task of increasing the competitiveness of EU countries.

In March 2000 the Lisbon European Council decided to launch a 'new strategic goal' aimed at economic, social and environmental renewal in the following ten years. The objective was to transform the EU into the '*most dynamic, competitive, knowledge-based economy in the world*' by 2010. EU training and education systems were to become a 'world quality reference'. The second part of this chapter deals with the main aspects of the Lisbon Agenda and its criticisms, revision and outlook.

The chapter then describes the replacement of the Lisbon Agenda in 2010 with the Europe 2020 strategy, which calls for smart, sustainable and inclusive growth. Smart growth relates to policies for innovation and knowledge. Sustainable growth is dealt with in Chapter 14 on environmental policy. Inclusive growth entails enhancing labour market participation, skills acquisition and the fight against poverty, and so builds on the tradition of EU social policy. As will be shown below in the final part of the chapter, although EU social policy and, in particular, efforts to increase employment, had a very different starting point, ultimately there was a confluence with the inclusive growth element of the Lisbon Agenda first, and Europe 2020 after.

7.2 The diagnosis: lagging growth and productivity

European Commission (2009c: 18) defines competitiveness in terms of the 'overall economic performance of a nation measured in terms of its ability to provide its citizens with growing living standards on a sustainable basis and broad access for jobs to those willing to work'.[1]

Within the EU, and in particular the eurozone, divergences in competitiveness create strains. If, for example a country such as Greece loses competitiveness vis-à-vis other EU countries the probable solution before adopting the euro would have been to devalue the drachma and render Greek exports cheaper. With the euro the only option for the less competitive country is to reduce costs and increase productivity. As discussed below in the context of the Europe 2020 strategy (and in Chapter 11 on EMU), one of the proposals to emerge in the debate about improving economic governance was that of an increased role for the EU in monitoring the competitiveness of individual member states.

In considering the international standing of the EU, the USA is a useful benchmark for comparison, and has probably the economy most similar to that of the EU (European Commission, 2009c). In the short run, the US economy seems more flexible and in times of recession US output and employment tend to fall less, and recover more quickly, than in the EU (see the section on EU employment below).

Also in the longer run, differences between the EU and US economies seem to persist. As a result of the economic success of the early years of the Community, with growth and employment reaching unprecedented levels (see Chapter 2), the GDP per capita of the Community rose to about 70 per cent

---

[1] The quotation continues: 'At the roots of competitiveness we find the institutions and microeconomic conditions under which businesses can merge and thrive, and individual creativity and effort are rewarded. Of equal importance are macroeconomic policies to promote a safe stable framework for business activity and the development of a low-carbon economy to ensure environmental sustainability'.

of the US level by the mid-1970s. Subsequently this gap failed to narrow (see Table 7.1). In 1997 labour productivity per person employed in the USA was 139 per cent of that of the EU(27), and was forecast to be 140.8 per cent in 2009.[2] As shown in Table 7.2, according to two of the best-known indices of competitiveness, the USA still ranked higher than all the EU economies in 2009.[3] An ongoing query since the time of the 1979 oil crisis has been to explain why the EU has failed to close this gap, and what remedy could reverse the process.

Differences in per capita income can be due to differences in labour participation or varying levels of production per worker. According to European Commission (2009c), the hours worked per person in the USA were between 12 and 24 per cent higher than in EU countries.[4] GDP per hour worked in terms of purchasing power parity was $59.0 for the USA and $42.6 for the EU in 2009.[5]

Productivity per hour worked depends on labour quality, capital intensity and total factor productivity. The quality of labour can be measured by the educational attainment of those employed. Capital intensity indicates the capital stock per hour worked. Total factor productivity is a residual between total hourly labour productivity and the other two components, and indicates the impact of technological progress, knowledge and organizational changes.

According to the European Commission (2009c), labour quality appears to be lower in the EU than in the USA, with, for example, the EU investing 1.2 per cent of GDP in higher education compared

Table 7.1 Selected structural indicators of the EU and USA (2009 unless otherwise indicated)

	EU(27)	USA
GDP per capita (PPS, EU(27) = 100)	100	146
Labour productivity per person employed (PPS, EU(27) = 100)	100	140.8
Employment rate (%)	64.6	67.6
Employment rate females (%)	58.6	63.4
Employment rate (%) of older workers (aged 55–64)	46.0	60.6
Comparative price levels of final consumption by private households	100	88.8
Energy intensity of the economy[a]	167.11	180.60

PPS: purchasing power standards
[a]Gross inland consumption of energy divided by GDP (kilogram of oil equivalent per euro).

Source: Eurostat, www.epp.eurostat.ec.europa.eu (accessed 13 September 2010), © European Union, 2011.

[2] According to European Commission (2009c), of the EU member states only Luxembourg had higher GDP per capita in purchasing power standards than the USA.

[3] The IMD in Switzerland carries out annual studies of competitiveness taking into account more than 300 variables. These reflect current economic performance, business surveys and factors such as infrastructure and innovation. The rankings of the World Economic Forum are calculated from both publicly available data and an annual opinion survey conducted by the World Economic Forum together with its network of partner institutes (research institutes and business organizations). In 2007 over 11,000 business leaders were polled in 131 countries.

[4] According to European Commission (2009c), in 2006 the average US employee worked 1,775 hours per year, while the corresponding figures were 1,571 for Belgium, 1,540 for France and 1,431 for Germany. See the section on employment below for a discussion of different preferences with regard to leisure.

[5] These data are taken from the Centre for International Comparisons of the University of Pennsylvania, http://pwt.econ.upenn.edu/ (accessed 26 October 2010).

Table 7.2 World competitiveness

Overall ranking International Institute for Management Development 2010				Overall ranking World Economic Forum 2010/11				
Country	Rank	Country	Rank	Country	Rank	Country	Rank
Singapore	1	Ireland	21	Switzerland	1	Estonia	33
Hong Kong	2	UK	22	Sweden	2	Cz. Rep.	36
USA	3	France	24	Singapore	3	Poland	39
Switzerland	4	Belgium	25	USA	4	Cyprus	40
Australia	5	Cz. Rep.	29	Germany	5	Spain	42
Sweden	6	Poland	32	Japan	6	Slovenia	45
Canada	7	Estonia	34	Finland	7	Portugal	46
Taiwan	8	Spain	36	Netherlands	8	Lithuania	47
Norway	9	Portugal	37	Denmark	9	Italy	48
Malaysia	10	Italy	40	Canada	10	Malta	50
Luxembourg	11	Hungary	42	UK	12	Hungary	52
Netherlands	12	Lithuania	43	France	15	Slovakia	60
Denmark	13	Greece	46	Austria	18	Romania	67
Austria	14	Slovakia	49	Belgium	19	Latvia	70
Germany	16	Slovenia	52	Luxembourg	20	Bulgaria	71
Finland	19	Bulgaria	53	Ireland	29	Greece	83
		Romania	54				

Source: *The Institute for Management Development data are reproduced with the permission of IMD International, Switzerland, World Competitiveness Center, www.imd.ch/wcc (accessed 13 September 2010). The statistics on world competitiveness ranking of the World Economic Forum are available at http://www.weforum.org/issues/global-competitiveness (accessed 31 August 2011), and are reproduced with permission of Palgrave Macmillan.*

with 2.9 per cent in the USA. Capital intensity is higher in the EU than USA, but further analysis would be necessary to assess whether there is a gap in the quality of capital relative to the USA. However, most of the labour productivity gap between the EU and USA seems to be explained by total factor productivity. The policy implication is that to close the productivity gap the EU should give priority to policies increasing total factor productivity such as information and communication technology (ICT), research, innovation, competition and better regulation, as well as measures to improve human capital.

According to European Commission (2009c), productivity growth in the EU is higher in manufacturing than in services, and the EU tends to perform relatively well in the world market for high-tech commodities compared with rivals such as the USA, Japan or the emerging economies. However, the share of services in EU output and employment is increasing, as is the case in other major industrialized economies. The faster productivity growth of EU manufacturing is attributed to relatively high levels of capital intensity and to outsourcing (see the section on globalization below).

Productivity on its own is insufficient to make international comparisons of competitiveness. A more useful measure is unit labour costs, which indicates the cost of labour input per unit of value added. When calculated at a sectoral level, unit labour costs can help to identify which sectors have a comparative advantage. However, most US–EU trade is intra-industry (see Chapter 4) and driven by economies of scale and product differentiation, so no clear structure in relative sectoral unit labour costs seems to emerge, though the EU appears to have a cost advantage for certain services such as financial intermediation (European Commission, 2009c).

7.3 The economic crisis and competitiveness

As explained in European Commission (2009c), the impact of the economic crisis on competitiveness is ambivalent: though a negative impact on competitiveness is likely in the short run, in the long run the crisis may also have positive effects by providing momentum for structural change.[6] In the short run, certain 'mechanical' effects of the recession tend to reduce productivity. There may be labour hoarding (workers are not laid off) because human capital may be firm specific due to learning-by-doing, or in order to preserve good matches which are sometimes difficult to obtain in labour markets with asymmetric information on vacancies and job seekers. Alternatively, labour market regulations may hinder shedding of jobs. As a result, with the recession the same number of workers may be producing lower output so labour productivity falls.

In the longer term, firms may delay taking on new labour, postpone investment projects, and cut back on R&D expenditures and innovative activities in general. The higher and more prolonged levels of unemployment may lead to depreciation of human capital. On the other hand, if workers cannot find jobs they may be encouraged to extend their education or training. Postponed investment decreases future productivity and extends the life of relatively obsolete equipment, in particular in sectors characterized by rapid technological change. However, by keeping installed capacity, and using it less intensively firms will slow the physical depreciation of capital. If some companies fail, firms may have to devote resources to rebuilding networks and distribution channels. Against this, Schumpeter (1975) refers to the process of 'creative destruction', and in times of economic recession firms may restructure or adopt better technologies to survive the downturn.

In order to maintain competitiveness and face the crisis (see also Chapter 11), the European Economic Recovery Plan (EERP) agreed in December 2008 incorporates two pillars. The first involves injections of fiscal stimulus to raise demand (through tax cuts, transfers and direct spending, in particular in environmental projects). This is to involve a fiscal package of 1.2 per cent of GDP by member states and 0.3 per cent of EU GDP by the EU. The second pillar aims at raising long-tem competitiveness with measures to encourage investment in R&D, human capital, energy efficiency, environmental improvements, small and medium enterprises, and infrastructure.

7.4 The challenges of international trade and globalization

In 2009 the level of world trade fell by 12 per cent in volume terms, the largest fall in seventy years, though it was expected to recover by 9.5 per cent in 2010.[7] In part, protectionist measures explain this fall in trade, but it was largely due to a synchronized fall in demand across countries, in particular for consumer durables and investment goods.[8]

In addition to competing in this more difficult international economic environment, other challenges for the EU arise from the ongoing process of globalization (understood here as increasing

---

[6] See Chapter 11 for a description of the economic crisis and a discussion of its implications for the eurozone.

[7] These data are taken from WTO 2010 press releases at http://www.wto.org/english/news_e/pres10_e/pr598_e.htm (accessed 27 October 2010).

[8] See Baldwin (2009) for a discussion of the reasons for this collapse in world trade.

worldwide economic integration),[9] with trade in goods and services, and cross-border capital flows rising substantially relative to GDP.

Various studies indicate that globalization has increased living standards worldwide, but not for everybody: there have been winners and losers from globalization (World Bank (2007), Della Posta et al. (2009), see also Stiglitz (2002) and the criticisms made against him by Bhagwati (2004)). Empirical evidence suggests that developing countries that experienced substantial poverty reduction have generally been those most integrated into the global economy through trade and foreign direct investment. However, though beyond the scope of the present discussion, studies such as World Bank (2007) point to the share of world income falling for countries less well able to participate in the process of globalization such as sub-Saharan Africa.

The economic crisis illustrates how the globalization of international capital movements has added a new urgency to the need for adequate supervision and regulation of financial markets (see Chapter 6), and appropriate macroeconomic policies (see Chapter 11).

In the context of globalization, Schumpeter's process of 'creative destruction' would seem to suggest a shift of EU production away from traditional, low-skilled tasks and sectors towards new competitive activities and specializations. According to economic theory,[10] when developed countries compete with low-wage economies such as China and India there will be downward pressure on wages, in particular for unskilled work, and there may also be adjustment costs and/or increased unemployment if there are labour market rigidities. In what is known as the 'Australian case' for protection (Irwin, 2002) unskilled workers in developed countries may lose their jobs and experience difficulty in finding a new occupation.

According to IMF (2007), globalization has reduced the share of national income going to workers in advanced economies, but has left them better off overall in absolute terms. On balance these workers have benefited from globalization because it has increased productivity and reduced the price of traded goods (consumers are the great beneficiaries from globalization). Many authors also attribute the falling share of workers in the national income of advanced economies to other factors such as labour-saving technology or tax systems.

A related issue is the impact of outsourcing on employment and wages in developed countries. Outsourcing (sometimes called offshore outsourcing or offshoring) is the international fragmentation of production of goods and services, which entails previously integrated production activities being segmented and spread over an international network of production sites (Baldone et al., 2001). In other words, there is trade in tasks within manufacturing and services. The digital revolution permits the unbundling of production to an unprecedented extent, rendering obsolete the idea that all services are non-tradable. The rapid growth of information technology services being produced in India is an example of this phenomenon. The number of tasks that can be outsourced is changing over time.

There are attenuating arguments to the presages of the dire consequences of outsourcing for the wages and jobs of workers in developed countries. As Venables (2006) and Krugman (1991b) point out,[11] there are still advantages arising from the agglomeration of economic activities, with firms finding gains from locating in proximity to concentrations of business. An example of this is the dominance of a few large cities in the world of international finance. Moreover, as Grossman and Rossi-Hansberg (2006) suggest, outsourcing has the effect of raising productivity, improving terms of trade (as export prices rise relative to imports), and releasing labour from previous tasks, so the overall impact on workers in developed countries may be more complex than is sometimes supposed.

---

[9] In economic terms, globalization can be associated with the four freedoms: of movement of goods, services, capital and labour.

[10] The process of factor price equalization of the Heckscher–Ohlin–Samuelson theorem described in Chapter 4 is relevant here.

[11] See also the discussion of Krugman (1991b) in Chapter 15.

The internationalization of production through outsourcing means that EU competitiveness has to be addressed in a new way, by looking at tasks within the supply chain. The issue becomes how far the EU is able to hold on to core competences and activities that add most value.[12]

The challenge for the EU is to provide an institutional framework capable of stimulating the competitiveness of tasks and of sectors, and of fostering flexible adjustment, and this was the aim first of the Lisbon Strategy and then of Europe 2020. Flexible adjustment means 'learning how to learn' (Baldwin, 2006b), so requires attention to labour market, social and education policies, as well as emphasis on research and innovation. At the same time, on equity grounds there may be a case for compensation for the losers from globalization. Various options are possible: subsidies for retraining or to raise the wages of the unskilled, or longer-term policies aimed at employability such as improving education and training. An initiative of this type is the European Globalisation Adjustment Fund, which provides up to €500 million a year for workers who have suffered as a result of major structural changes in the pattern of world trade.

7.5 The original Lisbon Agenda

In 2000 the Lisbon European Council argued that a 'radical transformation of the European Economy' was necessary to meet the challenges of globalization and the need to create a knowledge-driven economy based on ICT. Various goals were indicated:[13] better policies for the information society and R&D; making EU training and education systems a 'world quality reference' by 2010; completing the internal market; ensuring full employment; establishing an inclusive labour market in which unemployment is reduced and social and regional disparities are narrowed by 'modernizing the European social model, investing in people and combating social exclusion'; improving transport, telecommunications and energy networks; applying an appropriate macro-policy mix; and protecting the environment (this objective was added at the Gothenburg European Council of 2001).

The Agenda relied on a new 'open method of co-ordination' (OMC) for its implementation. This entails guidelines with specific timetables for reaching goals; establishing, where appropriate, quantitative and qualitative indicators and benchmarks against the best in the world. These guidelines are then adapted to national and regional policies by setting specific targets, and are subject to periodic monitoring, evaluation and peer review. The EU role is therefore to ensure that member states achieve certain policy targets through a mutual learning process. Kay and Ackrill (2007) argue that, in contrast with the Community method (see Chapter 3), the OMC allows issues to be given high EU priority while preserving national autonomy. Though the OMC is designed to bring about changes in national legislation, it does not involve a formal or fully fledged transfer of competences.

In 2002 a Competitiveness Council was created with the aim of relaunching the competitive drive of the EU. The role of the Competitiveness Council was to give an opinion on all matters affecting competitiveness, and in this way it was hoped to co-ordinate the efforts of different policies such as the internal market, industrial policy, competition policy and research and development.[14]

---

[12] See, for instance, the article by Giovannetti (2009) which describes how successful firms in Italy in sectors such as textiles and clothing, which faced high levels of international competition adopted a mix of strategies, including outsourcing low-valued tasks, increasing average skills, innovation and cutting costs, and sought new markets and adopted new marketing strategies.

[13] Presidency conclusions of the 2000 Lisbon European Council, http://www.europarl.europa.eu/summits/lis1_en.htm (accessed 29 October 2010).

[14] See the website of the Council for an account of the activities of the Competitiveness Council, http://www.consilium. europa.eu/policies/council-configurations/competitiveness.aspx (accessed 7 March 2011).

7.6 The Sapir Report

One of the criticisms made of the Lisbon Strategy at the time was that it lacked an intellectual basis, unlike the Single Market Programme, which relied on the Cecchini Report, or EMU, which drew on the Commission document 'One market, one money' (European Commission, 1990a; see Chapter 9 below). To meet this gap an independent high-level study group was set up, which published what became known as the Sapir Report (Sapir et al., 2004). The report carried out a comprehensive analysis of the growth and the catching-up problem of the EU, pointing out that both labour utilization and productivity had fallen in absolute terms and relative to the USA since the mid-1970s.

The Sapir Report agreed that the objectives of the Lisbon Strategy were rightly ambitious, but maintained that it rested on an excessive number of targets and a weak method. To meet these drawbacks the Sapir Report recommended focusing on growth (reflected in its title *An Agenda for a Growing Europe*), and called for coherence between EU policies and instruments on the one hand, and between decision makers at the EU and national levels at the other. The report repeated calls for completion of the Single Market, boosting investment in knowledge, funding restructuring and improving the macroeconomic framework. However, it also called for more focus of the EU budget on the priorities of the Lisbon Strategy, and measures to increase effectiveness (with more EU power to oversee Single Market rules, wider use of qualified majority voting on economic matters, and, where necessary, the creation of independent EU bodies for specific policy areas).

The Sapir Report stimulated a wide-reaching debate on the economic future of the EU. It shaped the Commission proposals for the 2007–13 financial perspective,[15] though as explained in Chapter 12, in the final agreement, spending on increasing competitiveness was scaled back.

The Sapir Report was influential in the debate leading to reform of the Stability and Growth Pact in 2005 (see Chapter 11), and in the creation of a Globalisation Adjustment Fund (see above and Chapter 12). It was also instrumental in creating the European Research Council to encourage scientific research in the EU.

7.7 The Kok Report

The European Commission regularly published documents assessing progress in realizing the Lisbon Strategy, and in November 2004 a high-level group led by the former Dutch prime minister Wim Kok, also presented a report (Kok Report, 2004). The picture that emerged from these stocktaking efforts is rather negative, with accusations of missed objectives and failed promises. According to the Kok Report the blame lies with national leaders, and four reasons for the poor EU performance were given: an overloaded agenda; poor co-ordination; conflicting priorities; and lack of determined political action.

The diagnosis presented by the Kok Report was better than the therapy it proposed. The goal of overtaking the USA as the world's most competitive economy was rephrased as making Europe 'a single, competitive, dynamic, knowledge-based economy that is among the best in the world' (Kok Report, (2004: 16). The proposed solution was to focus on growth and employment and to reshape the EU budget to reflect the Lisbon priorities. However, the Report still favoured maintaining too many priorities. Assessment of progress in the Lisbon Strategy had been based on over one hundred indicators, and the Kok Report proposed cutting these to fourteen, which is not exactly a reduced agenda. If member states are faced with too many targets, attention is not focused and they can generally claim that progress has been made in some areas and ignore the rest.

---

[15] European Commission Financial Programming and Budget, http://ec.europa.eu/budget/library/documents/multiannual_framework/2007_2013/comm_2010_0072_en.pdf (accessed 7 March 2011).

The report also called for benchmarking of the progress of individual countries with the 'naming and shaming' of those making slow progress. However, the European Council of November 2004 failed to accept this suggestion and the German chancellor, Gerhard Schroeder, argued that member states needed to adapt reforms to national circumstances. Proposing increased supervision by the European Commission was a sensitive issue at a time when there were differences of opinion over the Stability and Growth Pact (see Chapter 11).

7.8 The 2005 revision of the Lisbon Agenda

The Commission accepted the recommendations of the Kok Report, and in a speech to the European Parliament of February 2005, President Barroso called for a new and stronger focus to the Lisbon Strategy.[16] In the same year the Commission presented the communication *Working Together for Growth and Jobs: A New Start to the Lisbon Strategy*,[17] which indicated four main objectives: making the internal market work better; more and better jobs and increased social cohesion; knowledge and innovation;[18] and improved implementation.

However, the revision of the Lisbon Agenda failed to overcome its shortcomings, and in particular the lack of political will of many member states to meet the objectives they paid lip service to at the EU level. The emphasis remained on co-operation between member states and peer pressure rather than 'naming and shaming' and formal sanctions.

7.9 The Europe 2020 programme

In 2010 the EU launched the Europe 2020 strategy to replace the Lisbon Agenda. The new strategy identified three drivers for growth to be supported by actions at the EU and national levels:[19]

- **Smart growth**: fostering knowledge, innovation, education and the digital society;
- **Sustainable growth**: making EU production greener and more resource efficient while boosting competitiveness;
- **Inclusive growth**: enhancing labour market participation, skills acquisition and the fight against poverty.

The objectives of smart growth and inclusive growth (including its link to EU social policy) are discussed in the following sections, while sustainable growth is taken up in Chapter 14 on EU environmental policy.

To realize the priorities of Europe 2020 the European Commission indicated headline targets:[20]

- 75 per cent of the population aged 20–64 should be employed;
- 3 per cent of the GDP of the EU should be invested in R&D;

---

[16] For accounts of the speech see EurActiv, http://www.euractiv.com/en/future-eu/mid-term-review-lisbon-sons/article-134971 or Eironline, European Industrial Relations Observatory Online, http://www.eurofound.europa.eu/eiro/2005/02/inbrief/eu0502204n.htm (accessed 9 March 2011).

[17] European Commission (2005).

[18] This included the proposal to create a 'European Institute of Technology' (EIT), which was initially rejected by the member states as duplicating existing structures, but was eventually agreed in 2007 (see Chapter 17).

[19] European Commission (2010e).

[20] Eurostat publishes statistics on these headline targets for all the member states at http://epp.eurostat.ec.europa.eu/portal/page/portal/europe_2020_indicators/headline_indicators (accessed 9 March 2011).

- The 20-20-20 targets in terms of reduction of greenhouse gas emissions (see Chapter 14), renewable energy production and energy efficiency should be met;
- The share of school dropouts should be under 10 per cent and at least 40 per cent of the population between the ages of 30 and 34 should have a degree or a diploma;
- 20 million fewer people should be living below the poverty line.

In order to meet the targets, seven 'flagship initiatives' were launched: an innovation union (refocusing of R&D and innovation policies); youth on the move (by promoting the mobility of students and young professionals); a digital agenda for Europe; resource-efficient Europe (encouraging a shift to a low carbon economy); an industrial policy for green growth; an agenda for new skills and jobs; and a European platform against poverty.

In September 2010 at the opening of the European Parliament, President Barroso announced new initiatives involving an EU bond to finance infrastructure projects, and a European vacancy monitor to guide the unemployed to unfilled vacancies.[21]

One of the aims of the Europe 2020 strategy was to overcome the implementation weakness of the Lisbon Agenda. As will be explained in Chapter 11, in September 2010 the European Commission presented proposals for reform of the economic governance of the EU with simultaneous monitoring and evaluation of Europe 2020 and fiscal stabilization programmes.[22] After much debate, in March 2011 the European Council reached agreement on reform and announced its commitment to the Commission's proposals.[23] These include establishing an alert mechanism and a scoreboard covering a wide range of indicators to identify countries with potentially problematic levels of macroeconomic imbalances, including deteriorating competitiveness. Member states would have to set out policy measures to correct macroeconomic imbalances and to move towards the Europe 2020 targets.[24] However, the scoreboards used to monitor the Single Market had a limited effect, and it remains to be seen whether those for Europe 2020 will be more effective.

7.10 Smart growth: better policies for the information society and research and development

Like the Lisbon Strategy, Europe 2020 calls for measures to encourage smart growth by boosting R&D spending of each member state to 3 per cent of GDP (of which, private investment should account for 2 per cent of GDP); and improved education and human capital by halving the number of early school leavers, fostering lifelong learning and facilitating mobility.

As can be seen from Table 7.3, nearly ten years after the launch of the Lisbon Strategy the reality was still rather distant from these objectives. In 2008, on the basis of Eurostat estimates, the EU(27) spent 1.9 per cent of GDP on R&D, while the equivalent US figure was 2.8 per cent. Moreover, Gros (2007) argues that in addition to the quantitative lag of the EU behind the USA there is also a qualitative or efficiency lag. This relates to the rate at which R&D spending generates commercially exploitable ideas as measured by the number of patent applications filed per worker.[25] On this basis US knowledge workers emerge as twice as productive on average as their EU counterparts. The relative inefficiency of European R&D is attributed to the segmentation of public research efforts, the overlapping of competing research programmes, and consequently the underutilization of available human resources.

---

[21] As reported in the *Financial Times* of 8 September 2010.

[22] The package of all the proposals on governance is available at European Commission, Economic and Financial Affairs, 'A new EU economic governance – a comprehensive Commission Package of proposals', http://ec.europa.eu/economy_finance/articles/eu_economic_situation/2010-09-eu_economic_governance_proposals_en.htm (accessed 3 March 2011).

[23] See European Council (2011) for the summit conclusions. Agreement was also reached on the Euro-Plus Pact (see Chapter 11).

[24] See Chapter 11 for a detailed description of these measures.

[25] In 2009 the European patents Office registered a total of 134,542 patent applications of which 61,744 were from EU(27) countries and 32,966 were from the USA. In the same period the United States Patent and Trademark Office registered 485,500 applications, with just under half from the USA.

Table 7.3   Indicators for the member states relating to creation of a knowledge-based economy

	Early leavers from education[a] 2009	Tertiary educational attainment[b] 2009	Gross domestic expenditure on R&D as % GDP in 2009
BE	11.1	42.0	1.96p
BG	14.7	27.9	0.53p
CZ	5.4	17.5	1.53
DK	10.6	48.1	3.02e
DE	11.1	29.4	2.82e
EE	13.9	35.9	1.42p
IE	11.3	49.0	1.77p
EL	14.5	26.5	0.58e (2007)
ES	31.2	39.4	1.38
FR	12.3	43.4	2.21p
IT	19.2	19.0	1.27p
CY	11.7	44.7	0.46p
LT	13.9	30.1	0.46
LI	8.7	40.6	0.84
LU	7.7p	46.6p	1.68p
HU	11.2	23.9	1.15
MA	36.8	21.1p	0.55
NL	10.9	40.5	1.84p
AU	8.7	23.5	2.75pe
PL	5.3	32.8	0.59p
PT	31.2	21.1	1.66p
RO	16.6	16.8	0.48
SL	5.3	31.6	1.86
SK	4.9	17.6	0.48
FI	9.9	45.9	3.96
SW	10.7p	43.9p	3.6p
UK	15.7	41.5	1.87p
EU(27)	14.4	32.3	2.01e

e estimate   p provisional

[a] Percentage of the population aged 18–24 with at most secondary education and not in further education or training.

[b] Percentage of the population aged 30–34 years who have successfully completed university.

Source: Eurostat, www.epp.eurostat.ec.europa.eu (accessed 9 March 2011), © European Union, 2011.

7.11 Inclusive growth: the link to EU social policy

The Europe 2020 objective of inclusive growth involves enhancing labour market participation, skills acquisition and the fight against poverty. EU social policy predates the Lisbon Agenda and Europe 2020, and has different origins, but it converges on their objective of inclusive growth.

EU social policy has evolved over the years, but includes measures for: employment and working conditions; social exclusion (or the fight against poverty); equality between men and women (see Box 7.1); the involvement of the so-called social partners (trade unions and employers) in the legislative process; and the participation of workers in the decision making of a firm. As can be seen from the list, the term 'social policy' covers a wide range of issues whose boundaries are at times indistinct.

Box 7.1

Gender equality in the EU

Article 119 of the Treaty of Rome (now Article 157 TFEU) guarantees equal pay for men and women. As some member states were failing to comply with Article 119, the Community introduced directives on equal pay (1975), equal treatment (1976) and the elimination of discrimination in pension schemes (1986). The Court of Justice also reinforced EU gender policy in judgments such as *Defrenne v. Sabena* on equal pay (1976), and the *Marschall* judgment of 1997, which allowed priority to be given to the woman in the event of male and female candidates possessing the same qualifications.

In 1996 the Commission adopted the gender mainstreaming approach that involves 'incorporating equal opportunities for women and men into all Community policies and activities' (COM(96) 67 final). The European Social Fund is used to promote gender equality as was the Community initiative EQUAL over the 2000–06 period. Since 2007 the Community programme for social solidarity, PROGRESS (see below), has also provided funding for gender equality. The European Employment Strategy provides the member states with guidelines on how to attract more women into the labour force and narrow the gap between men and women with regard to pay, employment (see also Figure 7.2 below) and unemployment. The strategy for equality for women and men for the 2010–15 period uses a dual approach of specific initiatives and gender mainstreaming. However, in 2010 women continued to earn 17.8 per cent less than men for every hour worked and this figure has remained stable for some time.*

* European Commission, DG Employment, Social Affairs and Inclusion, http://ec.europa.eu/social/main.jsp?catId=418 (accessed 3 February 2011). From 1 January 2011 responsibility for gender equality was moved to Justice, Fundamental Rights and Citizenship.

European social policy includes the social policies of the member states and EU, and so has to be distinguished from EU social policy. EU social policy covers a relatively limited range of issues and amounts to just a small fraction of welfare expenditure by the member states, tending simply to complement national measures.

Despite the increasing role of the EU in the social sphere, there remain several obstacles to developing a fully fledged EU social policy:

- Differences in the demographic and socio-economic conditions of the member states;
- The contentious nature of social policy issues, with strong ideological differences about what the role of the state should be;
- The diversity of national social policy regimes;
- The reluctance of member states to give up control of social policy;
- The scale of budgetary transfers necessary for an extensive EU social policy;
- The even greater diversity of social policy requirements and regimes in an enlarged EU.

7.12   The early years of EC social policy

The origins of EU social policy are to be found in all three of the original treaties founding the European Communities. Article 46 of the Treaty of Paris establishing the European Coal and Steel Community refers to the improvement of the living and working standards of workers in the coal and steel industries. The Euratom Treaty sets out provisions for the health and safety of workers in the civilian atomic energy industry. By far the most extensive treatment of social policy is to be found in the Treaty of Rome, which refers to: free movement of workers (Articles 48 to 51); improvement in working conditions and in standards of living (Articles 117 to 128); equal opportunities for men and women (Article 119; see Box 7.1 above); and the creation of the European Social Fund (Article 123).

However, there was a dichotomy between the very ambitious objectives set out in the Treaty of Rome and the very limited means to achieve these aims. The commitments set out in the Treaty were far from being precise, and there was no fixed timetable for action. For instance, it was envisaged that improved working standards and conditions of work would be realized through operation of the common market.

Despite the introduction of a Social Action Plan in 1974, until the mid-1980s the social policy of the Community maintained a low profile. EC social policy was still concentrated on the co-ordination of national social security systems to permit the freedom of movement of labour and the operation of the European Social Fund (ESF). In its early years, the ESF (see Chapter 15) was mainly concerned with facilitating labour movement, but in the 1970s became more directed towards the fight against youth and long-term unemployment, in particular by promoting training schemes. EC policy was characterized by a lack of flexibility in selecting programmes and a tendency to rubber-stamp decisions already taken at the national level. Moreover, in many cases it seems likely that EC measures simply replaced national financing (the so-called additionality problem; see Chapter 15).

7.13   EU social policy since the Single Market Programme

Given the limited success of earlier measures, many of the social policy objectives of the Treaty of Rome still had not been realized when the Single Market Programme was introduced in 1985. Although social policy was not mentioned in the White Paper of 1985, debate about a 'social dimension' to the Single Market was soon to emerge.

Proponents of a more active EC role in social policy argued that this was necessary because the adjustment implied by the Single Market project could lead to higher unemployment and that deregulation could lead to a risk of social dumping as a result of differences in the level of social protection between the member states. Social dumping arises because firms may have an incentive to locate in countries where wages and the cost of social protection are lower (usually the poorer member states). To counter this tendency, countries with higher social standards may be forced to reduce social standards, giving rise to the risk of a 'race to the bottom'. One way of tackling the risk of social dumping is by setting certain minimum standards for working conditions, health and safety in all member states.

Though the debate about EC social policy was linked to the Single Market project, its ideological basis was wider, reflecting different views of the role of the state in the economy. The case for an increased role for the Community was generally based on a fundamental belief that the workings of the market had to be corrected on grounds of equity and consensus. Social cohesion was necessary to correct the possible negative impact of increased competition on the weaker and more vulnerable regions and sections of the population. Minimum social standards had to be introduced to prevent the risk of social dumping. Increased participation of the workers in the decisions of firms, and of the so-called social partners (employers and trade unions) in EC decision making, were ways of achieving consensus. Social policy was seen by some as a necessary progression in a neo-functionalist framework to carry economic integration forward successfully (see Chapter 1).

Those in favour of this type of approach included the Socialist president of the Commission, Jacques Delors, centre-left members of the European Parliament and the Socialist governments in France and

some of the southern EC countries (Tsoukalis, 1997). Most Christian Democratic parties were in favour of legislation to protect welfare and employment. In Germany there was a long tradition of worker participation in the decisions of the firm and attempts to find consensus between the social partners.

Perhaps the main opposition in the ideological debate was to be found in the British Conservative Party, and in Margaret Thatcher in particular. Increased government regulation of working conditions was considered to add to labour market rigidities, reducing competitiveness and increasing unemployment. The poor British performance when the Conservatives took office was interpreted as being largely the result of excessive trade union influence. Worse still, the attempt to strengthen the Community role in this area was considered an attack on national sovereignty and a violation of the principle of subsidiarity. The UK government found support for this position among EC employers' federations and its own businesspeople.

Delors was among the main proponents of a more active EC social policy, or 'European Social Space', and four aspects of this position can be distinguished:[26]

- **Social dialogue, or the involvement of the social partners in the EC decision-making process.** In 1985 Delors arranged a meeting of associations at the Belgian chateau of Val Duchesse to promote social dialogue between the Commission, employers and employees. This subsequently became known as the Val Duchesse Process and was institutionalized by the Single European Act (Article 118b) and the Maastricht Treaty (Article 3 of the Social Protocol). An institution that has played a growing role in social dialogue is the European Economic and Social Committee (EESC, or Ecosoc; see Chapter 3), which has evolved from a mere consultative body into an important institutional forum for social partners to engage in key discussions of different aspects of integration that affect the lives of EU consumers and citizens;

- **The Social Charter, or Community Charter of the Fundamental Social Rights of Workers.** This was drawn up as a non-binding declaration of intent at the request of the Commission, European Parliament and EESC. It builds on the Social Charter of the Council of Europe and similar documents of the International Labour Office. An action programme accompanied the Charter, with specific measures designed to assist realization of the objectives. As can be seen from Box 7.2, the objectives are couched in very general terms, but some were still the subject of heated controversy. For instance, the aim of achieving an 'equitable wage' was interpreted in certain quarters as implying the introduction of a minimum wage. Measures to protect seasonal, temporary and part-time workers were seen as an attempt to extend full social protection to such forms of atypical work, so adding to labour market rigidities. Although amended to take account of British objections, the Charter was not accepted by the UK, but it was adopted by the other eleven member states in 1989;

- **The creation of a 'Europe of the citizens'**, aimed at reducing the democratic deficit and bringing the Community closer to the people (see also Chapter 1);

- **The introduction of an EC company statute** that would ensure the participation of workers in the decisions of the firm along the lines of the German and Dutch models. In December 2000 the Council agreed on the introduction of a European Company Statute which would enable a company with a European dimension to set up as a single company under EU law with a unified set of rules, management and reporting system, and provisions for safeguarding workers' rights.

Though the Single European Act contained relatively few increases in the EC role in social policy, reference was first made to the need for economic and social cohesion, social dialogue (Article 118b) and improvements in health and safety at the workplace (Article 118a).

The Social Charter was subsequently to form the basis of the Social Chapter of the Treaty of Maastricht, which covered issues such as minimum hours of work, social security, health and safety requirements and consultation of the social partners.

---

[26] Delors presented his vision of a European Social Space, *inter alia*, to the European Trade Union Confederation in 1988.

Following its earlier refusal to sign the Social Charter, the UK initially also opted out of the Maastricht Social Chapter, and only signed it in 1997 under the Blair government. The Social Chapter was therefore added to the Maastricht Treaty as a separate protocol, and was only incorporated into the Community pillar under the Amsterdam Treaty. However, certain other aspects of social policy (such as protection of public health) were included in the Maastricht Treaty and were applicable in all member states.

As part of the relaunching of the Lisbon Strategy in 2005, the EU also agreed the Social Agenda (renewed in 2008), which aimed at providing jobs, improving living and working conditions, fighting poverty and promoting equal opportunities for all. The Social Agenda involved national, regional and local authorities, the social partners (representatives of employers and workers) and non-governmental organizations. It aimed at supporting member states in their efforts to reform pension and health care systems, tackle poverty, meet the demographic challenge and foster equal opportunities.

7.14   EU social policy in the Lisbon Treaty

In the Lisbon Treaty, Articles 151 and 161 TFEU deal with social policy and Articles 145 to 150 with employment. The Treaty contains a 'social clause', which entails mainstreaming of social policy so the promotion of employment, social protection, the fight against social exclusion, and so on, have to be taken into account in framing and implementing all EU policies. The Treaty recognizes fundamental human rights by making a legally binding reference to the Charter of Fundamental Human Rights (though the UK and Poland obtained opt-outs; see Chapter 3). It also states that the EU shall support and complement the activities of member states in areas such as working conditions, social security and the protection of workers, the information and consultation of workers, collective action, combating social exclusion, and so on (Article 153 TFEU). In addition, the Treaty confirms the role of social partners and enhances social dialogue (Articles 154 and 155 TFEU).

With regard to financial assistance from the EU, the European Social Fund has €77 billion for the 2007–13 period to increase the adaptability of workers and enterprises, enhance access to the labour market, combat discrimination, improve education and training systems, and improve institutional capacity in disadvantaged regions.

7.15 Employment in the treaties

At the time of the Treaty of Rome, unemployment was relatively low in the Community, so the Treaty contained few provisions on employment. The Commission published White Papers in 1993 and 1994 aimed at promoting employment, competitiveness and growth without compromising social protection. However, it was not until the Amsterdam Treaty that the legal basis of employment as a major area of EU policy was established. The Treaty called for a development of a co-ordinated strategy of the member states towards employment, and the 'mainstreaming' of employment policy, requiring it to be taken into account in the formulation of all EU policies and strategies.

These objectives were confirmed in the Treaty of Lisbon, which calls for the development of a 'co-ordinated strategy for improving employment and particularly for promoting a skilled, trained and adaptable workforce and labour markets responsive to economic change' (Article 145 TFEU).

7.16 The European Employment Strategy

Given persistent high levels of unemployment during the early 1990s, which were attributed to structural problems in labour markets, the 1997 Luxembourg European Council agreed that it was necessary to act collectively at the EU level to find solutions through more co-ordination and convergence of policies. This marks the beginning of the European Employment Strategy (EES), also known as the Luxembourg Process. The strategy aimed at:

- improving 'employability' (through active labour-market policies such as training schemes for the young and long-term unemployed to enable people to take up employment opportunities, increase skills and keep the unemployed in touch with the labour market; see Box 7.3);
- encouraging the adaptability of businesses and their employees (through union-negotiated work reorganization);
- strengthening policies for equal opportunities (between men and women, and also increasing job possibilities for the disabled); and
- developing entrepreneurship (in particular through deregulation and simplification of market access for small firms).

The EU adopted a dual approach to achieve these aims: setting the policy framework and guidelines, and providing financing for programmes through the Structural Funds (see Chapter 15). However, EU employment policy remains very much a complement to national measures.

The European Employment Strategy was reinforced and streamlined in 2003 to underpin the Lisbon Process, and the 2005 revision of the Lisbon Strategy set out guidelines for growth and jobs for the 2005–08 period.

As described above, in 2010 the Europe 2020 strategy indicated headline targets, three of which relate to the EES: 75 per cent of people aged 20–64 in work (see Figure 7.1 below); school dropout rates below 10 per cent and at least 40 per cent of 30–34-year-olds completing third-level education (see Table 7.3 above); and at least 20 million fewer people in or at risk of poverty and social exclusion. It also established the flagship initiative 'An Agenda for New Skills and Jobs', indicating actions necessary to meet these targets. These include measures to increase flexicurity (combining flexibility and security in the labour market), incentives to invest in training; improvement in employment legislation; and tax and administrative reforms to improve labour market conditions.[27]

---

[27] See European Commission DG Employment, Social Affairs and Inclusion, http://europa.eu/pol/socio/index_en.htm; http://ec.europa.eu/social/home.jsp (accessed 4 February 2011).

Box 7.3

An example of a project to combat long-term unemployment financed by the European Social Fund

A French project, CREATIVE, co-ordinated by the National Employment Agency, was established to encourage the long-term unemployed to find work or set up small businesses of their own. Operating through seven employment agencies, the project involved a micro-finance organization for individuals with a business idea but without the financial guarantees necessary to get a loan through a traditional bank. The loans offered were less than €5,000 in value, but in 2003, they helped 75 participants to set up their own business. The project also helps those with few qualifications to get a driver's licence as an additional skill for the job market. Successful participants, accompanied by a trainer, provide services to the community by giving lifts to people who have mobility problems. A further initiative teaches skills to job seekers by running courses giving practical training in arts and crafts. One course resulted in the successful transformation of a hallway in a residential building of a deprived area. Total funding for the project was €1,380,000, of which €450,000 came from the European Social Fund.

PROGRESS (the EU Programme for Employment and Social Solidarity) has a budget of €743 million for the 2007–13 period and supports measures in five main fields of action: employment, social protection and inclusion, working conditions, anti-discrimination and diversity, and gender equality.

Like the Lisbon Strategy, the EES is based on the open method of co-ordination, which provides a framework for the member states to share information, exchange knowledge of good practice, and discuss and co-ordinate their employment policies. Each year the EU and national governments meet in an Employment Committee to produce an Employment Package, which consists of: guidelines for national employment policies; targets and flagship initiatives; and a Commission report, with recommendations, if appropriate to member states.

In addition to this procedure there is an ongoing dialogue between the Commission, national governments, trade unions, employers' associations and other EU institutions such as the European Parliament, the EESC and the Committee of the Regions.

7.17   Assessment of the European Employment Strategy

Assessing the effects of the EES encounters the usual difficulty of isolating the impact of EU policies from other factors (such as growth) influencing employment levels. The question is further complicated in that national employment policies may not always be co-ordinated with those of the EU, though, as described above, over time there have been various initiatives to reduce such disparities.

The EU has not met the various targets with regard to employment set out in the Lisbon Strategy and Europe 2020 (see Figures 7.1–7.3). Eurostat calculates the employment rate by dividing the number of persons aged 15–64 by employment in the total population of the same age group. Total employment for the EU(27) rose from 60.7 per cent in 1997 to 65.7 per cent in 2008 and 64.6 per cent in 2009 (see also Figure 7.1), but is still well below the target of 70 per cent for 2010, or 75 per cent for 2020.

EU unemployment remained consistently higher than that of the USA from the mid-1970s on, while, as mentioned above, participation rates in the labour force have been lower (see also Table 7.1 above). Prescott (2004) argues that the lower utilization of labour in the EU is largely due to differences in the tax systems, while more generous unemployment schemes probably also play a role. Blanchard (2004) maintains the cause is a higher preference for leisure (with shorter working

hours and a lower rate of participation in the labour force in the EU). However, developments in demography are forcing changes in pension systems and choices about leisure.

A major ongoing debate is how far the higher level of participation in the USA is the result of greater labour market flexibility. The dilemma for the EU is how to reconcile a relatively high level of social protection with international competitiveness. The question that arises is whether competitiveness should remain a primary goal of the EU or whether it might threaten the European 'social model'.[28]

There are relatively few studies of the effects of EU spending on employment through the Structural Funds (see Chapter 15 for a description of these Funds). De la Fuente (2002) estimated that spending on the Structural Funds over the 1993–99 period added 0.4 per cent to employment growth in Spain. Martin and Tyler (2006) suggest that EU regional policy created some extra 1 million jobs in Objective 1 regions. According to the European Commission, cohesion policy for the 2000–06 period helped to create 1.4 million jobs. In contrast, Becker et al. (2008) found that while spending through the Structural Funds had a positive effect on growth, it failed to deliver employment effects. They maintain that this may be because the Objective 1 transfers mainly target investment, or that the creation of jobs takes longer than a programming period of five or seven years.

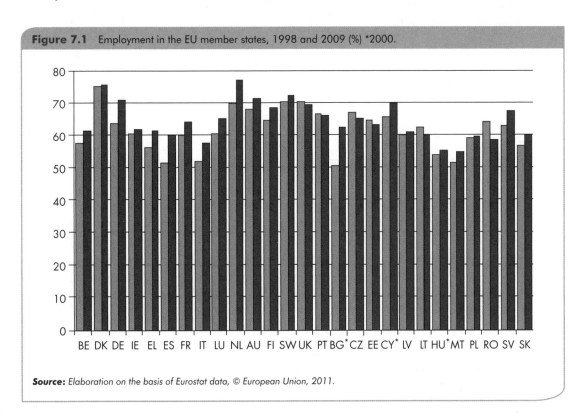

Figure 7.1   Employment in the EU member states, 1998 and 2009 (%) *2000.

Source: *Elaboration on the basis of Eurostat data,* © *European Union, 2011.*

---

[28] For example, in an article in the *Financial Times* of 8 October 2004, the famous professor of political science at Princeton University, Andrew Moravcsik, praises the European role model, which he maintains is more egalitarian, more communitarian and more cosmopolitan than that of the USA. Egalitarianism is evident in a welfare state that guarantees a certain minimum living standard, not only in cash, but also through health care, pensions and unemployment insurance. Europeans tend to be more committed to culturally diverse communal traditions and less convinced by the work ethic (a major reason behind the disparity in per capita income). At an international level Europeans seem more committed to conflict resolution through peaceful means. See also Moravcsik (1998).

Figure 7.2 Employment of women in the EU member states, 2000 and 2009 (%)

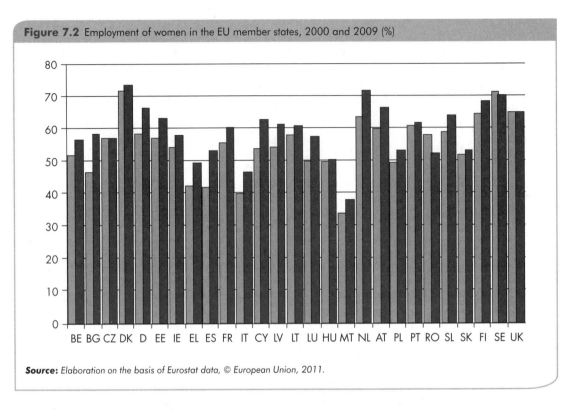

Source: *Elaboration on the basis of Eurostat data, © European Union, 2011.*

Figure 7.3 Employment of older workers (aged 55–64) in the EU member states, 2000 and 2009 (%)

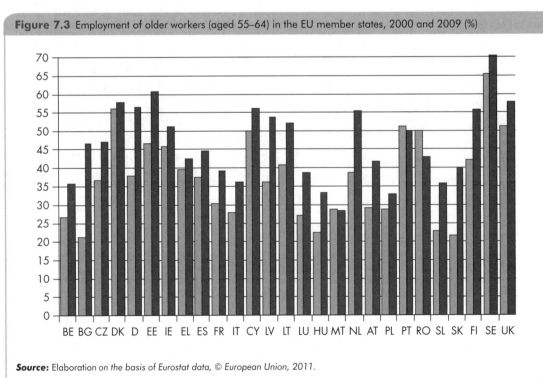

Source: *Elaboration on the basis of Eurostat data, © European Union, 2011.*

7.18 Inclusive growth: fighting poverty and social exclusion in the EU

'Social exclusion' is the term used by the Commission for poverty and marginalization. The definition of poverty adopted by the EU is having a disposable income less than 60 per cent of median income in the country concerned (see Table 7.4).[29] Despite having some of the most developed social protection systems, some 16.4 per cent of the EU population, or 84 million people, remained at risk of poverty in 2009, with higher rates for children, older people (see also Box 7.4) and the unemployed.[30] In the difficult economic transition process experienced by some of the new member states, an effective social protection system can play a key role in keeping the level of poverty low, and the experience of the Czech Republic is noteworthy.

Although between 1975 and 1994 the Community introduced three 'poverty' programmes, EU financing of such measures has always been limited, mainly because the richer member states insist

Table 7.4 Population at risk of poverty after social transfers, 2009[a]

Country	After social transfers (%)	Country	After social transfers (%)	Country	After social transfers (%)
Belgium	14.6	Austria	12.0	Latvia	25.7
Denmark	13.1	Portugal	17.9	Lithuania	20.6
Germany	15.5	Finland	13.8	Malta	15.1
Ireland	15.0	Sweden	13.3	Poland	17.1
Greece	19.7	UK	17.3	Romania	22.4
Spain	19.5	Bulgaria	21.8	Slovakia	15.1
France	12.9	Czech Rep.	8.6	Slovenia	11.3
Italy	18.1	Estonia	19.7		
Luxembourg	14.9	Hungary	12.4	EU(27)	16.3
Netherlands	11.1	Cyprus	16.2	EU(15)	16.1

[a] Less than 60 per cent of median income in the country concerned.

Source: Eurostat, http://epp.eurostat.ec.europa.eu/tgm/table.do?tab=table&init=1&plugin=1&language=en&pcode=tsdsc280 (accessed 9 March 2011), © European Union.

[29] Those at risk of poverty are defined as having an 'equivalized' income (which takes into account the household size and composition) below 60 per cent of the national median level. Retirement and survivor's pensions are counted as income before transfers and not as social transfers. See also the discussion of measures of disparity such as the Gini coefficient in note 13 of Chapter 15. The Stiglitz–Sen–Fitoussi Report (2009) points to the growing awareness of the shortcomings of GDP measures in indicating societal well-being and social progress. European Commission (2010f) therefore discusses various other quality of life measures, including life expectancy and health, ageing, security and unemployment.

[30] According to European Commission (2010f), 20 per cent of children, 19 per cent of people over 65 and 44 per cent of the unemployed were at risk of poverty in 2008 compared with 17 per cent of the total population. In Greece, Spain and Portugal the difference in the risk of poverty whether employed or unemployed is significantly lower than elsewhere. This is mainly due to a large number of the unemployed living in households where somebody is employed, rather than a reflection of the level of employment benefits.

that this is primarily a policy area for national competences. The year 2010 was declared European Year for Combating Poverty and Social Exclusion.

At the same time as the Lisbon Strategy, in 2000 the European Council decided to set up a Social Inclusion Process providing an EU framework to fight poverty and social exclusion, also based on the open method of co-ordination. This entails common objectives and indicators; national strategic reports against poverty and social exclusion, which are assessed in joint reports of the Commission

---

Box 7.4

The ageing of the EU population

According to Eurostat projections based on assumptions about future trends in fertility, mortality and immigration, the total population of the EU will grow from a provisional estimate of 501 million in January 2010 to 515 million in 2050, after which it is expected to fall. The median age in the EU is expected to rise from 40 years in 2008 to 45 years in 2030 and the share of those aged 65 and over is forecast to rise from 17 per cent to 24 per cent over the same period.* In 2007 pensions in the EU were on average 10.2 per cent of GDP, ranging from 5.2 of GDP in Ireland to 14.0 per cent in Italy.

According to Oksanen (forthcoming), work relating to population and ageing gained momentum in the EU when the Stockholm European Council of 2000 declared that 'the aging society calls for clear strategies for ensuring the adequacy of pension systems as well as of health care systems and care of the elderly, while at the same time maintaining the sustainability of public finances and intergenerational solidarity'.

Measures used to offset the effects of ageing of the population in the EU include immigration policies (see Chapter 8), raising the retirement age and encouraging continued participation in the labour force by women and older workers.

European Commission (2010f).

---

and Council; efforts to encourage a mutual learning process, also through peer review groups; a Social Protection Committee to encourage co-operation between the Commission and member states; and monitoring through Commission social situation reports and the European Observatory on the social situation.

According to the European Commission, the approach has increased awareness of poverty and social exclusion, created more consensus about what needs to be done, and encouraged EU member states to place these challenges higher on the political agenda.[31] However, the EU still appears to rely more on co-ordination than financial support: a more effective policy would need more funding from national governments and an increased allocation in the EU budget.

7.19   Evaluation

Despite the continued efforts of the Commission, there is a risk that the Europe 2020 strategy will end up being like 'Lisbon as usual', with all the associated shortcomings. As explained above, the Commission proposals for the Lisbon Agenda received various setbacks from the European Council, and spending on competitiveness and growth was less than initially envisaged in the 2007–13 financial perspective. The Lisbon Strategy before, and Europe 2020 after, still receive little more than lip service

---

[31] European Commission DG Employment, Social Affairs and Inclusion, http://ec.europa.eu/social/main. jsp?catId=758&langId=en (accessed 3 February 2011).

from the governments of many EU member states, and have failed to capture the imagination of the European public. Even before the economic crisis, in various member states additional funds for education, training and R&D failed to materialize, and job creation projects were on a relatively limited scale.

Europe 2020 needs restored credibility. Increasing EU competitiveness and promoting growth are crucial, but it seems that the cash-strapped governments of some of the member states still have to be convinced that higher priority and increased expenditure should be devoted to these aims, and that the EU is an appropriate framework for co-ordinating efforts.

Since the 1990s the EU has launched various strategies to combat unemployment and increase employment. Though at times the rhetoric and statements of intent and solidarity seem to exceed the results, there has been a slight reduction in unemployment and increase in participation in the labour force since the EES was launched in 1997. The EU approach relies heavily on active labour market measures (such as training and the creation of job opportunities), but financing is limited, and the effectiveness of this type of approach has sometimes been called into question. At least formal EU frameworks for the formulation, development and review of strategies to increase employment and combat social exclusion have been set in place, but progress remains slow.

Bongardt and Torres (2007a) argue that working together through the open method of co-ordination in the EU has conditioned the economic policy framework and set in motion new governance patterns. From this point of view the Lisbon Strategy and Europe 2020 can be regarded as an exercise in policy co-ordination with a view to stimulating interdependencies and policy learning. The effort to meet the Lisbon and Europe 2020 goals has required co-ordination of policies at the EU and member state levels and this has triggered improvements in governance methods.

As will be explained in Chapter 11, the EU is engaged in a fundamental debate about reform of its economic governance. In this debate, monitoring and possible sanctions both with regard to competitiveness and the Stability and Growth Pact have been linked. However, as will be shown in Chapter 11, the prospect of increased EU control of national economic policies has encountered the opposition of various member states, so it is doubtful how stringent the new system of EU economic governance will prove in practice. Without effective carrots and/or sticks, compliance is difficult to ensure, so it is open to question whether the member states will be more galvanized by Europe 2020 than they were by the Lisbon Agenda.

Summary of key concepts

- **Competitiveness** can be defined as improving the overall economic performance of a nation measured in terms of ability to provide growing living standards on a sustainable basis and broad access to jobs.

- The GDP per capita of the Community rose to about 70 per cent of the US level by the mid-1970s, but subsequently this gap failed to narrow.

- **Differences in per capita income** may be due to varying levels of production per worker, or differences in labour participation. Productivity on its own is insufficient to make international comparisons of competitiveness. A more useful measure is **unit labour costs**, which indicate the cost of labour input per unit of value added.

- The long-run impact of the economic crisis on competitiveness is ambivalent.

- **Globalization** has led to overall gains, but there have been **winners and losers** in the process. There are fears that workers in developed countries will suffer from downward pressure on wages and/or higher unemployment.

- In addition to the gap compared with US economic performance, there was also growing concern regarding the **challenge posed by the BRICs,** with China emerging as a major economic actor, and India becoming an increasingly important location for outsourcing.

- The **Lisbon European Council** of 2000 attributed poor EU economic performance to lack of completion of the Single Market, labour market rigidities, insufficient investment in education and training, and a technology gap between the EU and USA, in particular with regard to information science. It indicated goals and a new open method of co-ordination to overcome these shortcomings.

- The **Sapir Report** agreed that the objectives of the Lisbon Agenda were rightly ambitious, but maintained that the Agenda rested on an excessive number of targets and a weak method. To meet these drawbacks the Sapir Report recommended focusing on growth, and improving governance of the Agenda.

- The **Kok Report** also criticized the Lisbon Strategy for an overloaded agenda and insufficient political commitment. It proposed focusing on growth and employment, but still favoured maintaining too many priorities. The Kok Report also suggested benchmarking to assess progress of individual member states in realizing the strategy.

- The Barroso Commission attempted to **revise the Lisbon Agenda in 2005**, focusing on completion of the Single Market, more and better jobs, knowledge and innovation, and improved implementation.

- The European Council cut back the Commission's proposal for spending on competitiveness in the Financial Perspective, and rejected the Kok proposal of benchmarking of Lisbon Strategy progress.

- In 2010 the **Europe 2020 strategy** replaced the Lisbon Agenda and set out a programme for: **smart growth** (fostering knowledge, innovation, education and the digital society), **sustainable growth**, and **inclusive growth** (enhancing labour market participation, skills acquisition and the fight against poverty). Economic governance was to be reinforced, in particular through tighter country surveillance.

- The **shortcomings of the Europe 2020 strategy** seem likely to be the same as those of the Lisbon Agenda: an excessive number of targets, lack of political will, and reliance on the member states to implement measures (in a worse economic climate than before) in the absence of adequate incentives or sanctions to encourage compliance.

- **EU social policy** has evolved over the years, but includes measures for: employment and working conditions; social exclusion, or the fight against poverty; equality between men and women; the involvement of the so-called social partners (trade unions and employers) in the legislative process; and the participation of workers in the decision making of a firm.

- **Obstacles to developing a fully fledged EU social policy** include: differences in the conditions of the member states; the contentious, ideological nature of social policy issues; the diversity of national social policy regimes; the reluctance of member states to give up control of social policy; the scale of budgetary transfers necessary for EU social policy; and the even greater diversity of social policy requirements after enlargement.

- With the introduction of the Europe 2020 strategy in 2010, three **headline targets were set for the EES**: 75 per cent of people aged 20–64 in work; school drop out rates below 10 per cent and at least 40 per cent of 30–34-year-olds completing third level education; and at least 20 million fewer people in or at risk of poverty and social exclusion.

Questions for study and review

1 What do we mean by competitiveness and how can it be measured?
2 What is the effect of the economic crisis on competitiveness?
3 What are the negative aspects of globalization?
4 What are the main objectives of the Lisbon Strategy?
5 Describe the principal aspects of the Europe 2020 strategy.
6 What criticisms have been made of the Lisbon Strategy and of Europe 2020?
7 What measures do you think should be introduced to promote growth and the increased competitiveness of the EU?
8 Do you consider GDP an adequate measure for international comparisons between countries?
9 What do we mean by social dumping? To what extent do you think that it poses the risk of a 'race to the bottom'?
10 What are the obstacles to developing a fully fledged EU social policy?
11 What do we mean by the 'social dimension' of the Single Market Programme?
12 Indicate the main features of EU employment policy. What does the EES entail?
13 What policies do you think the EU should use to increase employment?
14 What policies do you think the EU should use to reduce poverty?

Online
Learning **Centre**

When you have read this chapter, log on to the Online Learning Centre website at *www.mcgraw-hill.co.uk/textbooks/senior* to explore weblinks, chapter-by-chapter test questions, case studies and more online study tools.

Chapter 8

Movement of Labour, Immigration and Asylum

Learning Objectives

By the end of this chapter you should be able to understand:

- ✓ The main advantages said to arise from freedom of labour movement
- ✓ The most frequent justifications given for introducing restrictions on immigration
- ✓ The main factors influencing the decision to migrate
- ✓ How migration may influence wage levels and unemployment
- ✓ The most common forms of immigration
- ✓ The barriers to freedom of movement of labour in the EU
- ✓ Immigration patterns within the EU
- ✓ The difficulties in establishing a common EU policy with regard to immigration and asylum
- ✓ How the pattern of immigration from the rest of the world to the EU has changed over time

8.1 Introduction

Ensuring freedom of labour movement within the Community was one of the main objectives of the Treaty of Rome, subsequently reinforced by the 1993 Single Market Programme. In practice, barriers to labour movement remain within the EU, and this was even more the case after the 2004 and 2007 enlargements.

Over the years, immigration from third countries to the EU has acquired new forms and dimensions, and urgently requires co-ordination of the positions of EU member states and the introduction of common policies. However, geographical, historical and cultural differences between

the member states have rendered the creation of a common EU policy towards immigration and asylum difficult.[1]

The aim of this chapter is first to provide a brief account of some of the theoretical aspects of labour movement. Then follows a description of the evolution of EU policies, before outlining the main developments in migratory flows both within the EU and from third countries.

8.2 The effects of migration

Freedom of movement of labour on an international scale is generally advocated because the removal of restrictions is said to increase efficiency and improve the allocation of resources. Workers will have higher chances of using their qualifications in the best possible way. Employers will be able to overcome eventual labour shortages and increase their possibilities of finding labour with the skills required.

More specific arguments are also advanced in favour of immigration. For example, in the country of destination it is sometimes claimed that the inflow of young workers can be used to offset possible negative effects of ageing of the population, or immigrants can be used to cover a skills shortage. Labour-exporting countries may favour emigration so that the balance of payments can benefit from workers' remittances (which in some countries are larger than foreign aid or inward investment), though these often tend to be invested in housing and consumption and may have limited lasting positive effect on the home economy.

The effects of migration can be analysed using a simple model. It is assumed that there are two factors of production, capital (C) and labour (L); two countries, home and foreign; that both countries produce one good and that there is perfect competition. The marginal product of labour shows how the output of a product increases when one additional unit of labour is used. Diminishing returns means that as additional units of labour are added to a given amount of capital, output will increase but by ever smaller amounts for each additional unit of labour.

Figure 8.1 shows the marginal product of labour in the home country MPLh. With the stock of home labour Lh, the equilibrium wage in the home country is Wh. Total earnings by home labour are given by the wage Wh multiplied by the amount of labour Lh. Under perfect competition the payments to the two factors of production will just equal the value of total production. The area under the curve indicates the total output of the home country. The payment to capital is therefore given by the area under the MPLh curve minus the payment to labour.

In order to show the effects of migration the marginal product of labour curves for both the home and foreign countries can be shown in a single graph. Assume initially that immigration is not allowed. Figure 8.2 reproduces the MPLh curve for home labour from Figure 8.1 but adds a second vertical axis and shows the marginal product of labour curve for the foreign country running right to left. The total horizontal distance between the two axes indicates the total amount of labour in the two countries (Lh + Lf).

With stock of labour Lf (total labour minus Lh), the equilibrium wage in the foreign country will be Wf. As can be seen from the graph, the equilibrium wage Wh in the home country is higher than Wf, so if migration is now allowed, there will be an incentive for workers to move from the foreign country to the home country to earn higher wages. The immigration will cause the wage at home to fall, and the wage in the foreign country to rise until they reach the same level W′. Equilibrium is reached when Lf − L′f workers have moved from the foreign country to the home country.

---

[1] The issue is further complicated in that allowing free movement of people involves a trade-off: control of international crime, terrorism, drug trafficking and migration becomes more difficult. EU policy has gradually shifted towards increased co-operation on home affairs, and police and judicial matters. As described on the Online Learning Centre (OLC) for this book, labour movement and immigration policy are intrinsically linked to the evolution of the EU as an area of Freedom, Security and Justice. The OLC provides an account of the changes in what was the third pillar of the EU over time.

Figure 8.1   The income shares of capital and labour

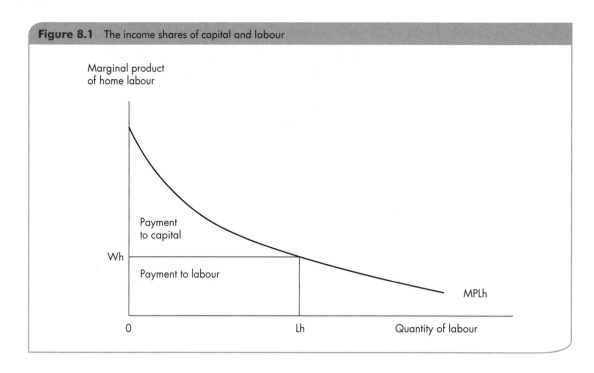

Figure 8.2   The causes and effects of immigration

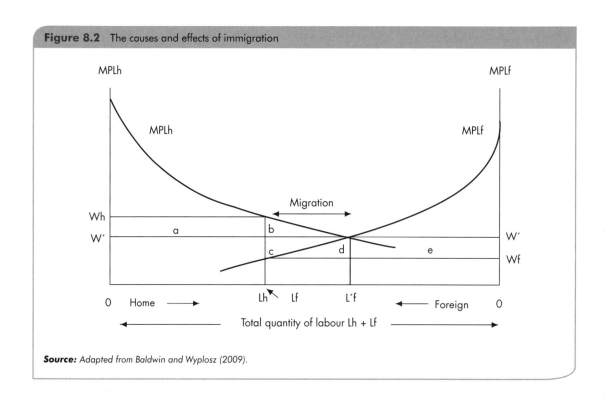

Source: Adapted from Baldwin and Wyplosz (2009).

The welfare effects of migration can also be seen from Figure 8.2:

- Home labour loses earnings of area a.
- Home capital gains earnings of a + b.
- The total gain to the home country is therefore b.
- Payments to labour remaining in the foreign county rise by e.
- Earning by capital in the foreign country fall by d + e.
- If foreigners now working in the home country are also taken into account, the earnings to foreign workers rise by c + d + e, the earnings of foreign capital fall by d + e, so there is a net gain of c.

Various effects of migration are, therefore, shown by this simple model:

- There is convergence of wages in the two countries, with wages falling at home and rising in the foreign country.
- Total world output, which is given by the area under the two curves MPLh and MPLf, rises. This is because migration has the effect of increasing efficiency.
- There are winners and losers from the migration.

8.3 The causes of migration

The simple model above attributes migration to wage differences, but in practice many other factors influence the decision to migrate (and pattern of migration), so the list becomes:

- The wage gap between the home and host country.
- Political and ethnic disturbances (which emerge as the main cause of major large-scale migration flows in Europe).
- The employment possibilities in both countries.[2]
- Economic expectations.
- The geographical proximity of the two countries.
- Emigration traditions.
- Ethnic and family networks.
- Cultural and linguistic factors.

Migration involves economic and psychological costs to the person involved. Individuals have a preference for living in their own country for social, cultural and linguistic reasons. Migration entails costs of travel, finding a house, job and so on. An individual will only undertake migration when the expected benefit is large enough to offset the costs of migration.[3]

8.4 Restrictions on migration

In practice most countries use restrictions on immigration, and as Boeri and Brücker (2005) state, international migration is the 'great absentee' in the era of globalization, as barriers to trade and international capital movements have been reduced substantially. Restrictions on immigration

---

[2] Faini (1995) also argued that, *ceteris paribus*, countries with a large informal sector tend to be attractive to immigrants because lower skills are generally required for employment.

[3] As Faini and Venturini (1994) argued, migration is an 'inferior' good, and staying at home is the 'normal' good.

generally consist of border controls and work or residence permits, but may also take other forms such as limited access to certain jobs and professions, or financial disincentives such as limits on access to social security benefits, long and/or difficult administrative procedures for admission, or unfavourable tax treatment. Other factors such as inability to find housing may also inhibit migration.

In the case of countries receiving immigrants the most frequently cited negative effects are:

- Increased government expenditure in order to provide the necessary social provisions for foreigners.[4]
- Societal disruption due to cultural differences and so on.
- Increased regional disparities as the foreign workers tend to be attracted to urban agglomerations where jobs are more readily available. Against this, where internal labour mobility in a country is low, immigration may 'grease the wheels' in reducing regional disparities as immigrants move to richer regions and may exert downward pressure on wages and higher unemployment of native workers in those areas.
- A worsening of the balance of payments as foreign workers send their earnings home.
- The downward pressure on wages (see next section).
- Increased unemployment (see next section).

In practice the importance of the political effects of immigration often outweigh the economic impact, because populist and nationalist political parties may exploit societal tensions, as has been the case in various EU countries.

In countries of emigration the most frequent justification for restrictions is that they are said to be necessary to avoid the possible negative effects of migration. These include the loss of human capital necessary for the development of the country as, in general, the younger, more dynamic and better skilled workers tend to leave (the so-called brain drain).

8.5 The impact of migration on wages and employment

One of the main debates about migratory flows relates to their impact on wages. Neo-classical economic theory argues that freedom of labour movement will lead to convergence of wages, as suggested by the model above. If costs of migration are also taken into account, the migratory flow will continue until the difference in wages between the two countries just matches the costs of migration.

According to the neo-classical view a similar mechanism is in operation for unemployment, and in the long run unemployment rates are likely to be independent of the size of the labour force. In the short run an increase in migration may lead to an increase in unemployment in the receiving country. Rising unemployment in the country of destination puts downward pressure on wages, inducing firms to take on more labour, and eventually unemployment will revert to its original level. The difficulty lies in assessing how long this process of adjustment will take.

However, the view that migration will lead to wage convergence and will not influence the long-run level of employment is based on some rather restrictive assumptions. Institutional barriers, such as restrictions on labour movement, may prevent adjustment from taking place. For example, trade unions or employee associations may prevent access to certain jobs, or employers may discriminate against certain types of workers on grounds of race or gender. Moreover, in practice the adjustment process may take some time, and in the meantime immigration may lead to lower wages and higher unemployment.

---

[4] Empirical studies such as Boeri and Brücker (2005) find that the income of natives in countries receiving immigrants will fall as the level of welfare benefits available also to immigrants rises, but conclude that the effect is relatively limited. The limited scale of the effect is confirmed by European Integration Consortium (2009), which maintains that immigrants from the new member states to the UK and Ireland after enlargement made a net contribution to public budgets due to their low age, good health and high employment rates. However, in other countries such as Germany, immigrants from the new member states are found to be more than proportionally affected by unemployment.

The impact of migration on wages and unemployment therefore becomes a question for empirical research. Analysing the EU labour market after enlargement, Boeri and Brücker (2005), updated as European Integration Consortium (2009), both find that wages will decline slightly in receiving countries and increase in the sending countries in the short run, while the overall impact on the aggregate wage level is neutral in the long run.[5] The aggregate unemployment is found to increase slightly in receiving countries and fall slightly in the sending countries in the short run. European Integration Consortium (2009) finds the overall level of unemployment to shrink slightly in the enlarged EU.

Kahanec and Zimmermann (2010) confirm that the effects of the 2004 and 2007 enlargements on wages and employment are small and hard to detect, and also argue that the issue of whether immigrants are high-skilled or low-skilled labour is crucial to the analysis of the impact of immigration on the economy of the recipient country.

The question here is one of complementarity versus substitutability. In many West European countries there is a shortage of unskilled workers. In Italy, for instance, unskilled immigrant labour is essential during the harvest and in helping in restaurants and bars during the tourist season. The unskilled work of immigrants therefore complements the skilled work of the Italian owners and managers of hotels, farms and so on. High-skilled labour can be regarded as a form of human capital, and so could be included as part of capital in Figure 8.2. Immigration of high-skilled labour to a country can therefore be seen as an increase in human capital, which tends to increase the marginal product (and hence wages) of low-skilled labour.

8.6 Types of immigration

Various categories of immigrants are generally distinguished:

- Economic immigrants seeking permanent residence to improve their living standards.
- Asylum seekers looking for refuge from war or oppression.
- Illegal immigrants.
- Seasonal or temporary workers.

As it is becoming ever more difficult to enter the EU from a third country as a long-term economic immigrant, there has been a growing tendency to seek other forms of access. The 1951 Geneva Convention provided a definition of refugees as those who are fleeing persecution for 'reasons of race, religion, nationality, membership of a social group or political opinion'. However, in practice it is very difficult to distinguish whether refugees are fleeing poverty rather than persecution. The number of those seeking asylum remained fairly stable in the 1980s but increased dramatically in Europe following the collapse of the Eastern bloc and the Balkan wars, and again in 2011 with the unrest in North Africa.

The treatment of requests for asylum varies considerably among the EU member states with regard both to percentage of asylum cases accepted and to the treatment of applicants while procedures are being carried out. From 1993, Germany became more restrictive in accepting requests for asylum,[6] but few refugees were sent home. In 1997 the UN High Commissioner for Refugees (UNHCR) estimated that Germany was harbouring about 1.3 million people who had requested asylum, creating a form of

---

[5] These results are similar to those of an earlier study by Boeri, Brücker et al. (2000) on the impact of immigration from the CEEC(10), which suggests that a 1 per cent increase in the share of foreign workers from these countries would lead to a fall in wages by 0.25 per cent in Austria and by 0.6 per cent in Germany, and to an increase in the risk of dismissal by 0.8 per cent in Austria and 1.6 per cent in Germany. According to Boeri, Brücker et al. (2000), the negative employment and wage effects from CEEC immigrants would be concentrated on less qualified, blue-collar workers. Initially immigrants from Central and Eastern Europe were considered to be relatively well qualified, but a closer analysis revealed that, in particular, the skills obtained in vocational schools under the old regime were often not suited to operating in a market economy.

[6] Between 1989 and 1994 some 2 million ethnic Germans or *Aussiedlers*, mainly from Russia, Poland and Romania, benefited from the provisions of the German constitution to move to Germany. In 1993 Germany introduced quotas of some 222,000 of such persons per year.

covert immigration. When Germany became more restrictive about asylum, the number of requests in the UK and Ireland rose as these were considered countries with a higher record of accepting claims, but they in their turn tightened restrictions.

To prevent asylum seekers 'shopping around', the 1990 Dublin Convention requires asylum seekers to apply for asylum in the first EU country they enter. The Convention was extended and updated as Regulation No. 343/2003 of February 2003 and became known as Dublin II. This indicates the competences for deciding which member state is responsible for implementing asylum proceedings.

In 2010 certain member states, such as the UK and Sweden, suspended application of Dublin II. The underlying reason was a large influx of refugees to Greece from Africa and Asia via Turkey. In October 2010 the European Commission agreed to co-ordinate emergency border controls.[7]

Faced with the huge influx of immigrants in the wake of North African unrest, in 2011 Italy attempted to get around the Dublin Convention by issuing humanitarian temporary residence permits to Tunisian refugees, many of whom wanted to proceed to France. In response, France and Belgium threatened to suspend Schengen.[8]

Temporary immigration generally involves a fixed-term contract, usually of less than one year. As permanent immigration to the EU has become more difficult, there has been a considerable increase in temporary immigration, which may take various forms: guest workers, seasonal workers, project-tied workers, border-commuters, or exchanges of trainees (Boeri, Brücker et al., 2000).

With the economic boom in Germany, from 1961 *Gastarbeiter*, or temporary guest workers, were recruited from Turkey and the former Yugoslavia. Many of these Turkish workers, in particular, failed to return home and were joined by their families. It is estimated that there are still some 2 million people of Turkish origin in Germany.

Seasonal workers are mainly employed in agriculture and tourism. They are generally taken on at times of the year when extra labour is necessary, for example during the harvest, so the employment of these workers tends to have complementary effects on the incomes of workers in the host country.

Tied-project programmes permit firms in the host country to subcontract parts of a project to foreign firms that employ workers with the wages and social security conditions of their own country, and are covered by the Posted Workers Directive described in Chapter 6.

Border commuting was frequent in countries such as Poland, the Czech Republic and Hungary, and the main countries of destination were Germany and Austria (Boeri, Brücker et al., 2000).

8.7 EU policies towards internal labour movement

Distinction must be made between freedom of movement of labour, which constitutes (at least in theory) one of the four fundamental freedoms of the Single Market, and common EU policies with regard to immigration and asylum from the rest of the world (discussed below).

The free movement of workers within the Community was one of the main objectives set out in the Treaty of Rome. The Treaty distinguished between workers and self-employed or independent persons:

- Articles 48 to 51 of the Treaty of Rome (now Articles 45 to 48 TFEU) refer to the free movement of workers, which should entail the abolition of any discrimination based on nationality between workers from member states with regard to employment, remuneration and other conditions of work.

- Articles 52 to 58 of the Treaty of Rome (now Articles 49 to 55 TFEU) deal with the freedom of establishment, or the right of self-employed or independent citizens of member states to set up businesses (including agencies, branches and subsidiaries) in other member states.

---

[7] In a number of cases the courts of other EU member states ruled against transfers of refugees to back to Greece under the Dublin Convention as treatment of asylum seekers was deemed inadequate on human rights grounds. About one thousand cases were taken to the Council of Europe, which in January 2011 ruled that conditions at Greek migrant detention centres were so squalid as to breach the ban on 'torture or inhuman or degrading treatment' (*Financial Times*, 20 December 2010 and *The Economist*' 19 February 2011).

[8] *Financial Times*, 12 April 2011.

Both the free movement of labour and the freedom of establishment were to be based on the principle of national treatment, which entails the same conditions for citizens of other EU member states and the nationals of that country. The Treaty of Rome (Articles 117 to 128, now Articles 151 to 161 TFEU) also included references to social policy (see Chapter 7), including the improvement of working conditions, equal pay for men and women, and paid holidays. The European Social Fund was set up with the aim of 'rendering the employment of workers easier and increasing their geographical and occupational mobility' (Article 123 of the Treaty of Rome, now Articles 162 to 164 TFEU).[9]

The legislation covering freedom of movement of workers was completed in 1968 (at the same time as the legal basis of the customs union), and extended to the European Economic Area in 1994. The Single Market Programme (see Chapter 6) gave a new impetus to the task of eliminating frontier controls and permitting the free movement of people (notably through the Schengen Agreement).

Under Article 48 of the Treaty of Rome (now Article 45 TFEU), freedom of movement of workers entails the right to move freely and to stay in a member state for the purposes of employment, subject to limitations on grounds of public policy, public security or public health. However, as explained below, fears that the 2004 and 2007 enlargements would lead to wide-scale immigration to the EU(15) from the new Central and East European member states led to derogations of up to seven years on the movement of labour from these countries.

Numerous measures have also been introduced aimed at eliminating intra-EU barriers to movement of people, relating *inter alia* to the aggregation of social security rights (including pensions), the recognition of qualifications, harmonization of regulation relating to residence permits, working conditions and so on, and providing information about job opportunities and working conditions in the various member states.

Despite these various EU initiatives, differences in labour market regulations and social security systems among the member states remain a major factor continuing to discourage labour movement within the EU. These regulations include laws on minimum wages, collective contracting, hiring and firing, the duration of the working week, flexible labour contracts and so on. Given the diversity and complexity of these laws, workers often have inadequate information to assess the various opportunities and risks in other member states. Together with natural barriers to labour mobility such as language, social and cultural differences between member states, and the ageing of the workforce (younger workers tend to be more mobile), these factors explain why labour mobility within the EU has been relatively low (see the statistics below).

8.8 The pattern of labour movement within the EU

In the first years of the Community, growth was rapid and, with the exception of Italy, the labour markets of the member states tended to be tight. During the 1958–73 period the only substantial migration flow within the Community was from Italy to Northern Europe.

Over time, with the growth of the Italian economy and the process of catching up with the other member states, the number of Italians migrating to Northern Europe dwindled. Italian emigration shrank still further after the 1973 oil crisis when employment opportunities in Northern Europe became scarce. The subsequent revival of the EC economy failed to bring about a corresponding return to earlier levels of migration and, indeed, many Italians, Spanish and Portuguese returned home. This suggests that when income and employment conditions at home reach a certain minimum threshold, most workers are unwilling to undertake the costs of migration.

During the 1973–89 period, other main categories of intra-EC migration included those working in multinational and international organizations, and Irish working in the UK. In 1973 these two categories, together with Italian emigrants in other EC states, amounted to some 3 million persons (Molle, 2006), so the degree of labour movement within the Community was relatively limited.

---

[9] See Chapter 15.

After 1989 some experts predicted large migration flows from CEECs to Western Europe as a result of lower levels of income in those countries, and the new-found freedom of citizens of those countries to travel abroad.[10] These fears grew as the prospect of EU enlargement drew closer.

According to European Integration Consortium (2009), in 2001 there were about 755,000 from the CEEC(8) that joined the EU in 2004 residing in the EU(15), most of whom were concentrated in Germany, Italy and Austria (see Table 8.1). This rose to about 1.9 million in 2007. During the same period the number of foreign residents from Bulgaria and Romania (CEEC(2)) increased to almost 1.9 million.

Table 8.1 Regional breakdown of migrants from the CEEC(10) across the EU(15) before enlargement

	Residents from CEEC(10) 2001	2001 residents as % population	Residents from CEEC(8) in 2007	Residents from CEEC(2) in 2007
Austria	80,184	1.0	89,940	36,792
Belgium	16,744	0.2	42,918	23,810
Denmark	11,027	0.2	22,146	3,316
Finland	14,714	0.3	23,957	1,388
France	53,707	0.1	36,971	43,652
Germany	579,355	0.7	554,372	131,402
Greece	30,039	0.3	20,257	52,567
Ireland	12,235[a]	0.4	178,504	24,496
Italy	121,552	0.2	117,042	658,755
Luxembourg	1,547	0.3	5,101	1,085
Netherlands	13,716	0.1	36,317	11,272
Portugal	963[b]	0.0	N/a	N/a
Spain	127,018	0.3	131,118	828,772
Sweden	23,198	0.4	42,312	6,280
UK	114,787	0.2	609,415	40,023
EU(15)	1,131,884[c]	0.3	1,910,370	1,863,610

[a] 2002.

[b] Boeri and Brücker (2005).

[c] European Integration Consortium (2009), excludes the estimate for Portugal.

Source: Elaboration on the basis of Boeri and Brücker (2005), and European Integration Consortium (2009), © European Union, 2011.

---

[10] Many Roma also left Bulgaria and Romania after 1989, and the Czech Republic and Slovakia subsequently. Racial discrimination, poverty and nomadic traditions all contributed to the exodus from the East.

Various studies attempted to estimate the long-run effect of migration from these new member states. Many of these studies estimated the long-run migration potential from the CEECs to the EU(15) as being between 3 and 4 per cent of the CEEC population and, therefore, manageable.[11]

European Integration Consortium (2009) estimated that the stock of migrants from the CEEC(8) would increase from 1.9 million in 2007 to 3.8 million in 2020 under existing institutional arrangements, and to 4.4 million when freedom of labour movement is introduced by all member states. The stock of migrants from Romania and Bulgaria was estimated to rise from almost 1.9 million in 2007 to 3.9 million in 2020 under existing immigration arrangements and slightly more than 4.0 million with free movement of workers.[12]

Although emigration from the CEEC(10) was expected to be limited, transitional periods of up to seven years were introduced after the 2004 and 2007 enlargements, which permit restrictions on freedom of labour movement under certain conditions. Under these transitional arrangements a formula of two years, plus three years, plus two years was introduced for the new CEEC members states.[13] For the first two years following the 2004 and 2007 enlargements the national law and policy of countries that were EU member states before the respective enlargements governed access of CEEC workers to their labour markets. National measures could be extended for a further three years. Subsequently, a member state applying the national measures could be authorized to continue such measures for a further two years, but only if serious disturbances on its labour market were experienced.

During the first two-year phase after the 2004 enlargement only Ireland, Sweden and the UK liberalized access to their labour markets under national law. However, the UK adopted a mandatory Worker's Registration Scheme, and both Ireland and the UK applied two-year residency restrictions before access to social welfare. The remaining member states of the EU(15) maintained work permit systems, in certain cases with modifications, and some countries also applied quota systems.[14] Austria and Germany applied restrictions on the posting of workers (see Chapter 6) in certain sensitive sectors. Poland, Slovenia and Hungary applied reciprocity to EU(15) member states implementing restrictions.

During the second phase from 2006 a further seven member states joined Ireland, Sweden and the UK in opening their labour markets,[15] but from 2009 only Austria and Germany continued to apply restrictions.

Following the 2007 enlargement, ten of the EU(25) countries liberalized access of Romanian and Bulgarian workers to their labour markets under national law.[16] The remaining member states (including the UK and Ireland which had liberalized after the 2004 enlargement) maintained work permits, although frequently with modifications and simplified procedures. Germany and Austria also applied restrictions on posting of workers. Bulgaria and Romania decided against applying reciprocal measures. In the second phase from 2009 a further five member states allowed free access.[17]

---

[11] See for example, Layard et al. (1992) and Boeri, Brücker et al. (2000), updated subsequently as Alvarez-Plata et al. (2003), Boeri and Brücker (2005) and European Integration Consortium (2009).

[12] These forecasts are roughly in line with the earlier estimates of Boeri, Brücker et al. (2000) Alvarez-Plata et al. (2003) and Boeri, Brücker et al. (2005).

[13] Cyprus and Malta have labour shortages so Cyprus was excluded from these arrangements and for Malta there is only the possibility of invoking a safeguard clause. See http://ec.europa.eu/social/main.jsp?langId=en&catId=466 (accessed 21 Decmber 2010) for a description of all the arrangements.

[14] Quota systems were applied by Austria, Denmark, Italy, the Netherlands and Portugal.

[15] Spain, Italy Finland, Greece, Portugal, the Netherlands and Luxembourg. Hungary (but not Poland or Slovenia) continued to apply reciprocal measures during the second phase, but these were removed from 2009.

[16] The Czech Republic, Estonia, Cyprus, Latvia, Lithuania, Poland, Slovenia, Slovakia, Finland and Sweden. Of these, Cyprus, Finland and Slovenia required that employment must be registered for monitoring purposes.

[17] Restrictions (in some cases with simplifications) continued to be applied by: Belgium, Germany, Ireland, France, Italy, Luxembourg, the Netherlands, Austria, the UK and Malta. The huge increase in Romanian immigration to Italy in these years was possible because the freedom of movement was applied in 'strategic sectors' (such as construction, metalworking, domestic and personal care, hotel-related sectors, agriculture, and maritime activities and fishing), though in other sectors workers had to apply for a visa.

Boeri, Brücker et al. (2005), and the European Integration Consortium (2009) predicted diversion of migration flows if only some member states opened their labour markets after enlargement, as occurred under the transitional arrangements. As shown in Table 8.1 above, Austria and Germany received most of the immigration before enlargement, but were replaced in the case of the CEEC(8) by the UK (with a large share coming from Poland) and Ireland. Spain and Italy became the main destinations of immigrants from Romania and Bulgaria.

In the summer of 2010 France closed over four hundred camps made by Roma immigrants and deported some eight thousand back to Central and East European member states. This led to criticism from various circles, including the Commissioner for Justice, Fundamental Rights and Citizenship, Viviane Reding, who likened the move to the atrocities of the Second World War.[18] The Commission considered taking France to the European Court of Justice, but in September 2010 decided that there was not sufficient evidence of French discrimination against the Roma on ethnic grounds.

8.9 The development of EU policies with regard to immigration and asylum from the rest of the world

The policies of the member states on asylum and immigration from third countries have generally evolved separately, and reaching common EU positions has not proved easy. The approach to EU immigration policy has generally been that of 'unity in diversity'.

Economic theory suggests strong reasons for policy co-ordination in this field relating to spillovers from national jurisdictions (with the fear that tightening of restrictions in a neighbouring country could lead to a diversion of flows of migration), economies of scale and potential free-riding in the enforcement of border controls.

Various factors may explain the different attitudes of the member states to immigration policy, and the extent to which they consider that common EU policies are opportune:

- Geographical differences between the member states (with, for instance porous external borders of countries such as Italy, Malta and Spain, which are among the main destinations of thousands of illegal immigrants on perilous boat journeys).
- Cultural and historical factors may shape national attitudes to immigration.
- National politicians may prefer to maintain jurisdiction for immigration policy as it is often a highly emotive issue, and has at times been exploited for populist motives.

Given the rise in number of legal and illegal immigrants (including asylum seekers), and the role that immigrant workers could play in meeting the demographic challenge in the EU, in 1999 the European Council at Tampere in Finland agreed on the basic elements for creating a common EU immigration policy, namely:

- A comprehensive approach to management of migratory flows so as to find a balance between humanitarian and economic admission.
- Fair treatment for third-country nationals.
- The creation of partnerships with countries of origin, including policies of co-development.

The 1999 Tampere European Council also agreed on the principles of a common EU asylum policy. A scoreboard was drawn up to spell out the respective responsibilities of the member states, the Commission and the Council. Legislation to implement the Tampere Programme included directives on: family reunification (2003); long-term resident status; and the admission of students and researchers from third countries.[19] Other measures included: networks to facilitate integration of

---

[18] *Financial Times*, 30 September 2010.

[19] Council Directive 2003/86/EC, Council Directive 2003/109/EC, Council Directives 2003/109/EC and 2005/72/EC respectively.

immigrants; an action plan on illegal immigration agreed in 2002, and readmission agreements with various countries. Mainstreaming of immigration was introduced, so it is taken into account in all EU policies. A programme for financial and technical assistance to third countries in the area of migration and asylum (AENEAS) covered the 2004–2008 period with a budget of €250 million. Subsequently a European Refugee Fund was set up to cover the period 2008–13.

In 2003 the EU, Iceland and Norway launched Eurodac, a system to fingerprint all asylum seekers and to exchange information. This enables member states to determine whether an individual has already applied for asylum in another EU country or whether that person was apprehended for attempting to enter the EU illegally.

In 2004 Common Basic Principles for Immigration Integration Policy were agreed and the Hague Programme was launched. This aimed at creating a Common European Asylum System by 2010 with practical co-operation (including exchange of information) between member states in a framework of rules set by the EU. Regional Protection Programmes were to be developed to increase the capacity for protection in the country of origin, and to permit resettlement. Immigration was also a priority of the Hampton Court European Council of 2005.

In 2005 Frontex was set up in Warsaw as an EU agency responsible for managing operational co-operation at the external borders of the EU. In 2007 it was also agreed to give Frontex the power to decide on the deployment of rapid-reaction border intervention teams including guards from other member states for limited periods. However, concerns have been expressed about the transparency and democratic accountability of Frontex.

In 2008 agreement was reached on a European Pact on Immigration and Asylum, whose aim was to:

- promote the better organization of immigration (with exchanges of information and best practices);
- control irregular immigration (through co-operation and incentive systems to cover voluntary return);
- improve effective control of the external borders of the EU;
- create a common system of asylum (with a single procedure and uniform status, thereby helping to remove disparities that continue to exist even though common minimum standards had been agreed); and
- encourage collaboration with countries of origin and transit (with EU or bilateral agreements covering legal and illegal migration, readmission and development of these countries).

In 2007 the Commission proposed a blue-card system, similar to the US green cards, to offer skilled immigrants a fast-track procedure for obtaining work permits. This was eventually agreed in 2009, and member states were given two years to incorporate the new provisions into their national legislation. Commission President Barroso maintained that the EU needed to attract more high-skilled workers to increase competitiveness and growth and to tackle the demographic challenge. In 2007, high-skilled foreigners accounted for about 10 per cent of the workforce in Australia, over 7 per cent in Canada and over 3 per cent in the USA. The equivalent figure for the EU was 1.7 per cent or about 70,000 highly skilled workers.[20] The blue card is a special residence and work permit. The system is demand-driven and offers fast-track procedures to skilled workers with job offers. It respects the jurisdiction of the member states to decide on the numbers of persons admitted. The system offers a series of socio-economic rights including easier family reunification and facilitated access to other jobs.

The Stockholm Programme for the 2010–14 period aimed at the development of integrated external border management and visa policies by the EU, and further efforts to establish a comprehensive common migration policy. It was again proposed to set up a Common European Asylum System, this time by 2012, with the assistance of a European Asylum Support Office.

---

[20] These statistics are taken from *The Economist*, 27 October 2007.

8.10 Immigration to the EU from the rest of the world

It is notoriously difficult to find accurate statistics on migration. Collection practices vary between countries, and illegal immigration poses a challenge. In recent years the data available have improved thanks to a concerted effort of the Development Research Centre of the University of Sussex and World Bank,[21] and to the dissemination of information by the International Organization for Migration (IOM).

Table 8.2 indicates the main countries of immigration and emigration in the world in 2010 (including intra-EU migration). As can be seen from Table 8.3, the main destinations in the EU were Germany, the UK, Spain, France and Italy. According to the International Organization for Migration

Table 8.2 Principal recipient and origin countries of world migration, 2010

Country of immigration	Number (million)	Country of emigration	Number (million)
USA	42.8	Mexico	11.9
Russian Federation	12.3	India	11.4
Germany	10.8	Russian Federation	11.1
Saudi Arabia	7.3	China	8.3
Canada	7.2	Ukraine	6.6
UK	7.0	Bangladesh	5.4
Spain	6.9	Pakistan	4.7
France	6.7	UK	4.7
Australia	5.5	Philippines	4.3
India	5.4	Turkey	4.3
Ukraine	5.3	Egypt Arab Rep.	3.7
Italy	4.5	Kazakhistan	3.7
Pakistan	4.3	Germany	3.5
United Arab Emirates	3.3	Italy	3.5
Kazakhistan	3.1	Poland	3.1
Jordan	3.0	Morocco	3.0
Israel	2.9	West Bank and Gaza	3.0
		Romania	2.8

Source: World Bank (2011).

[21] See also the contributions of Parsons et al. (2007) and Winters (2007).

Table 8.3 Migrant stocks in the EU(27)

	Immigrant stock 2010		Refugees as % immigrants 2010	Emigrant stock 2010	
	'000	% population		'000	% population
BE	1,465	13.7	1.2	455	4.3
BG	107	1.4	4.4	1,201	16.0
CZ	453	4.4	0.4	371	3.6
DK	484	8.8	7.7	260	4.7
DE	10,758	13.1	5.5	3,541	4.3
EE	182	13.6	0	169	12.7
EL	1,133	10.1	0.2	1,210	10.8
ES	6,900	15.2	0.1	1,373	3.0
FR	6,685	10.7	2.2	1,742	2.8
IE	899	19.6	1.0	737	16.1
IT	4,463	7.4	0.7	3,482	5.8
CY	154	17.5	0.7	150	17.0
LV	335	15.0	0	273	12.2
LT	129	4.0	0.5	440	13.5
LU	173	35.2	1.4	58	11.8
HU	368	3.7	2.0	463	4.6
MT	15	3.8	17.5	107	26.2
NL	1,753	10.5	5.3	993	6.0
AT	1,310	15.6	2.2	598	7.1
PL	827	2.2	1.0	3,103	8.2
PT	919	8.6	0	2,230	20.8
RO	133	0.6	1.3	2,769	13.1
SL	164	8.1	0.2	132	6.5
SK	131	2.4	0.2	520	9.6
FI	226	4.2	3.8	329	6.2
SE	1,306	14.1	5.7	318	3.4
UK	6,956	11.2	4.3	4,668	7.5

Source: *World Bank (2011).*

(2010), between 2000 and 2010 the number of immigrants to the EU rose, with the highest increase in Spain (up from 1.7 million in 2000) and Italy (2.1 million in 2000).

According to Eurostat data, the most numerous groups of foreign (including EU) citizens usually resident in the EU member states were from Turkey (2.4 million in 2009), Romania, Morocco, Poland, Italy, Portugal and Albania. In most member states (and notably Austria, Denmark, France, Germany, Poland, Portugal, the Netherlands, Sweden, and the UK) many immigrants acquired nationality, so foreign-born citizens are more numerous than non-nationals.

The historical evolution of immigration from the rest of the world to the EU can be divided into three phases.

Between 1960 and 1973 the number workers from third countries in the Community doubled from 3 per cent to 6 per cent of the workforce.[22] In particular, there was immigration from:

- Turkey and the former Yugoslavia as guest workers to Germany;[23]
- the Mediterranean countries then outside the EC to Northern Europe. These included flows from Franco's Spain (mainly to France, Germany and Switzerland), Greece (to Germany and to a lesser extent the UK) and Portugal (mainly to France);
- colonies of EC countries which gained independence, in particular to, France and the UK, which granted relatively open access to citizens of former colonies.

Between 1973 and 1989 the main trends in migration from third countries included: migration from Spain, Greece and Portugal (though this dropped drastically with EC membership, and many immigrants returned home); immigration from North Africa, Turkey and, to a lesser extent, Yugoslavia (also as a result of residence permits granted for family reunification); and continuing immigration from other former colonies.

From 1989 immigration from the rest of the world increased, in particular from the Mediterranean basin, the Middle East, Asia, sub-Saharan Africa, Latin America, Central and Eastern Europe (see above), and the former Soviet Republics. Immigrants were at times subject to unscrupulous human trafficking, as for example when 58 Chinese were found dead in a lorry at the UK port of Dover in 2000.

The end of the Cold War was marked by a rise in the number of ethnic conflicts, including those in the former Soviet Union and ex-Yugoslavia (in particular Bosnia and Kosovo), with an increase in the number of people fleeing from conflict at home.

According to the Frontex Report (2009), 102,600 illegal border crossings to the EU were detected in 2009, a decrease of 33 per cent with respect to 2008. However, the unrest in Tunisia, Libya and elsewhere led to fears of what, in a speech of 21 February 2011, the Italian foreign minister Franco Frattini described as immigration of 'epochal dimensions' towards the EU. Illegal boat immigrants to Italy had fallen from 36,951 in 2008 to 4,406 in 2010,[24] thanks also to bilateral co-operation with third countries of departure, but many of these agreements were subsequently suspended. According to the Lisbon Treaty (Article 77 TFEU), the EU should adopt 'any measure necessary for the gradual establishment of an integrated management system for external borders'. In May 2011 it was agreed that EU goverments in the Schengen zone could reimpose border checks when faced with extraordinary flows of immigrants (see Chapter 6). Denmark reintroduced guards and spot checks at its frontiers. In 2011 Italy and Malta repeatedly appealed to the EU for a concerted response to the situation.

8.11   Evaluation

Economic theory tells us that freedom of labour movement leads to increased efficiency, but in practice all countries apply restrictions on access to their labour markets. Empirical studies suggest

---

[22] Hall (2000).

[23] Hall (2000) estimates that in the 25 years following 1960 the number of foreigners (nearly half Turks) rose by 4 million.

[24] *The Economist*, 5 March 2011.

that immigration could have negative effects on the wages of less-skilled blue-collar workers, unemployment in the receiving country, and on the bill for welfare payments, although these effects are probably on a limited scale and may be temporary.

Although freedom of labour movement is one of the fundamental freedoms of the EU, in practice there are various barriers to the movement of labour within the EU. In part these are because of language, social and cultural factors, but they are also due to differences in labour market regulations and social security systems among the member states, and to the derogations on labour movement after the 2004 and 2007 enlargements.

In recent years there has been a tendency towards tightening of the immigration and asylum policies of the member states. Though there is a strong case for co-ordinating these policies, in practice the evolution of a common EU immigration and asylum policy as envisaged by the Tampere, Hague and Stockholm programmes has proved slow and piecemeal. Geographical, historical and cultural factors may explain why member states wish to retain responsibility for immigration policy, but the interests of populist politicians may also play a role. The unrest in North Africa and elsewhere in 2011 led to pleas by some southern member states for a more concerted EU reaction to immigration, while other countries favoured the reintroduction of frontier controls within Schengen.

Summary of key concepts

- **Freedom of movement of labour** on an international scale is generally advocated because it is said to lead to increased efficiency. More specific arguments are also advanced, such as to offset possible negative effects of ageing of the population or skill shortages.

- **Restrictions on immigration** include border controls and work or residence permits, limited access to certain jobs and professions, inability to find housing, financial disincentives, limits on access to social security benefits, or unfavourable tax treatment.

- Various factors influence the **decision to migrate:** the income gap between the home and host country; employment possibilities in both countries; the geographical proximity of the two countries; emigration traditions; ethnic and family networks; political and ethnic disturbances; cultural and linguistic factors; and economic expectations.

- The **impact of migration on wages and unemployment** is a question for empirical research. Some studies suggest that in the receiving countries in the short run the wages may fall, unemployment may rise and the cost of welfare benefits may increase, but these effects are likely to be on a limited scale.

- The **different kinds of immigrant** are: economic immigrants, asylum seekers, illegal immigrants and seasonal or temporary workers.

- To prevent asylum seekers 'shopping around', the **Dublin Convention** requires them to apply for asylum in the first EU country they enter.

- **Temporary immigration** may take various forms: guest workers, seasonal workers, project-tied workers, border commuters and exchanges of trainees.

- The Treaty of Rome and later treaties envisage the **free movement of workers,** and the **freedom of establishment.**

- In practice there are barriers to the movement of labour in the EU as a result of the derogations after the 2004 and 2007 enlargements, and because of differences in social security systems and labour market regulations of the member states.

- Member states applied **different policies with regard restrictions on workers from the new member states** after the 2004 and 2007 enlargements, and this appears to have caused immigration diversion, with inflows from the CEEC(8) higher than expected in the UK and Ireland. Spain and Italy have become the main destinations of immigrants from Romania and Bulgaria.

- In 1999 the European Council at Tampere in Finland agreed on the basic elements for creating a **common EU immigration policy**. At Tampere, the Hague in 2004 and Stockholm in 2010 it was agreed to work towards a **common EU asylum policy**. The aim is to co-ordinate the policies of the member states within a framework of EU legislation.
- Progress has been slow in developing common policies towards asylum and immigration from the rest of the world.

Questions for study and review

1 What are the main arguments in favour of freedom of labour movement?
2 What are the main arguments used by governments to justify restrictions on immigration? To what extent do you consider that these arguments are justified?
3 What is the effect of immigration on wages and unemployment?
4 Describe the main forms of immigration.
5 What are the remaining barriers to freedom of labour movement in the EU?
6 How has the pattern of immigration within the EU altered over the years?
7 What changes in the policy towards movement of labour in the EU occurred with enlargement?
8 What common policies do you consider that the EU should introduce with regard to immigration and asylum? Why is it so difficult to agree on common policies?

Online Learning **Centre**

When you have read this chapter, log on to the Online Learning Centre website at ***www.mcgraw-hill.co.uk/textbooks/senior*** to explore weblinks, chapter-by-chapter test questions, case studies and more online study tools.

Chapter 9

The Theory of Economic and Monetary Union

Learning Objectives

By the end of this chapter you should be able to understand:

- ✓ What we mean by an optimum currency area
- ✓ The main expected costs and benefits of introducing the euro ✗
- ✓ What we mean by an asymmetric shock
- ✓ How the exchange rate mechanism may be used to address the problem of asymmetric shocks
- ✓ Whether the likelihood of asymmetric shocks increases or decreases as the level of integration rises
- ✓ What other instruments can be used to address asymmetric shocks
- ✓ What the conditions are for joining an optimum currency area
- ✓ What the difference is between the 'monetarist', and 'economist' views of economic and monetary union
- ✓ Whether the EU constitutes an optimal currency area
- ✓ What the conditions are for Britain to join the euro ✗
- ✓ Whether the EU could become an optimal currency area

9.1 Introduction

From 1 January 2002 twelve EU countries replaced their national currencies with euro notes and coins.[1] Only three of the member states of that time remained out of what became known as the 'eurozone' or 'euro area': the UK, Denmark and Sweden. In May 1998 the decision concerning which countries could

---

[1] Austria, Belgium, France, Finland, Germany, Greece, Ireland, Italy, Luxembourg, the Netherlands, Portugal and Spain.

join the euro was taken (later for Greece which became a member from 1 January 2001) and, as will be shown, the verdict on which countries were ready to join was ultimately political. In June 1998 the European Central Bank (ECB) came into operation in Frankfurt. Slovenia joined the eurozone in January 2007, Cyprus and Malta in 2008, Slovakia in 2009 and Estonia in 2011. The countries of the eurozone adopted a common interest rate and (at least in theory) close co-ordination of their fiscal policies.

What were the expected advantages of adopting a single currency, and what were the possible costs of giving up exchange rate changes? Which countries were ready to adopt the euro? This chapter presents the theory used in attempting to address these questions.

9.2   The theory of optimum currency areas

Early theoretical assessments of whether countries should join together to form an economic and monetary union (EMU) generally make use of the concept of an optimum currency area (OCA).[2] A currency area may be defined as either a group of countries that maintain their separate currencies but fix the exchange rates between themselves permanently (see Box 9.1 for a description of different exchange rate regimes and Appendix 1 to this chapter for an explanation of the effects of monetary and fiscal policies with different exchange rate regimes). They also maintain full convertibility among their currencies and flexible exchange rates towards third countries. Alternatively, the member states may adopt a common currency, which floats against that of third currencies. The problem then becomes determining the optimum size of the currency area and, more specifically, deciding whether it is to the advantage of a particular country to enter or remain in a currency area.

Box 9.1

Different exchange rate regimes

Free floating. Movements of the exchange rate depend at all times and in all places on the market. This is generally the case for currencies such as the euro, dollar, yen or Canadian dollar (also known as 'loonie' after the bird or common loon that appears on the coin).

Managed floating (at times also called dirty floating) is between free and fixed exchange rates and involves occasional intervention by the central bank to buy their currency when it is considered too weak, and sell it if it is considered too strong. Examples include Romania or Croatia.

Crawling pegs. The authorities (as, for example, those of Nicaragua and Costa Rica) declare central parity and margin of fluctuation, but both the central parity and the margin of fluctuation are allowed to move regularly or 'crawl'.

Fixed, but adjustable parities. The authorities fix the official parity against some other currency such as the euro or dollar. In general there is a margin of fluctuation around the central parity and the central bank intervenes to keep the exchange rate within the margins of fluctuation. If necessary, realignment of the central parity is possible. The exchange rate mechanism adopted by the European Monetary System described in the next chapter is an example of this type of arrangement.

A **currency board** entails that domestic currency is at least 100 per cent backed by foreign reserves and the central bank loses autonomy in respect of monetary policy. If the central bank spends foreign reserves it must reduce the amount of domestic currency in circulation by at least the same amount. Examples include Bulgaria and Lithuania.

Euroization or dollarization involves adopting a foreign currency in parallel or instead of the national currency, as occurs with the euro in Kosovo and Montenegro, and in Panama with the US dollar.

---

[2] This concept was introduced by Mundell in 1961, and developed by McKinnon (1963) and Kenen (1969).

The early literature in this field concentrates on finding individual criteria that are necessary and sufficient to identify optimum currency areas. This involves indicating alternatives which could act as substitutes for exchange rate policies vis-à-vis other member countries, or which would render exchange rate adjustment within the area unnecessary. Possible candidates include trade integration, international factor mobility, financial integration, the diversification of production, convergence of inflation rates and integration of economic policies (see Mongelli, 2005). As can be seen, most of these also indicate the degree of integration between the member countries.

9.3 Cost/benefit analyses of economic and monetary union

Later authors adopt the traditional optimal currency area approach as a starting point but attempt to evolve a global framework that takes the various criteria into account. This involves using cost/benefit analysis to assess whether a country or group of countries should form an EMU. In order to decide whether membership is advantageous or not, it is necessary to identify the different costs and benefits involved and attach weights to each of these. The evaluation of whether countries should form an EMU will depend on the weight attributed to the various costs and benefits, and this can be very subjective as in practice some of these costs and benefits are extremely difficult to quantify.

According to Krugman (1990), the benefits of forming an EMU will increase, and the costs will decline, as the level of integration rises. The level of integration can be measured by, for example, the ratio of intra-EU trade to GDP.[3]

It is useful at this stage to identify the various possible costs and benefits of EMU.

9.4 The benefits of economic and monetary union

The benefits of EMU include the following:

- In changing from one currency to another, not only does a customer have to pay a commission but the price paid for buying a currency is higher than that received for selling at any given time. According to European Commission (1990a), if a citizen changed a certain sum of money successively into each of the former currencies of the EU, at the end of the process less than half the money would remain.[4] The 'transaction costs' of changing money reflect the fact that real resources are used up in the provision of foreign exchange services. The bank or bureau de change, has to pay the overheads for maintaining an office, the salaries of staff and so on. The benefit from elimination of transaction costs rises with the level of integration, as the savings will tend to be greater as the level of trade increases. According to the Commission (1990a), the reduction in foreign exchange transactions as a result of EMU could amount to some €13–€20 billion, or between 0.25 and 0.5 per cent of GDP each year.

- Economic and monetary union represents a further step towards completion of the Single Market. Quoting all prices in a single currency was expected to provide a further stimulus to price convergence in the EU (see Chapter 6).[5] However, it seems likely that in Europe differences in tastes, habits, culture and language will prevent the eurozone from becoming a single homogeneous market (see Box 9.2). In part, price differences between countries may also exist because much of the retail trade is organized on a national basis.

---

[3] This issue is taken up again below when costs and benefits are compared.

[4] The example given was of ECU 10,000 in Belgian francs being changed into the then ten other currencies of member states and back into Belgian francs.

[5] Engel and Rogers (2004) analysed price convergence for 100 identical products in eighteen cities in the eurozone between 1990 and 2003. They found that most convergence took place before 1999, and then stopped.

> ### Box 9.2
>
> ## Product differences in the EU
>
> Even in the case of multinational firms, surprisingly few homogeneous products are sold from one end of Europe to another. For instance, in the USA the same brands of soap powder are sold throughout the country, but in the EU even detergents are different from country to country to suit local conditions. As a representative from Henkel maintained, stains in the Scandinavian countries are different from those in Southern Europe because of 'the special challenges of olive oil and tomatoes'.*
>
> *As reported in the *Financial Times*, 5–6 January 2002.

- Introduction of the single currency could encourage the creation of a deeper, wider, more liquid capital market. Portes and Rey (1998) describe a circular mechanism by which this might come about. As euro markets for money and securities become more integrated and liquid, transaction costs will fall, rendering euro-denominated assets more attractive. Increased holdings of euro-denominated assets, and use of the euro as a vehicle currency, make the EU financial market deeper, broader and more liquid and so on. The shortcoming in this argument is that one of the main European financial centres, the City of London, remains outside the euro area, but, even here, trading in euros has been expanding rapidly (European Central Bank, 2010).

- Following the pioneering work of Andrew Rose (Rose, 2000, 2002; also Frankel and Rose, 2000), various studies have shown how introducing a common currency encourages trade growth. Rose (2000) found that countries with the same legal tender have trade flows between each other on average 100 per cent higher than those between pairs of countries that are not members of a monetary union.[6] This result spawned a vast literature. In a review of studies of the Rose result, Baldwin (2005) found an effect of 50 per cent or more for smaller countries. On the basis of a survey of the literature, Rose (2008) suggests that EMU could have increased trade in the eurozone by between 8 and 23 per cent. A later study by Baldwin et al. (2008) concludes that the euro has probably increased trade by about 5 per cent, which was less than previously thought, but still substantial.

- The euro has become an international reserve currency (European Central Bank, 2010), so is able to reap some benefits of seigniorage as part of the printed money ends up as international reserves.[7]

---

[6] The Rose (2000) analysis was based on a cross-country dataset covering bilateral trade between 186 economic systems at five-year intervals, using a linear gravity model. One of the surprising outcomes of Rose's study is that exchange rate volatility plays little significant role in the picture. Rose (2002) considers 24 studies of the impact of currency unions on trade, and despite the differences in approach and coverage of the studies, all seem to confirm that currency unions have a positive impact on trade.

[7] For a discussion of the euro as a reserve currency see the section on the euro in the international financial system in the next chapter. Seigniorage refers to the capacity of governments to increase their budget receipts as a result of their right to print money. The term 'seigniorage' derives from the benefits to the *seigneur* or lord of the manor in issuing coins. The gold content of such coins was generally less than their face value. In other words, if there were confidence in holding such coins, the *seigneur* could 'clip' part of their gold content.

A government may cover a budget deficit by printing money. The question that then arises is why the public is prepared to hold a greater stock of money, or even a stock of money that is increasing in size year after year. In part this willingness may be the consequence of real growth of the economy, but it is generally also the result of inflation. Assuming that there is no real growth in an economy, the public will want to hold a constant stock of money in real terms. However, with inflation the purchasing power of a given nominal stock of money will decline. In order to maintain the real value of money holdings unchanged, the public will have to hold an increasing stock of nominal money to compensate for the inflation rate. Inflation can therefore be regarded as a type of tax insofar as the public can only spend a smaller share of its income and has to pay the difference to the government in exchange for money. In other words, if the government sector is financing its deficit by printing money, and the public is prepared to hold this extra money to maintain the real value of its money holdings constant, the government is imposing a kind of 'inflation tax'.

Insofar as non-euro countries hold euros, they will also have to pay some of the costs of seigniorage. However, the benefits of having an international currency are relatively small. Over half of the US dollars issued by the Federal Reserve were held outside the USA, but the seigniorage earned was only about 3 per cent of GDP (Baldwin and Wyplosz, 2009).

- A monetary union entails the introduction of a common monetary policy, which, according to some, is a benefit, and to others a cost (see below). Some studies present the likely reduction of inflation and interest rates as one of the main advantages of a monetary union. This argument in favour of EMU rests on the assumption that the ECB is committed to low inflation, and that inflation-prone countries are incapable of pursuing the policies necessary to keep inflation low outside the EMU. A distinction can be made between the political and credibility constraints on governments in this context (see, for example, Torres, 2008). Political constraints arise as a result of differences over ultimate policy goals. Credibility constraints arise because of the temptation of governments to deviate from pre-announced plans (for instance, because of the pressures of interest groups the government may manipulate economic policies for electoral purposes).[8] Torres (2006) argues that the experience of co-operation in the creation and operation of EMU has led to a process of convergence of preferences with regard to political goals. Moreover, in the EU context a common monetary policy allowed other EU countries more say than was the case in the 'German policy leadership' model of the European Monetary System up until 1992 (see Chapter 10). With regard to credibility constraints, a common monetary policy might be considered an advantage in providing external discipline and 'borrowed' credibility for inflation-prone countries (see the discussion of the monetarist view below).[9]

- Exchange rate uncertainty is taken into account by firms in their location decisions. If this uncertainty is removed, firms are likely to have better long-run information about future prices, rendering decisions about investment and production easier. Firms will be able to locate where their unit costs are lowest, and where they can best exploit economies of scale. This is another reason why the benefits curve is assumed to slope up to the right as the level of integration increases (see Figure 9.1 below). Baldwin et al. (2008) attribute an increase in cross-border investments, mergers and acquisitions to the common currency.

- According to the neo-functionalist approach (see Chapter 1), introducing an EMU might further the integration process through spillover into other policy areas. For instance, the need for democratic control of a central bank could lead to institutional reform and further steps towards political union.[10]

- It seems likely that members of a monetary union will carry more weight at a world level in their dealings with third countries.

9.5 The main costs of economic and monetary union

The main costs of EMU include the following:

- Joining an EMU entails loss of an autonomous monetary policy, which also implies that a country loses the power to change the exchange rate mechanism.

---

[8] See Mueller (2003) for a review of the literature on these issues. The seminal work by Barro and Gordon (1983) indicates the role that can be played by rules and reputation.

[9] If governments take advantage of the temporary trade-off between inflation and unemployment and raise inflation to reduce unemployment, agents will come to expect them to do so and will predict a higher level of inflation. What is needed is a way of making commitment to lower inflation credible, and an independent ECB committed to curbing inflation may perform this function and bring about a lower rate of inflation. In this way the inflation-prone country may 'borrow' credibility.

[10] See the discussion on the independence and accountability of the ECB in the next chapter.

A single interest rate may be unsuited to the differing economic situation in individual member states, being too tight for some and too loose for others if their business cycles are not synchronized. For example, low interest rates contributed to the sovereign debt crisis in Greece, and overheating and the property bubbles in Ireland and Spain.[11] However, some economists have argued that the experience of participating together in EMU will bring the business cycles of the euro countries more in line with each other and so reduce this problem of 'one size fits all'.[12]

According to economic textbooks, the role of the exchange rate mechanism is to act as a shock absorber in the event of asymmetric shocks, that is, disturbances that affect the countries involved in different ways. Asymmetric shocks arise because countries are different in some important ways, often relating to their legal or political systems, or to differences in national labour market legislation and organization.

Differences between countries may also mean that the same, identical shock has asymmetric effects in different countries. For instance, a rise in oil prices will affect countries differently according to their oil dependency. Similarly, a single action by the ECB may have differing effects in various euro countries depending on their banking systems, financial markets or the size of firms and their ability to borrow. The analysis of asymmetric shocks here can also be applied to the asymmetric effects of a symmetric shock.[13]

It is useful to take an example to consider the effects of an asymmetric shock. For instance, if it is assumed that France is relatively intensive in the production of wine, and Germany is relatively intensive in the production of beer, an asymmetric shock could take the form of a health scare concerning wine that causes consumers to start drinking beer in place of wine. Output declines in France and rises in Germany, and this is likely to lead to increased unemployment in France, and lower unemployment in Germany. In this simple model there will be an incentive for French workers to move to Germany. To meet this situation France could try to increase competitiveness by reducing prices and wages. If this is not possible, before introduction of the euro France could have devalued the franc against the German D-mark, rendering French output cheaper relative to German output. As a result it is likely that people will again start drinking more wine and less beer, so it should therefore be possible to use the devaluation to return to the original situation in each country.[14] Appendix 2 at the end of the chapter provides a more formal treatment of this question.

- The introduction of a new, single currency is likely to involve psychological costs. A survey carried out by Eurobarometer suggested that in November 1997 the share of public opinion opposed to introducing the single money was highest in Finland, Denmark, Britain and Sweden. The countries with the largest share of public opinion in favour of the single money initially were Italy, Ireland, Luxembourg and Spain. This situation was soon to change and according to a survey carried out by Cetelem,[15] 59 per cent of 5,000 people surveyed in 2003 said they were worried about the effects of the euro, compared with one-third of respondents in 1999. Italians were the most critical, with 78 per cent expressing concern, probably because of the widespread conviction that the euro added to inflation (see Box 9.3 and Tables 9.1 and 9.2).

- The transition to the new system involves 'technical' costs such as the printing of new money (see also Box 9.4), the adjustment of slot machines, changes in accountancy etc.

---

[11] See the discussion in the next chapter.

[12] See, for instance, the empirical evidence of Frankel and Rose (1998) and Artis and Zhang (1995), or Bongardt and Torres (2007b) and Torres (2006) discussed below in the text.

[13] For example, Dornbusch et al. (1998) estimated that the initial impact of a rise in short-term interest rates was twice as high in Italy as in Germany.

[14] Alternatively, in a country with a flexible exchange rate such as the UK, the country can manipulate the interest rate to achieve the same objective.

[15] As reported in the *Financial Times*, 8 January 2004.

Box 9.3

The euro and inflation in Italy

In all eurozone countries, and in Italy in particular, introduction of the euro was believed to have caused large price increases. A first reaction of the Italian authorities was to deny such charges, and then the official consumer price index was adjusted, bringing the basket on which it was based up to date, but the increase in the consumer price index was only 2.6 per cent for 2002.* A common complaint of the public was that what had cost 10,000 lira now cost €10 (roughly 20,000 lira). As Table 9.2 illustrates, Italian food prices certainly increased substantially in the year the euro was introduced. However, the Italian authorities maintained that the weight of food in the consumption of households was low so this had little impact on the rate of inflation.

Although the price elasticity of demand for food is low, food is generally sold in competitive markets so it is difficult for retailers to exploit this low elasticity by raising price. A price rise requires simultaneous action by all suppliers, but in general it is difficult to reach agreement on this type of collective action. The introduction of the euro provided a window of opportunity, lowering the costs of collective action so all could raise the price together (De Grauwe, 2009a). This was not simply the rounding up of prices that economists expected.

There was speculation about Italy leaving the eurozone after the Italian minister of welfare, Roberto Maroni, voiced the possibility in June 2005. The idea was to return to the lira and use devaluation as an instrument for regaining competitiveness. However, much of Italy's large public debt is in euro, and leaving the common currency would probably lead to higher interest rates, adding substantially to the burden of debt.

On 3 March 2006 *Leggo*, an Italian newspaper distributed free, ran the headline 'About turn: From June 1st the lira will return!' According to the hoax article, Italy's request to leave the euro had been agreed by the Ecofin, while the UK, France and Germany were threatening to leave the EU.

*Eurostat data.

Table 9.1 Attitudes to the euro

Country	In favour (EB, 2010a)	Inflation higher than before introduction of the euro (EB, 2009)	Country	In favour (EB, 2010a)	The euro will increase prices (EB, 2010b)
Ireland	84	62	Bulgaria	55	69
Finland	77	65	Czech Rep.	36	69
Luxembourg	79	71	Denmark	52	
Austria	64	63	Estonia	57	77
Belgium	78	72	Latvia	55	62
Spain	64	73	Lithuania	50	73
France	65	83	Poland	43	77
Germany	46	65	Romania	64	47
Portugal	53	77	Hungary	67	62
Italy	64	62	Sweden	34	

Table 9.1 continued

Country	In favour (EB, 2010a)	Inflation higher than before introduction of the euro (EB, 2009)	Country	In favour (EB, 2010a)	Will euro increase prices? (EB 2010b)
Netherlands	71	59	UK	19	
Greece	64	66			
Slovenia	82	56			
Slovakia	87	37			
Cyprus	57	62			
Malta	66	67			

Source: Eurobarometer (EB) (2009, 2010a, b), © European Union, 2011.

Table 9.2 Price increases of food products in Italy between November 2001 and November 2002

Breakfast items (bread, snacks)	23.3%
Pasta, bread, rice	20.1%
Beverages	32.9%
Meat, eggs and fresh fish	22.1%
Cold cuts	27.5%
Canned food	30.9%
Fruit and vegetables	50.8%
Frozen food	23.6%
Average	29.2%

Source: Table 7.3 (p.161) The Economics of Monitary Union (2009) by Paul De Grauwe. By permission of Oxford University Press.

Box 9.4

What happened to the notes and coins not traded in?

It was estimated that central banks and governments in the eurozone were likely to collect a windfall of up to €15 billion from old currency notes and coins not handed in after introduction of the euro.*

The euro area central banks are responsible for the physical issuing of euros. The introduction of the euro required old coins to be rounded up and eventually melted down so their metal could be recycled. In order to guard against theft, a German firm, Eurocoin, introduced a machine known as the 'decoiner' which squashes and corrugates higher denomination coins, rendering them useless to thieves.† Eurocoin provides coin blanks for the euro and also for other currencies such as the Thai baht and Malaysian ringgit.

* Financial Times, 20 December 2001.
† Financial Times, 4 December 2001.

■ Monetary union entailed a loss of seigniorage for some EU member states. On 9 December 2001 the ECB indicated how the estimated €13 billion seigniorage was to be allocated among the central banks of the euro members. The allocation was based on each central bank's share in the capital of the ECB, with France, Greece and Finland standing to gain most among the countries initially adopting the euro, while Germany, Spain and Italy were the greatest losers.[16]

Seigniorage may be an important source of revenue in countries with a high level of inflation. During the 1980s, revenues from seigniorage accounted for about 2–3 per cent of GNP in countries such as Greece, Portugal, Spain and Italy, but declined substantially in the 1990s due to lower inflation so there was little need to replace seigniorage revenues with tax when EMU was introduced.

9.6 How effective is the exchange rate mechanism in correcting asymmetric shocks?

The effectiveness of the exchange rate mechanism in correcting asymmetric shocks has been questioned (see also Appendix 2 to this chapter). Even if French domestic prices remain the same, the devaluation will increase the franc price of German beer bought by French workers. If there is a high level of integration between the French and German economies, a large share of products in France will be imported from Germany. This means that a French devaluation will have a substantial effect in raising consumer prices in France.

These higher prices reduce real wages, and may lead to requests by French workers to increase nominal wages. There is even a risk that repeated devaluations lead to a wage–price–devaluation spiral. With a higher level of integration, an exchange rate change is more likely to alter consumer prices and lead to this kind of price–wage reaction. The higher the level of integration, the less is the cost of forgoing the exchange rate mechanism.

This observation was the basis of the important contribution of McKinnon (1963) to the theory of optimal currency areas. The effect of an exchange rate change on the aggregate price level will be greater in a small open economy than in a relatively closed one.[17] This is a major reason that the cost curve of monetary union with respect to trade integration is assumed to slope down to the right (see also Figure 9.1 below). For instance, a 10 per cent devaluation is likely to have more impact on a country that exports 90 per cent of its output, than on one that exports only 10 per cent. A small open economy has little power to change the price on international markets so the cost of giving up the currency is less. Similarly, if the country has a high level of import dependency, devaluation is likely to lead to a larger increase in prices. According to the McKinnon criterion, countries with very open economies and which trade heavily with each other should join a currency union.

Although this type of price–wage reaction reduces the effectiveness of the exchange rate instrument, few economists would argue that it loses all its effectiveness. The reactions may not be immediate, so that devaluation can give governments a breathing space while other policies are introduced.

In the more recent literature the view has emerged that rather than neutralizing asymmetric shocks, exchange rate changes might actually cause them. For instance, Buiter (2000: 236) maintains that with very high international financial capital mobility, market-determined exchange rates are primarily a source of shocks and instability, arguing: 'The potential advantages of nominal exchange rate flexibility as an effective adjustment mechanism or shock absorber are bundled with the undoubted disadvantages of excessive noise and unwarranted movements in the exchange rate, inflicting unnecessary real adjustments on the rest of the economy'.[18]

---

[16] *Financial Times*, 20 December 2001. France stood to gain most: although the franc accounted for only 12 per cent of issuance across the euro area, under the capital key the economic size and population of France entailed an estimated share of 20 per cent.

[17] In terms of the aggregate demand and aggregate supply analysis of the Appendix 2 of this chapter, a devaluation is likely to lead to a larger shift in the aggregate demand and supply curves.

[18] Mundell (1973) also made the point about exchange rates being a source of instability.

9.7　Does the likelihood of asymmetric shocks increase or decrease as the level of integration rises?

A further question that arises is whether a higher level of integration makes the likelihood of asymmetric shocks greater or less. It seems likely that a higher level of integration will lead to some convergence of consumer tastes and preferences. If this were the case, on the demand side the shocks would be more likely to affect all the partners, reducing the role for a shock absorber such as adjustment of exchange rates between the member states.

The implications for the production side are less clear. If integration leads to specialization,[19] the economies of the member states will become less similar and more vulnerable to asymmetric shocks. Against this, most trade within the EU is intra-industry and is usually explained in terms of economies of scale and imperfect competition (see Chapter 4). If this is the case it seems likely that shocks would be more likely to affect all the member states. If, however, as Krugman (1990, 1993b) argues, integration implies centrifugal forces leading to the concentration of industry,[20] asymmetric shocks may affect the poles of development. However, these agglomerations may not necessarily respect national boundaries, and may transgress one or more border.

If countries are specialized in the production of a narrow range of products they are more vulnerable to asymmetric shocks (Kenen, 1969). The Kenen criterion for a country to join a monetary union is therefore that the production and exports of member states should be diversified and of a similar structure.[21]

The issue of how increased integration affects asymmetric shocks is essentially an empirical question. Frankel and Rose (1998) found that more trade integration is strongly associated with more correlated economic activities between countries. Artis and Zhang (1995) also found that as European countries became more integrated, their business cycles became more synchronized. If this is the case, forming a currency union can help to create the conditions for its functioning.[22]

However, the problem of asymmetric shocks seems likely to remain in the EU, also because member states are responsible for many areas of economic policy, and this may be a source of such shocks. Taxation and spending decisions are taken largely by national authorities and may give rise to asymmetric shocks. The issue of fiscal policy in a monetary union is taken up in the next chapter. Wage bargaining also differs and may create asymmetric disturbances, while differences in legal systems mean that shocks may have asymmetric effects on financial markets between countries. Some economists (such as De Grauwe, 2009a) therefore argue that political union is a solution to the problem of asymmetric shocks.

9.8　Alternative mechanisms to the exchange rate instrument

The cost of forgoing the exchange rate mechanism will also be less if it can be replaced by alternative mechanisms. These could include:

- wage–price flexibility;
- factor mobility;
- transfers from the EU budget to compensate regions or countries that have been adversely affected.

Wage–price flexibility implies that in the case of a permanent adverse asymmetric shock the real wages and relative prices in that country (or region, if the production is concentrated in a particular area) will

---

[19] In terms of international trade theories, this would be the case with specialization according to a Ricardian concept of comparative advantage.

[20] These agglomeration effects are discussed in Chapter 15.

[21] For examples see the discussion of whether the EU is an optimal currency area below.

[22] See Mongelli (2005) for a review of the literature on this issue.

fall. There will be a strong incentive for workers to move to other regions or countries where real wages are higher. The Mundell criterion for joining a currency union is that movement of people between member states is relatively easy. Similarly, if there is sufficient capital mobility among the member states, in the example above there will be a reduced incentive to invest in the French wine industry and a tendency towards increased investment in German beer production. If factors of production were sufficiently mobile, this process would continue until differences in the remuneration of factors in different regions are eliminated. Although much progress has been made in increasing factor mobility in the EU, as the discussion in Chapter 8 shows, this process is far from complete, particularly in the case of labour.[23] If labour is not mobile in a currency area, it is likely that in the event of asymmetric shocks employment will have to take more of the burden. Similarly, if wages and prices are sticky the adjustment will take some time, imposing hardship.

In the case of a single country, if the demand for a good whose production is concentrated in a particular region falls, transfers from the government budget may be used to compensate producers in that region for the loss of income. This may, however, give rise to moral hazard by encouraging people in the region to assume that they will be bailed out, thereby reducing the incentive for adjustment. The compensation should therefore be used for temporary shocks, or in a temporary way for permanent shocks to avoid hindering the adjustment process.

In the case of the USA, at times individual states have experienced asymmetric shocks as, for example, did Texas with the fall in oil prices in the mid-1980s, and California with the collapse of the defence industry in the late 1980s and early 1990s. In the USA, not only do people tend to be more mobile, and willing to change state, but transfers from the federal government play an important role. Any fall in the income of a state will lead to higher benefits received from the federal authorities and lower taxes paid to them. According to Sachs and Sala-i-Martin (1992), for every $1 decline in state income the federal budget transferred back 40 cents, though subsequent studies suggest that this figure should be revised downwards and may be in the order of 10–40 per cent (Baldwin and Wyplosz, 2009).

At least in theory, EU regional or budgetary policies could be used in a similar way to offset the repercussions of asymmetric shocks among the member states.[24] However, the scale of the EU budget is too limited to enable the EU to carry out this kind of stabilizing role between member states effectively.[25]

9.9 A comparison of costs and benefits

As argued above, it is difficult to quantify and give relative weights to the various costs and benefits of EMU. None the less is it useful here to attempt to compare the costs and benefits, which have been identified.

Figure 9.1 illustrates the relationship between costs and benefits of monetary union and the openness of a country as measured by trade as a percentage of GDP. As the level of trade integration increases so too will the gains from elimination of transaction costs and the reduction in decision errors by firms and consumers as a result of exchange rate uncertainty, so the benefit line is assumed to slope up to the right. In accordance with the McKinnon (1963) criterion explained above, with more trade openness the cost of giving up an independent currency is less, so the cost line is assumed to slope down to the right.

---

[23] Baldwin and Wyplosz (2009) argue that one reason why currency areas often coincide with nation states is that labour mobility is likely to be higher within a country for reasons of language, culture, information and so on.

[24] The MacDougall Report (1977) advocated an increase in the Community budget to 7 per cent of GDP to enable it to perform this stabilizing role. Later work such as that by Danson et al. (2000) has suggested that a dedicated budget function may be significantly less costly, however.

[25] Moreover, as explained in Chapters 10 and 11, the need to meet the Maastricht criteria and the constraints imposed by the Stability and Growth Pact, together with austerity measures introduced in response to the economic crisis, limit the scope for increased contributions to the EU budget.

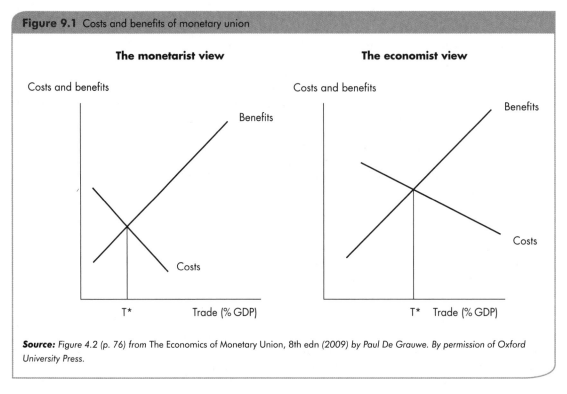

Figure 9.1 Costs and benefits of monetary union

Source: Figure 4.2 (p. 76) from The Economics of Monetary Union, 8th edn (2009) by Paul De Grauwe. By permission of Oxford University Press.

At the point of intersection between the cost and benefit lines it becomes worthwhile for a country to join a currency area.

The shape and position of the cost curve will depend on views about the effectiveness of monetary policy, including exchange rate policies.[26] At one extreme, according to the 'monetarist' view, the exchange rate is an ineffective corrective for different developments between countries, and the cost curve is close to the origin (see Figure 9.1). Monetary integration is considered the best way to commit national governments to taking the steps necessary to reduce inflation (for instance by cutting the budget deficit or curbing the wage claims of trade unions). It is assumed that once a monetary union is formed, past expectations are irrelevant and inflation is not sticky. The credibility of the common central bank will shape expectations and will deliver low inflation to all member states. As a result the cost of reducing inflation is assumed to be high before joining the monetary union, but almost negligible afterwards. According to this view, many countries would gain by giving up their national currencies and joining a monetary union. As a result the emphasis should be on building strong institutions rather than having demanding criteria and a lengthy convergence period before creating a monetary union. In the long debate about introducing a monetary union (see Chapter 10), countries such as France, Belgium, Italy and Luxembourg generally held monetarist views.

In contrast, the 'economist' view maintains that a higher level of co-ordination of economic policies and integration is necessary before creating a monetary union.[27] This view stresses rigidities (of wages and prices, and labour is considered immobile), arguing that the exchange rate is an effective instrument.

---

[26] The account here is based on De Grauwe (2009a).

[27] Wyplosz (2006) calls the use of the two terms 'economists' and 'monetarists' bizarre and questions the reasons behind them. Torres (2008) criticizes the mistaken tendency at times in the literature to identify the 'economist' view with the Keynesian approach, pointing out that West Germany (namely the Bundesbank) did not have a Keynesian perspective of macroeconomics, but simply wanted clearly defined rules before embarking on monetary union.

The assumption that inflation is sticky means that countries with a history of high inflation will not support tight monetary policy once they have a representative in the common central bank. Moreover, as these high-inflation countries see nominal interest rates decline, the low (or even negative) real interest rate that results might fuel demand causing further inflationary pressures. Low-inflation countries may import higher inflation from non-converged countries. This view is sometimes called the coronation theory as monetary union is regarded as the final step in a long process, occurring only when monetary policies have become fully aligned and national currencies are indistinguishable. The cost and benefit curves are considered to intersect a long way from the origin, implying that it would be in the interests of relatively few countries to join a monetary union. Typically countries such as Germany and the Netherlands maintained 'economist' views.

According to Wyplosz (2006: 217), the Maastricht Treaty reflects the 'economist' or German view, and all the monetarists obtained was a timetable for introducing EMU, but, in practice in 1998 when the initial decision was taken on which countries could join the euro, 'the monetarists carried the day on the ground'.

9.10 Is the EU an optimal currency area?

There is a large and growing literature about whether the EU, or at least a smaller group of its member states, form part of an OCA. Although the results of different studies vary, there seems to be a certain consensus among economists that the EU as a whole does not form a monetary union.[28] However, in general from empirical studies a 'core' group of countries emerges for which it was easy to recommend EMU membership. Usually these include Germany, Austria, the Benelux countries and sometimes also France. In contrast there is another group of countries, the 'periphery', for which membership is less easy to recommend, but the list of countries that fall into the category of periphery varies considerably between different studies. The distinction between core and periphery does not correspond to the initial participation or not in the euro because in many cases the latter was ultimately decided on a political basis (see Chapter 10).

The first articulated study of the optimal currency approach was reported in the Commission document 'One market, one money' (European Commission, 1990a). However, the theory was not sufficiently developed to render the approach operational, and, as explained in Chapter 10, played little role in the early stages of adopting the euro, though later it became more important in monitoring the progress of the EMU project.

Bayoumi and Eichengreen (1997) developed an OCA index based on the question of how far, given past experience, countries would have adjusted their exchange rate against the German D-mark to deal with asymmetric shocks. The countries that emerged as most suitable to join were Belgium, the Netherlands, Austria (long linked to the German D-mark), Ireland (the study pre-dates the economic crisis), and Switzerland (not even an EU member). The group with little convergence consisted of the UK, Finland, Norway, Denmark and, rather surprisingly, France.

Korhonen and Fidrmuc (2001) examined the correlation of demand and supply shocks between the new Central and East European member states and the euro area during the 1990s. Hungary and Estonia emerged as the countries most suited to join the euro area.

Horvàth (2005, 2007) elaborated on the approach used by Bayoumi and Eichengreen (1997) and developed an OCA index based on the intensity of trade with Germany or the eurozone (to capture the McKinnon criterion), dissimilarity of trade structures (to capture the Kenen criterion), a general measure of openness, and the level of financial development. The Central and East European countries emerged as the member states least fulfilling the OCA criteria, though the Czech Republic, Slovakia, Slovenia,

---

[28] See De Grauwe (2009a) for a review of the literature.

Hungary and Estonia appear (in that order) the most suited of these countries to join the euro. The five countries found to fulfil the OCA criteria best were the same as those of the Bayoumi and Eichengreen (1997) study (see above).

As argued above, the McKinnon criterion indicates that openness should be taken into account in deciding whether a country forms part of a currency area. Figure 9.2 uses exports as a percentage of GDP to measure openness, and illustrates that openness varied considerably between EU member states.[29]

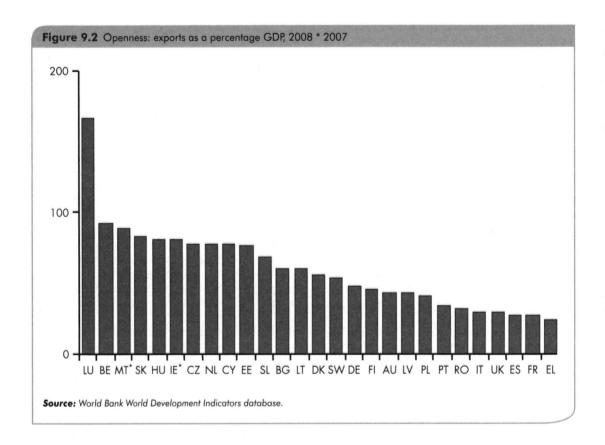

Figure 9.2 Openness: exports as a percentage GDP, 2008 * 2007

Source: *World Bank World Development Indicators database.*

An alternative measure is that of trade intensity or share of trade with other members of the monetary union as a share of total trade. Horvàth (2005) used trade of EU member states with the centre country, Germany, as an indicator of trade openness and found that bilateral trade links were strongest for Belgium, the Netherlands, Austria, Ireland, Denmark, France and Slovakia (in that order).

As stated above, Kenen (1969) maintained that asymmetric shocks are less likely among countries that share a similar production and export structure. Bayoumi and Eichengreen (1997) constructed a trade dissimilarity index compared with Germany, and found greatest dissimilarity for Norway (whose trade is dominated by oil and fish), Greece, Netherlands (with a large component of energy products) and Denmark. Horvàth (2005) found the greatest dissimilarity for Latvia, Denmark, Netherlands, Lithuania, Ireland and Bulgaria (in that order).

---

[29] A similar picture emerges if trade (exports plus imports) as a share of GDP is used, as shown in Senior Nello (2009: 217) with data for 2005. See also European Commission (2010g) for statistics on imports as a share of GDP for eurozone countries.

The creation of an OCA is facilitated by the existence of alternative adjustment mechanisms such as labour movement or the possibility of transfers through the common budget, but, as argued above (see also Chapters 8 and 12), the EU fares badly on both these counts.

Political considerations also play a role in deciding whether countries should form a monetary union. When an asymmetric shock occurs there may be differences of opinion as to what is the appropriate response. Some countries may give priority to keeping inflation low, while others may attach more importance to unemployment. For a monetary union to survive (or survive without excess strain), these differences should not be too wide and there should be a degree of homogeneity of preferences. Among the benefits of EMU for high-inflation countries indicated above was the possibility of gaining credibility, rendering it easier to reduce inflation. However, preferences with regard to inflation and unemployment still appear to differ between member states and continue to be a source of tension (see Chapter 11).

Some authors (see, for example, Bongardt and Torres, 2007b, or Torres, 2006) stress the importance of institutional factors, arguing that the ongoing negotiation and discussion of economic policies at the EU, national and regional levels and the repeated confronting of positions has led to a convergence of preferences so tending to reduce the likelihood of asymmetric shocks as a result of differences in policies and market structures.

Even if there are differences in the policy preferences of countries, a further political condition for a monetary union is that all the member states are ultimately committed to its continued existence. Without a sense of solidarity and common purpose a monetary union cannot survive.

As mentioned in Chapter 1, Eurobarometer carries out annual surveys about which decisions EU citizens believe are best carried out at the national or EU level. Though considerable differences emerge between member states,[30] there seems to be a considerable commitment on the part of eurozone countries to maintaining the common currency (if only because the costs of leaving the euro are so high, see also Box 9.3 above and Chapter 11).

9.11 Evaluation

The theory of OCAs has attracted much attention and debate, but is difficult to apply in practice. The theory would suggest that the choice of countries to join the euro should be made on the basis of real convergence as measured by criteria such as openness and similarity of the structure of production and exports, but, as explained in Chapter 10, the Maastricht criteria relate to nominal variables such as inflation and public deficits.[31] The choice of initial countries to join the third phase of EMU was essentially political.

Most economists agree that the EU(27) do not constitute an OCA. But they generally disagree over the division of countries into the core and periphery categories.

Though the EU is not now an OCA, the mere creation of EMU could help progress in this direction. Joining a monetary union encourages rapid growth of trade, speeding up the integration process. Authors such as Frankel and Rose (1998) and Artis and Zhang (1995) found empirical evidence for increased integration reducing the likelihood of asymmetric shocks, though there is debate about this issue. The decision to join a monetary union may therefore lower the costs relative to the benefits, so it is possible that the criteria for joining an OCA assume an endogenous nature.

---

[30] See the Standard Eurobarometer reports at http://ec.europa.eu/public_opinion/archives/eb_arch_en.htm (accessed 22 November 2010).

[31] In contrast, as will be shown in Chapters 10 and 11, the British assessment was based more closely on the optimal currency approach.

Summary of key concepts

- Most theoretical assessments of whether countries should join together to form an economic and monetary union take the traditional **optimal currency area approach** as a starting point but attempt to assess the various costs and benefits.

- The main **benefits** of EMU are: a saving in transaction costs; increased transparency in comparing prices; encouraging the creation of deeper and wider capital markets; increased trade; the use of the euro as an international reserve could yield seigniorage; the introduction of a common monetary policy which may permit countries to 'borrow credibility'; improved location of industry; neo-functionalist spillover into other integration areas; and increased weight of the member countries at a world level.

- The main **costs** of EMU are: loss of monetary policy autonomy, including the possibility of exchange rate changes among the member states; the psychological cost of losing a national currency; the technical costs of changeover, and loss of seignorage for some member states.

- The role of the exchange rate mechanism is to compensate **asymmetric shocks**, that is, shocks that affect in different ways the countries involved.

- When a country is small and open to trade, according to the **McKinnon criterion**, the cost of giving up the exchange rate mechanism is lower.

- Countries whose production and exports are diversified and of similar structure are more suited to forming a currency union (the **Kenen criterion**).

- The cost of forgoing the exchange rate mechanism will be less if other instruments such as **wage/price flexibility and/or factor movements, or budget transfers** can replace it. The **Mundell criterion** maintains that easier movement of people is a condition for OCAs.

- In general it is assumed that the costs of forming an EMU will fall, and the benefits will rise, as the level of integration increases. At the point of intersection between the cost and benefit lines it becomes worthwhile for a country to join a currency area.

- The shape and position of the cost curve will depend on views about the effectiveness of monetary policy, including exchange rate policies. At one extreme, according to the **monetarist view**, the exchange rate is an ineffective corrective for different developments between countries, and the intersection of benefit and cost curves is close to the origin. The **economist view** maintains that a higher level of co-ordination of economic policies and integration is necessary before creating a monetary union. The Maastricht Treaty reflects the 'economist' or German view, and all the monetarists obtained was a timetable for introducing EMU, but the initial decision in 1998 on which countries could join the euro largely reflected the monetarist view.

- The main criteria in deciding whether a country should form part of a currency area include: openness; the degree of similarity of the structure of production and trade; existence of alternative adjustment mechanisms such as labour movement or the possibility of transfers; a certain degree of homogeneity of preferences with regard to economic policies and common objectives.

- The results of different studies vary, but there seems to be a certain consensus among economists that the **EU(27) should not form a currency union**.

- Though the EU is not now an OCA, the mere creation of EMU could help progress in this direction. Joining a monetary union encourages rapid growth of trade, speeding up the integration process. Some authors have found empirical evidence that increased integration reduces the likelihood of asymmetric shocks so facilitating the creation of a currency union.

Questions for study and review

1 What do you consider the main costs and benefits of introducing a single currency?
2 How effective is the exchange rate instrument in correcting asymmetric shocks? What other instruments could be used?
3 Does the likelihood of asymmetric shocks increase or decrease as the level of integration rises?
4 What are the conditions for forming an optimal currency area?
5 Is the eurozone an optimal currency area?
6 Could the EU become an optimal currency area?

Online
Learning **Centre**

When you have read this chapter, log on to the Online Learning Centre website at *www.mcgraw-hill.co.uk/textbooks/senior* to explore weblinks, chapter-by-chapter test questions, case studies and more online study tools.

Chapter 9 Appendices

Appendix 1: The Mundell–Fleming model

The Mundell–Fleming model can be used to show the effects of monetary policy and fiscal policy with fixed and floating exchange rates and perfect capital mobility.[32]

Figure A9.1 presents the usual textbook version of IS and LM curves. The IS curve illustrates the various combinations of interest rates (i) and national income (Y) that yield equilibrium in the goods market. It is negatively sloped, since lower interest rates are associated with higher levels of investment and income (and higher saving and imports) for the quantities of goods and services demanded and supplied to remain equal. The LM curve illustrates all the points at which the money market is in equilibrium. As can be seen from Figure A9.1, the curve is positively sloped. The derivation of the LM curve is based on the assumption that the money supply is fixed. Higher incomes imply higher transaction demand for money. Higher incomes will therefore have to be associated with higher interest rates to ensure lower demand for money for speculative purposes (the opportunity cost of holding speculative money balances is greater with high interest rates), and thereby ensure that the total amount of money demanded remains equal to the fixed amount of money supplied.

An expansionary monetary policy will shift the LM curve to the right (from LM to LM' in Figure A9.1) since at each level of interest rate the level of national income must be higher to absorb the increase in

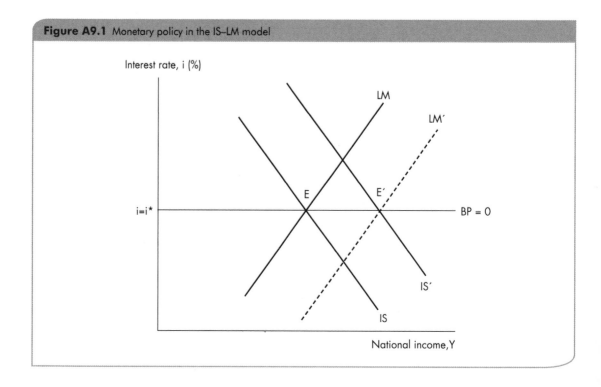

Figure A9.1 Monetary policy in the IS–LM model

---

[32] For a more complete discussion of these issues see a macroeconomic textbook such as Begg et al. (2008a).

money supply. With perfect capital mobility, assume that the interest rate prevailing on international markets is i*. Along the BP curve the balance of payments is in equilibrium, but this will only occur when the domestic interest rate i is equal to that prevailing on international markets. If, for example, the government attempts monetary expansion, moving the LM curve to LM', at the intersection of IS and LM' the domestic interest rate is below i*. Perfect capital movement means that this will cause an outflow of capital. What happens depends on the exchange rate regime.

If the exchange rate is freely floating, the balance of payments will be in deficit and there will be pressure towards depreciation of the exchange rate. The improvement in competitiveness means increased exports and falling imports, raising demand for domestic products. This will push the IS curve to the right until it reaches IS' where i = i* and capital outflows stop. The new equilibrium will be E'. In the case of flexible exchange rates monetary policy will be effective.

If the exchange rate is fixed, the central bank will have to intervene on the foreign exchange market, selling foreign currency and buying national currency until the LM curve has moved back to its original position, LM. The new equilibrium will be E. According to the model, monetary policy is ineffective with fixed exchange rates and free capital movements.

The same figure can be used to illustrate the effects of fiscal policy, which involves changes in taxation or government spending. An increase in public spending or a cut in taxes will raise demand, causing a shift of the IS' curve upwards to the right to IS', as shown in Figure A9.1. If there is no change in monetary policy the LM curve remains in the same place. At the new intersection of the IS and LM curves both output and the interest rate have risen. The interest rate rises as the increase in the budget deficit means that government borrowing has risen, pushing up interest rates. In a small open economy with perfect capital movement, interest rates cannot prevail at levels above i*. What happens depends on the exchange rate regime.

If the exchange rate is fixed, capital inflows create pressure for an appreciation of the currency. The central bank must therefore intervene to sell domestic currency to counteract the capital inflows and this will increase the money supply, shifting the LM curve to the right. The process stops only when the domestic interest rate has returned to i* with the new curve LM'. The new equilibrium is E'.

If the exchange rate is freely floating, the capital inflows lead to an appreciation of the exchange rate. If prices are sticky, the nominal appreciation leads to a real appreciation, and there is a loss of competitiveness and deterioration of the domestic account. The IS curve will shift to the left, returning to its initial position. The equilibrium is again E. In this case fiscal policy is ineffective.

These results are summarized in Table A9.1.

Table A9.1   The effects of fiscal and monetary policy in different exchange rate regimes

	Fixed exchange rate	Flexible exchange rate
Monetary policy	Ineffective	Effective
Fiscal policy	Effective	Ineffective

Appendix 2: An illustration of the role of the exchange rate mechanism using aggregate demand and supply curves

The role of the exchange rate as a shock absorber can be analysed using the concepts of aggregate demand and aggregate supply.[33] For simplicity, initially it is assumed that nominal wages are fixed.

---

[33] The analysis here is based on the standard forms of aggregate supply and demand curves explained in any basic macroeconomics textbook (see, for example, Begg et al. 2008a; Blanchard, 2009; Dornbusch et al., 2011).

Figure A9.2 presents the aggregate demand and supply curves for two countries, say France and Germany prior to EMU.

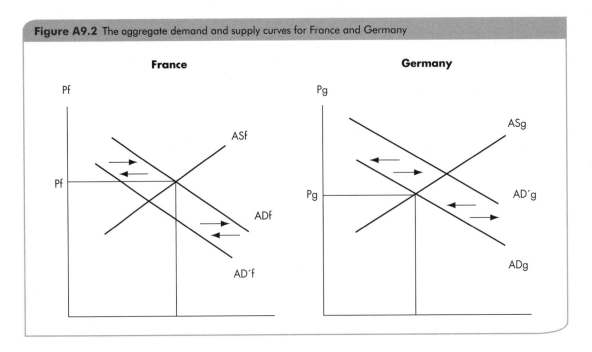

Figure A9.2 The aggregate demand and supply curves for France and Germany

The aggregate demand curve slopes down from left to right. This is because with lower prices the economy is more competitive, increasing the demand for domestic products, with a tendency to raise exports and reduce imports. At the same time, for a given money stock, lower prices will increase the value of real money balances, leading to an excess supply of money and an excess demand for bonds. This will raise the price of bonds and reduce the interest rate, leading to increased investment and a higher level of production.

The aggregate supply curve is assumed to slope upwards to the right. A possible explanation is that as prices rise, real wage costs fall and firms will take on more labour, increasing output. According to this view, the upward-sloping curve is based on the assumption that there is some money illusion on the labour supply side. This implies that an increase in money wages is perceived as an increase in real wages so more labour is offered. If prices rise, but money wages rise less quickly, there will still be an increase in the labour supply.

Assume that the initial position of the aggregate demand curves in France and Germany are ADf and ADg respectively.[34] An asymmetric shock then takes place because consumers' preferences change, possibly in response to a health scare. For instance, it is assumed that France is relatively intensive in the production of wine, and Germany is relatively intensive in the production of beer. As a result of a health scare concerning wine, consumers may start drinking beer in place of wine. This will shift the aggregate demand curve in France downwards to the left to AD'f, and that in Germany up to the right to AD'g, as shown in Figure A9.2.

Prior to introduction of the euro, to meet this situation the French franc might be devalued against the German D-mark, rendering French output cheaper relative to German output. This will have the effect of moving the French aggregate demand curve out to the right and the German curve in to the

---

[34] The example here is taken from Artis (1994), and owes much to the work of Mundell (1961). *Source*: pp. 351–2 from *The Economics of the European Union* (1994) by M. Artis and N. Lee. By permission of Oxford University Press.

left. According to textbook analysis, it should therefore be possible to use the devaluation to return to the original situation in each country, ADf and ADg.

Alternatively, if France and Germany had flexible exchange rates, France could have lowered its interest rate thereby simulating aggregate demand, while Germany would have raised its interest rate, reducing domestic demand. It is probable that these changes in monetary policy would have led to a depreciation of the French franc and an appreciation of the German D-mark. These changes would make German products sold in France more expensive. The effect would again be to raise aggregate demand in France and to lower aggregate demand in Germany.

However, the price levels so far considered are the domestic price levels in France and Germany (Pf and Pg respectively). Workers are not interested in the prices of domestically produced goods, but in the consumer price index, and this is also based on the price of imported goods. For instance, even if French domestic prices remain the same, the devaluation will increase the franc price of German beer bought by French workers. The French consumer price index PcF can be expressed by the following formula:

$$PcF = aPf + (1 - a)e\, Pg$$

where e is the exchange rate for converting D-marks into francs, a is the share of domestic products, and (1 – a) is the share of imported goods.

Even if Pf and Pg remain unchanged, a devaluation of the franc will increase PcF. If there is a high level of integration between the French and German economies, a large share of French products will be imported from Germany. This means that (1 – a) will be high, and a French devaluation will have a substantial effect in raising consumer prices in France.

These higher prices reduce real wages and may lead to requests by French workers to increase nominal wages. If these are granted, the aggregate supply curve will shift to the left, offsetting part of the effect of the devaluation. Prices will be higher and French output has not returned to its original level. There is even a risk that repeated devaluations lead to a wage–price–devaluation spiral.

With a higher level of integration, an exchange rate change is more likely to alter consumer prices and lead to this kind of price–wage reaction. The cost of forgoing the exchange rate mechanism is less the higher the level of integration, and this is a major reason that the cost curve of monetary union is assumed to slope down to the right.

Chapter **10**

The Long Road to Economic and Monetary Union

Learning Objectives

By the end of this chapter you should be able to understand:

☑ Why the aim of the 1969 Hague Summit to introduce economic and monetary union failed

☑ What we mean by the snake in the tunnel

☑ What the main features of the European Monetary System (EMS) were

☑ What we mean by the impossible trinity

☑ How the Maastricht Treaty set out the conditions for joining the single currency, the timing of its introduction and its main institutional features

☑ The arrangements used for EU countries outside the euro area

10.1 Introduction

Although there was no precise commitment to EMU in the Treaty of Rome, various initiatives were subsequently taken in this direction. For many years these initiatives met with mixed success, but they created a framework of institutions and arrangements on which EMU could eventually be built. This chapter therefore adopts a historical approach in discussing the long road to EMU. The objective of EMU was revived during the 1980s and, following the collapse of the Eastern bloc, was carried out with a surprising momentum so that theory could hardly keep pace with the political developments. Though little use was made initially of the optimum currency area theory (also because it was still in a fairly rudimentary stage), the approach was subsequently used to assess progress in the EMU project.

10.2 The international monetary system in the early years of the Community

As described in Chapter 3, the Treaty of Rome contains no specific commitment to EMU, partly because of the importance of the dollar in the international monetary system at the time. During

the late 1950s and 1960s international monetary arrangements were still based on the agreement reached at the 1944 Bretton Woods Conference. This entailed that members decided to make their currencies convertible into other currencies and gold at fixed exchange rates, and agreed not to impose import controls without permission of the International Monetary Fund (IMF, which was also set up as a result of Bretton Woods).

Gold continued to play an important role in the international monetary system in the 1950s and 1960s, and was used in settlement of imbalances. The price of gold remained fixed for many years at $35 per ounce, but the supply of gold was not rising fast enough to keep pace with the rapid increase in world trade.

After the Second World War the dollar became increasingly important as the main reserve currency. During the 1950s and 1960s the USA ran large and persistent payments deficits, thereby increasing dollar balances, since surplus countries were prepared to hold short-run debt in dollars. The US deficits therefore had the effect of increasing international liquidity as long as foreigners were prepared to hold dollars.

In 1970 and 1971 the US balance of payments deficit reached record levels partly because of large-scale investment by US firms abroad but also because of financing of the Vietnam War. At home the fiscal deficit was also growing, in part because of Lyndon B. Johnson's 'War on Poverty'. There was widespread speculation against the dollar, and pressure on the 'stronger' EC currencies, the German D-mark and the Dutch guilder.

10.3   The Hague Summit: 'EMU by 1980'

One of the most optimistic beliefs of the founding fathers of the Common Agricultural Policy (CAP) was that the introduction of a common system of prices for agricultural products (see Chapter 13) would render exchange rate adjustments between the EC currencies impossible. Theoretical support for this view was drawn from the neo-functionalist approach to integration: progress in harmonizing agricultural policy would spill over into the economic and monetary sphere. The optimism was to prove short-lived: common agricultural prices began to operate from 1967, and by 1969, with the French devaluation and the German revaluation, exchange rate instability had arrived in the Community.

In order to resolve this situation, in 1969 the European Commission submitted the Barre Plan to create a distinct monetary identity in the Community.[1] As part of the package for 'completion, deepening and enlargement' of the EC, at the 1969 Hague Summit the Community announced its intention to proceed towards EMU as a long-term objective.

Differences of opinion were soon to emerge: in particular, the 'economist' group of countries (see Chapter 9), including Germany and the Netherlands, maintained that before proceeding to monetary unification it was first necessary to reach a certain level of convergence of economic performance by setting common targets and co-ordinating economic policies. In contrast, the 'monetarist' countries (France, Belgium, Italy and Luxembourg) argued that the first step should be to narrow exchange rate fluctuations, as this would itself promote a certain degree of convergence.

A special study group was set up to examine EMU, and the results presented in 1970 are known as the Werner Report.[2] This proposed a three-stage move to full EMU by 1980. The exchange rates of the EC member states would be irrevocably fixed and a single currency would eventually be adopted (though this was considered desirable, but not strictly necessary for the project).

---

[1] European Commission (1969).

[2] European Commission (1970).

10.4   The snake in the tunnel

In the event the proposals of the Werner Report were overtaken by the situation of international monetary turbulence.[3] To meet the heavy speculation against the dollar in 1971, the USA had to suspend dollar convertibility and introduce a 10 per cent surcharge on imports. A solution to the US dollar and balance of payments problem was reached with the 1971 Smithsonian Accords. These involved a devaluation of the dollar by 7.9 per cent against gold, an adjustment of the EC currencies against the dollar[4] and a return to fixed exchange rates with margins of fluctuation of ±2.25 per cent around central rates. The US import surcharge was ended, and it was hoped that there would be an eventual return to dollar convertibility.

It was against this background that in 1972 the EC Six, together with the UK, Denmark, Ireland and Norway (which were expected to become the new EC members), decided to create what is known as 'the snake in the tunnel'.[5] For the EC currencies this entailed two margins of fluctuation:

- ± 2.25 per cent against the dollar.
- The maximum divergence between the strongest and the weakest EC currency was 2.25 per cent. Italy was allowed a wider margin of fluctuation of 6 per cent, and this was also offered to Ireland, though refused as a condition of more favourable credit.

However, speculation against currencies continued, and in 1972 the UK and Ireland were forced to float their currencies. Italy began to float in 1973, and France floated between 1974 and 1975, and again from 1976. By 1977 the snake members were Benelux, Germany, Denmark, Norway and (after 1973) Sweden, so the 'snake' had lost its EC character. In 1973 the 'tunnel' collapsed, and a 'joint float' of the snake against the dollar began.

10.5   The launching of EMS

Far from reaching EMU by 1980, the Community was no nearer this objective in the late 1970s than it had been in 1969. Moreover, the volatility of exchange rates was threatening to undermine such progress as had been made in integration. Exchange rate uncertainty acts as a barrier to trade and posed difficulties for the CAP.[6]

Partly as a reaction to the years of 'Eurosclerosis', by the late 1970s there was growing support for the idea of setting up a regional system of exchange rates as a first step towards EMU. The initiative would also help to bolster EC countries from the negative consequences of the US policy of benign neglect in international monetary matters.

The origins of the EMS date from a speech by Roy Jenkins at the European University Institute in Florence in 1977, calling for efforts to relaunch monetary integration. With strong support from President Giscard d'Estaing and Chancellor Helmut Schmidt, the idea of creating a zone of monetary stability in Europe gained ground (Ludlow, 1982). For the French this offered the prospect of escape from US dominance and a renewed role for France in integration initiatives, while for Germany reduced speculative pressure on the D-mark should lower inflationary pressures.

---

[3] For a more detailed account of these events see Gros and Thygesen (1998), or Swann (2000).

[4] The D-mark and guilder were revalued, sterling and the French franc remained unchanged, and the lira was devalued by 1 per cent.

[5] The attempt has been made here to explain the jargon associated with the EU as far as possible, but if additional information is necessary see the Europa Glossary of the EU at http://europa.eu/scadplus/glossary/index_it.htm (accessed 23 November 2010), or the website of Baldwin and Wyplosz (2009) at www.mcgraw-hill.co.uk/textbooks/baldwin (accessed 23 November 2010).

[6] As discussed in Chapter 13, the operation of the agrimonetary system meant that at times during the 1970s the difference in agricultural price levels in the national currencies of EC countries was greater than it had been prior to introduction of the CAP.

In drawing up the EMS proposals, the other EC countries implicitly accepted the traditional German priority attached to combating inflation, and both France and Italy considered participation in the EMS part of an anti-inflation strategy. The members of the former snake were pleased to see the area of exchange rate stability extended. Ireland was in favour of external discipline of monetary policy, independence from the UK and the credits offered as part of the new system. The UK only became a full member eleven years later, in part because it was wary of the political objectives of the EMS, and feared its deflationary consequences.

10.6 The EMS mechanisms

The EMS was introduced in 1979 and its membership comprised all the then EC members, although the UK participated in the provisions regarding exchange rates only from 1990. The EMS built on the snake, but included new characteristics, namely:

- the exchange rate mechanism (ERM);
- the introduction of the European Currency Unit (ECU);
- a divergence indicator designed to ensure that adjustment was symmetrical;
- a system of monetary co-operation with very short-, short- and medium-term credits to defend fixed interest rates.

There are two systems that can be used to peg fixed exchange rates: a parity grid and a basket of currencies. A **parity grid** is based on bilateral exchange rates between all the participating countries.[7] A **basket of currencies** is a monetary unit made up of fixed quantities of the currencies of participating countries. For instance, the ECU[8] was composed of given quantities of each of the EU currencies, including those (such as the UK up until 1990) that did not participate in the exchange rate mechanism. The ECU consisted of so many D-marks, so many francs, so many lira etc. The quantity of each currency in the basket is decided by some agreed criterion, and in the case of the ECU it roughly reflected the share of each member state in EC GDP and intra-EC trade. The central rates of each EC currency in ECU were used to establish a parity grid of cross-rates between the participating currencies. This constituted the basis of the **exchange rate mechanism.**

The EMS was a system of fixed but adjustable exchange rates. Member countries participating in the ERM were obliged to maintain their exchange rate with each other within a target band of fluctuation around their central rates. Between 1979 and 1993 the band of fluctuation for most participating currencies was ±2.25 per cent. A wider band of ±6 per cent was allowed for Italy between 1979 and 1990, and for the countries that joined later: Spain (1989), the UK (1990) and Portugal (1992). As described below, Italy and the UK were forced to abandon the ERM in September 1992, and Greece remained out of the ERM because of its higher level of inflation. The bands of fluctuation for countries participating in the ERM were widened to ±15 per cent from August 1993, when only the exchange rate between the D-mark and Dutch guilder maintained the narrow ±2.25 per cent band.

The EMS was a hybrid system since the introduction of a currency basket, the ECU, is not strictly necessary for the operation of a parity grid. One of the main reasons for the introduction of the ECU was its importance as a symbol, indicating commitment to the ultimate objective of EMU. Later the ECU provided the basis of what was to become the euro.

---

[7] If n countries participate, each country will have $n - 1$ exchange rates against the other currencies. The total number of exchange rates among participating countries will be $n(n - 1)$, but it is sufficient to know $n - 1$ rates to calculate them all.

[8] ECU indicates both the acronym in English and a coin formerly used in France.

The ECU performed the following functions:

- It acted as the numeraire for defining the central rates of the parity grid.
- The ECU was the unit of account used for the EU budget, including all payments and credits granted by the Community.
- It was used as a means of payment, initially by the EC authorities, and subsequently also by member states, international organizations and for private use.[9]
- It provided the basis for a divergence indicator aimed at ensuring early and symmetrical intervention. When a country's currency was out of line, the divergence indicator was intended to act as an alarm bell and there was a 'presumption' (not obligation) that the country would take corrective action.

The aim of the **divergence indicator** was to signal the direction and extent of divergence of a currency from its central rate in ECU. It was hoped that the divergence threshold would require adjustment by both strong and weak currency countries equally. If one currency reached the trigger point against another, both countries were expected to intervene. If, however, policies to maintain an exchange rate were unsustainable, or the balance of payments indicated that a parity was out of line, then by mutual agreement exchange rates could be realigned.

Given the obligations to maintain currencies within the bands of fluctuation, if necessary through unlimited intervention on exchange markets, the EMS was accompanied by provisions to ensure **monetary co-operation** among the participating countries.[10] These operated through the European Monetary Co-operation Fund (EMCF) which was superseded by the European Monetary Institute (EMI) in 1994. The central banks of EMS participants were required to pool 20 per cent of their gold and foreign exchange reserves with the EMCF in exchange for ECU. The EMI later provided the framework for what became the ECB.

10.7 The problem of asymmetry in the operation of the EMS

At the time of its inception, the EMS was envisaged as a symmetrical system, with the introduction of the divergence threshold aimed at ensuring intervention by the authorities responsible both for strong and for weak currencies. However, given the dominant role of Germany, it soon became apparent that the system was operating in an asymmetrical way.

Germany provided the anchor for the system, using the money supply to control German inflation. The high-inflation members of the ERM used their monetary policy to maintain their exchange rates with the D-mark with the aim of 'importing' low German inflation rates.[11]

The strong economic performance of Germany, and the implicit acceptance of German leadership after 1983, meant that other EMS members tended to co-ordinate their monetary policies with that of Germany. Increases in German interest rates aimed at domestic stabilization were generally followed by a rise in other European interest rates (including those of countries outside the ERM). At times, countries such as Italy and France introduced controls on capital movements to secure a certain

---

[9] Following the 1985 Basel Agreement.

[10] The monetary co-operation for countries in difficulty consisted of credit provisions for the very short run (45 days, but extended to 60 days with the Basle–Nyborg Agreement of 1987), the short run (up to 75 days but renewable up to three months) and the medium term (2–5 years). With the Basle–Nyborg Agreement the use of the credit facilities was extended to intra-marginal intervention, and many of the restrictions on use of the ECU were removed.

[11] Barro and Gordon (1983) developed the theoretical underpinning of this point. The cost in terms of output of an anti-inflationary policy depends on the ability of the authorities to convince the public that they will not renege on their policy commitments. If governments succeed in announcing a credible anti-inflationary policy, inflationary expectations will be lower. In this way a reduction in inflation can be achieved with a lower level of unemployment than would otherwise be possible.

degree of autonomy in monetary policy, but with the liberalization of capital movements from 1990 this was no longer possible.

All the ERM currency realignments carried out between 1979 and 1987 involved revaluation of the D-mark against other EC currencies and only the guilder–D-mark exchange rate remained unchanged over the 1984–87 period. The West German central bank, the Bundesbank, was hostile to unlimited intervention to support weak currencies. The divergence indicator never functioned particularly well in practice, and even when the divergence threshold was triggered, the Bundesbank rarely carried out intra-marginal intervention. Most of the burden of intervention and adjustment was borne by the weaker currency countries.

The weight of West Germany in the system, and the importance of the D-mark as a reserve currency, meant that the Bundesbank was largely responsible for exchange rate policy with regard to third currencies (chiefly the dollar and the yen), while the other central banks were mainly concerned with intervention for adjustment within the system.

10.8 The phases of operation of the EMS

The literature generally divides the operation of the EMS into four periods: 1979–83, 1983–87, 1987–92, and from the 1992 crisis until introduction of the euro in December 1999.[12]

The 1979–83 period

The first period, from March 1979 until 1983, was characterized by an unstable international monetary environment following the second oil crisis. The frequency (seven) and size of realignments during this period was unexpected. Differentials in inflation between the EC countries were high, but from 1983 France and other EC countries adopted more determined counter-inflationary measures (Artis and Healey, 1995).

The 1983–87 period

The second phase of EMS covers the 1983–87 period and was characterized by relatively few realignments, and when these occurred few currencies were involved and the changes in central rates tended to be small. During this period (which dates from the French decision of 1983 to use the exchange rate anchor to bring and keep inflation down, and to align monetary policy with that of the Bundesbank), empirical evidence suggests that the EMS had a stabilizing effect on exchange rates, and that there was a convergence towards lower inflation rates. The average level of inflation in countries participating in the ERM fell from 11.6 per cent in 1983 to 2.3 per cent in 1986.

There has been considerable debate as to how far the EMS was responsible for this reduction in inflation, which was also experienced by countries not participating in the EMS. There seem to be two ways in which the EMS contributed to downward price convergence:

- Member states used the EMS as a scapegoat to justify unpopular policies to reduce inflation and to limit wage claims.
- The increased importance attached to the anti-inflationary objective implied an acceptance of the traditional German priority by other EMS members.

The 1987–92 period

The third period (1987–92), known also as the 'hard' EMS, was characterized by great stability, if not rigidity, of exchange rates. There was, however, a 'technical' realignment when Italy entered the narrow ±2.25 per cent band of fluctuation in 1990.

---

[12] For a more complete discussion of the phases of EMS see Bladen-Hovell (2007).

During this period there was a gradual extension of the ERM membership, to Spain, the UK and Portugal, so that Greece was the only EC country not participating. The decision of these countries to join seems likely to have been influenced by a mixture of economic and political motives, including the desire of the Southern European countries to demonstrate their commitment to the European cause. In the case of the UK, a major factor was undoubtedly fear of remaining outside the system because of the speculative pressures against sterling.

The currency crisis of September 1992

The currency crisis of September 1992 led to the widening of most ERM margins to ±15 per cent in August 1993. Three events which contributed to the 1992/93 crisis are:

- the liberalization of capital movements;
- the early difficulties encountered by the Maastricht Treaty and the decision to move to economic and monetary union; and
- German reunification.

Up until 1990, countries such as France and Italy were able to resort to capital controls to regain a certain degree of autonomy for monetary policy. The use of capital controls can limit the scale of a speculative attack on a weak currency and may help to isolate interest rates from fluctuations on international markets. This was especially important given the Bundesbank's objection to unlimited intervention to protect weak currencies. The liberalization of capital movements from 1990 removed this safety valve from the system.

In 1992 there was great uncertainty about the prospects for the Maastricht Treaty and the EMU programme. In July 1992 the Danish voted against Maastricht in a referendum, though this decision was reversed in 1993. Then followed the '*petit oui*' in France in which only 51 per cent voted in favour of the Maastricht Treaty. One of the main reasons that there were no currency realignments during the 1988–92 period was to prepare the way for EMU. In 1992 EMU seemed at risk, calling into question the credibility of the EMS and encouraging currency speculation.

The operation of the EMS in the years before 1992 rested on the acceptance of German policy leadership by the other EC countries. German unification represented a shock, leading to a tightening of German monetary policy that other EMS members were unwilling to follow.

The collapse of the Berlin Wall in November 1989 was followed at breakneck speed by the monetary unification of Germany in July 1990, and political unification in October. The German government hugely underestimated the cost of reunification, which entailed transfers to East Germany of $79 billion in 1991 and $105 billion in 1992 (Nuti, 1994). As a result the public sector deficit deteriorated by more than 3 per cent of GDP. Inflation rose from 1.3 per cent in 1988 to 4.8 per cent in 1992. During the 1990 elections Kohl had promised that reunification would not lead to an increase in taxes, and the main strategy for combating inflation was through an increase in interest rates, which reached 9.75 per cent in 1992.

At the same time, fear of recession meant that in the USA the Federal Reserve reduced interest rates to 3 per cent, and the prospect of elections limited attempts to cut the deficit. The difference of 6.75 per cent between German and US interest rates led to huge capital inflows to Germany, causing upward pressure on the D-mark and leading to widespread expectation that there would be an EMS realignment. Fear of deflation (in particular in France, the UK and Italy) meant that other countries were reluctant to raise their interest rates to German levels. However, they were no longer able to use capital controls to protect their currencies from speculation.

Pressure against sterling and the lira forced them to be 'temporarily' withdrawn from the ERM in September 1992. The French franc then came under attack but was defended by a combined effort of the French and German central banks. There was also speculation against the currencies of Spain, Denmark, Ireland, Portugal and Belgium.[13] When the French franc came under attack again in August 1993, it was decided to widen the

---

[13] The French franc was defended by massive intervention and by a joint statement by the French and German authorities concerning the importance of the franc–D-mark exchange rate to the EMS.

bands of fluctuation to ±15 per cent (with the exception of the D-mark–guilder rate, which had remained unscathed during the crisis). At the time many thought such wide bands were not very different from floating, but in practice EMS exchange rates did not fluctuate much more than they had previously (Bladen-Hovell, 2007). The crisis appears to have increased the commitment of policy makers to EMU.

10.9 The impossible trinity

Padoa Schioppa (1987) refers to the 'contradictory quartet' that no international monetary arrangement has been able to reconcile simultaneously:

- liberalized trade;
- free capital movements;
- fixed exchange rates; and
- autonomy of monetary policy.

As liberalized trade became generally taken for granted, the later literature refers to the impossible or 'unholy' trinity of the remaining three items.

During the first period of the EMS (1979–83), participating countries maintained controls on capital movements and there were frequent realignments of exchange rates. After 1983 Italy and France managed to acquire exchange rate stability but only through losing autonomy for monetary policy and recourse to capital controls. The UK realized free capital movements during the 1980s, but only at the cost of exchange rate stability.

The combination of the Single Market and EMS implied a commitment to free trade and capital movement with fixed exchange rates.[14] This system could survive only as long as the other ERM countries were prepared to sacrifice monetary autonomy and accept German policy leadership. After German reunification this was no longer the case and the system broke down. EC countries regained a degree of monetary autonomy but at the price of sacrificing fixed exchange rates from August 1993.

The way forward proposed by the Maastricht Treaty was to combine free capital movements and the decision to give up the ERM with a common monetary policy for the euro area.

10.10 The 1980s and 1990s: back to EMU

During the late 1980s, the objective of EMU was revived with a renewed vigour for a number of reasons:

- Exchange rate uncertainty between the EC currencies was another obstacle to trade that should be eliminated in order to complete the internal market. The increased trade and interdependency between the EC economies would render exchange rate adjustment less effective, and a common currency would confirm the reality of the Single Market.

- The aim was to take the relatively successful experience of co-operating in the EMS one step further.

- The boom of the late 1980s was beginning to flag, so methods of prolonging business confidence were being sought.

- According to the neo-functionalist approach, EMU was viewed as a means of pushing the integration process further in the direction of political union, since greater Community responsibility for economic and monetary policies would require more effective democratic control.

- The Commission, and Delors in particular, played an active role in relaunching the initiative, supported by the French and German governments (despite the hesitancy of the Bundesbank).

---

[14] As explained in Chapter 6, capital movements were only liberalized in 1992 for Ireland and Spain. Greece and Portugal had a derogation until 1996, but Portugal liberalized all capital controls in 1992.

- Following German reunification, Kohl was anxious to demonstrate that an even more powerful Germany remained firmly anchored in Western Europe, and commitment to EMU provided a means of demonstrating that this was the case.

For once the role of the CAP and the need for exchange rate stability to ensure the effective functioning of the price support system played a relatively minor role. Similarly, compared with the 1960s and 1970s, the revived EMU initiative seemed less of a response to worries about the international monetary system.[15] As the process gained momentum, a further reason for its continuation was that it would have been increasingly costly to abandon the whole initiative (an argument that again came to the fore with the crisis of the eurozone from 2010, see Chapter 11). The result would have been speculation and currency instability, and the probable collapse of attempts at fiscal discipline, at least in some of the Southern European countries.

The EMU project was formally launched at the 1988 Hannover Summit, when it was decided to set up a committee for the study of EMU under the president of the Commission, Jacques Delors. The Committee's results were presented as the Delors Report in 1989.[16] The document 'One market, one money' (European Commission, 1990a), which contained the first articulated study of the costs and benefits of EMU, was prepared as input to the Delors Report. However, this approach was not taken up at that stage, partly because optimum currency area theory was still not sufficiently developed to be applied in practice, but also because events were moving so quickly after the collapse of the Eastern bloc. The Delors Report makes use of the impossible trinity argument, maintaining that the Single Market required freedom of capital movement and exchange rate stability to promote trade, so the loss of monetary autonomy implied by the single money project was a necessary consequence. Many of the conclusions were similar to those of the earlier Werner Report, which is not surprising as several of the members of the two committees were the same. The Delors Report differs from the Werner Report in its emphasis on the institutional changes implied by EMU, and the need for transfer of authority to the Community. In particular, the central bankers in the Delors Committee seemed concerned to draw the attention of politicians to the need for some constraints on fiscal policy. The Delors Report also appears to be based on the conviction that a very tight exchange rate commitment was simply not as robust as a single money.

During the debate at that time only the UK expressed doubts about the overall objective of EMU. France wanted to fix early dates for the introduction of EMU in order to ensure continuing German commitment to the project. Germany stressed the importance of stringent fiscal criteria and independent institutions mirroring as far as possible the German model. The poorer member states such as Ireland, Portugal and Greece called for a link between EMU and cohesion for the weaker regions and countries of the Community and wanted more flexible criteria as a condition for entering the final phase of EMU. The final compromise combines the stringency of the criteria and institutional arrangements requested by Germany with the early deadlines favoured by France.

10.11 The Maastricht Treaty

The Maastricht Treaty followed the main indications of the Delors Report. Its main provisions with regard to EMU are:

- The Treaty set out convergence criteria to be met before a country could participate in EMU, though allowance was made for certain countries opting out.
- A timetable was fixed for the introduction of a single currency by 1 January 1999 'at the latest'. This was to occur in three stages, and the Treaty describes the objectives to be reached and fixes the dates for each of these stages.

---

[15] According to Tsoukalis (1997), this reflected a greater confidence on the part of the EC countries and, in particular, less fear that the EMS was vulnerable to fluctuations in the value of the dollar.

[16] The Delors Committee was composed of the governors of the central banks of the EC member states and a group of independent experts. See European Commission (1989).

- The Treaty indicates the main institutional features of EMU and, in particular, of the European Central Bank.

10.12 The convergence criteria

Any country wanting to participate fully in the final stage of EMU had to satisfy the Maastricht convergence criteria. These were introduced in an attempt to ensure that the constraints on policy implied by the EMU were acceptable to the country concerned. The aim is to avoid destabilizing the EMU by the premature admission of countries whose underlying economic performance is not yet compatible with permanently fixed exchange rates. As mentioned in Chapter 9, these are nominal convergence criteria, rather than the real criteria suggested by the optimal currency area theory.

The criteria entail that:

- Successful candidates must have inflation rates no more than 1.5 per cent above the average of the three EU countries with the lowest inflation rate.
- Long-term interest rates should be no more than 2 per cent above the average of that of the three lowest inflation countries in the EU. This is to ensure that inflation convergence is lasting, because otherwise higher than expected future inflation in a country would be reflected in higher long-term interest rates.
- The exchange rate of the country should remain within the 'normal' band of the ERM without tension and without initiating depreciation for two years. At the time of the Maastricht Treaty the 'normal' band referred to the margins of ±2.25 per cent, but from August 1993 it was taken to refer to ±15 per cent.[17]
- The public debt of the country should not exceed 60 per cent of GDP.
- The national budget deficit must not be higher than 3 per cent of GDP.

The last two on the list are referred to as the 'fiscal' criteria and are subject to an escape clause. A country may be granted a waiver if the excessive public deficit has 'declined substantially and continuously' or is 'exceptional and temporary', or if the excessive debt is 'sufficiently diminishing and approaching the reference value at a satisfactory pace' (Article 104c Maastricht Treaty). As is described below, in practice there has been rather flexible interpretation of whether various countries have met the criteria.

10.13 The three stages in the introduction of EMU

The first stage: July 1990 to December 1993

The first stage in the introduction of EMU covered the period July 1990 to December 1993. The main objectives of that stage were to liberalize capital movements between EU members, to introduce long-run convergence programmes and to adopt multilateral monitoring of economic policies and performance through the Ecofin (the Council of Economic and Finance Ministers).

The second stage: 1 January 1994 to December 1998

The second stage in the introduction of EMU was to cover the period from 1 January 1994 until December 1996 or 1998. In the event the later date was chosen, and the 1995 Madrid European Council announced that the third stage would be launched from 1999 and adopted the name 'euro' for the single currency (see Box 10.1).

---

[17] The new member states which joined the EU in 2004 and 2007 had to respect the margin of ±2.25 per cent.

Box 10.1

Key dates in the EMU programme

1989	Delors Report on EMU.
1990	Beginning of stage 1 and abolition of capital controls in July for most member states.
1993	Maastricht Treaty.
1994	Stage 2 of EMU begins with the creation of the EMI.
1995	The Madrid European Council announces that the third stage would be launched from 1999, and adopts the name 'euro' for the single currency.
1996	Stability and Growth Pact agreed at the Dublin European Council.
1998	The European Council of May decides on the euro members, and fixed the exchange rates between the currencies of the participating countries irrevocably.
May/June 1998	The president and Executive Board of the ECB are chosen; the ECB comes into operation in June.
1999	The ECU is converted into the euro, and the third stage of EMU begins.
2001	Greece joins.
2002	Euro notes and coins introduced, and national currencies withdrawn.
2007	Slovenia adopts the euro.
2008	Cyprus and Malta adopt the euro.
2009	Slovakia joins the euro.
2011	Estonia joins the euro.

The main aims of the second phase were to encourage convergence and to prepare for the final stage, in particular by putting in place the necessary institutions and deciding which countries were to participate in the final stage. Temporary derogations were to be granted for countries deemed not yet ready. States subject to derogation would be reconsidered every two years. The EMI was set up in Frankfurt as the forerunner of the ECB, which came into operation in June 1998.

The selection of the countries participating in the euro took place at the May 1998 European Council.[18] Contrary to earlier expectations, when it was thought that several member states would fail to meet the Maastricht convergence criteria, this was the case only for Greece.[19] All countries had made serious efforts to meet the criteria. None the less, the generous final interpretation of who

---

[18] This summit took place in Brussels since, rather ironically, the country holding the Presidency at the time was the UK, who chose not to participate fully in stage 3 of EMU.

[19] In most of the participating countries certain 'cosmetic' measures were introduced to enable the Maastricht criteria to be met. These included a payment by France Télécom, a refundable 'eurotax' in Italy and an attempt by Germany to adjust the value of its gold reserves.

was able to satisfy the criteria probably owes much to the weakness of the German economy at the time. Germany had insisted on introduction of the fiscal criteria and their strict interpretation, but, following German reunification, could not meet them to the letter when the time came.

The argument that high-inflation countries could benefit from the borrowed credibility of a common monetary policy and monetary institution (see Chapter 9) explains the motivation of such countries to join the euro, so the question became why countries such as Germany, with credible monetary institutions and low inflation, were prepared to share their monetary autonomy with high-inflation countries. As Torres (2008) describes, a 1993 ruling of the German Federal Constitutional Court made it possible for Germany to withdraw from EMU if monetary stability were not delivered, and Germany insisted on prior agreement to basic economic principles and guarantees of the independence and commitment to price stability of the ECB. It was probably also felt that limited participation in stage 3 of EMU might undermine the achievements so far attained in monetary co-operation and with regard to the Single Market (if, for example, currency misalignments disrupted trade). Moreover, if some countries were left out of the third phase of EMU because perceived as laggards, it was considered likely to be more difficult for them to join later, especially if currency speculation distanced them still further from the Maastricht entry requirements.

It was agreed to grant the UK an 'opt-out' clause so that the decision to participate or not in the final stage would be left to future governments. Tony Blair subsequently announced that when certain economic conditions for membership had been met, British participation would be decided in a referendum (see Box 10.2). Denmark secured a milder version of the 'opt-out', and in 2000 the Danish people voted against participation in the euro in a referendum. In 2007 the Danish government announced that a further referendum would be held on all the Danish opt-outs, including that on EMU, but this was put on hold in the uncertain climate following the Irish rejection of the Lisbon Treaty in 2008. In 1998 Sweden also decided to remain outside on technical grounds (by not entering

Box 10.2

Should the UK adopt the euro?

When Gordon Brown was Chancellor of the Exchequer, an extensive cost/benefit analysis was carried out to assess whether the UK should join the euro. The decision was to be taken on the basis of five economic tests:

- **Convergence.** Are business cycles and economic structures compatible so that the UK can live comfortably with common eurozone interest rates on a permanent basis?
- **Flexibility.** If problems emerge, is there sufficient flexibility to deal with them?
- **Investment.** Would adopting the euro create better conditions for firms taking long-term decisions to invest in the UK?
- **The City of London.** How would adopting the euro affect UK financial services?
- **Stability, growth and employment.** Would adopting the euro help to promote higher growth, stability and a lasting increase in jobs?

The conclusions were presented in 2003 and were rather pessimistic. The convergence and flexibility conditions were not found to have been satisfied, the investment and financial services tests were met, and the growth, stability and employment condition was said to require fulfilment of the first two tests. Brown stated that structural reforms would be undertaken to enable the UK to join the euro in the future, and Tony Blair promised a referendum before the UK could join. An opinion poll carried out by Cetelem suggested that the share of British citizens expressing misgivings about the euro rose from 48 per cent in 1999 to 65 per cent in 2003.*

*As reported in the Financial Times of 8 January 2004.

the ERM), and in a referendum of September 2003, 56 per cent of the Swedish people voted against adopting the euro.[20]

One of the negative consequences of remaining out of the euro is that a member state's influence over certain decisions of importance to the future of the EU economy is likely to be reduced, especially as many important decisions are taken in the monthly informal meetings of the Eurogroup,[21] which take place the evening before Ecofin meetings. After September 2003 the UK, Denmark and Sweden were no longer able even to send senior officials to help prepare Eurogroup meetings.

At the May 1998 European Council it was also decided to fix the exchange rates between the currencies of the participating countries irrevocably. Conversion rates into the euro had to wait until 31 December 1998, because the euro was to replace the ECU (with one euro being equal to one ECU) and the ECU included currencies that were not then being replaced by the euro (those of the UK, Denmark, Greece and Sweden). These decisions account for the rather awkward numbers for converting the various national currencies into the euro (see Box 10.3).

Box 10.3

The conversion rates for the currencies participating in the euro

(See text for an explanation of how the conversion rates were derived).

€1 =

BEF 40.3399	DEM 1.95583	ITL 1,936.27	CYP 0.585274
FRF 6.55957	IEP 0.787564	ATS 13.7603	MTL 0.4293
LUF 40.3399	NLG 2.20371	ELD 340.750	SKK 30.1260
PTE 200.482	FIM 5.94573	SLT 239.640	EEK 15.6466
ESP 166.386			

The third stage: from 1 January 1999

The third stage of EMU began on 1 January 1999 and entailed a three-year transition period during which the currencies of the countries participating fully in EMU continued to exist but only as subdivisions of the euro.[22] Financial markets were encouraged to use the euro increasingly. It is perhaps a reflection of how strong the political commitment to EMU was during this period that the process proceeded smoothly and without strong speculative attacks against currencies. From 1 January 2002 euro notes and coins were introduced, and national banknotes and coins were withdrawn in the first two months of that year.[23]

---

[20] In Sweden 42 per cent voted in favour of the euro. Three days before the referendum the Swedish foreign minister, Anna Lindh, was stabbed to death in a department store. She had been strongly in favour of the euro, but the expected surge in yes votes as a reaction failed to take place. According to exit polls carried out at the time (and reported in *The Economist*, 20 September 2003), the Swedish people feared the loss of democracy, sovereignty, national control of interest rates and threats to their welfare state (in that order).

[21] The Eurogroup is composed only of economics and finance ministers from countries participating in the euro.

[22] From 1999 the euro began its existence as a largely virtual or non-cash currency appearing in accounting systems. In theory, from this date banks were to exchange euro currencies, and in particular euros, into those currencies without a commission, but in practice commissions continued to be charged.

[23] Initially, 1 July was indicated for the date when national notes and coins were to cease being national tender, but subsequently it was decided to shorten the time period for the changeover on practical grounds.

10.14 Countries outside the euro area

Even without participating fully in stage 3 of EMU, all EU countries are obliged to treat their economic policies as a matter of common interest and co-ordinate them in the Council (Article 121 TFEU, ex Article 99 TEC). This involves participation in the procedures to monitor economic performance in the EU and its member states. It also entails the co-ordination of economic policies through national convergence programmes, broad guidelines and multilateral surveillance to assess the consistency of the policies of the EU and its member states with the broad policy guidelines (though, as explained below, the system of economic governance of all the EU is likely to be changed from 2011).

The new member states were not given the possibility of opt-outs and will have to join the euro when they meet the Maastricht criteria.

To cater for countries outside the euro area, in 1999 the ERM was replaced with a new ERM II linking the currencies of non-euro member states to the euro (though participation in this mechanism is voluntary). Many of the arrangements of ERM II are simply a continuation of the earlier ERM. Central rates were defined in terms of the euro and ERM member states are obliged to keep their currencies within a ±15 per cent margin of their central rate, though narrower margins can be set by the country concerned. There was to be automatic intervention at the margins, and very short-term credit facilities were available. The ECB is also committed to intervention, provided this does not jeopardize price stability in the eurozone. Unlike in the earlier EMS, there was no attempt to impose symmetry of intervention.

Denmark, which joined ERM II in January 1999, keeps its currency within a narrower band of ±2.25 per cent. The UK and Sweden have remained out of ERM II (which is how Sweden managed to avoid joining the euro). Estonia, Lithuania and Slovenia joined in 2004, with Estonia and Lithuania maintaining currency boards. As explained in Chapter 9, a currency board entails that the outstanding liabilities of the central bank are backed at least 100 per cent by its foreign currency reserves. Cyprus, Latvia, Malta and Slovakia joined in 2005, with Latvia maintaining a margin of ±1 per cent, and Malta keeping its currency at the central rate.

The Maastricht criterion on exchange rates entails that a country should remain within the 'normal' band of the exchange rate mechanism (ERM II) without tension and without initiating depreciation for two years. For the new member states, this meant that full participation in the third stage of EMU had to wait for at least two years after joining the EU, and only Slovenia was deemed ready to join in 2007. Lithuania's inflation rate was slightly above the then benchmark of 2.6 per cent, but was predicted to rise to 3.5 per cent in the following year. The benchmark entails inflation not being more than 1.5 per cent above that of the three best performers in the EU. These were then Sweden, Finland and either the Netherlands or Poland, and the fact that the benchmark referred to at least one non-euro country was a matter of controversy. Cyprus and Malta joined the euro in January 2008, Slovakia in 2009 and Estonia in 2011.

The other Central and East European member states could have difficulties meeting the Maastricht criteria on fiscal deficits and inflation. These countries face pressure for government spending from a number of sources, including completing the implementation of the *acquis*; reform of pensions, social security, health care and education; and improvements in infrastructure and the environment. As described in Chapter 11, the economic crisis from 2007 posed additional pressures, in particular for the Baltic states, and Romania (see Dandashly et al, 2009). Poland was the only EU country with positive growth in 2009 (of 1.7 per cent, see also Figure 11.5 in Chapter 11). Fiscal imbalances led Hungary to seek IMF assistance in 2008.

When the formerly closed and inefficient centrally planned economies were opened up to market forces, a process of catching up occurred, with rapid gains in productivity. If the productivity gains are faster in the traded than in the non–traded sector, this can also generate inflation according to what is known as the Balassa–Samuelson effect. When a small economy opens to international trade its export prices are set at the world level. If the country is on its production possibility frontier, increased productivity in traded goods leads to increased wages in the traded goods sector. However, if wages

are equalized between the traded and non–traded goods sectors, and the non-traded goods sector has lower productivity, inflation will result. If the Central and East European countries attempt to peg their exchange rate when inflation is higher than in their main trading partners they may suffer a loss of competitiveness, which may result in currency crises. Ongoing higher inflation in some of these countries could be a source of tension when they join the euro.

10.15   Evaluation

Though the Treaty of Rome did not envisage economic and monetary union, the 1969 Hague Summit called for EMU by 1980. The unstable international monetary environment during the 1970s rendered this goal impossible, but the discussions of the time laid the basis for what was eventually to become the euro system. The launching of the EMS in 1979 provided a framework for ongoing monetary co-operation, created the ECU that evolved into the euro, and set up the EMCF that became the EMI and was subsequently transformed into the ECB.

Progress in implementing the three stages of EMU set out in the Maastricht Treaty proceeded surprisingly smoothly, though the number of countries fully participating in stage 3 was larger than initially foreseen. As will be shown in the next chapter, the celebrations to mark the first ten years of the euro were mainly positive, and it was only with the economic crisis that the serious consequences of certain unresolved questions began to emerge.

Summary of key concepts

- The **1969 Hague Summit** envisaged EMU by 1980, but the initiative failed in the face of the monetary instability of the 1970s.

- The **snake in the tunnel** was created in 1972, but by 1973 this had become a 'joint float' of currencies linked to the D-mark against the dollar.

- The **European Monetary System** was launched in 1979 and entailed: the exchange rate mechanism, introduction of the ECU, a divergence indicator and monetary co-operation. The ECU was the forerunner of the euro, and the European Monetary Institute provided the institutional basis on which to build the future European Central Bank.

- The operation of EMS can be divided into four periods: 1979–83, 1983–87, 1987–92 and the 1992 crisis and after. From August 1993, the bands of fluctuation were widened to ±15 per cent.

- According to the **impossible trinity**, no international monetary arrangement has been able to reconcile simultaneously: free capital movements, fixed exchange rates and autonomy of monetary policy.

- The 1993 **Maastricht Treaty** set out the criteria for joining the single currency, the timetable for its introduction and the main institutional features of EMU.

- The **Maastricht criteria** entail that successful candidates must have: inflation rates no more than 1.5 per cent above the average of the three countries with the lowest-inflation rate in the EU; long-term interest rates no more than 2 per cent above the average of the three lowest-inflation countries; an exchange rate within the 'normal' band of the ERM without tension and without initiating depreciation for two years; a public debt of no more than 60 per cent of GDP; and a national budget deficit of no more than 3 per cent of GDP.

- The decision about which countries could join the euro was made in May 1998 (though Greece joined later), and from that time no further exchange rate changes were made between their currencies. Britain, Sweden and Denmark remained outside the euro.

- The euro replaced the ECU from 1 January 1999. The European Central Bank began to operate from June 1998. Euro notes and coins were introduced from 1 January 2002.
- In January 2007 Slovenia joined, Cyprus and Malta adopted the euro from January 2008, Slovakia in 2009, and Estonia in 2011.
- Even without participating fully in stage 3 of EMU, all EU countries are obliged to respect the **EMU** *acquis* and treat their economic policies as a matter of common interest and co-ordinate them in the Council. To cater for countries outside the euro area, the ERM was replaced in 1999 with a new **ERM II** linking the currencies of some non-euro member states to the euro.
- The new member states were not given the possibility of opt-outs and will have to join the euro when they meet the Maastricht criteria.

Questions for study and review

1 Why do you think that the objective of introducing EMU by 1980 failed?
2 What are the main features of the EMS?
3 In what ways did the EMS set the stage for introduction of the euro?
4 How does the idea of an impossible trinity explain the main developments in each of the phases of EMS?
5 What were the motives for a return to the objective of EMU in the late 1980s?
6 Describe the main features of EMU as set out in the Maastricht Treaty.
7 What was the aim of the Maastricht criteria?
8 Describe the main steps in introducing the euro.
9 Should the UK adopt the euro?

Online Learning **Centre**

When you have read this chapter, log on to the Online Learning Centre website at ***www.mcgraw-hill.co.uk/textbooks/senior*** to explore weblinks, chapter-by-chapter test questions, case studies and more online study tools.

Chapter 11

The Eurozone: Structure, Performance and Outlook

Learning Objectives

By the end of this chapter you should be able to understand:

- ✓ What the tasks of the Eurosystem are
- ✓ The discussion about independence and accountability of the ECB
- ✓ The debate about the role of fiscal policy in a monetary union
- ✓ What problems the Stability and Growth Pact has encountered and the attempts at its reform
- ✓ The record of the Eurosystem until the eurozone crisis
- ✓ How the role of the euro in the international financial system is evolving
- ✓ The main features of the international economic crisis
- ✓ The strains imposed on the eurozone by the economic crisis

11.1 Introduction

The first part of this chapter deals with the institutional structure of EMU, indicating the main features of the Eurosystem (ECB and national central banks of the euro area countries), and the difficulty in reconciling the objectives of independence and accountability of the ECB. The debate about the necessity or desirability of fiscal co-ordination in a monetary union is then described before illustrating the vicissitudes of the Stability and Growth Pact. After a brief assessment of the record of EMU and of the problem of ongoing divergences between euro countries, the increasing role of the euro in the international financial system is then assessed. The final part of the chapter provides a brief description of the economic crisis and indicates some of the strains it has imposed on the eurozone.

11.2 The Eurosystem and the European System of Central Banks

The European System of Central Banks (ESCB) is composed of the ECB and the national central banks (NCBs) of all EU member states. A different name, the 'Eurosystem' is the term used to refer to the ECB and NCBs of the countries that have adopted the euro. The NCBs of member states that do not participate in the euro area are members of the ESCB with a special status since they do not take part in decision making with regard to the single monetary policy for the euro area.

The Governing Council is the main decision-making body of the Eurosystem, formulating monetary policies, taking decisions on interest rates, reserve requirements and the amount of liquidity in the system. The Governing Council is composed of the Executive Board and the governors of the NCBs of the euro area member states (see Figure 11.1). The Executive Board has six members (a president, vice-president and four other members).[1]

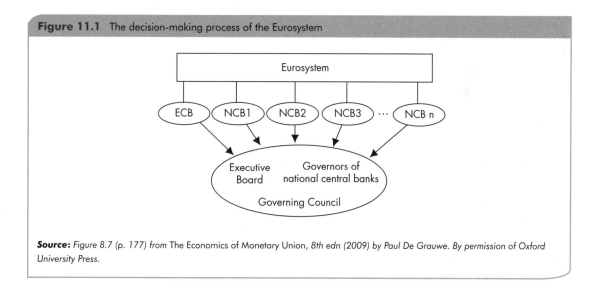

Figure 11.1 The decision-making process of the Eurosystem

Source: Figure 8.7 (p. 177) from The Economics of Monetary Union, 8th edn (2009) by Paul De Grauwe. By permission of Oxford University Press.

As the Governing Council is assumed to be independent of national interests and to reflect the interests of the Eurosystem as a whole, except on certain financial issues, the Maastricht Treaty made no provision for weighting of votes by the size of country.[2] The Governing Council can act by a simple majority of the votes cast by members who are present, but in practice consensus appears the rule and voting is an exception.

---

[1] There was a difference of opinion over the appointment of the first president between the French who favoured their own candidate, Trichet, and the Germans who wanted Duisenberg from the Netherlands. A compromise was reached whereby Duisenberg was appointed but seemed to agree that he stand down after four years on grounds of age. Subsequently, differences arose over the interpretation of this deal, but in November 2003 Trichet became the second president of the ECB. He is due to be replaced by Mario Draghi in 2011.

[2] According to the *Financial Times* (26 November 2010), the system of one nation one vote overrepresents prudent member states. Using an index of prudence based on recent deficits and public debt, prudent countries are found to account for 40 per cent of the eurozone GDP, but 56.3 per cent of national representatives in the Governing Council. This is largely due to the presence of three small but prudent countries: Cyprus, Malta and Slovenia.

The relationship between the ECB and the Eurosystem resembles the federal banking system of Germany or the USA, though in practice it seemed likely that there would be more decentralization. This was probable given the small initial size of the ECB, with a staff of less than 600 (though subsequently it began to expand), compared with the 60,000 working in the NCBs of the euro countries.[3] The number of governors of NCBs also outnumber the Executive Board in the Governing Council. However, De Grauwe (2009a) maintains that the Executive Board occupies a strategic position in the Governing Council, so its proposals are likely to prevail,[4] though with enlargement of the euro area to more of the new member states this situation could change.

In 2003 the European Council agreed a reform of the voting system of the Governing Council. This entailed that the number of NCB governors holding a voting right would be restricted to a maximum of 15. The new system should have come into operation from 2009 when Slovakia joined, but has been postponed until the number of euro members exceeds 18 (probably because certain member states feared a reduction in their voting rights). The reform entails the six members of the Executive Board maintaining permanent voting rights, while the governors of the NCBs would vote on the basis of a rotation system. Countries will be divided into tiers on the basis of the size of their GDP (on which five-sixths of their weighting would be based), and their share in the assets of the monetary financial institutions (determining one-sixth of their weighting). On the basis of the country rankings, larger member states would be entitled to vote more often.[5]

11.3 The tasks of the Eurosystem

The main tasks of the Eurosystem are:[6]

- '*To maintain price stability*'. According to the Treaty this is to be the '*primary objective*'. The ECB has adopted two policy guides to carry out this task: a reference value for monetary policy and an inflation target of 2 per cent or less over the medium term;

- '*To support the general economic policies in the Union*'. This is a secondary function, only to be carried out without prejudice to price stability;

- '*To define and implement the monetary policy of the Union*'. The Governing Council of the ECB was to set interest rates but not decide them unilaterally. The ECB would not normally engage in market operations, and the ESCB would be responsible for implementing monetary policy;

- '*To conduct foreign exchange operations*'. Decisions with regard to the exchange rate are to be taken by Ecofin but subject to consultation with the ECB, the European Parliament and the Commission in order to ensure accountability;

- '*To hold and manage the official foreign reserves of the member states*';

- '*To promote the smooth operation of payments systems*' (which included the introduction of a euro-payments mechanism called TARGET);

- To contribute to '*the smooth conduct of policies pursued by the competent authorities relating to the prudential supervision of credit institutions, and the stability of the financial system*'. However, the ECB

---

[3] Baldwin et al. (2001).

[4] According to the Taylor rule first elaborated by Taylor (1999), central banks will set interest rates on the basis of deviations of inflation and output from their desired levels. De Grauwe (2009a) used this rule to illustrate how, in 2003, the Executive Board was able to prevail in the choice of interest rates reflecting eurozone aggregates, despite the fact that various smaller countries would have preferred higher interest rates.

[5] See Scheller (2006). For example, with 22 countries there would be three tiers with the largest countries voting 80 per cent of the time, the middle tier 73 per cent and the smallest countries voting 50 per cent of the time.

[6] The reference is to Article 127 TFEU (ex Article 105 TEC).

is not responsible for the supervision of banks and financial institutions. This policy has been criticized in that the ECB is likely to obtain much information in carrying out its monetary policy operations, and this information will be wasted if it is not responsible for supervision. Chapter 6 describes the need for reform of supervision and regulation of the financial sector of the EU, and this question is closely linked to the difficulties that the eurozone encountered with the economic crisis (see below).[7]

One of the criticisms of the interpretation of the ECB of its role in its early years was that it seemed to concentrate almost exclusively on the primary priority of price stability, and appeared to pay less attention to the secondary and less well-defined objective of supporting general economic policies, covering goals such as stabilization of the business cycle and financial stability.

The Maastricht Treaty failed to define the primary goal of price stability precisely. It was subsequently defined by the ECB as an annual growth in the harmonized consumer price index of a rate of below 2 per cent in the medium term. It was not clear whether all rates in this range were equally desirable. Various observers, such as Fitoussi and Creel (2003), recommended moving to a more explicit inflation targeting procedure with a point target for inflation in the centre of a symmetrical range. Inflation targeting involves announcing a target, publishing an inflation forecast for a specific time horizon (usually one or two years ahead) and adjusting the interest rate according to the difference between the forecast and the target. In 2003 the Governing Council of the ECB clarified that its aim was to maintain inflation below, but 'close to 2 per cent in the medium term'.

Initially the Eurosystem adopted a two-pillar strategy composed of a monetary pillar, defined as a 'prominent role for money' based on the evolution of monetary aggregates, and a second pillar, which entailed a 'broadly-based assessment' of all other factors influencing inflation. This approach came under considerable criticism partly because most central banks had abandoned the use of monetary aggregates as not being a reliable guide. Moreover, at the time, inflation targeting was becoming popular.

Like the US Federal Reserve and the Central Bank of Japan, the Eurosystem rejected explicit inflation targeting. This was probably not only because it had adopted the money rule strategy of the Bundesbank, though in practice the Bundesbank had effectively abandoned this strategy since the mid-1990s (Wyplosz, 2006), but also to avoid the impression that the ECB acts mechanically. However, in practice the ECB has become what Wyplosz (2006) terms a 'closet' inflation targeter.

In 2003 the strategy of the Eurosystem was reformed, with the order of the two pillars being swapped and their names changed. The Eurosystem also renounced its practice of reviewing its rules for monetary growth each year. The new pillars became:

- Economic analysis aimed at the short to medium run and including everything (such as growth, employment, prices, exchange rates and foreign conditions) apart from monetary aggregates;
- Monetary analysis aimed at the medium to longer term and relying on monetary aggregates, in particular M3.[8]

Various authors have argued that the ECB should take more account of movements in bank credit and assets prices (such as stock prices and property prices) in setting its monetary policy.[9] This would help in providing the ECB with an early warning system of bubbles such as those that emerged in the economic crisis, and the proposals discussed below for a new system of EU economic governance from 2011 seem a step in this direction.

Like most other modern central banks the ECB implements this strategy essentially by the setting of one policy rate of interest, the Main Refinancing Rate, using the instruments of open market operations, standing facilities (credit lines) and minimum reserve requirements.[10]

---

[7] The narrow supervisory function of the ECB may reflect the German system in which the Bundesbank plays a limited role and supervision is carried out by a small number of large, private universal banks. However, the different institutional reality of the EU meant that the system was more open and deregulated.

[8] M3 includes cash in circulation, sight deposits, private sector time deposits, and certificates of deposit.

[9] See, for example, De Grauwe (2009b), Cecchetti et al. (2000) and Bernanke and Gertler (2001).

[10] See Artis (2007) or De Grauwe (2009a) for more detailed discussions of this issue.

The division of responsibility among the ECB, Ecofin, the Eurogroup and national governments is complex. The ECB is to define and implement monetary policy and hold foreign reserves. However, decisions with regard to the exchange rate are to be taken by Ecofin but subject to consultation with the ECB, the European Parliament and the Commission. National governments are to conduct fiscal policy, though, as discussed below, subject to the constraints of the Stability and Growth Pact.

The method of representing the euro countries on the international scene was decided at the Vienna European Council of December 1998. The president of the Ecofin was to participate in meetings of the G8, but if the president were from a non-euro state, representation would be by the president of the Eurogroup assisted by the Commission. The Council acting on a proposal from the Commission and consulting the ECB can take 'appropriate measures to ensure unified representation in international financial institutions and conferences' (Article 138 TFEU).

11.4 The independence and accountability of the European Central Bank

One of the main debates over the statute of the ECB centred on the issue of how far that bank should be independent and insulated from political pressure, or the extent to which it should be politically accountable.

France and some members of the UK government favoured the idea of a politically accountable bank that could act directly in the name of the EU countries and would be answerable to the governments of the member states. It was argued that certain functions of the ECB had important implications for the economic performance of the member states and, in particular, for politically sensitive issues such as unemployment. The activities of the bank should therefore be subject to adequate political control, and transparency was considered essential.

Germany, in contrast, wanted an independent bank modelled as far as possible on the Bundesbank. The theoretical justification for this type of institution draws on the economic literature on credibility (see Chapter 9), which takes for granted the technical ability of a central bank to pursue an anti-inflationary policy and concentrates instead on the political will of governments to do so. It was feared that a political bank would be open to political pressure to reflate, and so would be 'soft' on inflation.

What institutional arrangements can be used to meet the credibility constraint while at the same time ensuring that the decision-making process is democratically accountable?

In a democracy, politicians are elected on the basis of a certain mandate, but once in power have a certain independence to carry out policies. Ultimately, however, their accountability is ensured by having to face the electorate again. There may be a second phase in this process in that the politicians may delegate authority for a particular policy to a specialized agency. The politician will indicate the objectives and means of achieving them, but will have to monitor and oversee the activities of the agency to ensure that the objectives are realized. The Public Choice or New Political Economy literature sometimes makes use of the terms 'principal' and 'agent' to analyse this relationship. The principal delegates responsibility to the agent, but ultimately has to ensure the accountability of the agent.

In the case of the ECB the initial principals were the national governments of member states operating through the European Council and Council of Ministers to decide on the objectives, rules and institutional arrangements of EMU. They delegated responsibility for monetary authority to an agent (the ECB), and to meet the credibility constraint institutional arrangements were introduced to ensure that the principal could not exert political pressure on the agent. In other words, according to Giavazzi and Pagano (1988), there was an advantage in 'tying the hands' of the principal to avoid political interference. A series of institutional arrangements was also introduced to ensure the accountability and transparency of the agent, and the European Parliament was given a key role in this process.

In order to meet the credibility constraint the treaties attempt to ring-fence the independence of ECB by:

■ stipulating that the ECB shall not *'seek or take instructions from Union institutions, bodies, offices or agencies, from any government of a Member State or from any other body'* (Article 130 TFEU);

- forbidding the ECB to lend to *'Union institutions, bodies, offices or agencies, central governments, regional, local or other public authorities …'* (Article 123 TFEU), though, as explained below, interpretation of this prohibition became the subject of controversy during the economic crisis;

- requiring that members of its Executive Board be appointed for eight-year non-renewable terms by the heads of government of the euro area following consultation by the European Parliament and Governing Council (Article 283 TFEU).

At least on paper, the ECB appears one of the most independent central banks in the world.

With regard to accountability, the president of the ECB has to present an annual report to the European Parliament (EP),[11] the EP can hold a debate on that basis, and relevant committees can hear the ECB Executive Board. The European Council has to consult the EP about nominations to the Executive Board. However, though the power of the EP has been increasing, its effective control of the ECB is limited, and while the US Congress can change the statutes of the Federal Reserve by a simple majority vote, in the case of the ECB this requires a revision of the treaties.

Accountability is also weakened by the fact that the task of the ECB *'to support the general economic policies in the Union'* is not well defined, and the ECB tends to concentrate on its primary task of price stability. This was the basis of the attacks by the French president, Nicolas Sarkozy, who maintained that the ECB should give more weight to other general economic policies such as employment and growth (see also Chapter 17).

Transparency can play an important role in ensuring accountability. Though detailed minutes of the meetings of the Governing Council are not made public, press conferences are held immediately afterwards. The ECB has made a considerable effort to explain its decisions, and publishes widely about its positions (in, for instance, its *Monthly Bulletin*, see also Box 11.1).

Box 11.1

Communication by the ECB

During the early years of the ECB when Wim Duisenberg was president, the ECB was sometimes criticized for its haphazard communication style. In the first years of President Trichet, a traffic light system of code words signalling a rise in interest rates came into operation. Two months ahead of a rate rise President Trichet would announce that the ECB would 'monitor very carefully' inflation risks. The term 'strong vigilance' indicated a rate rise a month later. In 2007, with the economic slowdown, Trichet made it clear that 'monitor very carefully' would no longer be used. The use of such key words was useful during a phase of raising interest rates in times of economic growth, but less so with persistent low interest rates (of 1 per cent from May 2009 until April 2011). In March 2011 Trichet again referred to 'strong vigilance' being warranted to keep price expectations under control, and soon after rates were increased.

11.5 Fiscal policy in a monetary union

In order to understand the role of fiscal policy in a monetary union it is useful to return to the example of the asymmetric shock described in Chapter 9.[12] With the wine scare there is a fall in output and an increase in unemployment in France. The opposite occurs in Germany. With a common federal budget, the tax contributions will fall and unemployment benefits will rise in France. The German tax

---

[11] Article 284 TFEU.

[12] The analysis can also be presented using the framework of aggregate supply and aggregate demand curves presented in Appendix 2 to Chapter 9. According to early versions of the theory, fiscal policy could be used to offset the shift in the aggregate demand curve.

contributions will rise and unemployment benefit payments will fall, so the net effect is a transfer to France through the federal budget.[13]

What, however, would occur if there were no federal budget? The lower taxes and higher benefit payments in France will lead to an increased government deficit that will have to be covered by borrowing. In Germany, higher taxes and lower unemployment payments will reduce the deficit or increase the government surplus. With freedom of capital movement, the higher savings of Germany could cover the increased borrowing requirement of France.

The lessons of traditional optimal currency theory suggest either:

- that it is preferable to have a large enough federal budget to compensate for the asymmetric shock; or, if this is impossible;

- that fiscal policy should be used in a flexible way to compensate for the asymmetric shock (in this case with an increased deficit in France).

However, in the example above, the use of a government deficit by France to accommodate the negative demand shock will lead to an increase in indebtedness. This increase in debt will have to be serviced in future, and this will imply higher taxes or lower spending. Continued use of fiscal policy to accommodate negative shocks will therefore run into a problem of sustainability.[14]

Distinction also has to be made between 'automatic stabilizers' and discretionary fiscal policy. As in the case described above, when there is a slowdown in the economy, automatic stabilizers come into play, with taxes falling and spending rising, increasing the government deficit. In this way fiscal policy will work in a counter-cyclical way. Discretionary fiscal policy involves explicit attempts by government to change the amount of taxes and spending. However, discretionary changes in fiscal policy run into the long and complex budgetary process, with compromises having to be reached and approved by parliament over the various changes in spending and taxes. As a result, there may be lags and uncertainties in the application of discretionary fiscal policy.[15] Moreover, during the budgetary process the government is also likely to be subject to intense lobbying activity with pressure to increase spending and cut taxes.[16] In consequence the budgetary process generally entails a bias in favour of deficits.

What are the implications for fiscal policy in a monetary union? In general the literature justifies co-ordination of fiscal policy as being necessary in a monetary union to deal with interdependencies or spillovers. Baldwin and Wyplosz (2009) identify various forms of spillovers:[17]

- **Spillovers associated with excessive deficits.** As argued above, persistent deficits can lead to a problem of sustainability of debt. If, on international financial markets, the public deficit of a member country is judged unsustainable, this could lead to instability on financial markets with risk of contagion and speculation against other countries considered weaker (see the section on the economic crisis and the eurozone below), and possibly lack of confidence in the euro and capital outflows. There is also the risk of default by a country if its debt becomes unsustainable. This was recognized by the Maastricht Treaty, which contained a no bail-out clause, expressly forbidding the ECB to bail out a member state (as described above, now Article 123 TFEU).

---

[13] This account assumes either that the asymmetric shock is temporary, or, if the shock is permanent, that the transfer should only be used in a temporary way to avoid hindering the necessary adjustment of wages and prices and/or labour movement.

[14] Reinhart and Rogoff (2009) have shown that high levels of debt (over 90 per cent) are associated with slower growth.

[15] As any macroeconomic textbook explains, the debate about the effectiveness of fiscal policy is at the heart of the differences between Keynesian and neo-classical economists. There have been various challenges to the Keynesian view that an active fiscal policy can stabilize economic fluctuations. Barro (1974), for example, picked up an argument first noted by David Ricardo, which maintains that taxpayers may not spend debt-financed transfers as they expect higher taxation in the future to finance the debt.

[16] The New Political Economy literature discussed in Chapter 4 provides insights into this lobbying process. See Mueller (2003) for a discussion of the political business cycle.

[17] See Beetsma et al. (2005) for an attempt to quantify these spillovers.

According to McKinnon (1996), the risk of a debt default increases in a monetary union as the option of inflation and devaluation is not available to a country.

- **Cyclical income spillovers.** Business cycles may be transmitted through exports and imports. For example, if a country is in an expansionary phase, it is likely to import more, and this will have a knock-on effect on the country from which it is importing. If the business cycles of the two countries are synchronized and both adopt expansionary fiscal measures, in the absence of co-ordination between the two countries the measures may be excessive. If cycles are not synchronized, an expansionary fiscal policy in a country with a recession may contribute to overheating in the country with a boom.
- **Borrowing cost spillovers.** An increased deficit requires higher government spending and this may increase interest rates in the euro area.

In addition to dealing with spillovers, a further argument in favour of some form of co-ordination of fiscal policy in a monetary union is that it might provide a scapegoat to contain the requests of lobbies that push in the direction of a deficit bias. This argument is likely to be particularly strong in countries with weak political institutions.

Against such views, co-ordination of fiscal policies may involve a sacrifice of sovereignty. Member states may argue that tax and spending decisions are better taken at the national level to reflect the preferences of citizens, and where understanding of the issues involved may also be better.[18] The principle of subsidiarity (see Chapter 1) may also require decisions to be taken at a more decentralized level.

The EU solution to the question of fiscal policy was for the member states to retain responsibility, subject to detailed rules and procedures, at least in theory, through the Stability and Growth Pact.

11.6 The Stability and Growth Pact

In line with the logic of the convergence criteria for euro membership, Article 104 of the Maastricht Treaty required countries to avoid excessive deficits, and outlined an excessive deficit procedure. The details of the procedure were to be worked out later, and this took place when the Stability and Growth Pact (SGP) was agreed at the Dublin Council of 1996 and confirmed at Amsterdam in 1997.

According to the initial version of the Pact, budget deficits would be limited to 3 per cent of GDP, except if the country experienced a fall in GDP of over 2 per cent. Countries were invited to strive for a 'close to balanced budget', so that the margin between 0 and –3 per cent could be used for counter-cyclical policies in times of economic downturn. The excessive deficit procedure was designed to ensure conformity with the Stability and Growth Pact. If the Council decides that a country has an excessive deficit and insufficient action has been taken, sanctions can be imposed.[19] European Union countries outside the eurozone must keep their deficits below 3 per cent, but they are not subject to disciplinary proceedings should they break the Pact.

The SGP was largely introduced in response to German beliefs about the need to create a system that would ensure co-ordination of budgetary policies (Heipertz and Verdun, 2010). It was felt

---

[18] See the discussion on fiscal federalism in Chapter 12, which deals with the problem of the 'appropriate' level (local, regional, national or EU) for taking decisions.

[19] The country in question would have to make a non-interest-bearing deposit of 0.2 per cent of GDP plus 0.1 per cent for each point of the excess deficit, up to a maximum deposit of 0.5 per cent of GDP. The deposit would be returned when the deficit falls below 3 per cent of GDP, but if the excess deficit lasts for over two years the deposit could become a fine. If a country deviates substantially from its path, the Council could issue a recommendation to bring the country back on track.

that the Pact could encourage consolidation of fiscal policy, would help to avoid possible negative effects of fiscal spillovers between increasingly interdependent countries and would prevent excessive deficits undermining the independence of the ECB (despite the no bail-out clause).

With the slowdown of the EU economy from 2002, the SGP came under attack for being excessively rigid (relying on rather arbitrary numbers), or 'stupid' in the words of the then Commission president Romano Prodi.[20] By late 2002 the excessive deficit procedure had been initiated for Portugal, France and Germany. Portugal subsequently brought its deficit below the ceiling, but France and Germany were expected to break the Pact for the third year running in 2004. Germany announced measures to bring the deficit below 3 per cent, though the Commission considered these inadequate. The German finance minister, Hans Eichel, maintained that Germany had implemented the Commission's recommendations but only failed to respect the fiscal ceiling because exogenous factors had turned out to be less favourable than expected with the sluggish economy.

The Commission considered that it was legally obliged to move to the next stage in the procedure (that is, nearer to potential sanctions), but Germany, supported by France, favoured revising the previous recommendations (Beetsma and Oksanen, 2008; Heipertz and Verdun, 2010). This dispute caused deadlock in the Council as a qualified majority under the correct legal procedure could not be found for a decision. In November 2003 the EU finance ministers adopted 'conclusions' on their own initiative, that is, political declarations that were not legally binding and which effectively changed the text of the original Commission recommendations. A qualified majority in the Council endorsed these conclusions, and the sanctions mechanism of the Pact against France and Germany was declared to be in abeyance.

The ECB warned that this *de facto* suspension of the Pact could lead to 'serious dangers', including, higher interest rates. Smaller countries that had introduced fiscal consolidation (notably Austria, Finland, the Netherlands, Sweden and Denmark) attacked the failure of the two larger member states to respect the fiscal constraints.

In 2004 Commissioner for Monetary Affairs Pedro Solbes took the Council to the Court of Justice for not respecting the Treaty (and, in particular Article 104 TEC relating to the excessive deficit procedure). In July 2004 the Court ruled that the Council can indeed amend recommendations at a later stage, provided the Commission first puts an amended recommendation on the table (see Heipertz and Verdun (2010) for a detailed account of this ruling). The Court maintained that responsibility for enforcing budgetary discipline lies essentially with the Council, but that decisions under the excessive deficit procedure require a prior Commission recommendation. In adopting the November 2003 conclusions, the Council had operated in a legal void and had made a procedural error. Thus under the original SGP, initiating a revision was possible, and if the Commission did so, the Council could amend the recommendation by qualified majority. According to Oksanen (2010), this legal dispute undermined the credibility of the SGP because it allowed recommendations to be revised and deadlines for correcting excessive deficits to be extended if adverse economic events occurred.

In 2005 the Ecofin agreed on a reform of the SGP. The ceilings of 3 per cent for the budget deficit and 60 per cent for public debt were maintained, but the decision to declare a country in excessive deficit was to rely on a series of parameters, including the behaviour of the cyclically adjusted budget, the level of debt, the duration of the slow growth period, and the possibility that the deficit is related to productivity-enhancing procedures.

By October 2010 only three EU countries were not in violation of the excessive deficit procedure, having fiscal deficits below 3 per cent of GDP: Sweden, Luxembourg and Estonia (see also Table 11.1).

As explained below, in the context of the reform of EU economic governance, the debate about revision of the SGP moved to centre stage from late 2010.

---

[20] In a speech on 18 October 2002.

Table 11.1 Public deficit and debt in the EU, 2009

	Government deficit/surplus (% GDP)	Government debt (% GDP)		Government deficit/surplus (% GDP)	Government debt (% GDP)
BE	−6.0	96.7	LU	−0.7	14.5
BG	−4.7	14.8	HU	−4.4	78.3
CZ	−5.8	35.4	MA	−3.8	69.1
DK	−2.7	41.6	NL	−5.4	60.9
DE	−3.0	73.2	AU	−3.5	66.5
EE	−1.7	7.2	PL	−7.2	51.0
IE	−14.4	64.0	PT	−9.3	76.8
EL	−15.4	115.1	RO	−8.6	23.7
ES	−11.1	53.2	SL	−5.8	35.9
FR	−7.5	77.6	SK	−7.9	35.7
IT	−5.3	115.8	FI	−2.5	44.0
CY	−6.0	56.2	SW	−0.9	42.3
LT	−10.2	36.1	UK	−11.4	68.1
LI	−9.2	29.3			

Source: Eurostat, http://epp.eurostat.ec.europa.eu/cache/ITY_PUBLIC/2-22042010-BP/EN/2-22042010-BP-EN.PDF (accessed 24 March 2011), © European Union, 2011.

11.7 The first decade of the Eurosystem

In its early years the Eurosystem was relatively successful in realizing its primary objective of price stability, partly because of the efforts of its member states to meet the Maastricht criteria. Between 1999 and 2008 the average inflation rate in the eurozone was 2.2 per cent. The higher inflation in 2000–01 (see Figure 11.2) was probably due to an increase in energy prices, worsened by depreciation of the euro. The steep rise in inflation in 2007, before its dramatic fall, reflects the asset bubble, which subsequently burst (see the discussion of the economic crisis below).

Although at times inflation has been above the ceiling of 2 per cent, this is a target for the medium term. Official inflation statistics probably overestimate inflation as they fail to take full account of quality improvements. A low (rather than zero) level of inflation may permit more flexible adjustment of real wages.

Between 2001 and 2009 growth was relatively low, and generally worse than US performance (see Figure 11.3). The explanation probably lies largely in the structural weaknesses of the EU economy (see Chapter 7), and perhaps not surprisingly the ECB denied that the cause was an over-restrictive monetary policy stance. Although average growth was slow in the eurozone and EU(27), in some countries (such as Ireland, Luxembourg, Greece, Spain and Finland before the crisis) it was relatively high.

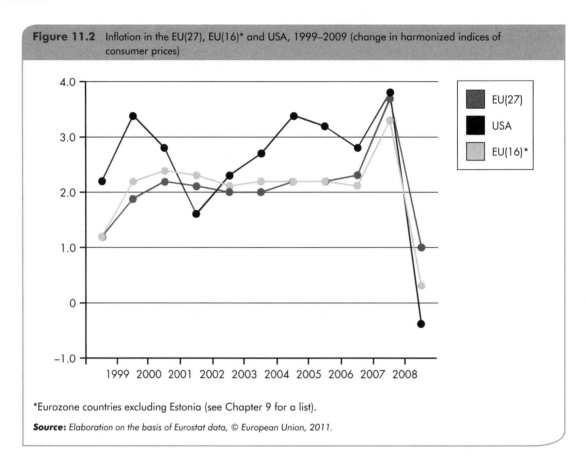

Figure 11.2 Inflation in the EU(27), EU(16)* and USA, 1999–2009 (change in harmonized indices of consumer prices)

*Eurozone countries excluding Estonia (see Chapter 9 for a list).

Source: Elaboration on the basis of Eurostat data, © European Union, 2011.

The movements of the euro in its early years defied the predictions of many observers, with an initial fall,[21] followed by a substantial rise against the dollar after 2002 (when Sarkozy, among others, accused the euro system of allowing overvaluation of the euro to the detriment of EU exporters). Further falls took place in 2008 and in 2010. The Eurosystem made it clear at the start that it would not take responsibility for the exchange rate, and that blind neglect was the best policy, but at times intervened (such as in 2000) to support the euro.

The optimal currency area theory suggests that, to be sustainable, a monetary union such as the eurozone should not experience too much divergence of major economic variables. However, as Figures 11.4 to 11.6 (and the tables for unemployment in Chapter 2) illustrate, there were differences between the eurozone member states.

The eurozone countries were characterized by divergences with respect to:

- public sector deficits, and thereby public debt levels (see Table 11.1 above);

- private sector deficits (and therefore private debt levels). The private sector balance is taken to be indicated by the sum of net borrowing by households and the non-financial corporate sector; and

- international competitiveness, and consequently current account deficits and foreign debts.

---

[21] Various explanations of the initial weakness of the euro were given: the faster productivity increase and more flexible markets of the USA; a few untimely statements by the first ECB president, Duisenberg; capital outflows from the EU; and the untested and cumbersome nature of EMU institutions. Some observers have also argued that market nervousness about EU enlargement also contributed to the weakening of the euro. Subsequently the strength of the euro was said to reflect factors such as international portfolio adjustment (Della Posta, 2006), relatively high interest rates in the eurozone and falling confidence in the dollar (spurred also by the large US current account and fiscal deficits).

Figure 11.3 Growth in the EU, euro area* and the USA, 1999–2009 (real GDP growth rate)

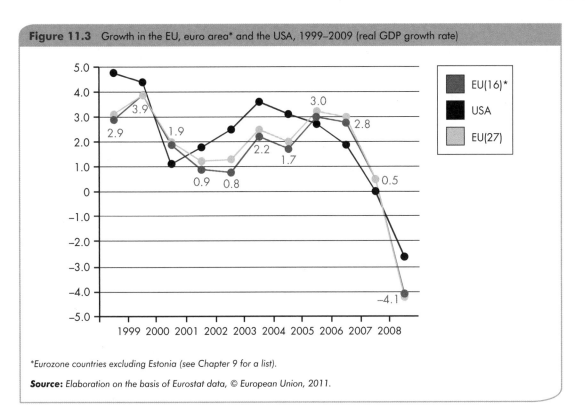

*Eurozone countries excluding Estonia (see Chapter 9 for a list).

Source: Elaboration on the basis of Eurostat data, © European Union, 2011.

Figure 11.4 Inflation in the EU, 2009

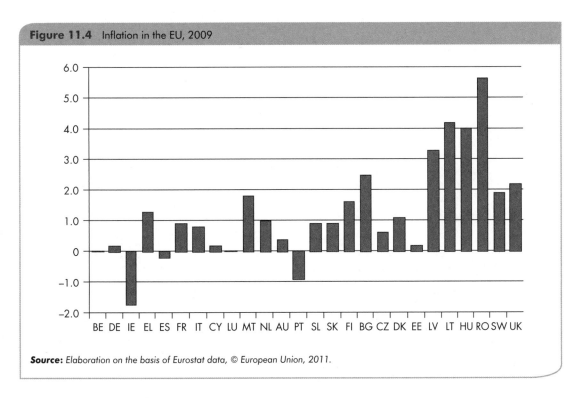

Source: Elaboration on the basis of Eurostat data, © European Union, 2011.

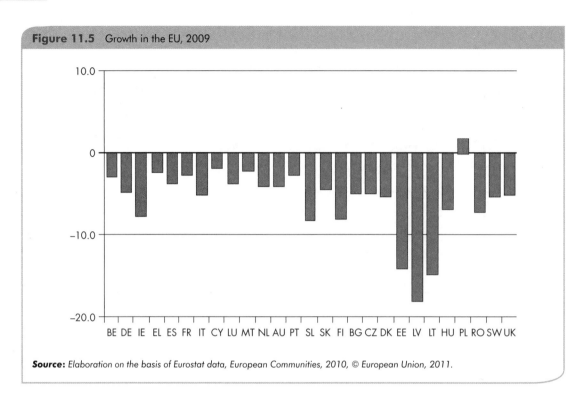

Figure 11.5   Growth in the EU, 2009

Source: Elaboration on the basis of Eurostat data, European Communities, 2010, © European Union, 2011.

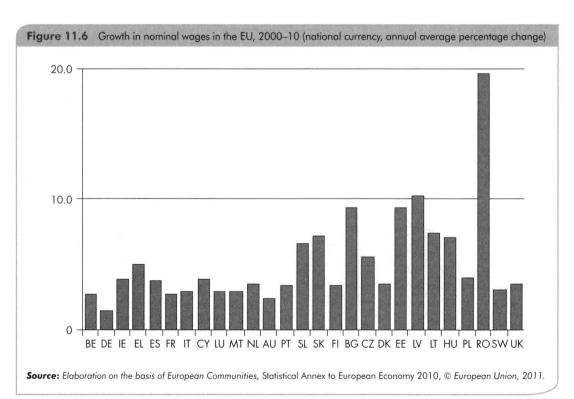

Figure 11.6   Growth in nominal wages in the EU, 2000–10 (national currency, annual average percentage change)

Source: Elaboration on the basis of European Communities, Statistical Annex to European Economy 2010, © European Union, 2011.

In practice when a problem initiates in one sector it is transmitted to others, and generally major difficulties end up on the books of the public sector. As will be explained below in the section on the economic crisis and the eurozone, initially public debt was the main problem for Greece, though a private deficit and loss of international competitiveness added to the weakness (Nomura, 2011). Long-term loss of competitiveness and structural problems accompanied public and private deficit issues in Portugal.

In Ireland and Spain private sector indebtedness was 236 per cent and 211 per cent of GDP respectively in 2009, fuelled by cheap credit, encouraged by the banking sector, and resulting in old-fashioned property bubbles.[22] Public indebtedness subsequently became a problem also thanks to private indebtedness in these two countries.

The level of public deficit and debt was high in Italy (see Table 11.1 above), but private indebtedness was relatively low (101 per cent of GDP in 2007 though rising slightly subsequently).

With regard to competitiveness, some of the more vulnerable Mediterranean countries had made huge efforts to qualify for joining the euro, but subsequently the pace of structural reform of their economies slowed. During the 1990s wage inflation led to loss of competitiveness in Portugal, Ireland, Italy, Greece and Spain.[23] In contrast, though the initial conversion rate of the D-mark appears to have been overvalued, Germany slowly managed to regain competitiveness by keeping wage growth below consumer price inflation (see also Figure 11.6 above).

The so-called imbalances were an ongoing source of tension in the eurozone: countries such as Greece and Spain had large current account deficits (though these fell after 2007), while others such as Germany had large surpluses, reflecting diverging competitiveness. While a country such as Greece has to reform its labour market to bring about adjustments in real wages, it was argued that Germany should also increase its long stagnant domestic consumption (an unlikely change requiring a shift in long-term patterns of behaviour). In an interview with the *Financial Times* of 14 March 2010, French finance minister Christine Lagarde called on 'those with surpluses to do a little something' to increase consumption to help weaker eurozone countries to boost exports and improve their finances, a suggestion that found little support in Germany.

11.8   The euro in the international financial system

There has been much speculation about future relations between the euro and the dollar, and whether the euro represents a challenge to the dollar in the international financial system. However, the extent to which the euro can challenge the dollar as an international currency will depend on how far the money and securities markets of the EU become effectively integrated, and on confidence in the euro as a stable currency. According to ECB (2010) volatile developments in international markets during the economic crisis had relatively limited impact on currency preferences, and the euro remained the second most important currency globally after the dollar.

The international role of money as a medium of exchange means that it is used to invoice trade. According to ECB (2010) the use of the euro in settlement and/or invoicing of merchandise exports of euro countries to non-euro area countries in 2009 varied between 97.3 per cent for Slovakia and 11.8 per cent for Cyprus. For merchandise imports it ranged between 86.3 per cent for Slovakia and 2.5 per cent for Cyprus.[24] Widespread use of the dollar in invoicing in international trade seems likely to continue, in particular in oil and commodity markets.

Transactions on international financial markets often take place in a vehicle currency to reduce the number of bilateral trades between currencies. Several euro area neighbouring

---

[22] The statistics here are taken from Nomura (2011). Private indebtedness also rose to 187 per cent of GDP for Portugal in 2009.

[23] These are sometimes called the 'PIGS', and though the 'I' initially indicated Ireland, subsequently it was often taken to refer to Italy.

[24] The relatively large share of trade with the UK, and the high percentage of petroleum and petroleum-based products in its trade, largely explain the case of Cyprus.

countries (including non-euro EU member states, candidate countries and Russia) continued to intervene frequently on foreign exchange markets using the euro. ECB (2010) estimated that the euro share of daily foreign exchange trading through Continuous Link Settlement amounted to 42.8 per cent in 2009 (of a total of 200 per cent as the two currencies involved are counted separately).

All central banks hold foreign exchange reserves to back their currency and, if necessary, intervene on foreign exchange markets. In 1997, 57 per cent of all official foreign exchange reserves were held in dollars, with a further 20 per cent being held in EU currencies and the ECU, and about 4.9 per cent in yen (IMF, 1998). The time horizon over which a shift into using the euro might occur is extremely uncertain as inertia is an important force, and, for example, the pound sterling continued to play an important role as a reserve currency long after the UK's decline as a hegemonic power.[25] According to ECB (2010), in December 2009 the share of the euro in global international foreign exchange reserves was 27.3 per cent, while that of the dollar was 62.1 per cent of an estimated total of about $8,200 billion.

The ECB defines international debt securities as long-term securities such as notes and bonds, and short-term securities such as money market instruments, and makes a distinction between a narrow measure of just international transactions, and a wider 'global' measure of domestic and international debt. Considering the narrower measure of just international debt securities, according to ECB (2010), the share denominated in euro amounted to $3,248 billion at the end of 2009, or 31.4 per cent of the total (slightly down from a peak in 2005, but up from about 23 per cent in 1999), whereas that denominated in US dollars was 38 per cent. If domestic as well as international debt is considered the respective shares were 30 per cent for the euro and almost 46 per cent for the dollar.

According to ECB (2010), in 2009 the euro accounted for 20.3 per cent of cross-border loans and 22.0 of cross-border deposits to non-financial firms and households.

As shown in Box 11.2, the euro also acts as an anchor to which other countries may tie their currency. Apart from the case of ERM II, this link is based on a unilateral decision and often reflects geographical or historical ties.

A foreign currency may sometimes be used as a parallel currency, operating alongside national money in a role of currency and asset substitution. Though it is difficult to obtain reliable data, according to ECB (2010), about 20–25 per cent of euro banks notes were circulating outside the euro area, in particular in neighbouring countries.

As explained in Chapter 9, aside from the prestige, the financial gains of having an international currency are relatively small. About half of all dollars are held outside the USA but the benefit of these expatriate dollars to the USA is only about 3 per cent of GDP (Baldwin and Wyplosz, 2009).

11.9 The economic crisis from 2007

The economic crisis, with turmoil on international financial markets from 2007,[26] and the sharpest drop in economic activity since the Second World War in 2008, is frequently likened the to the Great Depression of the 1930s. Much of the literature dates the origin of the crisis to the bursting of the real estate bubble in the USA in 2007 when higher interest rates and failure of house prices to rise as

---

[25] See Kindleberger (1984) and Eichengreen (1989).

[26] The rise in international economic uncertainty had begun earlier. A major setback in terms of promoting the creation of a fully fledged 'knowledge-based economy' was the series of technology, media and telecoms (TMT) stock crashes that occurred between March 2000 and late 2002 and had a massive impact on investors' confidence around the world. Add to this the string of accounting scandals (Worldcom, Enron and so on) and the resulting stringent regulatory environment in major countries. The overall impact was to undermine confidence in the robustness of Western economies.

Box 11.2

Currency arrangements of non-euro EU member states, candidate and potential candidate countries, and other countries linked to the euro

- ERM II membership: Denmark, Latvia, Lithuania.

- Euro-based currency boards: Bosnia and Herzegovina, Bulgaria.

- Managed floating based on the euro: Croatia, FYR Macedonia, Romania, Serbia, the CFA franc zone (Communauté Financière Africaine using the West African CFA franc or the Central African CFA franc),* French overseas territories (French Polynesia, New Caledonia, Wallis and Fortuna) , Cape Verde, Comoros, São Tomé e Principé;

- Euroization: Kosovo, Montenegro,[†] the European microstates and French territorial communities.

- Managed floating based on the Special Drawing Right (SDR) or other currency baskets in which the euro is included: Algeria, Azerbaijan, Botswana, Fiji, Kuwait, Libya, Morocco, Russian Federation, Samoa, Singapore, Syria, Tunisia, Vanuatu.

Pro memoria: independent floating by EU members, and potential and actual EU candidates: Czech Republic, Hungary, Poland, Sweden, UK, Albania, Turkey.

Source: *Adapted from ECB (2010), pp. 29–30, © European Union, 2011.*

*This includes countries belonging to the Central African Economic and Monetary Community and the West African Economic and Monetary Union.

[†]In October 2007 Ecofin announced that unilateral euroization on the part of Montenegro was not compatible with the EC Treaty, which envisages eventual adoption of the euro as the endpoint of a convergence process in a multilateral framework.

expected led to a dramatic increase in default rates in the US subprime mortgage market.[27] The prices of securities linked to US real estate prices plummeted, causing distress in global financial markets. What initially appeared to be primarily a US problem soon spread more widely as a result of complex linkages among international financial markets, and led in late 2008 to fears of meltdown of the international financial system.

The aim in this section is to provide a very brief outline of the main events in this crisis as it shaped many developments in the EU, including the introduction of new measures to improve financial supervision and regulation (see Chapter 6), and reinforced programmes to increase growth and employment (see Chapter 7) as well as EMU.

The literature generally indicates various factors as contributing to the rapid degeneration of the situation of the international financial system from 2007.[28] A long period of low real interest rates, easy credit conditions and increases in asset prices led to a credit boom in the USA and certain other

---

[26] The rise in international economic uncertainty had begun earlier. A major setback in terms of promoting the creation of a fully fledged 'knowledge-based economy' was the series of technology, media and telecoms (TMT) stock crashes that occurred between March 2000 and late 2002 and had a massive impact on investors' confidence around the world. Add to this the string of accounting scandals (Worldcom, Enron and so on) and the resulting stringent regulatory environment in major countries. The overall impact was to undermine confidence in the robustness of Western economies.

[27] The term subprime refers to the quality of the borrowers, who have a poor credit history and greater risk of default than 'prime' borrowers. See Kindleberger (2000) or Minsky (1980) for a typology of crises

[28] The literature is vast and growing rapidly. See, for example, BIS (2009, 2010), Brunnermeier (2009), European Commission (2009d), IMF (2010a, b), the OECD (2010), Vercelli (2010), Nomura (2011) and various issues of the *Financial Times* (where Martin Wolf, in particular, attaches much importance to the problem of global imbalances). See http://www.ft.com/comment/columnists/martinwolf (accessed 10 February 2011).

developed countries, with a dramatic rise in purchases of houses and consumer durables. Protracted low returns on interest rates encouraged the financial sector to take on higher risks with the aim of increasing returns and remaining profitable. At the same time, 'global imbalances' contributed to overheating of the US financial system, with large end persistent current US account deficits (see Table 1.2 in Chapter 1) being accompanied by huge capital inflows from capital-poor emerging countries. At the same time, China was running a huge surplus and was accused of keeping its currency low to promote exports.

At a microeconomic level, factors contributing to the crisis include: the transformation of the financial sector; defects in the techniques for measuring and managing risk; flawed incentives and weaknesses in corporate governance; and failures of the regulatory system.[29]

The subprime mortgage crisis was preceded by the rapid growth of the weight of the financial sector in the US economy and a qualitative as well as quantitative change in the financial system (Vercelli, 2010). The increasing importance of new types of institutions belonging to a 'shadow banking system' (such as hedge funds) rendered it easier to move activities outside the scope of supervision and regulation by the authorities.

Financial innovation, with the development of new types of instrument, many of which were linked to US mortgage payments and housing prices increased the vulnerability of the system.[30] There was little experience of assessing the risk of these instruments, or of regulating them. There was a tendency to underestimate risk, partly because before the crisis there had been a prolonged period of relative stability with low volatility of financial markets, and models often failed to take adequate account of infrequent events.[31] There was also a widespread failure to realize how linkages between financial instruments could increase systemic risk.

With regard to incentives, consumers and investors could not cope with the complexity and opacity of the system and were unable to safeguard their own interests. Financial institutions aimed at raising returns and this encouraged them to accumulate risk and increase leverage. Compensation of asset managers was often linked to short-term returns and the volume of affairs. Even if managers of financial institutions suspected an asset bubble, fear of sparking a chain reaction discouraged withdrawal of funds. Rating agencies often found it difficult to evaluate complex structured products, but were reluctant to pass up business, and at times had to rely on the risk management assessment of their clients. Rating agencies were also often paid by those being assessed, leading to distorted incentives and conflict of interest. A widespread belief in the efficiency of markets and in market discipline encouraged some of the authorities at the centre of the global financial system to adopt an extremely light legislative touch.

---

[29] See the annual reports of the Bank for International Settlements (BIS, 2009, 2010) for a discussion of these various causes.

[30] The increasing use of securitization or the transformation of non-traded assets and liabilities into traded securities entailed transformation from a banking model of 'originate and hold' to one of 'originate and distribute'. Securities such as mortgage-based securities (MBS), which involved bundling mortgages of increasingly high risk, played a key role in transmitting the housing crisis to financial markets. Collateralized debt obligations (CDOs) involved forming a diversified portfolio of mortgages, other types of loan, government bonds etc. The portfolios were then divided into 'tranches' and sold to investors with differing propensity for risk. Those buying tranches and bonds could also cover themselves by buying credit default swaps (CDSs), or contracts to insure against the default of a particular bond or tranche. In practice the opacity and complexity of these securities often meant that the market failed to price them accurately, and underestimated their systemic risk. The US authorities allowed the self-regulation of this over-the-counter 'derivatives' market. In 2003 Warren Buffett, the 'Sage of Omaha' or famous economic commentator, referred to these derivatives as 'weapons of mass destruction'. See Brunnermeier (2009) for a description of these instruments, and the risks involved.

[31] Models often assumed that the distribution of returns on many different assets was normal and so had thin tails. As Taleb (2010) pointed out, what was needed was 'black swan rationalisation' with adequate account being taken of high impact rare developments ('fat tails').

Box 11.3 sets out key dates in the evolution of the economic crisis, while Box 11.4 (see next section) deals with events from 2010 in the eurozone crisis. Widespread defaults in the US subprime market from June 2007 triggered disruption in interbank markets from August 2007 (with banks being reluctant or unable to lend to each other). Bank losses and write-downs in asset prices led to growing risks of outright bank failures. In March 2008 the investment bank Bear Stearns ran into a severe liquidity crisis, and the US authorities stepped in to facilitate its takeover by JPMorgan Chase.

After a mild recession and continuing difficulties in the interbank and US mortgage markets in the following months, the situation deteriorated rapidly following the default by the large US investment bank Lehman Brothers on 15 September 2008. The solvency of large parts of the global financial system seemed at stake, and the US government stepped in to rescue the largest US insurance company, AIG (American Insurance Group), the following day.

The crisis of confidence quickly spread across markets and countries, leading to intervention on an unprecedented scale by the USA and other governments. Some major financial institutions in both the EU and USA were allowed to fail, but others were taken over under duress, or were nationalized (see Box 11.3 for specific examples). Major central banks announced co-ordinated measures to address shortages in US dollar short-term lending and the USA presented early proposals of a $700 billion package to take on troubled assets of financial institutions.

By October 2008, despite the default of the three main Icelandic banks, there were signs that the unprecedented a co-ordinated intervention across countries was beginning to stem the crisis of confidence. On 8 October six central banks, including the ECB, the Federal Reserve and the Bank of

Box 11.3

Key dates in the international economic crisis

2007

9 August	Problems in the US mortgage market spill over into the interbank market.
12 December	Central banks in five main currency areas announce measures to ease problems in short-term funding markets.

2008

22 February	UK bank, Northern Rock, is nationalized.
16 March	JPMorgan Chase agrees to purchase Bear Stearns in a transaction facilitated by the US authorities.
4 June	US government announces support measures for mortgage finance agencies Freddy Mac and Fannie Mae.
7 September	US government formally takes control of Freddy Mac and Fannie Mae.
15 September	Default by Lehman Brothers.
16 September	US government steps in to support AIG.
18 September	The UK bank HBOS is forced into a government-brokered merger with the Lloyds TSB. The UK (and subsequently US) authorities suspend short-selling (that is, selling assets borrowed from a third party with the intention of buying identical assets to return to the lender later).
Late September	Co-ordinated central bank measures to address the squeeze in US funding.

29 September	Near simultaneous demise of the three main Icelandic commercial banks.
	UK mortgage lender Bradford and Bingley is nationalized. Three EU governments step in with a capital injection for Fortis, the insurance company. The German authorities provide a facilitated credit line for Hypo Real Estate.
30 September	The Irish government introduces guarantees for six Irish banks, and other countries introduce similar measures in the following weeks.
3 October	The US Congress passes a revised version of TARP (the Troubled Asset Relief Program), after an earlier version was rejected on 29 September.
8 October	UK announces comprehensive measures to recapitalize banks. Major central banks co-ordinated a cut in interest rates.
13 October	Major central banks jointly announce that they were prepared to inject US dollars to ease tensions in money markets. European authorities pledge recapitalization of banks system-wide.
28 October	IMF package for Hungary.
15 November	The G20 countries pledge increased co-operation and efforts to encourage growth and reform the international financial system.
25 November	USA creates $200 billion facility to support consumer and small business loans, and up to $500 billion for purchases of bonds and mortgage-backed securities issued by US housing agencies.
2009	
19 January	As part of a more general rescue package, the UK authorities increase their stake in Royal Bank of Scotland. Other national authorities introduce similar measures in the next few days.
10 February	USA presents plans for a support package including up to $1 trillion in a Public–Private Investment Program to purchase troubled assets.
5 March	Bank of England introduces a programme of about $100 billion aimed at purchases of private sector assets and government bonds over a three-month period.
2 April	G20 communiqué pledges joint measures to restore confidence and growth, and to strengthen the financial system.
7 May	USA publishes results of stress tests on the largest US financial institutions, and identifies ten banks with a capital shortfall to be covered primarily by additions to equity.
2010	
May	Greek bail-out agreed (see text).
21 July	US president Obama signed the Dodd–Frank Wall Street Reform and Consumer Protection Act (the 'Reform Act') relating to the regulation and supervision of the US financial system.
12 September	Agreement reached on Basel III setting a new capital ratio for banks of 4.5 per cent (more than double the previous 2 per cent level) with a new buffer of 2.5 per cent. The new rules are to be phased in from January 2013.

Source: Elaborated on the basis of BIS (2009, 2010) and Financial Times (various issues).

England announced co-ordinated interest rate cuts. However, when official statistics in early 2009 revealed the scale of the global economic slowdown (also in emerging markets), the price of financial assets again fell. They recovered from March 2009 when major central banks (including the Bank of England and the Federal Reserve) announced their commitment to purchases of assets and bonds. In May 2009 the ECB stated that it would start purchasing euro-denominated bonds. Despite the USA releasing the results of stress tests of banks in May 2009, the fragility of financial markets continued. Unemployment rose, in particular in countries such as Ireland, Spain and the USA that had experienced a construction boom before the crisis.

The combination of financial rescue and support packages and lower tax returns led to high levels of government budget deficits and public debt in most industrial countries. In addition to doubts about the effectiveness of support packages (which could lead to dependence of the financial system on financial assistance, delays in adjustment, and possible moral hazard), there were worries about the sustainability of the high and growing level of public debt in some countries. These were exacerbated in November 2009 when Dubai World (one of the country's three strategic investment vehicles) announced that it was seeking a moratorium on debt repayments.

In September 2010 after months of discussion, international agreement was finally reached on Basel III to strengthen the international regulatory framework. This entails setting a new capital ratio for banks of 4.5 per cent (more than double the previous 2 per cent level) with a new buffer of 2.5 per cent. The new rules are to be phased in from January 2013. Though limited in scale, the aim of the agreement is to increase transparency and constrain the build-up of excessive leverage and maturity mismatches in order to ensure that banks maintain more liquidity to face market crises, while at the same time avoiding reduced lending which could stifle economic recovery.

11.10 The eurozone crisis

The ECB was one of the early and most active actors in taking measures against the crisis, injecting €95 billion into markets in August 2007 (see Box 11.4), and €348.6 billion in December 2007 to address fears of insufficient short-term credit.

Following the collapse of Lehman Brothers, in October 2008 the EU countries agreed a rescue plan of €1873 billion to shore up their financial sectors. The EU set out principles for bank guarantees and, as explained in Chapter 7 recommended a co-ordinated fiscal stimulus by an amount equivalent to

---

Box 11.4

Key dates from 2010 onwards in the eurozone crisis

January 2010	Greek sovereign debt crisis worsens: deficits are at least double those reported.
February 2010	Greece given a timetable to solve its debt problem.
	The EU approves the Irish NAMA (National Assets Management Agency) or bad banks scheme.
March 2010	German chancellor, Angela Merkel, says that countries failing to respect budget discipline should be expelled from the eurozone.
	Van Rompuy task force set up to look into economic governance.
May 2010	Agreement reached on an EU/IMF package of assistance of up to €110 billion for Greece.

	Bail-out fund for eurozone countries of up to €750 billion, including a special-purpose European Financial Stability Facility (EFSF) of up to €440 billion; €60 billion from the European Financial Stabilisation Mechanism; and up to €250 billion from the IMF. The ECB decides to intervene in markets to buy government bonds, and to exempt the Greek government from minimum credit requirements on collateral used in its liquidity-providing operations. The ECB also reopens credit lines set up in autumn 2008 with the other major central banks, including the Federal Reserve.
	A fundamental debate on economic governance of the euro and EU is launched.
July 2010	Results of stress tests of EU banks released, with 7 out of 91 banks failing (5 in Spain, 2 in Germany, but surprisingly none in Ireland).
	France and Germany announce they are in favour of neutralization of voting rights for eurozone countries with excessive deficits.
September 2010	European Commission presents economic governance proposals to reinforce surveillance of fiscal and other macroeconomic policies, and structural measures.
October 2010	Franco-German agreement at Deauville on a permanent 'crisis resolution mechanism' making bondholders share in the cost of future bail-outs from 2013.
	Task force under European Council president Van Rompuy presents proposals on economic governance of the EU and reform of the Stability and Growth Pact.
	At a European Council Germany wins agreement for a Treaty change to introduce a permanent replacement to the EFSF.
	Portugal presents austerity budget.
November 2010	At the G20 in Seoul finance ministers of the five largest EU economies clarify that current bondholders would not be responsible for future bail-outs.
	Irish budget and four-year austerity plan announced.
	IMF, ECB and European Commission agree €85 billion bail-out package for Ireland, and the Eurogroup decides on a permanent European Stability Mechanism for dealing with debt crises in the eurozone, with bondholders paying for part of a future default.
December 2010	European Council declares that it is 'ready to do whatever [is] required' to protect the euro.
February 2011	Germany, backed by France, presents a proposal for a Competitiveness Pact at the European Council.
March 2010	Portuguese government resigns over failure to pass austerity budget.
	European Council agrees the Euro-Plus Pact.
May 2011	EU/IMF agree €78 billion bail-out for Portugal.

Source: *Elaborated on the basis of BIS (2009, 2010) and* Financial Times *(various issues).*

1.5 per cent of EU GDP (though views on fiscal stimulus varied considerably both between and within countries). In May 2009 the ECB cut its principal interest rate to a record low of 1 per cent.

Between 1999 and 2008, in what has been described as one of the 'most extraordinary mis-pricings in modern financial history' (Nomura, 2011:38), investors had been treating all euro-denominated bonds (from German to Greek) as if they carried almost the same credit risk. From late 2008, and in particular from 2010, doubts about the ability of some of the peripheral countries to service their debt led to a rise in the yields on their sovereign bonds (see Figure 11.7).

Though initially Portugal seemed the weak link in the eurozone, the crisis was eventually set off by high levels of public deficit and debt in Greece, leading to fear of default. From the early days of Greek qualification to join the euro there was a suspicion of creative accounting to meet the Maastricht

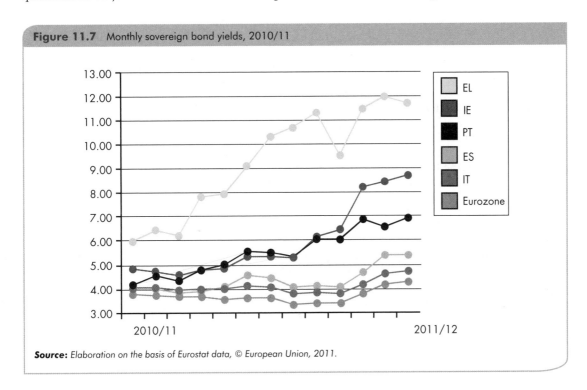

Figure 11.7 Monthly sovereign bond yields, 2010/11

Source: *Elaboration on the basis of Eurostat data, © European Union, 2011.*

criteria. In January 2010 the new Greek government stated that Greek official statistics had seriously underestimated the size of the government deficit, which was adjusted up to 13.6 per cent of GDP for the year (double what had earlier been predicted). After months of delay and debate about whether the IMF should be involved,[32] on 1 May 2010 agreement was reached on an EU/IMF package of assistance of up to €110 billion for Greece (of which €30 billion was from the IMF), conditional on Greek implementation of a stringent austerity package. In May 2010 it was also decided to exempt the Greek government from minimum credit requirements on collateral used in its liquidity-providing operations. The following months were marked by protests, riots and strikes in Greece against the fiscal tightening.

On 10 May 2010 the EU decided on a bail-out fund for eurozone countries of up to €750 billion. This included a special-purpose European Financial Stability Facility (EFSF) of up to €440 billion (though in practice the lending capacity was limited to about €250 billion because of the need to keep

---

[32] Some economists such as Daniel Gros and Thomas Mayer called for the creation of a European Monetary Fund; see their article in *The Economist*, 20 February 2010.

large cash buffers to maintain its triple A rating), which was set up for three years. In addition there was €60 billion from the European Financial Stabilisation Mechanism, and up to €250 billion from the IMF. The EFSF can raise funds on financial markets and make loans to eurozone countries in need. In January 2011 the EFSF went ahead with its first issue of bonds. The European Financial Stabilisation Mechanism depends on funds raised by the Commission using the EU budget as collateral.

In a somewhat controversial move, the ECB also decided to intervene in markets to buy government bonds. Some were opposed to this measure, including Axel Weber, then president of the Bundesbank and so also a member of the Governing Council of the ECB. Though considered a front-runner to replace Trichet as president of the ECB, he subsequently resigned from the Bundesbank because of disagreement with the ECB policy and, in particular, insistence on tighter interpretation of the no bail-out clause.

There was growing concern in Germany that its Constitutional Court would declare rescue plans illegal, and against the no bail-out clause introduced by the Maastricht Treaty (now Article 123 TFEU, as described above). Fear of an adverse ruling by the Court in Kahlsruhe explained the delay before German approval of the Greek package. The Court was also investigating the legality of the EFSF. Limited Treaty change would be a way around this difficulty and the UK was also prepared to accept this in return for tighter curbs on spending from the EU budget (see Chapter 12).

At a meeting in Deauville in October 2010 Angela Merkel and Nicolas Sarkozy published a joint statement in favour of giving national politicians more authority to delay or block sanctions (the German concession to France), the possible suspension of voting rights for a country that failed to respect the SGP, and Treaty change to establish a permanent 'crisis resolution mechanism' to replace the EFSF when it came to an end in 2013. This would share the cost of future rescue plans between private creditors and taxpayers. The ECB president, Trichet, warned that talk of debt restructuring and forcing private creditors to bear part of the burden would unsettle bond markets (as in fact occurred, helping to spark the Irish crisis).

Despite the high level of public deficit (11.9 per cent of GDP in 2009), bond yields for Ireland remained relatively stable during 2009 and early 2010, probably as a reaction to the severe austerity measures introduced in successive budgets by the Irish government from March 2009 on. The results of the stress tests published in July 2010 were positive for all the Irish banks (though Anglo Irish Bank was excluded from the tests), but with the benefit of hindsight, were based on excessively optimistic forecasts, in particular relating to the property market. Irish sovereign bond yields began to rise rapidly from mid-2010 (see Figure 11.7) as awareness grew of the huge scale of financing necessary for the Irish government to honour its guarantees to Irish banks in the wake of collapse of the property boom.[33]

In November 2010 officials disclosed that the Irish Central Bank had lent €20 billion to the banks in addition to the €120 billion from the ECB (about one-quarter of all ECB lending).[34]

---

[33] Following Ireland's entry into the eurozone in 1999, low interest rates and inflows of foreign capital allowed Irish banks to borrow heavily to finance the Irish property boom. Loans of the six main Irish Banks doubled in four years to reach €409 billion in 2007 when the Irish property market turned (*Irish Times*, 31 May 2010). Politicians who relied on developers, builders and bankers for electoral support helped to fuel the construction bubble with tax breaks and failure to tighten regulation. In September 2009 the Irish government introduced guarantees for the debts of six Irish banks, maintaining this was necessary to prevent systemic collapse. In January 2009 Anglo Irish Bank, the financial institution most exposed to the property boom, was nationalized. By September 2010 Allied Irish Bank was also 90 per cent owned by the state (*Financial Times*, 4 October 2010). In November 2010 the possibility of majority state ownership of Bank of Ireland (up from 36 per cent) was voiced, but in the event did not occur. Though considered one of the stronger Irish banks, Bank of Ireland revealed that it had lost €10 billion in corporate deposits in September 2010 alone. In March 2010 the NAMA (the National Assets Management Agency) came into operation as a 'bad bank' to acquire bad property loans at a steep discount from the banks (67 per cent discount for Anglo Irish in September 2010 (*Financial Times*, 4 October 2010)). In addition to ECB assistance, the National Pensions Reserve Fund was also used to underwrite the bank rescue. If the bank bail-out costs are also included, the Irish budget deficit was estimated at about 32 per cent of GDP in 2010, with public debt of 98.6 per cent. See also Kinsella and Leddin (2010).

[34] Initially some of Ireland's major politicians denied that external assistance was being discussed, but a team of IMF, ECB and European Commission officials arrived in Dublin and the governor of the Irish Central Bank, Patrick Honohan, eventually announced that a rescue package was being negotiated.

The temporary liquidity provided by the ECB was beginning to look like a more permanent arrangement, and by November 2010 the ECB was placing pressure on the Irish government to accept a bail-out.

The financial turmoil also precipitated a fall of government in Ireland, and the question of loss of national sovereignty was hotly debated in the Irish press. One of the most contested issues was the request by other EU partners for Ireland to raise its level of corporation tax from 12.5 per cent (a request refused on various occasions).[35] Ireland had long been accused of unfair tax competition, but maintained that the issue was not directly related to the banking crisis, and that low corporation tax was central to economic recovery and the ability to attract FDI.[36]

In November 2010 the Irish government announced a four-year austerity plan and a decrease of 12 per cent in the minimum wage. A few days later agreement was reached on an €85 billion bail-out package for Ireland,[37] and the Eurogroup (composed of eurozone finance ministers) agreed on a permanent European Stability Mechanism for dealing with debt crises in the eurozone. This will come into operation from 2013 when the EFSF ends. The new mechanism will involve collective action clauses that would involve bondholders in any eventual debt restructuring.

There were various calls (such as that by the Luxembourg prime minister Jean-Claude Juncker and the Italian finance minister Giulio Tremonti) for eurozone countries to issue a common bond.[38] This would have the advantage of lowering borrowing costs for peripheral countries, but was opposed by the German finance minister, Wolfgang Schäuble.

In March 2011 the Portuguese prime minister, José Sócrates, resigned when the national parliament rejected the fourth set of austerity measures in a year, and in May 2011 the EU and IMF agreed a €78 billion bail-out for Portugal.

In 2010 it was estimated that Ireland accounted for 1.7 per cent of eurozone GDP, Portugal for 1.9 per cent, Greece for 2.6 per cent and Spain for 11.4 per cent,[39] so the real worry is of contagion with the crisis extending to larger eurozone countries such as Spain or Italy.

11.11 Reform of EU economic governance

The Irish example illustrates the limitations of the Maastricht criteria and unreformed SGP. In 2007 Irish net public debt was only 12 per cent of GDP (compared with 27 per cent in Spain, 50 per cent in Germany and 80 per cent in Greece). The subsequent deterioration in the Irish fiscal situation was a consequence rather than a cause of the crisis. The Irish economy was ranked second in the EU for productivity and flexibility,[40] and was classed in the top ten countries for ease of doing business by the World Bank. Low interest rates (the 'one size' did not fit all), rapacious banks, and insufficient official

---

[35] See also Chapter 6.

[36] In particular, because exports were performing relatively well and grew by 6 per cent in 2010.

[37] The UK also participated in the bail-out (though, in the face of controversy, figures indicating the extent of its involvement were not initially released), and agreed direct bilateral loans of £3.2 billion. This action was in part motivated by the importance of British exports to Ireland and the exposure of certain UK banks to the risks of the Irish banking system. It was estimated that UK lenders (in particular Royal Bank of Scotland and Lloyds Banking Group) accounted for about $148.5 billion or 30 per cent of the total exposure of European banks to Ireland (*Financial Times*, 2 December 2010).

[38] The proposal to introduce a euro-wide bond and the German opposition are reported in the *Financial Times* of 6 December 2010. See also a similar proposal by Lorenzo Bini Smaghi (*Financial Times*, 12–13 March 2011).

[39] *Financial Times*, 3 March 2011.

[40] *Financial Times*, 25 November 2010.

regulation fuelled the Irish and Spanish property bubbles. This suggests that trends in bank credit and asset prices should also be taken into account in monitoring the economic performance of member states. This was one of the suggestions to emerge in the debate on the reform of economic governance of the eurozone and EU.

In May and June 2010 the Commission published communications on this reform, and a package of six legislative proposals (known as the 'six pack') was presented in September 2010.[41] In July it was also agreed to give Eurostat greater power in checking whether countries respect the SGP.

According to the Commission package, there should be a 'European semester' in the first half of the year with member states presenting their draft budgetary plans in April of each year so there would be time for surveillance. If necessary the Commission could recommend revision and budgets would be finalized in the second half of the year. Surveillance would be of all EU members but tighter for the eurozone.

The Commission also proposed an alert mechanism and a scoreboard to identify countries with potentially problematic levels of macroeconomic imbalances, including deteriorating competitiveness. The Council (on the basis of a Commission recommendation) could recommend corrective action to the country. In the event of non-compliance by euro members, a fine, generally of 0.1 per cent, could be applied through the excessive imbalances procedure. It was proposed that a 'reverse voting mechanism' should be used in applying sanctions, that is, the Commission's proposal for a sanction would be adopted unless turned down by a qualified majority in the Council.

With regard to the preventative arm of the SGP, the Commission proposed rendering the debt criterion operational with benchmarks to assess whether the debt level is diminishing towards the 60 per cent level. There would also be minimum requirements for national fiscal frameworks to ensure prudent fiscal policy making and convergence towards the medium-term objectives, closer monitoring and tighter sanctions. Slightly higher deficits and debts might be tolerated for countries with pension reforms already in place.

The sanction for an excessive deficit under the corrective arm of the SGP would consist of an 'interest-bearing deposit' of 0.2 per cent convertible into a fine in the case of non-compliance.[42] Again use of the 'reverse voting mechanism' was proposed for sanctions.

Though its recommendations are rather bland, the final report in October 2010 of a task force on economic governance under Van Rompuy (European Council, 2010) also advocated increased consideration of debt, the European semester, scoreboards, and stricter application of 'reputational' and financial sanctions in both the preventative and corrective arms of the SGP. It also recommended the extension of the threat of sanctions gradually to all EU members except the UK (whose opt-out was covered by Protocol No. 15 of the Lisbon Treaty).

By early 2011 the European Parliament had presented about two thousand amendments to the Commission proposals. Rather surprisingly, the president of the ECB, Trichet, was relying on the EP to help produce a 'quantum leap' in economic governance with stricter fiscal compliance, and tighter economic and financial co-ordination.[43]

At a European Council meeting of February 2011 initially intended to focus on energy and innovation, Germany, with the backing of France, tabled a 'Competitiveness Pact' to address the

---

[41] The package of all the proposals is available at European Commission, Economic and Financial Affairs, 'A new EU economic governance – a comprehensive Commission package of proposals', http://ec.europa.eu/economy_finance/articles/eu_economic_situation/2010-09-eu_economic_governance_proposals_en.htm (accessed 3 March 2011).

[42] During the debate about the proposals, other possible sanctions had been voiced such as withholding EU payments for regional policy and the CAP.

[43] See EurActiv of 18 March 2011 and *Financial Times* of 7 March 2011.

difficulties of the eurozone.[44] This entailed indicators and monitoring of price competitiveness, stability of public finance, and minimum rates for investment on research and development. In return, Germany was expected to agree increased financing for the EFSF. What aroused most controversy was a list of measures to be implemented nationally within twelve months, namely: the abolition of wage and salary indexation; mutual recognition of educational diplomas and vocational qualifications; a common assessment basis for corporate income tax; pension reform; a 'debt alert mechanism' in the constitutions of the member states; and a national crisis management scheme for banks. The underlying view was that it was necessary to complete monetary union with economic union. It was proposed that the European Council review the application of the Competitiveness Pact on a regular basis. To adopt the measures, France and Germany advocated using Article 136 TFEU of the Lisbon Treaty, which allows eurozone countries to 'strengthen the co-ordination and surveillance of their budgetary discipline' without requiring the approval of all EU member states.

The proposed Competitiveness Pact was criticized on a number of counts. Italy and Ireland were opposed to tax harmonization; Belgium and Luxembourg were against abolishing wage indexation; and Austria did not want to raise the retirement age. The use of an intergovernmental approach with a limited role for the Commission was criticized.[45] It was feared that the initiative could lead to a two-speed Europe and might disrupt debate on the Commission's proposals for reform of economic governance. A widespread complaint was also that Germany was attempting to impose its economic model on other eurozone countries.

In February 2011 work began under the presidents of the Commission (Barroso) and European Council (Van Rompuy) on a revised proposal to increase competitiveness. In March 2011 eurozone leaders, and subsequently the European Council, reached an agreement on a Euro-Plus Pact as an alternative to the Competitiveness Pact, and the European Council also expressed its commitment to the six legislative proposals of the Commission.

Though watered down with respect to the Franco-German proposal, the essence of the Euro-Plus Pact was to accept tighter economic co-ordination as a *quid pro quo* for German agreement to boost the funds for bail-outs of peripheral countries. Four non-eurozone member states, Britain, the Czech Republic, Hungary and Sweden, decided to remain out of the Pact and the European Stability Mechanism (ESM), but the other non-eurozone countries will participate. The Pact remains open for other member states to join.

Agreement was reached on the funding structure of the ESM from 2013, which will comprise €80 billion of capital paid in by member states, and €620 billion in callable capital in the form of guarantees. On 11 March 2011 eurozone leaders agreed that €40 billion of the upfront capital would be paid in 2013 and the remaining €40 billion in three annual payments. In the face of opposition at home, Merkel subsequently convinced the European Council meeting of 25 March 2011 to allow slower payment over five annual instalments of the German contribution of €22 billion to the upfront capital (also because 2013 is an election year).[46] It seems likely that other member states (such as Italy) may also encounter difficulties with their contributions. The EFSF and the ESM will be allowed to buy government bonds (relieving the pressure on the ECB). The decision to increase the EFSF so that it

---

[44] The text of the proposed Pact is available at EurActiv, http://www.euractiv.com/sites/all/euractiv/files/BRNEDA224_004512.pdf (accessed 24 February 2011).

[45] See, for instance, the letter of Belgian MEP and former prime minister Verhofstadt, and former Commission presidents Delors and Prodi in the *Financial Times* of 3 March 2011 criticizing the 'indelicate manner of presentation' of the Pact, and calling for the use of the 'Community' method (see Chapter 3 for a description of this method).

[46] The change in the German position after only a few days placed so much pressure on the chain-smoking head of the eurogroup, Jean-Claude Juncker, that he was asked to leave the room by security for smoking too much (EurActiv, 25 March 2011, http://www.euractiv.com/en/euro-finance/eu-leaders-thrash-deal-permanent-euro-shield-news-503505 (accessed 28 March 2011).

could use its full lending capacity of €440 billion was postponed until June largely because two net contributors, Germany and Finland, faced elections.[47]

The Euro-Plus Pact recommends greater tax co-ordination, lowering tax on labour, raising retirement ages and linking salaries to productivity, but leaves the decision on how and when to implement such measures to member states. Countries are expected to develop a common corporate tax base (CCCTB, see Chapter 6) as a revenue-neutral way to ensure consistency among national tax systems.

In July 2011 eurozone leaders agreed a second EU/IMF bail-out for Greece worth €109 billion. At German insistence (because of popular opposition to the EU becoming a 'transfer Union'), about a third of the burden will be borne by the private sector through voluantry debt swaps and roll-overs of Greek debt. It was estimated that this world entail about a 20 per cent cut on average in the net value of present bond holdings. There was a discussion of a variety of credit enhancements to provide incentives to participants, including other forms of collateral than Greek goverment guarantees to ensure repayment. The ECB president Trichet had resisted measures that might lead to what rating agencies considered a default. He was reassured when it was made clear thar such bondholder plans would be limited to Greece.

Interest rates are to be lowered, and maturities are to be extended on EFSF loans to Greece, Portugal and Ireland (despite no firm commitment to reduce corporation tax). To address the problem of contgion the EFSF will be able to help countries (such as Spain or Italy) not currently in bail-outs. It will also be able to buy bonds in secondary markets in 'exceptional cicumstances'.

While the agreements certainly bought time, it is doubtful that it will put an end to the eurozone difficulties.

11.12   Evaluation and outlook for the euro

The celebrations to mark the first ten years of the euro were mainly upbeat about the fair-weather decade, and it was only with the economic crisis that the serious consequences of certain unresolved questions began to emerge. The initial selection of countries to join the euro was clearly too generous, and the one-size interest rate did not fit all. Supervision and regulation of the financial sector was inadequate (see also Chapter 6), there was insufficient co-ordination of fiscal policies and, particularly after its reform, the Stability and Growth Pact was unable to guarantee discipline with regard to deficits and debts.

On 16 November 2010 the president of the European Council, Herman Van Rompuy, made the unfortunate statement that a 'survival crisis' could tear apart the EU, further destabilizing markets. In the same month, Angela Merkel announced that the euro was in an 'exceptionally serious' situation, and stated that the EU and the euro were inextricably linked.[48]

So, what then are the prospects for the euro? No country can be forced out of EMU: exit is voluntary. A peripheral country leaving the euro would probably have to default on its euro debt and would incur the cost of re-denominating all contracts. It could be that Germany, tired of bail-outs of peripheral countries, would want to leave the euro, but this would cancel the long effort to regain competitiveness, evident also from Figure 11.6 above. It seems unlikely that the eurozone will split up.

However, the outlook for the eurozone is not rosy. There have been protests against austerity measures in Greece, Ireland and Portugal. Spain has a relatively low level of public debt, but private debt is high, the financial sector remains fragile and further falls in property prices seem likely. In Italy, private debt is low, but the public debt was 120 per cent of GDP in 2011. Cyprus was vulnerable because of the exposure of its banks to Greece, difficulties in passing austerity measures, and an explosion at a power station in July 2011 which knocked out half of the island's power supply. The

---

[47] In the event the anti-EU party True Finn gained seats in Finland.

[48] *Financial Times*, 19 November 2010.

contributions of countries such as Germany and Finland to the EFSF and future ESM have not proved popular with their electorates, and Germany is also wary of challenge to bail-outs by its Constitutional Court.

It seems likely that the proposed reforms for economic governance will be watered down and, as the experience of the Single Market shows, scoreboards are limited as coercive measures. There is little reason to suppose that the revised SGP will be much more effective than its predecessor. In short, the usual practice of muddling through seems likely to prevail.

Summary of key concepts

- The **European System of Central Banks** is composed of the European Central Bank and the national central banks of all EU member states. The **Eurosystem** is the term used to refer to the ECB and NCBs of the countries that have adopted the euro.

- The main priority of the Eurosystem is to maintain **price stability.** It is responsible for supporting general economic policies, defining and implementing monetary policy for the euro area and holding foreign reserves. It also has to ensure the smooth operation of the payments system and supervision by the relevant authorities. On paper at least, the ECB appears one of the most independent central banks in the world.

- In the case of the eurozone there has been much debate about whether and what form of co-ordination of **fiscal policies** is necessary or desirable. The EU solution is for the member states to retain responsibility for fiscal policy, though subject to detailed rules and procedures.

- According to the **Stability and Growth Pact**, budget deficits should generally be limited to a maximum of 3 per cent of GDP and countries should aim at balanced budgets in the medium term. The Pact was reformed in 2005 to take more account of the business cycle, the level of public debt, and the extent to which deficits promoted productivity-enhancing activities.

- The early years of the euro were associated with relatively low inflation (though the ceiling of 2 per cent was often exceeded), but rather sluggish growth. It seems likely that there will be lasting **divergences** between euro member states for some time.

- The **international role of the euro** in the invoicing of trade, and in official reserves and private holdings of international financial assets has been increasing and is now second to that of the US dollar.

- Many date the beginning of **international economic crisis** to the collapse of the US subprime mortgage market in 2007, though the situation deteriorated rapidly after the collapse of Lehman Brothers in 2008.

- With the economic crisis, **bail-outs were organized for Greece, Ireland and Portugal.** The ECB was active with assistance for banks, and from May 2010 also with purchases of government bonds.

- In May 2010 a three-year rescue fund, the **European Stability Stability Facility**, for eurozone countries of up to €750 billion, was set up. Germany and France and subsequently the Eurogroup agreed on a Treaty change to set up a permanent **European Stability Mechanism** for crisis resolution in the eurozone, with creditors bearing part of the cost of bail-outs from 2013.

- In 2010 the European Commission presented proposals for **reform of economic governance** with broader and enhanced surveillance of fiscal and other macroeconomic policies and structural reforms (including deteriorating competitiveness trends), and reform of the SGP.

- In March 2011 the European Council agreed the **Euro-Plus Pact** to tighten economic co-operation in return for German agreement to increase bail-out funds.

Questions for study and review

1 What are the chief functions of the European Central Bank, and what criticisms can be made of its operation?

2 Explain why there is a tension between independence and accountability of the ECB.

3 What are the arguments in favour of or against co-ordination of fiscal policies in a monetary union?

4 How useful do you consider the Stability and Growth Pact?

5 How do you think the role of the euro in the world economy will change?

6 Describe the tensions that arose for the euro with the economic crisis.

7 What do you consider the outlook for the eurozone?

Online
Learning **Centre**

When you have read this chapter, log on to the Online Learning Centre website at **www.mcgraw-hill.co.uk/textbooks/senior** to explore weblinks, chapter-by-chapter test questions, case studies and more online study tools.

Chapter 12

The EU Budget

Learning Objectives

By the end of this chapter you should be able to understand:

- ✓ That although the Treaty of Rome envisaged the Community budget as having contributions and receipts roughly in balance, some member states have emerged as net beneficiaries and others as net losers
- ✓ The main items of expenditure from the EU budget and how these have changed over the years
- ✓ The basic principles of the EU budget
- ✓ How the financing of the budget has changed over time
- ✓ Why and when financial perspectives and multiannual financial forecasts were introduced
- ✓ The main features of the 2007–13 financial perspective
- ✓ The debate on the future of the EU budget

12.1 Introduction

The changing nature of the EU with its widening and deepening processes has been reflected in the evolution of its budget. Budgetary considerations have played an important role in much of the history of the EU, and the budgetary procedure is the outcome of many disputes and finely balanced compromises. There have been controversies about whether the Community first and EU later should have its own resources, about the respective roles of EU institutions in the budgetary process, and over the redistributive effects of the budget on different member states. The European Parliament, like most parliaments in history, has used its budgetary powers to increase its role and influence and to wrest concessions from the Commission and Council.[1]

---

[1] For instance, the 1999 institutional crisis described in Chapter 3 began with the European Parliament's refusal to approve the 1996 budget accounts.

12.2 The main features of the EU budget

In the early years of the Community some redistribution was expected to occur through the European Investment Bank, which was established with the main objective of encouraging development in the Italian South or Mezzogiorno. As can be seen from Figures 12.1 and 12.2, over the years some countries have emerged as net beneficiaries, others as net losers, and the respective shares have frequently been the subject of heated disputes.

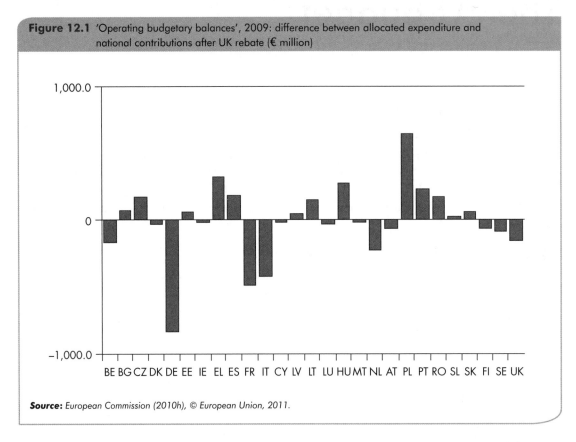

Figure 12.1 'Operating budgetary balances', 2009: difference between allocated expenditure and national contributions after UK rebate (€ million)

Source: *European Commission (2010h), © European Union, 2011.*

On the expenditure side, in the early years of the Community, agriculture accounted for some 90 per cent of spending from the Community budget. The share remained as high as 73 per cent in 1985, and natural resources (that is, agriculture, fisheries and the environment) were allocated 41.3 per cent of spending in 2011. The share spent on structural operations steadily increased over the years, from 6 per cent in 1965 to 17.2 per cent in 1988, and 36 per cent of the EU budget in 2011.[2]

From 2007 there was a change in the way in which the various budgetary headings for expenditure from the EU budget were classified (see Figures 12.3, 12.4 and 12.5), and five main categories were indicated:

---

[2] European Commission (2010h). Up until the term 'structural operations' covered spending on the Structural Funds (the European Social Fund; the European Regional Development Fund (ERDF); the Guidance Section of the European Guidance and Guarantee Fund (for agriculture), and the Fisheries Guidance Instrument), and the Cohesion Fund. In 2007 the term 'economic and social cohesion' was adopted and the three financial instruments for cohesion became the European Social Fund, the European Regional Development Fund and the Cohesion Fund (see Chapter 15).

Figure 12.2 'Operating budgetary balances', 2009: difference between allocated expenditure and national contributions after UK rebate, as a percentage of gross national income

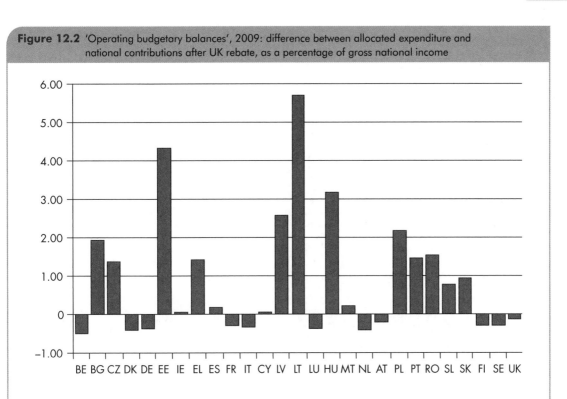

Source: *European Commission (2010h), © European Union, 2011.*

Figure 12.3 Expenditure from the 2011 budget: commitment appropriations

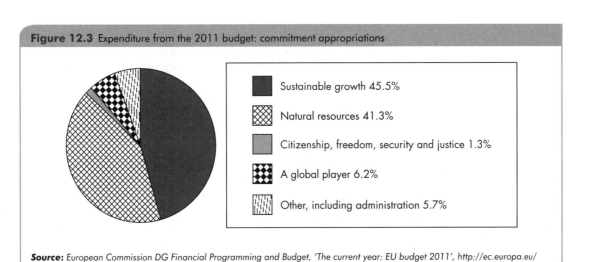

Sustainable growth 45.5%

Natural resources 41.3%

Citizenship, freedom, security and justice 1.3%

A global player 6.2%

Other, including administration 5.7%

Source: *European Commission DG Financial Programming and Budget, 'The current year: EU budget 2011', http://ec.europa.eu/budget/budget_detail/current_year_en.htm (accessed 24 January 2011), © European Union, 2011.*

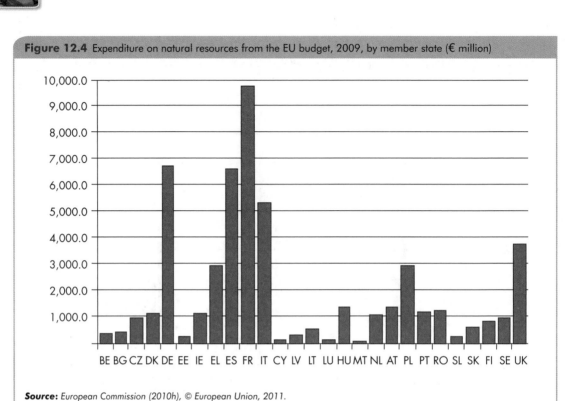

Figure 12.4 Expenditure on natural resources from the EU budget, 2009, by member state (€ million)

Source: *European Commission (2010h), © European Union, 2011.*

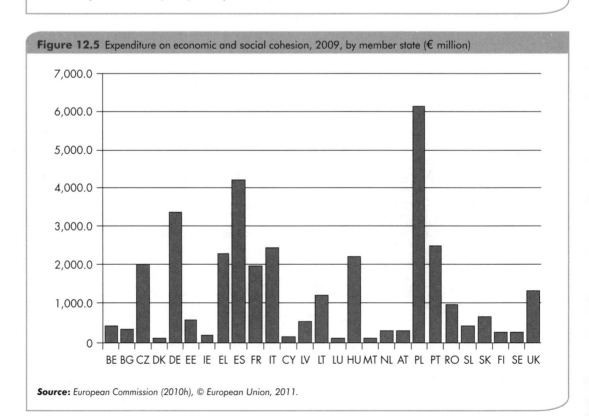

Figure 12.5 Expenditure on economic and social cohesion, 2009, by member state (€ million)

Source: *European Commission (2010h), © European Union, 2011.*

- **Competitiveness and cohesion for sustainable growth.** This reflects the priorities of the Lisbon Strategy relaunched as Europe 2020,[3] and is broken down into two subheadings: (i) investing in competitiveness for growth and employment, and (ii) cohesion for growth and employment. Spending on competitiveness includes the categories of: education and training, research and the information society (which were previously under internal policies), and energy and transport. Spending on cohesion includes regional development, the Cohesion Fund, and employment and social affairs, and so covers most of the former heading 'structural operations'.

- **Preservation and management of natural resources.** The previous heading of agriculture and rural development was expanded to cover fisheries (under structural actions before) and environmental policy (which was previously under internal policies).

- **Citizenship, freedom, security and justice.** Spending on 'freedom, security and justice' also includes sectors such as culture, the media, public health and consumer protection.

- **The EU as a global player.** The heading 'global player' covers enlargement, relations with third countries and humanitarian aid.

- **Administration.** At 5.7 per cent of the budget in 2011 this category absorbs less of the budget than the general public often thinks (as reflected in successive Eurobarometer opinion polls).

Overall the scale of budgetary spending as a share of the GDP of the EU has remained small, increasing from 0.3 per cent in 1960 to 0.53 per cent in 1973, and being fixed as a ceiling of 1.05 per cent of gross national income (GNI) for the 2007–13 period (see below).[4] Despite successive enlargements and extension of EU competences to new policy areas, the share of the EU budget in GNI, both in terms of ceiling and actual expenditure, has fallen in recent years. Payments effectively executed fell from 1.05 per cent of GNI for the 1993–99 period to 0.92 per cent for 2000–06. By way of comparison, about 45–50 per cent of the EU's GNI goes to national, regional and local public expenditure in the member states.[5]

12.3 The basic principles of the EU budget

Throughout its history the EU budget has been guided by certain basic principles:

Unity and universality

According to Article 310 of the Treaty on the Functioning of the European Union (ex Article 268 TEC), all revenues and expenditures have to be entered into the budget. Individual revenues must not be assigned to any particular expenditure, and all revenues and expenditure have to be entered in full in the budget without any adjustment against each other.

In practice there have always been certain exceptions to this rule and, for example, the activities of the European Investment Bank are outside the budget. The European Development Fund, which provides financial aid to developing countries (see Chapter 18), is also not in the budget despite a proposal to include it from 2007.

---

[3] See Chapter 7 for a discussion of the Lisbon Strategy and Europe 2020.

[4] Gross national product is the total income earned by domestic citizens regardless of the country where their factor services are applied, and is equal to GDP plus net property from abroad. Gross national income is GNP minus depreciation.

[5] Europe Media, Portal on EU Funding, Frequently asked questions on the 2007–13 budgetary period, http://www.2007-2013.eu/faq.php (accessed 24 January 2011).

Equilibrium

According to Article 310 TFEU (ex Article 268 TEC), the budget has to balance, that is, estimated revenues for a financial year have to equal expenditure for that year.[6]

Annuality

The budget runs for a financial year from 1 January to 31 December. In 1984 and 1985 financial difficulties led to budgets covering only the ten months up to October in order to satisfy the principle of equilibrium, with supplementary budgets being voted for the remaining period. The European Court of Justice ruled against this expedient as being contrary to the principle of annuality.

Specification

Although revenues cannot be earmarked for particular items of expenditure, all items of expenditure must be specified in the budget.

A common unit of account

All items of revenue and expenditure have to be indicated in a common unit of account rather than in national currencies. From 1981 the unit of account used was the European Currency Unit (ECU), and this was replaced by the euro from 1 January 1999.

Parallel to the debate on subsidiarity in the context of EU institutions, in the field of public finance a similar theoretical literature has emerged on what is referred to as fiscal federalism. This literature deals with the criteria for deciding the appropriate level of government (EU, national, regional or local) for decisions with regard to expenditure and revenue.[7] A central concept of the literature is the idea of congruence, according to which each level of government has to have its own source of revenue to match its expenditure responsibilities.

Criteria for assigning functions to higher levels of government could include the presence of externalities (for example, in fighting pollution), indivisibility or economies of scale (such as in R&D programmes) or ensuring minimum standards of services or of prosperity (as in the case of the Cohesion Fund). Criteria for assigning functions to lower levels of government could include the need for democratic control or to bring decisions closer to the citizens, flexibility, competition among units, or the aim of reflecting preferences more accurately, given the greater political homogeneity that often characterizes smaller communities.

12.4 The financing of the Community up until 1980

The Treaty of Rome envisaged a transition period until 1970 during which financing of the Community was to consist essentially of contributions from the member states. The basic contribution of the three large members (France, Germany and Italy) was fixed at 28 per cent of total budget revenue, while that of the Netherlands and Belgium was 7.9 per cent, with 0.2 per cent for Luxembourg. However, the basic financing rule was adjusted according to the importance of the policy in question for each member state. For instance, Italy's contribution to the European

---

[6] This, together with the small size of the EU budget, limits the ability to correct for asymmetric shocks (see Chapter 9).

[7] A difficulty with the *sui generis* nature of the EU is that much fiscal federalism literature assumes a clear hierarchical delimitation of power between the highest level of governance (central government) and lower layers (regional or local authorities). The EU is in some sense the 'highest level', but in many respects is also the least autonomous because of the role of member states. See also the discussion of competences in Chapter 1.

Social Fund was reduced to 20 per cent, while those of France and Germany were raised to 32 per cent, Belgium to 8.8 per cent, with the Netherlands at 7 per cent and 0.2 per cent for Luxembourg. During the transitional period the system of financing was further complicated by the existence of separate institutions for the three Communities up until 1967.

According to Article 201 of the Treaty of Rome, a system of own resources (or self-financing) for the Community was to be introduced at the end of the transition period. Own resources consist of revenue allocated automatically to the Community without any need for further decisions by the member states.

The 1962 agreement on the basic principles of the Common Agricultural Policy (CAP) called for a decision on the rules for financing Community policies by 1965. The CAP was due to come into operation from 1967 and, backed by France and the Netherlands, the president of the Commission, Walter Hallstein, was pushing for the new system of financing to begin operation at the same time.

The Commission's proposals for the Community budget were presented in 1965 and, in line with the provisions of the Treaty of Rome and the logic of a customs union, the proposals entailed that the Community should be financed directly by proceeds from the common external tariff.

Federalists such as Hallstein, Jean Monnet and Altiero Spinelli regarded the introduction of own resources as a step in the process of building a united Europe, in which the European Parliament would exercise powers of budgetary control. For example, Monnet drew on his experience of international organizations and concluded that if such institutions relied on their members for financing, their powers tended to be more limited. This had been a major motive for his insistence on own resources for the European Coal and Steel Community. Spinelli used his knowledge of the history of the taxing power of the US federal government to argue that the power to tax directly was 'the essence of federal institutions'.[8]

However, the Commission's proposal to introduce own resources was opposed by France since it appeared to challenge de Gaulle's concept of national sovereignty. The budgetary issue was directly linked to the question of how Community institutions should evolve (and, in particular, the balance of power between the Commission and Council, parliamentary budgetary powers and the use of the qualified majority vote in the Council) and was at the heart of the 1965 'Empty Chair' crisis. The distinction between compulsory and non-compulsory expenditure for many years, and the limitation of the budgetary powers of the EP to the latter dates from this time (see Box 12.1).

It was only when de Gaulle resigned in 1969 and was replaced by Pompidou that the introduction of own resources could proceed as part of the 'completion' of the Community called for by the 1969 Hague Summit (see Chapter 2). The French government considered a solution to the budgetary question as being in its own interests as a means of ensuring adequate financing for the CAP.

Treaties on Community financing came into operation in 1970 and 1975, though practical difficulties meant that the full system of EC self-financing had to be delayed until 1980. In the meantime a hybrid system was adopted, based partly on contributions from the member states, and partly on own resources.

By the time agreement was reached on own resources, the system of financing envisaged by the Treaty of Rome, based on tariffs and levies on agricultural imports from third countries, was clearly inadequate to meet the growing expenditure needs of the Community and, in particular, the already high and growing cost of the CAP. It was therefore decided to introduce a common system of turnover tax from 1967 based on the French tax, VAT, or value added tax. Value added tax is paid at each stage in the production process (including marketing) on the value added at each stage. A major reason for delaying full implementation of the system was that the VAT base varied from country to country, with differences in the products covered and the rates of VAT applied (see Chapter 6).

The own resources system, which was applied fully from 1980, consisted of three elements: tariffs on manufactured imports from third countries;[9] levies on agricultural imports from the rest of the world, and on sugar and isoglucose; and a percentage of VAT, fixed at 1 per cent up until 1986.

---

[8] The initial federal system in the USA ran into difficulty because of the refusal of states to pay their contributions.

[9] Member states were granted a 10 per cent reimbursement on tariffs and agricultural levies to cover the administrative costs of collecting these resources.

The difference between compulsory and non-compulsory expenditure in the EU budget before the Lisbon Treaty

Up until the Lisbon Treaty the EP could adopt or reject the whole EU budget, but only propose amendments over what is called non-compulsory expenditure. Compulsory expenditure was defined as spending necessarily resulting from the treaties 'or from acts adopted in accordance therewith' (Article 272 TEC). Compulsory spending was said to have a priority claim as it was considered necessary for the Community to meet its internal and external obligations. Most compulsory spending related to agricultural price support and certain forms of foreign aid to third countries. The underlying logic was that when, for example, the level of common agricultural prices was decided, this became Community law, and the necessary financing should be forthcoming (and consequently not subject to possible cuts by the EP). The EP could only propose modifications of compulsory expenditure to the Council.

In contrast, non-compulsory expenditure was said not to emanate from the commitments of the treaties, or the conventions and contracts signed by the EU. The largest component of non-compulsory expenditure was spending on the Structural Funds (see Chapter 15). Other categories of non-compulsory expenditure included internal policies (education, the internal market, research and the environment), external programmes and administrative expenditure.

The distinction between compulsory and non-compulsory expenditure was essentially political and related to the balance of power between the EU institutions. France objected to transfers of sovereignty to the Community, but wanted to ensure adequate financing for the CAP. The compromise, involving the division of types expenditure and the inclusion of agricultural support under compulsory spending, ensured that the Council had the final say on most EC agricultural spending. This, together with the use of unanimity voting after the Luxembourg compromise (see Chapter 3), offered a guarantee that the interests of French farmers would not be overridden.

12.5 The continuing difficulties of the Community budget during the 1980s

During the 1980s, primarily because of excess spending on the CAP but also because of its widening membership and extension into new policy areas, inadequate budgetary resources continually plagued the Community. In 1980 and again in 1985 the European Parliament rejected the proposed budget on the grounds of excessive growth in agricultural spending.

One of the most heated controversies over the EC budget was the so-called British budget question, which dragged on for several years. When Britain joined the Community a large share of its agricultural imports traditionally came from the rest of the world, in particular Commonwealth countries such as New Zealand. This, together with its relatively small but efficient agricultural sector, meant that Britain would be a large net contributor to the EC budget. It was hoped that during the seven-year transition period following UK accession the weight of agriculture both in the Community budget and economy would decline, thereby reducing the bias against Britain. According to the terms of accession, if the situation remained unacceptable, an equitable solution would be negotiated.

An initial proposal to resolve the situation entailed establishing an ERDF that would provide transfers to the economically weaker areas of the Community, including the regions of industrial decline in the UK. However, the recession after the 1973 oil crises meant that funding for the ERDF was not forthcoming on the scale initially envisaged.[10] Following a not very successful attempt by the British Labour government

---

[10] Transfers through the ERDF amounted to only 300 million units of account in 1975 and 500 million units in 1976 and 1977.

to renegotiate the terms of accession, from 1979 there was a determined attempt by the prime minister, Margaret Thatcher, to get Britain's 'money back'.[11]

By 1984 an increase in the VAT ceiling was urgently needed to avoid bankruptcy of the EC budget and to provide the necessary financing to permit the accession of Spain and Portugal to the Community from 1986. Any change in the VAT ceiling required ratification by all the member states, and UK acquiescence was conditional on settlement of the British budget question. The UK negotiated ad hoc rebates for 1980–83, and in 1984 the Fontainebleau Agreement was reached. This entailed:

- a refund of two-thirds of the UK's net contribution to the budget;[12]
- an increase in the VAT contribution to 1.4 per cent from 1986;
- a limit on the growth of agricultural spending, which could not grow more than the increase in own resources;[13] and
- the introduction of quotas on the production of milk.

12.6 The evolution of the sources of revenue of the EU budget

The Fontainebleau Agreement failed to resolve the ongoing financial difficulties of the Community budget. On the expenditure side, CAP spending continued to grow, and the three countries that joined the EC in the 1980s (Greece, Spain and Portugal) were all net beneficiaries from the budget. The poorer regions of the Community feared the additional competitive pressure expected to arise from the Single Market Programme and were pressing for compensation in the form of a substantial increase in the Structural Funds.

On the revenue side, all three sources of EC budgetary financing had been subject to erosion. Successive GATT rounds had reduced the average level of tariffs, thereby cutting the tariff share in budget revenue, as shown in Table 12.1. The growing level of EC self-sufficiency in agricultural products meant a falling share of levies on agricultural imports in budget resources.

Although, as Table 12.1 illustrates, the VAT share in budget revenue rose between 1975 and 1987, the VAT base (that is, the goods and services on which VAT was levied) was not growing as rapidly as the overall economy. Savings and investment and spending on services such as health and education are not subject to VAT, and these are often relatively higher in richer countries. The VAT contributions of different member states also depended on the level and number of VAT rates applied in each country (see Chapter 6).

By 1987 it was estimated that to balance the budget an increase in the VAT ceiling from 1.4 per cent to 1.9 per cent would be necessary. However, the regressive nature of VAT and the fact that increases in the VAT contributions of the member states failed to reflect their respective GDP performance led in 1988 to the decision to introduce a new resource, or additional form of financing for the EC budget.

Since 1988 the sources of revenue of the EU budget (see also Table 12.1) have been:

- Tariffs on imports of industrial products from third countries.
- Variable levies (which became tariffs from 1995) on imports of agricultural products from third countries, and the levies on sugar and isoglucose.[14]

---

[11] For a discussion of these issues see Pinder (1995).

[12] According to the Agreement, *'any member state sustaining a budgetary burden which is excessive in relation to its relative prosperity may benefit from a correction at the appropriate time'*.

[13] This could be considered as a type of 'constitutional rule' to limit increases in government spending favoured by some members of the Public Choice school such as Buchanan and Tullock (1962).

[14] Minus a reimbursement to member states to cover the administrative costs of applying the levies, which was 10 per cent up until 1999 and 25 per cent subsequently.

Table 12.1   The share of different resources in EC budget revenue[a]

	1975 (%)	1980 (%)	1987 (%)	2002 (%)	2011[c] (%)
Tariffs	52.5	37.7	25.0	10.3	12
CAP levies and tariffs	11.0	14.8	8.7	1.6	note[d]
VAT contribution	36.5	47.5	65.7	28.8	11
GNP/GNI[b]	—	—	—	59.1	76

[a]Totals may be less than 100 per cent because of correction for budgetary imbalances and 'other' item, see also note c below.
[b]The GNP/GNI resource was not used before 1988; see text for explanation.
[c]An additional 'other' 1 per cent consists of contributions of EU staff, amounts from previous years, and fines on companies that breach competition or other laws.
[d]Agricultural duties and sugar levies are included under tariffs.
Source: European Commission (2010h), http://ec.europa.eu/budget/library/publications/budget_in_fig/budg_2011_en.pdf (accessed 24 January 2011), © European Union, 2011.

- A percentage of the total VAT levied by the member states, fixed at 0.5 per cent from 2004.[15]
- The 'fourth resource', which is based on the difference between VAT levies and the GNP of a member state and which can be levied up to a maximum percentage of the GNP of the Community if the budget financing from the other three resources proves inadequate. In 1995 the concept of GNP was replaced by the concept of GNI.[16] The ceiling was fixed at 1.27 per cent of GNI for the 2000–06 period and 1.05 per cent for the 2007–13 period.[17]

A frequent criticism of the fourth resource is that it is based on government contributions of EU member states and so runs counter to the Treaty obligation that the EU budget should be financed wholly from 'own resources' (Article 311 TFEU, ex Article 269 TEC). Gros and Micossi (2005) proposed meeting this difficulty by increasing the VAT percentage given to the EU to 2 per cent, which would yield an EU budget of about 1 per cent of GNI. However, as explained in Chapter 6, there are differences in the application of VAT, and the proposed reform would imply an increase in the contributions of some less well off member states such as Estonia, Hungary and Slovenia. The fourth resource reflects the economic performance of countries better than does VAT. As discussed below, the reform of resources for the EU budget is central to the debate about the future of the EU budget after 2013.

 12.7 Financial perspectives and multi-annual financial frameworks

The creation of the fourth resource formed part of the 'First Delors Package' or 'bill for the Single Market' agreed in 1988. The package established the precedent of a financial perspective of the Community setting out the priorities for several years to come, in this case the 1988–92 period. To realize those priorities a multi-annual financial framework fixes the maximum amount and composition of EU expenditure over the next few years. The Lisbon Treaty (Article 312 TFEU) formalized use of multi-annual financial

---

[15] The level were 1.4 per cent from 1986 to 1987, 1 per cent from 1988 to 2000, and 0.75 per cent from 2001 to 2004.

[16] See note 4 above for a definition of these terms. The fourth resource is a residual set at the level needed to ensure that the EU budget balances.

[17] This is the global level of commitment appropriations for the 2007–13 period. Commitment appropriations are legal pledges to provide finance in a year, whereas payment appropriations are the actual transfer to the beneficiary and may include commitments from the current year and/or earlier years. The margin between appropriations for payments and for commitments allows for flexibility with multi-annual programmes.

frameworks. The advantages of this approach are that it ensures adequate financing for projects extending over several years, improves financial discipline, and establishes objectives from the outset. The annual budgetary procedure then determines the exact level of expenditure and breakdown of expenditure between headings for the year in question. Successive financial perspectives cover the periods:

1988–92: the 'First Delors Package', or the bill for the Single Market

With the 1988–92 financial perspective the link between the Single Market and redistributive policies became explicit. The poorer regions and countries of the Community insisted on reform of the Structural Funds and a near doubling of their financing in order to assist their adjustment to the additional competitive pressures of a less fragmented market. The strategy for rendering the necessary financing available was two-pronged: creating new resources for the Community and redimensioning spending on the CAP.[18]

1993–99: 'Delors 2', or the bill for Maastricht

The main innovations of the second 'Delors Package', agreed in Edinburgh in 1992, included a further increase in spending on the Structural Funds and the creation of the Cohesion Fund to compensate the poorer areas and countries of the Community for the additional competition expected to result from introduction of the single currency. The British budget rebate was also continued. The relative importance of the VAT contributions and the fourth resource were also adjusted. With the reduction in the ceiling of the VAT contribution to 1 per cent and the gradual increase in the GNP ceiling of the budget to 1.27 per cent by 1999, it was hoped that resources paid by each of the member states to the EU budget would better reflect their overall economic performance.

2000–06: the Berlin Agreement on Agenda 2000

The financial perspective for the 2000–06 period was decided at the Berlin European Council of March 1999. The package is also known as Agenda 2000 after the document of July 1997 setting out the Commission's proposals (European Commission, 1997c). A main priority of the package was to prepare the way for enlargement of the EU, and the deal included agreements on reform of the CAP and Structural Funds (see Chapters 13 and 15).

The Berlin Agreement on Agenda 2000 entailed a total budget commitment of €640 billion for the 2000–06 period. At the insistence of the main contributor countries, and Germany in particular, the ceiling on budget spending as a percentage of GNI remained at 1.27 per cent. The VAT contribution was decreased from 1 per cent in 2000 to 0.75 per cent in 2001 and 0.5 per cent in 2004. This again had the effect in increasing the share of the fourth resource in total revenue, with the intention of bringing the relative contributions of the different member states closer in line with their overall economic performance. The percentage of tariffs and agricultural levies retained by the member states in order to cover administrative costs was raised from 10 per cent to 25 per cent.

The British budget rebate continued (and was worth about 4 billion euro per year), but the UK agreed to forgo certain windfall gains that it would otherwise have received.[19] The other main contributors to the EU budget (Germany, the Netherlands, Austria and Sweden) also requested a reduction in their net contribution, but in the final compromise accepted simply that their contribution to the UK rebate would be reduced. It was, however, agreed that there would be a revision of budgetary procedures before the next financial perspective.

---

[18] The 1988 budget package introduced the 'Stabilizers' (see Chapter 13), and placed a ceiling on the rate of increase in Guarantee spending of the European Agricultural Guidance and Guarantee Fund, which could not exceed 74 per cent of the growth of the GNP of the Community. The European Parliament was to be responsible for ensuring that this limit was not passed.

[19] These included: the benefits from reducing the VAT ceiling, which was expected to increase the relative contribution of Italy, Belgium, Denmark and France, and to decrease that of Germany and the UK; the increased reimbursement to member states to cover administrative costs on traditional financing (tariffs and agricultural levies) from 10 per cent to 25 per cent; and the expenditure on EU enlargement, which was excluded from calculation of the British rebate.

With regard to total spending on agriculture, the initial intention was to freeze annual expenditure in real terms at the 1999 level of €40.5 billion for the 2000–06 period,[20] but in the event an additional €3 billion was agreed.

The Agenda 2000 package also entailed reform of the Structural Funds. The financial perspective earmarked some €195 billion for the Structural Funds for the 2000–06 period, with a further €18 billion for the Cohesion Fund.

The 2000–06 multi-annual financial framework allocated €3.14 billion per year in pre-accession assistance to the applicant countries. This was to consist of €1.56 billion each year in PHARE (Poland and Hungary Assistance for the Restructuring of the Economy) programme.[21] Initially PHARE was aimed primarily at facilitating economic and political transition, but increasingly it became focused on preparing the applicant countries for EU accession. This entailed assistance for institution building, investment support, and economic and social cohesion (see Chapter 19). The pre-accession assistance also included an allocation of €1.04 billion for ISPA, or the Instrument for Structural Policies Pre-Accession, and a further €0.52 billion each year for SAPARD, or the Special Accession Programme for Agriculture and Rural Development.

The Berlin Agreement on Agenda 2000 also fixed a budgetary allocation for new EU members, which was to rise from €4.14 billion in 2002 to €14.21 billion in 2006. The Berlin estimates were based on the assumption of the six 'front-wave' candidates of the Luxembourg group joining in 2002,[22] even though by then accession negotiations had begun and such an early deadline was clearly unrealistic. Presumably, in confirming the hypothesis which had been set out in the initial 1997 Agenda 2000 document, the EU wished to leave a certain amount of room for manoeuvre, and avoid possible diplomatic incidents that might arise if the date were postponed.

The Copenhagen European Council of December 2002 agreed on a revised financial package for EU enlargement over the 2004–06 period. This was based on the assumption that ten countries would join in 2004, with Bulgaria and Romania joining in 2007. It was agreed that no new member state should be a net contributor (which might risk happening because of delays in spending) to the EU budget in the 2004–06 period.

The aim of the Copenhagen Agreement was to keep within the Berlin budgetary key. The annual budgetary allocation for enlarging to ten countries set out at Copenhagen was below the Berlin allocation for each year for only six new members. The total allocation for commitment appropriations for accession was €42,590 million in the 1999 financial perspective, and €37,468 million in the 2002 agreement.

12.8 The multi-annual financial framework for the 2007–13 period

In 2004 the European Commission (2004b) presented proposals for the multi-annual financial framework for the 2007–13 period. According to an Interinstitutional Agreement of 6 May 1999, if a new financial perspective could not be agreed, the existing spending framework would be extended automatically. The new member states had transitional arrangements for 2004–06 and had a strong interest in reaching agreement on a new financial framework as it was likely to mean higher transfers from the EU budget. After an initial failure at the Luxembourg European Council in June 2005, Tony Blair was concerned to reach an agreement during the UK presidency, and this was achieved with the December 2005 European Council. In May 2006 an Interinstitutional Agreement between the EP, the Council and the Commission formalized the new financial framework and the rules for its management.

The 2007–13 financial perspective had to resolve certain controversial issues:

- The resources for the EU budget and the budget ceiling;
- The British rebate;
- Spending priorities (in particular, CAP reform and policies for economic and social cohesion).

---

[20] Allowance was made for 2 per cent inflation each year.

[21] The PHARE programme began in 1989, and the acronym soon became a misnomer as assistance was extended to other countries in Central and Eastern Europe (see Chapter 19).

[22] Cyprus, the Czech Republic, Estonia, Hungary, Poland and Slovenia (see Chapter 19).

The Commission initially proposed fixing the own resources ceiling at 1.24 per cent of GNI for the 2007–13 period. In December 2003 the six main contributors to the EU budget (Germany, Austria, France, the Netherlands, Sweden and the UK) published a letter calling for a ceiling of 1 per cent of GNI on expenditure from the EU budget. The Commission proposal was cut significantly by the European Council agreement of December 2005, but subsequently increased slightly (by €4 billion) by the Interinstitutional Agreement of May 2006 to reach €864 billion in 2004 prices for 2007–13, or 1.05 per cent of EU GNI.[23]

Over the 2007–13 period a number of financial instruments are available outside the expenditure ceiling in order to face unforeseen events. They include:

- The EU Solidarity Fund (maximum €1 million a year) to allow rapid financial assistance in the event of natural disasters in a member state or candidate country;
- The Instrument for Flexibility (maximum €200 million a year) to allow additional expenditure in defined circumstances;
- The Emergency Aid Reserve (maximum €221 million a year) to allow a rapid response to specific unforeseen aid requirements of third countries.

In addition, the European Globalisation Adjustment Fund can mobilize unused appropriations from the previous year to provide additional support for workers who have suffered as a result of major structural changes in the pattern of world trade (see Chapter 7).

A key is published indicating how much each of the other member states must contribute each year to the British rebate, pitting the UK against all the other member states.

The Commission proposed a possible general rebate from 2007, extended to other net contributors. A generalized corrective mechanism could be used to reflect the principle of *juste retour* by which each country gets back roughly what it puts in. This has the consequence that net contributors attempt to limit transfer of resources to net recipients, while the latter try to keep thier receipts as high as possible.

According to the Commission (2004b), when the UK was granted the rebate it was one of the poorest EU countries, with a GNI per capita of only 91 per cent of the EC average, but by 2003 this percentage had risen to 111 per cent, second only to Luxembourg. Without correction the UK rebate would have risen from €4.3 billion a year over the 1997–2003 period (when spending on enlargement was excluded) to €7.1 billion a year for the 2007–13 period, and the new member states would also have had to pay part of the British rebate. Under the correction mechanism proposed by the Commission, the UK would have contributed 0.51 per cent of GDP to the EU budget, becoming the highest contributor in terms of share of GDP. Not surprisingly this proposal was strongly contested by the UK. In the event, at the December 2005 European Council Britain agreed to give up about one-fifth of its rebate, or a maximum of €10.5 billion, attributable to Eastern enlargement.[24] Reduced VAT-based contributions were also agreed for all member states, with additional discounts for the other main contributors (Germany, the Netherlands, Sweden and Austria).

As shown in Table 12.2, despite the lip service paid to the Lisbon Strategy (and subsequently Europe 2020), the initial Commission proposal for spending on competitiveness was whittled away substantially in the budgetary decision-making process. The outcomes for spending on citizenship, freedom, security and justice, and the EU as a global actor were also less than initially proposed. In contrast, cohesion (covering the former category of structural operations) and natural resources (covering the previous agriculture and rural development heading) were cut far less, suggesting some inertia in spending patterns of the EU budget.[25]

---

[23] The financial framework may be revised in the event of unforeseen circumstances on a proposal of the Commission in compliance with ceilings defined in the own resource decision setting the maximum potential level of financing of the EU (1.24 per cent of GNI for payments and 1.31 per cent for commitments). Any revision requires unanimity in the Council.

[24] The rebate continues to apply on expenditures from the EU(15) and CAP, and part of the rural development funds for the new member states. The then UK Chancellor of the Exchequer, Gordon Brown, was consulted throughout the negotiations, but according to the *Financial Times* (26 June 2006) was dismayed by the outcome, and later argued that the UK rebate should also apply on UK payments to compensate the reduced contributions of Austria, Germany, the Netherlands and Sweden.

[25] See also Kay and Ackrill (2007) for a discussion of this issue.

Table 12.2 Changes in the proposed expenditure of the 2007–13 financial perspective (€ billion, 2004 prices)

	Commission proposal	European Council agreement	Interinstitutional agreement
Competitiveness	121	72	74
Cohesion	336	308	308
Natural resources	400	362	371
Citizenship, freedom, security and justice	15	10	11
Global partner	62	50	49
Administration	58	50	50

Source: Elaboration on the basis of Commission data, © European Union, 2011.

In 2010 there was a heated debate over the draft EU budget for 2011. The European Parliament was in favour of a 6.2 per cent increase in expenditure to fund additional EU tasks arising from the Lisbon Treaty such as the European External Action Service (see Chapter 1), and support for the ITER experimental nuclear fusion reactor in France. The EP also wanted to increase its influence over budgetary decisions. In the absence of an agreement, the 2010 levels of expenditure would have been rolled over (see Box 12.2). At a European Council meeting of October 2010 the UK prime minister gained support from eleven member states for a cap of €126.5 billion (equivalent to a 2.91 per cent increase), and this was the basis for a compromise reached in December 2010. The debate over the 2011 budget was a warm-up for discussions about the financial perspective after 2013.

Box 12.2

The budgetary procedure as established by the Lisbon Treaty (Article 314 TFEU)

- Establishment of the preliminary draft budget by the Commission and transmission to the EP and Council by 1 September. In practice the Commission attempts to submit the draft budget by the end of April/beginning of May
- First reading of the preliminary draft by the Council, which adopts its position with amendments if any and passes it to the EP before October 1.
- First reading by the EP, which has 42 days either to adopt the budget, or to hand its amendments to the Council.
- If the Council does not accept the EP's amendment a Conciliation Committee is set up (see Chapter 3). The Conciliation Committee has to present a joint text in 21 days, and if it fails the Commission has to produce a new draft budget. Once a joint text is agreed by the Conciliation Committee in early November, the EP and the Council have 14 days to accept it or reject it
- If a budget has not been agreed by the beginning of the financial year, a sum of one- twelfth of the budgetary appropriations for the preceding year may be spent each month.

Source: European Commission DG Financial Programming and Budget, http://ec.europa.eu/budget/budget_detail/deciding_en.htm (accessed 26 January 2011).

12.9 The post-2013 multi-annual financial framework

At the June 2005 European Council Tony Blair linked the question of the UK budget rebate to reduced spending on agriculture, but France, in particular, opposed further CAP reform. At the Brussels European Council of October 2002 the French president, Chirac (a former minister of agriculture), had convinced Germany and the European Council to accept a limit of 1 per cent per year on the increase in nominal spending on the CAP from 2007 until 2013 (see Chapter 13). By way of compromise the December 2005 European Council agreed a full, wide-ranging review of all aspects of EU spending, including the CAP, and of revenue, covering also the UK rebate. This was initially envisaged for 2008/09.

In order to begin the debate on the budget review and the multi-annual financial framework after 2013, the European Commission carried out a vast public consultation and organized a conference in 2008.[26] However, subsequently the fundamental review of all aspects of the EU budget was postponed as the Lisbon Treaty was not yet ratified, and the new Commission and EP were not yet in place. In October 2010 the Commission published a communication identifying principles, ideas and options for the future EU financial perspective, ways in which its functioning could be improved, and suggestions as to how the resources of the EU budget could be reformed.[27]

On the spending side, the issues raised in the debate and the 2010 communication by the Commission include the following:

- More **flexibility** is needed to react to unforeseen contingencies such as natural disasters, economic crises and so on. Under the present system even a limited shift in the use of funds requires a lengthy and cumbersome process.

- There should be less emphasis on inputs and more on **effective results.** To date, EU budget negotiations have been guided more by the need to satisfy all member states that they are receiving their fair share of the EU budget than by trying to ensure adequate funding for policy priority areas. More attention should be paid to identifying policies with EU added value.

- **Solidarity** through the EU budget is an indispensable element of the EU approach.

- Higher priority has to be given to the **smart, sustainable and inclusive growth** envisaged by the Europe 2020 strategy (see Chapter 7). This implies financing of research and innovation, key cross-border infrastructure, and energy and climate policies at the EU level.

- **CAP reform.** The options range from limited measures to improve the functioning and allocation of direct payments, to a further major shift from income and market support towards rural development (including environmental) measures, in other words pillar 2 of the CAP. However, as Chapter 13 indicates, pillar 2 policies are frequently not above criticism on efficiency and equity grounds.

- **Cohesion policy** should be less concerned with simply reducing the gap between rich and poor, and better geared to realizing the overall priorities of the EU such as those of the Europe 2020 strategy. There should be greater concentration of EU and national resources on agreed priorities, and more coherence and co-ordination between different policy areas.

- There should be more integration into a single programme of different measures to consolidate **EU citizenship.** It is suggested that the Solidarity Fund could be used for civil protection and all kinds of disasters, and not simply natural ones.

- The EU should continue to meet its **external commitments** such as those to raise development aid to 0.7 per cent of GNI by 2015, and improve its co-ordination and governance (see Chapter 18). In addition there should be continued efforts to tackle issues such as migration, competition, climate change, energy, terrorism and organized crime in an international context.

---

[26] See the material from the consultation and conference on the website of the European Commission: 'Reforming the budget, changing Europe', http://ec.europa.eu/budget/reform/index_en.htm (accessed 25 January 2011), and, in particular, Begg et al. (2008b), ECORYS Nederland BV et al. (2006), and Euréval and Ramboll Management (2008). For a treatment of the underlying issues see also Begg and Grimwade (1998) .

[27] European Commission (2010i). Formal Commission proposals were premature at this stage.

- More transparency and stricter discipline should be introduced with regard to **administrative expenditure.**
- The EU could increase its **efficiency** through more co-operation with partners such as the European Investment Bank, development banks in the member states and the European Bank for Reconstruction and Development (see Chapter 19), and through the use of new financial instruments such as EU project bonds. A ten-year financial framework with a mid-term review could be used to increase flexibility.

Also, on the revenue side of the EU budget, member states tend to favour instruments that improve their net position (in line with the principle of *juste retour*) rather than those with the greatest value added for the EU as a whole. The resources system is complex and far from being transparent, and issues such as the UK budget rebate and similar (though smaller) correction mechanisms for other countries pit member states against each other.

As mentioned above, the fourth resource now accounts for about three-quarters of EU budget revenue and is based on national contributions so is not in line with the spirit of the Rome or Lisbon treaties. Despite the Single Market Programme, VAT systems vary considerably between member states and the VAT contribution performs badly in reflecting relative economic performance. The 2010 communication by the European Commission (and other contributions to the debate) suggest abolishing the VAT-based own resource and introducing one or more new own resources as a replacement, such as:[28]

- a transaction or financial activities tax;
- a kind of carbon tax, such as using the proceeds from auctioning of emissions trading allowances (though the practical difficulties encountered by the system as described in Chapter 14 do not bode well for this option);
- an EU charge related to air transport (popular with airlines such as Ryanair!);
- a separate EU VAT rate; and/or
- a share of an EU energy or corporate income tax.

The debate on the next financial perspective and the changing priorities for policies it implies is likely to absorb a large share of EU energies in 2011 and 2012. Though a detailed discussion of these issues is beyond the present scope (and would require quite a degree of clairvoyance at this stage) the immense amount of material on the European Commission's 'Reforming the budget, changing Europe' is a good starting point for following the debate.[29]

12.10 Financial irregularities

In recent years there has been growing concern with financial irregularities in payments from the EU budget. According to Article 317 TFEU (ex Article 274 TEC), the Commission is responsible for implementing the budget, but in practice the Commission has to rely on the member states to put certain policies into practice. It is estimated that some 22 per cent of funds is managed centrally by the Commission, 76 per cent of funds is delegated to the member states by the Commission under 'shared management', while the rest is managed with international organizations or with third countries (European Commission, 2007d). In addition there is external control by the Court of Auditors (see Chapter 3) and a discharge from the European Parliament. The discharge procedure 'releases' the Commission from responsibility for management of a budget by marking the end of a budget's existence.

---

[28] See Begg et al. (2008b) and European Commission (2010i) for discussions of the advantages and shortcomings of these various measures.

[29] European Commission, 'Reforming the budget, changing Europe', http://ec.europa.eu/budget/reform/index_en.htm (accessed 25 January 2011).

Following the scandal that led to resignation of the Commission in 1999 (see Chapter 3), the new president of the Commission, Romano Prodi, announced a policy of 'zero tolerance' of corruption and set up an anti-fraud office, OLAF, to look into cases of financial irregularity. However, as Box 12.3 suggests, the EU continued to suffer shortcomings in financial accountability.

Box 12.3

An example of financial irregularities in the EU accounts

January 2002	Marta Andriessen appointed EU chief accountant.
March 2002	Andriessen argues with the Commission over a complete overhaul of the EU accounting system.
May 2002	Andriessen is removed from her job and offered a post in the personnel department.
August 2002	Andriessen is suspended on full pay for going public to the press and European Parliament. She is also banned from Commission buildings. Following Andriessen's suspension, the commissioner responsible for the budget, Michele Schreyer, promises a vigorous programme of reform and a switch to the modern accrual system of accounting by 2005. (Andriessen later became an MEP and a member of the EP's budget oversight committee.)
November 2002	The Court of Auditors strongly criticizes the 2001 accounts, arguing that it can only certify that 5 per cent of spending was legal and regular.
June 2003	The chief internal auditor of the Commission, Jules Muis, attacks the Commission's *'rudimentary financial control systems'* and announces that he will be leaving his job the following year. In a leaked paper, Muis accuses the Directorate-General for the budget of being *'a department haunted by a profound lack of qualified staff, a host of vacancies/absentees in crucial functions, a power ambience totally cater[ing] to the DG'* (*Financial Times*, 10 March 2003).

12.11 Evaluation and outlook

The history of the EU budget seems essentially a process of lurching from one crisis to another. Generally compromises have been reached to resolve these crises, though often with substantial concessions and delays. The arrangements that emerge from these compromises frequently seem messy and not very transparent, and are often difficult to justify on 'rational' grounds.

In line with the reform of the decision-making institutions, enlargement of the EU to 27 members or more also required changes in the budget. For this reason, since 2008 the EU has been scrutinizing the present system, taking into account topics such as CAP spending and the British rebate (or 'correction mechanism'). This led to the 2008 'health check' of the CAP (see Chapter 13), and attempts to evaluate cohesion policy and assess ways of further reducing regional disparities (see Chapter 15).

In 2010 the Commission published a communication (European Commission, 2010i) with the aim of opening debate on the question of EU budget reform. The document was not intended to provide numbers for the financial perspective from 2014, but to examine future spending priorities and the most effective ways of finding resources to finance them. On the expenditure side the aim was to look at questions such as: the focus of EU funding (whether a widespread approach is preferable to more concentration); ways of increasing transparency and accountability; the balance between stability and flexibility; the experiences and lessons to be learned from co-financing; and decisions concerning the levels of management (the degree of decentralization, and whether joint or shared mechanisms are more appropriate).

The sources and mechanisms of the EU budget are also to undergo review in order to meet principles such as economic efficiency, equity, stability, visibility and simplicity, administrative cost-effectiveness, financial autonomy and sufficiency.

The aim of the debate is to ensure that the EU budget is more responsive to changing needs, and that policy priorities are more closely reflected in spending priorities. In mid-2011 the European Commission is expected to present its proposals for the financial perspective after 2013 and a heated debate of these issues is certain to follow.

Summary of key concepts

- Over time, some countries have emerged as **net beneficiaries** of and others as **net losers** from the EU budget.

- The **share of agriculture** (now included under natural resources) in spending from the EU budget has been falling, while the **share of economic and social cohesion** (formerly called structural operations) in expenditure has been increasing steadily.

- Since 2007 the main items of **expenditure** from the EU budget are: competitiveness and cohesion for sustainable growth; preservation and management of natural resources; citizenship, freedom, security and justice; the EU as a global player, and administration.

- Overall the scale of **budgetary spending as a share of the GDP** of the EU has remained small, increasing from 0.3 per cent in 1960 to a ceiling of 1.05 per cent of GNI for the 2007–13 period.

- Throughout its history the budget of the EU has been guided by certain basic **principles**: unity and universality, equilibrium, annuality, specification and a common unit of account.

- **Fiscal federalism** deals with the criteria for deciding the appropriate level of government (European, national, regional or local) for decisions with regard to expenditure and revenue.

- The Treaty of Rome envisaged a **transition period until 1970** during which financing of the Community was to consist essentially of contributions from the member states to be followed by the introduction of a system of own resources.

- During the 1980s, excess spending on the CAP, widening membership and extension into new policy areas meant that **inadequate budgetary resources** continually plagued the Community.

- Since 1984 Britain has had a budget refund or 'correction', but this has been increasingly contested by other member states.

- The **own resources** consist of: tariffs on manufactured imports from third countries; agricultural tariffs and levies; a percentage of VAT and the fourth resource based on GNP/GNI.

- Since 1988 the **financial perspective** of the EU has been set out for several years to come. This was the case for the 1988–92 period (Delors 1, or the bill for the Single Market), 1993–99 (Delors 2, or the bill for Maastricht), 2000–06 (the Berlin Agreement on Agenda 2000, which can also be termed the bill for enlargement), and 2007–13 (the bill for the Lisbon Strategy and Europe 2020).
- A **fundamental debate** is under way on the future of the EU budget and the financial perspective after 2013.

Questions for study and review

1 What are the main principles underlying the EU budget, and how far have they been respected in practice?
2 Describe how the concept of fiscal federalism could be applied in the EU context.
3 Explain why the EU budget ran into difficulties on both the expenditure and the revenue sides.
4 Indicate the main changes in the EU budget over the years.
5 What changes were made in the EU budget as a result of enlargement?
6 What are the central issues in the debate about the future of the EU budget and the financial perspective after 2013?

Online
Learning **Centre**

When you have read this chapter, log on to the Online Learning Centre website at ***www.mcgraw-hill.co.uk/textbooks/senior*** to explore weblinks, chapter-by-chapter test questions, case studies and more online study tools.

Chapter 13

The Common Agricultural Policy

Learning Objectives

By the end of this chapter you should be able to understand:

- ✓ The reasons for public intervention in agriculture
- ✓ The objectives of the Common Agricultural Policy (CAP) set out in the Treaty of Rome and how they changed over time
- ✓ The three principles on which the CAP is based
- ✓ The main mechanisms used by the CAP and their changes through the years
- ✓ How the system of price support works
- ✓ The pressures for reform of the CAP
- ✓ The negative consequences of the price support policy
- ✓ The absence of an effective policy to improve farm structures for so many years
- ✓ The various attempts at CAP reform
- ✓ The outlook for the CAP after 2013

13.1 The reasons for public intervention in agriculture

Agriculture has always been one of the sectors most subject to state intervention, and this was also the case for the six founding members of the European Community.[1] There are various explanations for the scale of public intervention in agriculture. The dependence of agricultural production on biological

---

[1] For a history of the early formation of the CAP see Tracy (1989), Neville Rolfe (1984), Ackrill (2000) or Milward (2000).

cycles,[2] climate and natural phenomena (including epidemics) provide justification for government measures to stabilize farm prices and incomes. Empirical studies show that the elasticity of demand for food products is relatively low both with respect to price and income, meaning limited outlets for sales of foodstuffs over time, and rendering farmers more vulnerable to shocks on the supply side.[3] Difficulties may also arise for farmers because supply may be very inelastic in the short run. This may be because some output decisions (for example, sowing a crop) may be impossible to reverse in a changed market situation.[4] Farms in the EU are often of a relatively small dimension, which renders it difficult to exploit economies of scale, and may place the farmer at a bargaining disadvantage vis-à-vis larger producers in the food processing or farm input sectors. The economic and social difficulties many farmers have in leaving the sector have meant that, for protracted periods, farm incomes and living conditions may compare unfavourably with those in the rest of the economy.[5]

Public intervention may also be justified to deal with cases of 'market failure' as for instance may occur when information is costly or difficult to obtain. It may be extremely hard for consumers to acquire adequate information about the nature and safety of a food product even after that good has been consumed as, for instance, emerged clearly during the BSE or 'mad cow' crisis. Public intervention may be required to ensure standards are met, to carry out certification and testing, and to provide information through labelling, trademarks and so on.

Public intervention may also be justified when there are externalities, that is, when there is a difference between the costs and benefits to the individual and to the public. In other words, externalities are the positive or negative effects of the production or consumption by one individual on others, which are not reflected in prices (see Chapter 14 for an economic analysis of externalities). Negative externalities may arise, for example, from the impact of agriculture on the environment, with some forms of intensive production causing soil and water pollution, or the elimination of biodiversity. Positive externalities may occur when agriculture contributes to rural development, care of the landscape, protecting animal welfare or preservation of breeds in danger of extinction.

The activities of farm lobbies also help to explain the persistence and scale of state support for the farm sector.[6]

 ## 13.2 Agriculture in the Treaty of Rome

Given the tradition of intervention in agriculture in the founding members of the EC and the diversity of measures used, France, in particular, was adamant that the new Community policy could not simply be a collation of national policies and that some kind of common policy was necessary (see also Chapter 2).

---

[2] According to the Cobweb theory, if the quantity supplied adjusts with a lag to the market price a cycle may result (with an explosive cycle when supply is more elastic than demand in absolute terms), and government intervention may be necessary to stabilize prices and incomes. Though the theory is based on extremely simplifying assumptions, there does appear to be empirical evidence for cycles in the production of certain agricultural products such as beef or pig meat.

[3] According to Engel's law, as incomes rise the share of foodstuffs in household expenditure falls. Numerous empirical studies over time and across countries find support for this 'law'.

[4] There are various explanations of the low short-run elasticity of supply in agriculture. Fixed costs tend to be relatively high and while these have to be considered when expanding production, only variable costs are taken into account in deciding when to stop production (the shutdown point). According to Johnson and Quance (1972), the difference in the prices of certain factors of production (such as farm machinery on the new and used markets) may help to explain inelasticity of supply in the short run. If the price of second-hand factors of production is very low, they will continue to be used even when their marginal productivity in terms of value falls very low. Nerlove (1956) shows how elasticity of supply tends to increase over the time period considered.

[5] This is frequently referred to as 'the farm problem'.

[6] See Senior Nello (1984, 1989 and 1997) for more detailed descriptions of why farmers have been so successful in organizing pressure groups and how they manage to influence policy in their favour.

Articles 38 to 47 of the Treaty of Rome deal with agriculture (now in revised form as Articles 38 to 44 TFEU).[7] Article 39 is probably one of the most frequently quoted articles of the Treaty and sets out the **objectives of the CAP:**

> 1. (a) to increase agricultural productivity by promoting technical progress and by ensuring the rational development of agricultural production and the optimum utilization of factors of production, in particular, labour;
>
>   (b) thus to ensure a fair standard of living for the agricultural community, in particular by increasing individual earnings of persons engaged in agriculture;
>
>   (c) to stabilize markets;
>
>   (d) to ensure availability of supplies;
>
>   (e) to ensure that supplies reach consumers at reasonable prices.
>
> 2. In working out the Common Agricultural Policy and the special methods for its application, account shall be taken of:
>
>   (a) the particular nature of agricultural activity which results from the social structure of agriculture and from structural and natural disparities between the various agricultural regions;
>
>   (b) the need to effect the appropriate adjustments by degrees;
>
>   (c) the fact that in the Member States agriculture constitutes a sector closely linked with the economy as a whole.

Despite the importance that has always been attached to this statement of objectives, it is vague and lacking in precision on certain crucial points, and is not without contradictions. For instance, how is the increase in productivity mentioned in paragraph 1(a) to be achieved – by increases in output (which was the interpretation of the farm lobby at the time) or by reductions in the labour force? If, as turned out to be the case, support for agricultural prices is the main instrument used to achieve 'a fair standard of living' for farmers, how is this to be reconciled with 'reasonable prices' for consumers? The reference to the 'social structure of agriculture' can be interpreted as a commitment to the family farm (which has to be read in the context of the post-war collectivization in the Eastern bloc). However, given the small size of many farms at that time, the question of how to ensure their efficiency arises. The stress on availability of supplies reflects the post-war concern with shortages, even though surpluses had already emerged for certain Community agricultural products (such as grains, dairy products and sugar) by the late 1950s.

What is missing from the Treaty is a precise description of what form this CAP should take, and, in particular, there is little mention of the policy mechanisms to be used. These omissions from the Treaty reflect the ongoing differences among the member states about how a common policy should be constructed. After its earlier experiences of co-operation on agricultural policy matters with Luxembourg and Belgium, the Netherlands was anxious to ensure less restricted markets and effective guarantees against reintroducing restrictions on trade. In contrast, the French favoured a more interventionist approach in order to ensure adequate levels of support and protection.

13.3   The agreement on the CAP mechanisms

As many of the key questions were still unanswered, Article 43 of the Treaty of Rome called for a conference to work out the details of the future CAP. This led in 1958 to the Stresa Conference,

---

[7] Article 38 of the Treaty of Rome defined the field of action as 'plant, livestock and fish products, including those subject to the first stage of processing'. Articles 40 to 47 speak in very general terms about the policies to achieve these objectives, the institutions for agricultural decision making and the arrangements for the transitional period. See Fennel (1997) for a discussion of agriculture in the Treaty of Rome.

generally recognized to be one of the milestones in the creation of the European Community. However, the conference failed to resolve many issues, and heated debate about the future form of the CAP continued. Agreement was not reached until 1962.

The second stage of the transition period was due to come into operation from January 1962, with deadlines for more dismantling of tariffs between the member states and further progress in the creation of the common external tariff. While Germany was anxious for progress on trade issues, France and the Netherlands threatened to block the move to the second stage of the transitional period (due to begin in January 1962) if sufficient progress were not made on agriculture. The issue of what mechanisms to adopt for the CAP was hammered out in the famous 23-day marathon of the Council of Ministers, and failure to meet the January deadline led to the expedient of 'stopping the clocks' until agreement was finally reached on 14 January 1962.

The package eventually agreed by the Council of Ministers included what subsequently became known as the three fundamental principles of the CAP:

1 **Unity of markets.** Trade would be progressively liberalized between the member states and common prices would be introduced for the main agricultural products throughout the Community.

2 **Community preference.** Barriers on trade between member states were to be removed, but common levies on imports of agricultural products from the rest of the world meant that EC producers would be at an advantage vis-à-vis those from third countries in selling their agricultural produce on Community markets.

3 **Financial solidarity.** A European Agricultural Guidance and Guarantee Fund (EAGGF, or FEOGA after its French acronym) would finance agricultural policy measures. The Guidance section would cover expenditure on structural measures, while the Guarantee section of the EAGGF would be responsible for market intervention and export refunds.

Agreement was also reached on the market organization to use for cereals and the so-called cereal-based products: poultry and pig meat.[8] Similar mechanisms were subsequently extended to about three-quarters of all agricultural products. Figure 13.1 sets out the **basic price support mechanism**. Though not shown in the diagram, target prices for each year were agreed by the Council of Ministers as the basis for calculating all the other common prices. Initially target prices were calculated according to the 'objective method', which involved taking account of the evolution of costs and revenue in order to ensure that developments in farm incomes were in line with those in other sectors. This method was abandoned from the mid-1980s when a policy of price restraint for agricultural products had to be introduced.

Each year intervention prices, or minimum guaranteed prices, are also agreed. Intervention agencies have to stand ready to buy up the product to ensure that prices do not fall below this floor level.[9] The intervention agencies are organized on a national basis, with, for example, the AIMA (L'Azienda Italiana per i Mercati Agricoli) and subsequently the AGEA (Agenzia per le Erogazioni in Agricoltura) in Italy. The Intervention Board in Britain was replaced in 2001 by the Rural Payments Agency responsible for CAP payment schemes in England and for certain schemes throughout the UK.

The threshold price is a minimum entry price applied on imports from the rest of the world at the point of entry to the EU. In the first years of the CAP the threshold price was calculated as the target price minus the cost of transport from the main port of entry (Rotterdam) to the main consumption

---

[8] The introduction of the variable levy in mid-1962 on imports from the rest of the world led to the 'chicken war', or first trade dispute between the Community and the USA.

[9] Initially the intervention prices were calculated on the basis of the target price minus the cost of transport from the point of major production of grain (Ormès in France) to the point of main consumption in the Community (Duisburg in Germany), also taking into account margins of distribution, but subsequently the ratio of intervention price to the other common prices has become a matter for political compromise.

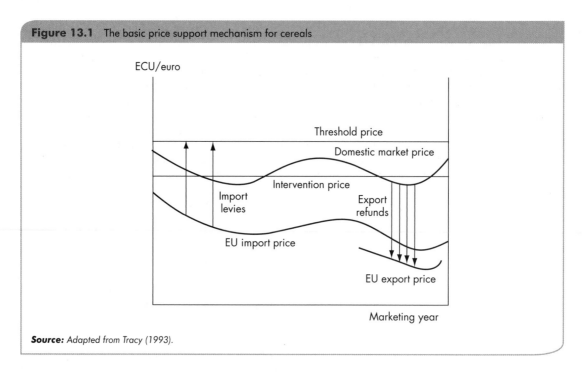

Figure 13.1 The basic price support mechanism for cereals

Source: Adapted from Tracy (1993).

area (Duisburg), and was estimated at 10 per cent below the target price. In later years the ratio of threshold to other common prices also became subject to negotiation.

The level of Community preference, or advantage, that EU farmers have on Community markets over producers from the rest of the world is given by the difference between threshold and intervention price. In general the market price in the EU will oscillate between these two limits, but weakening of the intervention system in subsequent years (with, for example, disincentives and time and quality restrictions before intervention could take place) meant that, at times, market prices could descend below intervention levels.

Variable import levies were applied on imports from the rest of the world in order to bring their prices up to the threshold price. If prices on world markets fell while Community prices remained unchanged, the variable levy would simply increase, and this was regarded by the USA, in particular, as a particularly insidious form of protection. In 1995, as a result of the 1994 General Agreement on Tariffs and Trade (GATT) Uruguay Round Agreement on Agriculture, variable import levies were replaced with tariffs on imports of agricultural products from the rest of the world (see the OLC to this book for a description of the GATT/WTO agricultural negotiations).

For exports, **export refunds** (also called restitutions) or subsidies generally cover the gap between domestic EU prices and prices on world markets. Each week, management committees in the Commission calculate the difference between EU and world prices in order to set the level of export refunds, though there is a certain leeway to take account of market conditions. On numerous occasions the EU was criticized for its 'generous' calculation of the level of export refunds.

13.4 The 1964 agreement on common price levels

The 1962 decision on the mechanisms of the CAP failed to give any indication of what the common levels of prices would be, and clearly the level of prices has crucial implications for the evolution of output and consumption in the Community.

Again the difficulties in reaching agreement reflected different national positions. At the time, agricultural prices were relatively high in Germany, Luxembourg and Italy, and lower in France, Netherlands and Belgium. The solution of the Commission in document COM(60) 105 was to propose that an average price be applied as the basis for the new common policy.

However, the national farm lobbies, and COPA (Comité des Organisations des Producteurs Agricoles, the umbrella organization of national farm associations which had been established in September 1958) were strongly opposed to the Commission proposal. The Agricultural Committee of the European Parliament (composed mainly of farmers) also called for an increase in prices to the level of those in the main consumer country, Germany (Tracy, 1989).

In May 1964 the Kennedy Round of GATT negotiations opened formally, but France made progress on reaching a common Community position conditional on resolution of the question of grain prices.[10] In November 1964 Germany accepted a wheat price slightly below the German level, but obtained agreement that the new prices would apply only from 1967/68; that prices for barley, maize and rye (of which Germany was a major producer) would be fixed relatively close to wheat, and that there would be temporary, degressive payments to compensate for the agricultural price cuts in the high-price countries: Germany, Italy and Luxembourg.

13.5 The effects of EU price support policy

The effects of the traditional Community price support system can be analysed using a partial equilibrium framework similar to that used for tariffs in Chapter 4. The world supply curve of a particular product is assumed to be perfectly elastic at Pw in Figure 13.2. The demand and supply curves (assumed linear for simplicity) of the Community for the traded product are indicated by D and S in the diagram. Without price support, the domestic price of the product in the EC is assumed equal to the initial world price Pw. At the world price Pw the Community would produce Qs and demand Qd of the product, so the EC would import Qs – Qd (equivalent to the excess demand) of the product.

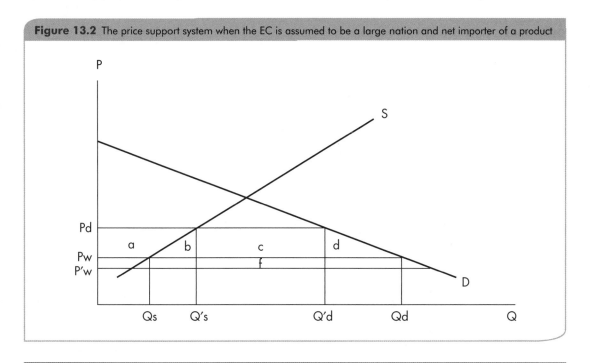

Figure 13.2 The price support system when the EC is assumed to be a large nation and net importer of a product

---

[10] See Tracy (1989) or Fanfani (1998).

For simplicity, the EC threshold and intervention prices are assumed to be the same and are both Pd. At Pd the Community will import Q's – Q'd of the product. As can be seen from the figure, the level of EC prices is shown to be considerably higher than the world price level, as was generally the case for many products (grain prices, for instance, were often over twice as high as world levels).

The EC is assumed to be a large nation. As can be seen from the diagram, the application of Community price support reduces net imports from Qs – Qd to Q's – Q'd. *Ceteris paribus* in the case of a large nation, the fall in net imports would have the effect of reducing demand on world markets, causing the world price level to fall. Conversely, the reduction or elimination of price support would increase EC net imports causing the world price to rise. The gap between the new world price P'w and the EC minimum import (or threshold) price Pd was covered by a variable import levy until 1995. Subsequently tariffs (the difference is explained below) were applied on EU agricultural imports.

The variable import levy or tariff is a source of revenue for a government budget.[11] The total revenue for the budget will be equal to the unit value of the variable import levy or tariff (Pd – P'w) multiplied by the quantity imported after introduction of the tariff (Q'd – Q's). In the diagram this corresponds to the area of the rectangles c and f, or (Pd – P'w) × (Q'd – Q's). If this revenue is used in a socially useful way, it represents a welfare benefit to a country. This benefit could be considered an increase in the income of taxpayers in that *ceteris paribus* in the absence of the tariff the government would have to charge higher taxes.[12]

With the introduction of price support, producer surplus rises by area a, consumer surplus falls by a + b + c + d and the revenue for the budget is areas c + f. As the EU is assumed to be a net importer, the fall in world price from Pw to P'w as a result of the introduction of price support causes a transfer from producers in the rest of the world to consumers in the EU of area f (given by the quantity of imports Q'd – Q's times the fall in world price Pw – P'w). The net welfare effect for the EC of introducing price support is therefore area f minus areas b and d.

Figure 13.3 illustrates the difference between a variable import levy and a tariff. Again the EU is assumed to be a net importer of the product, and a large nation. Introduction of price support will

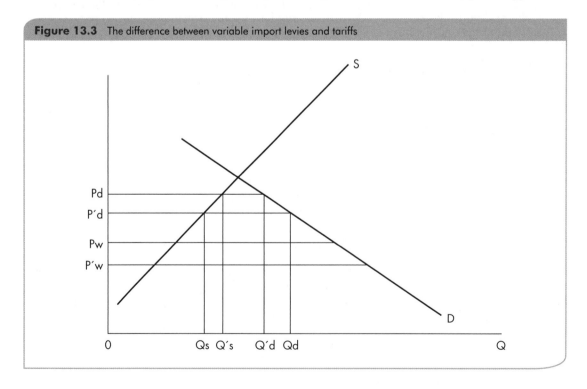

Figure 13.3 The difference between variable import levies and tariffs

---

[11] See the discussion on the sources of revenue of the EU budget in Chapter 12.

[12] See Chapter 4 for a description of these effects.

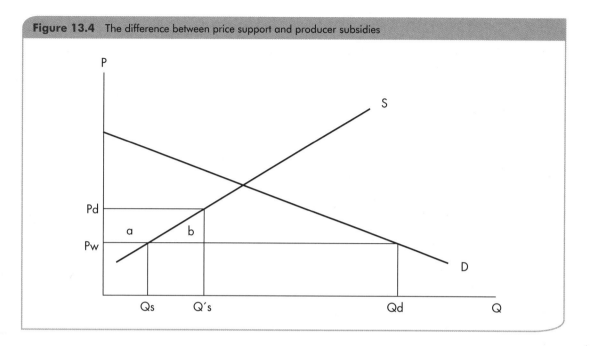

Figure 13.4 The difference between price support and producer subsidies

reduce the world price from Pw to P'w. Under the traditional price support system of the Community the threshold price Pd was fixed for the year and did not change even if world prices fell (by Pw – P'w). All that happens is that the variable import levy increases to cover the gap between the new world price and the threshold price, so the unit value of the variable levy becomes Pd – P'w.

In contrast, with an ad valorem tariff following the fall in the world price, the internal EU price becomes P'd. With a tariff EU domestic prices are therefore more sensitive to movements in world price levels, and this was why the USA, in particular, criticized the Community's variable import levies. From 1995 variable import levies were converted into tariffs as a result of the 1994 GATT Uruguay Round Agreement on Agriculture.

The difference between the price support system and **producer subsidies** can be seen from Figure 13.4. In agriculture these producer subsidies are often also referred to as 'deficiency payments' after the system applied in Britain before joining the EC. The main difference between the EU price support system and producer subsidies is that the introduction of producer subsidies leaves the domestic price unchanged for consumers. As Figure 13.4 shows, with the producer subsidy the domestic price to producers rises to Pd, while the price paid by consumers remains Pw. Producer surplus rises by area a, the cost of the surplus to budget contributors is area a + b (that is, the unit cost of the subsidy, Pd – Pw times the new quantity of output Q's). The net welfare loss is triangle b.

The impact of high and stable prices was to turn the EU from a net importer into a net exporter of many temperate agricultural products. As explained above, export subsidies or restitutions were used to cover the difference between the internal EU market price and the world price. Figure 13.5 shows the effect of EU export subsidies. D and S are the EU demand and supply curves for the product. With price support the internal EU price Pd is above the world price Pw, and the EU will export Q's – Q'd. The unit value of the export subsidy is Pd – Pw, and it is applied on the exports of the product Q's – Q'd. The export subsidy increases producer surplus by areas a, b and c, reduces consumer surplus by areas a and b and costs the budget areas b, c and d. The net welfare loss as a result of the export subsidy is equivalent to areas b and d. The Online Learning Centre for this textbook provides a numerical example of the effects of an export subsidy as an exercise.

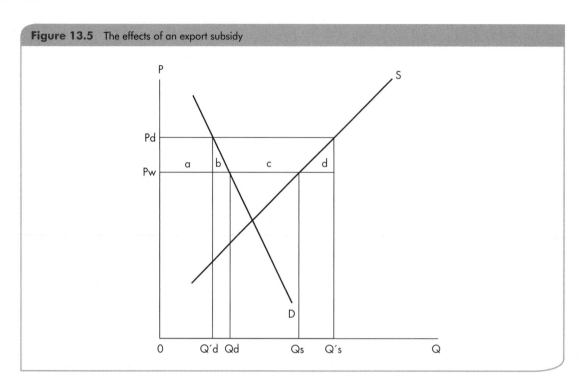

Figure 13.5 The effects of an export subsidy

13.6 The 1968 Mansholt Plan

The 1968 Mansholt Plan was probably one of the most controversial documents ever produced relating to the CAP. Published in December 1968 as Commission document COM(68) 1000, the plan set out proposals to resolve the problems of surpluses and inadequate farm incomes over the following decade, so was also known as 'Agriculture 1980'.

The plan involved a dual approach, with price policy being used to achieve market balance, while structural measures (expected to account for about one-third of the agricultural budget) would be used to create large, efficient farms. A central concept of the plan was the 'modern farm enterprise' that could ensure farm incomes and working conditions (including working hours, holidays and so on) comparable with those in other sectors. A modern farm enterprise could be formed out of a single farm or by a group of farmers coming together. The plan also introduced the concept of production units, or the dimension of production required to ensure efficiency and the use of modern technology. The creation of co-operatives was to be encouraged in order to concentrate supply and render prices more stable.

The Mansholt Plan also aimed at the reduction of surpluses and the improvement of the structure of production by cutting the number of factors of production in the sector. The objective was to induce 5 million people to leave farming, 4 million of whom would be persuaded to retire, while a further 1 million would be found alternative jobs in other sectors.

It was expected that the reduction in the labour force would release 20 million hectares, most of which could be used to restructure farms. However, to cut surpluses some 5 million hectares would be withdrawn from agricultural production and used for forestry, recreational purposes and so forth. To meet the problem of dairy surpluses, 3 million cows would also be put down.

The plan also encouraged the formation of co-operatives and producer associations to improve marketing. Account was to be taken of regional diversity (a proposal opposed by the member states) arising because farmers were operating under different natural conditions.

The reaction of the farming community to the plan was violent outrage. The proposals were thought to be too radical, and the dimension of farms proposed was considered too far removed from reality. The Commission was accused of being 'technocratic' and of attacking the family farm through back-door collectivization. Particular concern was expressed about the proposed reduction in the labour force, and about whether the means to ensure employment in other sectors would prove adequate.

In 1972 the Council finally agreed three directives on structural measures, but these were far removed from the original Mansholt Plan.[13] The financial allocation for the directives was extremely limited (and in general the Community contribution was only 25 per cent), and the extent to which they were taken up was far less than expected. The use of the directives also seemed to depend more on the administrative capacity of the member state in question than on structural needs. The whittling down of the Mansholt Plan is a major factor explaining the evolution of the CAP with its almost exclusive reliance on price support for many years. As late as 1983, Guarantee spending (on price support) accounted for 95 per cent of EAGGF spending, and in 1995 the share had only fallen to 92 per cent.[14]

13.7 The agrimonetary system

What was considered to be one of the early achievements of the CAP, the introduction of common prices, was soon undermined by changes in exchange rates between the member states. Common prices were set in units of account so had to be converted into national currencies. According to the neo-functionalist approach to integration (see Chapter 1), it was hoped that the introduction of common agricultural prices would spill over into economic and monetary union in order to avoid complications to the system as a result of exchange rate changes.

This optimism was soon to prove unfounded, and beginning with a French devaluation and a German revaluation in 1969, changes between EC currencies became a frequent occurrence. Special 'green' exchange rates were introduced for agriculture. Changes in these green rates lagged behind those in the central rates of EC currencies, since in that way it was possible to delay adjustment of agricultural prices in national currencies. This meant that a system of taxes and subsidies had to be set up at the border between EC countries to avoid speculative trade flows, and as a result market unity was undermined.[15] The operation of this 'agrimonetary system' led at times to price divergences between member states in national currencies larger than before the CAP had been introduced. In 1976, for example, for a time the gap between prices in the UK and Germany was over 50 per cent. It was only with the introduction of the euro that these difficulties were finally resolved (at least for euro members).

13.8 The ongoing need for reform of the CAP

During the 1970s and 1980s, the CAP seemed increasingly to be transformed from the cornerstone to the stumbling block of the Community. The negative effects of what had begun as a high price policy were accentuated each year by substantial increases in prices for the main agricultural products (see Table 13.1). High and stable prices encouraged production leading to surpluses. Grain and butter

---

[13] The three structural directives of 1972 relate to modernization of farms (72/159), early retirement (72/160) and socio-economic advice to farmers whether to continue farming or not (72/161).

[14] European Commission, *The Agricultural Situation in the Community*, various years.

[15] The system of subsidies and taxes at the borders were called monetary compensatory amounts (MCAs). See Senior Nello (1985) for a more complete account of the system and its effects.

Table 13.1 Average increase in Community agricultural prices (percentage variation)

	Commission proposal (1)	Council decision (2)	Difference (2) – (1)	COPA proposal
Community of six				
1968–69		–1.3		
1969–70		0.0		
1970–71		0.5		
1971–72		4.0		
1972–73		4.7		
Community of nine				
1973–74	2.8	5.0	2.2	
1974–75	11.8	13.9	2.5	12.4
1975–76	9.2	9.6	0.4	15.0
1976–77	7.5	7.5	0.0	10.6
1977–78	3.0	3.9	0.9	7.4
1978–79	2.0	2.1	0.1	5.0
1979–80	0.0	1.3	1.3	4.0
1980–81	2.5	4.8	2.3	7.9
1981–82	7.8	9.2	1.4	15.3
Community of ten				
1982–83	8.4	10.4	2.0	16.3
1983–84	4.2	4.2	0.0	
1984–85	0.8	–0.5	–1.3	
1985–86	–0.1	0.1	0.2	
1986–87	–0.3	–0.3	0.0	
Community of twelve				
1987–88	–0.5	–0.2	0.3	
1988–89	0.0	–0.1	–0.1	
1989–90	–0.2	–0.2	0.0	
1990–91	–1.1			

Source: Fanfani (1998).

mountains and wine lakes were the visible symbols of the malfunctioning of the CAP. According to the Commission (COM(91) 100), between 1973 and 1988 EC agricultural production rose by 2 per cent per year, while consumption rose by only 0.5 per cent each year.

These surpluses either had to be held in public storage, or sold on world markets with the help of export subsidies. Public storage was expensive, unpopular and involved the deterioration of foodstuffs over time, while the use of export subsidies antagonized other agricultural exporters, and the USA in particular.

Although the successive reforms of the CAP described below attempted to address its various shortcomings, then as now the main criticisms of the CAP were:

- the cost to the EU budget;
- the burden on consumers;
- tensions with third countries, and, in particular, agricultural exporters;
- disparities in the level of support with a bias in favour of larger farmers and those in Northern Europe; and
- adverse consequences for the environment.

The high and rising level of agricultural prices posed an excessive burden on the EC budget (see Chapter 12). EAGGF Guarantee spending rose from ECU 4.5 billion in 1975 to ECU 11.3 billion in 1980 and ECU 31.5 billion in 1991. In 2009, spending on agriculture and rural development was €55.3 billion, or about 42 per cent of the EU budget but, 68 per cent of this was direct aids to farmers (see below) and about 26 per cent was for rural development.

The CAP entails heavy costs to consumers as a result of the higher prices that have to be paid for food and agricultural products. Because the share of food in household expenditure is higher for less well-off households, price support hits the poorest disproportionately. As Marsh and Tarditi (2003) argue, although more than 70 per cent of consumer expenditure on food and beverages relates to processing, distribution and so on,[16] the burden of the CAP on consumers remains substantial and varies between products. According to the OECD, between 1986 and 1988 the **Consumer Support Estimate** (CSE) or annual monetary value of gross transfers (measured at the level of farm gate) from consumers of agricultural commodities as a result of policy measures that support agriculture was €68,272 million, or 37 per cent of the value of farm production in the EC. Even after the successive reforms of the CAP described below, according to the OECD in 2009 transfers from consumers to farmers in the EU(27) were an estimated €19,952 million, or 7.24 per cent of the value of the value of production at the farm gate.

As well as the CSE, the OECD publishes two other indicators annually, which can be used to compare support to agriculture in different countries: the **Producer Support Estimate** (PSE), and the sum of the most production- and trade-distorting forms of support. The PSE adds up the monetary value of government interventions that result in financial transfers from consumers and taxpayers to support agricultural producers. When expressed as a percentage of total farm receipts the PSE allows comparisons of support across countries and commodities (see Figure 13.6). Following the various CAP reforms the share of most distorting forms of support in total CAP support fell from 97 per cent in 1986–88 to 54 per cent in 2005–07.[17]

The growing EC self-sufficiency in the major foodstuffs lowered imports from the rest of the world and increased exports, thereby reducing prices of these products on world markets. Less developed

---

[16] Data of Coldiretti, an Italian farmers' association, suggest that in 2004 the share going to farmers was 7 per cent for pasta, 9 per cent for tomato sauce, 27 per cent for wine and 40 per cent for beef. By 2009 the situation had not improved, with 60 per cent going to distribution, 23 per cent to processing and only 17 per cent to farmers for food products in general; http://www.cuneo.coldiretti.it/prezzi-generi-alimentari-forbice-insostenibile-tra-campo-e-tavola.aspx?KeyPub= 17232532%7C17233991&Cod_Oggetto=16311848&subskintype=Detail (accessed 16 July 2010).

[17] This consisted of market price support, plus payments based on input use, and payments based on output: http:// www.oecd.org/dataoecd/57/5/43411396.pdf (accessed 16 July 2010). See Anania (2010) for a discussion of this issue.

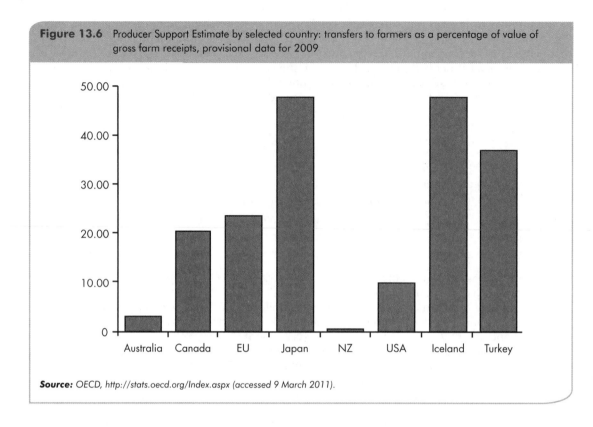

Figure 13.6 Producer Support Estimate by selected country: transfers to farmers as a percentage of value of gross farm receipts, provisional data for 2009

Source: OECD, http://stats.oecd.org/Index.aspx (accessed 9 March 2011).

countries accused the Community of agricultural protectionism, increasing instability on world markets and lowering prices for their agricultural exports.

Linking support to prices meant that those farmers who produced more benefited most from the system. According to the European Commission (1991), it was estimated that between 1970 and 1990, 80 per cent of support from the EAGGF went to the 20 per cent of farmers with the largest farms. As explained below, when price support was reduced, the largest farms were compensated most so the new system also failed to resolve the problem of income disparities.

The CAP also tended to favour Northern European producers over Mediterranean farmers. For instance, in 1986 dairy products, which are produced mainly in Northern Europe, accounted for 20 per cent of the value of production, but 27 per cent of CAP spending, while grains were 13 per cent of production and 16 per cent of spending. In contrast the equivalent figures for typical Mediterranean products were 6 per cent for production and 3 per cent of spending for wine and 15 per cent of production and 5 per cent of spending for fruit and vegetables. The exceptions were tobacco and olive oil, which were relatively expensive regimes.[18]

The almost exclusive reliance on price support encouraged specialization and intensive methods of production, with negative implications for the environment and biodiversity. There has been growing public concern about water and soil pollution by fertilizers, pesticides and intensive livestock units, destruction of wildlife habitats and changes in the appearance of the countryside.

---

[18] Tobacco accounted for 0.6 per cent of production and 3.7 per cent of spending in 1986, while olive oil was 1.6 per cent of production and 2.9 per cent of spending. These data are taken from European Commission, *The Agricultural Situation in the European Community* (1987).

13.9   Attempts at reform in the 1970s and 1980s

During the early years of the 1970s reform of the CAP was still a taboo subject. It was thought that by undermining the progress achieved in the only functioning common policy, the whole fragile edifice of European integration might come tumbling down. Discussion documents of the Commission at this time refer to 'improvement of the CAP' (1973) or 'stocktaking of the CAP' (1975).

Over time it became increasingly difficult to deny the need for change, and there were early and not very successful attempts at price restraint during the late 1970s.[19] In addition there were various reform attempts to tackle the problems of surpluses and excessive budgetary expenditure and, in particular: co-responsibility levies; milk quotas; stabilizers; and the 1988 reform package.

The aim of the **co-responsibility levies** was to render farmers 'responsible' by involving them in bearing the cost of surpluses. Each year a certain level of production for an agricultural good would be fixed, and the cost of any excess production over that level would be totally or partially borne by farmers. Co-responsibility levies were introduced for milk from 1977 and for cereals from 1986. In both cases the measures had a positive impact on the budget but failed to resolve the problem of surpluses largely because in practice their application became subject to negotiation.

The dairy sector was proving one of the most expensive CAP regimes, accounting for over 40 per cent of EAGGF Guarantee spending between 1976 and 1980. In 1983 the Commission document COM(83) 500 called for reform of the sector, arguing that a price cut of 12 per cent would be necessary to restore market balance. The member states were reluctant to accept such a large price cut and agreed on a system of **milk quotas** as a lesser evil.

The aim of the quota system was to freeze milk production at 1981 levels (1983 for Italy which imported 40 per cent of its milk and for Ireland, which is a major exporter). The EC quota was then broken down by country, and the member states could decide on two methods of application. System A involved dividing the national quota by single farms. If a farm exceeded its quota, it would have to pay a fine of 75 per cent (100 per cent from 1987). According to system B, quotas were granted to dairies and or other processors which paid a supplementary levy of 100 per cent if the quota was exceeded. From 1992 the two systems were fused, with quotas being allocated to farms, and dairies being responsible for paying a levy of 115 per cent if quotas were exceeded. Initially, quotas could only be transferred through the renting or sale of a farm, but from 1992 unused quotas could be reallocated to other producers.

Figure 13.7 uses a partial equilibrium approach to compare the welfare effects of production quotas and reductions in price support. The situation is shown for a net exporter, say the EU, even though certain member states (such as Italy) were net importers of dairy products. A reduction of support prices from Pd to P'd would have caused EU net exports of dairy products to fall from Qs – Qd to Q's – Q'd. The budgetary cost of export subsidies as a result of the reduction in price support would fall by the area b + c + f + e + d + h + g. Consumer surplus would rise by a + b, while producer surplus would fall by area a + b + c + f + e. The net improvement in welfare from reduction of price support would therefore be area b + d + h + g.

In contrast, assume that a quota of Q* for total production of milk in the EU was introduced. The EU supply curve would then become SS'S* because at Q* the EU supply curve would become perfectly inelastic. Consumers would continue to buy quantity Qd at prices well above world levels, and consumer surplus would remain unchanged. The loss in producer surplus from introduction of the quota would be area e.

Burrell (1989) has presented a more realistic version of the model, with an initial loss of producer surplus of e + f + k in Figure 13.7. Area e is lost because the quota restricts output, but areas f and k are lost because of the way quotas are allocated to individual producers. If a transfer of a quota is permitted (as was the case from 1992), the purchase of quotas by low-cost producers from high-cost producers would enable k + f of producer surplus to be recovered.

---

[19] Gundelach, the Commissioner for Agricultural over the 1977–81 period, favoured a prudent price policy.

Figure 13.7   The comparison of the effects of quotas and price support reduction

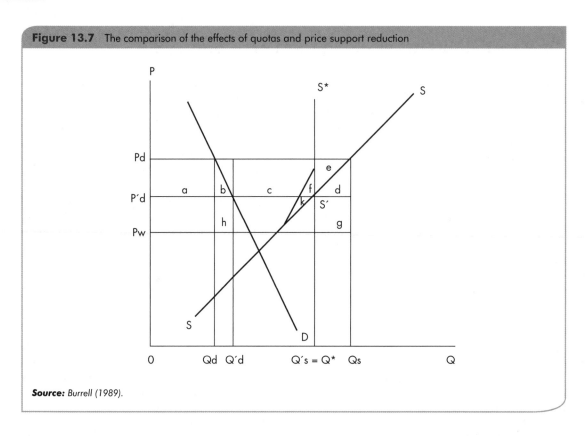

Source: Burrell (1989).

Budgetary savings as a result of introduction of the quota amount to area e + d + g. The total welfare effect of introducing a quota when transferability of quotas is permitted is therefore only a welfare gain of d + g. The question then becomes, why were quotas introduced if the net welfare gain (d + g) was likely to be less than that of a price cut (b + h + d + g)? The answer is that probably quotas were more politically acceptable to the farm lobby since, while restraining the budgetary cost of milk support, they entailed less dislocation to producers (Colman, 2007).

The quota system involves freezing the structure of production, so introducing an element of economic inefficiency (though this was somewhat attenuated by introducing the transferability of quotas in 1992). It tends to be costly to administer (see Box 13.1) and may enable cuts in milk prices to be deferred. The operation of quotas may also entail windfall gains for existing producers from the sale or rent of quotas. Moreover, the operation of quotas may exert upward pressure on land prices. However, the operation of milk quotas in the EU made a substantial contribution to reducing the problem of surpluses and slowing the rate of price increases. Milk quotas are to be phased out in the EU by 2015 (see below).

The **Green Paper of 1985** (COM(85) 333), published by the European Commission, marks the beginning of a change in priorities of the CAP. The document calls for a diversification of policy instruments in order to realize a number of objectives that cannot be reached through the almost exclusive reliance on price support. The Green Paper lists the priorities of the CAP as: reducing surpluses, promoting the quality and variety of agricultural production, improving the incomes of small family farms, supporting agriculture in areas where it is necessary for rural development, promoting awareness by farmers of environmental questions, and assisting the processing industry.

The aims of the 1985 Green Paper were to some extent taken up by the package of reforms introduced in 1988. As explained in Chapter 12, these reforms were adopted in the context of the financial perspective for the 1988–92 period and involved reform of the Structural Funds, a ceiling on the growth of CAP spending and the introduction of the stabilizers and accompanying measures.

Box 13.1

The Italian milk quotas

The history of the Italian milk quotas is one of long delays in applying Community legislation, huge fines, fraudulent activity and violent farm protests. One of the main complaints of Italian milk producers was that it was difficult for honest farmers to operate in such an environment.

Italy was granted a quota of 9.9 million tonnes on the basis of national statistics, and in 1984 the Italian minister for agriculture argued that there was a discrepancy between the quota and actual production of 11.4 million tonnes. Disagreements over the actual level of production and number of producers were to continue for many years.

Since Italy imports 40 per cent of its milk requirement, in order to exploit the full national quota it was decided to treat the whole country as a single national entity for two years, and not allocate individual quotas. In 1985 Italy applied to adopt system A, but 'administrative problems' delayed its implementation. In 1988, in order to use the quota fully, it was decided to allocate the quota to producer associations who would act as a 'single producer', and Unalat was created for this purpose. Unalat decided to apply the legislation on a voluntary basis. Unofficially Unalat and the Ministry were encouraging farmers to exceed their quotas since Italy was a deficit country, and the exact level of production had not yet been established.

The non-application of the system meant that Italy was running up a fine of about 300 billion lira (roughly 150 million ECU) each year. In 1991 the European Court of Justice stopped 330 billion from payments to Italy through the EAGGF, but by 1992 the fine had reached 4,000 billion (2 billion ECU). Italy maintained that the quota was inadequate and requested a backdated increase. In 1994 a compromise was reached whereby the Italian quota was increased (not retroactively) and the fine was reduced to 3,620 billion lira. In the logic of a supply-control measure, this fine should be paid by farmers, but in the face of protest by Italian farmers was passed on to taxpayers.

In 1993, nine years after the measure was introduced, a first attempt was made to collect data to establish quotas. Individual quotas were published, but their sum exceeded the national quota. It was decided to rely on a system of *autocertificazione* whereby farmers provided their own data on production. Such a system was an invitation to irregular practices, with quotas representing herds of cows that existed only on paper. One famous case involved a herd of 1,500 cattle based in Piazza Navona in the centre of Rome, which was said to have been rented out twelve times.

In a further moratorium in 2003, Italian dairy farmers were given 30 years to pay off the backlog of their fines.

The **stabilizers** were intended to introduce an automatic check on agricultural spending. In general these entailed fixing a maximum guaranteed quantity (MGQ) for a product, and if that quantity were exceeded, the following year there would be a cut in prices or subsidies. The effectiveness of the stabilizers as a supply-control measure was undermined by the fact that the MGQs tended to be set at relatively high levels, and the price cuts involved were small relative to the level of price support.[20] In practice there was also a tendency to challenge the 'automatic' nature of the price or subsidy cut and attempt to negotiate a compromise measure.[21]

With the benefit of hindsight, the most lasting and radical change for agriculture introduced by the 1988 package was that of the accompanying measures. These included incentives for early retirement, more extensive production methods, reforestation and set-aside.

---

[20] The maximum guaranteed quantity for cereals was fixed at 160 million tonnes in 1988 compared with a 1987 EC production of 154 million tonnes. Stabilizers, imposed at most a price cut of a few per cent at a time when support prices were many times world levels.

[21] Stabilizers had first been introduced for cereals in 1982 and should have brought about a 5 per cent cut in prices in 1985/86. A compromise was reached whereby prices were cut by only 1.8 per cent.

The set-aside scheme was voluntary and involved compensation for farms withdrawing at least 20 per cent of their arable land for at least five years. The land set aside could be left totally idle; used for forestry or non-food production (such as linen); included in a land rotation scheme or used for pasture or the production of selected crops such as chickpeas, lentils or vetches. It was hoped that set-aside would improve soil conservation and would contribute to the reduction of surpluses. However, the impact of set-aside on production is undermined by the phenomenon of 'slippage' whereby marginal land tends to be removed from production, and labour and capital tend to be used more intensively on the land that remains in production.

13.10 The 1992 MacSharry Reform

The stabilizer package failed to resolve the problem of surpluses of the main CAP products, and by 1991 reform had again acquired a new urgency. The EC became increasingly aware that CAP reform was necessary to avoid collapse of the GATT Uruguay Round negotiations.[22] A new financial perspective was due from 1993 and spending on agriculture would have to be redimensioned. Reform of the CAP was essential to permit eastward extension of the CAP with enlargement (see below). The aim was to reinforce the new priorities set out in the 1985 Green Paper, including rural development, environmental objectives and fairer distribution of support for farm incomes.

A central element of the reform was cuts in administered prices for certain key products, compensated by the introduction of direct payments to farmers. For cereals, the intervention price was to be cut by 29 per cent over three years, reaching ECU 100/tonne in 1995/96.[23] For farmers claiming compensation for an area producing less than 92 tonnes of cereals, compensation was available unconditionally in what was called the 'simplified scheme'. Farmers claiming a higher level of compensation through the 'general scheme' were required to set aside a certain percentage of their land. The percentage of land that had to be set aside varied with market conditions, and, for example, was 15 per cent in 1993/94.[24]

Oilseeds (such as soya, sunflower and colza) were at the centre of a protracted dispute between the USA and the EU. In the early years of the Community, oilseed production was small, and in 1962 an EC–USA deal agreed duty-free access. Given the relatively high prices for grains in the Community, oilseeds had increasingly been replacing grains in animal foodstuffs, and production of pigmeat and poultry grew rapidly around the main ports where oilseeds were imported, such as Rotterdam, Bremen and Antwerp. The EC introduced relatively low tariffs on oilseed imports (maximum 15 per cent) and subsidies for 'crushers' to ensure domestic producers a return compatible with that from cereals (Tracy, 1993). The USA maintained that this system ran counter to the 1962 agreement, and two successive GATT panels ruled in their favour. In 1992 the USA threatened to introduce prohibitive duties on imports worth $300 million from the EC (including pasta and white wine) if the oilseed dispute were not resolved, and for a time the whole GATT Uruguay Round appeared threatened by this dispute. As a concession to the USA the MacSharry package reformed the oilseeds sector, and the EC fixed a separate base area for oilseeds, on which a minimum set-aside area of 10 per cent was to be levied.[25]

---

[22] See Chapter 18 for a description of the GATT/WTO negotiations, and Anania (2010) or the Online Learning Centre of this book (www.mcgraw-hill. co.uk/textbooks/senior) for the agricultural negotiations.

[23] Common prices were then fixed in terms of ECU, which, as explained in Chapter 12, was subsequently replaced by the euro. The intervention price was to be cut to ECU 100/tonne in 1995/96. The target price was to be reduced to ECU 155/tonne, leaving a substantial Community preference. Farmers were compensated for the price cut by direct payments on a per hectare basis. The compensation was calculated by multiplying a basic rate (ECU 45/tonne in 1995/96) by average yields in the past in each region. The use of the hectare as the basis for calculating arable compensation led to an increase in land prices.

[24] The percentages of compulsory set-aside were: 12 per cent for 1994, 10 per cent for 1995, 17.5 per cent for 1996 and 5 per cent for 1997. Initially set-aside was to be rotational, but this obligation was dropped in 1996 (also because the administrative costs involved were substantial).

[25] The reform fixed the ratio of prices between cereals and oilseeds (1 to 2.1) as a basis for calculating per hectare compensatory payments for oilseeds.

The MacSharry Reform also included reforms in other sectors such as beef, milk and tobacco.[26] and accompanying measures which entailed a series of financial incentives for early retirement, reforestation and protection of the environment. The environmental measures were numerous, and included incentives to reduce the use of fertilizers and pesticides; to encourage extensive production methods and voluntary set-aside; to encourage the creation of natural parks, and to protect endangered species.

The MacSharry Reform represents a radical break with the past and sets a precedent for the shape of successive CAP reforms. From the point of view of economic efficiency, direct payments are preferable to price support and have the advantage of being more transparent. The reform recognizes the role of farmers in rural development and protection of the environment, but the funds allocated to these objectives were limited.

The MacSharry Reform was instrumental in permitting a successful outcome to the GATT Uruguay Round, though at the time the Commission was adamant that the reform was not introduced in response to US pressure. The reform failed to ease the pressure of agricultural spending on the Community budget, also because there was overcompensation for the price cuts.[27]

Although the compensation for price cuts was initially intended to be temporary, a date for its elimination was never fixed. Over time it became increasingly difficult to justify continued compensation for a once-and-for-all cut in prices. One of the objectives of the MacSharry Reform was to correct the inequity in the distribution of CAP transfers. However, compensation was highest for those who produced most, so the iniquity of the system was protracted.

13.11 The 1999 Berlin Agreement on Agenda 2000

The lengthy document *Agenda 2000*, published by the Commission in July 1997, was intended to prepare the EU for enlargement, *inter alia* by setting out the financial perspective for the 2000–06 period and proposals for the reform of the CAP and Structural Funds (see Chapter 15).

Agenda 2000 refers to new concepts in the agricultural policy debate, including 'multifunctionality' and the 'European model of agriculture'. **Multifunctionality** entails that farmers should not simply be considered producers of agricultural goods but account should be taken of the role they can play in pursuing other objectives such as rural development, protecting the environment, safeguarding the countryside, guaranteeing the safety and quality of food and promoting animal welfare (see Box 13.2). The **European model of agriculture** requires social, historical and environmental considerations to be taken into account, and not just economic factors (and is sometimes seen by the USA as an excuse by the EU not to cut farm subsidies).

In March 1999 the Berlin European Council reached agreement on the Agenda 2000 package (overruling an earlier agreement of the Council of Agricultural Ministers). The agricultural aspects of the final agreement included three main elements:

1 Reform of the common market organizations for products such as cereals, oilseeds, beef, milk and wine.[28] Prices were cut with partial compensation for farmers in the form of direct aids.

---

[26] Since beef producers would benefit from the lower grain prices, the intervention price for beef was also cut by 15 per cent, and premia per head of cattle were introduced to encourage more extensive forms of production. The quota system remained for milk, and there was a cut of 5 per cent in the institutional price for butter. The tobacco regime (which was one of the most expensive common market organizations relative to the amount of production) was simplified and updated. Intervention and export refunds were abolished for tobacco, the number of varieties classified was reduced to eight, and each group was subject to a quota.

[27] According to Buckwell et al. (1997: 30), the overcompensation for cereals between 1992 and 1996 was 16 per cent. This overcompensation amounted to ECU 2.0, 4.2 and 5.0 billion for the three years 1993 to 1996.

[28] Cereal prices were cut by 15 per cent, with farmers being compensated with direct payments for 50 per cent of the price reduction. Arable area payments on oilseeds and linseed were reduced and brought in line with those of cereals from 2002. Supplementary payments were made to Finland and Arctic regions of Sweden to compensate for extra drying costs.

Box 13.2

Animal welfare

Problems for animal welfare may arise from intensive farming methods in view of the confinement and restricted movements imposed on animals, and the increased use of antibiotics. More integrated markets may subject animals to lengthy travel, with increased risk of spreading disease (as, for example, in the outbreak of foot and mouth disease in the UK in 2001). Many of the consequences of new developments such as genetically modified organisms and growth-producing hormones for animal health and biodiversity are still unknown.

The issue of animal welfare may have ethical, health, environmental and quality implications. The Lisbon Treaty (Article 13 TFEU) insists on 'full regard for the welfare requirements of animals', but certain aspects of animal protection (such as those relating to the use of animals in competitions or shows) remain national competences. EU Directive 98/58 of 20 June 1998 fixes minimum animal welfare standards for all animals reared for food production. Member states must ensure that the conditions under which animals are kept and bred correspond to the needs of their species as well as their physiological and ethological needs. Later directives set out minimum standards for the protection of calves, pigs and chickens. In 2007, a new EU regulation on the protection of animals during transport came into operation. All these rules are based on the European Convention for the Protection of Animals kept for Farming Purposes, a framework convention agreed by the Council of Europe in 1976.

However, implementation of legislation may be difficult in view of the following:

■ The implications for trade and international trade agreements. It may be claimed that animal welfare measures are being used as a non-tariff barrier, and agreement on such issues may be difficult to reach at an international level.

■ The additional costs of production (increased expenditure on feed, energy, housing and so on), though at times this may be offset by technology and, at the level of overall welfare, may be compensated by the reduction in negative externalities.

■ Detailed labelling and traceability may be costly.

Compulsory set-aside of land for large farmers (that is, those claiming direct payments on more than 92 tonnes of cereals) was to continue and was set at 10 per cent.

2 Increased flexibility for the member states in the use of funds through measures such as cross-compliance and modulation. **Cross-compliance** is a form of conditionality whereby farmers have to meet certain environmental requirements to receive their direct payments in full. **Modulation** entails reductions in the payments to a farm on the basis of total amount of aid paid to the holding, overall prosperity of the holding or overall employment on the farm. The funds saved in this way can be used for environmental and related measures. Use of cross-compliance and modulation after the 1999 reform was extremely limited. By 2001 only France, the UK and Portugal had implemented modulation.

3 Rural development policy was to become the **second pillar** of the CAP (see also Box 13.3 below). The term 'rural development' is intended in the widest sense as many measures are not strictly

The milk price was cut by 15 per cent with direct aids compensating farmers for 65 per cent of the price cut. Milk quotas were to continue until 2006, with a 0.9 per cent increase in the size of the quota for Ireland, Northern Ireland, Italy, Spain and Greece from 2000, and a further 1.5 per cent increase in quotas for all member states from 2005. There was a 20 per cent reduction in beef prices, with 85 per cent compensation for farmers, and certain increases in the premia per head of cattle. For wine there was a block on planting new vines until 2010 with limited exceptions. Quality improvement was encouraged, and there was a grubbing programme. Voluntary distillation and 'crisis' distillation in times of surplus were permitted.

concerned with 'development' as such. Spending on such measures continued to account for only 10 per cent of the agricultural budget. Tighter conditions were imposed on member states in the administration of rural development schemes. Money not utilized the first year could not be carried forward. New legislation was introduced in order to promote environmentally friendly measures through the use of 'good farming practices'. The definition of good farming practice was flexible, but was to be based on the usual good farming practice in the area to which the measure applies.

13.12 The CAP and the enlargements of 2004 and 2007

Agriculture frequently threatened to prove a stumbling block in the enlargement process. As shown in Table 13.2, agriculture continues to play an important role in many of the new member states. With the 2004 enlargement the numbers employed in agriculture in the EU increased from about 7 million to 11 million. At the same time the share of agriculture in employment rose from 4 per cent to 5.5 per cent, becoming 7.5 per cent with Bulgaria and Romania in 2007.

The new member states had the complex task of adapting to EU policies and standards (food and agricultural measures account for roughly half the *acquis communautaire*), while the EU wanted to ensure that enlargement did not result in excessive transfers from the EU budget.

There was considerable debate about extending direct income payments to farmers in countries joining the EU. At least initially, such payments were introduced as compensation for the reductions in price support. At first the Commission argued that farmers in applicant countries would not generally experience price cuts and so should not benefit from direct payments.[29]

According to the Commission, prices for most agricultural products were below EU levels,[30] and it was argued that farmers in the Central and Eastern European countries (CEECs) would receive the benefit of higher prices when they joined the EU, so compensation in the form of direct payments was superfluous. However, this argument was somewhat undermined by rapid price increases for agricultural products in the CEECs. The proposed differential treatment between 'rich' Western farmers and their poorer counterparts in the CEECs was subject to fierce criticism in those countries.

In March 2002 the Commission published an extensive study of the impact of enlargement on agricultural markets and incomes,[31] confirming the view that immediate payment of 100 per cent direct payments on accession of the CEECs would lead to social distortions and inequalities. Moreover there would be non-rural beneficiaries who had generally become landowners as a result of the privatization process that included restitution in most CEECs. The report took into account four different policy scenarios: no enlargement; application of the 1999 CAP without direct payments; introduction of the CAP with full, immediate direct payments; and acceptance of the candidate countries' negotiating positions.

The working assumption of the analysis was accession of eight CEEC candidates from 2007 (Bulgaria and Romania were assumed to join later). According to the Commission report, even without direct payments the CEEC farmers would benefit on average from a 30 per cent increase in income as a result of EU market support. With the scenario of full application of direct payments in the new member states, the average expected income gain tripled, reaching a level of 89 per cent, while assuming that the applicant countries' negotiating positions were accepted, the predicted gain quadrupled to reach an estimated 123 per cent.

At the Copenhagen European Council of December 2002 it was agreed that direct aids for the new member states would be phased in gradually over ten years. These countries would receive direct

[29] See, for example, the *Agricultural Strategy Paper* (European Commission, 1995) and *Agenda 2000* (European Commission, 1997c). See also Tarditi et al. (1995) for a discussion of this issue.

[30] European Commission (1995) maintained that, depending on the product, CEEC prices were between 40 and 80 per cent of EU levels.

[31] European Commission (2002).

Table 13.2   Basic data on agriculture in the new member states

	Utilized agricultural area (m. ha) 2008	Gross value added in ag. at basic prices (€billion) 2008	Agriculture as % GDP 2008	Employment in agriculture, fishing and forestry('000) 2008	Ag. as % total civilian working population 2008	Food expenditures (% income) 2008
Bulgaria	5.1	1.8	5.5	251	7.5	N/a
Czech Rep.	3.6	1.2	0.8	166	3.3	23.3
Slovakia	1.9	0.6	1.0	98	4.0	22.8
Hungary	5.8	2.6	2.5	173	4.5	26.7
Poland	15.6	7.9	2.2	2,206	14.0	N/a
Romania	13.7	8.4	6.0	2,694	28.8	31.5
Slovenia	0.5	0.6	1.0	85	8.6	19.3
Estonia	0.8	0.2	1.4	25	3.9	24.8
Latvia	1.8	0.3	1.3	89	7.9	24.6
Lithuania	2.7	0.7	2.3	121	7.9	30.9
Cyprus	.1	0.3	1.7	17	4.3	21.6
Malta	.01	0.06	1.0	3	2.0	19.9
EU(15)	127.1	127.9	1.1	5,918	3.4	15.2
EU(27)	178.8	152.5	1.2	11,846	5.4	16.0

Source: European Commission DG Agriculture and Rural Development, http://ec.europa.eu/agriculture/agrista/2009/table_en/index.htm (accessed 9 March 2011), © European Union 2011.

payments equivalent to 25 per cent of the existing system in 2004, 30 per cent in 2005 and 35 per cent in 2006, rising to 100 per cent only in 2013. The new member states were offered the possibility of topping up direct payments through national funds and their rural development funds to 55 per cent in 2004, 60 per cent in 2005 and 65 per cent in 2006.

In order to meet problems of administrative costs and fraud, the new member states could opt for a **simplified single payments scheme** for three years, renewable for up to two more years. This would entail area payments per hectare on the whole of the agricultural area of the new member states. There would be no obligation for farmers to produce in order to receive these payments. The possibility of continuing this system was subsequently extended until 2013 for the CEECs that joined the EU in 2004, and 2019 for Bulgaria and Romania.

Difficulties also arose in deciding on production quotas for milk and sugar for the new member states. The Commission proposed taking 1995–99 as the reference period, but this was contested by some of the CEECs as not being representative. For instance, since milk production fell during these years due to the process of restructuring, countries such as Poland and the Czech Republic argued in favour of a quota based on production in the 1980s or some estimate of 'productive potential'. The Copenhagen European Council agreed on production quotas on the basis of 'the most recent historical reference periods for which data is available', though in fact some concessions were granted.

A further sensitive issue was whether the CEECs would be allowed a derogation on land ownership. Land prices were much lower in the CEECs, and though a general derogation of seven years, with the option of extending the derogation for a further three years, was eventually agreed (twelve years for Poland), the initial requests were higher (eighteen years in the case of Poland).

13.13 The Mid-term Review or Fischler Reform

The Berlin Agreement envisaged a Mid-term Review of progress in implementing the 1999 reform. The debate over the Mid-term Review was often acrimonious, and the final compromise reached in 2003 is also called the Fischler Reform as the agreement owes much to the personal efforts of the then Commissioner for Agriculture. Some member states (and notably France under President Chirac) had insisted that the Mid-term Review should be limited to mere revision of policies and should not introduce substantial changes, but the Commission rightly called the agreement a 'fundamental reform' of the CAP.

The 2003 reform entailed the introduction of a **Single Farm Payment** (SFP) for most EU farmers, and the aim was to render this **decoupled** from, or independent of, the level of production. Decoupled support is considered to have the advantage of causing less distortion of international trade, but subsequently debate emerged as to how far the SFP was in effect 'decoupled' and modifications have been introduced to reduce the risk of challenge in the WTO.[32] In its 'historical' form the SFP was based on a reference amount of the annual average of the arable crop and meat direct payments that the farmer received during the 2000–02 period. The farmer would receive the SFP regardless of whether land were used to produce anything (except fruit, vegetables or permanent crops apart from olives in the initial version of the reform), or were left idle (but maintained in good agronomic condition). After the 2003 reform member states wanting to reduce the risks of abandonment of production could continue to pay limited per hectare payments for production of certain arable crops, and some premia per head of animal (partial decoupling). The aim of the reform was to render the system simpler and more transparent, and to allow market forces again to play a role in influencing what (or whether) farmers decide to produce.

The member states had the option of introducing a system of regionalization of the direct payments. Regions would be defined on the basis of homogeneous production conditions, and all farmers in the region would receive the same basic payment per hectare, regardless of what they received or produced during the 2000–02 period. The aim of regionalization is to reduce distortions between the single payments made to farmers, which might arise under the historical system because of the different choices made in the base period. In the new member states the flat rate of per hectare payments was continued.

The SFP is linked to respect of environmental, food safety, and animal health and welfare standards, and to the requirement to keep all farmland in good agricultural and environmental condition (cross-compliance). Failure to respect these objectives would entail reduction of the direct payments to farmers.

There were also revisions in the cereals, durum wheat, dairy, rice, nuts and dry fodder sectors.[33] Subsequently similar reforms were introduced for sectors such as olive oil, tobacco, fruit and vegetables, wine, and, partly in response to disputes in the WTO framework, for cotton, sugar and bananas. In all cases support was to become at least partially decoupled and included in the SFP system.

---

[32] See Daugbjerg and Swinbank (2008).

[33] See the Commission website for a discussion of these measures (http://ec.europa.eu/agriculture (accessed 9 March 2011)). Though the current intervention for cereals was to be maintained, monthly increments were to be cut by a half. Milk quotas were confirmed until 2015, but intervention prices for butter were cut by 25 per cent and for skimmed milk powder by 15 per cent by 2007/08, with compensation through the SFP. Intervention for butter was limited to 30,000 tonnes.

The 2003 reform strengthened rural development policy (the second pillar of the CAP) with increased EU financing, reshaping of all measures into a single Rural Development Regulation covering the 2007–13 period (see Box 13.3), and new measures to promote the environment, quality, animal welfare, and to help farmers to meet EU production standards. EU co-financing of agri-environmental measures was increased to up to 85 per cent in Objective 1 regions (see Chapter 15 for an explanation and map of these regions) and up to 60 per cent elsewhere.

As part of the 2003 reform a subsidy of €45 per hectare to stimulate bioenergy production on up to 1.5 million hectares in the EU was introduced, but it was abolished in 2008 because of growing doubts about the consequences of such a policy (see Chapter 14).

The 2003 package introduced wide scope for choices to be made by member states in deciding how the reform is to be applied. It was hoped that this additional flexibility would allow the CAP to be adapted better to national and local conditions. The reform also introduced national envelopes that enable the member states to cut total direct aids and use the funds saved for specific objectives. Total direct aids could be cut by up to 10 per cent to finance additional spending on environmental objectives or measures to improve the quality of agricultural products. Alternatively, total aids could be cut by 3 per cent to resolve 'particular situations' and allow certain categories of farmers also to receive single payments.

A mechanism for financial discipline was introduced to ensure that during the period 2007–13 the agricultural budget is not overshot. Excessive spending is to induce an automatic reduction in total spending on direct payments. Measures to stabilize markets and improve common market organizations were also introduced.

As part of the 1999 reform, the Commission had proposed a ceiling, whereby if the sum total of acreage and headage to a single holding exceeded €100,000, it would have been reduced. However, the Council rejected this proposal as larger farmers, in particular in Britain and East Germany, did not want limits on their transfers.

The 2003 reform introduced compulsory modulation, with reductions in the direct payments to farmers of 3 per cent in 2005, 4 per cent in 2006, and 5 per cent from 2007 (the initial proposal of the Commission had been 20 per cent). The first €5,000 received by a farm was exempt from this reduction. The funds released were to be used to improve the environment, ensure the quality and safety of foodstuffs, or to protect animal welfare. A reduction of 5 per cent a year in direct payments was expected to release an additional €1.2 billion a year to finance these objectives. The European Council subsequently agreed on voluntary modulation of 20 per cent.[34]

13.14 The ongoing CAP reform process

As explained in Chapter 12, in 2002 it was agreed to limit the increase in CAP spending to 1 per cent per year in nominal terms between 2007 and 2013.[35] Phasing in of the CAP in Bulgaria and Romania (which joined the EU in 2007) also had to be covered by this budgetary guideline, but spending on rural development was excluded. At the 2005 European Council it was agreed that there would be a comprehensive review of all expenditure and resources of the EU budget by 2008/09, including a review of spending on the CAP.

---

[34] The European Parliament twice rejected the Commission proposal to render this measure compulsory on the grounds that it would distort competition and implied a renationalization of the CAP.

[35] '... total annual expenditure for market-related expenditure and direct payments in a Union of 25 cannot, in the period 2007–2013, exceed the amount in real terms of the ceiling of category 1A for 2006 agreed in Berlin for the EU(15) and the proposed corresponding expenditure ceiling for the new member states for the year 2006. The overall expenditure in nominal terms for market-related expenditure and direct payments for each year in the period 2007–2013 shall be kept below this 2006 figure increased by 1 per cent per year.' Conclusions of the Brussels European Council of October 2002 (Doc. 14702/02).

Box 13.3

Rural development measures 2007–13

Axis 1 COMPETITIVENESS

Human resources

Vocational training, young farmers, early retirement, farm advisory services, setting up farm management services etc.

Physical capital

Farm/forestry investments, processing/marketing, co-operation for innovation, agriculture/forestry infrastructure, restoring agricultural production potential

Quality of agricultural production and products

Transitional measures

Semi-subsistence, setting up producer groups

Axis 2 LAND MANAGEMENT

Sustainable use of agricultural land

Sustainable use of forestry land

Axis 3 WIDER RURAL DEVELOPMENT

Quality of life

Basic services for the rural economy, renovation and development of villages, protection and conservation of the rural heritage

Economic diversification

Diversification to non-agricultural activities, support for micro enterprises, encouragement of tourism

Training skills and animation

Leader Axis

A Community Initiative involving a number of states and aimed at specific groups and targets. Local Action Groups draw up strategies for the sustainable development of local areas

Source: *European Commission DG Agriculture and Rural Development, www.ec.europa.eu/agriculture (accessed 9 March 2011),* © *European Union, 2011.*

The Commission maintained that the future of the CAP was to be determined by 'one vision, but two steps'. The first was a 'Health Check' of the CAP until 2013. This was said to be simply an adjustment and simplification of the CAP, but as can be seen from the next section, the agreement reached in 2008 implied profound changes in the CAP. The second stage is a fundamental debate on

the future of the CAP in the context of the new financial perspective from 2013. Mariann Fisher Boel, Commissioner for Agriculture and Rural Development from 2004 to 2009, seemed determined to arrive at that debate with a more transparent, rational CAP that would be easier to defend.

13.15 The CAP Health Check

In November 2008 the Council reached agreement on the CAP Health Check, which in effect completed the Fischler Reform package. A central aim was to render the Single Farm Payment scheme more effective and simpler by moving from the historical system (which becomes harder to defend over time) by giving member states the possibility of shifting to the flatter rate regional system (see the 2003 reform above). Virtually all direct payments were to be decoupled as the scope for member states to choose partial decoupling was reduced. The simplified single area payment scheme (which applies on the whole of the agricultural area) was to be replaced by the SFP system by 2013 in the CEECs that joined the EU in 2004, and by 2019 for Bulgaria and Romania. The operation of cross-compliance (in particular, to meet technical concerns about controls and sanctions) was to be improved. Entitlements to SFPs were to be harmonized.

The reform also aimed at providing a 'soft landing' for the abolition of milk quotas in 2015 by, for instance, increasing the size of quotas and using rural development measures if necessary for areas heavily dependent on milk production. Set-aside was abolished, though rural development measures could be used to maintain its positive environmental effects. The price support for commodities provided by intervention was to be limited, or in some cases eliminated. More flexible use was to be made of Article 68 measures, or the 10 per cent of national budget ceilings for direct payments that may be retained for environmental policies, to improve food quality or marketing, or for farmers with special needs;[36] The percentage of modulation was doubled by adding a further 5 per cent over four years, thereby transferring more resources from direct farm payments to rural development policies. The first €5,000 received by a farm continued to be exempt from this reduction. 'Progressive modulation', which implies an additional 4 per cent reduction in payments for amounts above €300,000 per farm, was introduced. There was to be increased funding and innovation for the 'new challenges' of rural development: climate change, renewable energies, water management, biodiversity and some dairy measures.

The increased modulation under the Health Check was aimed at addressing the bias of direct payments in favour of larger farmers (see Table 13.3). As in 2003, the Commission proposed either a cap or a mechanism to reduce direct payments to larger farms, but the Council blocked this measure.

From 2005 member states were obliged to publish data on beneficiaries from CAP spending.[37] This was subsequently suspended when, in November 2010, the European Court of Justice declared partially invalid the legal basis for the publication of this information. The ruling was in response to an appeal by German farmers who challenged the publication of the name, address and amount an individual received on privacy grounds.

To reduce administrative costs, the Health Check established a lower limit of €100 or 1 hectare under which direct payments are not paid, though member states can adjust the minimum threshold to amounts that reflect their agricultural structures. The reform also allowed member states to withhold payments from applicants whose farming activity is marginal.

---

[36] Formerly called Article 69 measures under the 2003 reform.

[37] According to Article 44A of Regulation (EC) No. 1290/2005.

Table 13.3 The inequity of direct payments in the EU(27), receipts of all direct payments per farm, 2008

Size class (€)	% of EU(27) payments to size class	Number of farms in size class, '000	% of EU(27) farms in size class
< 0 €[a]	–0.11	6.31	0.08
≥,0 and < 500	2.13	3910.22	48.14
≥ 500 and < 1,250	2.94	1383.01	17.03
≥ 1,250 and < 2,000	2.30	544.16	6.70
≥ 2,000 and < 5,000	7.32	855.92	10.54
≥ 5,000 and < 10,000	10.24	541.24	6.66
≥ 10,000 and < 20,000	15.87	419.35	5.16
≥ 20,000 and < 50,000	28.22	345.73	4.26
≥ 50,000 and < 100,000	15.81	88.57	1.09
≥ 100,000 and < 200,000	7.39	21.00	0.26
≥ 200,000 and < 300,000	2.41	3.74	0.05
≥ 300,000 and < 500,000	2.14	2.13	0.03
≥ 500,000	3.34	1.30	0.02
Total	100	8122.68	100

[a]Beneficiaries in this category had to reimburse money to the European Agricultural Guarantee Fund.

Source: European Commission DG Agriculture and Rural Development, http://ec.europa.eu/agriculture/funding/index_en.htm (accessed 20 July 2010), © European Union, 2010.

13.16 The CAP post-2013

In 2010 the debate on the future of the CAP post-2013 began to heat up.[38] The Commission launched a massive public consultation on the topic in April 2010, contacting the general public, stakeholders, think tanks, research institutes and so on.[39] The aim of the consultation was to address four main questions: why we need a CAP; what citizens expect from agriculture; why reform the CAP; and what tools are needed for the CAP of tomorrow.

---

[38] See Senior Nello and Pierani (2010) for some of the contributions to this debate.

[39] See European Commission (2010j) and European Commission, DG Agriculture and Rural Development, http://ec.europa. eu/agriculture/cap-post-2013/debate/index_en.htm (accessed 10 March 2011).

With regard to why we need a CAP, most respondents were in favour of having an agricultural policy at the EU level, and many, though not all, felt that recent reforms had moved the CAP in the right direction.

At times the need for any agricultural policy at all is called into question, but as argued at the beginning of this chapter, the specific characteristics of supply and demand of agriculture and the need to correct market failure provide strong motives for public intervention in agriculture. Following the hike in world food prices in 2007/08 and again in 2010/11, concerns about future food security seem likely to remain an issue. Climate change (with more extreme weather events) also points in the direction of increased need for management of risk.

According to the 2010 consultation, many felt that having an agricultural policy at the EU level offers the advantages of a single market, and the hope of guaranteeing a level playing field.

Turning to what citizens expect from agriculture, the 2010 consultation confirms earlier Eurobarometer opinion polls in finding that citizens are in favour of the CAP providing safe and healthy food at affordable prices; sustainable use of the land; activities that maintain rural communities and the countryside; and security of food supply. The recent reforms have moved the CAP in the direction of provision of such public goods, and spillovers suggest that the wider EU level is more appropriate to realize such aims.

However, the consultation confirms the widespread feeling that further CAP reform is necessary to: cope with increased instability and volatility of food and agricultural prices; increase the equity of direct payments; simplify administrative procedures; concentrate more on the provision of public goods; respond more effectively to climate change; take into account the higher expectations of consumers; increase the competitiveness of EU agriculture; and ensure better co-ordination with other policies for rural areas.

With regard to tools for the CAP of tomorrow, a wide spectrum of views emerged from the consultation. These ranged between two poles: one in favour of maintaining the current direction of reform of the CAP with very little change, and the other wanting to refocus the CAP in order to link production and the compensation of farmers more closely to the provision of public goods associated with the second pillar of the CAP.

In November 2010 the European Commission published a blueprint for the CAP after 2013.[40] This built on the outcome of the 2010 consultation, and attempted to ensure that agricultural policy could contribute to the Europe 2020 objectives of sustainable, smart and inclusive growth (see Chapter 7). The communication of the Commission also considers the instruments that might contribute best to realizing these aims, indicating three possible options:

- Option 1 would continue with the present system of direct payments but introduce more equity in their distribution; streamline and simplify existing market measures and strengthen risk management tools; and continue in the direction of the Health Check with regard to the second pillar of the CAP.

- Option 2 would introduce more radical change for direct payments, also to render them more equitable. Direct payments would consist of: a basic rate; compulsory additional aid for agri-environmental actions; an extra payment to compensate for specific natural constraints; and voluntary coupled support for specific sectors and regions. Existing market instruments would be streamlined and simplified, and risk management tools would be strengthened.

- Option 3 would focus on environmental public goods and climate change, abolishing market measures apart from those to be used in times of severe crisis, and phasing out direct payments in their present form.

---

[40] See European Commission (2010k).

13.17 Evaluation and outlook

Since the mid-1980s the CAP has changed fundamentally. One of the first indications of this change was the 1985 Green Paper published by the Commission. This document called for an end to the almost exclusive reliance on price support and listed among the priorities of the CAP: the reduction of surpluses, the promotion of the quality and variety of agricultural production, rural development and environmental objectives.

After a rather limited attempt to move the CAP in this direction with a package of reforms in 1988, radical changes followed with the 1992 MacSharry Reform, the 1999 Berlin Agreement, the Fischler Reform or Mid-term Review of the CAP of 2003, and the 2008 Health Check.

In 2009 direct payments accounted for about 68 per cent of CAP spending, rural development had become the second pillar of the CAP with 26 per cent of all spending (while interventions in agricultural markets amounted to only 6 per cent of spending). The 'multifunctionality' of farmers was recognized as a central tenet of EU policy.

Three developments influenced (and continue to influence) the pace and shape of CAP reform: the weight of agricultural spending in the EU budget; GATT/WTO commitments; and the concern of the public for safer food, and more environmentally friendly agriculture.

In order to finance other increasingly important EU policy areas (and notably the Single Market and EMU, which were accompanied by higher spending on economic and social cohesion), the CAP share of the EU budget had to be redimensioned, at least in relative terms. The October 2002 European Council agreed on an annual increase in nominal terms in CAP spending over the 2007–13 period, but the allocation now has to be shared among 27 countries.

As explained above, agriculture continues to play an important role in some CEEC economies and the discrimination in treatment between old and new member states with regard to CAP payments is due to come to an end in 2013. Given the constraints of the EU budget ceiling, which seem likely to continue for the new financial perspective after 2013, a probable solution to this dilemma is to move further in the direction of co-financing of agricultural policy by the member states.

A second factor that influenced CAP reform was the GATT/WTO framework. The agricultural negotiations of the 1986–94 Uruguay Round were focused on three pillars: cuts in domestic support; reductions in export subsidies; and easier market access.[41] The 1992 MacSharry Reform has to be read against the background of fear of collapse of the negotiations because of disputes on agriculture, in particular between the EU and the USA. In order to reach a compromise, the solution of the EU was to transform price support into direct payments, reducing the need for export subsidies. It was also hoped that the MacSharry direct payments would be exonerated from the obligation to reduce domestic support.[42] The 1999, 2003 and 2008 CAP reforms represent further steps in this direction, with the attempt to 'decouple' support from production, thus rendering it more compatible with GATT/WTO commitments. Despite the collapse of Doha Round negotiations, WTO dispute settlements and the growing proliferation of regional trade blocs that

---

[41] See Anania (2010) or the Online Learning Centre of this book (www.mcgraw-hill. co.uk/textbooks/senior) for discussions of the agricultural trade negotiations.

[42] The GATT/WTO classification of policies follows a traffic-light analogy: red measures must be stopped (but no agricultural policies are included in this category), amber box policies should slow down (by means of reduction), while green measures can go ahead. Green box measures must meet the 'fundamental requirement that they have no or at most minimal trade-distorting effects or effects on production' (Annex 2, Article 1 of the Uruguay Round Agreement on Agriculture). The EU hoped that the MacSharry direct payments would fall into the green box and so be exempt from the commitment to reduce domestic support. In the event, a blue box was created to cover the MacSharry direct payments (which were considered to be only partially decoupled) and the US deficiency payments.

increasingly cover agriculture in a more systematic way will continue to stimulate the process of CAP reform.[43]

The third factor behind reform was the growing public insistence (as confirmed by 2010 public consultation described above and repeated public opinion surveys such as Eurobarometer (2007a)) on increased priority for rural development, environmental objectives and guaranteeing the safety and quality of food. Cross-compliance represents an attempt to meet these objectives, though its practical application encounters many difficulties. Despite the widespread popularity of the second pillar of the CAP, care must be taken to ensure the economic efficiency and equity of its measures. Weaknesses in implementation, conflicting objectives and lack of effective controls often characterize rural development policies.[44]

It is also necessary to increase competitiveness, while at the same time preparing the EU to respond better to the challenges of climate change and greater volatility of food prices. In addition there is a need for increased equity in CAP payments, with a shift in favour of smaller farmers, disadvantaged regions and new member states. There is also much scope for simplification of administrative procedures.

It is unrealistic to expect that a CAP based more on these new priorities will cost less. Health and quality controls involve high administrative costs, in particular when associated with measures such as effective labelling, animal passports and the traceability of all stages of the production and distribution processes. EU budgetary constraints are likely to become even tighter. The increased emphasis on rural development and environmental measures implies a shift towards measures that are already co-financed by national governments. A partial renationalization of the CAP seems difficult to avoid.

It seems likely that the 'tools' that will be considered most appropriate for the CAP post-2013 will be a fine-tuned version of the measures introduced in recent reforms. After the upheaval entailed by the 2003 and 2008 packages, and the ongoing reform resistance of the CAP (thanks to the pressure of lobbies and certain member states), a radical change in instruments seems unlikely. Probably the most fundamental change after 2013 will be in the source of financing of the CAP, with a shift of more of the burden towards member states.

---

[43] See Daugbjerg and Swinbank (2008, Ackrill and Kay (2009)), the website of European Commission DG Trade, http://trade.ec.europa.eu/doclib/html/134652.htm or the website of the WTO, www.wto.org. Some of the disputes are described on Online Learning Centre of this book (www.mcgraw-hill. co.uk/textbooks/senior).

[44] For an account of the inefficiencies and waste associated with the second pillar of the CAP, see Koester and Senior Nello (2010).

Summary of key concepts

- The scale of **public intervention in agriculture** can be explained by: the dependence of agricultural production on biological cycles, climate and natural phenomena (including epidemics); low elasticity of demand with respect to price and income; the inelasticity of supply in the short run; the small size of many EU farms; the economic and social difficulties many farmers face in leaving the agricultural sector; the need to provide consumers with adequate information and guarantees about the quality and safety of food; and the role farmers may play in protecting the environment, safeguarding the countryside, ensuring animal welfare and promoting rural development.

- The activities of **farm lobbies** also help to explain the persistence and scale of state support for the farm sector.

- Article 39 of the Treaty of Rome set out the initial **objectives of the CAP**.

- In 1962 there was agreement on the **three fundamental principles of the CAP**: unity of markets, Community preference and financial solidarity. There was also agreement on the price support mechanisms.

- Until 1995 **variable import levies** were applied on imports from the rest of the world, but as a result of the 1994 GATT Uruguay Round most variable import levies were replaced with tariffs.

- **Export refunds** (also called restitutions) cover the gap between domestic EU prices and prices on world markets.

- The failure of the **1968 Mansholt Plan** meant that for many years structural measures played a very limited role in the EC.

- During the 1970s and 1980s, high and stable EC agricultural prices encouraged production leading to surpluses. The **criticisms of the traditional CAP** are that it weighed excessively on the Community budget, caused tensions with other agricultural exporters, imposed a heavy burden on consumers, failed to improve the relative income situation of small farmers and encouraged intensive farming methods that had a negative impact on the environment.

- **Early attempts at CAP reform** included co-responsibility levies, milk quotas and stabilizers. The 1988 reform package introduced accompanying measures, which included incentives for early retirement, more extensive production methods, reforestation and set-aside.

- The **1992 MacSharry Reform** and the **1999 Berlin Agreement on Agenda 2000** cut prices for certain key products and introduced direct payments for farmers. The MacSharry Reform also introduced measures for early retirement, reforestation and protection of the environment. With the Berlin Agreement rural development policy became the **second pillar of the CAP**.

- Since the late 1990s EU agricultural policy has increasingly been based on the concept of **multifunctionality,** which entails that farmers should not simply be considered producers of agricultural goods but account should be taken of the role they can play in pursuing other objectives such as rural development, protecting the environment, safeguarding the countryside, guaranteeing the safety and quality of food, and promoting animal welfare.

- The **Mid-term Review or Fischler Reform of 2003** introduced the **Single Farm Payment** aimed at rendering support more **decoupled** from, or independent of, the level of production. Decoupled support is considered to have the advantage of causing less distortion of international trade. Rural development was again given a higher priority, with a single Rural Development Regulation covering the 2007–13 period.

- The **Health Check of 2008** completed the Fischler Reform encouraging regionalization of the SFP; reducing decoupling, ending set aside, reducing intervention, preparing for abolition of milk quotas and strengthening the second pillar of the CAP.

- The fundamental debate on the future of the CAP from 2013 has begun.

Questions for study and review

1 Why has the CAP always played such a central role in the EC/EU?
2 What are the main defects of a price support policy?
3 Why did structural policy play such a minor role in the EC for so long?
4 What were the objectives of the CAP set out in the Treaty of Rome, and to what extent have they been realized? How have the objectives of the CAP changed over time?
5 Why has the CAP proved so resistant to reform over the years?
6 Describe the early attempts to reform the CAP.
7 The 1992, 1999, 2003 and 2008 reforms changed the mechanisms used by the CAP. Describe the fundamental aspects of these reforms.
8 What criticisms can be made of EU rural development policy?
9 What are the advantages and disadvantages of 'decoupling' support from production? How far is the Single Farm Payment decoupled?
10 Describe the main sources of pressure for further reform of the CAP.
11 How do you envisage the CAP post-2013?
12 Exercise on the introduction of an export subsidy in a large nation (see Chapter 4 and the Online Learning Centre of this textbook for examples of how to carry out the exercise). Assume that in conditions of free trade with a world price Pw of €100 tonne for a product, the quantity of that product demanded Qd by a country is 1,500 tonnes and the quantity supplied Qs is 2,500 tonnes. Assume that the price elasticity of demand for the product in that country is –0.4, and the price elasticity of supply is 0.3. The country then introduces an export subsidy of €20/tonne which causes a change in world prices (that is, the terms of trade of that country) of €30/tonne. Calculate the effects of introducing the export subsidy on consumer expenditure, producer revenue, the trade balance and the total welfare of the country.

Online
Learning **Centre**

When you have read this chapter, log on to the Online Learning Centre website at ***www.mcgraw-hill.co.uk/textbooks/senior*** to explore weblinks, chapter-by-chapter test questions, case studies and more online study tools.

Chapter 14

Environmental and Energy Policies

Learning Objectives

By the end of this chapter you should be able to understand:

- ✓ The economic basis of environmental policy
- ✓ The main instruments used in environmental policy
- ✓ How EU measures have evolved over the years
- ✓ The five principles of EU environmental policy
- ✓ The role of the European Environmental Agency
- ✓ The international dimension of EU environmental policy, in particular with regard to the Kyoto Protocol and after
- ✓ The main features of the EU energy market
- ✓ The evolution of EU energy policy

14.1 Introduction

During the German presidency of 2007 Angela Merkel singled out environmental policy as a way of relaunching the integration process, announcing that the EU was at the vanguard of the battle against climate change. The choice seemed strategic as a way of injecting new adrenaline into the EU fifty years after its foundation: environmental measures are widely favoured by the public, and action at the regional or national level is generally not considered effective. According to a Eurobarometer survey of 2010, 69 per cent of EU citizens would like to see protection of the environment dealt with at

the EU level.[1] EU initiatives may provide an incentive to reaching agreement at a wider international level, and may also act as a way of increasing the weight of the EU as a global actor.

After a slow start, since the early 1970s the EU has developed a wide range of environmental policies. The main stepping stones in the development of EU environmental policy include the introduction of six Environmental Action Programmes, successive Treaty changes increasing the EU role in environmental issues, and the creation of a European Environmental Agency based in Copenhagen, which started its activities in 1994. The EU and its member states operate a common negotiating position on environmental issues at an international level. EU environmental and energy policies are closely linked, in particular in the task of tackling climate change. As explained in Chapter 7, EU environmental policy is a central element of the objective of the Europe 2020 project to ensure sustainable growth.

Energy policy has returned to centre stage in the integration process in recent years, with a renewed effort to tackle national champions and complete the internal market in this sector. With the Lisbon Treaty, for the first time the treaties contain a section on energy. This sets out the objective of ensuring proper functioning of the energy market, including promotion of energy efficiency, increasing the security of energy supply and the development of new and renewable forms of energy.

This chapter first sets out the economic basis of public intervention and the various types of instrument used in environmental policy, before describing the various EU measures, with particular reference to the policies towards climate change. Then follows an analysis of the EU energy market, and a description of the evolution of EU energy policy, focusing on recent developments, including attempts at 'unbundling' or the separation of companies dealing with transmission and the distribution of energy.

14.2   The economic basis of environmental policy

The economic basis of environmental policy can be explained with the help of Figure 14.1.[2] In the figure there are two horizontal axes. The higher axis indicates the level of output Q of a firm that pollutes. The lower axis shows the level of pollution or waste W associated with each level of output. It is assumed that as the level of output Q increases, so too does the level of pollution W. One of the main aims of environmental policy is to 'decouple' negative environmental effects from the level of economic activity.

The vertical axis indicates money units in euros. The line MNPB sloping downwards from A to Qp shows the marginal net private benefit to a firm, or the additional profit on an extra unit of output. As output increases, the marginal net private benefit is assumed to fall, finally reaching zero at Qp. The area under the MNPB line gives total profits, so at Qp the firm maximizes profits. Wp is the level of pollution associated with Qp, the profit-maximizing level of output for the firm.

The pollution causes externalities to third parties. An externality in production occurs when the activity of a firm has an unintended impact on the utility or production function of another individual or firm. The externality may be positive or negative. The diagram here illustrates the situation for negative externalities, such as the impact upon others of the firm's polluting water or the air. The marginal external cost line MEC shows the additional damage to third parties from each extra unit of pollution. The MEC line slopes up from 0 to C in the diagram because it is assumed that each extra unit of pollution will cause more damage (though in practice the line may take various shapes). The marginal external cost is also measured in money units, or euros.

The diagram can be used to show the **optimum level of pollution** from the point of view of society as a whole. If a firm aims at maximizing profits, and fails to take into account the effect of its

---

[1] This is 1 per cent down on the equivalent Eurobarometer survey for 2009. According to Eurobarometer (2007b), 88 per cent affirmed that the EU should deal with global warming as a matter of urgency. Eighty-nine per cent of the same poll unequivocally welcomed EU policies to reduce greenhouse gases by 20 per cent by 2020.

[2] The explanation here is based on Pearce (2003).

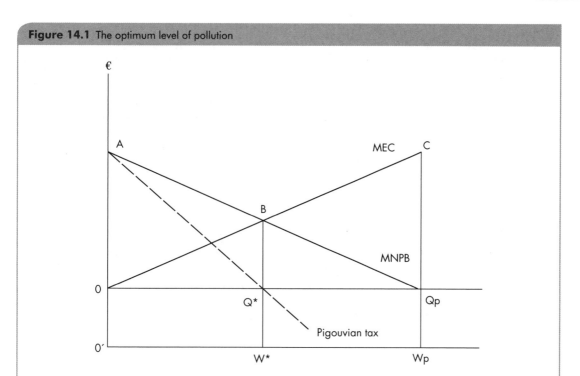

Figure 14.1 The optimum level of pollution

Source: Figure 9.1 (p. 217) from The Economics of the European Union, 3rd edn (2003) by M. Artis and F. Nixson. By permission of Oxford University Press.

pollution on others, it will produce at Qp with total profits of 0AQp. However, at Qp the total external cost of the pollution on others is 0CQp. The overall impact on society (that is, taking into account the impact on the firm and on those suffering the pollution) will therefore be a net gain of 0AB and a cost of BCQp.[3] This is not an optimum, because it fails to maximize the gains to society as a whole.

The optimum level of output is at output Q* with a waste level W*, where the net gain to society 0AB is at a maximum. At levels of output below Q*, the net marginal private benefit to the firm is greater than the marginal external cost (the MNPB line is above the MEC line), so the net social gain could be increased by expanding output. At levels of output above Q*, the MEC line is higher then the MNPB line, so the total gain to society could be increased by cutting output. It is important to note that the optimum level of pollution is not zero since society would forgo the gain 0AB. The 'optimum' from the point of view of economic theory may therefore differ from that of ecologists who set an intrinsic value on aspects of the environment such as biodiversity or continuation of the species even if no humans are involved.

The problem then becomes how to ensure that the firm will produce at level of output Q*, and this can be achieved in various ways:

- Bargaining can occur between the firm and those suffering from pollution in situations where the firm is given the right to pollute.[4] As long as the marginal external cost to sufferers is greater

---

[3] From the point of view of society, the benefit of 0BQp to the firm and the cost 0BQp of pollution on others cancel out.

[4] The classic article by Coase (1960) provides the framework for this type of analysis.

than the net marginal benefit to the firm (that is, the MEC line is above the MNPB line), those suffering from pollution will have an incentive to pay the firm to cut back pollution, and the firm will have an incentive to accept those payments. These payments will continue until the marginal external cost equals the marginal net private benefit (that is, the MEC line intersects the MNPB line), which occurs at level of output Q*. In practice, high transaction costs may prevent bargaining between sufferers and the firm reaching the optimal level of pollution. There may also be a tendency for individuals suffering from pollution to 'free ride' and not pay their contribution to stop the firm polluting, in particular if the sufferers are numerous. Individual sufferers assume that their non-payment to the firm will not be noticed and that others will bear the cost of inducing the firm to cut production and pollution.

- In the absence of transaction costs, bargaining between the firm and those suffering from pollution will also lead to the optimum level of output Q* in situations where the firm is obliged to pay compensation for pollution. Starting from a level of output 0, the firm will have an incentive to pay compensation to those suffering from pollution as long as the marginal net private benefit of the firm is higher than the marginal external cost (that is, the MNPB line is above the MEC line), and this is the case up to level of output Q*.

- The government may prohibit firms from emitting more than a certain level of pollution, or require them to use a particular technology, and impose sanctions (such as fines) on firms failing to comply with the legislation. This type of intervention is usually called 'command and control' (see below), though strictly the term entails the government fixing both the level of pollution and the means of achieving this goal as is usually the case in fixing technology requirements. To achieve the optimum level of pollution, the government would fix the level of pollution at W*.

- The government may require the firm to pay a tax equal to the marginal external cost. This is called a **Pigouvian tax** after the economist Alfred Pigou who first proposed this type of tax. It is shown by the dotted line in Figure 14.1. At each level of output, the MNPB line of the firm is reduced by an amount equal to the MEC.[5] The firm will have an incentive to produce at Q*, because this is the level of output which maximizes output after tax.

In practice it is difficult to calculate the level of a Pigouvian tax, so it is not frequently used. However, other kinds of tax and subsidy are often used to promote environmental objectives. For example, landfill taxes tax waste going to landfills to encourage more efficient means of waste disposal. These are forms of market-based instruments and offer firms financial incentives or penalties to encourage them to realize the objective.

14.3   Instruments of environmental policy

In general, environmental measures may be divided into three broad categories, though in practice the distinction between these categories is not always absolutely clear:

- **Command and control** entails introducing legislation to fix norms and environmental standards that have to be complied with. These may take the form of the prohibition of certain products or substances, or emission standards combined with requirements to use certain types of technology. Strictly, the term 'command and control' entails public intervention to fix both the level of pollution and the means of achieving this goal, but in practice the term is often used more widely. The Community relied heavily on command and control in the early years of its environmental policy, and an example of the approach

---

[5] In other words, the vertical distance from the horizontal axis to the MEC line is subtracted from the vertical distance from the horizontal axis to the MNPB line.

was the strict standards for the quality of drinking water introduced in the 1970s and 1980s which included measures relating to the discharge of dangerous substances into rivers and seas.

- **Market-based instruments** set standards (in theory on the basis of an analysis of the costs and benefits involved) and offer firms a financial incentive or penalty to encourage them to realize the objectives. These instruments give a firm a choice of how to reduce pollution. Examples of market-based instruments include charges on emissions, products and users; environmentally related taxes (see below); subsidies to encourage environmentally friendly production methods (which, as described in Chapter 13, are widely used in the CAP), and tradable permits. Tradable or transferable permits involve the authority issuing a number of permits to pollute and allowing firms to trade these permits. Tradable permits are widely used in the USA. In the past the EU tended to rely more on environmental taxes and subsidies, but, as explained below, from 2005 an Emissions Trading System was introduced.

- **Voluntary agreements** (in general between a public authority and private enterprise) may be introduced to encourage environmentally friendly measures. An example of an EU measure of this type is the Eco-Management and Audit Scheme (EMAS).[6] According to this scheme a firm or public organizations voluntarily chooses to introduce an environmental programme, which is subject to external audit and publication of the results. The firm may gain from increased competitiveness and an improved image with customers, suppliers and public institutions.

14.4 The evolution of EU environmental policy

The number and variety of instruments now used in EU environmental policy render their description difficult. However, in recent years there has been a growing tendency to use market-based instruments rather than the strategy of command and control. Such instruments generally involve lower implementation costs than command and control.

There is no mention of a role for the Community in the Treaty of Rome, reflecting the rather low priority given to such questions at the time, and creating difficulties in finding a legal basis for Community initiatives for some years. Though some environmental measures were implemented at a national level by the member states, it was not until the early 1970s that environmental objectives appeared on the Community agenda.

According to Pearce (2003), the 1972 study by the Club of Rome, 'Limits to growth', marks a growing international awareness of environmental questions. This study drew attention to the limits of natural resources and of the Earth to absorb waste. In the same year at the Paris Summit the EC member states called for environmental issues to be included in the Community agenda.

In 1973 the Community embarked on the first of what are now six **Environmental Action Programmes** (EAPs). These are indicative programmes, even though many of their guidelines were subsequently translated into Community legislation.

The First EAP covered the period 1973–76 and set out the general principles and goals of environmental policy.[7] In order to achieve these objectives the First EAP attempted to increase awareness of environmental problems, conduct impact studies, reduce pollution and improve waste management (see Box 14.1).

The following three EAPs (1977–81, 1982–87 and 1987–92) were mainly concerned with consolidating the aims of the First EAP. Given the limited success of these programmes, the Fifth EAP (1993–01) reflected a change in approach with a shift to emphasis on prevention rather than

---

[6] Introduced in 1993 with Regulation No. 1836/93 and updated in 2001 with Regulation No. 761/2001 and in 2009 with Regulation No. 1221/2009.

[7] These included the first four of the five principles subsequently included in the Maastricht Treaty, as described below.

Box 14.1

EU policy towards waste

According to the European Environment Agency, each year every EU citizen throws away 445 kg of household waste and this is expected to increase. The EU throws away roughly 1.3 billion tonnes of waste a year, 40 million tonnes of which is hazardous. EU municipal waste is burnt in incinerators (19 per cent), recycled or composted (39 per cent), or dumped in landfill sites (39.5 per cent). Landfilling occupies land space and discharges chemicals such as carbon dioxide and methane into the atmosphere, and chemicals and pesticides into the soil and groundwater. Landfills are becoming so difficult to site that the term 'nimby' or 'not in my back yard' has been coined.

In 2003 the European Commission presented a thematic strategy on waste. This was updated as a proposal for a new thematic strategy and directive in December 2005, based on the following principles:

- **A life-cycle approach.** This involves looking beyond the pollution caused by waste to consider its potential contribution to a more sustainable use of natural resources and raw materials.

- **Prevention of waste.** Member states are required to develop waste prevention policies and 'reach out to the individuals and businesses' responsible for waste generation.

- **Recycling and reuse.** EU-wide standards are to cover waste collection, reuse and recycling.

- **Improving final disposal and monitoring.** Energy recovery from municipal incinerators is to be improved, and landfills should be used only as a last resort. The EU has introduced a directive on landfill management, which bans certain types of waste such as used tyres.

- **Simplifying existing legislation and targets.** The EU strategy does not set specific targets on waste recycling or prevention so, according to the Commission, is not expected to impose any 'quantifiable financial costs' on businesses or member states.

Source: Statistics from European Environment Agency, http://www.eea.europa.eu/themes/waste/about-waste-and-material-resources (accessed 28 December 2010).

---

correction of the damage, and from the top-down command and control approach based on regulatory legislation to a bottom-up approach based on a wider range of policies, in particular on market-based instruments involving a larger number of socioeconomic actors.

The Sixth EAP, 'Environment 2010: Our future, our choice', covering the 2002–12 period, aims at using a wide range of instruments to influence decisions made by 'business, consumers, policy-planners and citizens'.[8] This is to be achieved by: improving the implementation of existing legislation; integrating environmental concerns into other policies; working more closely with the market; empowering people as private citizens and helping them to change behaviour; and taking account of the environment in land-use planning and management decisions.

The programme identifies four priority areas: climate change; nature and biodiversity; environment and health (see Box 14.2); and management of natural resources and waste. It is difficult to imagine a wider agenda, and the European Commission has at times been criticized for being too ambitious in setting objectives. There is to be an assessment of the Sixth EAP in 2011 before deciding whether to introduce a seventh action programme.

---

[8] The Sixth EAP, 'Environment 2010: Our future, our choice', http://ec.europa.eu/environment/newprg/index.htm (accessed 11 January 2011).

Box 14.2

The REACH legislation

In 2006, after much controversy, Regulation No. 1907/2006 on **REACH**, or Registration, Evaluation, Authorisation and Restriction of Chemical Substances, was passed. This requires manufacturers and importers to gather information on chemicals used in their products, and to register some 30,000 substances in a central database of the European Chemicals Agency in Helsinki. The Agency will help in the better and earlier identification of the intrinsic properties of chemical substances, and in the co-ordination of in-depth analysis of potentially dangerous chemicals. The regulation requires progressive substitution of the most dangerous chemicals when alternatives have been identified. The REACH legislation was drawn up on the basis of extensive consultation with stakeholders, and will be phased in over eleven years. As a result of intensive lobbying by industry, numerous exceptions were allowed, and the list of hazardous substances for which alternatives should be found was reduced to between 1,500 to 2,000. According to the European Commission, the cost to industry of abiding by the regulation could be in the order of €2.6–5.2 billion over eleven years, but by reducing exposure to hazardous materials savings in health care could be as much as €50 billion over the next thirty years.*

*As reported in The Economist, 26 November 2005.

14.5 Environmental policy in the treaties

The first explicit statutory mandate in the treaties for Community environmental policy came in 1987 with the Single European Act. The Maastricht Treaty strengthened the role of the EU in environmental policy, and revised Article 2 of the Treaty of Rome, which sets out the objectives of the Community. The expression 'continuous and balanced expansion' was replaced with 'sustainable and non-inflationary growth respecting the environment'.

The Treaty of Amsterdam again changed the wording of Article 2 of the EC Treaty. The rather imprecise concept of 'sustainable growth' respecting the environment was replaced by 'sustainable development', though again the concept was not defined in the Treaty. The concept of sustainable development was raised in the UN Bruntland Report of 1987 and is generally interpreted to mean economic and social development that is sustained over time. As a result future generations will have the same amount of assets per capita as the present generation. The assets in question are capital (plant and machinery), human capital (the stock of knowledge and skills), natural capital (the environment yields flows of services over time) and social capital (relations between people and between people and institutions). If the total stock of these assets per capita remains constant over time, development is said to be sustainable, even though environmental damage may be increasing. In 2001 the European Council adopted the EU Sustainable Development Strategy, which has the long-run aim of combining a dynamic economy with social cohesion and high environmental standards.

Building on earlier treaties, the Treaty of Lisbon confirmed the following:

- **Environmental mainstreaming**, which requires environmental issues to be taken into account in defining and implementing all EU policies. The Cardiff Process (named after the European Council of 1998) obliges the different Councils to integrate environmental considerations into their activities.
- The **objectives** of environmental policy.
- The **principles** of EU environmental policy.
- The **requisites** the EU must take into account in developing environmental policy.

The objectives of EU environmental policy entail: preserving, protecting and improving the quality of the environment; protecting human health; prudent and rational utilization of resources, and promoting measures at international level to deal with regional or worldwide environmental problems (Article 191 TFEU).

The Maastricht Treaty confirmed the four principles of Community environmental policy that had been set out in the Single European Act and added a fifth, the precautionary principle. Ever since, the **principles of EU environmental policy** have been:

- **The principle of prevention**. Prevention is preferable to correction of damage.

- **The polluter pays principle**. The polluter should bear the cost of prevention and correction of the damage.

- **The principle of correction at source**. As a priority, actions in one member state should not be allowed to affect the environment in another member state.

- **The principle of subsidiarity**.

- **The precautionary principle**. The precautionary principle implies that lack of scientific evidence linking cause and effect should not be deemed sufficient reason to take no action when there are considered to be significant risks.[9]

Assessment of requisites of environmental policy may be carried out on the basis of cost/benefit analysis. This entails a formal comparison of the costs and benefits of a policy (or investment). The assessment may, for example, consist of a formal appraisal of the expenditure involved in adapting to the legislation, an estimate of the risks associated with the pollution addressed and an analysis of how effective the measure is likely to prove in practice. A policy should only be introduced where the expected benefits exceed the costs and, where different policies are being compared, that producing the highest net benefits should be chosen. In assessing the effectiveness of environmental measures, account has to be taken not only of their impact on the environment, but also of their economic and equity implications.

The Maastricht Treaty required EU environmental measures to take into account the potential benefits and costs of action or lack of action. Although this was interpreted as not necessarily requiring a fully fledged cost/benefit analysis before introducing EU measures, some form of assessment was necessary. It is only since the early 1990s that the Commission has been using cost/benefit analysis in a routine way. The Amsterdam Treaty required the Commission to prepare assessments of the environmental impact for policy proposals with significant environmental implications. This was taken up in the Lisbon Treaty (Article 191 TFEU) and involves taking account of: available scientific and technical data; environmental conditions in the various regions of the EU; the potential benefits and costs of action or lack of action; and the economic and social development of the EU as a whole and the balanced development of its regions.

14.6 The European Environment Agency

Situated in Copenhagen, the European Environment Agency (EEA) came into operation in 1994. The aim of the Agency is to support sustainable development and to help achieve a significant and measurable improvement in Europe's environment through the provision of information to policy-making agents and to the public. The EEA is at the centre of the European Environmental Information and Observation Network (Eionet). Eionet is composed of national institutes in Europe through which it collects and disseminates environment-related information and data. The EEA is an EU body open to other members, and in 2010 had 32 member states.

---

[9] The precautionary principle is also discussed on the Online Learning Centre of this book.

14.7   The international dimension

Since pollution is an international phenomenon, EU policy also has a wider dimension. The EU (the member states and European Commission acting collectively as a negotiating bloc) takes part in global attempts to tackle transnational environmental problems such as depletion of the ozone layer, climate change and the destruction of tropical rainforests.[10]

In 1987 the Community signed the **Montreal Protocol** aimed at reducing depletion of the ozone layer. Among the main causes of ozone depletion were CFCs (chlorofluorocarbons) which were used in refrigerators, aerosol spray cans and air conditioning systems (see Box 14.3). In 1985 a hole in the ozone layer had been noted over the Antarctic. A thinner ozone layer allows more UVB (harmful ultraviolet rays) to pass through, increasing the risks of skin cancer, premature ageing of skin, eye cataracts and threats to biodiversity. International compliance with the Montreal and subsequent CFC protocols succeeded in reducing the use of CFCs, also because relatively cheap substitutes were generally available. This also had positive implications for climate change, as many of the ozone-depleting substances are also greenhouse gases (see below). However, the process of halting ozone depletion is slow because of the existing levels of ozone-depleting chemicals in the stratosphere. By 2010, 196 parties had signed the Montreal Protocol, and it is generally regarded as the most successful multilateral environmental agreement.

Box 14.3

Ozone depletion

In the 1930s the DuPont Corporation, one of the oldest chemical firms in the USA, developed a new form of chemical refrigerant. This relied on simple chemicals containing chlorine, fluorine and carbon, hence the name CFCs. CFCs are non-toxic stable substances which functioned significantly better than earlier substances used as refrigerants such as ammonia.

CFCs (together with halons) are referred to as 'ozone-depleting' substances. They may accidentally escape and disperse into the troposphere, and because they are stable, they may persist in the troposphere long enough to escape into the stratosphere. In the stratosphere these substances may react with ozone under the influence of intense solar radiation.

Initially the DuPont Corporation denied that there was a scientific connection between CFCs and the ozone layer. In 1983 the US Academy of Sciences released a report illustrating that CFCs had contributed to ozone depletion. Based on the Report, DuPont agreed to reduce CFC production, and in 1987 announced its commitment to developing ozone-friendly substitutes for CFCs.

In 1992 at the Earth Summit at Rio de Janeiro two international agreements were signed: the Convention on Biological Diversity and the United Nations Framework Convention on Climate Change (UNFCCC), which entered into force in 1994. In 1997 the **Kyoto Protocol** to the UNFCCC was agreed. Under the Kyoto Protocol industrialized countries are required to limit or reduce their emissions of six greenhouse gases (see Box 14.4).

With the ratification in 2004 by Russia (under EU pressure), the threshold was crossed for the Kyoto Protocol to come into effect (namely, ratification by developed countries emitting more than 55 per cent of greenhouse gases in the world), and it entered into force in February 2005. Emerging economies such as China and India were exempt from the Protocol, and it was not ratified by the USA as the Bush Administration maintained that it would cause serious harm to the US economy.

---

[10] The EU has also played an active role in noise abatement policies related to aircraft noise. The unilateral ban in the past on hush-kitted aircraft in the EU was a major source of tension with the USA.

Box 14.4

Climate change

Climate change refers not just to global warming but also to more extreme weather events such as more frequent storms, floods, droughts and heatwaves. Possible effects for the EU include: changes in rainfall putting pressure on water resources in many regions and leading to desertification in Southern European areas; melting snow and ice (with glaciers in retreat) causing a rise in sea levels and creating difficulties for coastal areas, and geographical shifts in the occurrence of different species and/or the extinction of species.

Greenhouse gases such as carbon dioxide (CO_2), methane (CH_4), nitrous oxide (N_2O), hydrofluorocarbons (HFC), perfluorocarbons (PFC) and sulphur hexafluoride (SF_6) can contribute to global warming. When visible light is scattered and absorbed at the Earth's surface it changes into heat, part of which is trapped in the lower atmosphere by gases such as carbon dioxide and then radiated back to the surface of the Earth. Carbon dioxide accounts for 55–60 per cent of present heat-trapping gases and is the main worry of policy makers. The quantity of carbon dioxide in the atmosphere has increased as a result of the combustion of oil, gas and coal, and also because of reduced absorption arising from deforestation, in particular in tropical areas.

The **Intergovernmental Panel on Climate Control** (IPCC) probably reflects the most authoritative global scientific consensus on climate change, and in 2007 the Panel won the Nobel Peace Prize together with Al Gore for his film *An Inconvenient Truth*. Although it is difficult to isolate the effect of greenhouse gases from other factors having an impact on climate change, or the long-term natural variability of climate, there is growing consensus among the world's leading scientists that human activity has contributed to climate change. According to the Fourth Assessment Report of the IPCC of 2007, 'most of the observed increase in globally averaged temperature since the mid-twentieth century is very likely due to the observed increase in anthropogenic (human) greenhouse gas concentrations'.* In IPCC terminology the assertion 'very likely' implies a 90 per cent probability that increased man-made emissions have caused most of the temperature rise since the mid-twentieth century, and is stronger than the conclusions of the 2001 IPCC Report, which refer to a 66 per cent probability.

According to the 2007 IPCC Report, the Earth's average temperature has risen by 0.76 degrees Celsius since 1850, with Europe warming faster than average, by about 1 degree Celsius. Fifteen of the hottest years on record occurred in the last twenty years. Assuming that no further action is taken to reduce emissions, the average temperature could rise by between 1.8 and 4.0 degrees Celsius this century. Even the lower end of that range would take the temperature increase to above 2 degrees since pre-industrial times, the threshold beyond which strong scientific evidence indicates that the risk of irreversible and possibly catastrophic changes greatly increases. It is projected that global warming could cause a further rise in sea levels by between 18 and 59 mm this century, although this could be an underestimate as it fails to take full account of changes in ice flows.

In November 2009 controversy arose following the hacking of a server at the University of East Anglia, and the publication of a series of emails that appeared to show certain climate scientists criticizing and planning to manipulate the peer review process. This was followed in early 2010 by a revelation that a claim in the 2007 IPCC Report had not been subjected to peer review and was inaccurate. The statement that the Himalayan glaciers would disappear by 2035 was traced by the journal *New Scientist* to an interview with an Indian glaciologist in 1999. However, the claim was not repeated in any peer reviewed journals and was challenged by other glaciologists, who maintained that the process would be much slower. After a short delay, the IPCC said that it regretted the poor application of its procedures in this case.

One of the more controversial aspects of the climate change debate is that it might cost more for some countries (such as the USA or Japan) to cut carbon dioxide emissions than to adapt to climate change. Moreover, powerful lobbies are opposed to reduction in carbon dioxide emissions and the reduced energy consumption it implies. It is sometimes argued that certain

countries, such as Russia and Canada, might benefit from global warming, but this view probably fails to take full account of the possibility of more extreme weather events.

The economic costs of climate change and the economic advantages of taking early preventative action were set out in the Stern Review (Stern, 2006), commissioned by the UK government. According to the Review, without further action to limit emissions, climate change could reduce global GDP by between 5 and 20 per cent a year. The Review estimated that early action to stabilize greenhouse gas emissions to prevent climate change reaching dangerous proportions could cost about 1 per cent of GDP. The Stern Review was criticized on three main counts: overestimation of the economic costs of global warming; underestimation of the costs of mitigating action; and the discount rate used for comparing present costs of mitigating action with the long-term costs of continuing with present action was said to be wrong.[†] The debate over the Review confirmed the difficulty of evaluation of the losses from climate change, but added to the growing consensus on the need for present action.[‡]

Building on an earlier 2007 study by McKinsey & Co., the McKinsey Report (2009) argued that the cost of moving to a low-carbon economy would be less than the cost of inaction as presented in the Stern Review. According to the Report, urgent implementation of the most cost-effective green technologies throughout the world could keep global warming below the 2 degree threshold for as little as 0.5 per cent of global GDP. The main reductions in greenhouse gases would come from energy efficiency improvements of vehicles, electrical appliances and buildings, low-carbon energy supply, and halting tropical deforestation.

[*] Available at the IPCC website, http://www.ipcc.ch/publications_and_data/publications_and_data_reports.shtml#1 (accessed 23 December 2010).

[†] See, for example, Dasgupta (2006) or Nordhaus (2006) on this debate.

[‡] For dissenting views see Lomborg (2001) or Lawson (2008).

The USA, however, embarked on a campaign to encourage research into improved technology such as carbon sequestration and began to sign bilateral international deals on climate change, but many observers criticized these moves as inadequate. Some individual states in the USA, such as California, introduced measures to limit emissions. With the change in government, Australia ratified the Protocol in December 2007.

The EU(15) countries that were member states at the time of ratification of the Kyoto Protocol in 2002 agreed to cut their emissions to 8 per cent below base year levels (generally 1990) between 2008 and 2012. In the CEECs, emissions fell after 1989, largely because of the decline in heavy industries. Cyprus and Malta do not have Kyoto targets, but the other new member states negotiated individual reduction commitments of 6 per cent (Poland and Hungary) or 8 per cent. The target set out under the Kyoto Protocol is for the EU as a whole, and the EU Burden Sharing Agreement allows some countries to increase emissions provided these are offset by reductions in other member states. The EU must ensure that the actions of the member states are consistent with the Protocol. If a party fails to meet its emissions target the Kyoto Protocol requires it to make up the difference in the second commitment period (after 2012), with an additional 30 per cent penalty. As can be seen from Table 14.1, there are considerable differences in performance between countries, but also thanks to the recession, most EU member states seem likely to meet their Kyoto goals.

In 2012 Kyoto's targets expire and after that date a new initiative is needed to limit global warming. In June 2007, as host of the G8 Summit, the German chancellor Angela Merkel was instrumental in enabling the G8 to pledge to begin discussions on a successor to the Kyoto Protocol after 2012 (see Box 14.5). At the G8 Summit, President Bush promised that the USA would 'be actively involved, if not taking the lead, in a post-Kyoto framework, post-Kyoto agreement'. In October 2007 he reversed his earlier position by acknowledging climate change as 'one of the greatest challenges of our time' and calling for long-term goals to cut emissions.[11]

[11] Financial Times, 2 October 2007.

Table 14.1 Greenhouse gas emissions, 2008

	2008	Target		2008	Target
EU(27)	88.7	N/a	Netherlands	97.6	94.0
Belgium	92.9	92.5	Austria	110.8	87.0
Bulgaria	62.6	92.0	Poland	87.3	94.0
Czech Rep.	72.5	92.0	Portugal	132.2	127.0
Denmark	92.6	79.0	Romania	60.3	92.0
Germany[a]	77.8	79.0	Slovenia	115.2	92.0
Estonia	49.6	92.0	Slovakia	66.1	92.0
Ireland	123.0	113.0	Finland	99.7	100.0
Greece	122.8	125.0	Sweden	88.3	104.0
Spain	142.3	115.0	UK	81.4	87.5
France	93.6	100.0			
Italy	104.7	93.5	Croatia	99.1	95.0
Cyprus	193.9	N/a	Turkey	196	N/a
Latvia	44.4	92.0	Iceland	142.9	110
Lithuania	48.9	92.0			
Luxembourg	95.2	72.0			
Hungary	75.1	94.0			
Malta	144.2	N/a			

N/a not applicable

In general, the base year is 1990 for the non-fluorinated gases (carbon dioxide (CO_2), methane (CH_4), nitrous oxide (N_2O)) and the fluorinated gases (HFC, PFC and SF_6). Data exclude emissions due to landuse, land-use change and forestry, and to international aviation and international maritime transport.

[a]Including former East Germany.

Source: Eurostat, 'Total greenhouse gas emissions', http://epp.eurostat.ec.europa.eu/tgm/table.do?tab=table&init=1&plugin=1&language=en&pcode=tsien010 (accessed 23 December 2010), © European Union, 2011.

In December 2007 at the UN climate change conference in Bali, the UNFCCC agreed to complete the negotiations of a post-2012 global climate change agreement in Copenhagen in December 2009. In the event the meeting at Copenhagen ended in chaos and discord. There were criticisms about: the radical demands of non-governmental organizations (NGOs) rendering compromise impossible; the difficulties in reaching consensus between over 130 countries; and shortcomings in the Danish organization. Nevertheless, for the first time it was agreed that both developed and developing countries should curb their greenhouse gas emissions, and that developed countries should help to finance developing countries in coping with climate change. However, details on how such measures were to be implemented were missing. The refusal of countries such as Venezuela, Bolivia, Nicaragua

Box 14.5

Milestones in EU policies to meet climate change

1988	The UN forms the International Panel on Climate Change (IPCC).
1992	At the Earth Summit at Rio de Janeiro the United Nations Framework Convention on Climate Change (UNFCCC) signed.
1997	The Kyoto Protocol to the UNFCCC signed.
2005	The Kyoto Protocol comes into effect.
2005–07	The first phase of the Emissions Trading System of the EU.
2007	The IPCC presents its Fourth Assessment Report warning of the consequences of climate change unless emissions peak in 2015–20.
March 2007	Under the German presidency the European Council agrees to cut emissions by 20 per cent by 2020 compared with 1990 levels.
June 2007	The G8 (including the USA) pledge to begin discussions on a successor to the Kyoto Protocol after 2012.
2007	Australia ratifies the Kyoto Protocol.
December 2007	The UNFCCC in Bali agrees to complete the negotiations of a post-2012 global climate change agreement in Copenhagen in December 2009.
2008–12	The second phase of the EU Emissions Trading System.
2008	The EU agrees the Climate and Energy Package, endorsing targets for 2020.
December 2009	Copenhagen UNFCCC conference.
November–December 2010	Cancún UNFCCC conference.
November–December 2011	UNFCCC conference in South Africa.

and Sudan to agree to the Copenhagen Accord meant that it could not be formally adopted within the UN framework.

A successive meeting at Cancún proved more successful and, as only Bolivia continued to hold out, consensus was reached within the UN process, with China and the USA also participating. The main elements of the agreement were.

- A commitment within the UN process by developing and developed countries to curb emissions.
- A $100 billion a year green fund to help developing countries cope with the negative effects of climate change (recognizing the fact that developed countries produce more emissions per capita).
- A framework for co-operation on low-carbon technology (though developed countries rejected the request of some developing countries for free access to intellectual property on this issue).
- A framework agreement on deforestation.
- Some progress was made towards an agreement on how to monitor emissions.

However, despite the unexpected last minute success at Cancún, many questions remained open. A full legally binding treaty was not on the table at Cancún, but agreement still has to be reached on the form of a new climate deal, and in particular, on whether this is based on voluntary or legally binding (as in the case of Kyoto) commitments. It is still undecided whether there is to be a continuation of the Kyoto Protocol or a new agreement (as some developed countries prefer). There was no agreement on how the money for the green fund was to be raised. The scope of a $5 billion accord to protect forests is limited, and the details of how it is to operate in practice still have to be worked out. Details on how to monitor and verify emissions were also lacking.

Agreement at Cancún at least kept the climate change negotiations on track and left room for cautious optimism about a deal for the post-2012 period, possibly in South Africa in 2011.

14.8 EU policies: towards an integrated approach to energy and climate change

To assist in meeting its Kyoto obligations in 2000 the EU launched the European Climate Change Programme (ECCP). The ECCP entailed the introduction of a wide range of measures, such as initiatives to promote renewable energy sources, expand the use of biofuels in transport, and promote the energy performance of buildings, as well as the introduction of the Emissions Trading System (see below). Over time, EU policies for climate change and energy have become increasingly intrinsically linked. The ECCP has a stakeholder structure under which the Commission discusses with industry, national experts and NGOs in the preparation of new measures.

A second European Climate Change Programme began in 2005 with the aim of identifying further cost-effective ways of reducing emissions (see also Box 14.6). This led to various new measures, such as proposals to strengthen the ETS also by including the aviation sector (which should occur from 2012), and legislation to reduce carbon dioxide emissions from new cars.

Box 14.6

A proposal to save energy

As part of the fight against climate change, in July 2007 there was a proposal to allow the 11,700 male eurocrats working in the European Commission to come to work without ties. It was hoped that tie-less officials would be better able to tolerate heat in July and August and so reduce the need for air conditioning in the 64 offices of the Commission across Brussels.*

*Financial Times, 9 July 2007.

At the centre of EU policy towards climate change is the commitment to keep temperature increase to a maximum of 2 degrees above the pre-industrial level, the threshold beyond which scientific evidence suggests there is increased risk of irreversible and possible catastrophic changes (see Box 14.4 above). According to the European Commission (2007g), this would require global emissions to fall by almost 50 per cent compared with 1990 levels by 2050, which implied a cut by 60–80 per cent by developed countries and a gradual but significant effort by developing countries.

In 2008 a Strategic Energy Technology Plan to focus R&D activities on low-carbon technologies was agreed. In the same year the Strategic Energy Review set out an action plan to strengthen energy security, also in dealing with partners like Russia.

In 2009 the Climate and Energy Package brought into force what became known as the **20-20-20 goals**:

■ A unilateral cut in EU greenhouse gas emissions by 20 per cent by 2020 compared with 1990 levels (or 30 per cent if other developed countries reached similar commitments). This objective had already been agreed in 2007 as part of the first EU Energy Action Plan.

- Improving energy efficiency in order to save 20 per cent of the energy consumption of the EU compared with forecasts for 2020.
- Raising the share of renewable energy to 20 per cent of EU overall energy consumption by 2020, with an increase the share of biofuels to at least 10 per cent of total petrol and diesel consumption for transport in the EU by 2020 (see the next section).

The Package also entailed complementary legislation relating to:

- the revision and strengthening of the ETS (see below), including measures for sectors not covered by the ETS;
- binding national targets for renewable energy;
- a legal framework to promote carbon capture and storage, which entails a series of technologies that allow carbon dioxide emitted by industrial processes to be captured and stored underground where it cannot contribute to global warming. Revised guidelines for state aids will permit more government support for this type of initiative.

In presenting the Package, Commission president Barroso acknowledged that the EU(27) would face costs of an estimated €60 billion a year, or 0.45 per cent of GDP, as a result of implementing the measures, but argued that the cost of inaction (as indicated by the Stern Report, see Box 14.4) would be much higher.

Measures to further the 20-20-20 goals were agreed in successive EU energy programmes, and were embedded in the **Europe 2020** strategy agreed in 2010. As described in Chapter 7, the Europe 2020 programme also aims at sustainable growth, which entails a resource-efficient, low-carbon economy in which growth is decoupled, as far as possible, from resource and energy use.

14.9 Biofuels in the EU

In 2003 the EU agreed Directive 2003/30/EC to increase the use of energy from forestry, agriculture and waste materials, setting a 'reference value' of 5.75 per cent of transport fuel to be covered by biofuels and other renewable fuels by 31 December 2010.

As explained above, the 20-20-20 plan set a target of at least 10 per cent of transport fuel coming from bioenergy by 2020 (compared with about 1 per cent in 2007).

As part of the 2003 CAP reform (see Chapter 13), a subsidy of €45 per hectare to stimulate bioenergy production on up to 1.5 million hectares in the EU was introduced, but it was abolished in 2008 because of growing doubts about the consequences of such a policy.

The first-generation biofuels produced in the EU include ethanol from grain and sugar beet, and biodiesel from oilseeds. These are relatively costly, in particular when compared with Brazilian ethanol produced from sugar cane, and their impact on the environment has been questioned.[12] The advantage of biofuels is said to be that carbon emissions from use of the fuel is balanced and reabsorbed by new plant growth. However, in practice biofuels are not carbon neutral as energy is needed to grow crops and process them into fuel. The production of crops for biofuels may lead to a reduction in biodiversity or, in some parts of the world (such as Indonesia or Malaysia), to deforestation.

The OECD (2006) estimated that without imports of biofuels, 72 per cent of arable land in the EU would be needed to meet 10 per cent of current transport needs.[13]

---

[12] See OECD (2008) for a survey of 60 studies showing the environmental effects of biofuels.

[13] European Commission (2007f) estimated that only 15 per cent of arable land would be necessary, and the difference from the OECD figure is due to different assumptions about yields, the development of second-generation biofuels, imports and the price of petrol.

In 2007/08 world prices of certain agricultural commodities, such as corn, rose rapidly, partly because of bad weather and increased imports by China and certain other emerging countries, but also because of the demand for biofuels.[14] In 2008 the food price index of the Food and Agricultural Organisation (FAO) reached the highest level since it was launched in 1990, causing difficulties for the World Food Programme of the UN, a pasta boycott in Italy and food riots in Mexico. Again in 2010/11 there was a hike in world food prices (see Chapter 13).

Second-generation technologies, such as cellulosic ethanol made from plant waste, would not compete directly with food production, and would have a more positive effect on greenhouse gas emissions, but most will not be ready for commercial production for some years.

14.10 The EU Emissions Trading System

A core element of the efforts of the EU to meet its Kyoto objectives is the **Emissions Trading System** (or 'carbon trading'), which was introduced in 2005. This was the first, and to date largest, emissions trading scheme in the world, and applies in the 27 member states and in the three countries of the European Economic Area: Norway, Iceland and Liechtenstein. The first period (2005–07) was a 'learning by doing' phase, and the second period (2008–12) coincided with the first commitment period of the Kyoto Protocol.

In the first two phases of this 'cap and trade' system, member states set a National Allocation Plan or cap (subject to approval from the European Commission) on carbon dioxide emissions from over 10,000 energy-intensive plants (power plants, steel factories, oil refineries, paper mills, glass and cement producers and so on). These are responsible for close to half of the EU's emissions of carbon dioxide and 40 per cent of its other greenhouse gas emissions.[15]

Under the system each member state grants permission to individual companies to emit a certain amount of carbon dioxide each year within the limits of the national cap. Originally a fine of €40 per excess tonne of carbon dioxide was imposed on plants exceeding their individual targets, but this was increased to €100 per tonne in 2008. Companies that expect to more than meet their target can trade the right to carbon dioxide emissions with those who cannot meet their target. The idea is that, for climate, it does not matter who emits the carbon dioxide. If company A can cut its carbon dioxide emissions at a lower cost than company B, from the point of view of economic efficiency there is an advantage in company A cutting its emission more, and company B cutting less. Companies motivated by the profit they can make by selling their excess emission allowances will be encouraged to develop and use clean technologies.

The first phase of the ETS (2005–07) ran into difficulties when it emerged that companies had been issued with more permits than they needed. Member states had overestimated the need for emissions (also because they were subject to lobbying by industry), and as a result the price of carbon fell. Official EU data suggested that, for example, Germany was left with 44.1 million tonnes of extra carbon dioxide allowances for 2005.[16] In general the scheme failed in its aim of forcing companies either to reduce emissions or to buy permits from cleaner companies. In the second phase (2008–12) the Commission attempted to use verified emissions data to set caps on national allocations that would effectively cut emissions. In the event the recession further contributed to the excessive number of permits, leading to concerns that these unused allowances would continue to suppress prices even after economic recovery.

---

[14] OECD (2008) estimated that continuation of the policies such as those of the EU and USA used in 2007 to stimulate bioenergy production could increase prices of wheat by 5 per cent, corn by 7 per cent and oilseeds by 19 per cent by the 2013–17 period.

[15] European Commission Climate Action, http://ec.europa.eu/clima/policies/ets/index_en.htm (accessed 11 January 2011).

[16] EurActiv, 'EU Emissions Trading Scheme', http://www.euractiv.com/en/climate-change/eu-emissions-trading-scheme/article-133629 (accessed 11 January 2011).

The first two phases of the ETS also allowed for a number of exemptions, with whole sectors such as transport and building being excluded. Member states could apply for opt-outs for individual plants from the system, and additional emissions were allowed in cases of *force majeure*, such as exceptionally low winter temperatures.

In 2009 a new directive set out reform of the ETS for the period 2013–20.[17] The new measures aim at meeting the shortcomings of the first two phases and include the following:

- One EU-wide cap on the number of emissions allowed rather than the separate national caps. Permits would be reduced by 21 per cent from 2.1 billion tonnes of carbon dioxide in 2005 to 1.7 billion tonnes in 2020.[18] The cap will decrease by 1.74 per cent annually with respect to the average annual total of allowances for 2008–12. An EU cap should enable more harmonization of rules, which was widely agreed to be necessary as different national allocation methods were threatening fair competition.

- Other industries (such as aviation as well as that based in third countries from 2012, and bulk organic chemicals, hydrogen, aluminium and ammonia producers), and new gases (nitrous oxide and perfluorocarbons) will be included in the scheme so that it will cover 50 per cent of emissions. Road transport and shipping remain excluded, though the latter seems likely to be included at some stage. Agriculture and forestry were also left out because of difficulties in measuring emissions accurately.

- An Effort Sharing Decision for the reduction of greenhouse gases in sectors not covered by the ETS such as transport other than aviation, housing, agriculture and waste. Each member state has agreed to a binding emissions target by 2020 reflecting its relative wealth.[19] Emissions in these sectors were to be cut overall at the EU level by 10 per cent of 2005 levels by 2020.

- Member states will be allowed to exclude small installations (those that emit less than 25,000 tonnes of carbon dioxide per year) from the system, provided these are subject to equivalent alternative emission reduction measures.

- Industrial greenhouse gases prevented from entering the atmosphere through carbon capture and storage schemes can be credited under the ETS, though not for the power sector. The proceeds from auctioning 300 million allowances will be used to provide financial support for twelve carbon capture and storage demonstration schemes.

- A much larger share (from an estimated less than 4 per cent in phase 2 to over half in phase 3) of permits auctioned rather than granted free of charge, and full auctioning from 2013 for the power sector. This is expected to lead to a 10–15 per cent increase in electricity prices. Certain member states are allowed an optional and temporary derogation from the rule of no free allowances to electricity generators from 2013. Free allocation in other sectors is to be phased out between 2013 and 2027 (compared with 2013–20 in the original Commission proposal). Certain energy-intensive sectors would continue to receive their free allocation in the long term if the Commission deems there is a significant risk of 'carbon leakage' or relocation to countries with less stringent climate change legislation. At least half of revenues received from auction

[17] Directive 2009/29/EC of 23 April 2009. This account is also based on European Commission (2010m).

[18] The overall aim is for a 20 per cent reduction in emissions compared to 1990, which is equivalent to 14 per cent since 2005, but because reduction in sectors covered by the ETS is cheaper, the target for reduction is higher. In other sectors the target is a 10 per cent reduction. If an international agreement is reached and the EU implements a 30 per cent reduction in emissions compared with 1990, targets would have to be adjusted. Adjustments will also have to be made for changes in the scope of the ETS.

[19] Richer countries such as Denmark and Luxembourg would have to make cuts of 20 per cent, while poorer countries such as Portugal and the new member states except Cyprus could increase their emissions (by up to 19 per cent for Romania and 20 per cent for Bulgaria).

would be used to fight and adapt to climate change mainly in the EU, but also in developing countries.

- Ten per cent of the allowances for auctioning emissions would be redistributed through a solidarity fund from high- to lower-income member states to strengthen the capacity of the latter to invest in climate-friendly technologies. A further 2 per cent of allowances auctioned would be redistributed among member states whose emissions in 2005 were at least 20 per cent below their emissions in the Kyoto base year.

- The Commission is responsible for developing EU rules for a distribution method for free allowances. Member states would be responsible for auctions of allowances, though this sparked some concerns about the need to ensure harmonized arrangements.

- The risk of 'carbon leakage' (and consequently compensation for EU companies) is considered to depend on whether a global agreement on climate change is reached, subjecting third countries to similar climate mitigation changes. If an international deal is not reached, some form of 'carbon equalization scheme' would be introduced involving either additional free allocations or the inclusion of energy-intensive imports from third countries in the EU ETS.

- If a global climate-change agreement is reached, member states could continue to meet part of their target by financing emission reduction schemes in third countries, through the joint implementation and clean development mechanisms envisaged by the Kyoto Protocol. Member states could also gain access to additional credits and use types of credit and mechanisms covered by the international agreement. In the absence of a global deal, the final compromise on the directive allows for a top-up to the Commission's initial proposal to limit use of such credits to 3 per cent of member states' total emissions in 2005. Overall use of such credits would be limited to 50 per cent of EU-wide reductions in emissions for the 2008–12 period. It will not be possible to use credits from land-use change or forestry.

Environmentalists maintained that the proposals had been watered down in the face of industrial lobbies (with, for instance, a deferral of the date on which firms would have to start paying for their emissions permits with respect to the Commission's original proposals). They also argue that the EU is defeatist in introducing measures aimed at an overall reduction in emissions of 20 per cent rather than 30 per cent. However, business groups in sectors such as iron and steel argued that the measures would undermine their global competitiveness, in particular in the absence of a global climate change deal. The possibility of requiring importers to pay emission charges under some form of carbon equalization system has been criticized because of fears of provoking a trade war with retaliation and/or litigation in the WTO.

14.11   Evaluation of EU environmental policy

For many years environmental issues lacked the status of a fully fledged EU policy, and, even now, in practice the various measures do not always appear to be co-ordinated into a single approach. Successive treaties have attempted to raise the priority given to environmental issues in the EU, requiring the EU to introduce environmental mainstreaming and to take account of sustainable development, not always with complete success. Over the years there has been a shift away from the command and control approach in favour of market-based instruments, which tend to have lower implementation costs.

At the EU level, tensions frequently arise between environmental objectives and the Single Market, and northern member states often express fears that their higher environmental standards might be undermined in a 'race to the bottom'.

EU initiatives in environmental policy and mitigation of the effects of climate change have been presented as a way of reinventing the integration process. The public generally supports EU initiatives despite fears that more regulation might render the EU less competitive compared with countries

with fewer restrictions (leading to a risk of environmental dumping and/or a 'race to the bottom'). The EU seems intent on inventing a role for itself in promoting global initiatives with respect to the environment (and seems to have more success in reaching common positions than in foreign policy or defence issues). The 20-20-20 plan represents a landmark in this direction. However, the success of international agreements also depends on other key actors whose commitment is not always forthcoming.

14.12   The evolution of the EU energy market

During the first fifteen years of the Community, growth led to increased energy consumption, and the relatively low world prices for oil caused the gradual substitution of oil for coal. As a result the EC became increasingly dependent on imports of energy, and of oil in particular. In 1950 coal accounted for two-thirds of energy consumption and oil for 10 per cent in what were the original six EC countries, but by 1973 oil covered 67 per cent of consumption (Kengyel and Palankai, 2003). In 1960 domestic production accounted for 60 per cent of EC energy requirements (with coal being produced mainly in Germany, France and Belgium), but by 1973 this proportion had fallen to 37 per cent.[20]

When the OPEC (Organization of the Petroleum Exporting Countries) cartel increased oil prices by 475 per cent in 1973 and a further 134 per cent in 1979, the Community was very vulnerable. Despite a certain lack of co-ordination, the reaction of the Community was to introduce measures to reduce dependence on oil imports, encourage the development of alternative energy sources (such as nuclear, wind, solar, water, geothermal, bioenergy and so on), hold minimum stocks against emergencies and introduce energy-saving measures. Western industrialized countries (except France) joined the International Energy Agency (IEA), formed under the auspices of the OECD in 1974.

The policy of developing domestic energy sources and cutting consumption met with some success. North Sea oil production began in 1976, and the UK became a net exporter of oil. However, production met less than one-quarter of EC requirements and was relatively costly. The Netherlands became an important producer of natural gas, but again extraction costs were relatively high. Renewable energy sources were slow to develop, and the public in many member states increasingly opposed the use of nuclear power plants. Table 14.3 shows the gross inland consumption by energy source of the member states, and the difference in choices about nuclear energy emerges clearly from the table.[21] Coal production continues to be important in countries such as Spain, Germany, Poland and the Czech Republic. See Figure 14.2 and Tables 14.2 and 14.3 for breakdowns on energy consumption in the EU(27) by type of fuel.

In 2007 the EU(27) continued to rely on imports for 53.1 per cent of its energy requirements (82.6 per cent in the case of oil but 60.3 per cent for natural gas). The main sources of supply are shown in Table 14.4. The heavy dependence of the EU on Russia for oil and gas imports is at times a source of concern (see below). French import dependency fell from 79 per cent in 1980 to 50.4 per cent in 2007 (thanks also to its nuclear power programme). However, as can be seen from Table 14.5, even in 2005 the import dependency of other EU member states such as Luxembourg (97.5 per cent), Ireland (88.3 per cent), Italy (85.3 per cent) and Portugal (82.0 per cent), remained high. Apart from Malta (100.1 per cent) and Cyprus (95.9 per cent), in 2007 energy import dependency in the new member states was lower at, for example, 25.5 per cent for Poland and 25.1 per cent for the Czech Republic, also due to the production of coal in these two countries.

---

[20] Kengyel and Palankai (2003).

[21] The European Atomic Energy Community (Euratom) Treaty aimed at establishing the basic installations necessary for the development of nuclear energy in the Community, and ensuring that all users in the Community received a regular and equitable supply of ores and nuclear fuels. The Euratom Supply Agency, operative since 1960 and with a renewed statute since 2008, is the body established by the Euratom Treaty to ensure this supply by means of a common supply policy. The Euratom Supply Agency acts under the supervision of the European Commissioner responsible for energy.

Figure 14.2 Gross inland energy consumption of the EU(27) by fuel/products, 2007

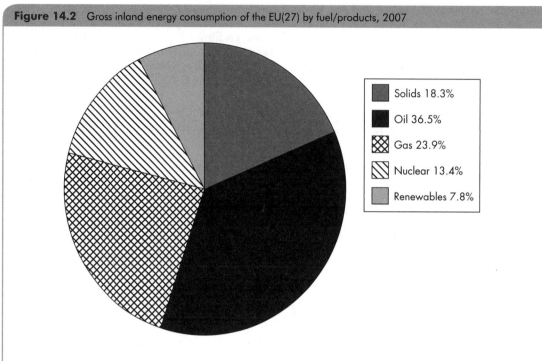

Solids 18.3%

Oil 36.5%

Gas 23.9%

Nuclear 13.4%

Renewables 7.8%

Source: European Commission (2010n), http://ec.europa.eu/energy/publications/statistics/doc/2009_energy_transport_figures.pdf (accessed 23 December 2010), © European Union, 2010.

Table 14.2 Fuel shares, 2007 (%)

	Solids	Oil	Gas	Nuclear	Hydro	Biomass	Other
EU(27)	18.3	36.4	23.9	13.4	1.5	5.4	1.1
USA	23.7	38.9	23.0	9.3	0.9	3.5	0.7
Japan	22.3	44.8	16.2	13.4	1.2	1.4	0.7
Russia	15.2	19.7	54.4	6.3	2.3	1.0	1.2
China[a]	65.6	18.2	3.1	0.8	2.1	9.9	0.2
India	40.8	23.7	5.6	0.7	1.8	27.2	0.3
World	26.5	34.0	20.9	5.9	2.2	9.8	0.7

[a]Includes Hong Kong.

Source: European Commission (2010n), http://ec.europa.eu/energy/publications/statistics/doc/2009_energy_transport_figures.pdf (accessed 23 December 2010), © European Union, 2011.

Table 14.3 Gross inland consumption by type of energy in the member states, 2007 (million tonnes)

	All fuels	Solid fuels	Oil	Natural gas	Nuclear	Renewables	Other[a]
EU(27)	1,806.4	331.2	656.9	432.4	241.3	141.0	3.5
	100%	18.3%	36.4%	23.9%	13.4%	7.8%	0.2%
BE	57.4	4.6	22.6	14.9	12.4	1.8	1.0
BG	20.3	7.8	5.1	3.0	3.8	1.0	–0.3
CZ	46.2	21.4	10.0	7.2	6.8	2.2	–1.3
DK	20.5	4.7	8.3	4.1		3.6	–0.1
DE	339.6	87.0	112.7	76.6	36.3	28.1	–1.1
EE	6.1	3.7	1.2	0.8		0.6	–0.2
IE	15.9	2.3	8.7	4.3		0.5	0.1
EL	33.5	10.8	17.2	3.3		1.7	0.4
ES	146.8	20.2	70.8	31.9	14.2	10.3	–0.5
FR	270.3	13.4	90.9	38.5	113.4	19.0	–4.9
IT	183.5	16.8	80.3	69.5		12.7	4.1
CY	2.7	0.0	2.6			0.1	0.0
LV	4.8	0.1	1.6	1.4		1.4	0.4
LT	9.2	0.3	2.8	2.9	2.5	0.8	–0.1
LU	4.7	0.1	2.9	1.2		0.1	0.3
HU	27.0	3.1	7.6	10.7	3.8	1.4	0.4
MT	0.9		0.9				
NL	84.5	8.4	37.2	33.4	1.1	3.0	1.5
AT	33.8	3.9	13.9	7.0		8.0	1.0
PL	98.0	55.5	25.1	12.4		5.0	0.0
PT	26.0	2.9	14.0	3.8		4.6	0.6
RO	40.1	10.2	10.2	13.0	2.0	4.8	–0.1
SL	7.3	1.6	2.6	0.9	1.5	0.7	0.0
SK	18.1	4.0	3.9	5.1	4.0	1.0	0.2
FI	37.6	7.2	11.0	3.7	6.0	8.5	1.1
SE	50.6	2.7	13.9	0.9	17.3	15.6	0.1
UK	221.1	38.7	78.7	82.0	16.3	4.6	0.8

[a]Electrical energy and industrial waste.

Note: Gaps indicate zero or insignificant amounts.

Source: European Commission (2010n), http://ec.europa.eu/energy/publications/statistics/doc/2009_energy_transport_figures.pdf (accessed 23 December 2010), © European Union, 2011.

Table 14.4 The main sources of EU(27) energy imports, 2007: main non-EU suppliers to the EU (% of EU imports)

Crude oil		Natural gas		Hard coal	
Russia	30.3	Russia	30.7	Russia	22.6
Norway	13.8	Norway	20.1	S. Africa	18.6
Libya	9.1	Algeria	12.8	Australia	11.7
Saudi Arabia	6.4	Nigeria	3.9	Colombia	11.7
Iran	5.6	Libya	2.5	USA	8.4
Iraq	3.1			Indonesia	7.1
Kazakhstan	3.0				

Source: *European Commission (2010n), http://epp.eurostat.ec.europa.eu/statistics_explained/index.php?title=File:Main_origin_of_ primary_energy_imports,_EU-27,_2000-2007_(%25_of_extra_EU-27_imports).PNG&filetimestamp=20100503141336 (accessed 23 December 2010), © European Union, 2011.*

Table 14.5 Import dependency[a] by type of energy, 2007 (%)

	All fuels	Solid fuels	Oil	Gas
EU(27)	53.1	41.2	82.6	60.3
BE	77.2	95.8	97.4	99.8
BG	51.9	39.4	100.8	91.5
CZ	25.1	−14.8	96.2	93.7
DK	−25.4	100.4	−67.9	−99.7
DE	58.9	37.2	94.3	80.6
EE	29.7	0.9	99.0	100.0
IE	88.3	65.1	97.0	91.4
EL	67.3	3.3	100.9	99.6
ES	79.5	66.6	99.7	98.9
FR	50.4	92.5	98.7	96.5
IT	85.3	99.2	92.5	87.0
CY	95.9	68.0	98.6	
LV	61.5	88.0	98.1	96.8
LT	62.3	87.2	93.3	102.9
LU	97.5	100.0	98.8	100.0
HU	61.4	44.0	82.7	79.9
MT	100.1		100.0	
NL	38.6	105.3	92.8	−64.3
AT	69.1	105.1	92.6	81.0
PL	25.5	−15.5	102.2	66.7
PT	82.0	100.5	98.9	98.7
RO	32.0	34.8	53.7	29.8
SL	52.5	21.0	98.9	99.7
SK	69.0	95.4	91.3	97.9
FI	53.8	62.8	97.8	100.0
SE	36.1	93.8	96.7	100.0
UK	20.1	69.5	0.9	20.3

[a]*Import dependency = Net imports / (Bunkers + Gross inland consumption)*

Source: *European Commission (2010n), http://ec.europa.eu/energy/publications/statistics/doc/2009_energy_transport_figures.pdf (accessed 23 December 2010), © European Union, 2011.*

14.13 The evolution of EU energy policy

Two of the initial Communities were set up to deal with energy: the European Coal and Steel Community and Euratom. Oil, gas and electricity fell within the scope of the EEC, though the Treaty of Rome did not list energy policy among the specific competences of the Community. Defence of national companies, differences in dependence on energy imports of the various member states and in the mix of energy sources used, have acted as obstacles to the development of a common policy.

There was a first effort at co-ordination of the energy policy of the member states with a Protocol on Agreement on Energy in 1964, and introduction of a common policy was again attempted in 1968 when the three Communities were merged, but with few practical results (Hitiris, 2003). After 1978 the Community tried to co-ordinate the national measures of the member states, set energy targets and fix a collective target for the rationalization of production, consumption and imports.

The Single Market Programme aimed at the liberalization of energy (which in the case of gas and electricity was generally controlled by national monopolies) and the promotion of investment in infrastructure and networks, but progress was slow, and over a decade later the Commission was still presenting proposals to liberalize the EU energy market.

The Maastricht Treaty confirmed the legal basis for Community measures in the sphere of energy and called for joint efforts in the creation of trans-European networks (TENs) in energy infrastructure.[22]

EU action for the development of TEN-Energy relates to the main transportation and transmission networks for electricity and natural gas. Priority measures for the electricity sector include the connection of isolated electricity networks and the development of interconnections between member states and with third countries. TEN-Energy gas priorities include the introduction of natural gas into new regions, the interconnection of isolated networks and increased capabilities for storage and transport. After the 2004 and 2007 enlargements, emphasis was placed on integrating the new member states into priorities and projects.

As with environmental policy the debate about energy in the EU acquired a greater urgency in the new century. Green Papers in 2001, 2005 and 2006 stimulated a lively debate and led to the Energy Package of 2007 (see below), and the 20-20-20 goals. EU energy policies were increasingly integrated with those on climate change.

In these measures certain key concerns of EU energy policy can be identified:

- The problem of ensuring security of supply, in particular given the dependence of the EU on imports from Russia.
- The need to reduce consumption, increase efficiency in the use of energy and promote renewable forms of energy.
- The environmental and social implications of energy policy.
- The need to complete the internal market for energy in order to increase competitiveness. Interconnections between countries may be necessary to increase efficiency and cut costs.

The EU continues to rely heavily on fossil fuels (oil, coal and natural gas) which make up four-fifths of its total energy consumption, almost two-thirds of which are imported (see Tables 14.3 and 14.5) and this seems likely to increase. The International Energy Agency estimated that world energy needs will be 40 per cent higher in 2030 than today, with China and India alone accounting for over 50 per cent of the increase in demand.[23] As shown in Table 14.4, a large

[22] Article 129b of the Treaty, which became Article 170 in the Lisbon Treaty.

[23] IEA, http://www.iea.org/press/pressdetail.asp?PRESS_REL_ID=294 (accessed 12 January 2011).

share of EU oil and gas imports come from Russia. The EU has had difficulty in agreeing on an energy strategy with Moscow, and Russia continues to sign bilateral agreements with individual member states, and has created various difficulties for EU companies operating energy projects in Siberia.

The EU has relatively little room to manoeuvre with regard to energy supplies because of its low or less-competitive (for example coal and North Sea oil) energy resources, so its adopted strategy relies heavily on demand management and the promotion of renewable energy.

14.14　The attempt at unbundling of the EU energy sector

The characteristics of certain industries are influenced by the technologies used. For electricity, supply is based on generation, transmission, distribution and retailing, and the situation is similar for gas. The existence of expensive infrastructure such as gas pipelines and an electricity grid is often advanced as a case of natural monopolies (see Chapters 4 and 16). Historically, in the EU, the provision of electricity and gas services has tended to be organized on the basis of vertical integration, with regional or national monopolists, and often public ownership.

According to the European Commission, structural failings (and, in particular, excessive vertical integration) of the EU gas and electricity industries led to high prices for consumers, and discrimination against new users of the network in favour of incumbent production and supply companies. There was also said to be insufficient investment in infrastructure, and a tendency to restrict capacity to protect parent companies. The idea was to open the energy sector, making it easier for smaller firms to operate, in the hopes that this would lower prices and that independent network companies might be more prepared to upgrade facilities by, for example, improving cross-border links.

Directives aimed at opening up the electricity and gas markets were passed in the late 1990s, and further directives agreed in 2003. However, the effect of these measures was limited and European Commission (2007h) estimated that between 1998 and 2006 in EU countries where the electricity networks were owned by the supply and generating companies, prices rose by 29 per cent compared with a price rise of 6 per cent where the networks were independent.

In January 2007, as part of the Energy Package, the European Commission set out proposals for liberalization of energy markets, including **unbundling** or the separation of companies responsible for transmission (the networks of pipes and wires) from those dealing with distribution (supply of gas and electricity). The proposal met with heated opposition from about half the EU member states and, in particular, from large power groups such as Eon and RWE in Germany and Gas de France and Electricité de France.

In the face of such opposition, in September 2007 the Commission presented a revised proposal (the third energy liberalization package), and after long negotiations the Council adopted the package in 2009. The final compromise offered three options:

- Ownership unbundling.
- An opt-out clause whereby countries not wanting to split up their large energy companies could choose to set up 'independent system operators', which are separate companies controlling access to, and investment in, networks that would still be owned by suppliers. The independent system operators would be designated by national governments subject to Commission approval.
- A third way was introduced in response to lobbying by France and Germany, in particular. Former state monopolies could retain ownership of their gas and electricity grids provided they are subject to outside supervision. Daily management of the grids would be given to an independent transmission operator.

The package also attempted to address the lack of coherence and remits of national energy regulators, which was identified as one of the main obstacles to functioning of the single energy market. The package envisaged increased powers and independence for national regulators, more co-operation between national transmission operators backed by a new EU network, and a new EU Agency for the Co-operation of Energy Regulators to facilitate cross-border energy trade. Under a 'reciprocity clause', non-EU firms would be able to control energy networks in the EU only if they met certain stringent conditions, and this was interpreted in some circles as a move to ensure reciprocal access to the Russian energy market for EU companies.

Even the watered-down proposal, together with the increased emphasis on transparency, could still imply substantial pressure on large groups to break up voluntarily. Not surprisingly, there was heated opposition from some member states which claimed that the EU needed power giants to stand up to large suppliers such as those in Russia and Algeria, while other countries were more in favour of liberalization. [24]

Parallel to its legislative proposals the European Commission also carried out antitrust actions (see Chapter 16) against large energy companies. This led in 2008 to a deal with the German group E.ON, which agreed to sell its electricity grid and 20 per cent of its power plant capacity (though E.ON denied that this was as a result of the Commission's inquiry).[25] Electricité de France, Belgium's Electrabel and Germany's RWE were also subject to investigation by the European Commission.

At the same time a series of mergers and acquisitions was changing the structure of the EU energy sector. Certain of these, such as the merger between the Belgian-French group Suez and Gas de France, increased market power concentration and were perceived by some as a threat to the liberalization of the EU energy market.

14.15 Evaluation of EU energy policy

The EU is frequently criticized for its slowness in developing an energy policy, but defence of large national firms, differences in the import dependency of the member states, and in the structure of energy sources used to meet consumption render it difficult to reach common positions.

In the early years of the Community, oil gradually replaced coal as the main source of energy, leading to increased import dependency. The EC member states were therefore vulnerable to the oil crises of the 1970s and reacted by attempting to reduce import dependency, develop alternative sources of domestic supply and reduce energy consumption.

Security of energy supply remains a key priority for the EU, and the present strategy relies heavily on the introduction of energy-saving measures and incentives to develop renewable energy sources. Commission proposals to harmonize taxation and liberalize energy markets in the EU have met with limited success, but in recent years there has been a growing consensus enabling measures to tackle climate change to be introduced. In contrast, attempts to liberalize EU gas and electricity markets by unbundling transmission and distribution networks have encountered opposition from large national companies, often backed by national governments such as those in France and Germany.

---

[24] Germany, France, Austria, Latvia, Bulgaria, Greece, Luxembourg and Slovakia were opposed, while the UK, the Netherlands, Italy, Spain and Poland were more in favour of liberalization.

[25] *Financial Times*, 1–2 March 2008.

Summary of key concepts

- **The evolution of EU environmental measures has encountered tensions** because of differing environmental standards in the EU member states; the fuzzy boundary between EU and national policies; difficulties in implementing policies; the persistence of environmental problems; difficulties in reconciling environmental measures with other EU policies and disagreements about how to share the financial burden for measures.

- **Environmental measures fall into three broad categories: command and control, market-based instruments and voluntary agreements.** In recent years there has been a growing tendency in the EU to use market-based instruments rather than the strategy of command and control.

- There is no mention of a role for the Community in environmental policy in the Treaty of Rome. In 1973 the Community embarked on the first of what are now six Environmental Action Programmes.

- The **principles of EU environmental policy** are: the principle of prevention; the 'polluter pays' principle; the principle of correction at source; the principle of subsidiarity; and the precautionary principle.

- **Environmental mainstreaming** requires that environmental issues should be taken into account in deciding all EU policies.

- The **European Environment** Agency came into operation in 1994.

- The EU takes part in global attempts to tackle transnational environmental problems such as depletion of the ozone layer (the **Montreal Protocol** of 1987 and subsequent agreements), climate change (the 1997 **Kyoto Protocol**) and the destruction of tropical rainforests.

- The EU introduced an **Emissions Trading System** (or 'carbon trading') in 2005, but difficulties arose during the first two phases (2005–07 and 2008–12) as too many permits were issued and there were many exceptions. In 2009 the EU agreed a reform of the system for the 2013–20 period, with a cap of EU emissions at 21 per cent of 2005 levels by 2020; inclusion of more sectors and gases; and a huge increase in auctioning of allowances rather than granting them free.

- In the early years of the Community, oil gradually replaced coal as the main source of energy, leading to increased import dependency.

- The EU is frequently criticized for its **slowness in developing an energy policy**, but large national firms, and differences in the import dependency of the member states and in the structure of energy sources used to meet consumption, render it difficult to reach common positions.

- **Security of energy supply** remains a key priority for the EU, and the present strategy relies heavily on the introduction of energy-saving measures and incentives to develop renewable energy sources.

Questions for study and review

1 What were the obstacles to developing an EU environmental policy?
2 Describe main types of instrument used in environmental policy.
3 Describe how EU environmental policy has evolved over time.
4 What difficulties arise in applying the principles of EU environmental policy?
5 What is sustainable development? How can it be ensured in practice?

6 What role has the EU played at an international level in deciding on environmental questions?

7 What are the limitations of the Kyoto Protocol? What aspects should a successor agreement to Kyoto have?

8 What are the likely effects of increased use of biofuels?

9 Describe the Emissions Trading System of the EU. What improvements could be made to this scheme?

10 Why do most countries introduce an energy policy?

11 Describe the different sources of energy the EU uses to meet its requirements. How have these changed over time?

12 Describe the evolution of EU energy policy.

13 What strategies is the EU adopting to ensure security of energy supplies?

Online
Learning **Centre**

When you have read this chapter, log on to the Online Learning Centre website at ***www.mcgraw-hill.co.uk/textbooks/senior*** to explore weblinks, chapter-by-chapter test questions, case studies and more online study tools.

Chapter 15

Regional Policy

Learning Objectives

By the end of this chapter you should be able to understand:

- ☑ Various views about the link between integration and regional disparities
- ☑ The problem of regional disparities in the EU
- ☑ The principal funds used by the EU to reduce regional disparities
- ☑ How EU regional policy has evolved over the years
- ☑ How EU cohesion policy operates in the 2007–13 period
- ☑ The extent to which there has been convergence between EU regions and countries
- ☑ How effective EU policies have been
- ☑ The ways in which regional policy might be rendered more effective

15.1 Introduction

Regional problems are the disparities in levels of income, in rates of growth of output and employment, and generally in levels of economic inequality between different regions. Public intervention may be considered necessary to reduce these disparities through redistribution. Over the years the EU has gradually evolved an active policy of redistribution between different regions and countries of the EU (the regional dimension), and different sections of the population (the social dimension, see Chapter 7).

The aims of EU regional policy figure among the objectives are set out in Article 3 TEU (ex Article 2 TEC), which requires the Union to:

- ■ *'work for the sustainable development of Europe based on balanced economic growth ...'*; and
- ■ *'Promote economic, social and territorial cohesion, and solidarity among Member States'*.

Articles 174 to 178 of the Lisbon Treaty (TFEU, ex Articles 158 to 162 TEC) deal with *'economic, social and territorial cohesion'*, and require the EU to reduce *'disparities between the levels of development of the various regions and the backwardness of the least favoured regions'*. Article 174 TFEU states that the EU should pay particular attention to *'rural areas, areas affected by industrial transition, and regions which suffer from severe*

and permanent natural or demographic handicaps such as the northernmost regions with very low population density and island, cross-border and mountain regions'.

While there is no clear definition of cohesion, it can be understood as *'the degree to which disparities in social and economic welfare between different regions or groups within the Community are politically and socially acceptable'* (Molle, 2006: 287).

Regional policies are often advocated on grounds of efficiency since they may help to remove bottlenecks and obstacles to development. For instance, public investment in infrastructure may encourage firms to move to a less favoured region, or programmes for retraining may help workers to find jobs. Regional policy may help to ease the problems of overcongestion or overheating in areas where economic activity is concentrated. The concept of social and economic cohesion also suggests a justification for redistributive policies on equity grounds: regional policies may be required to guarantee certain minimum levels of services, while social policy may ensure certain minimum incomes or living standards (see Chapter 7).

Various indicators can be taken into account in assessing the degree of disparity between different regions or countries:

- Income per capita (which is the indicator generally used by the EU).
- Labour productivity.
- The availability and accessibility of jobs.
- The standard of living, which involves also taking into account the environment, the health service, cultural infrastructure, leisure activities and so on.

A major, and still unresolved controversy is whether economic integration leads to greater or less convergence between different regions. The first part of this chapter reviews some of the main theories advanced on either side of the argument. Then follows a survey of the instruments of EU regional policy and how they evolved over the years. The final part of the chapter addresses the question of whether there has been convergence in the EU. This is complicated by the fact that convergence may take place both within and between countries. A further difficulty arises in attributing the causes of convergence (or lack of it). To what extent was convergence due to integration, and what was the role of EU cohesion policy? The last part of the chapter discusses the outlook for EU cohesion policy post-2013, and attempts to identify elements that make for a successful regional policy.

15.2 The view that integration leads to less income disparity

The view that integration will lead to greater convergence is generally based on faith in markets. Integration allows free operation of the market forces and sets in motion a process by which the return to labour and capital in different regions will tend to converge. The mechanisms by which this convergence comes about are:

- **Free trade,** which permits regions to specialize on the basis of comparative advantage (see Chapter 4). A region with surplus labour will specialize in labour-intensive goods, causing incomes to rise and unemployment to fall. The Heckscher–Ohlin–Samuelson theorem described in Chapter 4 provides an explanation of how the removal of barriers to trade may lead to the convergence of incomes in different regions. The limitation of this explanation arises from the restrictive assumptions on which the theorem is based.
- **Labour migration and capital mobility.** Labour will tend to leave regions with lower wage levels and move to regions where wages are higher, bringing about a process of wage equalization, as described in Chapter 8. A similar mechanism to that in Figure 8.2 can be used to explain capital movements by simply reversing the positions of capital and labour.[1] Capital will be attracted to the

---

[1] See Baldwin and Wyplosz (2009) for an example of how this approach is applied to capital movement.

regions where wages are lower and returns on capital are higher, setting in motion a process that leads to equalization of returns on capital in different regions.

■ **Capital accumulation.** According to orthodox neo-classical growth theory (see the description of the Solow model in Chapter 5), in regions with higher productivity and per capita incomes, growth will prove more difficult as capital accumulation runs into diminishing returns.

15.3 The view that integration leads to greater regional disparity

Various theories are advanced to explain why integration may lead to divergence or greater disparities between regions:

■ **Modern growth theory**, which was briefly described in Chapter 5, may explain why more prosperous areas can enjoy ongoing long-term growth. Important factors in explaining growth are market access, human capital, investment in R&D, technological change, economies of scale, institutional efficiency and so on, and these may be encouraged by integration. Some countries master good combinations and grow, others fail to do so and fall behind.

■ **Technology diffusion.** According to evolutionary economic theory, knowledge and innovation tend to concentrate in certain areas.

Evolutionary economics owes much to the pioneering work of Nelson and Winter (1982) and adds new insights into the role of knowledge and innovation.[2] According to the Schumpeterian view, the evolution of the economy is constantly being 'disrupted' by technological change in a process of 'creative destruction'. Learning and evolution are seen as a disequilibrium process, and dynamic selection and mutation lead to superior responses. Structural change and growth are the result of the irruption of new technologies in the economic system which provide opportunities for investment and the opening of new sectors. Drawing on Kondratiev's concept of waves of economic activity, Schumpeter argued that radical innovations tend to be concentrated in certain periods.

Knowledge is a key concept in this framework, and evolutionary economics makes the distinction between codified and tacit knowledge. Codified knowledge is formalized and can be stored and transmitted easily, whereas tacit knowledge is obtained through experience, requiring a process of learning-by-doing in order to be passed on.

According to evolutionary economics a large part of knowledge needed for innovation is tacit, so contacts between people are important, and location therefore counts. There will tend to be an agglomeration of innovation in geographic clusters. In contrast, codified knowledge can be transmitted easily so activities based on this knowledge can be moved to low-cost locations. According to the view that integration encourages economic concentration, by reducing barriers to the location of industry, integration will render it easier for firms to move to areas where there is an agglomeration of innovation.

■ The **New Economic Geography approach** developed by Krugman and Venables.[3] This approach involves a kind of circular causality. The possibility of exploiting scale economies is an incitement to the concentration of industry, while trade costs are reduced if firms locate close to large markets.[4] Where firms are concentrated, there will be large markets and large markets provide an incentive for firms to locate. The combination of opportunity to exploit economies of scale and reduce trade costs makes for this circular causality.

---

[2] This account is based on Navarro (2003).

[3] Krugman and Venables (1990) and Krugman (1991b).

[4] Trade costs include transport costs but also the more general costs of adapting to the local market, which depend on information, culture, distance and so on.

Supporters of the New Economic Geography approach argue that it explains the existence of centripetal forces in the EU. The central core area is said to lie in a so-called pentagon stretching from London, across to Hamburg, down to Munich, across to Milan and up to Paris.[5]

According to the view that integration encourages economic concentration, by freeing trade, creating a Single Market and introducing a common currency, the integration process will help remove various obstacles that could hinder the agglomeration process.

However, even when considering the various 'stages' of integration (see Chapter 1), different views emerge as to whether integration leads to more or less convergence. The customs union frees trade, creating opportunities for exploiting comparative advantage, but there may be rigidities in the process, and where adjustment takes place it may involve costs. These costs may be concentrated in certain sectors or regions. A common market introduces the four freedoms, enabling labour to move from less favoured regions, but in practice capital tends to move faster and may concentrate in faster-growing regions. Economic and monetary union removes the possibility of using the exchange rate and monetary policies for adjustment between countries. However, disparities also arise within countries, and with higher levels of integration the effectiveness of the exchange rate instrument has been challenged, and it has been argued that exchange rate changes may even be a source of shocks (see Chapter 9).

15.4 EU instruments for cohesion and regional policy

EU implementation of regional and social policy operates chiefly though what were traditionally called the Structural Funds and related instruments, though clearly other policies (such as the CAP) will have distributional implications.

Up until 2006 the term 'Structural Funds' referred to the European Social Fund (ESF), the European Regional Development Fund (ERDF), the Guidance section of EAGGF (or the European Agricultural Guidance and Guarantee Fund, often known by its French, or Italian, acronym, FEOGA, as the English equivalent is unpronounceable),[6] and the Financial Instrument for Fisheries Guidance (FIFG).[7] Related instruments are the European Cohesion Fund and the European Investment Bank (EIB).

The system was reformed for the 2007–13 period, with a reduction in the number of financial instruments for economic and social cohesion to three:

- The ESF
- The ERDF
- The Cohesion Fund.

The guidance section of EAGGF (or FEOGA) and the FIFG were transformed into a new European Agricultural Fund for Rural Development (EAFRD) and a European Fisheries Fund (EFF) respectively.

The European Social Fund

Created in 1960, according to the Treaty of Rome, the aim of the ESF is to increase employment opportunities and contribute to the improvement of living standards. The strategy for realizing this aim is dual: through creating jobs and assisting training. The ESF is now implemented in conjunction

---

[5] The earlier literature refers to a golden triangle in North-West Europe running from Paris to London and including most of Belgium and the Netherlands (Harrop, 2000), and a so-called 'blue banana' in the shape of a banana that runs from the golden triangle through West German cities such as Bonn and Frankfurt, parts of Austria and Switzerland to Milan (Williams, 1996).

[6] The Guidance section of EAGGF was established as a result of the 1962 agreement on CAP mechanisms (see Chapter 13) and traditionally financed measures to adapt and improve farm structures and the marketing of agricultural products, and to develop rural infrastructure.

[7] The FIFG was created in 1993 in order to modernize the EU fleet, safeguard certain marine areas and improve the structures for processing and marketing of fish in the EU (see the Online Learning Centre of this book for a discussion of the EU Fisheries Policy).

with the European Employment Strategy and the Europe 2020 programme (and previously the Lisbon Strategy, see Chapter 7). It is focused on four key areas:

1 Increasing adaptability of workers and enterprises.

2 Enhancing access to employment and participation in the labour market.

3 Reinforcing social inclusion by combating discrimination and facilitating access to the labour market for disadvantaged people.

4 Promoting partnership for reform in the fields of employment and inclusion.

The European Regional Development Fund

The ERDF is the largest of the financial instruments for cohesion. Created in 1975, the aim of the fund is to reduce disparities between various regions in the EU through the promotion of public and private investments. Following the 1973 enlargement and the entry of the UK with its difficulties in Northern Ireland, Scotland, Wales and the north of England (see Chapter 2), the ERDF was initially conceived as a means of assistance to regions facing industrial decline.

During the 2007–13 period the ERDF provides financing for programmes addressing general infrastructure, innovation and investments (see also Box 15.1). The ERDF finances projects in areas such as: research and innovation, infrastructure projects (for transport, telecommunications, energy and water supply), the information society, environmental protection, risk prevention, education and professional training, health services, tourism and culture.

Box 15.1

Examples of projects supported by EU cohesion policy

EU cohesion policy supported the extension of the Faculty of Mathematics and Computer Science of the Nicolas Copernicus University in Torun, Poland. With financing from the ERDF the centre was extended in a way consistent with the original 1930s architecture. The new wing consists of a lecture hall with capacity for 350 people, a conference room, 10 computer laboratories, and 40 rooms for academic staff.

Near Porto in Northern Portugal the Sousa Valley is famous for its Romanesque architecture. In 2003 a project was set up with support from the ERDF to restore buildings, highlight their cultural significance, and promote the area as an important tourist attraction. In 2006 promotional and marketing activities were launched to establish this 'Romanesque art road' as a principal tourist attraction in Portugal.

The *Financial Times* of 30 November 2010 describes an interesting case in which an estimated €1.5 million from the Structural Funds was allocated for machinery and training schemes to tobacco companies such as British American Tobacco and Japan Tobacco International. This occurred at a time when the EU is spending €16 million a year on its anti-smoking campaign.

Source: *The Polish and Portuguese examples are from Inforegio of December 2006, www.ec.europa.eu/regional_policy,* © *European Communities, 2008.*

The Cohesion Fund

Introduced as part of the Maastricht package, the Cohesion Fund provides assistance to those member states that fear that they will not be able to meet the additional competitive pressures resulting from economic and monetary union. The criterion for eligibility is that the country has a GDP per capita that is less than 90 per cent of the EU average. The countries receiving assistance through the Cohesion Fund are the new member states, Greece and Portugal. Spain is subject to a transitional phasing-out arrangement as it met the 90 per cent threshold for EU(15), but not EU(25) or EU(27),

and indeed a number of Spanish regions were well above the threshold. Ireland was also initially a cohesion country, but no longer qualifies, so aid has been phased out. Countries benefiting from the Cohesion Fund are obliged to adopt economic policies conducive to convergence. In return they receive financial assistance for projects in favour of the environment and trans-European networks to improve transport infrastructure. The contribution of the Fund may amount to up to 85 per cent of total financing of the project (see Table 15.1).

Table 15.1   EU co-financing rates for the 2007–13 period

Criteria	Member states, regions	ERDF, ESF	Cohesion Fund
(1) Member states whose average GDP per capita was below 85% of the EU(25) between 2001 and 2003	CZ, EE, GR, CY, LV, LT, HU, MT, PL, PT, SL, SK, BG, RO	85%	85%
(2) Member states other than those under (1) eligible to the Cohesion Fund	ES	80%/50%[a]	85%
(3) Member states other than those under (1) and (2)	AT, BE, DK, DE, FR, IE, IT, LU, NL, SE, FI, UK	75%/50%[a]	–
(4) Outermost regions referred to in Article 349 TFEU	Regions in ES, FR, PT	85%	85%[b]

[a] The first rate concerns regions eligible under the convergence objective; the second one those under the regional competitiveness and employment objective. See the text for a definition of these objectives.

[b] If applicable.

Source: European Commission, Regional Policy – Inforegio, http://ec.europa.eu/regional_policy (accessed 27 January 2011), © European Union, 2011.

The European Investment Bank

The Treaty of Rome (now Articles 308 and 309 TFEU of the Lisbon Treaty) envisaged the creation of the EIB. The EIB helps to finance projects in the member states and in certain third countries (such as those in the Mediterranean area, in Central and Eastern Europe and in the ACP group). The EIB raises funds on financial markets using its name as a guarantee, and provides subsidized loans to finance projects carried out by public authorities and private firms. In recent years the EIB has been involved in supporting the Lisbon Strategy and Europe 2020 with, for example, loans for investment in education, health care and high-technology sectors.

The European Union Solidarity Fund

Following the intense flooding in the EU in August 2002 it was decided to set up the European Union Solidarity Fund (EUSF). This is not one of the structural instruments, but member states and countries negotiating accession can request assistance from this Fund in the event of a major disaster.

Actions were taken in response to the 2002 flooding in Germany, Austria, the Czech Republic and France. Other interventions were for the *Prestige* oil spill in Spain, earthquakes in Molise and Poulles, the eruption of Mount Etna and forest fires in Portugal in 2003. By 2010 the Fund had been used for 33 catastrophic disasters in 20 countries, spending over €2.1 billion.

15.5   The evolution of EU regional policy

During the 1958–75 period, regional measures were widely implemented at a national level in the member states, but there was no real Community policy. The original six member states were a relatively homogeneous economic group, with the exception of the Mezzogiorno of Italy. The EIB was set up principally with the aim of resolving the problems of Southern Italy, but in practice its activities were on a relatively limited scale. It was hoped that measures to promote labour movement in the Community would also have the effect of reducing unemployment in the Mezzogiorno. It was also considered that the CAP could play a redistributive role since farm incomes were generally below those in other sectors.

Between 1975 and 1988 the regional policy of the Community was characterized by the introduction of new measures, the wider use of existing instruments and a gradual increase in the funds available for redistributive measures (Tsoukalis, 1997).

The ERDF was created in 1975 largely at British request. With a tradition of importing food from the rest of the world, and a small but efficient agricultural sector, the UK was expected to be a large net contributor to the EC budget (see Chapter 12). The ERDF was considered a mechanism for correcting this imbalance, though following the 1973 oil crisis its operation was on a far smaller scale than initially foreseen. The funds available for the ERDF increased over the years, but it was criticized for poor co-ordination, insufficient flexibility in the choice of project and of being used simply to replace funding by national authorities.

In 1978 a 'Mediterranean package' was introduced as a response to criticisms that the CAP had traditionally favoured northern farmers and fear that the Mediterranean enlargement would add to competitive pressures. Requested by France and Italy, the measures were also extended to Greece from 1981, and entailed increased price and market support for certain Mediterranean products, assistance for irrigation, the infrastructure and reforestation. From 1981 similar 'integrated development programmes' were introduced for other less favoured areas such as Lozère in France, Southern Belgium and the Western Isles of Scotland.

Building on these initiatives, and with a view to preparing for Spanish and Portuguese accession, in 1985 the Community introduced Integrated Mediterranean Programmes. These marked the beginning of a new strategy aimed at overcoming some of the shortcomings of earlier redistributive measures. There was to be more co-ordination both between the then three Structural Funds (the ESF, EAGGF Guidance and the ERDF) and with the EIB. Decentralization was to increase with more involvement of local and regional authorities. The measures were directed chiefly at rural areas, but it was argued that assistance should not simply be to agriculture in these regions but should take account of the wider economic and social environment. Between 1985 and 1992, ECU 4.1 billion was allocated to these programmes, but the change in approach was probably more important than the increase in funding available.

During the period since 1988 the current instruments of EU economic and social cohesion policy were gradually evolved. In 1985 when the internal market was announced, the less favoured peripheral regions and countries feared that they would not be able to meet the additional competitive pressures this involved. Disparities in the Community had increased since 1975 (Tondl, forthcoming), and a further rise following the accession of Greece, Spain and Portugal was expected. The separate operation of the various Structural Funds achieved limited results, and the need to increase their effectiveness was recognized.

In 1987, the Single European Act introduced the concept of economic and social cohesion and called for harmonious development, the reduction of regional disparities, and the co-ordination and rationalization of the Structural Funds (Articles 130a to 130e).

Reform of the Structural Funds was agreed in 1988 and covered the 1989–93 period. The underlying philosophy of this reform was confirmed and strengthened in the subsequent cycles of the Structural Funds covering the periods 1994–99, 2000–06 and 2007–13. The main aspects of the reform were:

- A doubling of the Structural Funds from ECU7 billion in 1989 to ECU14 billion in 1993.
- The creation of so-called Community Initiatives which involve a number of member states.

- The introduction of a series of **principles of operation.**
- The concentration of the Funds on priority **objectives.**

The aim of Community Initiatives was to encourage co-operation between different member states on matters of common interest. Community Initiatives accounted for about 10 per cent of spending under the Structural Funds. During the 1989–93 and 1994–99 periods there were a number of Community Initiatives aimed at specific groups and targets, but for the 2000–06 period they were reduced to four:[8] LEADER+ (rural development); INTERREG II (cross-border, transnational and interregional co-operation); URBAN (economic and social regeneration of cities and urban neighbourhoods); and EQUAL (transnational co-operation to combat all kinds of discrimination and inequalities in the labour market).

The 1988 reform introduced four principles for implementing cohesion policy, and these have applied ever since:

1 **Concentration.** Measures were to be concentrated on priority objectives to ensure close co-ordination of policies (see Box 15.1). Concentration is also intended to ensure that the effectiveness of measures is not undermined by resources being spread too thinly either geographically or by policy measure, but it does not always succeed in this aim.

2 **Partnership.** This implies close co-operation between the European Commission and the appropriate national, regional and local authorities at all stages. Horizontal co-operation between organizations at the regional and local levels is required, as well as the development of vertical aspects of multi-level governance and the interplay between different tiers of government. Partnership may help to disseminate information and to take a broader range of views into account in assessing needs and evaluating projects. The disadvantage of this approach is that procedures may be complex and heavily bureaucratic. Because allocation decisions are made primarily at the level of member states and their regional and local authorities (in line with the principle of subsidiarity) this appears to have changed little over the years despite efforts made to streamline the objectives and protocols for submitting proposals. See Hooghe (1996) for a good description of the mechanics of how funds are channelled down to regional and local beneficiaries.

3 **Programming.** The Structural Funds would be implemented through structured programmes lasting a number of years (1989–93, 1994–99, 2000–06 and 2007–13). The cycles generally coincide with successive financial perspectives. Programming is intended to encourage longer-term, more strategic planning, but at times difficulties are encountered with the length of time taken to approve programming documents and with their complexity.

4 **Additionality.** This aims at ensuring that allocations are additional to national financing and do not simply replace national measures. The aim is to stimulate an increase in finance (both public and private) available, and, at least before the economic crisis, in Objective 1 regions this objective appears to have been realized.[9]

The main changes introduced in the Structural Funds for the 1994–99 period were: the creation of the Cohesion Fund; an increase in financing through the Structural Funds; a change in the objectives (see Box 15.2); the introduction of the Financial Instrument for Fisheries Guidance; the simplification of procedures; and an increased role for regional and local authorities. However, the criticisms of complex procedures, lack of co-ordination and insufficient decentralization continued to be levelled at the Structural Funds.

---

[8] These were incorporated into the new objectives for the 2007–13 period, with URBAN II and EQUAL being integrated into the convergence and regional competitiveness and employment objectives, and INTERREG providing a basis for the European territorial integration objective (see below).

[9] As explained below, with the economic crisis the member states encountered difficulties with the co-financing requirement.

Box 15.2

Evolution of the objectives of the Structural Funds between 1989 and 2013

1989–93	1994–99	2000–06	2007–13
Objective 1: The less well developed areas of the Community, which are defined as those whose GDP per capita is less than 75% of the EU average in the previous three years.	*Objective 1*: The less well developed areas of the Community, which are defined as those whose GDP per capita is less than 75% of the EU average in the previous three years.	*Objective 1*: The less well developed areas of the EU, which are defined as those whose GDP per capita is less than 75% of the EU average.	*Objective 1*: Convergence regions, or the less well developed areas of the EU, which are defined as those whose GDP per capita is less than 75% of the EU average.
Objective 2: Regions affected by the decline of traditional industries.	*Objective 2*: The conversion of regions seriously affected by industrial decline.	*Objective 2*: The economic and social conversion of regions that were facing natural difficulties, including declining rural areas and those dependent on fishing.	*Objective 2*: Competitiveness and employment creation.
Objective 3: The fight against long-term unemployment.	*Objective 3*: Combating long-term unemployment (more than 12 months) and facilitating the integration into work of young people (under 25 years of age), women and persons exposed to exclusion from the labour market.	*Objective 3*: Improvement of human capital by promoting employment, education and professional training.	*Objective 3*: European territorial co-operation.
Objective 4: Integration into working life of young people.	*Objective 4*: Facilitating the adaptation of workers to industrial change and changes in production systems.		

Objective 5a: Assisting the structural adjustment of agriculture and fisheries.	*Objective 5a*: Assisting the structural adjustment of agriculture and fisheries.	Rural development became the second pillar of the CAP.
Objective 5b: Aid to rural areas.	*Objective 5b*: Aid to rural areas.	
	Objective 6: Regions with a low density of population in the extreme north of Finland and Sweden.	

Note: With the 1993 reform the previous Objectives 3 and 4 were integrated into a revised Objective 3, and new Objectives 4 and 6 were created. With the 1999 reform the old Objectives 1 and 6 were incorporated into the new Objective 1, the old Objectives 2 and 5a were included in the new Objective 2 and Objective 5b was transformed into rural development, which became the second pillar of the CAP.

At the Berlin European Council of 1999 agreement was reached on reform of the Structural Funds for the 2000–06 period, also with a view to EU enlargement (see Chapter 19). The reform aimed at simplification of the instruments, by reducing the number of regulations, objectives and sources of financing. The procedures of programming and financial management were also rendered less complex, and the instruments of control, monitoring and evaluation were reinforced. Subsidiarity was strengthened, with increased decentralization to regional and local authorities.

The objectives of the Structural Funds were reduced to three. In Objective 1 regions GDP per capita was less than 75 per cent of the EU average and these were allocated 69.7 per cent of all spending. A further 12.3 per cent of Structural Funds was earmarked to assist the economic and social conversion of Objective 2 regions which were facing change in industrial and service sectors or urban difficulties, declining rural areas and depressed regions dependent on fishing. The remaining funds were allocated to Objective 3, which was a so-called horizontal measure in the sense that it applied throughout the EU. Its aim was to improve human capital by promoting employment, education and professional training. Objective 3 schemes had to promote equal opportunities between men and women. It was hoped that by adopting these three objectives, priorities would be fixed, and the use of funds would be rendered more effective.

The European Council in Berlin agreed €195 billion for the Structural Funds and €18 billion for the Cohesion Fund for the 2000–06 period. Each year €1.04 billion was earmarked over the 2000–06 period for ISPA (the Instrument for Structural Policies Pre-Accession) for the CEECs, and the financial perspective contained a budgetary heading for Structural Funds for the new member states. There was much debate about the absorption capacity or ability of new member states to draw up and implement effective policies. In the event cohesion policy in the new member states was less generous than in earlier periods in the cohesion countries, and the latter also saw their aid density decrease.

15.6 EU cohesion and regional policy over the 2007–13 period

For the 2007–13 period the term 'cohesion policy' replaced the earlier expression 'structural actions' and various changes were introduced:

- Thirty-six per cent of spending from the EU budget over the 2007–13 period, or €308 billion, is to be allocated to cohesion policy (see Figure 15.1 for the division of this allocation by member state).

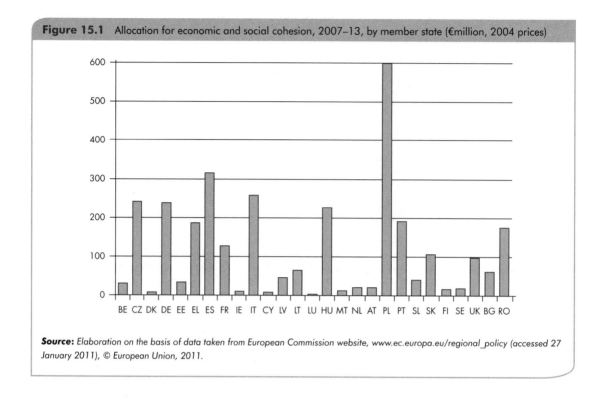

Figure 15.1 Allocation for economic and social cohesion, 2007–13, by member state (€million, 2004 prices)

Source: *Elaboration on the basis of data taken from European Commission website, www.ec.europa.eu/regional_policy (accessed 27 January 2011),* © European Union, 2011.

- A reduction in the number of financial instruments used for cohesion policy to three (the ESF, the ERDF and the Cohesion Fund, see above).
- Continuation of the principles of concentration, partnership, programming and additionality (see above).
- A tighter and more explicit linking of cohesion policy to the Lisbon Strategy and subsequently Europe 2020,[10] including earmarking of resources to support specific priorities of the Strategy and so ensure an adequate financial contribution for promoting growth and employment.
- New objectives for social and economic cohesion.
- Changes in operating procedures, with increased concentration and simplification of measures.
- A wider delegation of responsibility to member states and regions.
- The introduction of new measures (such as JASPERS for investment programmes and technical assistance, JESSICA to encourage sustainable development in urban areas, and JEREMIE, by which the EIB and Commission can provide repayable types of assistance to micro-to-medium firms).

Cohesion policy was to support the Lisbon Agenda and later Europe 2020 by: making countries more attractive for investments; encouraging innovation, entrepreneurship and the knowledge economy; and creating more and better jobs.

There were to be three new priority objectives for economic and social cohesion in the 2007–13 period (see Table 15.2):

---

[10] See Chapter 7.

Table 15.2 Financing the different cohesion policy objectives, 2007–13

Objectives	Financial instruments		
Convergence	ERDF	ESF	Cohesion Fund
Regional competitiveness and employment	ERDF	ESF	
European territorial co-operation	ERDF		

Source: European Commission, www.ec.europa.eu/regional_policy (accessed 27 January 2011), © European Union, 2011.

1 **Convergence**
2 **Competitiveness and employment co-operation**
3 **European territorial co-operation.**

The aim of the first objective is to speed up the economic convergence of less developed regions. The convergence objective will concern regions whose GDP per capita is less than 75 per cent of the average for the EU(25).[11] In the EU(27) this objective covers 84 regions with a total population of 154 million in 17 member states (see Figure 15.2).[12] This objective will receive 81.6 per cent of contributions for cohesion actions (or €283 billion) over the 2007–13 period compared with the 75 per cent for the previous Objective 1 over the 2000–06 period.

The average GDP per capita was reduced with the enlargements of 2004 and 2007. As a result, if the criterion for Objective 1 regions of being under 75 per cent of average EU GDP remained unchanged, some regions that previously qualified for Objective 1 status would no longer do so in an enlarged EU. A phasing-out system (see Figure 15.2) was therefore adopted for regions that would have been eligible for funding if the threshold had been calculated for EU(15) rather than EU(25).

The regional competitiveness and employment objective is to receive 15.9 per cent of resources for cohesion actions. It applies in 168 regions representing 314 million inhabitants. The aim of the objective is to implement regional development programmes to strengthen regional competitiveness and attractiveness by anticipating economic and social change and supporting innovation, the knowledge society, entrepreneurship, protection of the environment, accessibility and risk prevention. The new Objective 2 also envisages programmes financed by the ESF to help workers and companies on the basis of the European Employment Strategy. Some regions are to be covered by a 'phasing-in' arrangement (see Figure 15.2) as they were covered by the former Objective 1 for the 2000–06 period, but their GDP now exceeds 75 per cent of the average GDP of the EU(15).

The European territorial co-operation objective accounts for 2.5 per cent of the total allocation for cohesion over the 2007–13 period. The purpose of this objective is to strengthen co-operation at three levels: cross-border co-operation through joint programmes; co-operation between transnational zones; and networks for co-operation and the exchange of experiences throughout the EU. A European Grouping for Territorial Co-operation (EGTC) has been set up as a legal entity to promote cross-border, transnational and regional co-operation.

For the implementation of policy the Commission consults with the member states and draws up common Strategic Guidelines on cohesion. Each member state then prepares a National Strategic Programme Reference Framework. The Commission validates the parts of these frameworks which require a decision, as well as the Operating Programmes. The Operating Programmes present the priorities and methods of programming of the member states and/or regions.

---

[11] Bulgaria and Romania were not yet member states when agreement was reached in 2006 on cohesion policy for the 2007–13 period.

[12] The statistics in this section are taken from www.ec.europa.eu/regional_policy (accessed 27 January 2011).

Figure 15.2 Convergence objective and regional competitiveness and employment objective regions, 2007–13

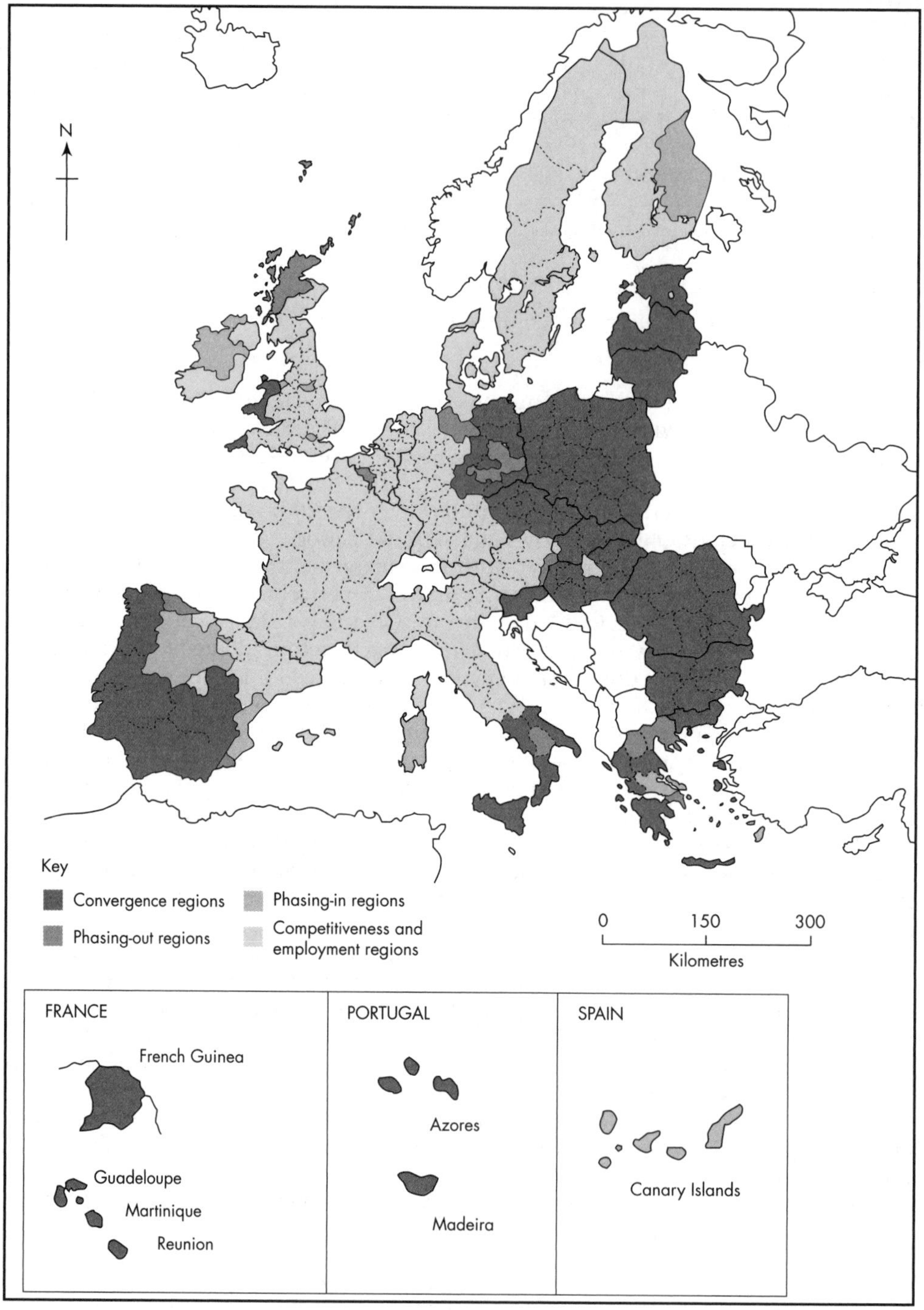

Key

■ Convergence regions   ▨ Phasing-in regions

■ Phasing-out regions   ▨ Competitiveness and
                           employment regions

0   150   300
Kilometres

FRANCE

French Guinea

Guadeloupe
Martinique
Reunion

PORTUGAL

Azores

Madeira

SPAIN

Canary Islands

Source: European Commission, www.europa.eu/regional_policy (accessed 27 January 2011), © European Union, 2010.

15.7 | Has there been convergence in the EU?

The question of whether there has been convergence in the EU has been extensively documented in the successive reports of the European Commission on economic, social and now also territorial cohesion (see, for instance, European Commission, 2010f). From these reports it emerges that the disparities in GDP per capita among EU countries have narrowed since the mid-1990s (but, as explained below, it is difficult to assess how far this was due to cohesion policy).[13] However, wide disparities between the less developed and highly developed EU regions remain.[14] Though regional disparities have decreased in the EU as a whole (see also Table 15.3 and Figure 15.3), they have increased in some countries, in particular in new member states such as Romania. A major cause of disparity within countries is the concentration of economic activity around capital cities.

The impact of the economic crisis was extreme in some regions, but it was no worse on average in less well-off EU regions than in highly developed ones, so regional disparities barely changed as a result of the crisis.[15]

Table 15.3 GDP per capita in the EU

	1950 GDP per capita EU(15)=100 (€)	1990 GDP per capita EU(15)=100 (€)	2000 GDP per capita EU(15)=100 (€)	1997 GDP per capita EU(27)=100 (PPS)	2009 GDP per capita EU(27)= 100 (PPS)		1997 GDP per capita EU(27)=100 (PPS)	2009 GDP per capita EU(27)=100 (PPS)
Germany	93	125	111	124.9	116	Bulgaria	26	44[a]
France	136	111	106	115.2	108	Cyprus	86	98
Italy	71	101	89	119.6	104	Czech Rep.	73	82
Netherlands	100	100	111	127.6	131	Estonia	42	64
Belgium	166	104	106	126.2	116	Hungary	53	65
Luxembourg	201	149	191	215.7	271	Latvia	35	52
UK	140	89	113	116.7	112	Lithuania	39	55

---

[13] For instance, European Commission (2010f) obtains this result for the 1996–2007 period using various measures of disparities: the coefficient of variation, the Gini index, and the S80/S20 ratio (the ratio of the top 20 per cent of regions to the bottom 20 per cent). The Gini index is based on the Lorenz curve which shows the proportion of the total income earned by the population (y-axis) that is cumulatively earned by the bottom x per cent of the population (x-axis). The 45° line indicates equality of incomes, and the Gini coefficient measures the ratio of the area between the Lorenz curve and the line of equality, to the total area under the line of equality. The Gini coefficient can take values between 0 (complete equality) and 1 (complete inequality).

[14] The regions with the highest GDP per capita in the EU in 2007 were: Inner London (334 per cent of the EU(27) average), Luxembourg (275 per cent), Brussels (221 per cent), Hamburg (192 per cent), Prague (172 per cent), l'Île de France (169 per cent), southern and eastern Ireland (166 per cent), Groningen (165 per cent), Oberbayern (165 per cent) and Stockholm (165 per cent).

[15] According to European Commission (2010f), some 64 convergence regions (that is, those eligible for support under this objective) and 15 transition regions (those eligible for phasing out or phasing in, see above in the text) were estimated to have fared better than the EU average in the crisis. Most Polish regions, Greek regions specialized in tourism, the East German *Länder* and the capital city regions of the new member states were relatively little affected. In contrast the Baltic States, West Hungarian regions, the Italian Mezzogiorno and Southern Spain suffered significant economic contraction. Some previously buoyant regions in Ireland, Southern Finland, and Central and Northern Italy were hard hit.

Table 15.3   continued

	1950 GDP per capita EU(15)=100 (€)	1990 GDP per capita EU(15)=100 (€)	2000 GDP per capita EU(15)=100 (€)	1997 GDP per capita EU(27)=100 (PPS)	2009 GDP per capita EU(27)= 100 (PPS)		1997 GDP per capita EU(27)=100 (PPS)	2009 GDP per capita EU(27)=100 (PPS)
Denmark	153	132	142	133.8	121	Malta	80	81
Ireland	81	71	112	115.4	127	Poland	47	61
Spain	35	69	67	93.7	103	Romania	29	46
Portugal	35	37	49	76.5	80	Slovakia	51	73
Greece	30	43	52	85.0	93p	Slovenia	78	88
Austria	58	109	112	133.2	124			
Sweden	170	142	122	122.6	118			
Finland	114	143	110	111.2	113			
(EU)15	100	100	100	115.5	110			

PPS purchasing power standards; p provisional

ᵃ 2008.

Source: European Commission (2004c) and European Commission Regional Policy – Inforegio, http://ec.europa.eu/regional_policy/index_en.htm (accessed 28 January 2011), and elaborations based on Eurostat data, © European Union, 2011.

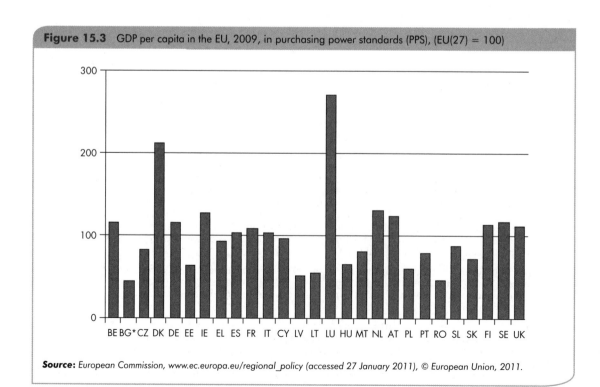

Figure 15.3   GDP per capita in the EU, 2009, in purchasing power standards (PPS), (EU(27) = 100)

Source: European Commission, www.ec.europa.eu/regional_policy (accessed 27 January 2011), © European Union, 2011.

Box 15.3

A case study of the catching-up process in the EU. From boom to bust: the Celtic Tiger

From the early 1990s until 2007 the Irish economy experienced consistently high growth compared with both the USA and average EU performances, leading to the term 'Celtic Tiger'. Irish GDP per capita increased from 64 per cent of the Community average in 1973 when Ireland joined, to 71 per cent in 1990, 147 per cent in 2007 (when the property boom ended, see Chapter 11), before falling to 127 in 2009 (see also Figure 15.3). Various explanations were advanced for the positive performance for so many years. In general, attention was drawn to the strategy to reduce unemployment adopted by successive Irish governments since the 1960s, which entailed attempts to attract foreign direct investment (FDI) and promote export-led growth. Ireland used low rates of corporation tax (which were much criticized by other EU members, see Chapters 6 and 11) and other financial incentives to encourage investment by foreign companies. Active intervention by, for example, the IDA Ireland (Industrial Development Agency, Ireland) was used to select investment in what were considered sectors with a global growth potential (such as electronics and the pharmaceutical industries). The FDI strategy also encouraged upstream linkages between foreign and indigenous companies, the creation of industrial clusters and the location of industry in the less developed areas of the country such as the West. The stability offered by EU membership and the advantage of an English-speaking labour force helped to attract foreign investors. An important role was also played by a policy of improving education and human capital during the 1960s and after, and by the introduction of appropriate macroeconomic policies and a restrained wage-setting environment in the 1980s (Sweeney, 2008).

Substantial financing through the EU Structural Funds contributed to the funding of regional investments and incentives at a time when the Irish economy could not have provided these resources without undermining its corrective macroeconomic policies (Braunerhjelm et al., 2000). A relatively efficient administration also favoured the successful implementation of measures financed with the EU Structural Funds, though insufficient attention was paid to developing infrastructure, in particular transport. Unfortunately, as explained in Chapter 11, inadequate regulation, in particular of the banking and building sectors, allowed the positive record of many years to develop into a property bubble, which eventually burst.

The level of GDP per capita of a country or region can be attributed to the output of each person working (labour productivity), and the number of people working (see also Chapter 7). According to European Commission (2010f), between 2000 and 2007 GDP per capita in the EU(27) grew by 1.8 per cent a year, of which 1.4 per cent was due to the annual productivity increase and 0.4 per cent was explained by the annual employment increase, while the share of working-age population in the total remained largely unchanged.

Labour productivity has been growing rapidly, in particular in the new member states (see Table 15.4) where output and employment in many regions have been shifting from less productive activities to those with higher value added. The ten fastest growing regions of the EU between 2000 and 2007 were all in the CEEC new member states, and experienced an increase of GDP of over 8 per cent a year.[16] The slowest growing regions of the EU were mainly in Italy and had an annual growth of GDP per capita of only 0.2 per cent. [17]

---

[16] These were regions in Romania, the three Baltic States and Slovakia (see European Commission, 2010f).

[17] Lombardia, Piemonte, Puglia, Emilia-Romagna, Abruzzo, Umbria and Trento in Italy, Franche-Compté in France, Berlin in Germany and the Balearic Islands in Spain (European Commission, 2010f)

Table 15.4 Labour productivity per person employed

	Labour productivity per person employed 2004 EU(27)=100	Labour productivity per person employed 2009 EU(27)=100		Labour productivity per person employed 2004 EU(27)=100	Labour productivity per person employed 2009 EU(27)=100
Bulgaria	34.6	40.0	Ireland	135.4	130.5
Cyprus	82.8	89.0	Portugal	69.2	75.3
Czech Rep.	68.0	72.9	Belgium	131.7	125.5
Estonia	57.4	105.1	Germany	108.1	109.2
Hungary	67.5	72.3	France	120.6	120.9
Latvia	45.7	53.2	Italy	112.2	111.8
Lithuania	53.3	57.3	Luxembourg	169.6	170.3
Malta	90.0	90.7	Netherlands	112.2	111.1
Poland	69.2	75.3	Austria	117.5	113.2
Romania	34.4	48.0	Finland	112.9	109.1
Slovakia	65.4	80.7	Denmark	108.6	103.3
Slovenia	81.5	81.6	Sweden	114.9	109.9
Greece	110.6p	98.0p	UK	113.8	106.6
Spain	102.0	109.8	EU(15)	111.0	109.6

p provisional

Source: Eurostat, http://epp.eurostat.ec.europa.eu/tgm/table.do?tab=table&init=1&plugin=1&language=en&pcode=tsieb030 (accessed 27 January 2011), © European Union, 2011.

There are substantial differences in employment rates between EU regions (see also Figures 7.1–7.3 for national employment rates in Chapter 7). According to European Commission (2010f), raising the employment rate to 75 per cent of people aged 20–64, a target set by the Europe 2020 strategy, would increase GDP per capita by more than 6 per cent in the EU as a whole, and by 17 per cent in the convergence regions.

Tondl (forthcoming) provides a survey of regional convergence studies for the EU. Studies such as Armstrong (1995), Fagerberg and Verspagen (1996) and Tondl (1999) found a strong European convergence process until the 1970s, with a subsequent standstill and some recovery at the beginning of the 1990s. Many later studies are concerned with the speed of the catching-up process of the new member states. LeSage and Fischer (2008), Eckey et al. (2009) and Crespo Cuaresam and Feldkircher (2009) find convergence in the EU(25). Niebuhr and Schlitte (2008) and Paas and Schlitte (2008) find divergence within the EU(10) with catching-up concentrated in areas around the capitals, but convergence in the EU(25). Bulgaria and Romania were not included in these studies.

15.8 Studies of the effects of EU cohesion policy

It is extremely difficult to assess the effectiveness of cohesion policy on a number of counts, and the following list does not pretend to be exhaustive:

- The impact of many projects and programmes (for example, infrastructure) can only be assessed in the long run.
- Problems arise in isolating the effects of regional policies from other factors (including other EU policies with regional implications such as the CAP, and competition, transport and environmental policies).
- It is difficult to separate the impact of national and EU regional policies.
- Recipients tend to overestimate the impact of regional measures.

Esposti (2008) and Tondl (forthcoming) provide a survey of studies on the effects of the Structural Funds. In general the studies concentrate on the effects on growth and two main approaches are used: [18]

- Econometric studies based on a growth model and regional convergence (which provide mixed evidence on growth effects. For studies of this type see Becker et al. (2008) or Busillo et al. (2009).
- Projections using macroeconomic model simulations, which generally indicate that the Structural Funds can potentially make a significant contribution to long-term growth. The studies by the European Commission described below fall into this category, but see also ESRI and GEFRA (2002) or Bradley (2008).

The European Commission and member states carry out regular in-depth assessment of cohesion policy. EU member states are responsible for *ex ante* evaluation, while the Commission carries out *ex post* assessment.

Many of the results of the studies of the Commission are presented in the reports on economic, social and (now) territorial cohesion. The econometric research carried out by the European Commission using two different macroeconomic models and presented in the most recent of these reports suggests that cohesion policy in the EU has had a significantly positive effect.[19] According to simulations using the HERMIN model, cohesion policy for the 2000–06 period is estimated to have increased GDP in the main recipient countries by 1.2 per cent each year until the end of 2009 when the implementation period finished. These effects are cumulative, leading to GDP in those countries in 2009 being about 11 per cent higher than it would have been without cohesion policy. Unlike the HERMIN model, the QUEST model also takes into account the financing costs of cohesion policy by the EU(15), so net receipts are smaller for those member states even though they are expected to benefit from higher exports of capital goods and services to net recipient countries as they develop. The QUEST model estimates the cumulative effect of the 2000–06 programme on the GDP of member states (excluding Bulgaria and Romania) to be 3.7 for the EU(10), and 0.7 per cent for the EU(25) in 2009, rising to 4 per cent in 2014. The difference in estimated effects between 2009 and 2014 arises because the QUEST model is an endogenous growth model so attempts to take account of the effect of investment in human capital and of research and technological development policy on growth. According to the HERMIN model, every euro invested under the 2000–06 programme resulted in a return of €2.1 on average. The QUEST model estimates suggest that the return on a euro was €1.2 in 2009, but €4.2 by

---

[18] See Chapter 7 for a discussion of estimates of the effects on employment.

[19] European Commission (2010f). See this report and earlier versions for descriptions of these models and the simulations. The HERMIN model is a macroeconomic model with neo-classical features on the supply side. QUEST is a neo-Keynesian micro-founded dynamic general equilibrium model with endogenous growth. The use of two models based on different assumptions about the working of the economy is intended to render the results more robust.

2014. Because cohesion funding in the new member states was increased for the 2007–13 period, both models forecast that it will lead to even higher gains in GDP.

In late 2010 the *Financial Times* and the non-profit Bureau of Investigative Journalism presented the results of an extensive analysis of the effectiveness of EU structural operations. The research was aimed at addressing two questions: how was the money allocated from the EU budget being spent, and how far did the policy succeed in realizing its objectives. EU cohesion policy was criticized on a number of counts:[20]

- By November 2010 only €35 billion, or roughly 10 per cent of the allocation for cohesion policy for the 2007–13 period, had been spent. At a time of economic crisis and budget austerity the principle of additionality was creating difficulties as member states could not match EU funding with co-financing. The Commission maintained that low take-up was normal, reflecting the time necessary for projects to be drawn up and implemented, and then for the funds to be reimbursed from Brussels. However, in 2009 the EU released €6.2 billion as pre-payments to kick start projects. The question of whether to reallocate unspent funds also arises, though this is complicated midway through the financial perspective.

- In 2009 some €109 million of spending on structural operations was the subject of suspected fraud. Payments had to be suspended in Bulgaria and Romania, and there were scandals about the siphoning off of funding to Mafia-type organizations in Italy.

- According to the 2009 report of the Court of Auditors, about one-third of projects audited were subject to error. Italy, Poland, the UK and Spain have high levels of irregularities. Procedures are slow, bureaucratic and lack transparency. The system of monitoring is complex and badly co-ordinated. OLAF, the EU's anti-fraud agency, is understaffed and appears to lack effectiveness.

- Although a priority for cohesion policy was assistance for small and medium enterprises, some of the main beneficiaries of financing were large multinationals such as American Tobacco, IBM, Coca-Cola, Fiat and H&M. For instance, McDonald's received almost €60,000 for 'skills training' in Uppsala in Sweden, and the project was said to be justified because it targeted a disproportionate number of women, young school-leavers, immigrants and people with disabilities. Many large firms appear to have used financing to relocate from Western to Eastern Europe.

15.9 Cohesion policy after 2013 and the need to select an appropriate development strategy

As described in Chapter 12, the EU has embarked on a fundamental debate on the future of the EU budget after 2013, a debate that covers all aspects of spending, including cohesion policy. Various issues can be identified with regard to cohesion policy:

- Whether structural operations should be primarily a redistributive tool or an instrument of a pan-European development programme.

- If a development strategy, what priorities for spending should be identified.

- This raises the related question of whether all EU regions should continue to benefit from EU funding, or whether financing should be concentrated on poorer regions.

- What is to be the overall level of spending on cohesion policy.

- How could governance and the implementation of measures be rendered more effective.

- How is responsibility to be divided between the European Commission, and national, regional and local authorities.

---

[20] See the *Financial Times*, 30 November 2010, and 1, 2 and 3 December 2010.

Although there is much debate about the role of structural operations (redistribution, resource allocation policy or *juste retour*, see, for example, Hardy et al. (1995), or even just a compensation instrument to the poorer countries for their support for integration), there seems widespread consensus that a low level of economic development should not be a sufficient condition for receiving transfers. Instead an effective cohesion policy should be based on a development strategy.

Successive European Commission reports on economic, social and now territorial cohesion have argued that cohesion policy can play a fundamental role in helping the EU to meet objectives such as overcoming the economic crisis, competing at a global level with countries like China and India, reducing social exclusion, and meeting new challenges such as ageng and climate change. The communication of European Commission to the EU budget review (European Commission, 2010i) maintains that these objectives will be realized best by linking cohesion policy to Europe 2020, and calls for the identification of a limited number of priorities of European importance. These could include encouraging investment, innovation and the knowledge society, and creating more jobs. The Commission would adopt a common Strategic Framework highlighting necessary reforms and indicating investment needs with regard to headline targets and flagship projects. Within this Framework, member states would present National Reform Programmes.

The Commission also envisages 'development and investment partnership contracts' between the Commission and member states setting out the commitments of partners at the national and regional levels in order to address the priorities of Europe 2020. This would introduce an element of competition and would allow the Commission more direct control over at least a part of spending. However, the proposal was not received well by national ministers in the Council, who probably fear increased interference and a threat to their authority.

In addition, as described in Chapter 7, there are doubts about the commitment of member states to the Europe 2020 programme, and differences of opinion about its priorities and approach. For instance, even if the idea of a development strategy is accepted, there is debate about whether industrial districts or clusters are preferable to more evenly spread growth. One of the criticisms mentioned above is that funding is given to multinationals, but this might be more effective from the point of view of encouraging training and structural adjustment.

The view of cohesion policy as a wider instrument of overall development suggests that the present approach of spreading funding across most if not all EU regions will be continued, though for solidarity reasons it will be concentrated on the poorest regions and countries. This also seems the probable outcome for political economy reasons because regions (also through the Committee of the Regions, see Chapter 3) and national governments are powerful lobbies, and strongly oppose cuts in their funding. However, cohesion spending will have to be balanced against competing claims for spending from the EU budget (such as the CAP), and the determination of net contributors to limit the dimension of the EU budget after 2013 (Bachtler et al., 2010).

The principles of partnership and subsidiarity imply decentralization of decision making with the involvement of national, regional and local authorities. At times this has the disadvantage of complex and bureaucratic procedures. Despite efforts to streamline the objectives and protocols for submitting proposals over the years, this shortcoming has proved rather intractable. Differences in administrative capacity of regions and member states appear to be a major factor in determining the effectiveness of measures (Bollen et al., 2000). Despite these difficulties, a priority for cohesion policy after 2013 must be to develop an appropriate system for selecting projects and programmes, for setting out clear objectives and targets, for carrying out effective evaluation and monitoring, and for strengthening administrative capacity at all levels. The system should also be able to withstand pressure from politicians and pressure groups.

15.10 Evaluation and outlook

With EU enlargement in 2004 and 2007, income disparities in the EU increased substantially. Disparities between regions in the new member states were similar to those in the EU(15), but at a lower level of income. The aim of EU cohesion policies is to reduce these regional income disparities throughout the

EU, and according to various studies carried out by the European Commission, intervention has had positive effects on GDP per capita and employment (a view not shared universally by the academic research).

For the 2007–13 period 36 per cent of EU spending has been allocated to cohesion policy, and the aim is to link that policy to the objectives of the Lisbon Strategy and Europe 2020. Nobody denies the validity of such aims, but often in practice inadequate funds are allocated for their realization, both at the national and at the EU level. The EU budget is little more than 1 per cent of GDP, but even here, as described in Chapter 12, cuts in the initial Commission proposals for cohesion spending were made.

The debate is now on to define EU cohesion policy post-2013, and it is necessary to develop a strategy for ensuring its effectiveness, which ideally should include the following elements:

- Evolving an overall approach to avoid the risk of piecemeal measures and lack of co-ordination.
- Ensuring adequate endowment of infrastructure of various types: physical (in the form of transport, energy and telecommunications networks), human (in the form of skills and know-how of the workforce), and social (in the form of care and other support services).
- Developing capacity for innovation, which encompasses human resource endowment, but also the resources devoted to R&D and the effectiveness with which they are used.
- Adopting a development path that is sustainable in order to protect the environment.
- Ensuring stable macroeconomic framework. This is also necessary to permit low interest rates that can stimulate investment and capital accumulation.
- Adopting robust selection procedures and effective monitoring of programmes.
- Developing an effective institutional framework for planning and implementing measures.

Summary of key concepts

- **Regional problems** are the disparities in levels of income, in rates of growth of output and employment, and in general in levels of economic inequality between different regions.
- The view that **integration will lead to greater convergence** assumes effective functioning of the market. Convergence is said to occur through free trade, labour migration, capital mobility and diminishing returns to capital accumulation.
- Theories explaining why **integration may lead to divergence** or greater disparities between regions include modern growth theories, the evolutionary economics view of knowledge diffusion, and the New Economic Geography approach.
- For the 2007–13 period the three funds for regional and cohesion policy are: the **European Social Fund**, the **European Regional Development Fund** and the **Cohesion Fund**. Related instruments are the European Investment Bank and the European Union Solidarity Fund.
- Between 1958 and 1975 EU regional policy was characterized mainly by national measures; over the 1975–88 period new EC initiatives were launched; and since 1988 EU regional policy has evolved with successive financial perspectives.
- The four **principles of operation** of the Structural Funds are: concentration, partnership, programming and additionality.
- The reform of **cohesion policy for the 2007–13 period** is tightly integrated with the objectives of the Lisbon Strategy and Europe 2020. It allocates 36 per cent of the EU budget to cohesion measures; changes the objectives of cohesion policy; aims at improving implementation and monitoring; and introduces new instruments.

- The **objectives of cohesion policy** have changed over the years. Since 2007 there have been three objectives. Objective 1 covers the convergence regions, which are defined as those whose GDP per capita is less than 75 per cent of the EU average. Objective 2 concerns regional competitiveness and employment, and Objective 3 promotes regional territorial co-operation.

- There appears to have been **convergence between EU countries and regions**, though large disparities remain.

- It is extremely difficult to assess **the effectiveness of structural measures** because: the impact of many projects can only be assessed in the long run; problems arise in isolating the effects of regional policies from other factors; and recipients tend to overestimate the impact of regional measures.

- To render regional policy effective, in particular post-2013, it is necessary: to develop an overall **strategy for regional and national development;** to ensure stable macroeconomic policies; and to develop an effective institutional framework for planning and implementing measures.

Questions for study and review

1 Do you think that integration leads to more or less income disparity?
2 Describe the various financial instruments used to implement EU cohesion policy?
3 What are the main stages in the evolution of EU regional and cohesion policy?
4 How well do you consider that the four principles for implementing cohesion policy function?
5 Has there been convergence between EU countries and regions?
6 How effective was the cohesion policy of the EU? Why is it so difficult to provide an assessment of its effectiveness?
7 In the context of the debate about EU cohesion policy post-2013, what strategies do you think can be used to render regional and cohesion policy more effective?

Online
Learning **Centre**

When you have read this chapter, log on to the Online Learning Centre website at ***www.mcgraw-hill.co.uk/textbooks/senior*** to explore weblinks, chapter-by-chapter test questions, case studies and more online study tools.

Chapter 16

Competition Policy

Learning Objectives

By the end of this chapter you should be able to understand:

☑ The ways in which distortions in competition may undermine the integration process

☑ The main features of EU antitrust policy

☑ How merger control operates in the EU

☑ What measures are used by the EU to prevent abuse of state aids on the part of national governments

☑ The criticisms made of the role of the European Commission in competition policy

☑ The ways in which EU competition policy could be rendered more effective

16.1 Introduction

Competition policy was envisaged as an essential part of the integration process both in the Treaty of Paris establishing the European Coal and Steel Community (ECSC) and in the Treaty of Rome. Competition policy is aimed at preventing distortions in competition caused either by private firms or by government actions, and can be regarded as 'policing the Single market'. EU competition policy is complementary to national measures, but in cases of conflict EU competition law prevails.

Central to the analysis of the likely benefits of integration are the cost and price reductions that were expected to accrue.[1] However, there is a risk that restrictive practices between otherwise independent firms, or the behaviour of dominant (or monopoly) firms, might prevent these price reductions from being realized. Integration is also expected to lead to increased competition, and to meet these additional pressures firms might be induced to form cartels or undertake mergers in order to reach dominant market positions. National governments may be tempted to help their firms face the additional competitive pressures by granting them state aids.

---

[1] See Chapter 6. For a discussion of the link between competition policy and integration see also Bongardt (2005).

To prevent such developments undermining competition, and as a necessary complement to the four freedoms, EU policy therefore covers:

- antitrust measures, or the fight against cartels and restrictive practices (Article 101 TFEU ex Article 81 TEC) and against dominant position (Article 102 TFEU ex Article 82 TEC);
- mergers (Regulation No. 4064/89 of 1989 and Regulation No. 139/2004 of 2004); and
- state aids and regulated industries (Articles 106 to 108 TFEU ex Articles 86 to 88 TEC).

To prepare for EU enlargement, the EU introduced new rules on competition policy, effective from 1 May 2004. Before discussing the various aspects of EU competition policy and its reform, it is useful to present the theoretical basis for introducing competition policy and a description of the institutions involved in EU competition policy.

16.2 The theoretical basis for competition policy

Although a complete analysis of different forms of behaviour by firms is beyond the present scope, the aim of this section is to compare the outcome of certain non-competitive models with a situation of perfect competition. Even these simple models can be used to show why competition policy may be necessary. Students familiar with models of monopoly and collusion can skip this section.

The simplest model of the non-competitive behaviour of a firm is that of monopoly. A monopoly entails that there is only a single seller of the product, so the firm does not have to take into account the behaviour of other suppliers. Perfect competition occurs where there are a large number of buyers and sellers, a homogeneous product, free entry of firms to the market and perfect information.

Since the monopolist is the only seller of the product, the demand curve of the firm and the demand curve of the industry are the same. The industry demand curve faced by the monopolist will slope downwards. The monopolist is a price maker. If the monopolist sets a higher price, less will be sold. For simplicity it is assumed that the aim of the monopolist is to maximize profits. In order to decide what quantity of output to produce in order to maximize profits, the monopolist will have to take into account the different revenues and costs associated with each level of output.

Marginal revenue (MR) can be defined as the change in total revenue when output is changed by one unit. When the demand curve slopes downward, MR will be less than price. This can be seen from Figure 16.1. When the price is €6 the firm can sell 2 units and total revenue is €12. To sell 3 units, the firm must reduce its price to €5 and total revenue becomes €15. When the firm increases its sales from 2 to 3 units, the first two units are sold for €5, and total revenue decreases by area a, which is equal to €2. At the same time, total revenue increases by area b, which indicates the addition to revenue from selling the third unit at €5. Area b is equal to the price of the product €5. When increasing output from 2 to 3 units, total revenue rises by area b minus area a. This increase in total revenue for a one-unit change in output is marginal revenue. Marginal revenue is therefore less than price.[2]

In order to maximize profits the monopolist will also have to take costs into account. Marginal cost (MC) is defined as the change in total costs of production when output is varied by one unit. The monopolist will maximize profits at the level of output where MC equals MR. At lower levels of output MR exceeds MC, so the monopolist can increase profits by producing more. Equilibrium occurs where MC and MR intersect at point Em in Figure 16.2, where the level of output is Qm.[3] The price Pm charged for level of output Qm is given by point C on the demand curve directly above Em.

---

[2] Another way of explaining this concept is to recall that the demand curve represents average revenue (AR). Average revenue is the total revenue divided by number of units sold. If the demand curve is negatively sloped, AR is falling, so MR must lie below the average.

[3] The same type of graphical analysis can be used for long- or short-term analysis, using long-term cost curves or short-term cost curves respectively. The difference between long and short run arises because in the short run a firm is not able to vary the quantities of all the inputs it uses.

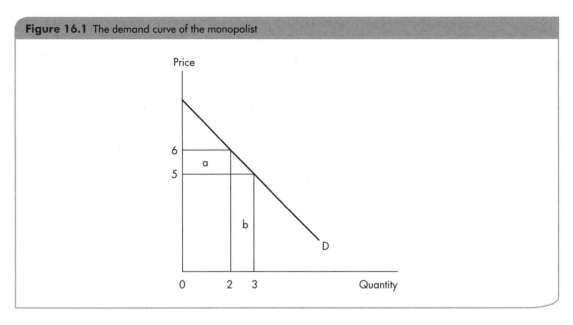

Figure 16.1 The demand curve of the monopolist

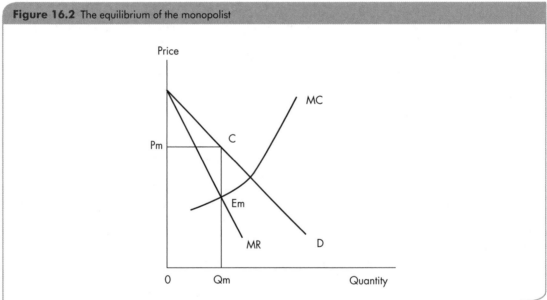

Figure 16.2 The equilibrium of the monopolist

The aim is now to show how the quantities produced and prices charged differ under conditions of monopoly and perfect competition. In order to render comparison simpler, a few additional assumptions are now introduced:[4]

- An industry is initially assumed to be operating under perfect competition and then a monopoly is introduced.
- The industry demand is assumed to be the same for the monopoly and the competitive industry.
- The long run is considered to be when firms have adjusted fully to each price.

---

[4] The analysis here follows Browning and Zupan (2009).

- The industry is assumed to operate under constant costs. Average costs are defined as the total costs of producing a given number of units output divided by the number of units of output. In a constant-cost industry, the long-run MC and AC curves will coincide. The assumption of constant costs implies that input costs will be the same under perfect competition and monopoly.
- All competitive firms are equally efficient.

The demand curve of the industry is D in Figure 16.3. With monopoly the demand curve of the industry is the demand curve of the firm. In contrast, under perfect competition the two are different. Under perfect competition the firm is a price taker, and the demand curve of the individual firm is a horizontal straight line at the going price. Price will therefore equal MR for the competitive firm. In the short run the perfectly competitive firm will maximize profits when MC equals price and MR.[5]

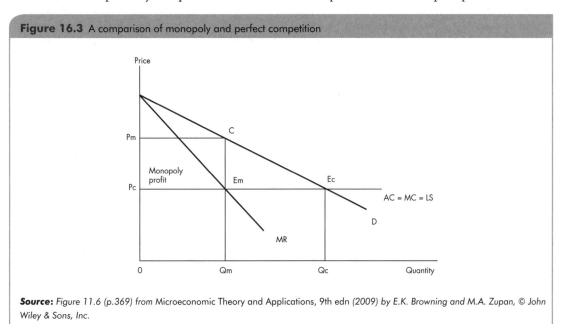

Figure 16.3 A comparison of monopoly and perfect competition

Source: Figure 11.6 (p.369) from Microeconomic Theory and Applications, 9th edn (2009) by E.K. Browning and M.A. Zupan, © John Wiley & Sons, Inc.

In the long run, for the competitive industry to be in equilibrium each firm must make zero profits, so there is no incentive for firms to enter or leave the industry.[6] The firm will earn zero profits if and only if the price for the product is equal to long-run MC and long-run AC.[7] The long-run competitive supply curve LS of the competitive industry will be a horizontal line as shown in Figure 16.3. In a constant-cost industry an increase in industry output will not raise factor prices. If industry output increases, the cost curves of firms do not change, and the expansion of industry output takes place at the same cost as new firms enter the market. Under perfect competition long-run equilibrium occurs where the industry demand curve intersects LS, the long-run supply curve. In Figure 16.3 this occurs at Ec, where output is Qc and price is Pc.

Assume now that the industry becomes a monopoly. In order to maximize profits the monopolist will produce quantity Qm, at which MC equals MR and the price charged will be Pm. At the level of output Qm, the difference between price Pm (or average revenue) and AC gives the average profit per unit of output. The total profit of the monopolist is given by average profit multiplied by the quantity of output Qm, or the rectangle PcEmCPm shown in Figure 16.3.

---

[5] For a review of this topic see, for example, Varian (2009) or Begg et al. (2008a).

[6] All competitive firms are assumed to be equally efficient.

[7] The condition for long-run equilibrium is: Pc = MR = LMC = LAC where Pc is price, MR is marginal revenue, LMC is long-run marginal cost and LAC is long-run average cost.

Since it is assumed that the monopolist faces the same costs in its different plants as did competitive firms, the long-run competitive supply curve LS is also the long-run MC curve of the monopolist. The assumption that the industry operates under constant costs means that the long-run MC curve and the long-run AC curve of the monopolist coincide, and both are equal to LS in Figure 16.3. At equilibrium the monopoly produces Qm at price Pm. When the industry was competitive, quantity Qc was produced and sold at price Pc. Under monopoly there is therefore a lower quantity of output and higher prices than in a competitive situation.

Figure 16.3 can also be used to illustrate the welfare costs of introducing a monopoly. The monopoly reduces output from Qc to Qm. The fall in output releases resources and these can be used to create other products. In competitive markets the resources released can be used to produce output worth rectangle QmQcEcEm. The increase in price under monopoly causes a fall in consumer surplus of PmCEcPc. Rectangle PcEmCPm showing the monopoly profit is simply a transfer from consumers to producers so does not represent a net welfare loss to society. The net welfare loss to society is indicated by triangle CEcEm.

As explained below, one of the main aims of EU competition policy is to avoid abuse of monopoly power by firms in a dominant position. The simplified analysis here shows that competition policy may be aimed at reducing or avoiding the net welfare loss to society as a whole that results from the reduction in output and the rise in price, and limiting or eliminating (generally on equity grounds) the transfer from consumers to the producer represented by monopoly profit.

Monopoly is an extreme case, and in practice firms generally face some form of competition. Though beyond the present scope, most texts on microeconomic theory deal with situations of duopoly, oligopoly and monopolistic competition[8] and consider how outcomes vary according to the different market structure and assumptions about the behaviour of the firm, in particular attitudes towards competitors. Here the discussion is limited to a model of collusion or cartel. As explained below, cartels are forbidden in the USA, but subject to heavy regulation in the EU.

The aim of collusion or the formation of a cartel by firms in a competitive industry is to co-ordinate their activities in order to earn monopoly profits. Figure 16.4 shows the downward-sloping industry demand curve D for the product, and the marginal revenue curve MR. SS is the short-run supply curve of the industry, that is, the sum of the short-run marginal cost curves of all the firms. Under conditions of perfect competition, industry equilibrium occurs at Ec, with price Pc and quantity of output Qc.

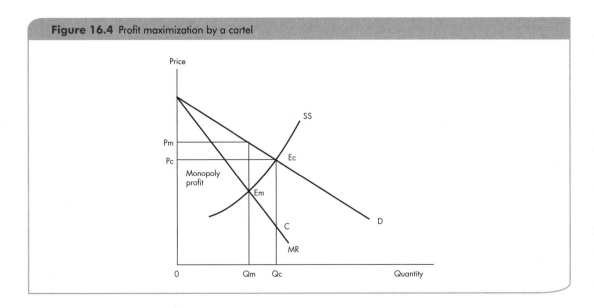

Figure 16.4 Profit maximization by a cartel

---

[8] A duopoly consists of an industry with two firms, whereas in an oligopoly a few firms produce all or most of the output of the industry. Monopolistic competition occurs where entry and exit to the industry are unrestricted but firms produce differentiated products.

Assume that the firms then form a cartel and agree to restrict output in order to raise prices. The firms will behave like a monopolist and will maximize their combined profits at Em, where the SS curve intersects the marginal revenue curve MR, with a combined output of Qm and a monopoly price of Pm. This outcome is the same as if a single monopoly controlled all the firms making up the cartel (see, for analogy, Figure 16.2 above).

Area EcEmC indicates the increase in total profits for all the firms in the cartel. By reducing the quantity produced from Qc to Qm, the firms eliminate all output for which their combined marginal costs exceed MR, and in this way the firms in the cartel can increase their combined profit.

However, as explained in Chapter 4, there are inherent economic reasons that cartels are unstable and tend to break down. As Figure 16.3 shows, the cartel can restrict output to raise prices, but at the higher prices each firm has an incentive to cheat since the individual firm could increase its profits by expanding output. Members of the cartel may find it difficult to reach agreement over price, output and profit sharing. Moreover, the monopoly profits earned by a cartel may encourage other firms to enter the industry.

16.3 The institutions responsible for EU competition policy

The Commission plays a central role in the implementation of EU competition policy. It may investigate rules at its own initiative, or upon the receipt of a complaint from an individual, company or member state. It can force firms to hand over documents and carry out raids on firms without prior warning (known as 'dawn raids' by the media). Decisions are prepared by the Directorate-General for Competition (DG COMP). If a case of infringement is found, the Commission will generally attempt to convince the company or government in question to bring practices in line with EU competition law voluntarily. If this is not possible, the Commission can order enforcement or, in some cases, impose a fine.

The European Court of Justice was responsible for appeals, but subsequently this role was taken over by the Court of First Instance. The role of the Council of Ministers is limited to deciding on regulations and directives in the EU decision-making process. As explained below, with the reform of 2004 national courts and national competition authorities assumed a more active role in competition policy in the EU.

16.4 Antitrust enforcement

Antitrust measures cover cartels and restrictive practices, and abuses of dominant position. Article 101 TFEU prohibits as *'incompatible with the internal market'* all agreements that affect trade between the member states and have the intention or effect of preventing, distorting or restricting competition. Fines of up to 10 per cent of their annual worldwide turnover may be imposed on the guilty parties (see Box 16.1). Collusive behaviour (or concerted action having the same effect as collusion) is considered contrary to consumer interests when it entails agreements to:[9]

- fix prices;
- limit or control production, markets, technical development or investment;
- share markets or sources of supply;
- apply dissimilar conditions to equivalent transactions with other trading parties; or
- make the conclusion of contracts subject to supplementary obligations.

One of the major difficulties in implementing EU policy with respect to Article 101 TFEU is that in practice it may be difficult to establish that collusive behaviour has taken place. In the Franco-Japanese ball bearings case of 1972, representatives of firms and trade associations from the two countries met in Paris and wrote minutes recording their agreement to fix prices.[10] The minutes ended in the hands of the European Commission competition authorities, but rarely is such information readily available.

---

[9] Article 101(1).

[10] *Official Journal* 343 of 21 December 1974.

Box 16.1

The ten largest fines imposed by the Commission on firms in cartel cases since 1969

Year	Firm	Case	Fine (€)
2008	Saint Gobain	Car glass	869,000,000
2009	E.ON	Gas	553,000,000
2009	GDF Suez	Gas	553,000,000
2007	ThyssenKrupp ENI SpA	Elevators and escalators	479,669,850
2001	Hoffmann-La Roche AG	Vitamins	462,000,000
2007	Siemens AG	Gas insulated switchgear	396,562,500
2008	Pilkington	Car glass	370,000,000
2010	Ideal Standard	Bathroom fittings	326,091,196
2008	Sasol Ltd	Candle waxes	318,200,000
2010[a]	Air France/KLM	Air freight	310,080,000

[a] Last change November 2010.

Source: European Competition, europa.eu/rapid/pressReleasesAction http://ec.europa.eu/competition/cartels/statistics/statistics. pdf (accessed 8 February 2011), © European Union, 2011.

The task of proving that collusive behaviour has taken place is further complicated by the fact that, for example, in a situation of oligopoly the outcome may appear collusive (with lower output and higher prices) without the firms actually having to collude in a legal sense (see Box 16.2).

One way around the cloak of secrecy of cartels is the leniency policy of the EU. This offers companies involved in a cartel full or partial immunity from fines if they self-report or hand over evidence. In this way the Commission may obtain inside information of cartel infringements. The leniency policy also acts as a deterrent to forming cartels and undermines existing ones by creating suspicion among cartel members.

Box 16.2

The difficulty of proving collusive behaviour: the *Wood Pulp* case

The difficulty in proving that there has been collusive behaviour was evident in the *Wood Pulp* case of 1993 described in Martin (2007). The EU was supplied largely by firms in Northern Europe and North America, which tended to adjust prices by similar amounts at about the same time. Most of these firms met regularly at a trade association in Switzerland. The Commission maintained that there was collusion but was overruled by the Court of Justice on the basis of insufficient evidence. According to the Court, the parallel pricing might be based on collusion, but it might simply be the consequence of transparent prices in an oligopoly market.

Horizontal co-operation involves firms at the same stage in the production process, and is generally found to violate EU competition policy when it can be established that there are agreements to set prices, impose entry barriers or reserve particular geographical areas for certain firms.

Vertical co-operation is between firms at different stages in the production process. The 1999 regulation on vertical restraints forbids agreements on:[11]

- exclusive purchasing;
- resale price maintenance (the distributor agrees to sell at or above the price indicated by the manufacturer).

These types of vertical restraint typically infringe EU competition policy by fragmenting the Single Market or by introducing price discrimination (see Box 16.3).

Box 16.3

Case study: The car distribution and repair system in the EU

An example of vertical restraint can be found in the car distribution system in the EU, which for many years allowed car manufacturers to sell through designated dealers in specific territories. The justification given was the repair and maintenance that cars require. Manufacturers were, however, obliged to allow dealers to sell cars to customers who were not resident in the designated sales area. On various occasions the Commission fined EU firms (Volkswagen in 1995 and 1999, and the Dutch General Motors in 2000) for attempting to block dealers from selling in other territories. In October 2002 a new car distribution regulation came into operation, which offers distributors greater freedom to operate multi-brand dealerships (Regulation No. 1400/2002 of 31 July 2002).

In May 2010, Block Exemption Regulation No. 461/2010 introduced a sector-specific regulatory framework for vehicle distribution and repair. The new rules aimed at increasing competition in the market for repair and maintenance by improving access to technical information needed for repairs, and by making it easier to use alternative spare parts. This follows four cases brought by the Commission against Daimler Chrysler, Fiat, Toyota and GM to ensure they allow independent garages adequate access to repair information. The new rules are important for consumers as repair bills account for about 40 per cent of the total cost of owning a car, and have been rising in recent years. It should also be easier for the Commission to tackle attempts by manufacturers to abuse warranties by requesting that cars only be serviced in authorized garages.

In recent years real car prices have been falling because of production overcapacities (in particular during the economic crisis) and technological improvements. However, distribution costs account for about 30 per cent of the price of a new car. From 2013 simplification of the rules and more scope for multi-brand dealers should enable these costs to be cut*.

* See also the work of the Commission on car prices to improve the working of the Single Market discussed in Chapter 6.

Source: Martin (2007) and the DG Competition website, http://europa.eu/rapid/pressReleasesAction.do?reference=IP/10/619& format=HTML&aged=0&language=EN&guiLanguage=en (accessed 9 February 2011), © European Union, 2011.

Although collusion is forbidden, Article 101(3) TFEU envisages exemptions and permits other forms of co-operation between firms, which improve the production or distribution of goods, promote technical progress and allow consumers a fair share of the resulting benefit.[12]

---

[11] *Official Journal* 336 of 29 December 1999.

[12] In the early years of competition policy, the Commission itself was responsible for granting exemptions, but the huge workload that this entailed meant that alternatives had to be developed. These include the block exemption system, and 'comfort letters' from the Commission, which indicated whether a firm was considered likely to qualify for an exemption or not (though, according to the Court of Justice, these letters were not legally binding). As explained below, the 2004 reform reinforced the trend towards a growing role for national competition authorities and courts.

Article 102 of the EC Treaty prohibits abuse of dominant position by one or more firms. Types of behaviour that are found to constitute such abuse are:

- directly or indirectly imposing unfair prices or trading conditions;
- limiting production, markets or technical development to the detriment of consumers;
- applying dissimilar conditions to equivalent transactions with other trading parties;
- making the conclusion of contracts subject to supplementary obligations.

There are no exemptions to Article 102. Examples of cases raised by the Commission against abuse of a dominant position were those against Microsoft (see Box 16.4), Google (Box 16.5), Unilever and Intel.[13]

Box 16.4

The Microsoft case

In 2004 the European Commission ruled against Microsoft for abusing its near-monopoly in the PC market (Windows was the operating system on more than 90 per cent of PCs) to extend its market power in two adjacent markets. According to the Commission, Microsoft had deliberately restricted interoperability between Windows PCs and non-Microsoft workgroup servers, and had tied sales of its Media Player to sales of the Windows operating system. As a result, the Commission claimed that Microsoft had used its PC market strength to acquire a dominant position in the workgroup server operating systems market and had significantly weakened competition in the Media Player market. The Commission fined Microsoft €437 million and required Microsoft to take remedial action. The latter included disclosing information to competitors about interfaces allowing non-Microsoft workgroup servers to interoperate with Windows PCs and offering a version of Windows client PC operating system without Media Player in the EU. The Commission stated that the fine was calculated on the basis of EU sales and not on worldwide sales in deference to the USA.

The Commission turned down an offer of settlement by Microsoft. Microsoft decided to appeal against the Commission's decision, arguing that it had invested substantially in developing Windows and that its corporate strategy was to increase the sales of Windows. Microsoft stated that being forced to disclose interface information for servers runs against this strategy and would act as a disincentive to innovation. The company also maintained that Windows might not be able to function properly without Media Player.

In September 2007 the Court of First Instance confirmed the Commission decision, maintaining that withholding information that is needed for servers and PCs to work together can constitute an abuse of dominant position if it prevents rival firms developing alternative software for which there is potential consumer demand. In February 2008 the Commission fined Microsoft a record additional €899 million for failure to comply with the 2004 decision. Microsoft again lodged an appeal with the Court of First Instance. For a discussion of the case see Vickers (2009).

In another Microsoft case in 2009 the Commission accused Microsoft of abuse of its dominant position through tying of Internet Explorer to Windows. In December 2009 an agreement was reached whereby the Commission accepted legal commitments from Microsoft to address allegations that it unlawfully bundled its software products. From March 2010 Microsoft agreed to offer PC users a browser Choice Screen within the Windows software allowing them to choose between a dozen rival browsers to access and surf the internet. This would be available for five years within the European Economic Area. If Microsoft breaks its commitments the Commission can impose a fine of 10 per cent of Microsoft's total annual turnover.

---

[13] Unilever provided freezer cabinets free to Irish distributors on condition they stocked only Unilever ice cream. This was found to limit the choice of Irish consumers. In 2009 the Commission adopted a decision that Intel had abused its dominant position for giving hidden rebates to computer manufacturers such as Dell, HP, NEC and Lenovo, and giving direct payments to computer manufacturers such as HP, Acer and Lenovo to stop or delay the launch of certain products. For the *Intel* case see http://ec.europa.eu/competition/sectors/ICT/intel.html (accessed 9 February 2011).

Box 16.5

The *Google* case

In December 2010 the European Commission announced investigations into allegations that Google had abused its dominant position in the online search market. This follows eight months of more informal inquiries into whether Google had given preferential treatment to its own services when ranking search results, and had discriminated against rivals. The inquiry will also deal with allegations about whether Google imposes exclusivity obligations and restricts advertisers from providing their data to competitors. The Commission inquiry followed complaints from three other companies providing internet services, including Microsoft.

Google challenged the claim that it was dominant in the online search market, maintaining that many users go directly to more specialized search sites. The search rankings of Google are based on its own algorithms, which have so far largely been kept secret.

16.5 The 2004 reform

From 1 May 2004 a 'modernization package' of EU competition policy came into operation, including a new EU enforcement regime on restrictive practices and dominant position. Routine *'notification of agreements and practices to the Commission for clearance'* is no longer required. Instead, companies make their own assessment. All agreements considered to have a net positive effect on the internal market are automatically valid. This will free the competition authorities to tackle serious violations, in particular the cases affecting cross-border trade. The fear was that, with enlargement, extension of the previous notification system to 27 member states would have led to a paralysis of enforcement activities.

The reform applies the notion of safe harbours for firms. If a company is below a certain market share threshold, it can benefit from a safe harbour and does not have to worry about the compatibility of agreements with EU competition law. At the same time, guidelines will help to define 'hardcore restrictions' relating to practices that are prohibited because they have a negative impact on the Single Market (such as agreements to fix prices, limit output, or share markets or consumers).

In order to ensure a more effective division of tasks, the Commission, national competition authorities and national courts are to share responsibility for enforcing EU antitrust rules. The Commission will focus on the infringements presenting the greatest risk of distortion at the EU level. To facilitate co-ordination between the various authorities a European Competition Network (ECN) has been set up. This is composed of the Commission and competition authorities of all the member states. The role of the ECN is to establish principles for the allocation of cases among the various authorities, exchange information, provide mutual assistance in investigations and co-ordinate the final decisions taken.

16.6 Merger control

While measures relating to restrictive practices and dominant position were already envisaged by the Treaty of Rome, the addition of merger control to EC competition policy came only in 1989. This was partly because the idea of promoting EC champions was popular in the 1970s and early 1980s, and there may be a tension between industrial policy and competition policy (see Chapter 17). However, it was also because the level of merger activity in the Community remained relatively low until the mid-1980s. During this period most mergers were between firms in the same country and were aimed chiefly at increasing market share on the domestic market.

The announcement of the Single Market Programme (see Chapter 6) was accompanied by a spectacular increase in the number of mergers in the Community, which rose from 200 in 1985 to 2,000 in 1989 (Tsoukalis, 1997). Mergers were increasingly cross-frontier and also involved firms from outside the EU in an attempt to strengthen positions on world markets. The composition of mergers also altered, with a growing number of mergers in service sectors (such as banking, insurance and the retail trade).

The 1989 Merger Control Regulation (Regulation No. 4064/89) gave the European Commission the authority to control mergers that met a specified size and multi-nationality conditions, including mergers between non-EU businesses with substantial sales in the EU. The aim of the Regulation was to provide a 'one-stop shop' where firms could request clearance for the mergers and acquisitions in the whole EU, thereby reducing the costs, legal uncertainty and bureaucracy associated with multiple filings. According to the 1989 Regulation, a merger should be blocked if it led to a potentially abusive dominant position and, therefore, was likely to result in higher prices, more limited choice for consumers and less innovation.

Between 1989 and 1995 the approach of the Commission to merger control was sometimes criticized as being too cautious and bland (Tsoukalis, 1997). Of 398 mergers considered during this period, only 4 were blocked. Many firms were not meeting the threshold for notification of the merger to the Commission so this led to a revision of the turnover threshold with Regulation No. 1310/1997.

In 2002 the Court of First Instance upheld three high-profile cases of appeal against the Commission's merger decisions (Airtours/First Choice, Schneider/Legrand and Tetra Laval/Sidel; see Box 16.6), giving rise to heated debate about the powers and procedures of the Commission.

Box 16.6

Examples of EU merger cases

In the case of the British Airtours proposed takeover of First Choice, the 1999 decision of the Commission argued that the merger would reduce the number of tour operators in the UK to three, and that their UK collective dominance could impede competition. In June 2002 the Court of First Instance overruled the decision, arguing that it was not clear that there were significant barriers to other (foreign) operators entering the market or that smaller operators would not have access to favourably priced seats. According to the Court, the Commission had not proved its case and the decision had been based on factual errors so the Court annulled the decision of the Commission.

In 2003 the European Commission blocked a deal to merge two French electrical equipment companies, Schneider and Legrand, maintaining that the deal would have a negative impact on competition. The Court of First Instance overturned the decision in 2002, stating that there were serious procedural errors, and in 2007 awarded damages to Schneider for some of the losses incurred as a result of the decision of the Commission. The compensation was to cover the losses from having to file a second merger case and sell Legrand later than would otherwise have been the case. According to the Court the Commission showed *'grave and manifest disregard'* for the limits of its powers of assessment.

In October 2002 the merger between Tetra Laval and Sidel was blocked because the Commission argued that Tetra Laval was carrying out leverage, that is, using its dominant position in the packaging sector to obtain a dominant position in another sector, that of machinery for making plastic (PET) bottles. While the Court did not rule out the underlying theoretical argument, it maintained that so far there had been no evidence of this type of behaviour.

Partly to address these reversals, the 2004 modernization package of EU competition policy also covered mergers. There was a reform of the internal working of the Commission (with the introduction of the post of chief economist, and a system of internal review by an independent panel before decisions are confirmed). In addition to adopting guidelines and a set of best practices, and increasing

the flexibility of timeframes, a new merger regulation (Council Regulation No. 139/2004) was introduced, which entailed the following measures:

- Reinforcing the one-stop shop concept to avoid the problem of multiple filings for authorization (that is, notification of the same operation having to be made to several competition authorities in the EU).

- Continuing the application of merger control to mergers having a 'Community dimension', including firms from third countries with a large presence in the EU.[14]

- Extending the authority of the Commission to investigate all types of harmful scenarios resulting from a merger and not just cases of market dominance. Now any merger that will *significantly impede effective competition in the common market or in a substantial part of it* is to be blocked. Dominance will remain a major concept, but the test is extended markets where the merged company may not be dominant. The central question becomes whether there is competition to provide consumers sufficient choice.

Over the period from September 1990 to 31 January 2011 the Commission examined 4,569 mergers of which 24 were stopped; in 4 cases there was an obligation to restore effective competition; and 9 cases involved a decision imposing fines.[15]

16.7 Liberalization and state aid

Whereas Articles 101 and 102 and the 1989 Merger Control Regulation relate to the behaviour of firms, Articles 106 to 108 TFEU attempt to prevent competition being undermined by government intervention.

Article 106 covers the monopoly rights granted by member states to private or public undertakings to perform services in sectors such as the postal service, energy, telecommunications and transport. However, the Commission argues that these special rights should not exceed what is necessary to provide the service, otherwise competition could be restricted. Many of these services require expensive infrastructure, and the Commission makes the distinction between infrastructure and services. While monopoly of the infrastructure is permitted, the monopolist must allow access to other competitors to provide the services. The European Commission has been instrumental in opening up such markets to competition (also known as liberalization, see Box 16.7).

Box 16.7

The *Telefónica* case

An example of an Article 106 TFEU ruling is that by the Commission against Spain in 1997 over the liberalization of the mobile phone market. A private company, Airtel Móvil, was charged €510 million to operate, while the state firm Telefónica could enter the market without payment. The Spanish government was required to introduce corrective measures.

In 2007 Telefónica again came into the limelight of EU competition policy when the European Commission fined it for keeping rivals out of the broadband market. The Commission found that for five years Telefónica had imposed unfair prices in the form of a margin squeeze between the wholesale prices it charged to competitors and the retail prices it charged to its own customers. Competitors had to make losses if they wanted to compete with Telefónica's retail prices. As a result, consumers were paying the highest prices in Europe for broadband and broadband diffusion was very low.

---

[14] The worldwide threshold based on the turnover of the companies involved amounted to €5 billion, and the EU-wide threshold to €250 million. Below these thresholds, the national authorities in the member states carried out merger control. Above the threshold the Commission had to be notified of the proposed merger.

[15] European Commission DG Competition, http://ec.europa.eu/competition/mergers/statistics.pdf (accessed 9 February 2011).

Article 107 prohibits state aids to business if they distort competition or intra-EU trade. State aid is defined as an advantage conferred on a selective basis to firms by national authorities, and may take various forms, including subsidies, capital investment, tax breaks and sales of assets at favourable prices. General measures applying to all firms regardless of size and location such as tax measures or employment legislation are not regarded as state aid.

Article 107(2) and (3) TFEU indicates that exceptions are allowed for state aid. Article 108 requires member states to give prior notification of state aid,[16] and gives the Commission control over the enforcement of rules preventing undue granting of state aid. Over the years the Commission has developed a framework for types of state aid that are allowed, and these include so-called horizontal measures for developing disadvantaged regions, promoting small and medium enterprises (SMEs), R&D, the protection of the environment, training, employment and culture. In contrast controversial types of aid, which are subject to investigation by the Commission, include rescue and restructuring aid (see the theoretical analysis of industrial policy in Chapter 17), and financial aid to sensitive sectors such as steel, shipbuilding and motor vehicles. The Commission maintains that large enterprises should make a substantial contribution to the financing of restructuring (see also Box 16.8).

State aid was a particularly sensitive issue in the new member states of Central and Eastern Europe, which needed to restructure their economies and to prepare for EU membership. Following the 2004

Box 16.8

The *Alstom* case

In August 2003 France informed the European Commission about a package of measures in favour of the Alstom engineering group, which (among other things) produces high-speed trains. The package included a commitment by the French state to subscribe irrevocably half of a capital increase worth €600 million. The package was to be put immediately into effect without waiting for clearance from the Commission and so, according to the Commission, violated the obligation of prior notification of aid.

In September 2003 the Commission began its investigation and considered introducing an injunction to suspend the participation in the capital increase because of its irreversible structural effects. In the event the Commission gave France five days to renounce the measure, and France agreed to introduce debt instruments instead, which would not have irreversible structural effects on the market. France also agreed to subject the envisaged entry into Alstom's equity to prior authorization by the Commission.

The Commission then began its analysis of whether the package was in line with the rescue and restructuring guidelines and, in particular, whether the restructuring plan would restore Alstom's viability and if compensatory measures were necessary to counterbalance the distortions of competition.

In 2004 (when Nicolas Sarkozy was involved in the negotiations as finance minister), the Commission agreed to a package of €3.2 billion government aid to Alstom, including an €800 million debt-for-equity swap on condition that Alstom disposed of businesses accounting for 10 per cent of revenues worth about €1.5 billion. The Commission argued that industrial partnerships were necessary to ensure the viability of Alstom and compensate for the distortions in competition caused by state aid.

---

enlargement the European Commission launched a State Aid Action Plan in 2005.[17] The Plan built on the objectives decided at the 2002 Barcelona European Council when the member states called for 'less and better state aid'. 'Better aid' is interpreted to mean the horizontal measures to correct market failures. Since 2005 a number of new regulatory texts have been adopted, including regional aid guidelines.

---

[16] There are exceptions to the notification requirement, such as aid to encourage training, employment, small and medium enterprises and R&D.

[17] COM(2005) 107 final.

In response to the economic crisis, in late 2008 the European Commission eased up on state aid rules and introduced a temporary framework that allowed governments to grant loans, state guarantees and direct aid to banks and companies hit by the financial turmoil and subsequent credit shortages. These measures were due to expire at the end of 2010, but were extended with some technical changes for a further year during which time they would gradually be phased out.[18]

The Commission publishes regular state aid scoreboards to monitor the amount and nature of state aid. According to the Autumn 2010 Scoreboard, over the 2002–07 period the level of state aid to industry and services decreased by an annual average of 2 per cent and amounted to less than 5 per cent of EU GDP in 2007.[19] With the economic crisis, state aid rose in 2008 and again in 2009 when it reached 3.6 per cent of GDP, or €427 billion. In absolute terms the largest grantors of aid in 2009 were Germany, France, Spain, Italy and the UK in that order. As a share of GDP the countries granting most state aid in 2009 were Malta, Hungary, Portugal, Denmark and Sweden.

16.8 Evaluation

In recent years the Commission has played an active role in merger control, cracking down on cartels, and carrying out inquiries into sectors such as energy, information technologies and financial services. However, at times the pace of EU investigations (on average over 35 months) was slow, and there was insufficient use of economic reasoning in some cases of investigation into alleged abuse of dominant position (Dumont and Holmes, forthcoming). With the economic crisis, rules on the granting of state aid had to be relaxed.

It is too early to assess how the 2004 reforms of competition policy will prove in practice. One of the initial aims of vesting so much power in the Commission was to limit the opportunities for political pressure and lobbying over decisions (in particular on state aid). Now responsibility is more decentralized, with a greater role for national authorities, many of which have limited experience in applying competition law. Decentralization could also increase uncertainty as rules and substantive tests still differ among member states.

In recent years there have been increased efforts to co-operate on competition policy and investigations with major trading partners such as the USA, Japan and Canada. However, relations with the USA were strained by the Commission's rulings over General Electric's proposed takeover of Honeywell in 2001 and the *Microsoft* case (see Box 16.4 above). US authorities had approved the General Electric–Honeywell merger, and though the Commission attempted to co-operate with US antitrust authorities over Microsoft, the USA maintained that its own settlement with Microsoft was the appropriate framework for dealing with the case.

Summary of key concepts

- **Competition policy** is aimed at preventing distortions in competition caused either by private firms or by government actions.

- Article 101 TFEU prohibits as 'incompatible with the internal market' all agreements that affect trade between the member states and have the intention or effect of preventing,

---

[18] *Financial Times*, 5 October 2010. For a description of the measures see European Commission DG Competition, http://ec.europa.eu/competition/consultations/2010_temporary_measures/index.html#docs (accessed 9 February 2011).

[19] The statistics in this paragraph are taken from European Commission DG Competition, http://ec.europa.eu/competition/state_aid/studies_reports/studies_reports.html (accessed 9 February 2011).

distorting or restricting competition. Although **collusive behaviour** is forbidden, the Treaty permits other forms of co-operation between firms that are not considered to threaten consumers.

■ Article 102 TFEU prohibits abuse of **dominant position** by one or more firms.

■ The **2004 reform** of competition policy entails that companies will no longer be subject to the obligation of routine notification to the Commission for antitrust clearance. National competition authorities and national courts are to share responsibility for enforcing EU antitrust rules

■ The announcement of the Single Market Programme was accompanied by a spectacular increase in the number of **mergers** in the Community. The merger regulations of 1989 and 2004 give the European Commission the authority to control mergers that meet a specified size and multi-nationality conditions. The 2004 legislation extends the authority of the Commission to investigate all types of harmful scenarios resulting from a merger and not just market dominance.

■ Article 106 TFEU covers the **monopoly rights** granted by member states to private or public undertakings to perform public services, but these rights should not go beyond what is necessary to provide the service, otherwise competition could be restricted.

■ Article 107 TFEU prohibits **state aids** to business having the effect of distorting competition. Exceptions are allowed for certain types of aid. The 2004 reform of competition policy aims at simplification and acceleration of procedures, and at encouraging member states to use a more economic approach in assessing state aids.

Questions for study and review

1 Explain how the integration process may be undermined by distortions in competition.
2 Describe the role of the various EU institutions with regard to competition policy.
3 What criticisms can be made of EU competition policy, and what reforms could be introduced?
4 Explain the difficulties in establishing whether collusive behaviour between firms has taken place.
5 Describe what kinds of behaviour by firms are considered evidence of abuse of dominant position. Explain why market definition may pose difficulties in this context.
6 How has EU merger control changed over the years?
7 How successful do you think that EU policy with regard to state aids has been?

Online Learning **Centre**

When you have read this chapter, log on to the Online Learning Centre website at ***www.mcgraw-hill.co.uk/textbooks/senior*** to explore weblinks, chapter-by-chapter test questions, case studies and more online study tools.

Chapter 17

Industrial Policy

Learning Objectives

By the end of this chapter you should be able to understand:

- ✓ The reasons for industrial policy
- ✓ How EU industrial policy has evolved over the years
- ✓ The main aspects of R&D policy in the EU
- ✓ The revived debate about supporting national and EU champions

17.1 Introduction

One of the difficulties in discussing industrial policy is that of separating industrial policy from all the other measures having an impact on industry. The European Commission defines industrial policy as relating to manufacturing industry, but in the literature a wider concept is sometimes used which includes agriculture and certain services. Most industrial policy is carried out by the member states rather than at the EU level.

In general the aim of industrial policy is to increase competitiveness, or the ability of an economy to provide its population with high and rising standards of living, and high rates of employment on a sustainable basis. There are very different views of how this is best achieved, depending on differing opinions about the effectiveness of the market mechanism. At the risk of oversimplification, it is useful to distinguish certain main tendencies.

According to the market-orientated approach to industrial policy, the most effective way of promoting competition and efficiency is by allowing the market mechanism to operate as fully as possible. The removal of trade barriers and the creation of a common market will intensify international competition. The role of policy is to allow the market to operate by preventing abuse of monopoly power and ensuring that state aids do not distort competition. The role of industrial policy is therefore 'negative' in the sense that it is mainly concerned with eliminating distortions to competition.

At the other end of the scale, a selective, interventionist industrial policy may be used to favour certain firms or industries (see next section). An active industrial policy is sometimes advocated in order to support declining industries and avoid loss of jobs. For instance, if a declining industry is important in a particular region, allowing it to fail could lead to a high level of long-term unemployment in that region, with a heavy social cost. However, in many cases it seems likely that a subsidy to the declining industry will simply postpone unemployment.

An active industrial policy may also be seen as a means of promoting key or strategic industries, such as aerospace, telecommunications and the audiovisual sector, in an effort to create national or EU champions. This is very similar to the strategic trade theory and infant industry arguments described in Chapter 4. According to this approach, public intervention may be used to create a competitive advantage for firms. However, there are numerous objections to these arguments on theoretical grounds. These include the negative implications of protection, insufficient information and the difficulty of picking winners, and the risk of retaliation by other countries.

Measures to encourage R&D and innovation are generally a central component of industrial policy. The traditional economic justification for such measures is in terms of externality. The social return on R&D and innovation is higher than the private return, so public intervention is justified to favour such activities.

An alternative justification for measures to promote R&D and innovation can be found on the basis of evolutionary economics. As described in Chapter 15, evolutionary economics makes the distinction between codified and tacit knowledge. Codified knowledge is formalized and can be stored and transmitted easily, whereas tacit knowledge is obtained through experience, so requires a process of learning-by-doing in order to be transferred. According to evolutionary economics a large part of knowledge needed for innovation is tacit, so contacts between people are important. As innovation depends on interaction between people, public intervention can be used to encourage that interaction. Measures may be introduced to encourage networking and co-operation on research and technological development between public authorities, firms, research institutions and universities. There may also be a case for favouring the creation of economic clusters, or networks of production of strongly interdependent firms. Highly skilled labour is often relatively mobile and may help to transmit tacit knowledge, so there may be a role for public intervention in attempts to attract highly qualified people to an area.

The instruments of industrial policy are various and include: financial assistance, tax breaks, aid for R&D, public contracts, trade barriers, export assistance and measures to encourage technology diffusion.

17.2 The theoretical basis of interventionist industrial policy

A simple framework can be used to explain the link between interventionist industrial policy and integration. The first step is to assume imperfect competition and a closed economy. As explained in Chapter 16, in the absence of perfect competition firms will charge a price that is above their marginal cost in order to maximize profit. The difference between prices and marginal cost constitutes the mark-up of the monopolist. If there are more firms in the market, competition will lower the mark-up that each firm can charge. In Figure 17.1 the competition curve showing the relationship between the number of firms and mark-up each firm can charge is therefore assumed to slope down to the right.[1]

With imperfect competition and increasing returns to scale only a given number of firms can survive in a market. The higher the mark-up (or gap between prices and marginal cost) the more firms can survive. The break-even curve (or zero profit curve) shows how many firms can break even at each level of mark-up. Intuitively, more firms can survive when the mark-up is high, so the break-even curve is assumed to slope up to the right.[2] In the short run, firms will not always be on the break-even curve, but, in the long term, firms can enter and leave the sector, so being on the curve will be a condition for equilibrium. Firms will be on the competition curve as they can adjust prices quickly in response to changes in the number of firms. The intersection of the competition and break-even curves indicates the equilibrium mark-up m-u and long-run number of firms n as shown in Figure 17.1.

---

[1] The discussion in this section follows Baldwin and Wyplosz (2009). The downward slope of the competition curve is intuitive, but for an analysis of the theoretical basis of this curve see these authors.

[2] Again, see Baldwin and Wyplosz (2009) for the theoretical derivation of this curve.

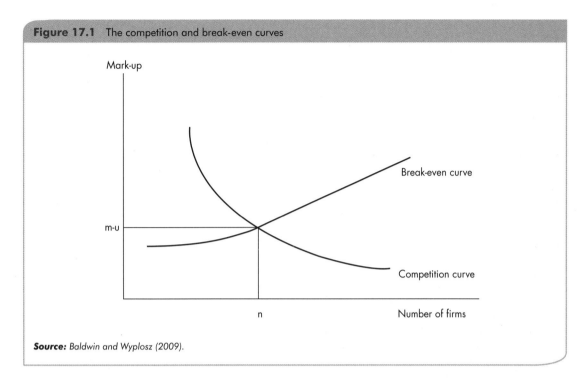

Figure 17.1 The competition and break-even curves

Source: Baldwin and Wyplosz (2009).

Figure 17.2 uses this result to establish the equilibrium price and firm size in a closed economy. The right-hand panel indicates that at equilibrium n firms would charge m-u mark-up. By definition, the equilibrium price p is the marginal cost plus the equilibrium mark-up (that is, MC + m-u). The left-hand panel in Figure 17.2 introduces the marginal and average cost curves of a typical firm in the sector. The equilibrium price is p, where price equals average cost AC. At p total revenue equals total costs and profit is zero (as required by equilibrium). As shown in the left-hand panel of Figure 17.2, at equilibrium, price is p and the size of the firm is x.

The middle diagram in Figure 17.2 shows the demand curve, which indicates that at price p total sales of the sector will equal c.

The framework can be used to analyse the effects of integration. For simplicity it is assumed that integration leads to trade liberalization between two countries: home and foreign. The impact of the trade liberalization implied by integration is to increase the size of the market, leading to more competition. Increased competition means that the typical firm will have to cut its mark-up. At the same time the larger market means that more firms can survive. This is because the larger market creates opportunities for higher sales, so with a given mark-up a larger number of firms can survive. As shown in Figure 17.3, this has the effect of shifting the break-even curve to the right.

The size of the shift of the break-even curve will depend on the number of firms in the integrated market. Assume that the number of firms increases to n', so the break-even curve passes through point T. The competition curve in Figure 17.3 indicates that n' firms will charge m-u' mark-up, and the price will be p'. However, point A is below the break-even curve, so there will be an incentive for firms to leave the sector. This will occur until the new long-term equilibrium of E'' with n'' firms is reached. At the long-term equilibrium, price will be p'', total sales are c'',[3] and sales per firm are x''. The increase in competition means that price–cost margins are m-u'', and so lower than in the pre-integration situation. The left-hand part of Figure 17.3 illustrates that the typical firm increases its sales and

---

[3] The centre panel shows the demand for the home country, but demand for the foreign partner is assumed to be identical so is left out.

Figure 17.2   Prices, output and equilibrium firm size in a closed economy

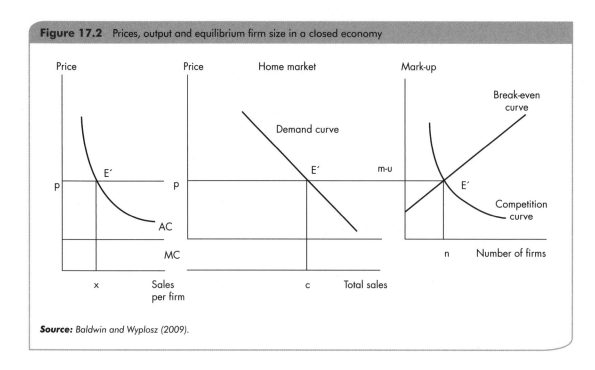

Source: *Baldwin and Wyplosz (2009).*

Figure 17.3   Prices, output and equilibrium firm size with integration

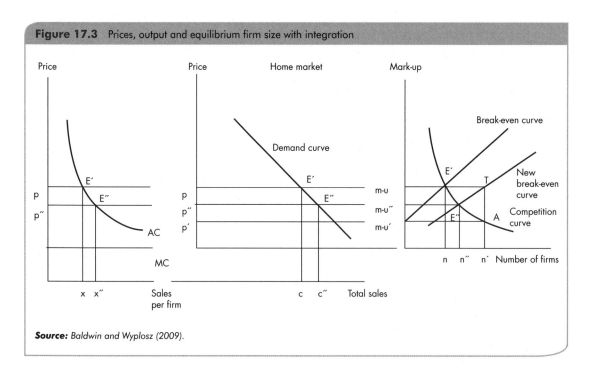

Source: *Baldwin and Wyplosz (2009).*

efficiency as average cost is lower at E″. The integration effect therefore has two components, a short-term move from E′ to A and a long-term move from A to E″.

The move to the long-term equilibrium after integration therefore increases competition and forces many firms to leave the sector, while remaining firms increase their size and become more efficient. This restructuring process involves adjustment costs, and is likely to involve to unemployment. Firms (and trade unions) may attempt to resist this pressure either by collusion,[4] or by exerting pressure on governments for subsidies.

In terms of Figure 17.2, at the limit these subsidies, or state aid as it is called in the EU context,[5] could avoid the move from A to E″ and would enable n′ firms to stay in business by receiving subsidies that cover their losses (the difference between m-u and m-u′).

Applying this framework to the EU, the subsidies to maintain loss-making firms in business and slow down the restructuring process could be given by the EU to firms from all member states. Alternatively, it might simply be given by one member state to its domestic firms. In this case the restructuring process will be forced on firms from other member states that do not subsidize giving rise to claims of unfair competition. It is for this reason, as explained in Chapter 16, the EU has rules on state aid.

17.3 Industrial policy in the treaties

Two of the original Communities, the European Coal and Steel Community (ECSC) and Euratom, covered key industrial sectors, and the approach used was essentially *dirigiste*, with an active role envisaged for public intervention. At the time, this type of approach was also deemed appropriate for sectors such as agriculture and transport, which were subject to intensive state intervention. It was considered easier to introduce a common policy for these sectors rather than attempt to harmonize the diverse national approaches.

The Treaty of Rome failed to make any mention of industrial policy, though a legal basis for industrial policy can be found in various articles. With the exception of the sectors mentioned above, the Treaty seems to be based on a market-orientated approach. The removal of trade barriers was seen as the means of promoting competition and efficiency, and the role of public intervention was to eliminate obstacles to the functioning of the market. Many of the articles in the Treaty of Rome considered most relevant for industrial policy were therefore those setting out competition policy. As discussed in Chapter 16, these articles dealt with cartels and restrictive practices, abuse of dominant position and state aids. Other articles were also intrinsically linked to industrial policy, such as those on the movement of capital and labour, the right of establishment and the creation of the common market. Industrial policy measures could also be justified on the basis of general treaty objectives set out in Article 235 (now Article 352 TFEU).

17.4 The early years: a market-orientated approach to industrial policy

In the 1960s the market-orientated view of the role of the Community continued to prevail, and industrial policy consisted mainly in removing barriers to operation of the common market. In 1967 the Directorate-General for Industry (DGIII) was set up to promote cross-border co-operation. However, the industry of the member states seemed to encounter difficulty in adapting to the enlarged market and was less active than US and Japanese firms in setting up FDI in the Community (Hitiris, 2003).

At the time there were considerable differences in prevailing ideologies with regard to industrial policy in the member states, with Germany favouring a neo-liberal approach, while France and Italy were traditionally more in favour of intervention. Under the laissez-faire approach of the Commission, national industrial policies of the member states failed to converge.

---

[4] See Figure 16.4 in Chapter 16.

[5] See Chapter 16.

As the market-orientated approach to Community industrial policy was not realizing the expected results, in 1970 the Commission published a Memorandum on Industrial Policy, also known as the Colonna Report. This called for a Community industrial policy aimed at economic expansion and technological development. However, the differing ideologies in the member states meant that there was little consensus on what Community industrial policy should be, and a change in approach failed to materialize.

In 1972, with the prospect of enlargement, the Paris Summit called for the establishment of 'a single industrial base for the Community as a whole'. In December 1973 the Commission published the Spinelli Memorandum proposing a competition-orientated Community policy based on harmonization of national regulations, company law and capital markets, the opening of public procurement, and measures to encourage the creation of EC-wide firms. Again the consensus necessary to implement the measures was not forthcoming.

17.5   Towards a more active Community industrial policy

As described in Chapter 6, the 1973 oil crisis was followed by the years of Europessimism, with stagflation and growing fragmentation of the Community market as member states attempted to assist their own industries. Many of the interventionist policies were taken over, at times reluctantly, by the Community in order to co-ordinate assistance and render it more transparent. Community industrial policy during these years was mainly characterized by crisis management for specific sectors such as steel (see Box 17.1), shipbuilding and textiles. These are 'problem' industries with excess supply at a world level and/or competition from lower-cost producers abroad.

Etienne Davignon, Commission vice-president with responsibility for industry from 1981 to 1985, attempted to 'build Europe' by increasing the competitiveness of Community firms and gained the support of industrialists for cross-border collaboration on technology. At the Copenhagen European Council of 1982 agreement was reached on strengthening the Single Market, increasing research related to industry and providing more funding for investment in industry, technology and energy. While interventionist measures for declining industries continued,[6] from about 1985 there was a shift in emphasis in Community policy away from saving declining industries towards promoting high-technology industries.

Despite the obvious advantages of pooling R&D, the Treaty of Rome made no mention of a common R&D effort. During the early 1980s the first Community R&D programmes were launched. The European Strategic Programme for Research and Development in Information Technology (ESPRIT) came into operation from 1984 in response to lobbying by prominent firms active in the information technology sector. ESPRIT was a joint Community and private sector programme to promote co-operation in research with potential industrial applications. The emphasis was on 'pre-competitive' or basic research in order to ensure compatibility with Community competition law. The private sector was required to make a substantial contribution to the financing of projects to ensure their commitment and avoid accusations, in particular on the part of the USA, that the Community was subsidizing industry.

Firms in other sectors soon became aware of Community financial support for information technology and began lobbying the Commission for similar measures in their favour. The Community responded by introducing the First Framework Programme covering the 1984–87 period. This aimed at providing coherence and continuity by incorporating all Community aid for R&D into a single instrument and by extending the programme over a number of years.

Programmes for other industries were also introduced including JET (Joint European Torus on thermonuclear fusion), BRITE/EURAM (Basic Research in Industrial Technologies for Europe/European Research in Advanced Materials) and RACE (Research into Advanced Communications for Europe).

---

[6] Davignon sponsored 'crisis cartels' for problem industries such as steel. In order to avoid chaotic price cutting, there were common scrapping programmes that entailed common and binding floor prices, or public intervention to fix prices.

Box 17.1

Measures to assist the EU steel industry

Concern with the steel industry was one of the reasons for creating the ECSC in 1951. During the 1950s and 1960s the problem was that of adjusting to meet growing demand, but during the 1970s the steel industry became characterized by overcapacity at a world level. Since 1974 output and employment in the EU steel industry have been falling. The situation was worsened by falling demand for steel products with the development of substitutes and the emergence of new competitors on world markets such as Japan, South Korea and Brazil. The Community implemented a series of restructuring plans in the 1970s (such as the Simonet Plan and the Davignon Plan) aimed at modernization and reductions in capacity, but state aids and resistance to capacity cuts at a national level continued. Following the second oil price increase in 1979, the Community was forced to declare the steel industry in 'manifest crisis'. The Community responded with mandatory production quotas on firms and restrictions on imports. The effort to restructure the industry and cut excess capacity continued, but one of the effects was to reinforce the oligopolistic structure of the sector.

Difficulties continued into the 1990s, with falling employment in the sector and rising EU trade deficits, in particular after the 1992–93 recession. The EU responded with financial incentives to cover some of the costs of restructuring, and foreign trade measures aimed at stabilizing the EU steel market. As these measures initially proved insufficient, the Commission tightened the application of state aids and controls on cartels in the steel sector. State aids were only to be tolerated if accompanied by capacity reductions. Social measures were introduced to assist workers who lost or changed jobs, support was given to R&D and to measures to reduce regional disparities, improve the environment, modernize economic and social infrastructure, and develop alternative economic activities.

After a long and costly adjustment, according to the Commission, the EU emerged with a modern and competitive steel sector. Over a twenty-year period the EU closed down 50 million tonnes of excess capacity and reduced manpower by 650,000. The EU enlargement of 2004 increased the steelmaking capacity by 40 million tonnes to 240 million tonnes, but since the mid-1990s there has been significant restructuring of the steel industry also in the new member states. In 2008 the sector employed about 410,000 people, or 1.25 per cent of employment in total EU manufacturing. Production was 200 million tonnes of crude steel in 2008, or about 16 per cent of world output, second only to China.

Source: *The data in the final paragraph is taken from European Commission DG Enterprise and Industry, http://ec.europa.eu/ enterprise/sectors/metals-minerals/steel/ (accessed 10 February 2011).*

RACE was subsequently replaced by ACTS (Advanced Communications Technology and Services), whose aims include the development of broadband technology.

In 1985 Eureka (European Research Co-ordination Agency) was set up partly as a response to President Reagan's Star Wars initiative in the USA. It was established as a French initiative to reduce the fragmentation of European industry. Eureka is pan-European, including members such as Norway, Switzerland, Iceland and Turkey, and involves public support for firms to launch new high-technology products and increase competitiveness in key areas for the future.

The early R&D programmes of the Community probably had a fairly limited impact on competitiveness, but they established the tradition of firms working with the Commission, and laid the basis for the Single Market. If the Commission were encouraging co-operation between firms and financing R&D to overcome the fragmentation of EC industry, why not tackle the causes of fragmentation directly?

This was the aim of the 1987 Single European Act, which also called for measures to promote research and technological development, to assist small and medium enterprises and to encourage co-operation between firms from different regions of the Community.

Not only did the prospect of the Single Market provoke the spate of cross-border mergers and acquisitions described in Chapter 6, but these changes in European industry in turn led to a reassessment of Community industrial policy. An intense debate ensued, with lobbying from industries in difficulty, such as electronics firms, and some member states (notably France) for Community support in favour of certain industries.

17.6 The Bangemann Memorandum and after

The Commission view was generally that effective competition was the best means of ensuring the success of industry, and this position was set out in the Bangemann Memorandum of 1990,[7] named after the commissioner responsible for industry. The report established the broad principles on which EU industrial policy has been based ever since. According to the Memorandum, the main role of the Community was not to provide selective intervention for individual firms or industries but rather to adopt a 'horizontal' approach aimed at: maintaining a competitive environment; providing catalysts for structural adjustment, including completion of the Single Market; and developing instruments to accelerate structural adjustment.

According to the Memorandum, a competitive position could best be ensured by measures to control state aids, avoid abuse of dominant position and eliminate barriers to international trade. The main responsibility for structural adjustment was said to lie with economic operators, but the Community could help to provide the necessary prerequisites for adjustment, including a high level of educational attainment, social cohesion and environmental protection. Community assistance was therefore to be aimed at ensuring a 'level playing field' through an appropriate combination of the Single Market and trade, competition, regional, social and environmental policies. In order to accelerate the process of structural adjustment, measures could be introduced to promote research and technology, encourage a better use of human resources, ensure the conditions for the development of business services and favour SMEs.

This view of the role of the EU also permeates the Maastricht Treaty, where the Community received explicit responsibility for industrial policy for the first time. Article 130 of the Maastricht Treaty called on the EU and its member states '*to ensure that the conditions needed to make the Community competitive are met in a system of open and competitive markets*'. However, unanimity voting was required in the Council, limiting the possibilities for the Community to extend its role.

In the years following the 1990 Bangemann Memorandum, the horizontal approach continued to characterize EU industrial policy. The EU moved away from selective industrial policy and greater emphasis was placed on helping to regenerate regions where declining industry was located (see Chapter 15). However, the EU continued to take measures aimed at the specific requirements of several sectors including: steel (see Box 17.1 above), textiles and clothing, shipbuilding, the automotive industry, and advanced technology industries such as aerospace, telecommunications, biotechnology and information technologies. The EU attempted to avoid direct intervention, instead relying on measures to: reduce capacity; limit the use of state aids; avoid cartels; promote technology; assist regional and social adjustment; promote environmental objectives; and control competing imports.

17.7 Promoting competitiveness

The Lisbon Treaty (Article 173 TFEU ex Article 157 TEC) calls on member states to ensure the conditions necessary for the competitiveness of EU industry, with action aimed at:

- speeding up the adjustment of industry to structural changes;

---

[7] European Commission (1990b).

- encouraging an environment favourable to initiative and to the development of undertakings throughout the Union, particularly SMEs;

- encouraging an environment favourable to co-operation between undertakings;

- fostering better exploitation of the industrial potential of policies of innovation, research and technological development.

As described in Chapter 7, these are objectives central to the Lisbon Agenda first and the Europe 2020 strategy later.

Promoting SMEs is considered a high priority, and by 2010 it was estimated that there were 20 million SMEs, accounting for 99 per cent of all enterprises in the EU.[8] In line with the European Charter for Small Enterprises adopted at the Fiera European Council of 2000, the Commission calls for a business environment conducive to SMEs, with improved entrepreneurship and skills; measures to encourage networks, consultation and dialogue; improved access to markets; increased growth potential (through better R&D capacity); and business support measures.

17.8 EU research and development policy

As explained in Chapter 7, the 2002 Barcelona European Council agreed the objective of increasing R&D spending to 3 per cent of GDP, but the EU is still a long way from this target.

EU funding of research continues to be covered by Framework Agreements, and the Seventh Framework Programme was introduced for the 2007–13 period. The budget amounted to €50.5 billion, an increase of 40 per cent compared with the Sixth Framework. An additional €3.6 billion was allocated to the Competitiveness and Innovation Programme over the same period. The aim is to create a European Research Area (ERA) with integrated cross-border and multi-disciplinary research programmes in order to overcome the fragmentation of research efforts in the EU.

Four priority areas for research were chosen:

- **Co-operation:** collaborative research in health, food, agriculture, fisheries, biotechnology, information and communication technologies, nanosciences, nanotechnologies, materials and new production technologies, energy, environment (including climate change), transport (including aeronautics), socio-economic sciences and the humanities, space and security. This is allocated €32.4 billion for the 2007–13 period.

- **Ideas:** including the establishment of the European Research Council (ERC) to support research at the frontiers of science (€7.5 billion).

- **People:** human resources, which has an allocation of €4.75 billion to be spent on training, research and so on (and so is linked to the European Employment Strategy, see Chapter 7).

- **Capacities:** research infrastructures, development of the potential research capacity of SMEs, developing knowledge and science clusters in Europe's regions (see also Chapter 15), and promoting science in society as a whole (€4.1 billion).

The EU normally pays for 50 per cent of the research, but SMEs can receive grants of up to 75 per cent, while research at the frontiers of knowledge can be fully funded. The creation of a European Institute of Technology or EIT (similar to the MIT or Massachusetts Institute of Technology in the USA), was eventually agreed in 2007 and set up in Budapest.

---

[8] The statistics are taken from the Directorate-General for Enterprise and Industry, http://ec.europa.eu/enterprise/policies/sme/index_en.htm (accessed 10 February 2011).

17.9   Evaluation and outlook

As described in Chapter 7, the EU is experiencing considerable difficulty in moving towards the goals of the Europe 2020 strategy. Productivity, in particular in high-technology sectors, remains lower than in the USA. The EU seems unlikely to meet the objective of R&D spending at 3 per cent of GDP. Slow growth and the increasing strength of emerging competitors at a world level, such as China and India, have led to questioning of the 'horizontal' approach to industrial policy adopted by the EU since 1990.

In this context the old debate about promoting national and European champions re-emerged, in what, in 2004, the commissioner then responsible for the internal market, Frits Bolkestein, called a 'time warp' reverting to the 1970s.[9] In 2004 French president Jacques Chirac and German chancellor Gerhard Schroeder called a meeting to discuss encouraging *'the creation of the industrial champions of the Europe of tomorrow, of which France and Germany could build a certain number'*.[10]

President Sarkozy continued in this direction, supporting French firms and becoming known as a 'liberal Colbertian'.[11] Jean-Baptiste Colbert was finance minister under Louis XIV in the seventeenth century. Colbert aimed at making France economically self-sufficient with active involvement of the state in industrial policy, and protectionism in order to maximize exports and minimize imports. Colbertism suggests less competition and more economic nationalism. In a speech to the European Parliament in 2007, Sarkozy maintained that Europe should not be alone in the world in making competition a 'religion'. He famously persuaded the European Council to drop the reference to *'free and undistorted competition'* in Article 2 of the Lisbon Treaty, and challenged the independence of the European Central Bank, calling for less emphasis on inflation and an exchange rate policy geared towards more promotion of EU exports.

The French government has also been active in support for national champions, though the emphasis seems more on nationality than on state ownership (hence the description as a 'liberal' Colbertian). When PepsiCo expressed interest in Danone, France declared dairy products a strategic sector.

France was not alone in this economic nationalism. Italy, Poland and Germany resisted foreign takeovers in the banking sector. The Italian government opposed foreign control of Alitalia and of its motorways, and resisted attempted French takeovers of the energy group Edison, the jeweller Bulgari and the dairy company Parmalat. Spain seemed determined to keep its electricity companies in national hands.

Revival of the debate on an activist industrial policy also found echo at the EU level. The 2003 Brussels European Council expressed concern that the EU was undergoing a process of deindustrialization, and maintained that EU industry was having increasing difficulties in the face of competition, which it perceived as *'unbeatable and sometimes unfair'*.

With the economic crisis, fears grew about the revival of interventionist policies by some of the member states. Such policies tend to breed rent-seeking activities and politicization of decisions; can lead to unfair competition; and are difficult to justify on the grounds of economic theory. Concentrating on the more traditional prescription of the Commission (see also Chapter 7) of promoting research and innovation, investing in human capital, favouring SMEs and improving the functioning of markets would seem a more promising way forward, but the main difficulty here is that words have generally failed to be matched by actions.

---

[9] *Financial Times*, 14 June 2004.

[10] *Financial Times*, 19 May 2004.

[11] A phrase used by Mario Monti, former Commissioner for Competition, as reported in the *Financial Times*, 9 May 2007. Monti and Sarkozy were involved in negotiating the *Alstom* case described in Box 16.8 of Chapter 16.

[12] For instance the French Government supported the creation of a power giant through the merger of state-owned Gaz de France and Suez to ward off foreign takeovers. Government support was also given to the state-owned Arena to ensure its dominance of the French market (and avoid a merger with the German firm Siemens). France also resisted EU efforts to open up its railways and postal market (see Chapter 6).

Summary of key concepts

- A **market-orientated industrial policy** aims at removing the barriers to the operation of competition.
- Selective **interventionist industrial policy** involves support for declining industries to avoid loss of jobs and the promotion of industries considered key or strategic.
- During the 1960s Community industrial policy was based on a market-orientated approach, but in the 1970s and 1980s more selective intervention was used in favour of specific sectors.
- Following the 1990 **Bangemann Memorandum**, the Community adopted a 'horizontal' approach to industrial policy.
- In recent years the debate about supporting **national and EU champions** has revived, and with the economic and financial crisis there was a fear of the revival of economic nationalism.

Questions for study and review

1 Describe the different forms industrial policy may take.
2 How successful has EU industrial policy proved to be?
3 What difficulties arise in the promotion of national and EU champions? Give some examples.

Online
Learning **Centre**

When you have read this chapter, log on to the Online Learning Centre website at ***www.mcgraw-hill.co.uk/textbooks/senior*** to explore weblinks, chapter-by-chapter test questions, case studies and more online study tools.

Chapter 18

EU Trade and Aid Policies

Learning Objectives

By the end of this chapter you should be able to understand:

- ✓ What we mean by the 'hierarchy' of trade preferences of the EU
- ✓ The main functions of the GATT/WTO
- ✓ What we mean by the Generalised System of Preferences
- ✓ What trade and aid measures the EU uses for developing countries
- ✓ The trade and investment relations between the EU and the USA
- ✓ What the institutional framework for the transatlantic dialogue involves
- ✓ Some possible explanations of the conflictual co-operation between the EU and the USA
- ✓ What are the main features of the European Neighbourhood Policy
- ✓ What the Euro-Mediterranean Partnership entails
- ✓ The main aspects of EU relations with Russia, Asia (including China, Japan and India), and Latin America

18.1 Introduction

Although the EU has primarily been concerned with promoting integration internally, it has also had to develop a trade policy towards the rest of the world. The Common Commercial Policy (CCP) of the EU was based on Article 113 of the Treaty of Rome, which required a common Community tariff regime and common trade agreements with third countries.[1] EU trade policy is intrinsically linked to other policy areas, and notably the Common Agricultural Policy (CAP), the Single Market and the

---

[1] According to Article 207 TFEU (ex-Article 133 Tec), the European Commission negotiates trade agreements on behalf of the member states, in consultation with a special committee known formerly as the 133 Committee and now the 207 Committee. The 207 Committee is made up of representatives of all the member states, and the European Commission The 207 Committee meets on a weekly basis to discuss all trade policy issues affecting the EU, from WTO negotiations, to trade problems with specific products, or trade implications of other EU policies. Since the Lisban Treaty the Council acts by qualified majority voting an trade agreements, but agreements involving services or intellectual property rights require a unanimous vote in the Council. Major treaty ratifications covering more than trade need assent by the European Parliment.

Common Foreign and Security Policy (CFSP). The EU participates in multilateral trade negotiations. Table 18.1 indicates the main trading partners of the EU.

Table 18.1 The major EU(27) trade partners (imports + exports) in extra-EU trade, 2009

Partner	%	Partner	%
USA	15.9	Brazil	2.1
China	12.9	Canada	1.8
Russia	7.9	Singapore	1.5
Switzerland	7.1	Algeria	1.4
Norway	4.6	South Africa	1.4
Japan	4.0	Saudi Arabia	1.3
Turkey	3.5	Australia	1.3
South Korea	2.3	Hong Kong	1.3
India	2.3	United Arab Emirates	1.3

Source: Eurostat, http://trade.ec.europa.eu/doclib/docs/2006/september/tradoc_113440.pdf (accessed 18 February 2011), © European Union, 2011.

At times the gradual extension of EU responsibility into questions of external relations not strictly related to trade has been hotly contested by the member states. The external aid policy of the EU has been influenced by historical and strategic considerations, with former French and British colonies receiving particularly favourable treatment, and continuation of this historical bias in policies has at times been challenged.

In line with the Lisbon Agenda (which was subsequently replaced with Europe 2020, see Chapter 7), in 2006 the Global Europe strategy was launched, which aimed at increasing the contribution of trade and FDI to EU competitiveness. This entailed a reorientation of EU policies towards a new generation of free trade agreements with growing economies in Asia, and increased focus on questions such as intellectual property rights and access to raw materials (European Commission, 2006e).

Over time the EU has developed a patchwork of preferential agreements with other countries or groups of countries (see Box 18.1). Reference is frequently made to the 'hierarchy of EU preferences' or the 'pyramid of privileges'. In practice it is no longer possible (if it ever was) to discern a clear hierarchical pattern since the system is complex, in flux, the concessions are generally riddled with exceptions and the agreements rarely refer exclusively to trade issues.

Box 18.1

The trade arrangements of the EU*

- The European Economic Area with Norway, Iceland and Liechtenstein (see Chapter 2).

- Customs unions with Turkey, Andorra and San Marino.

- Stabilisation and Association Agreements (SAAs) with South-East European countries (see Chapter 19): FYR Macedonia, Croatia, Albania, Montenegro and Bosnia and Herzegovina.

- An interim trade agreement with Serbia.

- Free trade agreements with other European partners such as the Faroe Islands and Switzerland.

- The Cotonou Convention covered relations with African, Caribbean and Pacific (ACP) countries, but since 2008 is being replaced with Economic Partnership Agreements (EPAs). These are agreements between the EU and groups of neighbouring ACP countries. The objective is to build free trade areas with different ACP regions (see text).

- Interim Economic Partnership Agreements with Ivory Coast and Cameroon and various regional groupings (see text).

- The Generalised System of Preferences (GSP) that entails the elimination or reduction of tariffs on imports from developing countries on a non-reciprocal basis.

- The 'Everything but Arms' (EBA) initiative for least developed countries, by which all other imports (with a few exceptions such as delayed implementation for bananas, sugar and rice) from these countries enter the EU duty free.

- The Euro-Mediterranean Partnership, which also involves Euro-Mediterranean Association Agreements (see text).

- Wider Europe or the European Neighbourhood Policy (ENP) with EU eastern and southern neighbours.

- Trade and Co-operation Agreements, and Co-operation and Partnership Agreements with Russia and other ex-Soviet Republics.

- Association Agreements with free trade agreement components with the Central American and Andean countries, Mercosur, Chile, and certain Overseas Countries and Territories (OCT/ PTOM II).

- An Economic Partnership Agreement with Cariforum.

- An Economic Partnership, Political Co-ordination and Co-operation agreement with free trade agreement components with Mexico.

- A Trade, Development and Co-operation Agreement with free trade agreement components with South Africa.

- MFN (most favoured nation, by which trade concessions already negotiated in the WTO framework are extended to all member states) treatment for countries such as the USA, Japan and Australia.

- Negotiations have started on free trade areas with ASEAN, Canada (a comprehensive Economic and Trade Agreement), the Gulf Co-operation Council (GCC), India, Korea, Singapore and Ukraine.

*See text for descriptions of the regional blocs.

Source: *European Commission DG Enterprise and Industry, http://ec.europa.eu/enterprise/policies/international/facilitating-trade/ free-trade/index_en.htm and http://ec.europa.eu/enterprise/policies/international/files/existing_trade_agreements_feb2010_en.pdf (accessed 15 February 2011), © European Union, 2011.*

The aim of this chapter is to describe certain of these arrangements and, in particular, those with developing countries, the USA, eastern and southern neighbours, Russia, Asia and Latin America.[2] Box 18.2 sets out EU relations with certain other trade blocs (some of which are discussed in the text). Countries involved in the EU enlargement process are discussed in the following chapter.

---

[2] For a further discussion of these issues see, for instance, Victor et al. (2007).

Box 18.2

EU relations with certain integration blocs

Integration bloc	Current membership	Characteristics/weaknesses of bloc	Links with EU
ASEAN (Association of Southeast Asian Nations) created in 1967.	10 countries: Indonesia, Malaysia, Philippines, Singapore, Thailand, Brunei/ Darussalam, Vietnam, Laos, Burma/Myanmar and Cambodia.	Differences between the countries meant that for many years it was difficult to move beyond co-operation to integration. The consensus-based approach to decision making helped to resolve political differences but has meant slow progress in integration. The ASEAN Economic Community aims to create an area with the free flow of goods, services and investment and the freer flow of capital by 2015.	In 2009 the EU accounted for 11.2% of ASEAN's trade.* The EU has regular ministerial meetings with ASEAN. Dialogue is based on a 1980 Co-operation Agreement. The EU has difficulties extending the Agreement to Myanmar (Burma).
SAARC (the South Asian Association for Regional Co-operation) set up in 1985.	Afghanistan, Bangladesh, Bhutan, India, the Maldives, Nepal, Pakistan and Sri Lanka. China and Japan have observer status.	There is an asymmetry between India (with about three-quarters of the population and regional GDP) and the other members. Slow and cumbersome procedures, and tensions between members have limited the effectiveness of this bloc.	The EU maintains that this bloc could play a useful role in encouraging regional co-operation.
Mercosur (El Mercado del Sur) set up in 1991.	Argentina, Brazil, Paraguay, Uruguay, and Venezuela (whose membership was ratified in 2010). Chile, Bolivia and Peru, Colombia and Ecuador are associate members.	After some success in promoting trade liberalization and export growth during the 1990s, economic crises first in Brazil and then in Argentina acted as a setback to further attempts at integration. Under current rules, in addition to the common external tariff, non-Mercosur goods transported between Mercosur countries are subject to a second tariff. In 2010 Mercosur leaders expressed a new determination to move towards a full customs union by 2012. This would also facilitate closer trade relations with the EU.	In 1995 the Madrid Treaty marked the beginning of negotiations to set up a free trade area between the Mercosur and the EU, but the treaty was too generic in its means and goals. Actual negotiations began in 1999 but stalled as the deterioration of the economic situation undermined the internal cohesion of Mercosur. In 2004 negotiations for an Association Agreement between the two blocs were suspended over differences on the trade chapter, but in 2010 it was decided that it should be possible to relaunch the negotiations.

In 1969 the Cartagena Agreement established the Andean Pact. In 1996 this became the Andean Community.

Bolivia, Colombia, Ecuador and Peru. Venezuela joined in 1973 but left in 2006, and Chile was an original member, but also left. Argentina, Brazil, Paraguay and Uruguay are associate members.

It is considered that regional integration could increase regulatory stability and create a market of sufficient size to attract trade and development. The EU maintains that tighter regional integration is a precondition for signing a free trade agreement with the bloc.

In 1998 a Framework Co-operation Agreement came into force between the EU and Andean Community. One of the highest priorities is the fight against drugs. A new Political Dialogue and Co-operation Agreement was signed in 2003 and aims at reinforcing political dialogue, including conflict prevention, good governance, migration and counter-terrorism. In 2007 negotiations of an Association Agreement between the two blocs were launched, but was suspended in 2008. Negotiations began again in 2009 reaching a successful conclusion between the EU and Colombia and Peru in 2010, but being suspended with Ecuador.

Caricom (the Caribbean Community and Common Market) was formed in 1973, replacing the Caribbean Free Trade Association (Carifta) of 1965–72.

Caricom consists of Antigua and Barbuda, The Bahamas, Barbados, Belize, Dominica, the Dominican Republic, Grenada, Guyana, Haiti, Jamaica, Monserrat, St Lucia, St Kitts and Nevis, St Vincent and the Grenadines, Suriname, Trinidad and Tobago. Various countries have associate or observer status.

The Caricom Single Market and Economy was launched in 1989 and was initially implemented in 2006 when 12 member states eventually adhered.

In 1984 the EU and Central American countries set up the San José Dialogue to promote democratization, peace and closer economic ties. A co-operation programme was established to address the socio-economic causes of unrest in Central America, and reduction of vulnerability to natural disasters. Cariforum is the forum of the EU and ACP Caribbean states. In 2008 an Economic Partnership Agreement with the EU was signed (2009 for Haiti).

SICA (Central American Integration System) established in 1991.

Belize, Costa Rica, El Salvador, Guatemala, Honduras, Nicaragua, and Panama. There are various associate and observer countries.

The intra-regional freeing of trade has proved beneficial, but the bloc has failed both to avoid disputes between members (such as Nicaragua and Honduras), and to enable the countries to present a common front towards third countries.

The EU participates in a specialized dialogue with SICA, and aims at strengthening regional integration and security in Central America.

*Statistics from European Commission DG Trade, http://ec.europa.eu/trade/creating-opportunities/bilateral-relations/ (accessed 15 February 2011).

18.2 The GATT/WTO

Given the importance of the EU as the world's largest trader, EU relations with the main organization regulating international trade – the WTO (World Trade Organization) and its predecessor the GATT (General Agreement on Tariffs and Trade) – are of paramount importance. As explained in Chapter 2, the need to present a common front in GATT negotiations was instrumental in driving forward the early integration process. Subsequently, the commitments made in the GATT/WTO shaped key aspects of EU policy, and notably the CAP (see Chapter 13). At the same time, the importance of the EU in world trade means that it is one of the main actors in trade negotiations and trade disputes taking place in the GATT/WTO framework. It is therefore useful at this point to give a brief explanation of the links between the EU and the GATT/WTO. The Online Learning Centre of this book provides a more detailed analysis of the GATT/WTO, including descriptions of the ongoing attempts to liberalize world trade, and of some of the major disputes in the GATT/WTO framework.

The GATT came into operation in 1948 with the aim of providing a framework for international trade negotiations, and attempts to regulate world trade.[3] The WTO replaced the GATT from 1995, and its framework was reinforced and extended. The GATT/WTO has three main functions:

- Setting out regulations governing the conduct of international trade.
- Making provisions for the settlements of disputes and retaliatory actions.
- Providing the framework for multilateral negotiations to liberalize world trade.

The GATT system has traditionally been based on three principles: tariff reductions, reciprocity and non-discrimination. Tariffs were preferred to other barriers on trade since they were considered the most transparent form of protection. Reciprocity implies that the concessions made by the parties should be more or less balanced. This generally involves matching tariff concession with tariff concession. When a country joined the GATT, it received the benefit of trade concessions already negotiated within that framework on the basis of the most favoured nation (MFN) principle.[4] The MFN clause was conceived as a means of ensuring non-discrimination.

Among the GATT rules with particular implications for the EC was Article XXIV dealing with regional groupings. By its nature a customs union is regional and the trade preferences involved are not extended to all GATT members, and this seems to run counter to the principle of non-discrimination.[5] To meet this difficulty Article XXIV sets out certain conditions for the creation of regional groupings. In particular, the Article requires that the move to implementation must take place within a reasonable time (defined by the WTO as a period that should exceed ten years only in exceptional cases), and that such arrangements should cover *'substantially all'* trade. The *'general incidence of duties and other regulations of commerce'* should also be no higher than before creation of the regional trade arrangement. The underlying assumption of the GATT therefore seemed to be that regional integration arrangements were a building block rather than a stumbling block to global liberalization of trade.[6]

---

[3] The original intention after the Second World War was to create an International Trade Organization, (ITO) but difficulties in ratification (in particular, by the US Congress) led to the ITO Convention being abandoned. In its place the 'temporary' GATT arrangement was adopted.

[4] In return the principle of reciprocity meant that the country had to offer 'equivalent' concessions.

[5] Controversy also arose over the trade preferences granted by the Community under the Association System. The preferences given by France, Italy, Belgium and the Netherlands to former dependencies were acceptable to the GATT because they had been granted before 1947. However, the GATT opposed the extension of these preferences so that all EC members could grant them. The question was examined in a working party with GATT and EC representatives, and it was decided that the EC should take mitigating action if damage to third parties were proved. For discussions of the implications of GATT Article XXIV see, for example, Goto and Hamada (2002) or McMillan (1993). See also the discussion the Cotonou Agreement and the Economic Partnership Agreements (EPAs) below.

[6] Bhagwati first used these expressions (see, for example, Bhagwati, 1993). See also Chapter 5.

Typically the liberalization of world trade proceeds in series of successive 'rounds' of negotiations. To date, eight such rounds have been completed (see Box 18.3).

Box 18.3

GATT/WTO rounds

Name of the Round	Year	Topic of negotiation
Geneva	1947	Tariffs
Annecy	1949	Tariffs
Torquay	1951	Tariffs
Geneva	1956	Tariffs
Dillon Round	1960–62	Tariffs
Kennedy Round	1964–67	Tariffs and anti-dumping
Tokyo Round	1973–79	Tariffs, non-tariff barriers, multilateral agreements
Uruguay Round	1986–94	Tariffs, creation of the WTO, agriculture, textiles, services, TRIMs, TRIPs and VERs*
Doha Round	2001–?	

*See text and the Online Learning Centre of this book for a more detailed explanation.

The Uruguay Round, launched in 1986 at Punta del Este, was far more ambitious than earlier GATT trade negotiations, which had been almost exclusively concerned with tariff reductions. The aim of the Uruguay Round was to further the process of tariff reduction, but also to extend fair trade disciplines to areas that hitherto had been largely exempt from GATT rules and regulations, including agriculture, textiles, services (through the GATS or General Agreement on Trade in Services), trade-related investment measures (TRIMs) and trade-related intellectual property rights (TRIPs). Despite initial US reluctance, it was also agreed to replace the GATT with the WTO. The Uruguay Round was protracted well beyond all initial deadlines, and during the seven tortuous years of negotiations the Round seemed near to breaking down on various occasions, usually over the question of agriculture. Though falling short of many expectations, the results were substantial (see the Online Learning Centre of this book for a more detailed discussion of the agreement).

Following the failed attempt to launch a new Round at Seattle in 1999, in November 2001 the Doha Development Agenda (DDA) began. After numerous difficulties, negotiations were eventually suspended in 2008, largely over differences about over US domestic subsidies to agriculture, and market access to countries such as India and Brazil (see Anania (2010) or the Online Learning Centre for discussions of the negotiations). Successive reforms of the Common Agricultural Policy meant that it was no longer the main obstacle to reaching agreement in the WTO negotiations. Despite subsequent attempts to revive the Doha Round, a successful conclusion in the near future seems unlikely.

The WTO replaced the GATT in 1995, and in 2008 it reached 153 members. It was considered that much of the future reputation of the WTO would depend on the performance of the new Disputes Settlement Mechanism (DSM). This established procedures for consultations, the setting up of panels, the presentation of panel reports and the possibility of appellate review, with precise deadlines for each. The consensus was to be against the establishment of panels, or the adoption of panel reports

for decisions not to be made, and so represented a reversal of the GATT condition. Moreover, the possibility of appeal against a decision was now introduced. The WTO may authorize sanctions if a member state is found to be in contradiction of the rules. Examples of disputes are provided below in the context of the discussion of EU–US relations and on the Online Learning Centre of this book.

18.3 The Generalised System of Preferences

As trade is generally considered one of the most effective tools in fostering development, in 1968 the UNCTAD (United Nations Conference on Trade and Development) called for a Generalised System of Preferences under which industrialized countries would grant preferences to all developing countries.[7] In 1971 the Community established a Generalised System of Preferences (GSP). Under the GSP the EU imports products either duty free, or with a tariff reduction, depending on the arrangement with the beneficiary country.[8] The GSP system of the EU is based on guidelines covering ten-year cycles. In 2004 the guidelines for the 2006–15 period were agreed, and on the basis of these, a new GSP system came into operation.[9] This increased the number of products on which preferences are granted to about 6,200, many of which are agricultural and fisheries products. The new system covered 176 countries and the number of GSP arrangements is reduced to three:

- General arrangements.
- The special incentive arrangement for sustainable development and good governance (the 'GSP+') provides additional benefits for countries implementing certain international standards in human and labour rights, environmental protection, the fight against drugs, and good governance;[10]
- Special arrangements for the least developed countries (LDCs), also known as EBA ('Everything but Arms').

Under the general arrangements products classed as 'non-sensitive' enter the EU duty free, whereas 'sensitive' products are subject to tariff reductions. The classification of products by sensitivity largely depends on the market situation of the product in the EU.

The special incentive arrangements for the protection of labour rights, the environment (in particular, those relating to tropical forests) and so on entail additional tariff reductions on sensitive goods for countries respecting core requirements. This arrangement is limited to lower-income economies, landlocked countries, small island countries, and those that can demonstrate that their economies are poorly diversified.[11]

The UN identifies 49 LDCs on the basis of their low GDP per capita, weak human assets and economic vulnerability. In 2001 the EU launched its EBA initiative for these countries. This implies that apart from arms and ammunition all imports from these countries enter the EU duty free and quota free. The removal of import duties was delayed until 2006 for bananas, and 2009 for sugar and rice.

---

[7] In order to implement the system, a waiver was required from Article 1 of the GATT, which prohibits discrimination. This waiver was granted in 1971 and originally for a period of ten years, but was renewed in 1979, for an indefinite period of time. According to the clause, preferential treatment under the GSP has to be non-discriminatory, non-reciprocal and autonomous. While discrimination in favour of developing countries is allowed, there should be no discrimination between them, except for the benefit of least developed countries.

[8] Up until 1995 the GSP system adopted quotas and ceilings for individual countries and products.

[9] Through Council Regulation No. 980/2005. For a description of the system see European Commission DG Trade, http://ec.europa.eu/trade/wider-agenda/development/generalised-system-of-preferences/ (accessed 18 February 2011).

[10] The list of countries receiving GSP+ is set out in Commission Decision 2005/924/EC.

[11] The list of countries is to ensure that the EU meets the WTO ruling that equal treatment should be given to all similarly situated GSP beneficiaries. India had raised a WTO complaint against the earlier EU scheme, which entailed trade preferences initially designed to discourage drug production in the Andes being extended to other countries, including Pakistan.

The GSP system has been criticized on a number of counts. The preferences given are relatively low, and concessions are often minimal on the products of most interest to the developing countries. In particular, this is the case for agricultural products, and though the 2006 reform increased their GSP coverage, even under the EBA, there were exceptions with delayed implementation. The system involves administrative costs and rules of origin, and often producers in developing countries consider that it is not worthwhile applying for preferences. The GSP scheme of the EU also envisages 'graduation' of more competitive countries (defined since the 2006 reform on the basis of the share of those countries in the exports of all GSP countries). Although the EU justifies this on the grounds of targeting preferences to those most in need, it also relieves the competitive pressures on EU producers.

18.4   The EU and developing countries

In 2000 the international community agreed on the Millennium Development Goals (MDGs) up to the year 2015. These entail:

- eradicating extreme poverty and hunger by halving between 1990 and 2015 the proportion of people whose income is less than US$1 a day;
- achieving universal primary education;
- promoting gender equality and empowering women;
- reducing child mortality by cutting the mortality rate of under-fives by two-thirds between 1990 and 2015;
- improving maternal health;
- combating HIV/AIDS, malaria and other diseases;
- ensuring environmental sustainability;
- developing a global partnership for development.

The EU worked with member states and other international organizations such as the OECD, the World Bank and the UNDP (United Nations Development Programme) to develop a core set of indicators to assess progress in meeting the MDGs. According to the 2010 World Development Indicators,[12] the number of people living on less than US$1.25 a day was falling, but only 49 of the 87 countries with data were on track to meet the poverty target. Most of the poverty reduction was in Asia, and sub-Saharan Africa remained off track to meet the poverty income goal. Child mortality in the world declined from 101 per 1,000 in 1990, to 73 per 1,000 in 2008. Countries in Africa and South Asia are still lagging behind with regard to the goals to improve maternal health and education.

In early 2011 the rise in world food prices led to concern that the number of chronically hungry people could increase to 1 billion, the level reached in the 2007/08 food crisis.[13] This represents an increase of 44 million people in extreme poverty associated with hunger. In 2009 at the G8 Summit at L'Aquila, the eight leading economies pledged $20 billion over three years to meet the problem, including a Global Agriculture and Food Security Program at the World Bank to administer much of the funding. However, by February 2011 the Fund had received only $350 million.[14]

The Monterrey Consensus of 2002 is the partnership between developed and developing countries to ensure financing to meet the MDGs. In 2002 at the Barcelona European Council, member states agreed to increase their official development aid (ODA) in order to reach the MDGs. In 2005 the EU adopted a timetable for the member states to reach the UN target of ODA equal to 0.7 per cent of

---

[12] The statistics in this paragraph are taken from World Development Indicators, http://data.worldbank.org/news/world-development-indicators-2010-released (accessed 18 February 2011). More detailed data by country is available at http://data.worldbank.org/indicator (accessed 18 February 2011).

[13] *Financial Times*, 16 February 2011.

[14] Jeffrey Sachs writing in the *Financial Times*, 16 February 2011.

gross national income (GNI) considered necessary to meet the MDGs. At the G8 Summit in Gleneagles in 2005, the UK prime minister, Tony Blair, obtained a commitment from the heads of government of the eight industrial countries present to spend $50 billion more each year on aid, with half the increase going to sub-Saharan Africa.

In 2009 the EU was the major source of development aid in the world, providing €9,654 million in 2009, or 56 per cent of total ODA reported to the Development Assistance Committee (DAC) of the OECD.[15] This compares with 24 per cent of total ODA for the USA, or 0.20 per cent of GNI. Table 18.2 presents the ODA of EU member states. The only countries to meet the UN target of 0.7 per cent of GNI were Denmark, Luxembourg, the Netherlands, Sweden and Norway.

Table 18.2 Official development aid of the EU member states, 2009

	% GNI		% GNI
Belgium	0.55	Luxembourg	1.01
Bulgaria	0.04	Hungary	0.09
Czech Rep.	0.12	Malta	0.20
Denmark	0.88	Netherlands	0.82
Germany	0.35	Austria	0.30
Estonia	0.11	Poland	0.08
Ireland	0.54	Portugal	0.23
Greece	0.19	Romania	0.08
Spain	0.46	Slovenia	0.15
France	0.46	Slovakia	0.08
Italy	0.16	Finland	0.54
Cyprus	0.17	Sweden	1.12
Latvia	0.08	UK	0.52
Lithuania	0.14	EU(27)	0.42

Source: Eurostat, http://epp.eurostat.ec.europa.eu/tgm/table.do?tab=table&init=1&language=en&pcode=tsdgp100 (accessed 18 February 2011), © European Union, 2011.

EU development assistance is a shared competence between the EU and its member states. At the EU level, development policy is implemented through instruments such as trade preferences, development finance and humanitarian aid. EU development policy is centred on the 79 ACP countries, many of which are former colonies of EU member states. However, aid is also given to other countries, such as those in the Mediterranean area, the former Eastern bloc, Latin America, Asia and Africa.

As much aid is organized on a geographical basis, historically it was disbursed through a number of different financial instruments. These include the European Development Fund (EDF) for ACP countries, which is funded not from the general Community budget but from direct contributions from the member states. The funding by member state is partly based on GDP and partly on their historical links with the

---

[15] The statistics in this paragraph are taken from OECD, http://stats.oecd.org/Index.aspx?DatasetCode=ODA_DONOR (accessed 18 February 2011).

ACP country concerned. The EDF allocates €22,682 million at current prices for the 2008–18 period, but the EDC will remain outside the EU budget despite a Commission proposal for its inclusion.

The 2007–13 financial perspective attempted to simplify and rationalize the way in which EU external co-operation is financed through the EU budget, reducing the number of financing instruments to nine. Six funds support policies with a geographic or thematic focus: the Pre-Accession Instrument (see Chapter 19); the European Neighbourhood and Partnership Instrument; the Development Co-operation Instrument; the Instrument for Co-operation with Industrialised Countries; the European Instrument for Democracy and Human Rights; and the Instrument for Nuclear Safety Co-operation. Three instruments address crisis situations: the Instrument for Stability; existing humanitarian aid, which will incorporate emergency food aid; and macro-financial assistance instruments.

The funds available for the Development Co-operation Instrument for the 2007–18 period amount to €10.1 billion for developing countries from Latin America, Asia, the Middle East and South Africa.

18.5   The evolution of EU policy towards the ACP countries

The evolution of EU development policy has been influenced by changes within the EU itself but also by the political, strategic and economic changes on the international scene, decolonialization, changing views of economic and social development, the ending of the Cold War, and globalization.

EU development policy dates from the Treaty of Rome when France wanted to maintain its links with its colonial territories but share some of the financial costs with other Community members (see Box 18.4). For this purpose, in 1958 the EDF was set up, and financed social and economic infrastructure projects mainly in French-speaking Overseas Countries and Territories. Subsequently the EDF financed aid to the ACP countries.

Box 18.4

The evolution of EU policy towards the ACP countries

Articles 131 and 136 of the Treaty of Rome provided for the association of non-European countries and territories with which the EEC states had particular relations.

1958   The EDF was established.

1963   Yaoundé I: trade concessions and financial aid to African ex-colonies.

1969   Yaoundé II.

1975   Lomé I: non-reciprocal trade preferences to ACP countries, equality of partners and introduction of Stabex.

1980   Lomé II: no major changes apart from the introduction of Sysmin.

1985   Lomé III: attention was shifted from the promotion of industrial development to self-reliant development on the basis of self-sufficiency and food security.

1990   Lomé IV (revised in 1995): covered a ten-year period and gave more emphasis to the promotion of human rights, democracy, good governance, the situation of women, protection of the environment (including forests), decentralization of co-operation and increased regional co-operation.

2000   Cotonou: intended to cover a twenty-year period using an approach based on politics, trade and development to tackle poverty.

Since 2008 Cotonou is being replaced by Economic Partnership Agreements.

During the 1960s many of the overseas territories gained independence, and a new framework of assistance was provided with the Yaoundé agreement of 1963 (renewed in 1969) covering trade and aid arrangements between the EC and former French colonies in Africa. The entry of the UK into the Community in 1973 led to a reappraisal of development policy, resulting in the first Lomé Convention of 1975. Subsequent Conventions followed in 1980, 1985 and 1990 (which covered a ten-year period) and the Cotonou Agreement of 2000.

In line with the then widely discussed objective of creating a New International Economic Order (NIEO), the initial ambitious aim of the Lomé conventions was to create a 'partnership of equals'. The main instruments adopted were non-reciprocal and included: tariff preferences; preferences for agricultural products; financial aid; and Stabex arrangements (subsequently also Sysmin for mining sectors), which are funds to stabilize export earnings.[16]

However, the global economic instability following the oil shocks of 1973 and 1979 hit sub-Saharan economies particularly hard and the ACP countries were disappointed with the Lomé conventions. The conventions were criticized for poor use of aid since projects were often badly designed and hindered by a hostile policy environment, and for weak management on the part of donors, with slow and cumbersome disbursement procedures and accusations of political interference.[17]

Although under the preferential system the ACP countries faced lower (often zero) tariffs than other developing countries, this failed to stem their decline in EU trade. According to Eurostat data, the ACP share in extra-EU imports fell from 6.7 per cent in 1976 to 2.8 per cent in 1999, rising to 4.5 per cent in 2009. Of these, imports from South Africa comprise roughly one-third, and about one-quarter is energy from Nigeria. The poor infrastructure, fractured markets and difficulties in meeting EU standards and technical restrictions of many of the ACP countries limit the impact of tariff reductions. Too often, trade promotion was regarded as an end in itself rather than as a means of favouring development.

The need to tackle poverty, instability and political conflict led to a renewed debate on EU development policy in the late 1990s. To facilitate discussion the Commission published a Green Paper in 1996 and a discussion paper in 1997 setting out its proposals for a post-Lomé agreement.[18] Negotiations began in 1998, and in 2000 the Cotonou Agreement was signed between the EU and the ACP countries. This was to cover a period of twenty years. It was based on a perspective that combines politics, trade and development. The central objective of the Agreement was the reduction and eventual eradication of poverty, and for that purpose five interdependent pillars were indicated: a comprehensive political dimension; participatory approaches; strengthening the focus on poverty reduction; a new framework for trade and co-operation; and a reform of financial co-operation.

The Cotonou Agreement envisaged a five-year review procedure, and the first revision of the Agreement took place in 2005.[19] The revised version of the Agreement entailed further emphasis on political dialogue, references to the fight against terrorism, co-operation in countering the proliferation of weapons of mass destruction, and tighter relations with the International Criminal Court. The 2005 revision also took participation under the second pillar (the CFSP) further by encouraging more involvement of non-state actors and local authorities.

The increased EU stress on the political dimension, and the need to promote respect for human rights, democratic institutions, the rule of law and avoidance of corruption is shared by other international organizations such as the World Bank and European Bank for Reconstruction and Development (EBRD).[20] Democratic elections and freedom of the media render politicians more answerable for their choices. Effective rule of law ensures that contracts are enforceable and, if necessary, redress is possible through the courts. Corruption and criminal activity may impede the establishment of new firms, and disrupt the activities of existing ones. Protection of property rights is necessary to ensure the

---

[16] Stabex applied to over 40 agricultural raw materials and guaranteed compensation for a fall in income from sales subject to maximum rates, and provided certain conditions were met.

[17] See Stevens (1990) for an early criticism of these agreements.

[18] European Commission (1996, 1997b).

[19] Council Decision of 21 June 2005, published in Official Journal L 209 of 11 August 2005.

[20] See, for example, EBRD Transition Report, 2003.

efficient allocation of resources, and to encourage innovation and investment. Participation is aimed at encouraging ownership of policies and implies the involvement of civil society and a wide range of economic and social actors in development co-operation.

Poverty is not defined simply as lack of income or financial resources, but encompasses the notion of vulnerability and factors such as lack of access to adequate food supplies, education, healthy drinking water, employment, and political involvement. The focus on poverty reduction requires measures to support: economic development (including private sector development and investment, macroeconomic and structural policies and reforms, and sectoral policies); social and human development; and regional co-operation and integration. At the same time three horizontal themes are to be taken into account in all areas of co-operation (in accordance with the principle of 'mainstreaming'): gender equality; environmental sustainability; and institutional development and capacity building.

The aim of EU development policy is also to ensure 'the three Cs': coherence, co-ordination and complementarity. Complementarity (of different aid measures) and co-ordination are necessary to render aid more effective, while coherence requires an integrated approach to external relations, security, economic and development policies.

18.6   The Economic Partnership Agreements

The special preferences granted by the EU to ACP countries were against WTO rules, which require reciprocal arrangements to cover '*substantially all trade*' and non-discrimination between similarly situated countries. The EU preferences to the ACP countries came under sustained attack during the banana dispute.[21] The EU obtained a five-year waiver for its ACP treatment, but this came to an end on 31 December 2007. The EU was against seeking further waivers, and decided to introduce WTO-compatible arrangements in the form of Economic Partnership Aggrement (EPAs) or reciprocal free trade areas with groups of ACP countries.

Negotiations on the EPAs began in 2002, and they were expected to come into operation from January 2008. The EU proposed EPAs with six groups of neighbouring ACP countries. The aim was to liberalize trade among the ACP members of the regional grouping, and gradually (over 15 years and in some cases up to 25 years) lower trade barriers against the EU, while providing protection for the most sensitive 20 per cent of imports. In return the EU would offer enhanced or almost free access to its market and simplification of procedures, including those relating to rules of origin. There would also be focus on ACP development, assistance to the ACP countries in implementing the agreements, and co-operation in areas such as standards.

In practice the EU was forced to modify radically its proposal for the EPAs. Initially the EU wanted to include services and foreign investment rules (two issues that caused much conflict in WTO negotiations, see the Online Learning Centre of this book), but in many cases had to drop these from the agenda. The only region to sign a comprehensive EPA by the 2008 deadline was the Caribbean area (Cariforum with the exception of Haiti). However, some interim agreements were signed, and various ACP countries signed individually or as small groups of countries rather than the comprehensive regional EPA groupings initially envisaged.[22]

18.7   The EPAs and the debate about the effectiveness of EU development policy

The introduction (or 'imposition' as some saw it) of EPAs was extremely controversial. There was a heated debate about whether the EPAs would benefit the ACPs, or whether, as claimed in some quarters, the EU was acting mainly in the interests of its own exporters and forcing ACP countries into

---

[21] See the Online Learning Centre of this book for a description of the banana dispute.

[22] See European Commission DG Trade, http://ec.europa.eu/trade/creating-opportunities/bilateral-relations/regions/africa-caribbean-pacific/ (accessed 18 February 2011).

premature liberalization. In addition to trying to place services and investment on the agenda, the EU also maintained that by the MFN clause the ACP countries could not have higher tariffs with other trading partners than with the EU.

Various academic studies suggested that the EPAs would lead to trade diversion. For instance, Bouët et al. (2007) of the International Food Policy Research Institute found that EPAs would lead to tariff and income losses for ACP countries, and would result in an increase in EU exports to the ACPs by $14.7 billion by 2018, compared with a fall of $3 billion for exports from the rest of the world.

Messerlin and Delpeuch (2007) suggested that the ACP countries should be allowed to make a counter-proposal in place of the EPAs, offering more limited trade liberalization for the EU in return for maintaining their preferential access to the EU market.

Other observers argued that the impact of the EPAs would be limited, pointing to the relatively small level of tariff cuts involved, and the long timescale for implementation.[23] Others objected to EU brinkmanship in trying to force the ACP countries to accept EPAs by the tight 2008 deadline, or be subject to GSP treatment (though the then Commissioner for Trade, Peter Mandelson, maintained that the EU had no choice under WTO rules). The EU Development Commissioner, Louis Michel, also offered the ACP countries compensation for eventual loss of tariff revenue and more development assistance, leading to accusations of bribery.

The debate extended to the more general issue of the effectiveness of EU development policy. Difficulties have been encountered in introducing common, simplified procedures, and ensuring co-ordination and that the different aid measures and activities of donors were complementary. Insufficient progress has also been made in realizing coherence with other EU policies, and ongoing attention is necessary to ensure that decisions in areas such as trade and agriculture are compatible with development co-operation. The organizational structure of EU policy is complex and divided between various offices (such as: European Commission Development and Cooperation EuropAid, European Commission Humanitarian Aid and Civil Protection, and the DGs responsible for trade, external relations and enlargement), so could be simplified. There would also seem a case for including the EDF under the EU budget.

Economic development is a complex process depending on a whole series of factors, including the internal situation of the recipient countries, the international economic environment, globalization, the evolution of EU policies (such as the CAP or CFSP) and the outcome of the Doha Round. As the quantity of ODA seems likely to remain limited, it is essential to ensure its quality (House of Lords, 2004). Candidates for ensuring the quality of aid include the following:

- Emphasis on promoting economic growth.
- Focusing on essential priorities such as reducing poverty and fighting disease.
- Building democratic institutions that can ensure the rule of law and respect for minorities, the reduction of corruption and guarantees of property rights.
- Applying conditionality so that building democratic institutions, rule of law and respect for human rights are consistently applied as conditions for receiving aid.
- Promoting sustainable development.
- Simplifying the procedures and ensuring better co-ordination of aid programmes.

18.8   EU–US trade and investment

Trade relations between the EU and the USA have at times been tense, degenerating into surprisingly acrimonious disputes over issues as varied as bananas, beef, genetically modified organisms (GMOs)

---

[23] See King and Campbell (2009) or Christopher Stevens as quoted in the *Financial Times* of 13 December 2007. See also Stevens et al. (2008) and Bilal and Stevens (2009). Fontagne et al. (2008) find benefits from increased ACP exports to the EU, but loss of tariff revenues for these countries. Swinnen et al. (2010) find that improved standards associated with EPAs can benefit poor rural households in ACP countries.

and subsidies to aircraft. At the same time there have been various initiatives to construct an institutional framework for transatlantic co-operation. The aim here is to describe and attempt to provide explanations of this conflictual co-operation.

In terms of economic dimension, the EU and the USA are roughly compatible. According to Eurostat statistics, in 2010 the EU(27) had a population of 501 million, while that of the USA was 318 million. The land area of the USA is considerably greater at 9.2 million square kilometres, while that of the EU(27) was 4.3 million in 2010. Compared with a GDP in purchasing power standards of the EU(27) of 100, that of the USA was 146 per cent in 2009.

The EU(27) share of world merchandise exports was 17.3 per cent in 2009, while that of the USA was 16.3 per cent. In 2008 the EU(27) accounted for about 30.4 per cent of world GDP, while the share of the USA was 23.4 per cent. The USA was the main destination of EU exports, receiving 18.7 per cent of all extra-EU exports in 2009, and was second to China in supplying EU imports, with a share of 13.3 per cent. The EU and USA are also each other's most important source and destination of FDI. In 2009 inward stocks of EU FDI from the USA amounted to €1,044 million, while outward stocks were €1,134 million. About one-quarter of all EU–US trade consists of transactions within firms based on their investments either side of the Atlantic.

18.9   The institutional framework for transatlantic co-operation

During the post-Second World War period, the USA demonstrated unequivocal support for the integration process in Europe. Marshall Aid was conditional on regional co-operation of the recipient countries and led to the creation of the Organization for European Economic Co-operation (OEEC).[24] The early European federalists hoped this would become a supranational institution, but in the event the OEEC and its successor, the OECD, were firmly based on intergovernmental co-operation (thanks largely to Britain and the Scandinavian countries, see Chapter 2). The USA also expressed strong support for the creation of the European Community and was disappointed when the West European integration split into two blocs with the establishment of the European Free Trade Association (EFTA) in 1960.

An ongoing feature is the rhetorical character of statements made about EU–US relations (even when they are conflictual).[25] This, for instance, is typified in Kennedy's 'Declaration of Interdependence', or 'Grand Design', announced at Independence Hall, Philadelphia, on 4 July 1962. The aim was to create a concrete Atlantic partnership based on a declaration of interdependence with a united Europe.[26] The EC was viewed as an ally that could be induced to assist in the fight against communism (both at an international level and internally in countries such as Greece and Italy) and to bear part of the bill for international security.

Recent years have been characterized by several concrete attempts to promote EU–US co-operation, as summarized in Box 18.5 and described below.

In 1990 the **Transatlantic Declaration** institutionalized a framework for consultation and co-operation, and led to the 1995 **New Transatlantic Agenda** (NTA), which entailed joint action in four areas: promoting peace, stability, democracy and development around the world; responding to global challenges; contributing to the expansion of world trade and closer economic relations; and 'building bridges' across the Atlantic (which implies promoting contacts at the level of individual citizens).

The institutional structure of the NTA entails twice-yearly meetings between the US president and the presidents of the EU Council and Commission, and an Action Plan to implement the above objectives. The NTA led to a number of bilateral agreements, covering, for example, co-operation and mutual assistance on customs matters (1997), science and technology (1997), competition laws (1998) and veterinary equivalence (1999).

---

[24] For a description of US attitudes towards European integration in the 1950s, see Chapter 2 of Guay (1999).

[25] On the negative side, in 2000, at the beginning of his term of office, the EU Commissioner for Trade, Pascal Lamy, referred to the need to replace megaphone with telephone diplomacy.

[26] For a more detailed description see Guay (1999: 32).

Box 18.5

Recent landmarks in EU–US relations

1990   Transatlantic Declaration

1995   New Transatlantic Agenda

1998   Transatlantic Economic Partnership

1999   Bonn Declaration

2002   Positive Economic Agenda

2004   Dromoland Summit in Ireland

2007   Transatlantic Economic Council between the USA and EU created.

In 1997 the Mutual Recognition Agreement was signed to meet complaints about customs formalities that often involve requests for additional documentation and information, and lengthy sampling and inspection procedures. Regulatory barriers are now the main obstacles to transatlantic business, and the agreement is a move towards reciprocal recognition of standards and technical regulations.

The NTA also established the Transatlantic Business Dialogue (TABD) that came into operation in 1995. The TABD involves top business people in a forum to discuss ways of reducing barriers to trade and investment. Annual meetings take place alternately in the EU and the USA, and business people have been called on to make recommendations relating to the evolution of common standards, the reduction of tariffs and the implementation of anti-corruption measures. Governments have subsequently endorsed many of the recommendations.

Under the aegis of the NTA, in 1998 it was proposed to create a New Transatlantic Marketplace in order to eliminate barriers to the flow of goods, services and investment between the EU and USA by 2010. The EU approved the New Transatlantic Marketplace, but France subsequently blocked it over concerns that that audiovisual services (which had sensitive cultural implications) and agriculture would not receive adequate special treatment.

Following this failure, in 1998 a **Transatlantic Economic Partnership** (TEP) was agreed. The TEP aimed at creating an open and more accessible world trading system, and improving economic relations between the EU and the USA. This involves tackling trade issues, and, in particular, regulatory barriers. The aim of the TEP is also to integrate labour, business, and environmental and consumer interests into the process.

In 1999 an EU–US summit resulted in the **Bonn Declaration** which aimed at developing an effective warning system to identify problems at an early stage and avoid the risk of conflicts undermining EU–US relations.

In 2002 the **Positive Economic Agenda** (PEA) was set up to enhance bilateral co-operation between the EU and the USA. It provides a framework for setting up new objectives, starting negotiations or increasing the momentum of existing dialogues. The PEA entails bilateral projects, with reports each year to the EU/US summit in order to take stock of progress.

In 2004 at the Dromoland Summit in Ireland, agreement was reached on a new commitment to furthering transatlantic integration. In 2007 a **Framework for Advancing Transatlantic Economic Integration between the USA and EU** was signed. This involved the establishment of a work programme, and the creation of a **Transatlantic Economic Council** (TEC) to oversee and accelerate implementation of the work programme. The annual meetings of the TEC aim at promoting transatlantic convergence, and the generation of growth and jobs by eliminating barriers and creating new business opportunities.

One of the worries in the early years of the Obama Administration was that more attention was being paid to Europe as a NATO partner than to the EU. Obama refused to attend an EU–US summit in Madrid in 2010 and appeared impatient at a 2009 summit in Prague with speeches from all 27 EU leaders.[27] At the December 2009 conference on climate change in Copenhagen the EU seemed to be bypassed by direct meetings between the USA and China (though this could simply reflect common interests of the two largest emitters of greenhouse gases).

18.10   Trade disputes between the EU and the USA

In addition to differences in the Uruguay Round and Doha Round negotiations,[28] many of the WTO trade disputes involved the EU and the USA. However, despite their high profile, according to the European Commission disputes only touched about 2 per cent of trade.

Between 1960 and 1985 the USA initiated 17 legal cases against the EC in the GATT, 13 of which (or 76 per cent) concerned agriculture and fisheries (Hudec, 1993).[29] More recent disputes cover a wide range of issues, including:

- genetically modified organisms;
- beef with growth-promoting hormones;
- geographical indications;
- the EU banana regime, which discriminated in favour of ACP countries;[30]
- the UN ban on imports of beef from the USA and Canada containing growth-promoting hormones;
- the US use of foreign sales corporations to reduce the taxes of US firms exporting abroad;
- the EU failure to authorize additional genetically modified organisms;
- US public procurement (the *Massachusetts–Burma* case raised by the EC in 1997);[31]
- US use of trade defence instruments (such as anti-dumping and safeguards);
- EU protection of trademarks and geographical indications for agricultural products and foodstuffs; and
- preferential loans for the development of a flight management system by the French government to Airbus, and the 2004 *Airbus–Boeing* case (see Box 18.6).[32]

The increasing number of disputes may simply reflect the interdependence and the higher level of international trade and FDI between the EU and the USA. It may also be an indication that countries

---

[28] See the Online Learning Centre of this book for a description of these negotiations.

[29] The first dispute, the 1962 US/EU 'chicken war', was the direct result of the 1962 EC agreement creating the CAP. The USA objected to the system of variable levies used by the EC on its imports of agricultural products from the rest of the world; the level of EC domestic support to agriculture and the use of export subsidies on agricultural products. See Chapter 13 for a more detailed discussion of these questions.

[30] As explained on the Online Learning Centre, the involvement of the USA was because the main distributors of Latin American bananas – Chiquita, Dole Foods and Del Monte – also contested the EU regime. In addition to the USA, South American countries producing bananas (such as Ecuador, Guatemala, Honduras and Panama) were also involved in the GATT/WTO banana disputes.

[31] The Commonwealth of Massachusetts forbade business with anyone having official relations with Burma (Myanmar). The EU maintained that subnational action violated international trade agreements signed by national governments. See http://www.wto.org/english/tratop_e/dispu_e/dispu_e.htm#disputes (accessed 18 February 2011).

[32] Other EU–US disputes (such as those over the EU banana regime, beef hormones, foreign sales corporations and GMOs) are taken up as case studies and discussed in more detail on the Online Learning Centre of this book. See also the WTO website, http://www.wto.org/english/tratop_e/dispu_e/dispu_e.htm#disputes (accessed 18 February 2011).

Box 18.6

The Airbus–Boeing dispute

The biggest and most expensive cases to date in the WTO were over EU and US subsidies to the civil aircraft makers Airbus and Boeing respectively. After unsuccessful attempts to reach a bilateral agreement, in 2004 the USA lodged a complaint (Dispute DS316) that Airbus had received illegal subsidies from the EU and a 'reimbursable launch investment' from France, Germany, Spain and the UK. These subsidies were said to have caused material harm to Boeing. The USA unilaterally abrogated a 1992 agreement with the EU to limit subsidies for aircraft manufacturers, maintaining that the EU had not respected the agreement. The 1992 agreement was somewhat ambiguous as to what forms of state aid were permitted (and the EU argued that it allowed the launch aid for Airbus). Boeing expressed support for the US complaint, though earlier it had indicated fears that a WTO case might alienate passengers. The US complaint was lodged a month before the presidential elections.

In return, the EU filed a counter-complaint, maintaining that Boeing had received about $23.7 billion in US federal, state and local subsidies in the two decades to 2004. The European Commission argued that this violated the 1992 agreement and that the subsidies were not consistent with WTO rules. The EU also filed a complaint over tax breaks worth $3.2 billion from Washington State to Boeing to finance the new 7E7 Dreamliner jet.

In a panel report of June 2010 the WTO found that Airbus had received illegal subsidies (Dispute DS316), and the EU appealed against the report to the Appellate Body of the WTO. In September 2010 an interim finding of a panel report was that Boeing had received illegal subsidies in the form of non-repayable grants though their contract work for NASA and the US Department of Defense.

Given the complexity of the cases, differences over Airbus and Boeing have been dragging on for years, and both parties appear to have lost. Exchanges have been acrimonious. Many observers have questioned the decision to take the disputes to the WTO, and have argued that the only feasible resolution would be a negotiated settlement, as otherwise the EU and USA could risk losing their market share to other competitors such as China or Russia.

---

are more willing to refer their conflicts to a multilateral forum, since the WTO is considered to be more effective in settling disputes than its predecessor, the GATT.

The increase in EU–US trade disputes may also reflect the changed international environment since 1989 with the end of the Cold War. Earlier reliance of West European countries on the US nuclear umbrella constrained the extent to which they could provoke the USA with bitter trade wars.

According to international relations theory, the increased strength and changing role of the EU could imply a decline in the hegemonic stability of the USA. The basic hypothesis of this type of approach is that the existence of a single hegemonic nation will lend stability to the international economic and political system, but if rival countries emerge to challenge the hegemony, the system may become unstable. The picture that emerges varies considerably according to the policy area considered. Few would contest the continued hegemonic role of the USA with regard to international security. In the international monetary sphere there has been much speculation as to whether the euro would challenge the dollar, both as a reserve currency and in the invoicing of international trade (see Chapter 11). However, it is in the area of international trade that the real discussion about possible decline of US hegemony emerges.

Domestic pressures and, in particular, interest groups and big business have generally played a role in the disputes. The USA challenged the EU banana regime, though bananas are not produced in the USA. However, the US government appeared subject to pressure from large multinationals, Chiquita and Dole, while in the EU the firms controlling banana licences had a vested interest in not reforming the regime. The banana lobby was also strong in some of the ACP countries. The GMO market is controlled by large multinationals, and in most cases producer lobbies (such as the National Cattlemen's Beef Association in the beef hormone case) were active in claiming compensation for their losses.

In certain cases sanctions were applied (as in the banana and beef hormone cases), and these took the form of tariffs on a certain value of imports. These sanctions hit consumers, but the general public may have been unaware of these effects. Alternatively, in the beef hormone case, EU authorities may have considered sanctions a worthwhile price to pay in view of the strong preferences of consumers with regard to possible health risks. It seems likely that other lobbies quite unconnected to the case in question influenced the choice of products on which to apply sanctions.

Disputes may arise from different regulatory approaches that reflect economic, social, historical and cultural diversity, or different sensitivities and societal values with regard to health, consumer and environmental protection. For instance, the EU public seems to have less confidence in the ability of food safety authorities to guarantee safe and healthy food. The increasing complexity of the issues renders it difficult to draw up clear and unambiguous rules, in particular when there may be conflicts between policy objectives, such as between free trade and the environment.

The EU has frequently complained about US attempts to apply extraterritoriality and unilateralism in trade policy. The EU objects to extraterritorial application of US domestic legislation when it requires individuals or companies in the EU to comply with US laws or policies. In general the EU and the USA also have different views about the effectiveness of linking strategic and commercial objectives. While the USA sees trade as a useful diplomatic weapon in dealing with rogue countries, the EU is more sceptical about the effectiveness of sanctions and tends to favour a policy of engagement.

18.11   Wider Europe: the European Neighbourhood Policy

In March 2003 the European Commission published the Communication on Wider Europe, setting out the European Neighbourhood Policy (ENP) to deal with relations between an enlarged EU and its eastern and southern neighbours.[33] The aim is to prevent new dividing lines emerging between the EU and its neighbours, to enhance security and narrow the prosperity gap on the new external borders of the EU.

The ENP is for countries with no immediate prospect of EU membership, covering countries such as the western NIS (newly independent states) and Southern Mediterranean countries, but not South-East Europe (see Chapter 19).

The approach is based on mutual commitment to values such as the rule of law, good governance, respect for human rights (including minority rights), the promotion of a market economy, sustainable development, and certain foreign policy goals. The ENP aims at establishing a pan-European integrated market, functioning on the basis of rules that are similar or harmonized with those of the EU.

Central to the policy are bilateral ENP Action Plans negotiated between the EU and individual partners, covering areas such as:

- political dialogue, including measures against terrorism, and to prevent the spread of weapons of mass destruction and the encouragement of regional co-operation;
- economic and social development policy, offering partner countries a stake in the EU internal market based on regulatory and legislative convergence, participation in certain EU programmes (such as education, training, research and innovation), and improved interconnections and physical links with the EU (in transport, energy, the environment and telecommunications);
- the promotion of trade, including convergence with EU standards;
- co-operation on issues such as border management, migration, the fight against terrorism, organized crime, trafficking in human beings, the drugs trade and so on.

From 2007 the European Neighbourhood and Partnership Instrument replaced the TACIS, MEDA and other assistance instruments used by the EU in these countries.

---

[33] European Commission (2003b). For a more recent description of the policy see European Commission, European Neighbourhood Policy, http://ec.europa.eu/world/enp/index_en.htm (accessed 18 February 2011).

The ENP builds on other regional and multilateral co-operation initiatives such as the Union for the Mediterranean (see below), the Eastern Partnership, and Black Sea Synergy. The Eastern Partnership was launched in Prague in 2009, and links the EU with Armenia, Azerbaijan, Belarus, Georgia, Moldova and Ukraine. It offers the prospect of association agreements with free trade components, easier travel and co-operation with countries able and willing to engage more closely with the EU. The Black Sea Synergy was launched in Kiev in 2008 and aims at promoting closer regional ties between countries around the Black Sea: Armenia, Azerbaijan, Georgia, Moldova, Russia, Turkey and Ukraine. Co-operation is aimed at promoting democracy and stability, resolving conflicts and encouraging economic development.

While it seems a positive move to avoid new divisions with neighbouring countries, it is difficult to see how a single policy, the ENP, can be applied to countries with such different characteristics and needs, even with a differentiated approach. The use of benchmarks in applying the ENP Action Plans seems to imply that the EU is attempting to introduce some form of conditionality, but as the experience of the former Yugoslav republics of South-East Europe and other countries (including those of the Mediterranean area) has shown, conditionality is a very blunt weapon without the prospect of EU membership. The idea that the ENP is extended to countries with no immediate prospect of EU membership might also be interpreted as a 'cold shoulder' by some of them.[34]

18.12 The Mediterranean region

The Euro-Mediterranean Partnership (Euromed) links the EU and sixteen Mediterranean countries.[35] Launched in 1995 as the Barcelona Process, under the prompting of Nicolas Sarkozy this was revived in 2008 as the Union for the Mediterranean (UFM). The relaunch aimed at rendering the process more visible and concrete with new regional and subregional projects. Since 2010 the UFM has a secretariat in Barcelona. Initiatives include: fighting pollution of the Mediterranean; improving transport links; increased prevention and improved response to national and man-made disasters; a Mediterranean solar energy plan; a Euro-Mediterranean university (set up in Slovenia), and the Mediterranean Business Development Initiative to favour small businesses.

The Euro-Mediterranean Partnership is composed of bilateral and regional relations. At the regional level the aim is to promote activities in all three domains of the Barcelona Declaration: the political and security dimension (with emphasis placed on creating a zone of peace and stability); the economic and financial dimension; and the social, cultural and human dimension. A key objective is to establish a Euro-Mediterranean Free Trade Area. This also involves encouraging 'horizontal' or 'South–South' integration through the creation of free trade areas among the Mediterranean partners themselves. For instance, in 2001 the Agadir Initiative entailed agreement to set up a free trade area between Egypt, Jordan, Morocco and Tunisia. However, to date Euromed resembles more of a hub-and-spoke arrangement with the EU.

At a bilateral level the EU carries out activities with individual countries, including those implemented through Euro-Mediterranean Association Agreements.[36] The Euro-Mediterranean Agreements differ between countries, but their main features include co-operation, and trade in goods, with additional measures being negotiated to open up trade in agriculture and services, and investment.

---

[34] See Chilosi (2007, 2009) for a critical analysis of the ENP.

[35] Albania, Algeria, Bosnia and Herzegovina, Croatia, Egypt, Israel, Jordan, Lebanon, Mauritania, Monaco, Montenegro, Morocco, the Palestinian Authority, Syria, Tunisia and Turkey. Turkey is a candidate country for EU membership, but (as was the case for Cyprus and Malta) can participate in Euro-Mediterranean regional co-operation until accession. Libya belongs to the UFM, but not the Euro-Mediterranean Partnership.

[36] Between 1998 and 2005 Association Agreements were signed with Egypt, Israel, Jordan, Lebanon, Morocco, Tunisia and Algeria. An agreement with Syria was initialled in 2008. See Chapter 19 for a discussion of EU relations with the former Yugoslav republics and Albania.

Financial support for Euromed is provided through the European Neighbourhood and Partnership Instrument.[37] In 2002 a facility for Euro-Mediterranean investment and partnership was set up under the EIB and invested €10 billion between 2002 and 2010.

Despite Euromed, the income gap between the Northern and Southern Mediterranean has been widening. The Mediterranean partners criticize the EU for limited concessions in the sectors that interest them most, namely agriculture and textiles and clothing. Progress in setting up the Union for the Mediterranean was slow, and few people even knew of its existence.

However, the main weakness of Euromed is that the aspiration of creating an area of peace, prosperity and progress around the Mediterranean is constantly threatened by the ongoing unsettled international situation. This came to the fore in early 2011 with disturbances in various countries such as Egypt, Tunisia and Libya, and a massive surge in immigrants trying to reach the EU (see also Chapter 8). The EU response was slow and badly co-ordinated, and the newly created External Action Service (see Chapter 1) was not much in evidence. In 2011 there were calls from some circles to set up an equivalent of the Marshall Fund to foster stability in the Mediterranean area.[38]

18.13   The Russian Federation

After the USA and China, Russia is the third main trading partner of the EU, while the EU is Russia's major trading partner and source of FDI. Energy and mineral fuels products account for about 77 per cent of Russian exports to the EU.[39] Sixty per cent of all Russian oil exports are to the EU, and amount to over 25 per cent of total EU oil consumption. Fifty per cent of Russian natural gas exports go to the EU and constitute over 25 per cent of total EU consumption of natural gas. Russia is also an important exporter of nuclear fuels to the EU. Almost 75 per cent of FDI in Russia is from EU member states. The exports of the EU to Russia are diversified and include machinery and transport equipment (43 per cent in 2008), chemicals, manufactured goods, and food and live animals.

The EU dependence on Russian energy conditions its attitude, and what has emerged since the early 1990s is a growing gap between what appears on paper as an extensive institutional framework for co-operation, and tensions in practice between Russia on the one hand, and the EU and various of its member states on the other.

The legal basis for EU relations with Russia is the Partnership and Co-operation Agreement (PCA), which came into operation in 1997. The PCA was extended to the new member states after EU enlargement. The Agreement covered a ten-year period, but initially Poland blocked negotiation of a new replacement agreement (probably over fears that the EU failed to present a sufficiently united front in the face of Russia). It was therefore decided to roll the existing agreement over annually. In 2008 negotiations of a new agreement began. It should cover political dialogue, trade, investment and energy, economic co-operation, research, education and culture, and co-operation to combat illegal activities, drug trafficking, money laundering and organized crime.

An Energy Dialogue was established in 2000 as a forum for discussion and co-operation on energy issues.

Since 1991 the EU has provided technical assistance to Russia through the TACIS Programme. By 2010 a total of €2.8 billion had been given through TACIS. Some projects will continue until 2013, but they are now carried out with co-financing by Russia.

In 2003 the Final Declaration of the EU–Russian Summit in St Petersburg defined four 'common spaces' or areas for co-operation within the framework of the PCA: the economy; liberty, security and justice; research, education and culture; and external security.

---

[37] This replaced the MEDA Programme from 2007.

[38] See, for example, the Italian minister of foreign affairs, Franco Frattini, writing in the *Financial Times* of 18 February 2011.

[39] Unless otherwise stated all the statistics in this chapter are taken from Eurostat.

Since EU enlargement, part of the Russian Federation, Kaliningrad, is surrounded by EU member states. This raised the sensitive question of how to guarantee transit between Kaliningrad and the rest of Russia. In 2002 at the Brussels Summit, agreement was reached on a package of measures addressing this problem, which included: a facilitated transit document; assessing the feasibility of a non-stop, high-speed train; discussions on the long-term goal of visa-free travel between the EU and Russia; and full use of existing international conventions to simplify transit of goods, including energy.

The implementation of these arrangements has led to high increases in transit figures. The EU also provides substantial financial assistance for the development of the Kaliningrad region.

Despite the institutional framework for co-operation, there have been numerous tensions between Russia and the EU and its member states. The worsening of relations was exacerbated by enlargement, with various countries formerly in the Soviet sphere of influence joining the EU. Some Russian circles also considered the creation of the Eastern Partnership in 2009 (see above) as encroachment by the EU into an area that had previously formed part of the Soviet bloc.

Disputes between Russia and the CEEC member states have covered a wide range of issues (some of which were subsequently resolved), including: a ban on Polish meat exports; a blockade of Lithuanian oil imports; a row with Estonia over moving a Soviet war memorial; criticism of Czech and Polish plans to host a US anti-missile system; and tensions with Poland over the causes of the April 2010 Katyn air crash in which 97 people died (including the Polish president) on their way to visit the site of a massacre of Polish officers during the Second World War.

There were also differences with the older EU member states over energy security, trade (Sweden and Italy), human rights, Georgia, and a Russian spying scandal with Spain. Following the killing of Alexander Litvinenko in 2006 and the dispute over British Council activities, relations between the UK and Russia seemed redolent of the Cold War. The EU was also concerned about human rights restrictions and violations of democracy in Russia, including the detention of former chess champion Gary Kasparov in 2007. Kosovo was a major source of tension, with Russia backing Serbia and threatening to block the 2006 proposal of UN envoy Martti Ahtisaari for gradual independence of Kosovo (see Chapter 19). Russia also backed separatist enclaves in Georgia and Moldova, and there were also differences over Ukrainian moves to draw closer to the EU. A dispute about the pricing of gas between Russia and Ukraine in 2009 led to gas supplies to part of the EU being cut for almost two weeks.

For a time EU leaders such as Chirac, Berlusconi and Schroeder appeared very pro-Russian (probably also because of the energy question). Subsequently both the German chancellor, Angela Merkel, and Commission president, Barroso, stressed that it was important for Russia to realize that the EU was based on solidarity, so the difficulties of countries such as Poland, Lithuania or Estonia with Russia were also EU problems.

18.14 EU relations with Asia

Trade between the EU and Asia has been growing rapidly, and now accounts for about one-third of total EU trade flows. EU FDI in Asia has also been increasing, and has reached about one-third third of EU FDI abroad. Strengthening relations with Asia has therefore become one of the highest priorities of EU foreign relations.

The Asia–Europe Meeting (ASEM) was set up in 1996, and encourages dialogue and co-operation between the EU and ASEAN (see Box 18.2), and what had become eighteen Asian countries in 2011. ASEM involves summits (which have taken place every two years), ministerial meetings, and conferences and seminars at expert level to discuss political, economic and cultural issues. Action Plans have been drawn up to facilitate trade and investment, and a Trans-Eurasia Information Network has been set up to encourage research and education. There are also meetings on a regular basis of civil society and of the private and public sectors in the Asia–Europe Business Forum, and of social movements and civil society organizations in the Asia–Europe People's Forum. The Asia–Europe Foundation was set up in 1997 in Singapore in order to promote cultural and intellectual meetings between the two regions. The dialogue encouraged by the ASEM process has recently concentrated more on political issues such as the fight against terrorism and transnational crime, and the management of international migration.

The EU also has relations with subregional Asian groupings such as ASEAN, and the South Asian Association for Regional Co-operation (SAARC), as described in Box 18.2 above, and bilateral relations with individual Asian countries.

18.15   EU relations with China

Trade between the EU and China has been growing dramatically, and China is the second trading partner of the EU (see Table 18.1 above), and has displaced the USA as the main source of EU imports. EU imports from China grew by about 16.5 per cent a year between 2004 and 2008, but fell by 13 per cent in 2009 due to the economic crisis.[40] Whereas the EU(15) had a surplus with China at the beginning of the 1980s, the deficit (including services) of €128 billion with China in 2009 was the largest bilateral trade deficit of the EU. In 2010 China was the main exporter in the world, ahead of Germany and the USA. The exports to the EU are mainly industrial goods: machinery and transport equipment, and miscellaneous manufactured articles. These categories, together with chemicals, are also the principal EU exports to China.

In 2009 EU companies invested €5.3 billion in China (up from €4.7 billion in 2008). The flow of Chinese investment in the EU was €0.3 billion in 2009 (compared with a net disinvestment of €1.8 billion in 2008).

The large EU deficit reflects what is claimed to be the artificially low value of the Chinese currency, and the difficulties EU companies still experience in accessing the Chinese market due to red tape and cumbersome procedures. In 2010 the EU had 52 anti-dumping cases against China, but according to the European Commission these covered only about 1 per cent of EU imports from China. Infringements of intellectual property rights remain a problem for EU businesses in China, and in 2008 about 54 per cent of counterfeit goods seized at the EU borders came from China.

The EU supported China's WTO membership (achieved in December 2001) and is now concerned to ensure implementation of China's WTO commitments, in particular with regard to market access and intellectual property rights.

In 2006 the EU adopted a Partnership and Competition strategy pledging the EU to accept sharp competition from China, while encouraging China to trade fairly. In 2008 a High Level Economic and Trade Dialogue between the EU and China was launched, and in 2007 negotiations of a Partnership and Co-operation Agreement began.

18.16   EU relations with Japan

After a decade of stagnation, Japan experienced annual growth of 2.1 per cent between 2005 and 2007, before a 1.2 per cent fall in GDP in 2008 and a 6.3 per cent fall in 2009. Even before the tsunami of 2011 and damage to the Fukushima nuclear reactor, entrenched deflation, and declines in bank lending and land prices suggested ongoing difficulties.

Historically, Japan had a large trade surplus with the EU, but from the 1990s trade with Japan became more balanced. The EU deficit with Japan fell from €47 billion in 2000 to €20 billion in 2009. Over the 2005–09 period EU exports of goods to Japan declined by 4.7 per cent per year on average (at a time of overall growth in EU exports of 1 per cent per year). In 2009 Japan accounted for 4.7 per cent of EU imports and was the sixth most important source of imports. At the end of 2009 about 5 per cent of the EU inward FDI stock was from Japan, and 2.3 per cent of the EU outward stock went to Japan. However, most EU investment in Japan is concentrated in a small number of large acquisitions in sectors such as telecommunications, car manufacturing, retailing and insurance.

---

[40] The statistics in this section are taken from European Commission DG Trade, *EU–China Trade in facts and figures*, http://trade.ec.europa.eu/doclib/docs/2009/september/tradoc_144591.pdf (accessed 23 February 2011).

In the past, EU relations with Japan tended to be dominated by trade disputes, and EU companies still complain of difficulties in market access. From the 1990s there was increased Japanese willingness to meet EU requests for structural reforms and deregulation. Since 1995 the Regulatory Reform Dialogue has provided a forum for reciprocal requests for reducing the number of unnecessary regulations that may obstruct trade. In 2002 the EU–Japan Mutual Recognition Agreement entered into force, and in 2003 an Agreement on Co-operation on Anti-Competitive Activities was adopted. In 2004 a Co-operation Framework for two-way investment promotion was agreed. Despite such initiatives, structural features of the Japanese economy and society continue to pose obstacles for foreign firms.

EU relations with Japan are covered by the 1991 Political Declaration, which set out common principles and shared objectives in the political, economic, and cultural areas, and other forms of co-operation. It also established a consultation framework for annual summits between the EU and Japan. In 2001 an Action Plan ('Shaping Our Common Future') was launched, covering EU–Japanese relations for a ten-year period to 2011. The Action Plan has four basic objectives: promoting peace and security (through measures such as arms control, non-proliferation, conflict prevention); strengthening the economic and trade partnership; coping with global and societal change; and bringing together people and cultures. The EU and Japan have also attempted to co-ordinate their positions in international organizations such as the UN and the WTO.

18.17 EU relations with India

With a market of 1.17 billion people in 2010 and an annual growth rate of 8.4 per cent between 2004 and 2010,[41] the importance of India as a trade partner for the EU has been increasing rapidly. Trade between the EU and India rose from €4.4 billion in 1980 to €28.6 billion in 2003 and about €53 billion in 2009. In 2009 EU imports of goods from India amounted to €25.3 billion, and exports to €27.6 billion. EU FDI stocks in India rose from €759 million in 2003 to €2.7 billion in 2009. EU exports in commercial services were €8.3 billion in 2009, while imports were worth €7.3 billion.

Indian tariff and non-tariff barriers (such as quantitative restrictions, import licences, testing and certification, and lengthy customs procedures) remain a problem. In 2008 the World Bank ranked India 120 (out of 178 countries) for 'ease of doing business'. In 2007 (also with the EU Global Europe strategy in mind[42]), the EU and India launched negotiations to create a free trade area, but progress has been slow.

EU–India relations date from the 1960s, and agreements were signed in 1973 and 1981. The current Co-operation Agreement, which dates from 1994, extends beyond trade and co-operation. In 2004 it was agreed to launch a Strategic Partnership between the EU and India. This is implemented through the EU–India Joint Action Plan launched in 2005 and revised in 2008. Regular meetings take place at all levels, up to the annual EU–India Summit. The EU provides an average of €67 million a year in financial assistance to India over the 2007–13 period.

18.18 EU–Latin American relations

With the entry of Spain and Portugal into the Community, relations with Latin America acquired a higher priority. Trade between the EU and Latin America more than doubled between 1990 and 2008. The EU is Latin America's second trading partner after the USA, with imports to the EU from Latin America and the Caribbean amounting to €102.4 billion, and exports to the region to €86.4 billion in 2008. The EU is the most important foreign investor and major source of foreign aid. In 2007 the total FDI stock of the EU in Latin America and the Caribbean amounted to €228 billion.

---

[41] According to national statistics.

[42] The Global Europe strategy aimed to increase the contribution of trade and FDI to EU competitiveness. See further the introduction to this chapter.

The EU is concerned that Latin America should maintain a balanced relationship between its two principal trade partners, even though the proposal to create a Free Trade Area of the Americas (FTAA) has stalled since 2005. The aim of this initiative was a geographical extension of the North American Free Trade Agreement (NAFTA), but differences arose over the liberalization of agricultural trade, and because developed countries wanted opening of trade in services and increased protection of intellectual property rights.

The EU has developed a parallel set of ties with Latin America and the Caribbean, with simultaneous relations at the regional, subregional and bilateral levels. At the regional (subcontinent) level, in 1986 six Latin American countries set up the Rio Group in order to discuss matters of common interest. Membership of this group has gradually expanded, and it now includes all the Latin American countries and a number of Caribbean countries.[43] Meetings are held between the EU and Rio Group every two years.

In 1999 at the Rio Summit it was decided to develop a strategic partnership between the EU, and Latin America and the Caribbean (EU–LAC) in order to develop political, economic and cultural understanding between the partners. Emphasis was traditionally placed on developing democracy, the rule of law, human rights, pluralism, peace and security and political stability. Over time, however, more priority has been given to international challenges such as such as energy security, climate change, financial stability and growth of the world economy.

At a subregional level, as shown in Box 18.2 above, the EU has relationships with the three main integration blocs in Latin America: Mercosur (El Mercado del Sur), the Andean Community, and Central America (the SICA, or Central American Integration System). The EU encourages regional integration as a means of ensuring economic development and security.

The EU also has bilateral links with individual countries and, in particular, Mexico and Chile, which are not full members of Latin American integration blocs. In 2005 an Association Agreement between the EU and Chile came into force and covers political and trade relations and co-operation. An Economic Partnership, Political Co-operation and Co-operation Agreement (Global Agreement) was signed between the EU and Mexico in 1997 and came into force in 2000. This entails a free trade area in goods and services, political dialogue, the mutual opening of the procurement markets, the liberalization of capital movements and payments, and the adoption of disciplines in the fields of competition and intellectual property rights.

18.19   Evaluation

A major fear in recent years is that the economic crisis would lead to a rise in economic protectionism. Despite the relatively high level of anti-dumping and anti-subsidy investigations (see Chapter 4), the EU seems to have continued attempts to tighten links with its main trading partners and encouraged the efforts of other regional integration blocs.

Through the GSP (and, in particular, the EBA) initiative the EU offers trade concessions to developing countries, but the impact of these in promoting development seems to have been limited. The foreign aid of the EU and its member states is still well below the levels required to reach the Millennium Development Goals. The decision to render trade relations with ACP countries WTO-compatible through the introduction of EPAs led to contention over the risk of trade diversion, and pressure on developing countries to open their markets. Against this, the negative effects may be limited, and trade liberalization and assistance in meeting standards seems to have increased some trade flows. The debate about the EPAs has fed into a wider discussion about the style and effectiveness of EU development policy.

In relations with Russia, despite the extensive institutional framework for co-operation, dealings have been tense. Though relations with other major trade partners are better, at times there have been

---

[43] Dominican Republic, Jamaica, Belize, Guyana and Haiti. Cuba joined the Rio Group in 2008. The other Caribbean countries are represented by one of the full Caribbean members.

conflicts, such as in the various WTO disputes with the USA, and the limitations on Chinese imports of textiles and clothing. The EU has criticized countries such as China, Japan and India over continued obstacles to market access, including the ongoing Chinese practice of keeping its currency low.

In part these tensions might simply reflect the consequences of globalization (see Chapter 7) and the economic slowdown. However, they may also be due to a growing awareness of the role of an enlarged EU in the world, and of the need to present a counterweight to other major actors and, in particular, the USA and China.

Summary of key concepts

- The **Common Commercial Policy** of the EU was based on Article 113 of the Treaty of Rome and entails a common EU tariff regime and common trade agreements with third countries. Over time the EU has developed a patchwork of preferential agreements with other countries or groups of countries.

- The **GATT** came into operation in 1948. The GATT was replaced by the **WTO** in 1995.

- The **functions of the GATT and subsequently the WTO** are: to set out regulations governing the conduct of international trade; to make provisions for the settlements of disputes and retaliatory actions and to provide the framework for multilateral negotiations to liberalize world trade.

- The GATT/WTO system has traditionally been based on **three principles**: tariff reductions, reciprocity and non-discrimination.

- The liberalization of world trade proceeds by **rounds** of negotiations, the last of which to be completed was the Uruguay Round (1986–94). Following the failure to launch a trade round at Seattle, the **Doha Development Agenda** eventually began in November 2001, but broke down in 2008.

- In 1971 the Community established a **Generalised System of Preferences**. This entails a list of products negotiated each year on which tariffs are reduced by an amount that depends on the 'sensitivity' of the product and degree of development of the exporting countries.

- **EU development policy** is centred on the ACP countries, most of which are former colonies of EU member states. However, policies to reduce world poverty have met with limited success.

- Following the four Lomé conventions, the 2000 **Cotonou Agreement** between the EU and ACP countries aimed at poverty reduction and covered a twenty-year period. It placed a new emphasis on the political dimension (respect for human rights, democracy and rule of law) and on improved implementation.

- The **Economic Partnership Agreements** introduced from 2008 unite the EU with regional groupings of ACP countries with the aim of eventually creating free trade areas. Their introduction has proved controversial.

- In terms of economic dimension, the **EU and the USA** are roughly compatible. The USA and the EU are each other's largest trading partner and most important source and destination of FDI.

- During the post-Second World War period, the USA demonstrated unequivocal support for the integration process in Europe. Marshall Aid was conditional on regional co-operation of the recipient countries and led to the creation of the OEEC.

- Recent years have been characterized by several concrete attempts to promote EU–US co-operation, but there have been numerous trade disputes between the EU and the USA on issues such as: subsidies to Airbus and Boeing, bananas, meat containing growth-promoting hormones, foreign sales corporations and genetically modified food.

- In March 2003 the European Commission launched the **European Neighbourhood Policy** to deal with relations between an enlarged EU and its eastern and southern neighbours. In 2008 the Black Sea Synergy was created, and in 2009 the Eastern Partnership was set up.
- The **Euro-Mediterranean Partnership** links the EU and other Mediterranean countries. Launched in 1995 as the Barcelona Process, this was revived in 2008 as the **Union for the Mediterranean**.
- The Partnership and Co-operation Agreement is the legal basis for **EU–Russian relations**. In 2003 Russia and the EU agreed on a framework for creating 'common spaces', but in practice relations have been tense.
- The **Asia–Europe Meeting** was set up in 1996 to encourage dialogue and co-operation between the EU and Asian countries.
- Despite various institutional arrangements to tighten bilateral economic relations, the EU has criticized countries such as **China, Japan and India** over continued obstacles to market access, including the ongoing Chinese practice of keeping its currency low.
- **EU relations with Latin America** are carried out simultaneously at regional, subregional and bilateral levels. The EU is concerned that Latin American countries maintain a balance in their links with major partners.

Questions for study and review

1 What are the main features of EU trade policy?
2 What were the main functions of the GATT, and how effective was it in meeting its objectives?
3 How is the WTO different from the GATT?
4 How has the GATT/WTO influenced the EU?
5 What are the main criticisms of EU development policy? How successful do you think that the Cotonou Agreement was in overcoming these shortcomings?
6 What is the link between economic development and democracy?
7 What are the main features of the EPAs? Why are they controversial?
8 What strategies should be used to ensure the effectiveness of development policies?
9 Indicate the main features of EU–US economic relations.
10 Describe the main attempts at EU–US co-operation. How successful do you consider these initiatives?
11 Describe some of the main trade disputes between the USA and the EU (see the Online Learning Centre of this book and the WTO website).
12 How can we account for the increase in trade disputes between the EU and the USA in recent years?
13 How successful do you consider the WTO in resolving these disputes?
14 How do you envisage the future of EU–US relations?
15 Do you think that the European Neighbourhood Policy will prove successful?
16 What criticisms can be made of the Euro-Mediterranean Partnership?
17 How could the EU reduce tensions in its relationship with Russia?
18 How could Europe–Asia relations be strengthened?
19 What are the main features of EU relations with China?
20 Describe EU and US rivalry in Latin and Central America.
21 Do you think that the EU is right to promote efforts at regional integration in other areas?

Online Learning **Centre**

When you have read this chapter, log on to the Online Learning Centre website at ***www.mcgraw-hill.co.uk/textbooks/senior*** to explore weblinks, chapter-by-chapter test questions, case studies and more online study tools.

Chapter 19

EU Enlargement

Learning Objectives

By the end of this chapter you should be able to understand:

- ✓ Where we are in the EU enlargement process
- ✓ How the theory of clubs has been used to analyse the question of EU enlargement
- ✓ What measures were introduced by Western countries to assist the transition process in Central and Eastern European countries (CEECs) and with what success
- ✓ The differences between aid for transition and the Marshall Plan
- ✓ The difficulties encountered in trying to apply the Copenhagen criteria
- ✓ The main steps involved in the pre-accession strategy
- ✓ EU policy towards South-Eastern Europe
- ✓ EU relations with the candidate countries: Croatia, the Former Yugoslav Republic of Macedonia, Iceland and Turkey
- ✓ EU relations with the pre-candidate countries

19.1 Introduction

In May 2004 ten new countries joined the EU, and Bulgaria and Romania became members in 2007. Croatia, the Former Yugoslav Republic of Macedonia, Iceland, Montenegro and Turkey are candidate countries. Potential candidate countries in the Western Balkans, which could eventually include Albania, Bosnia and Herzegovina, Kosovo and Serbia.

The ongoing EU enlargement process raises fundamental questions about the future of the Union. Will, for instance, expanding membership lead to a change in identity of the EU? Is widening on this scale compatible with deepening? Will there be endless arguing about the relative size of contributions to and receipts from the EU budget? Will an expanded membership require fundamental changes in EU economic and social cohesion policy and the CAP after 2013 (when a new financial perspective begins)? Will the Lisbon Treaty provide the EU with an institutional framework that enables it to avoid deadlock in decision making, and at the same time increase its transparency and democratic accountability? The EU is committed to further enlargements, but where should its borders end?

In order to address these questions, this chapter first provides some theoretical background. The main features of the 2004 and 2007 enlargements are described, also because these might provide insights into future enlargements. The present state of play of the enlargement process is then discussed before drawing conclusions about the future of the EU.

19.2 The theory of clubs

The EU enlargement process is frequently analysed using the economic theory of clubs.[1] Clubs are assumed to pursue a well-defined common interest. The problem is to determine the optimal number of members or size of the club, and this will entail defining the costs and benefits of increasing membership. For simplicity here it is assumed that clubs provide goods and services for their members, which are intermediate between private and public goods in that the clubs supply a product that is excludable (like a private good) but non-rival (as in the case of a public good). However, it is debatable how far each of the various common EU policies is non-rival (as for example the Common Fisheries Policy, see the Online Learning Centre of this book) or even in some cases excludable (for example, non-EU members have been able to share in the benefits of adopting common standards). It is probably more realistic to assume that the club supplies a semi-public or congestion good, with the marginal cost eventually increasing as the number of members rises.

The members of the club are assumed to be identical, so the marginal costs and marginal benefits of an additional member to existing members can be depicted in a single diagram as seen in Figure 19.1. If every member is different, a separate axis for the marginal costs and benefits of each member is necessary.

In the case of the EU, the benefits of membership include, for instance, the right to be a member of the EU and to participate in common policies such as the Single Market, economic and monetary union, economic and social cohesion and the CAP. Starting with a small number of members, in much of the literature the benefits to incumbents are assumed to rise initially as membership increases, but eventually decline as congestion grows (implying a decline in the benefits both to new and existing members), causing the marginal benefit curve to take the form shown in Figure 19.1.

For simplicity it is assumed that the total cost of providing these policies is fixed, that the members are identical, and costs are shared equally. As the number of members increases, each new member will bear a share of the total cost, but the share will gradually decrease as more members are added. The cost to existing members declines initially as membership increases, but in the literature is generally assumed eventually to rise. The increase in marginal costs is also the result of congestion and the greater difficulty of reaching agreement among more numerous members, and of sacrificing sovereignty.

The optimal number of members of the club M* occurs where the curves indicating marginal costs and marginal benefits to existing members (who are also responsible for deciding on the admission of new members) intersect. Changes in EU institutions and policies can be introduced to alter both the marginal costs and marginal benefits. For example, increased use of qualified majority voting could shift the marginal cost curve down (even though in practice consensus is usually used), so the optimal size of the club increases.

In practice the picture is more complex in that it is necessary to consider not only the costs and benefits at the time of enlargement, but also constellations of bargaining power and formal decision-making rules over time. These may enable a net loser at the time of enlargement to ensure a guarantee of compensation at a later stage from the winners (Schimmelfennig and Sedelmeier, 2005). What

---

[1] See Mueller (2003) for a discussion of this theory, which was initially elaborated by Buchanan (1965). For an application to EU enlargement see Gros and Steinherr (2004), De Benedictis and Padoan (1994), or Alesina and Spolaore (2003). For the latter authors, benefits may come from economies of scale and costs from increasing heterogeneity of preferences. Though the application of the theory is less developed, it is not without parallels to the theory of the optimal currency area discussed in Chapter 9.

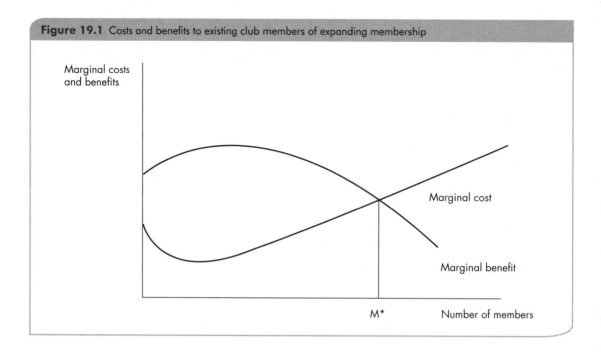

Figure 19.1 Costs and benefits to existing club members of expanding membership

then becomes more important in the accession negotiations is the voting power of the country in the European Council and Parliament (though the Council is decisive as the simple majority threshold in the Parliament on most questions is lower than that of the Council).

As applied to EU enlargement the theory of clubs raises interesting questions, but is difficult to apply in practice. For instance, it suggests that the net advantages of membership are greatest for the early members of the Community, but fell as more members were added. The framework can also be used to illustrate how reforms in areas such as EU decision making, the CAP or the EU budget could be used to shift the marginal cost and benefit curves, and increase the optimal size of EU membership. However, it is difficult to identify the various costs and benefits as a result of EU enlargement, or to give weights to them, and the shape and position of the marginal cost and benefit curves are not known with any precision. The members and potential members are clearly not identical, so separate analyses would have to be carried out for individual member states and potential candidates.

19.3   A brief chronology of the enlargement process

Before dealing with the main aspects of enlargement in more detail, it is useful to provide a brief chronology of the main steps in the process (see also the Online Learning Centre of this book for a list of key events).

As soon as the central planning system collapsed in 1989, many of the smaller CEECs were anxious for tighter links with, or membership of, the European Community. The Community responded with a series of trade and aid measures, but a strategy with regard to enlargement emerged only gradually.

It was as late as 1993 that the Copenhagen European Council set out the conditions applicant countries have to fulfil in order to join the EU. The 1994 Essen Summit established a 'pre-accession strategy' to help prepare the candidate countries for eventual membership. As described below, this entailed the PHARE programme of assistance (Poland and Hungary Assistance for the Restructuring of the Economy), the Europe or Association Agreements and a 'structured dialogue', bringing

together the EU and candidate countries to discuss questions of common interest. The Madrid European Council of 1995 stipulated that the candidate country must be able to put EU rules and procedures into place.

On the basis of the accession criteria, in July 1997 the EC Commission published opinions on the readiness of the applicant countries to join the EU. These opinions were included in the document *Agenda 2000* (European Commission, 2007e), which represents a milestone in the enlargement process. *Agenda 2000* analysed the steps necessary to prepare both the EU and accession countries for enlargement and set out the Commission's proposals for the 2000–06 financial perspective.

Following the decision of the Luxembourg European Council in December 1997, accession negotiations started with Cyprus and with five of the ten Central and East European countries in March 1998.[2] Each year the EC published Regular Reports on the progress made by applicant countries in preparing for EU membership. At the 1999 Helsinki European Summit it was decided to extend negotiations to a further six countries.[3] Malta's application lapsed in 1996 but was resumed in 1998, and Malta was included in the Helsinki group.

Turkey applied for EU membership in 1987. In December 1997 it was decided to establish the European Conference that would entail an annual meeting of the EU member states and the *'European states aspiring to accede to it and sharing its values and internal and external objectives'*.[4] The aim was to reassure those countries not included in the first wave of negotiations and, in particular, Turkey. However, Turkey was offended by the fact that it had been overtaken by so many countries in the accession queue, and refused to attend the first two meetings of the European Conference. At the Helsinki Summit of 1999 Turkey was declared a candidate, and Turkey began to participate in a reinforced pre-accession strategy similar to that of the other candidate countries.

At the Berlin European Council of March 1999 agreement was reached on the Agenda 2000 package, including the financial perspective for the 2000–06 period and reform of the CAP and Structural Funds.[5] Following the disappointing results of the Amsterdam and Nice treaties, the Lisbon Treaty entails further reforms of EU decision making, also with a view to enlargement.

In May 2004 ten new countries joined the EU, with the date being chosen so they could participate in the elections to the European Parliament of June 2004. In a referendum on 24 April the Greek Cypriots voted against a UN proposal for settlement and, as a result, in May 2004 only the Greek Cypriot part of the island joined the EU. Bulgaria and Romania became members in 2007.

In 2005 the EU began negotiations for membership with Croatia and Turkey (see Table 19.1), and the Former Yugoslav Republic of Macedonia was declared a candidate country. Iceland applied for membership in July 2009 and began negotiations in June 2010, and Montenegro achieved the status of candidate country in December 2010, but a date was not fixed for beginning negotiations.

Albania, Bosnia and Herzegovina, Kosovo and Serbia are all considered potential candidate countries.

---

[2] The Czech Republic, Estonia, Hungary, Poland and Slovenia. See Senior Nello and Smith (1998) for a discussion of this process.

[3] Bulgaria, Latvia, Lithuania, Romania, Slovakia and Malta.

[4] Conclusions of the European Council, Luxembourg, December 1997, where the decision to establish the European Conference was taken.

[5] The financial package for the new member states was subsequently amended at the 2002 Copenhagen European Council (see Chapter 12).

Table 19.1　Basic data on the candidate and potential candidate countries, 2009

	Population (millions)	Exports to EU(27) as % of total exports	Imports from EU(27) as % total imports	GDP (€ billion)
FYR Macedonia	2.0[a]	75	57	6.7
Turkey	71.5[a]	41	46	440.5
Croatia	4.4[a]	64	65	48.5
Albania	3.2	87	73	8.8
Bosnia and Herzegovina	3.9	72	67	12.2
Montenegro	0.6	56[c]	33[c]	3.0
Serbia	7.4	54	54	30.8
Kosovo	2.2[b]	29[b]	30[b]	3.4[b]
Iceland	0.3[a]	78	52	8.7
EU(27)	501.1	67	64	11,787

[a]2010.

[b]2007.

[c]Istituto nazionale per il commercio estero, Belgrade office, 2008 data, www.ice.it/paesi/europa/serbia/upload/094/CongiunturaMontenegro2009.pdf

Source: Elaborations on the basis of Eurostat and European Commission Trade data, http://trade.ec.europa.eu/doclib/docs (accessed 1 March 2011), © European Union, 2011.

19.4　Trade and aid arrangements between the EU and CEECS before enlargement

The 'first-generation' Trade and Co-operation Agreements

After a long history of stormy relations between the European Community and the Eastern integration bloc, the CMEA (Council for Mutual Economic Assistance), in June 1988 a Joint Declaration of Mutual Recognition was signed.[6] This opened the way for tighter links between the Community and individual CEECs.

In September 1988 Hungary signed a Trade and Co-operation Agreement with the Community, and similar 'first-generation agreements' with the other CEECs and the USSR soon followed. The agreements related to trade and to commercial and economic co-operation. The first-generation agreements were soon overtaken by events, but remain important as a milestone in EC–CEEC relations.

---

[6] Also known as the Comecon, the CMEA was founded in 1949 and formally dissolved in 1991. It was composed of the USSR, Bulgaria, Czechoslovakia, East Germany, Hungary, Poland, Romania, Cuba, Mongolia and Vietnam. Angola, Ethiopia, Laos and North Korea had observer status, while Yugoslavia participated only with regard to certain sectors. For a more detailed account of EC–CMEA relations up to 1988 and a description of the CMEA and its activities, see Senior Nello (1991).

Aid measures for the CEECs prior to accession

The question of whether to aid transition was decided in July 1989 when, encouraged by President Bush, the Commission chaired a meeting of the then 24 OECD countries (the G24) to seek ways of facilitating the process of moving towards democracy and market-orientated economies. Also involved in the programme were the EIB (European Investment Bank), the World Bank and the International Monetary Fund (IMF).

The main argument advanced in favour of giving aid to the CEECs and former Soviet republics was Western self-interest. Despite the low levels of East–West trade at the end of the 1980s, and the difficulties of transition, the CMEA countries represented a potential market of some 450 million consumers. For several generations, the objective of ensuring Western security vis-à-vis the Eastern bloc had entailed huge defence budgets, and now a different type of effort was needed to further peace and prosperity. If transition failed, the West could risk experiencing external costs in the form of migratory pressures and spillover of ethnic and nationalistic tensions.

The term 'PHARE' (Poland and Hungary Assistance for the Restructuring of the Economy) was adopted for the Community's programme, though this soon became something of a misnomer as aid was extended to the other CEECs. After a heated debate on possible political and economic consequences, assistance was also extended to the Soviet Union and, subsequently, to former Soviet republics through the TACIS programme (Technical Assistance for the Commonwealth of Independent States).

The PHARE programme came into operation from 1990 and was initially demand driven and based on the requests of the recipient countries. The measures included: food aid to Poland, Romania, Bulgaria and the USSR; agricultural assistance; training and human resources; energy and the environment; improved market access; assistance for privatization and restructuring (for small and medium enterprises, the financial system, technical assistance, investment guarantees and so on); and medical aid. In addition, loans were granted for stabilization and to cover balance of payments difficulties, and debt relief was extended to countries such as Poland and Bulgaria.

The European Bank for Reconstruction and Development (EBRD) was established in 1991 to encourage investment in transition countries and reduce financial risks. From 1993 PHARE became more concerned with preparing CEECs for accession. Increasingly, PHARE used the procedures of the Structural Funds in order to familiarize the CEECs so they could use the Structural Funds more efficiently upon accession.

One of the main mechanisms used in the task of institution building was 'twinning'. Twinning brings administrations and semi-public organizations in the EU and candidate countries together to work on common projects related to the *acquis*. Typically, twinning involves secondment of civil servants from the EU member states working on EU policies to a candidate country for a period of time.

The 1999 Berlin Council established the three pre-accession instruments for the 2000–06 period to help prepare the candidate countries for membership:

- PHARE, which had an allocation of €1.56 billion per year, 30 per cent of which was earmarked for institution building, 35 per cent for the regulatory infrastructure required for implementation of the *acquis*, and 35 per cent for economic and social cohesion.
- ISPA (Instrument for Structural Policies Pre-Accession), which was allocated €1.04 billion per year for assistance for the environment and transport infrastructure.
- SAPARD (Special Accession Programme for Agriculture and Regional Development), which received an allocation of €0.52 billion per year. Measures included improving quality, applying veterinary and plant controls, setting up producer groups and creating land registers.

There was much debate about whether Western assistance to the transition countries could be construed as a new Marshall Plan. However, there were substantial differences from the Marshall Plan:[7]

- Post-war reconstruction is very different from transition.
- Most of Marshall Aid came from one donor, so the co-ordination problems were fewer.
- The scale of financing, and the share of grants (80 per cent compared with 15 per cent, according to Mayhew (1998) were higher under the Marshall Plan.

---

[7] As reported in Mayhew (1998).

According to some observers,[8] the financial assistance under the Marshall Plan was probably less important than the conditionality imposed. In order to receive aid West European countries were encouraged to opt for market economies, liberalized trade and regional co-operation.

Western measures to assist the transition process were also conditional. For instance, PHARE aid to Romania was suspended on human rights grounds in 1990 and was not extended to Albania until 1991. However, as a substantial literature demonstrates, it is the prospect of EU membership that ultimately renders the conditionality effective.[9]

Regional co-operation was also a condition of EU assistance, and this was a major factor leading to the creation of arrangements such as the Central European Free Trade Area (CEFTA) in 1992,[10] the South East European Cooperation Process (SEECP) of 1996 and the Stability Pact for Southeast Europe of 1999, which later became the Regional Cooperation Council (RCC) and was transferred to Sarajevo.[11] However, a major shortcoming of these initiatives among transition countries was that they were generally more interested in co-operation with the EU than with each other.

Given the size and number of post-communist economies and the cost of transition, it was inevitable that the role played by external financial assistance would be relatively modest.[12] Much aid was in the form of loans, and much consisted of export credits, which also benefit Western firms. However, occasionally aid may arrive at a crucial, vulnerable time. The policy advice and training given was often criticized as being contradictory, inconsistent and not always tailored to the needs of the recipient country. Another complaint was that the main beneficiaries were often Western consultants. There was also criticism of the insufficient co-ordination and excessive bureaucracy in giving aid. With the benefit of hindsight, trade liberalization, FDI and the prospect of EU membership were probably more important catalysts in encouraging transition.

19.5 The 'second-generation' Europe Agreements

Between 1991 and 1996 the EU signed second-generation 'Europe Agreements' with ten CEECs deemed to have made sufficient progress in economic and political transition (these were the same ten as were subsequently the first to start accession negotiations).[13] The Europe Agreements were the basic legal instruments covering the relationship between the EU and the CEEC(10).[14] The Agreements covered trade-related issues, political dialogue, legal approximation, 'phased introduction' of the four freedoms (though the EU failed to grant any access to workers beyond what was guaranteed by its member states), and co-operation in other areas, including industry, environment, transport and customs (Mayhew, 1998).

The Europe Agreements created a free trade area between the EU and associated CEECs. Because the CEEC partners needed more time to become competitive, the tariff cuts were asymmetric, with

---

[8] De Long and Eichengreen (1993).

[9] See, for example, Smith (2001, 2003), Vachudova (2001) and Grabbe (2002).

[10] CEFTA was composed of the Czech Republic, Hungary, Poland and Slovakia; Bulgaria, Romania and Slovenia joined subsequently.

[11] The SEECP was composed of Albania, Bosnia and Herzegovina, Bulgaria, FYR Macedonia, Moldova, Hungary, Romania and Turkey, with Croatia as an observer. The Regional Co-operation Council consists of the members of the SEECP, Kosovo, the EU as well as donor countries, international organizations and international financial institutions engaged in regional co-operation in South-East Europe.

[12] However, the EU and international financial institutions (IFIs) played an important role in attracting additional financing from official sources, including debt relief through the Paris Club. They were rather less successful in attracting complementary private financing or private (London Club) debt relief.

[13] From 1992 negotiation began leading to the signing of less far-reaching 'trade and partnership' agreements with various former Soviet republics, including Russia, Belarus, Ukraine, Kazakhstan, Georgia and Kyrgyzstan.

[14] See Senior Nello (1991) for a more detailed description of these agreements.

the EU proceeding more rapidly. The removal of tariffs on certain sensitive sectors such as steel, and textiles and clothing was to be phased over several years, but by 1998 most restrictions on industrial products had been removed.[15] The concessions granted on agricultural trade were less favourable than in other sectors, and it was only in 2003 that agricultural trade with the new member states was liberalized for products meeting EU standards.

As a result of the provisions of the Europe Agreements, a free trade area was in place before enlargement. For the CEECs, joining the EU meant moving from a free trade area to a customs union (by adopting the Common Commercial Policy with its 'hierarchy' of trade preferences) and the Single Market.[16]

What is significant about the level of trade between the EU and CEECs is the speed of its reorientation from Eastern to Western markets, also thanks to the Europe Agreements.[17] By 2004 the EU accounted for 73 per cent of the trade of the new member states (rising to 76 per cent in 2007), a share similar to the old member states (European Commission, 2009e). Trade between the EU(15) and new member states tripled from around €150 billion to €450 billion in the decade to 2008 (European Commission, 2010p).

EU tariffs towards the rest of the world were also generally lower than those of the acceding countries, so it was widely believed that there would be little trade diversion (see Chapter 5). After enlargement, trade of the new member states with the rest of the world continued to expand, confirming the view that trade diversion was limited (European Commission, 2009e).

For many years the most dynamic part of FDI flows within the EU was between the EU(15) and the new member states (NMS). In 2006, FDI inflows from the old to the new member states amounted to €37 billion and represented 27 per cent of capital formation in the NMS (European Commission, 2009e). The NMS were able to attract FDI due to their geographical location and cost advantages, but also for reasons of market access. However, as a result of the economic crisis, FDI to the NMS halved in 2009, shrinking back to the 2005 level. FDI outflows from the NMS proved more resilient to the crisis than the inflows to these countries (also because of capital repatriation), falling by only a quarter in 2009. As a result overall outward FDI of the NMS was equivalent to 31 per cent of inward FDI in 2009 compared with 22 per cent in 2008.[18]

Many studies emphasize the overall positive impact of FDI and outward processing trade (or the international fragmentation of the production process) in the enlargement process.[19] Benefits include the stimulation of investment, exports and employment, as well as knowledge spillovers, better organization, competition, and improved quality and variety of products. FDI was also considered to offer opportunities to the EU(15) to increase global competitiveness by exploiting complementarities.

With regard to the costs to the EU(15) because of relocation of industry, the literature finds that results differ according to sector. For example, European Commission (2009e) finds that employment in the old member states is negatively correlated with the rise in employment as a result of FDI in some sectors (food, clothing, publishing, communication equipment, office machinery and vehicles), while the reverse is true for other sectors (machinery, furniture, medical instruments, chemicals and tobacco). With the economic crisis, fears of negative correlation have grown in the EU(15), while certain new member states have expressed concern at vulnerability because some sectors such as banking are so extensively foreign owned.

---

[15] See Mayhew (1998) or Senior Nello (2002) for descriptions of the timing of trade liberalization for various groups of products.

[16] In contrast, many empirical studies of integration effects are based on the assumption of a move from free trade to a customs union (see Chapter 5).

[17] See Senior Nello (2002) for a discussion of this issue.

[18] The data here are taken from EurActiv, www.euractiv.com/en/financial-services/new-eu-members-hit-by-fdi-outflow-analysis-495038 (accessed 6 July 2010).

[19] See European Commission (2009e) for a review of these studies.

19.6 The Copenhagen criteria

In 1993 the Copenhagen European Council agreed that *'accession will take place as soon as the applicant country is able to assume the obligations of membership by satisfying the economic and political conditions required'*. The conditions were first drawn up for the CEEC countries, but were subsequently extended to apply to all candidate countries and entail the following:

- The applicant state must have a functioning market economy with the capacity to cope with competitive pressures and market forces within the EU.
- The applicant state must have achieved stability of institutions, guaranteeing democracy, the rule of law, human rights and respect for and protection of minorities.
- The applicant state must be able to take on the obligations of membership, including adherence to the aims of political, and economic and monetary union.

At the Copenhagen Summit it was also stipulated that enlargement is subject to the condition that the EU is able to absorb new members and maintain the momentum of integration. The 1995 Madrid European Council also required the candidate countries to adopt adequate administrative and judicial capacity to put EU rules and procedures into effect.

The criteria are generally divided into political criteria, economic criteria, and ability to take on the *acquis communautaire* and to establish the administrative and judicial capacity to ensure its effective implementation.

There are three political criteria:

- Stability of institutions guaranteeing democracy, the rule of law, human rights and respect for and protection of minorities.
- Adherence to the objective of political union.
- Maintaining the momentum of integration.

The economic criteria are similarly divided into three:

- The existence of a functioning market economy.
- Capacity to cope with competitive pressures and market forces within the EU.
- Adherence to the aim of economic and monetary union.

The accession criteria are presumably intended to provide some kind of objective basis for selecting countries ready to join the EU, as well as indicating to the applicant countries the tasks they are expected to perform. The introduction of the Copenhagen criteria would therefore seem aimed at replicating the experience of the Maastricht criteria but in a different field, that of enlargement.

However, although there is a certain flexibility and political leeway in deciding whether the Maastricht criteria have been met, this is far more the case for the accession criteria. This arises from the number of criteria and, at times, from the vague and imprecise nature of the concepts involved. This is the case, for instance, in deciding whether a country has a 'a functioning market economy' or the 'capacity to cope with competitive pressures'. There are different models of market economies, and no indication is given as to which model is appropriate, or how to assess when an economy has 'arrived'. In deciding whether a country is ready to cope with competitive pressures in an enlarged EU, a detailed analysis of its economy is necessary, together with predictions about which sectors will be able to cope in the internal EU market.

For other criteria, such as the obligation to take on the aim of political union, or the requirement that the momentum of integration can be maintained (which presumably requires some form of enhanced co-operation or flexibility, see Chapter 3), the objectives in question were far from being clearly defined.

The simple rule 'when a country meets the accession criteria, it can join the EU' is misleading given the degree of discretion in deciding whether the accession criteria have been met. In the end, choice of who joins when becomes a political issue.

Although at the time of the Copenhagen European Council no indication was given with regard to the weights of the different criteria, subsequently the European Commission indicated that predominance was to be given to the political criteria, so a country must fulfil these before joining and must be making substantial progress towards meeting the economic criteria. *Agenda 2000* (European Commission (1997e: 40) stresses that '*the effective functioning of democracy is a primordial question in assessing the application of a country for membership of the Union*'.

Political criteria were introduced into the Amsterdam Treaty and taken up as Article 2 (TEU) of the Lisbon Treaty, which states: '*the Union is founded on the values of respect for human dignity, freedom, democracy, equality, the rule of law and respect for human rights, including the rights of persons belonging to minorities*'. According to Article 49 (TEU), any country that respects these values and is committed to promoting them may apply to become a member of the Union. It is mainly on the basis of the political criteria (including treatment of minorities) that the European Commission continues to express misgivings about Turkey (see below).

The EU has repeatedly emphasized the need for regional co-operation and good neighbourly relations before accession (though this was unhappily forgotten in the case of Cyprus, see below), and has stressed that this is also a condition for the former Yugoslav republics of South-Eastern Europe.

Partly as a result of the experience of the 2007 enlargement, greater emphasis is now placed on the need to combat crime and corruption in the candidate countries. A Special Co-operation and Verification Mechanism had to be set up in Bulgaria and Romania to assist in reform of the judiciary and the fight against crime and corruption after accession.

19.7 The pre-accession strategy

The Essen European Council of 1994 set out a pre-accession strategy to help the candidate countries prepare for EU membership, and an enhanced pre-accession strategy was launched from 1998. In addition to the Europe Agreements and pre-accession assistance (through PHARE, ISPA and SAPARD), the enhanced strategy included Accession Partnerships and National Programmes for the Adoption of the *Acquis* (NPAAs), the opening of Community programmes and agencies, and a review procedure.

The Accession Partnerships set out the main priorities for each of the candidate countries in preparing for EU membership and provided a single framework for co-ordinating the various forms of EU assistance. Each of the candidate countries drew up an NPAA that indicated in detail how the country aimed to meet the priorities of the Accession Partnership. The Commission also prepared Action Plans with the negotiating countries to reinforce their administrative and judicial capacity.

The opening of EU programmes and agencies was aimed at promoting co-operation between the member states and applicant countries in areas such as public health, the environment, energy, research, small and medium enterprises, culture, vocational training, and support for student and youth exchanges. In this way it was hoped that the new member states could be familiarized with the way in which EU policies and instruments are put into practice.

Following the opinions on the applications of the candidate countries for accession, each year, in order to assess progress in preparing for membership, the Commission submitted Regular Reports to the Council. Progress Reports continue to be published for the present candidate countries (usually in October or November), but are now generally incorporated into a composite Enlargement Strategy Paper (see, for example, European Commission, 2010p). While useful as a source of information, often the style of these publications is not far removed from school reports, though the comments 'could try harder', or 'could do better' were usually expressed in slightly more diplomatic terms.

19.8 The accession negotiations

A first step in preparing for the accession negotiations is the 'screening' of the *acquis*. In the case of the CEECs, screening began in March 1998 with all the candidate countries, whether negotiations had been opened or not. The purpose of the exercise is to identify issues likely to arise in the negotiations. It consists of a detailed presentation by Commission experts on the application of all the chapters of the *acquis* to the candidate countries. At the time of the screening of the CEECs the *acquis* consisted of 31 chapters, but it has subsequently been reorganized and the number of chapters has been increased to 35 (see Table 19.2). Though the Commission stressed that political criteria remained primordial, in the case of the CEECs the screening of the candidate countries to assess their progress in taking on the 'obligations of membership' encouraged a shift of emphasis away from the other Copenhagen criteria. The speed and progress of accession negotiations appeared to depend heavily on the ability of a country to adopt the *acquis* and its administrative and judicial capacity to implement the *acquis*.

Table 19.2 Chapters of the *acquis*

1. Free movement of goods	19. Social policy and employment
2. Freedom of movement for workers	20. Enterprise and industrial policy
3. Right of establishment and freedom to provide services	21. Trans-European networks
4. Free movement of capital	22. Regional policy and co-ordination of structural instruments
5. Public procurement	23. Judiciary and fundamental rights
6. Company law	24. Justice, freedom and security
7. Intellectual property law	25. Science and research
8. Competition policy	26. Education and training
9. Financial services	27. Environment
10. Information services and the media	28. Consumer and health protection
11. Agriculture and rural development	29. Customs union
12. Food safety, veterinary and phytosanitary policy	30. External relations
13. Fisheries	31. Foreign and security and defence policy
14. Transport policy	32. Financial control
15. Energy	33. Financial and budgetary provisions
16. Taxation	34. Institutions
17. Economic and monetary union	35. Other
18. Statistics	

Following the screening process, negotiations were opened with the candidate countries, chapter by chapter. A chapter was considered 'provisionally closed' with a candidate country when the EU considered that further negotiation was not required on the chapter, and the candidate concerned accepted the EU common position. The EU reserved the right to return to the chapter at a later stage during the negotiation if new *acquis* were adopted, or if the candidate country concerned failed to implement the commitments it had taken on the chapter. As a result, though chapters could be 'provisionally closed', the Commission's negotiating stance was based on the principle that 'nothing is agreed until everything is agreed' and that a final overall compromise deal was necessary to conclude negotiations.

For the areas linked to the functioning of the Single Market, according to the Commission, any transition periods were to be few and short (though there were exceptions to this general rule, for instance the derogation on movement of people requested by existing member states). For areas where considerable adaptations were necessary, and which required substantial effort (including large monetary outlays) such as the environment, energy and infrastructure, transition periods involving 'temporary derogations' were granted, but in some areas (nuclear safety, the fight against crime) the new members were expected to go 'beyond the *acquis*'.

The new member states criticized the Commission's attitude to the adoption of the *acquis* on a number of counts:

- The asymmetry of treatment compared with existing EU members (for example, the Nice Treaty did not require respect for minorities, whereas the Copenhagen criteria do, though this difference was rectified with the Lisbon Treaty).
- The CEECs were given little opportunity to voice objections to the conditions, and their preferences seemed to be marginalized at times (whereas the EU(15) have on occasion challenged the overriding nature of the *acquis*, see Chapter 1).
- Taking on the *acquis* does not always further transition.
- The *acquis* is constantly evolving.
- The insistence on taking on all the *acquis* might divert attention from the need for a hierarchy of priorities.

19.9 Extending EU policies to the new member states

As explained in the relevant chapters, the EU enlargements of 2004 and 2007 posed particular challenges for the EU budget, economic and social cohesion, the CAP, EMU and labour movement.

Despite the recognition that enlargement would require additional transfers from the EU budget, the main contributors to the budget (and Germany, in particular, after having to meet the bill for German unification) were reluctant to raise the ceiling of the financial perspective, which was fixed at 1.05 per cent of GNI for the 2007–13 period. As explained in Chapter 12, the main casualty of this financial stringency was the Lisbon Agenda (and subsequently Europe 2020). Although the new member states have been growing faster than the EU(15) since the mid-1990s (see also Chapter 15), Table 19.3 (see also Table 2.5 in Chapter 2) shows that in the new member states the per capita income in terms of purchasing power standards (PPS) remains well below the EU(27) average. Following enlargement, the gap between the most and the least prosperous member states widened. The average GDP per capita was reduced with the increase in the number of member states from 15 to 27. As a result, if the criterion (GDP less than 75 per cent of the EU average) for Objective 1 had remained unchanged, some regions that previously qualified for Objective 1 status would no longer do so in an enlarged EU. This was the case for four regions in Eastern Germany, four in the UK, four in Spain, and one each in Greece, Italy and Portugal. It is estimated that some 19 million people in the EU(15) lived in such regions. Certain of the EU(15) member states were concerned about a reduction in their transfers for economic and social cohesion as a result of this 'statistical effect' of enlargement. To meet these fears a phasing-out system (see Chapter 15) was therefore adopted for regions that would have been eligible for funding if the threshold had been calculated for EU(15) rather than EU(27).

Table 19.3 Selected economic indicators for the enlarged EU

	EU(27)	New member states
Population (millions) Jan. 2010	501.1	103.3
Average % change in population 2000–2007	0.4	−0.3
GDP current €billion 2010	12,284	947
GDP per capita in € 2007	24,810	8,330
GDP in PPS % average change 2000–07	2.5	6.2
Real GDP % average change 2000-07	2.1	4.7
Agricultural employment (AWU[a] '000) 2009	11,223	5,799
Agricultural employment % fall 2009/2000	−24.9	−31.2

[a]*Annual work unit (AWU), which is the equivalent of a full-time worker engaged in agricultural activities over an entire year.*

Source: *Eurostat and European Commission (2009e),© European Union, 2011.*

The new member states were allocated 50.5 per cent of total spending on economic and social cohesion for the 2007–13 period. This represents a substantial increase both compared with the pre-accession assistance and the temporary arrangements for the 2004–06 period reflecting the fact that in deciding the financial allocation for 2007–13, ten of the new member states had voting power in the Council of Ministers. As explained in Chapter 12, Kandogan (2000, 2005a) finds a distinct positive relation between the per capita vote shares of EU member states in the Council and their share in expenditure from the EU budget.

Agriculture frequently threatened to prove a stumbling block in the enlargement process. Agriculture continues to play an important role in many of the CEECs, both in terms of share in employment and contribution to GDP (see Table 19.3 and Chapter 13). At the same time, the CAP continues to absorb just under half of the EU budget, while food and agricultural measures account for roughly half the *acquis communautaire*. The new member states had the complex task of adapting to EU policies and standards, while the EU(15) wanted to ensure that enlargement did not result in excessive transfers from the EU budget.

As described in Chapter 13, the 1992, 1999, 2003 and 2008 reforms of the CAP entailed cuts in support prices for some of the main EU products. The impact of these price cuts for farmers in the EU(15) was (more or less, see Chapter 13) offset by direct payments. As explained in Chapter 13, the European Commission maintained that full, immediate payment of direct income support in the CEECs would have inequitable income effects. The solution was to phase in direct payments gradually so that full application of the system would not take place until 2013. Even partial payments of EU direct income support has led to substantial increases in farm incomes in some of these countries (by 47 per cent on average by 2007 compared with the period before accession according to European Commission (2010e)). As explained in Chapter 13, derogations on foreign land ownership were also allowed as land prices were lower in many CEEC countries.

Even without participating fully in the third stage of EMU, all EU member states have to adopt the relevant *acquis*, which includes respect of the Stability and Growth Pact; treatment of the exchange rate and of other economic policies as a matter of 'common concern'; liberalization of capital movements; and independence of the central bank.

The Maastricht criterion on exchange rates entails that a country should remain within the 'normal' band of the exchange rate mechanism (ERM II) without tension and without initiating depreciation for two years. For the new member states, this meant that full participation in the third stage of EMU had to wait for two years after joining the EU since they were not allowed to join the ERM II before they become EU members. Slovenia adopted the euro in 2007 and Cyprus and Malta joined in 2008, Slovakia in 2009 and Estonia in 2011.

There was some doubt about further enlargement of the eurozone with the economic crisis, in particular as the GDP of Estonia had fallen by over 14 per cent in 2009.[20] However, Estonia met all the Maastricht criteria and had a public debt of only 7.2 per cent of GDP in 2010. It was felt that rejection of Estonia would create a damaging precedent and send a negative signal to other CEEC countries. With the economic crisis the Czech Republic, Hungary and Poland were able to use depreciation to maintain competitiveness, and postponed the likely date for joining the euro (also because of the negative situation of public finances in Hungary). Latvia, Hungary and Romania were able to reach agreements with the IMF quickly (unlike Greece). However, as small open economies, Lithuania and Latvia remain in favour of joining the euro as soon as possible. Lithuania and Bulgaria have currency boards, and Latvia has a similar arrangement pegged to the euro, so all three have had to adjust prices and wages to maintain competitiveness. As a member of the eurozone heavily reliant on exports, Slovakia's GDP fell by 4.8 per cent in 2009, but the cost of borrowing on international markets was cheaper than for the Czech Republic, and though wages were higher than in Poland or Hungary, they were still lower than those in Western Europe.

As explained in Chapter 8, although labour movement from the new member states was predicted to be on a manageable scale (see European Integration Consortium, 2009), after the 2004 and 2007 enlargements the EU applied transition periods of two plus three years, renewable for a further two on workers coming from the new CEEC member states. During this time the EU member states could continue to apply their differing policies with regard to access to their labour markets for workers from the CEEC member states.

There have at times been tensions between 'old' and 'new' member states, as, for instance, over the Service Directive and that on posted workers (see Chapter 6), the derogations for labour movement (see Chapter 8), the interpretation of the Maastricht inflation criterion for Lithuania in 2007 (Chapter 10), and the bargaining tactics over the Lisbon Treaty of the Polish government (Chapter 3).

19.10 EU policy towards the Western Balkans

The EU generally uses the term 'Western Balkans' to refer to Croatia, Montenegro, and FYR Macedonia (which are candidates for EU accession), and other countries with potential candidate status: Albania, Bosnia and Herzegovina, Kosovo, and Serbia. South-Eastern Europe (SEE) is generally taken to refer to the Western Balkan countries and the two EU member states Bulgaria and Romania.

The poor long-term economic performance of the Western Balkans has been compounded by the series of wars that resulted from the disintegration of Yugoslavia. The instability in the Western Balkans also imposed costs on the EU in terms of military intervention, migration, trade disruption, ecological damage and the need for humanitarian and other aid. Between 1991 and 1999 EU assistance (including EBRD measures) to the five Western Balkan countries amounted to €8.2 billion, of which roughly half was humanitarian aid (Uvalic, 2002, 2010). In 2009, €1.5 billion of EU funds was committed, with priority to state building, good governance, rule of law and civil society (European Commission, 2010p).

Initially the EU underestimated the political problems arising from the collapse of Yugoslavia and failed to develop a long-term strategy towards the area, relying instead on ad hoc measures and 'day after' actions. It was only after the Dayton Peace Agreement of 1995 that the EU began to evolve a regional approach to SEE. In 1995 the EU launched the Royaumont Process aimed at

---

[20] The statistics in this paragraph are taken from Eurostat.

promoting stability and good neighbourly relations in SEE. In 1996 the Regional Approach of the EU was introduced, but it was not well defined, had limited financial resources, arrived late, and failed to offer the SEE countries any incentive for compliance.

In 1999 the EU attempted to bring an end to its crisis-by-crisis approach by introducing the Stability Pact, which aimed at fostering peace, democracy, human rights and economic prosperity as a means of bringing stability to the region. Importantly, the EU attempted to reinforce its leverage in SEE by offering the prospect of eventual EU membership. The EU insisted that its approach would be differentiated according to the compliance of a country to the relevant conditions, including increased emphasis on regional co-operation.[21] Central to the approach was the Stabilisation and Association Process (SAP) which offered eligible Western Balkan countries the possibility of signing Stabilisation and Association Agreements (SAAs).

In 2003 the 'Thessaloniki Approach' was agreed, which entailed extending some of the more successful instruments of the pre-accession process to the SEE countries. In particular, European Partnerships were introduced to set out the short- and medium-term priorities these countries need to address. Over time it was expected that these Partnerships would be increasingly geared to the task of taking on the *acquis*, and when countries gain candidate status they would be replaced with Accession Partnerships. The European Commission publishes an annual Enlargement Strategy paper, which also monitors progress in these countries.

EU assistance to the Western Balkans was provided mainly through the CARDS (Community Assistance for Reconstruction, Development and Stabilisation) Programme over the 2000–06 period, and about €5 billion was earmarked for this purpose. From 2007 all pre-accession support was unified into a single instrument, the IPA or Instrument for Pre-Accession Assistance (see Table 19.4). This covers both the candidate countries and countries with potential candidate status. The IPA covers: transition assistance and institution building; cross-border co-operation; regional development; human resources development and rural development.

Table 19.4 EU financial assistance under the Instrument for Pre-Accession Assistance (IPA) for potential candidate countries (€ million)

	2007	2008	2009	2010	2011	**2007–11**
Albania	61.0	70.7	81.2	93.2	95.0	**401.1**
Bosnia and Herzegovina	62.1	74.8	89.1	106.0	108.1	**440.1**
Serbia	189.7	190.9	194.8	198.7	202.7	**976.8**
Kosovo	68.3	124.7	66.1	67.3	68.7	**395.1**
Total	**412.5**	**493.7**	**464.5**	**499.2**	**509.2**	**2,379.1**

Source: European Commission DG Enlargement, www.ec.europa.eu/enlargement (accessed 27 January 2011), © European Union, 2011.

At times, bilateral differences, including those over the status of Kosovo (see below), placed strains on the operation of the Stabilisation and Association Process. By mid-2008 all Western Balkans countries had signed SAA agreements with the EU, but in some cases there were delays before

[21] Regional co-operation has led to the creation of the Regional Cooperation Council, based in Sarajevo, the Transport Observatory in Belgrade, the Sava River Commission in Zagreb, and the Regional Centre of the Migration, Asylum, and Refugees Regional Initiative, in Skopje. Other initiatives include the Black Sea Economic Cooperation (BSEC), including Russia and Turkey, the Adriatic–Ionian Initiative (AII) with the participation of all seven countries bordering these seas, and the South East European Cooperation Process (SEECP).

implementation. As emerges from the discussion here, individual countries are at different stages of the integration process.

So-called 'White Schengen' Agreements permitting visits to the Schengen area without short-term visas were signed with the FYR Macedonia, Montenegro and Serbia in 2009, and with Albania and Bosnia and Herzegovina in 2010.

Turning to individual countries, **Albania** signed an SAA with the EU in 2006, which entered into force in 2009. In 2009 Albania applied for EU membership. In November 2010 the Commission published an opinion (see European Commission, 2010p), which echoed criticisms made in earlier Progress Reports and called on Albania to make 'further efforts' to meet the Copenhagen criteria. Despite acknowledging some improvements, the opinion maintained that the effectiveness and stability of democratic institutions had not been sufficiently achieved; reforms establishing the rule of law were incomplete; the fight against corruption and organized crime had to be intensified; and concrete steps were needed to ensure greater protection of human rights. With regard to the economic criteria the opinion called for further efforts to reinforce governance and the rule of law; improve the functioning of the labour market; ensure the recognition of property rights; and strengthen physical infrastructure (in particular for energy) and human capital.

In 1995 the Dayton Peace Agreement brought an end to the 1992–95 war in **Bosnia and Herzegovina**. The Agreement created two entities within the state of Bosnia and Herzegovina: the Bosniak/Croat Federation of Bosnia and Herzegovina, and the Bosnian Serb-led Republica Srpska. In accordance with the Dayton Peace Agreement, a UN-mandated office of the High Representative, who was also EU Special Representative, was created in order to restore peace in Bosnia and oversee implementation of civilian aspects of the Agreement. According to the EU, the authorities of Bosnia and Herzegovina have not demonstrated the capacity to take responsibility from the Office of the High Representative so its closure has been postponed. The EU is unable to accept an application by Bosnia and Herzegovina for EU membership as long this Office remains. The EU also provides aid and a peacekeeping force. An SAA with Bosnia and Herzegovina was signed in 2008, when an Interim Agreement on Trade and Trade-related Matters came into effect.

Successive Progress Reports stress: the lack of consensus and of a shared view of political leaders on the main features of state building; limited progress in creating democratic institutions; ethnic tensions; corruption; the need for further progress in creating a market economy and single economic space; and deteriorating public finances since the economic crisis. According to European Commission (2010p), elections in 2010 were largely in line with international standards, but were characterized by nationalistic rhetoric, and the constitution still had not been brought in line with the European Convention of Human Rights.

For many years as an autonomous province within Serbia and as part of the former Yugoslavia, **Kosovo** enjoyed a considerable degree of autonomy, but this was ended by the Milosevic regime in 1989. After years of mainly non-violent protest, conflict erupted in 1998/99. In 1999 NATO intervened on humanitarian grounds to end ethnic cleansing of Albanian Kosovars and wide-scale displacement of the civilian population. Institutional arrangements in Kosovo are covered by United Nations Security Council Resolution (UNSCR) 1244, which established an interim civilian administration United Nations Mission in Kosovo (UNMIK). The constitutional framework divided responsibilities between UNMIK and the provisional institutions of self-government pending a final settlement.

United Nations Special Envoy Martti Ahtisaari spent a year trying to negotiate a settlement, but Serbia wanted to reassert sovereignty over Kosovo, while the Albanian Kosovars (estimated as being over 90 per cent of the population) insisted on independence. In March 2007 Ahtisaari presented a comprehensive proposal to the UN Security Council, maintaining that 'supervised independence' was the only viable option. The Security Council began considering a draft resolution, which would endorse this proposal, but Russia backed Serbia and threatened a Security Council veto. The Albanian Kosovar government announced that it would declare independence even without a UN resolution, but Russia warned that this would set a dangerous precedent for international law.

In February 2008 the EU agreed the financial and legal apparatus for a mission under which police officers, judges, prosecutors and customs officials would be sent to bolster stability in Kosovo after independence. The initiative was attacked by Russia on the grounds that any changes to the presence of the international community required a UN Security Council mandate. On 18 February 2008 Kosovo declared independence. Serbs (including those in Kosovo) protested against this unilateral declaration of independence of what was traditionally an integral part of Serbia, maintaining that it ran counter to international law, and that they were being punished for the acts of Milosevic. While the USA, many EU member states and other countries recognized an independent Kosovo, others such as Cyprus, Greece, Romania, Slovakia and Spain feared knock-on effects for unilateral separatist movements. Local elections were held in November 2009, and a part of the ethnic Serb minority participated in some areas despite Belgrade's recommendation of a boycott. Parliamentary elections were held in December 2010, but there were criticisms of widespread fraud. Two days later the Council of Europe released a report by Dick Marty, Swiss politician and former prosecutor, allegedly implicating the prime minister of Kosovo, Hashim Thaci, in drug smuggling and murder.

The SAA with **Serbia** was signed in 2008, but was blocked by the Netherlands until there was improved co-operation with the International Criminal Tribunal on the former Yugoslavia (ICTY). In particular, there were calls for the transfer to The Hague of all remaining fugitives such as Hadzic and Mladic, the Bosnian Serb former commander accused of ordering the 1995 Srebrenica massacre (which had taken place despite the presence of four hundred Dutch peacekeepers in the area). The two were eventually arrested and transferred to The Hague in 2011. Improved co-operation led to an unfreezing of the Interim Agreement on Trade and Trade-related Matters in 2009 (which came into force in February 2010), and opened the way to Serbia's application for EU membership in December 2009. The ratification process of the SAA was launched in 2010.

The Progress Reports of the European Commission have noted the new constitution of 2006, and parliamentary elections, but continue to criticize the slow pace of judicial reform, corruption, the need to enforce human rights and reduce ethnic tensions, and (despite some progress in dialogue) continuing differences with the EU over Kosovo.

 19.11   The candidate countries

Croatia

Croatia formally applied for EU membership in February 2003, and, following a favourable opinion by the European Commission, was granted candidate status by the European Council in June 2004. The EU interpreted Croatia's failure to deliver General Ante Gotovina to the International Criminal Tribunal on the former Yugoslavia as lack of respect for the Copenhagen political criteria, and the European Council of March 2005 decided to postpone the start of accession negotiations. Screening only began in October 2005 after General Gotovina had been handed over to the ICTY, and during the course of 2005 support for EU membership as measured in opinion polls of the Croatian population fell substantially.[22] Settlement of a border dispute with Slovenia in 2009 helped to open the path towards accession. Accessign to the EU is foreseen for 1 July 2013.

In the past the political criteria had created difficulties for Croatia. Issues such as refugee return and human rights, and respect for democratic institutions meant that the EU was unwilling to negotiate the SAA with Croatia under the Croatian Democratic Union led by President Tudjman, and negotiations began only after he left office. The SAA was signed in 2001 and entered into force in February 2005. It envisaged the creation of a free trade area by 2007 for industrial products and most agricultural products. In December 2002 Croatia adopted the first National Programme for the Integration of the Republic of Croatia as a roadmap for legal harmonization, and in 2008 an Accession Partnership was introduced.

According to European Commission (2010p), problems still remain over: the capacity of the opposition to scrutinize legislation; the ability to guarantee free and fair elections; reform of public

---

[22] See, for instance, Eurobarometer surveys of Croatia. This conditionality was also applied in the negotiation of the SAA.

administration and of the judiciary; punishment of war crimes; corruption (in 2010 the former Croatian prime minister Ivo Sanader was arrested in connection with an anti-corruption investigation); treatment of minorities and co-operation with the ICTY. The European Commission stressed that Croatia would have to improve its track record in appointing independent judges, protecting human rights and prosecuting high-level corruption before membership.

The economic criteria for EU membership do not seem to pose particular problems for Croatia, and the macroeconomic response to the economic crisis was considered by and large appropriate, though unemployment was high, growth was weak and the external debt burden remained heavy.

As a candidate country Croatia benefited from the three pre-accession instruments – PHARE, ISPA and SAPARD – and from the CARDS regional programme up until 2006, but from 2007 the IPA replaced these instruments (see Table 19.5).

Table 19.5 EU financial assistance under the Instrument for Pre-Accession Assistance (IPA) for the candidate countries (€ million)

	2007	2008	2009	2010	2011	**Total 2007–11**
Croatia	141.2	146.0	151.2	154.2	157.2	**749.8**
FYR Macedonia	58.5	70.2	81.8	92.3	98.7	**401.5**
Montenegro	31.4	32.6	33.3	34.0	34.7	**166.0**
Turkey	497.2	538.7	566.4	653.7	781.9	**3,037.9**
Total	**696.9**	**754.9**	**799.4**	**900.2**	**1,037.8**	**4,189.2**

Source: European Commission DG Enlargement, www.ec.europa.eu/enlargement (accessed 27 January 2011), © European Union, 2011.

The Former Yugoslav Republic of Macedonia

The Former Yugoslav Republic of Macedonia applied for EU membership in 2004, received a favourable opinion from the Commission in November 2005, and obtained candidate status in December 2005. However, negotiations for EU membership have yet to start because of a dispute with Greece over the name of the country.

The Ohrid Framework Agreement of 2001 aims at contributing to the consolidation of democracy and the rule of law, in particular, by ensuring equitable representation of the country's ethnic communities in public administration, and transferring more responsibility to local communities. An SAA was signed in 2001 and entered into force in 2004. In 2008 an Accession Partnership replaced the previous European Partnership.

According to European Commission (2010p), some advance has been made in the implementation of the Ohrid Agreement, and the 2009 elections met most international standards. Further progress was necessary in the fight against corruption, independence of the judiciary, reform of the public administration and freedom of expression in the media, but the FYR Macedonia was deemed to have largely met the political criteria. The economic crisis had a negative impact on the economy, with very high unemployment and deteriorating public finances.

Montenegro

In May 2006, in line with the provisions of Article 60 of the Constitutional Charter of Serbia and Montenegro, Montenegro held a referendum on independence. A majority (55.5 per cent) of voters were in favour of independence, which was declared in June 2006.

Montenegro signed an SAA with the EU in 2007, which entered into force in 2010. Montenegro applied for EU membership in 2008 and the Commission published an opinion in November

2010, which was in favour of granting candidate status, but called for continuing efforts to meet the Copenhagen criteria. In particular, the opinion indicated the need to: improve the legislative framework for elections; further public administration reform; strengthen the rule of law; intensify the fight against corruption and organized crime; enhance media freedom; and improve the treatment of displaced persons (European Commission, 2010p).

Despite Dutch misgivings about corruption and organized crime, in December 2010 the European Council decided to give Montenegro candidate status, though without setting a date for the opening of negotiations.

Iceland

Gaining independence from Denmark only in 1944, Iceland was reluctant to lose its sovereignty, and had a long-standing opposition to becoming an EU member. The 2008 financial and economic crisis led to collapse of the Icelandic banks, devaluation and recession. It was widely felt in Iceland that the euro would have been a safe haven, leading to calls for its unilateral adoption (though subsequently with the experience of Ireland doubts began to creep in). Both the European Commission and the ECB insisted that EU membership was a condition for adopting the euro.

In July 2009 Iceland applied for EU membership and on the basis of a favourable opinion by the European Commission, in June 2010 the European Council decided to open accession negotiations with Iceland. Economies of scale in the ratification process suggest that the Commission had a preference for treating Iceland and Croatia together.

With its advanced economy and well-established democratic tradition, Iceland has been a member of the European Economic Area since 1994, taking part in the Single Market and contributing to economic and social cohesion in the EU. Iceland is also a member of Schengen and participates in a number of EU agencies and programmes covering areas such as enterprises, the environment, education and research, though without voting rights.[23] Iceland has adopted about two-thirds of the *acquis*,[24] has signed the Dublin Convention on asylum policy in Europe, and is a member of NATO.

However, the accession process raises certain concerns, including agriculture and fisheries. Iceland unilaterally extended its fishing limits (causing 'cod wars' in the past, see also the Online Learning Centre of this book) and operates a successful policy to preserve stocks through measures such as quotas and cutting the size of its fleet. It is therefore reluctant to grant access to its waters to EU members. Fishing accounted for about 40 per cent of exports in 2007 and employed some 8,000 people (of a population of 320,000).[25] Iceland also dropped out of the International Whaling Moratorium, though there have not been large hunts in recent years.

Tensions with the UK and the Netherlands arose over the collapse of the Icesave internet accounts of Landsbanki. President Grimsson rejected a bill passed by the Icelandic Parliament in December 2009 to pay €3.9 billion (equivalent to roughly half the GDP of Iceland) to the Dutch and British governments to compensate savers in these countries for their losses, and his decision was subsequently upheld in a referendum in Iceland in March 2010.[26] In February 2011 the President again blocked a deal to repay the UK and the Netherlands, and the decision was upheld in a second referendum in April 2011. The two countries threatened to hold up Iceland's EU accession process until they had been paid, and it seems likely the case will be taken to the EFTA court in Luxembourg.

---

[23] Unless otherwise stated the information here is taken from the website of the European Commission, http://ec.europa.eu/enlargement/candidate-countries/iceland/relation/index_en.htm (accessed 9 July 2010).

[24] *The Economist*, 24 January 2009.

[25] *Financial Times*, www.ft.com/iceland (accessed 27 January 2010).

[26] For a defence of the outcome of the referendum see the blog of Mario Nuti, http://dmarionuti.blogspot.com/2010/03/iceland-three-cheers-for-democracy.html (accessed 9 July 2010).

Turkey

A brief chronology of relations between the EU and Turkey is provided as Appendix 1 to this chapter, but it is useful to recall certain events in the enlargement process here; then the principal arguments put forward in favour and against Turkish membership of the EU will be discussed.[27] A short account of the Cyprus issue is provided in Appendix 2 to this chapter.

At the Brussels European Council of December 2004 it was agreed that Turkey could start accession negotiations with the EU from 3 October 2005. The negotiations are proving lengthy and even 2015 mentioned at the 2004 summit as the earliest expected date for accession seems optimistic.[28] The conclusions of the European Council also refer to the possibility of long transition periods, derogations, and specific arrangements or safeguard clauses. These could cover areas such as freedom of movement of persons, economic and social cohesion, and agriculture.

The European Council reiterated the 1999 Helsinki conclusions that Turkey was a candidate destined to join the EU on the basis of the same criteria as applied to other countries. However, it called for more progress in political and economic reforms. As a condition for opening negotiations Turkey was required to introduce six pieces of legislation enhancing human rights and the functioning of the judiciary, and sign a protocol extending its existing SAA with the EU to all new member states, including the Republic of Cyprus (see Appendix 2 to this chapter). This created difficulties as Turkey recognizes only the Turkish Republic of Northern Cyprus (TRNC). The compromise eventually agreed was a verbal declaration that Turkey would extend its SAA with the EU to all new member states, including the Republic of Cyprus before beginning accession negotiations.

At the December 2004 European Council, the Greek Cypriots were isolated and were persuaded not to veto the possibility of Turkish accession. However, the president of the Republic of Cyprus, Tassos Papadopoulos, announced that he had 64 opportunities to veto Turkish accession: at the beginning and end of the accession negotiation process and before opening or closing each of the then 31 chapters of the *acquis*. Austria and France have expressed the intention of holding referenda on Turkish EU accession.

Following screening in 2005, in June 2006 Turkish accession negotiations began, and the chapter of the *acquis* on science and research was opened and provisionally closed. However, the November 2006 Regular Report criticized Turkey for letting the pace of reforms slow, and Turkey was given a month to open its ports and airports to Greek Cypriots. Turkey argued this should be part of a package with the EU fulfilling its promise to help end the isolation of Northern Cyprus (see Appendix 2 to this chapter). Under the Finnish presidency there was an attempt to broker a deal,[29] but agreement was not reached. In December 2006 EU foreign ministers decided to suspend (in other words, not open) negotiations on 8 out of 35 chapters of the *acquis*, and not to provisionally close any chapter until Turkey has fulfilled its commitment. The suspended chapters related to the failure to recognize the Republic of Cyprus (the customs union, free movement of goods, transport, agriculture, fishing, external relations, and financial services). In practice the Greek Cypriots had effectively blocked negotiations since June 2006. Olli Rehn, the Commissioner for Enlargement, maintained that a 'train crash' had been avoided, and negotiations on other chapters of the *acquis* could continue.[30]

---

[27] See the Progress Reports of the European Commission on Turkey, and Hughes (2004) for more detailed discussions of these issues.

[28] A date occasionally mentioned with the idea of giving a firm, though distant, goal is 2023, the centenary of the Turkish Republic.

[29] According to the Finnish proposal, the port of Famagusta in the north would come under EU management and be opened for trade with the rest of the EU; the UN would take charge of the ghost tourist town of Varosha in the north, and access for the original Greek owners would be allowed; Turkey would have to include the Republic of Cyprus in its customs union and open ports. In response the Turkish government sent an informal transcript offering to open one major port and one airport provisionally for a year as part of a package in which the EU would back the goals of reaching a comprehensive settlement and reduce the isolation of Northern Cyprus. However, the office of the then Turkish president, Sezer, said that it had not been informed of the offer and the army complained about it. The EU rejected the Turkish offer as inadequate (too vague and conditional).

[30] In 2006 one new chapter was opened and provisionally closed, in 2007 five new chapters were opened, a further two in 2008 and one in June 2010. As shown in Table 19.5 above, from 2007 EU pre-accession instruments to assist Turkey were replaced with the IPA. In 2008 a revised Accession Partnership was adopted for Turkey.

In late 2009 Cyprus threatened to block the opening of a further five chapters of the *acquis* unless Turkey opened its ports and airports to Greek Cypriots. France declared that it was against proceeding with the five chapters, as President Sarkozy preferred a 'privileged partnership', or 'special relationship' for Turkey rather than EU membership. It was rumoured that he was planning to propose a Franco-German initiative to this end, though Chancellor Merkel was said to accept that EU countries had recognized Turkey as an official candidate in 1999 so could not renege on commitments.[31] By early 2011 thirteen chapters of the *acquis* had been opened, but only one had been provisionally closed.

In September 2009 a commission under Martti Ahtisaari published a report maintaining that negative reactions from some EU leaders and growing hesitation by the public had all but derailed the process of accession (Independent Commission on Turkey, 2009). The report accused public discourse in the context of electoral campaigns of using the Turkey–EU process as a proxy for popular fears about immigration, loss of jobs, Islam and a general dissatisfaction with the EU. Support for the EU accession process and for reform had faded in Turkey, and slowing of reform triggered more EU opposition to Turkey's accession, leading to a 'vicious circle' according to the report.

Fear of this vicious circle is one of the main reasons usually advocated in favour of Turkish membership of the EU. Turkey formally applied for EC membership in 1987, and was put off for a long time, so a further delay could create disillusion with the EU, and might jeopardize the reform process in Turkey.

Encouraged by the prospect of EU membership, between 2000 and 2005 Turkey rewrote about one-third of its constitution, introducing a series of radical political reforms, including: increased civilian control over the army; reform of the judiciary; attempts at more respect for human and minority rights; attempts to eliminate torture and ill-treatment in prisons; abolition of the death penalty; greater protection of freedom of expression, association and the media; and improved treatment of the Kurdish minority.

This wave of reform coincided with six years of 7 per cent growth and unprecedented foreign direct investment (Independent Commission on Turkey, 2009). Ironically the reform process began to slow in 2005 when accession negotiations started. As well as being a reaction to cold-shouldering of Turkish accession by the EU, the slowing of reform was also due to the government of the moderate Islamic AKP (Justice and Development Party) under Erdogan missing opportunities, and being subject to domestic constraints.

The statesman Mustafa Kemal Atatürk (1880–1938) left Turkey with the tradition of a modern secular state. Many members of the establishment see EU membership as a means of extending this goal. However, others, including certain elements of the military and nationalists, object to the extent of EU leverage over what are considered internal Turkish matters. Although the Turkish government had pushed for a settlement to the Cyprus issue, the fact that it was being placed under pressure to recognize the Greek Cypriot Republic of Cyprus also caused resentment in some circles. Members of the secular elites were used to being those associated with the reform process, and many remain sceptical of the Islamic leanings of the AKP. In 2007 the General Staff of the Turkish Armed Forces criticized the AKP and in 2008 the chief prosecutor of the Supreme Court called for its demise. In 2007 and again in 2010 alleged conspiracies to topple the government were discovered. In 2008 a proposal by the AKP government to allow women to wear headscarves in universities caused secular outrage.

In 2008 Turkey rendered it harder to open cases against dissidents and intellectuals under Article 301 of the criminal code relating to '*denigration of Turkishness, the Republic, and state organs and institutions*'. This had been used against journalists and writers (such as Orhan Pamuk, the Nobel prize winner) for mentioning sensitive topics such as the Armenian massacres and the Kurdish question. However, even in its amended form, the report by the Independent Commission on Turkey (2009) feared the Article could still be open to abuse.

In 2009 Turkey signed an agreement with Armenia recognizing the 1915 massacre of up to 1.5 million Armenians by Ottoman Turks, but tensions remained, and Erdogan stated that implementation was conditional on Armenian withdrawal from Nagorno Karabakh (a mainly Armenian enclave in Azerbaijan).

---

[31] *Financial Times*, 16 October 2009.

Despite attempts to improve the situation of the Kurdish minority, terrorist attacks by the PKK (Kurdistan Workers' Party) continue.

The 2010 Progress Report on Turkey recognized that further constitutional reform in 2010 had created the conditions for progress in areas such as reform of the judiciary and fundamental rights.[32] However, it pointed out that implementation of the package would be the key to its success, and called for further efforts in the areas such as: treatment of minorities (in particular the Kurds) and cultural rights; judicial guarantees for all suspects and a reduction of the high proportion of prisoners in pre-trial detention; civilian oversight of the military; corruption; rights of non-Muslim religious communities; freedom of expression; and excessive use of force by law enforcement authorities.

Despite such difficulties, a major argument advanced in favour of Turkish EU accession is that it could increase security in an unstable part of the world. Turkey has borders with countries such as Syria, Iraq, Iran, Armenia and Georgia. With its large Muslim population and tradition of a secular state, there are strong geostrategic reasons for encouraging the political and economic stability of Turkey as a regional diplomatic power, energy hub and bridge to the Muslim world. Turkey is a long-standing NATO member, so there may be an interest in including Turkey in EU initiatives relating to defence and foreign policy.

However, in recent years there has been growing concern in the West that Turkey has been looking increasingly eastwards. In 2010 Turkey opposed UN security sanctions against Iran, and relations with Israel deteriorated after killings of civilians on a Turkish-registered ship carrying aid to Gaza. Tensions with Iraq gave way to political accommodation, visa-free travel was introduced with Syria, and ties with Saudi Arabia and the Gulf states were tightened. The US reaction was to blame the EU and argue in favour of Turkish accession, a position not appreciated in Brussels and certain member states.[33] Turkey's reaction was simply to argue that it wanted a 'zero problem' foreign policy with its neighbours.

The principal reasons given against EU membership are that Turkey is too big in terms of population (see Table 19.1 above), too poor and agricultural, still has to make much progress in political and economic reform, is too Muslim and would fundamentally change the nature of the EU and undermine the momentum of the integration process. Concerns are still also expressed about the treatment of the Kurdish minority, and tensions remain over Cyprus (see Appendix 2 to this chapter).

According to forecasts of the UN World Population Division, Turkey would have a population of 82 million in 2015, but this would rise to 87 million by 2025, making Turkey the largest member of the EU. The fears associated with having such a large new member state in terms of population relate to the possibility of labour migration (though a derogation would probably be applied), the weight of Turkey in EU decision making, and the change in nature of the EU. However, the fast-growing Turkish population (with about half the population under 25) could help to resolve the problem of ageing in the EU.

Evaluation and outlook for an enlarged EU

Though the EU was slow to respond to the requests of the CEECs for membership, there were few illusions that transition and preparing for accession could prove other than lengthy and complex. Many aspects of transition (such as those relating to infrastructure, energy, the environment, human capital, social capital and institution building) continued long after enlargement.

Though an enlargement on the scale of that of 2004 has never again been attempted, it seems likely to become simply one in an ongoing process. In addition to the accession of Bulgaria and Romania in 2007, Croatia, FYR Macedonia, Iceland, Montenegro and Turkey are candidate countries. Croatia is expected to join in 2013 and Iceland could as well if it resolves the problems of Icesave Bank with the UK and the Netherlands, and ratifies EU accession. As part of the Stabilisation and

---

[32] European Commission (2010p).

[33] President Sarkozy was reputed to have said that President Obama should mind his own business, *Financial Times*, 24 November 2009.

Association Process, other countries of the Western Balkans have been granted potential candidate status. European Neighbourhood Policy foresees tighter links with eastern and southern neighbours, and even if the prospect of enlargement has been ruled out for the present, eventual enlargement or at least some kind of privileged relationship cannot be indefinitely excluded for at least some of these countries.

In 2008, largely at the instigation of French president Sarkozy, a Reflection (or 'Wise Man') Group on the future of the EU in 2030 was set up under the former Spanish prime minister Felipe Gonzales to study the long-term future of the EU. However, the group was not given an explicit mandate to decide where the ultimate borders of the EU should be as this was considered too divisive.[34]

With regard to EU widening, the case of Turkey is undoubtedly the most contentious, sparking intense differences in opinion. It is difficult to pretend that accession will not pose difficulties for the EU, given the size of the Turkish population, the overwhelmingly Muslim population, the level of GDP per capita and the share of agriculture in the economy. Against this, the urgent need to provide security in such an unstable corner of the globe could prove overriding. The prospect of EU membership has encouraged the Turkish government to undertake an active policy of democratization, and there are strong reasons for continuing this process. Similar arguments apply for many of the countries in South-Eastern Europe, though at least in some cases the relatively small size of these countries means that fewer problems are posed for the EU.

With previous enlargements (and those of 1973 and with the Mediterranean countries, in particular) there were fears that larger membership would profoundly change the nature of the Community. Is this still the case, and what kinds of changes can be expected?

The fear of deadlock of decision making with enlargement led to the main energies and efforts of the EU being absorbed by the debate on institutional reform for many years. First the inconclusive Amsterdam and Nice treaties, and then the long process of evolution of earlier the Constitutional Treaty, and later the Lisbon Treaty, were at the centre of the debate on the future of the EU for some time.

How much difference is the Lisbon Treaty likely to make to efficiency of decision making in an enlarged EU? To date, decisions in the EU have generally been taken on the basis of consensus, and this has usually been the case even after the 2004 and 2007 enlargements. Even on issues where qualified majority voting (QMV) is foreseen in the Council, votes are rarely taken and efforts are made to find a compromise. Since Lisbon there has been a shift in lobbying activities towards the European Parliament reflecting the increased powers of that institution. In a larger EU confrontational politics will probably be more difficult to avoid, and efforts to find a compromise could lead to a slowing of the integration process. There may be a shift to more application of the QMV rule, but even with the Lisbon Treaty, various sensitive policy areas remain subject to unanimity. Confrontational tactics could lead to a return to situations like the 'Empty Chair' crisis of 1965 or the Eurosclerosis of the 1970s.

However, Eurosclerosis forty years later would be a different animal. The *acquis* has grown, and achievements like the Single Market seem irreversible, though less stringent application of, for example, competition or industrial policy (with the growing tendency to promote national champions) or of Schengen could erode some of the advantages.

Despite the threats posed by the difficulties of Greece, Ireland, Portugal and other 'peripheral' countries, the euro also seems here to stay, if only because of the cost and complexity of a country leaving the single currency. The tasks of the ECB have been extended in response to the eurozone crisis and frequently the Bank has had to enter uncharted waters. Differing traditions of regulation in the member states have rendered the task of strengthening financial supervision difficult. A reformed system of economic governance will come into operation for the eurozone and more generally to increase EU competitiveness, but the need to find a compromise between very different positions has entailed considerable watering down of proposals.

---

[34] The results of the Reflection Group on the Future of the EU in 2030 were published as *Project Europe 2030: Challenges and Opportunities*, May 2010, http://www.reflectiongroup.eu/wp-content/uploads/2010/05/reflection_en_web.pdf (accessed 4 April 2011).

Member states will continue to benefit from the advantages of a larger market with more price transparency, but the aim of first the Lisbon Strategy and subsequently Europe 2020 is to move beyond this and to create a competitive, knowledge-based economy. Part of the difficulty is that the goals of the Lisbon Strategy and Europe 2020 are disparate and rely on the efforts of national governments and private business for their realization. Insufficient resources are still devoted to education and research, and to reaching the goals of the European Employment Strategy, which include increasing employment, the improving the quality of work and more social cohesion.

Immigration could help the EU in meeting the demographic challenge, but different traditions and geographical situations render it difficult to reach common positions. Ongoing tensions in North Africa and elsewhere underline the urgency of reaching common EU positions to such questions.

One of the main aims of the 2007–13 financial perspective was to give goals such as increasing competitiveness and cohesion a higher priority. However, the member states that are net contributors to the EU budget opposed any increase in spending (and, indeed, the share of GNI for competitiveness and cohesion was reduced for the 2007–13 period). The Lisbon Strategy was the main casualty of tighter EU budgetary stringency.

The October 2002 European Council precluded the possibility of releasing substantial resources from the CAP for other spending before 2013. There have been calls for radical cuts, if not the elimination of the CAP, from some quarters. However, as argued in Chapter 12, there are well-founded reasons for public intervention in agriculture, rural development and related issues. The public has repeatedly expressed a strong preference for safe and high-quality food, and a healthy environment. Though there is still much space for improvement in gearing policy to these objectives, the CAP has been radically transformed by the 1992, 1999, 2003 and 2008 reforms. Goals such as food safety and protection of the environment are not achieved cheaply, but it seems likely that more of the burden will be shifted to national governments, with a partial renationalization of the CAP. The debate on the future of the CAP post-2013 is warming up.

So too is that on the future of economic and social cohesion. Since the scope for increased spending is limited, the emphasis will have to be on increasing the effectiveness of measures. As argued in Chapters 7 and 15, more effort must be devoted to the task of identifying appropriate strategies to raise competitiveness and cohesion.

One of the main challenges for the EU remains establishing its democratic legitimacy. When consulted in referenda or opinion polls the people of Europe have frequently expressed negative opinions of the integration process (for instance, the Danish and Swedish votes against the euro, the Irish votes on the Nice and Lisbon treaties, or the French and Dutch votes on the Constitutional Treaty). Anyone who has attempted to consult it can verify that the Lisbon Treaty has severe limitations as an attempt to 'sell Europe' to its citizens. As Siedentop (2000:1) argues, ongoing debate about the future of the EU is the only way to convince Europeans that '*what is happening in Europe today is not merely the result of inexorable market forces or the machinations of élites, which have escaped from democratic control*'.

New forms of privileged relationships with neighbouring countries will probably be set up. Given the energy dependency of the EU a better working relationship will have to be evolved with its prickly neighbour, Russia. The 'conflictual co-operation' with the USA seems likely to continue, but more dialogue and an improved institutional framework could help to reduce the scope for disputes. The EU will also have to intensify its efforts if the Millennium Development Goals are to be met.

Clearly prescriptions concerning the future of the EU are beyond the present scope, but further forms of flexibility, and enhanced co-operation, are likely to emerge. They will probably do so in the time-honoured, piecemeal EU method of reaching compromises and allowing exceptions. Grand designs for Europe invariably have to be whittled down and adjusted so that one size is stretched into shape to fit all.

Summary of key concepts

- In May 2004 ten countries joined the EU: Cyprus, Czech Republic, Estonia, Hungary, Latvia, Lithuania, Malta, Poland, Slovakia and Slovenia. Bulgaria and Romania joined in 2007. Croatia, Iceland, Montenegro, the Former Yugoslav Republic of Macedonia and Turkey are candidate countries. The EU has granted potential candidate status to countries in the Western Balkans: Albania, Bosnia and Herzegovina, Kosovo and Serbia.

- According to the **theory of clubs**, the optimal size of membership occurs when marginal costs and marginal benefits to incumbent members are equal. The theory yields insights, but in practice is difficult to apply to the EU.

- The PHARE programme that came into operation from 1990 was initially demand driven and based on the requests of the recipient countries. From 1993 PHARE became increasingly concerned with preparing CEECs for accession. PHARE was one of the three **pre-accession instruments** for the 2000–06 period. The other two instruments were ISPA and SAPARD. In the 2007–13 period the IPA, or Instrument for Pre-Accession Assistance, replaced these.

- Western assistance to the transition countries was different from the Marshall Plan. Postwar reconstruction is very different from transition, while the co-ordination problems were fewer, the scale of financing was higher and the conditionality was tighter under the Marshall Plan.

- The **Copenhagen criteria** for accession set out in 1993 are: a functioning market economy with the capacity to cope with competitive pressures and market forces within the EU; stability of institutions guaranteeing democracy, the rule of law, human rights and respect for and protection of minorities; and ability to take on the obligations of membership, including adherence to the aims of political, and economic and monetary union. It was also stipulated that enlargement is subject to the condition that the EU is able to absorb new members and maintain the momentum of integration.

- Difficulties arise in applying the Copenhagen criteria because of the number of criteria and, in some cases, the vague and imprecise nature of the concepts involved.

- EU policy towards the **Western Balkans** covers countries with potential candidate status: Albania, Bosnia and Herzegovina, Kosovo and Serbia. In 1999 the EU introduced the Stabilisation and Association Process, which offered eligible West Balkan countries the possibility of signing Stabilisation and Association Agreements and eventual EU membership.

- **Croatia** is foreseen to join the EU in 2013. **Iceland** could also join soon if the problem of banks is resolved, and the Icelandic population votes in favour of EU membership in the event of a referendum.

- The **Former Yugoslav Republic of Macedonia** obtained candidate status in December 2005, but is in a dispute with Greece over its name. **Montenegro** was granted candidate status in 2010.

- **Turkey** started accession negotiations with the EU in October 2005, but the process is proving lengthy. Even with membership, long transition periods, derogations and specific arrangements are likely for areas such as freedom of movement of persons, economic and social cohesion, and agriculture.

- One of the main **reasons in favour of Turkish EU membership** is that Turkey formally applied for EC membership in 1987, and has been put off for a long time, so a further refusal could create disillusion with the EU, and might jeopardize the reform process in Turkey. Turkish accession could also increase security in an unstable part of the world.

- The principal **reasons given against Turkish EU membership** are that Turkey is too big in terms of population, too poor and agricultural, still has to make much progress in political and economic reform, is too Muslim, and would fundamentally change the nature of the EU and undermine the momentum of the integration process. Concerns are also expressed about the treatment of the Kurdish minority and ongoing tensions over Cyprus.

Questions for study and review

1 What criticisms can be made of Western measures to assist transition?
2 How far can Western measures to facilitate transition be considered a new Marshall Plan?
3 Discuss the conditionality applied by the EU in its dealings with the CEECs.
4 Describe the main features of the Europe Agreements.
5 When the CEECs joined the EU, they passed from a free trade area to membership of the Single Market. What does this imply?
6 What criticisms can be made of the Copenhagen criteria?
7 Describe the main features and limitations of the policy of the EU towards the Western Balkans.
8 Why did the accession of Cyprus to the EU create difficulties (see Appendix 2 below)?
9 What are the arguments advanced in favour of and against Turkey joining the EU?
10 Where do you consider that the boundaries of the EU should end?
11 What is your view of the future of an enlarged EU?

Online
Learning **Centre**

When you have read this chapter, log on to the Online Learning Centre website at ***www.mcgraw-hill.co.uk/textbooks/senior*** to explore weblinks, chapter-by-chapter test questions, case studies and more online study tools.

Chapter 19 Appendices

Appendix 1: EU–Turkish relations

Turkey became a member of the OECD in 1948, the Council of Europe in 1949 and of NATO in 1952. It applied for Associate Membership of the EEC in 1959 (a few days after Greece), but following the coup in 1960, talks were suspended for two years.

In 1963 Turkey signed an Association Agreement, the Ankara Treaty, with the Community, which came into force in 1964. Since being European is one of the conditions of Community membership, in 1963 the then president of the European Commission, Hallstein, ruled in favour of Turkey, confirming its 'European vocation', and announcing that it was 'part of Europe'. However, debate about the dual European and Muslim identities of Turkey and the implications for EU membership continues.

An Additional Protocol modifying the Association Agreement was signed in 1970 and came into force in 1974. It called for the creation of a customs union by 1995 and legal harmonization in economic matters. However, during the 1970s, tensions arose over the 1974 Cyprus crisis and the Greek application of 1975 for full membership. In 1978 Turkey requested participation in European Political Co-operation (EPC) in order to prevent Greece using its position to hinder the development of tighter Turkish–EC relations. This request was rejected, and in 1978 Turkey issued a unilateral declaration freezing its relations with the EC. The military took over in Turkey in 1980, and relations with the EU remained suspended. Relations were resumed in 1986, leading to a reactivation of the Association Agreement from 1988.

Turkey presented a formal request for EU membership in 1987, and received a negative reply two years later. The official reason given by the Commission was the need to complete the Single Market Programme. In 1990 the EC implemented a package to improve relations with Turkey, which included financial and technical assistance and the creation of a customs union by 1995.

At the Luxembourg European Council of December 1997 Turkey was not even included among the slow-track countries being considered for EU accession. The Council decided to establish the European Conference, but Turkey refused to attend its first two meetings. In 1999, meetings were suspended, but were resumed with Turkish participation after the 1999 Helsinki European Council. At the 1999 Helsinki European Council Turkey was declared a candidate. The 2002 Copenhagen Summit agreed that a decision on whether Turkey was ready to join the EU would be taken in December 2004, and if so that negotiations would begin 'without delay'. As explained in the main text of this chapter, negotiations began in 2006, but soon ran into difficulties.

Appendix 2: The EU and Cyprus

Since 1974 the island of Cyprus has been divided into the Greek Republic of Cyprus and what in 1983 was declared the Turkish Republic of Northern Cyprus (TRNC), recognized only by Turkey.

Cyprus obtained its independence from Great Britain in 1960, and the Treaty of Guarantee placed the independence, territorial integrity and security of the island under the joint guarantee of Greece, Turkey and the UK. The Treaty envisaged a complex power-sharing arrangement and a bi-communal structure. The Turkish Cypriots claimed that representation in municipal authorities and the army failed to conform to planned ethnic proportions and began to exercise their veto rights. In 1963 President Makarios proposed constitutional amendments to reduce the opportunities for the Turkish Cypriots to block legislation, and there was a political crisis. Intercommunal violence broke out, Turkish Cypriots moved into enclaves and withdrew from the common institutions.

In 1964 the UNFICYP (United Nations Peacekeeping Force in Cyprus) was established to prevent a recurrence of fighting and to contribute to the maintenance of law and order.

In 1974 the Greek junta staged a coup against President Archbishop Makarios and claimed annexation of Cyprus to Greece. Also committed to the protection of Cypriot independence, Turkey intervened on 20 July 1974. Two conferences were held in Geneva between Greece, Turkey and the UK, with the second also attended by Greek and Turkish Cypriots. The talks were inconclusive, and on 14 August the Turkish army launched a second offensive. According to the Greek Cypriots, this second invasion was not justified by the Treaty of Guarantee since the constitutional order had already been restored.

In 1974 Cyprus was divided by a 'Green Line', with the Turkish Cypriots holding almost 37 per cent of the island. In 1974 some 140,000–160,000 Greek Cypriots moved to the South, while an estimated 30,000–40,000 Turkish Cypriots fled to the North (Brewen, 2000). It is estimated that some 50,000 Turkish Cypriots left the island, while between 85,000 and 115,000 settlers (in particular from Anatolia) came over from the Turkish mainland, though the statistics are controversial.[35] A large Turkish force (estimated at 35,000) remained in Northern Cyprus.

The division of Cyprus left scars that are enduringly difficult to eradicate. Any proposed settlement of the Cyprus issue has a long list of questions to resolve, and these include:[36]

- the institutions of the federal state;
- the adjustments to the map of Cyprus;
- movement of people after the adjustments to the map of Cyprus;
- return of property or compensation payments;
- resolution of the problem of people missing during the 1963–74 period;
- progressive demilitarization, while at the same time guaranteeing the security of both communities on the island;
- the duration and shape of peacekeeping forces; and
- improvement of trust and personal links across communities.

In 1990 the Republic of Cyprus applied for EC membership. In 1993 the EC Commission published its opinion on application for EC membership, which appeared to make accession conditional on internal political settlement.

In 1994 Greece threatened to veto negotiations for a customs union between the EU and Turkey if Cyprus were not included in the next EU enlargement process, and at the 1997 Luxembourg European Council it was agreed to include Cyprus among the first-wave countries.

The EU continued to push for a settlement, but the presidency conclusions of the 1999 Helsinki European Council announced that 'if no settlement has been reached by the completion of accession negotiations, the Council's decision will be made without the above being a pre-condition'.

There have been numerous attempts by the UN to resolve the Cyprus issue. These include the detailed proposal of November 2002 by the then UN Secretary-General, Kofi Annan, to set up a Swiss-type confederation between the two parts of the island, which would also permit Northern Cyprus to join the EU. On 24 April 2004 a referendum was held in the two parts of the island over a revised version of the UN proposal. Had agreement been reached, the European Commission stated that the whole island could have acceded without any further need to renegotiate the terms of membership. However, although 65 per cent of Turkish Cypriots voted in favour of the proposal, it was rejected by 75.83 per cent of the Greek Cypriots. As a result, only the Greek Cypriot part of the island joined the EU in May 2004.

As their EU membership was assured, the Greek Cypriots were free to express their dissatisfaction with various aspects of the UN proposal or Annan Plan. Aside from resentment at a settlement

---

[35] The data here are taken from www.un.int/cyprus/cyissue.htm.

[36] For a more detailed discussion of these issues see Senior Nello (2004).

being imposed from 'outside', the Greek Cypriots were concerned about security and the costs of reunification. They objected to the continued presence of what they considered too many Turkish troops and settlers in the North. The arrangements with regard to territorial adjustment and property were thought inadequate, and the Greek Cypriots also criticized the limits on their right to residence in the North. Possibly many hoped for more favourable treatment by appealing to the European Court of Human Rights in Strasbourg. The situation was further changed in favour of the Greek Cypriots in 2010 when, obeying a ruling of the European Court of Justice that courts anywhere in the EU should enforce a Greek Cypriot judgment, a UK court ordered a British couple to demolish their holiday home and hand the property back to its original owner.[37]

Though the Turkish Cypriots also had misgivings about the Annan Plan, these were evidently overcome by the economic prosperity, end to isolation and stability EU accession promised.

The whole of the island is now considered to be part of the EU, but in the North EU legislation is suspended in line with Protocol No. 10 of the Accession Treaty. These areas are therefore outside the customs and fiscal territory of the EU, though the personal rights of Turkish Cypriots as EU citizens are not affected.

In reaction to the referendum result, a General Affairs Council of 26 April 2004 announced that measures would be introduced to end the isolation of the Turkish Cypriots. A Green Line Resolution was passed with the aim of making the Green Line as flexible as possible, with more border crossings being opened.

The Commission was also in favour of resuming direct flights to Northern Cyprus. Regulations on aid and direct trade were proposed. Goods certified by the Turkish Cypriot Chamber of Commerce were to be recognized and a wide variety of goods (including commodities, agricultural goods and fish) were to enter the South duty free. When the Republic of Cyprus became an EU member it blocked such measures, though eventually in 2006 the aid regulation was passed. The Greek Cypriots have resisted pressures to allow direct trade between North and South Cyprus on the pretext that if the Turkish Cypriots became more prosperous they would be less inclined to accept a settlement.

Following elections in 2008, the new president of the republic of Cyprus, Demetris Christofias, agreed to meet his Turkish Cypriot counterpart, Mehmet Ali Talat, for fully fledged negotiations under UN auspices. The aim was to establish a bi-zonal, bi-communal federation, but there was little progress on some of the toughest issues: the occupation by Turkish troops, the division of the island and property claims.

In 2010 the hard-line nationalist Dervis Eroglu won Turkish Cypriot elections, ending any immediate hopes that a settlement would be reached. The UN continued to broker negotiations in late 2010 and early 2011 but there seemed little hope of reaching agreement on property or territorial division of the island. The formal division of the island began to emerge as a real prospect (in particular after the ruling by the International Court of Justice that Kosovo's declaration of independence was not a violation of international law).

---

[37] *Financial Times*, 2 February 2010.

References

Ackrill, R. (2000) *The Common Agricultural Policy*, Sheffield Academic Press, Sheffield.

Ackrill, R. and A. Kay (2006) 'Historical-institutionalist perspectives on the development of the EU budget system', *Journal of European Public Policy*, 13(1): 113–33.

Ackrill, R. and A. Kay (2009) 'Historical learning in the design of WTO rules: The EC sugar case'; *The World Economy*, 32(5); 754–71.

Aitken, N.D. (1973) 'The effects of the EEC and EFTA on European trade: a temporal cross-section analysis', *American Economic Review*, 68: 881–92.

Alesina, A. and F. Giavazzi (2006) *The Future of Europe: Reform or Decline*, MIT Press, Cambridge, MA.

Alesina, A. and E. Spolaore (2003) *The Size of Nations*. MIT Press, Cambridge, MA.

Alvarez-Plata, P., H. Brücker and B. Siliverstovs (2003) *Potential Migration from Central and Eastern Europe into the EU-15 – An Update*, Report for the European Commission DG Employment and Social Affairs, http://europa.eu.int/comm/employment_social (accessed 21 December 2010).

Anania, G. (2010) 'Multilateral negotiations and the CAP', in S. Senior Nello and P. Pierani (eds) *International Trade, Consumer Interests and Reform of the Common Agricultural Policy*, Routledge, Abingdon.

Ardy, B. and A. El-Agraa (2007) 'Tax harmonisation', in A. El-Agraa (ed.) *The European Union: Economics and Policies*, 8th edn, Cambridge University Press, Cambridge.

Armstrong, H.W. (1995) *Convergence among Regions of the European Union, 1950–1990*, Papers in Regional Science, 74(2): 143–52.

Artis, M. (1994) 'European Monetary Union', in M. Artis and N. Lee (eds) *The Economics of the European Union: Policy and Analysis*, Oxford University Press, Oxford.

Artis, M. (2007) 'The ECB's Monetary Policy' in M. Artis and F. Nixson (eds) *The Economics of the European Union. Policy and Analysis*, 4th edn, Oxford University Press, Oxford.

Artis, M. and F. Nixson (eds) (2007 and earlier editions) *The Economics of the European Union. Policy and Analysis*, 4th edn, Oxford University Press, Oxford.

Artis, M. and W. Zhang (1995) *International Business Cycle and the ERM: Is there a European Business Cycle?* CEPR Discussion Paper No. 1191, London.

Bache, I., S. George and S. Bulmer (2011) *Politics in the European Union*, 3rd edn, Oxford University Press, Oxford.

Bachtler, J., C. Mendez and F. Wishlade (2010) *Challenges, Consultations and Concepts: Preparing for the Cohesion Policy Debate*, European Policy Research Paper 74, European Policies Research Centre, Glasgow.

Bainbridge, T. (2002) *The Penguin Companion to European Union*, 3rd edn, Penguin Books, London.

Balassa, B. (1961) *The Theory of Economic Integration*, Irwin, Homewood, IL.

Balassa, B. (1967) 'Trade creation and trade diversion in the European common market', *Economic Journal*, 77: 1–21.

Balassa, B. (1974) 'Trade creation and trade diversion in the European Common Market: an appraisal of the evidence', *Manchester School*, 42: 93–135.

Balassa, B. (ed.) (1975) *European Economic Integration*, North-Holland, Amsterdam.

Baldone, S., F. Sdogati and L. Tajoli (2001) 'Patterns and determinants of international fragmentation of production: evidence from outward-processing trade between the EU and Central Eastern European countries', *Weltwirtschaftliches Archiv*, 137(1): 80–104.

Baldwin, R. (1989) 'The growth effects of 1992', *Economic Policy*, 2: 247–81.

Baldwin, R. (1993) *A Domino Theory of Regionalism*, CEPR Working Paper No. 857, London.

Baldwin, R. (1994) *Towards an Integrated Europe*, Centre for Economic Policy Research, London.

Baldwin, R. (2005) *The Euro's Trade Effect*, http://hei.unige.ch/~baldwin/RoseEffect/Euros_Trade_Effect_Baldwin_31May05.pdf (accessed 2 August 2010).

Baldwin, R. (2006a) *Multilateralising Regionalism: Spaghetti Bowls and Building Blocs on the Path to Global Free Trade*, CEPR Discussion Paper No. 5775, www.cepr.org (accessed 15 April 2011).

Baldwin, R. (2006b) *Globalisation: The Great Unbundling*, www.hei.unige.ch/baldwin (accessed 13 September 2010).

Baldwin, R. (2007) *Poland's Fight on Voting Rules Matters for EU Budget Allocation*, http://www.voxeu.org/index.php?q=node/279 (accessed 18 May 2010).

Baldwin, R. (ed.) (2009) *The Great Trade Collapse: Causes, Consequences and Prospects*, a VoxEU.org publication, Centre for Economic Policy Research, London, http://www.voxeu.org/reports/great_trade_collapse.pdf (accessed 26 October 2010).

Baldwin, R. and A. Venables (1995) 'Regional economic integration', in G.M. Grossman and K. Rogoff (eds) *Handbook of International Economics*, Vol. 3, North-Holland, Amsterdam.

Baldwin, R. and C. Wyplosz (2009 and earlier editions) *The Economics of European Integration*, 3rd edn, McGraw-Hill, Maidenhead.

Baldwin, R., E. Berglof, F. Giavazzi and M. Widgren (2001) *EU Reforms for Tomorrow's Europe*, CEPR, London.

Baldwin, R., V. Di Nino, L. Fontagné, R. De Santis and D. Taglioni (2008) 'Study on the impact of the euro on trade and foreign direct investment', Economic Papers 321, *European Economy*, European Commission, http://www.graduateinstitute.ch/webdav/site/ctei/shared/CTEI/Baldwin/Publications/Chapters/European%20Integration/Study%20on%20the%20Impact%20of%20the%20Euro%20on%20Trade%20and%20Foreign%20Direct%20Investment.pdf (accessed 22 November 2010).

Barro, R. (1974) 'Are governments' bonds net wealth?' *Journal of Political Economy*, 82: 1095–117.

Barro, R. and D. Gordon (1983) 'Rules, discretion and reputation in a model of monetary policy', *Journal of Monetary Economics*, 12: 101–21.

Bayoumi, T. and B. Eichengreen (1997) 'Ever closer to heaven: an optimum currency area index for European countries', *European Economic Review*, 41(3–5): 761–70.

Becker, S., P. Egger, M. von Ehrlich and R. Fenge (2008) *Going NUTS: The Effect of EU Structural Funds on Regional Performance*, Stirling Economics Discussion Paper, https://dspace.stir.ac.uk/bitstream/1893/572/1/SEDP-2008-27-Becker-Egger-vonEhrlich-Fenge.pdf (accessed 3 February 2011).

Beetsma, R. and H. Oksanen (2008) 'Pensions under aging populations and the EU Stability and Growth Pact', *CESifo Economic Studies*, 54: 563–92.

Beetsma, R., M. Giuliodori and F. Klaasen (2005) *Trade Spillovers of Fiscal Policy in the European Union: A Panel Analysis*, CEPR Discussion Paper No. 5222.

Begg, I. and N. Grimwade (1998) *Paying for Europe*, Sheffield Academic Press, Sheffield.

Begg, D., S. Fischer and R. Dornbusch (2008a and earlier editions) *Economics*, 9th edn, McGraw-Hill, Maidenhead.

Begg, I., H. Enderlein, J. Le Cacheux and M. Mrak (2008b) *Financing of the European Union Budget*, http://ec.europa.eu/budget/reform/library/issue_paper/study_financingEU_de_en_fr.pdf (accessed 25 January 2011).

Bellak, C., M. Leibrecht and A. Riedl (2008) 'Labour costs and FDI flows to the CEECs: A survey of the literature and some empirical evidence', *Structural Change and Economic Dynamics*, 19: 17–37.

Bernanke, B. and M. Gertler (2001) 'Should central banks respond to movements in asset prices?' *American Economic Review*, 91: 253–7.

Bevan, A.A. and S. Estrin (2004) 'The determinants of foreign direct investment into European transition economies', *Journal of Comparative Economics*, 32: 229–48.

Bhagwati, J. (1993) 'Regionalism and multilateralism: an overview', in **I. de Melo and A. Panagariya** (eds) *New Dimensions in Regional Integration*, Cambridge University Press, Cambridge.

Bhagwati, J. (2004) *In Defense of Globalisation*, Oxford University Press, Oxford.

Bhagwati, J. and A. Panagariya (1996) 'Preferential trading areas and multilateralism: strangers, friends or foes?' in **J. Bhagwati and A. Panagariya** (eds) *The Economics of Preferential Trading Arrangements*, AEI Press, Washington, DC.

Bhagwati, J., D. Greenaway and A. Panagariya (1998) 'Trading preferentially: theory and policy', *The Economic Journal*, 108: 1128–48.

Bilal, S. and C. Stevens (2009) *The Interim Economic Partnership Agreement between the EU and African States: Contents, challenges, and prospects*, ECDPM and ODI, http://www.ecdpm.org/Web_ECDPM/Web/Content/Download.nsf/0/B6CB574AC6DA08AAC125760400322BDE/$FILE/pmr17-def.pdf (accessed 23 February 2011).

BIS (Bank for International Settlements) (2009) *Annual Report 2008/2009*, http://www.bis.org/publ/arpdf/ar2009e.htm (accessed 7 October 2010).

BIS (Bank for International Settlements) (2010) *Annual Report 2009/2010*, http://www.bis.org/publ/arpdf/ar2009e.htm (accessed 7 October 2010).

Bladen-Hovell, R. (2007) 'The creation of EMU', in **M. Artis and F. Nixson** (eds) *The Economics of the European Union: Policy and Analysis*, 4th edn, Oxford University Press, Oxford.

Blanchard, O. (2004) 'The economic future of Europe', *Journal of Economic Perspectives*, 18: 3–26.

Blanchard, O. (2009 and earlier editions) *Macroeconomics*, 5th edn, Prentice Hall, New Jersey.

Boeri, T. and H. Brücker (2005) *Migration, Co-ordination Failures and EU Enlargement*, Discussion Paper 481, DIW (Deutsches Institut für Wirtschaftsforschung, Berlin, www.diw.de/deutsch/produkte/publikationen/discussionpapiere/docs/papers/dp481.pdf (accessed 22 December 2010).

Boeri, T., H. Brücker et al. (2000) *The Impact of Eastern Enlargement on Employment and Wages in the EU Member States*, Report for the European Commission, http://europa.eu.int/comm/employment_social (accessed 22 December 2010).

Bojnec, S. and I. Ferto (2007) *European Enlargement, Trade Creation and Dynamics in Agro-food Trade*, www.econ.core.hu (accessed 2 August 2010).

Bollen, F., I. Hartwig and P. Nicolaides (2000) *EU Structural Funds beyond Agenda 2000: Reform and Implications for the Current and Future Member States*, European Institute of Public Administration, Maastricht.

Bongardt, A. (ed.) (2005) *Competition in the European Union: Experiences and*

Challenges Ahead, National Institute of Administration, Oeiras, Portugal.

Bongardt, A. and F. Torres (2007a) 'Is the "European Model" viable in a globalized world?' NIPE WP 20/2007, http://ideas.repec.org/p/ave/wpaper/462007.html (accessed 13 September 2010), also published in P. Della Posta, M. Uvalic and A. Verdun (eds) (2009) *Globalization, Development and Integration: A European Perspective*, Palgrave Macmillan, Basingstoke.

Bongardt, A. and F. Torres (2007b) 'Institutions, governance and economic growth in the EU: is there a role for the Lisbon Strategy?' *Intereconomics: Review of European Economic Policy*, 42(1): 32–42.

Bouët, A. (2006) *What can the Poor Expect from Trade Liberalization? Opening the Black Box*, MTID Discussion Paper No. 93, International Food Policy Research Institute, Washington, DC.

Bouët; A., D. Laborde and S. Mevel (2007) 'Searching for an alternative to economic partnership agreements', International Food Policy Research Institute, www.ifpiri.org (accessed 18 February 2011).

Bradley, J. (2008) 'EU cohesion policy: the debate on Structural Funds', *International Journal of Public Policy* 3(3/4): 246–60.

Braunerhjelm, P., R. Faini, V. Norman, F. Ruane and P. Seabright (2000) *Integration and the Regions of Europe: How the Right Policies Can Prevent Polarization*, Monitoring European Integration 10, Centre for Economic Policy Research, London.

Brewen, C. (2000) *The European Union and Cyprus*, Eothen Press, Huntingdon, UK.

Browning, E.K. and M.A. Zupan (2009 and earlier editions) *Microeconomic Theory and Applications*, 9th edn, John Wiley & Sons, Hoboken, NJ.

Brunnermeier M.K. (2009) 'Deciphering the liquidity and credit crunch 2007–2008', *Journal of Economic Perspectives*, 23(1): 77–100.

Buchanan, J.M. and G. Tullock (1962) *The Calculus of Consent*, University of Michigan Press, Ann Arbor.

Buchanan, J.M. (1965) 'An economic theory of clubs', *Economica*, 32 (February): 1–14.

Buckwell, A. et al. (1997) 'Towards a common agricultural and rural policy for Europe', *European Economy Reports and Studies*, No. 5.

Buiter, W.H. (2000) 'Optimal currency areas'. Scottish Economic Society/Royal Bank of Scotland Annual Lecture, *Scottish Journal of Political Economy*, 47(3): 213–50.

Burfisher, M.E., R. Robinson and K. Thierfelder (2004) 'Regionalism: old and new, theory and practice', in G. Anania, M.E. Bohman, C.A Carter and A.F. McCalla (eds) *Agricultural Policy Reform and the WTO: Where are we Heading?* Edward Elgar, Cheltenham.

Burrell, A. (1989) *Milk Quotas in the European Community*, CAB International, Wallingford.

Busillo, F., T. Muccigrosso, G. Pellegrini, O. Tarola and F. Terribile (2009) *Measuring the impact of European regional policy on economic growth: a regression discontinuity design approach*, http://homes.stat.unipd.it/mgri/SIS2010/Program/contributedpaper/742-1333-1-DR.pdf (accessed 2 February 2010).

Cecchini, P. (1988) *The European Challenge: The Benefits of a Single Market*, Wildwood House, Aldershot.

Cecchetti, S.G., H. Genberg, J. Lipsky and S. Wadhwani (2000) *Asset Prices and Central Bank Policy*, International Centre for Money and Banking, Geneva.

CEPS, EGMONT and EPC Joint Study (2007) *The Treaty of Lisbon: Implementing Institutional Innovations*, http://shop.ceps.eu (accessed 11 February 2011).

Chilosi, A. (2007) 'The European Union and its neighbours: "Everything but Institutions"?' *European Journal of Comparative Economics*, 4(1): 25–38.

Chilosi, A. (2009) 'Perspectives of the ENP, and perspectives of the EU: neighbourhood, enlargement and unanimity', *Aussenwirtschaft*, 3: 253–68.

Cini, M. and N. Perez-Solorzano Borragan (2009) *European Union Politics*, Oxford University Press, Oxford.

Coase, R. (1960) 'The problem of social cost', *Journal of Law and Economics*, October, 1–44.

Colman, D. (2007) 'The Common Agricultural Policy', in M. Artis and F. Nixson (eds) *The Economics of the European Union. Policy and Analysis*, 4th edn, Oxford University Press, Oxford.

Commons (2002) 'Crossborder shopping and smuggling', *House of Commons Library*, Research Paper 02/40, London.

Coombes, P. and H. Overman (2004) 'The special distribution of economic activity in the EU', in V. Henderson and J.F. Thisse (eds) *Handbook of Regional and Urban Economics*, Vol. 4, Elsevier, Amsterdam.

Cooper, C.A. and B.F. Massell (1965) 'A new look at customs union theory', *Economic Journal*, 75: 742–75.

Coudenhove-Kalergi, R.N. (1926) *Pan-Europe*, Knopf, New York.

Crafts, N. and G.Toniolo (1996) *Economic Growth in Europe since 1945*, Cambridge University Press, Cambridge

Craig, P. and G. De Burca (2007) *EU Law: Text, Cases and Material*, 4th edn, Oxford University Press, Oxford.

Crespo Cuaresma, J. and M. Feldkircher (2009) *Spatial Filtering, Model Uncertainty and the Speed of Income Convergence in Europe*, Working Papers in Economics and Statistics 2009–17, University of Innsbruck.

Dandashly, A., A. Surdej and H. Tendera-Wlaszzczuk (2009) *Global Financial Crisis and Euro Zone Enlargement*, Wydawnictwo Adam Marszalek, Krakow.

Danson, M., H. Halker and G. Cameron (2000) *Second Report on Economic and Social Cohesion*, European Commission, Brussels.

Dasgupta, P. (2006) *Comments on the Stern Review's Economics of Climate Change*, http://www.econ.cam.ac.uk/faculty/dasgupta/STERN.pdf (accessed 28 December 2010).

Daugbjerg, C. and A. Swinbank (2008) 'Curbing agricultural exceptionalism: the EU's response to external challenge', *The World Economy*, 31(5): 631–52.

De Benedictis, L. and P.L. Padoan (1994) 'The integration of Eastern Europe into the EC: a club theory interest groups approach', in S. Lombardini and P.L. Padoan (eds) *Europe between East and South*, Kluwer Academic, Dordrecht.

De Grauwe, P. (2009a and earlier editions) *The Economics of Monetary Union*, 8th edn, Oxford University Press, Oxford.

De Grauwe, P. (2009b) 'The fragility of the eurozone's institutions', *Open Economic Review*, http://www.econ.kuleuven.be/ew/academic/intecon/Degrauwe/PDG-papers/Recently_published_articles/Fragility-eurozone-OER.pdf (accessed 26 November 2010).

De la Fuente (2002) *The Effect of Structural Fund Spending on the Spanish Regions: An Assessment of the 1994–99 Objective 1 CSF*, CEPR Discussion Papers No. 3673, London.

De Long, B. and B. Eichengreen (1993) 'The Marshall Plan: history's most successful structural adjustment programme', in R. Dornbusch, W. Nölling and R. Layard (eds) *Postwar Economic Reconstruction and Lessons for the East Today*, MIT Press, Cambridge, MA.

Deardorff, A. and R. Stern (2002) *EU Expansion and EU Growth*, Ford School of Public Policy Working Paper No. 487, University of Michigan, Ann Arbor.

Delgrado, J. (2006) *Single Market Trails Home Bias*, Breugel Policy Brief 5, www.breugel.org (accessed 15 April 2011).

Della Posta, P. (2006) 'Fundamentals, international role of the euro and "framing" of expectations: What are the determinants of the dollar/euro exchange rate?' in F. Torres, A. Verdun and H. Zimmermann

(eds) *EMU Rules: The Political and Economic Consequences of European Monetary Integration*, Nomos, Baden–Baden.

Della Posta, P., M. Uvalic and A. Verdun (eds) (2009) *Globalization, Development and Integration: A European Perspective*, Palgrave Macmillan, Basingstoke.

Demekas, D.G., B. Horvath, E. Ribakova and Y. Wu (2007) 'Foreign direct investment in European transition economies – the role of policies', *Journal of Comparative Economics*, 35(2): 369–86.

Deutsch, K.W. (1968) *The Analysis of International Relations*, Prentice Hall, Englewood Cliffs, NJ.

Dinan, D. (2005) *Ever Closer Union: An Introduction to European Integration*, Palgrave Macmillan, Basingstoke.

Dornbusch, R., C. Favero and F. Giavazzi (1998) 'Immediate challenges for the European Central Bank', *Economic Policy*, 26.

Dornbusch, R., S. Fischer and R. Startz (2011 and earlier editions) *Macroeconomics*, 11th edn, McGraw-Hill, Maidenhead.

Downs, A. (1957) *An Economic Theory of Democracy*, Harper & Row, New York.

Dumont, B. and P. Holmes (forthcoming) 'EU competition policy from an economic perspective: shaping policy or shaped by policy?' in A. Tovias and A. Verdun (eds) *Mapping European Integration*, Palgrave Macmillan, Basingstoke.

Eckey, H.F., C. Dreger and M. Türck (2009) 'Regional convergence in the enlarged European Union', *Applied Economics Letters*, 16(18): 1805–8.

ECORYS Nederland BV, Netherlands Bureau for Economic Policy Analysis (CPB) and Institute for Economic Research (IFO) (2008) *A Study on EU Spending*, ec.europa.eu/budget/reform/library/issue.../study_EUspending_en.pdf (accessed 25 January 2011).

Eichengreen, B.J. (1989) 'Hegemonic stability theories

of the international monetary system', in R.N. Cooper, B.J. Eichengreen and C.R. Henning (eds) *Can Nations Agree? Issues in International Economic Co-operation*, The Brookings Institution, Washington, DC.

El-Agraa, A.M. (2007) 'The theory of economic integration', in A.M. El-Agraa (ed.) *The European Union: Economics and Policies*, 8th edn, Cambridge University Press, Cambridge.

Emerson, E. M. Aujean, M. Catinat, P. Goybet and A. Jacquemin (1989) *The Economics of 1992: The EC Commission's Assessment of the Economic Effects of Completing the Single Market*, Oxford University Press, Oxford.

Engel, C. and J. Rogers (2004) 'European product market integration after the euro', *Economic Policy*, CEPR and CESifo, July.

Esposti, R. (2008) 'Regional growth convergence and EU policies: empirical evidence and measurement problems', *CESifo Forum*, 9(1): 14–22.

ESRI with GEFRA (2002) *An Examination of the ex-post Macroeconomic Impacts of CSF 1994–99 on Objective 1 Countries and Regions, Final Report*, Economic and Social Research Institute, Gesellschaft für Finanz- und Regionalanalysen, Dublin.

Ethier, W.J. (1998a) 'The new regionalism', *The Economic Journal*, 108: 1149–61.

Ethier, W.J. (1998b) 'Regionalism in a multilateral world', *Journal of Political Economy*, 106(6): 1214–45

Euréval and Ramboll Management (2008) *Meta-study on Lessons from Existing Evaluations as an Input to the Review of EU Spending*, ec.europa.eu/budget/reform/.../study_meta_evaluation_long_en.pdf (accessed 25 January 2011).

Eurobarometer (2007a) *Europeans, Agriculture and the Common Agricultural Policy*, Report 03/07, www. ec.europa.eu/public_opinion (accessed 2 August 2010).

Eurobarometer (2007b) *Public Opinion in the EU*, No. 67

(Spring), www.ec.europa.eu/ public_opinion/archives/eb (accessed 28 December 2010).

Eurobarometer (2009) *The Euro Area: Public Attitudes and Perceptions, Analytic Report*, http://ec.europa.eu/public_ opinion/flash/fl_279_en.pdf (accessed 12 November 2010).

Eurobarometer (2010a) *Public Opinion in the EU*, No. 73, http://ec.europa.eu/public_ opinion/archives/eb/eb73/ eb73_vol1_fr.pdf (accessed 28 December 2010).

Eurobarometer (2010b) *The Introduction of the Euro in the New Member States, Analytic Report*, http://ec.europa.eu/ public_opinion/flash/fl_296_ en.pdf (accessed 12 November 2010).

European Bank for Reconstruction and Development (various years) *Transition Report*.

European Central Bank (ECB) (2010) *Review of the International Role of the Euro*, June 2007, http://www.ecb. int/pub/pdf/other/euro-international-role201007en.pdf (accessed 2 December 2010).

European Commission (1969) *Commission memorandum to the Council on the co-ordination of economic policies and monetary co-operation within the Community* (Barre Plan), COM(69) 150 of 12 December 1969, Supplement to EC Bulletin No. 3–1969.

European Commission (1970) *Presentation by the Werner group to the Council and the Commission of the final report on the attainment by stages of economic and monetary union in the Community* (Werner Report), document 9.504/II/70, OJ C 136, 11 November 1970, Supplement to EC Bulletin No. 11–70.

European Commission (1985) *Completing the Internal Market*, COM(85) 310, http://europa. eu/documents/comm/white_ papers/pdf/com1985_0310_f_ en.pdf (accessed 3 March 2011).

European Commission (1989) *Report on Economic and Monetary Union in the European Community* (Delors Report), available at http://aei.pitt. edu/1007/1/monetary_delors.

pdf (accessed 17 February 2011).

European Commission (1990a) 'One market, one money', *European Economy*, 44.

European Commission (1990b) *Industrial Policy in an Open and Competitive Environment: Guidelines for a Community Approach*, COM(90) 556.

European Commission (1991) *The Development and Future of the CAP: Reflections Paper of the Commission*, COM(91) 100 final.

European Commission (1992) *The Future Development of the Common Transport Policy*, COM(92) 0494.

European Commission (1995) *The Agricultural Strategy Paper*, CSE(95) 607.

European Commission (1996) *Green Paper on the relations between the European Union and the ACP countries on the eve of the 21st century – Challenges and options for a new partnership*, COM(96) 570, 20 November.

European Commission (1997a) *Single Market Review*, Vol. 2, Luxembourg and Kogan Page, London.

European Commission (1997b) *Guidelines for the negotiation of new co-operation agreements with the African, Caribbean and Pacific countries*, COM(97) 537, 29 October.

European Commission (1997c) *Agenda 2000 For a Stronger and Wider Union*, COM(97) 2000, http://eur-lex.europa.eu/ smartapi/cgi/sga_doc?smartapi! celexplus!prod!DocNumber&lg =en&type_doc=COMfinal&an_ doc=1997&nu_doc=2000 (accessed 15 April 2011).

European Commission (2001) *European Transport Policy for 2010: Time to Decide*, COM(2001) 370 final, www. europa.eu/scadplus/leg (accessed 3 March 2011).

European Commission (2002) *Enlargement and Agriculture: Successfully Integrating the New Member States into the CAP*, Issues Paper, SEC(2002) 95, Brussels, January.

European Commission (2003a) *The Internal Market: Ten Years without Frontiers*, www.europa. eu.int/comm/internal_market (accessed 3 March 2011).

European Commission (2003b) *Internal Market strategy. Priorities 2003–2006*, COM(2003) 238 final, www.europa.eu.int/ comm/internal_market (accessed 3 March 2011).

European Commission (2003c) *Wider Europe – Neighbourhood: A New Framework for our relations with our Eastern and Southern Neighbours*, COM(2003) 104 final.

European Commission (2004a) *Building our Common Future: Policy Challenges and Budgetary Means of the Enlarged Union 2007–13*, COM(2004) 101, 10 February 2004.

European Commission (2004b) *Proposal for a Council Decision on the System of the European Communities Own Resources*, COM(2004) 501 final, 14 July 2004.

European Commission (2004c) *Third Report on Economic and Social Cohesion*, http:// ec.europa.eu/regional_policy/ sources/docoffic/official/ reports/cohesion3/cohesion3_ en.htm (accessed 2 February 2010).

European Commission (2005) *Working Together for Growth and Jobs: A New Start to the Lisbon Strategy*, http://eur-lex.europa. eu/LexUriServ/LexUriServ. do?uri=COM:2005:0024:FIN: EN: PDF (accessed 13 September 2010).

European Commission (2006a) *Survey on a Future Single Market Policy*, SEC(2006).

European Commission (2006b) *Guidance on the Posting of Workers in the Framework of the Provision of Services*, COM(2006) 159 final.

European Commission (2006c) *Public Consultation on a Future Single Market Policy*, SEC(2006) 1215/2.

European Commission (2006d) *Keep Europe Moving – Sustainable Mobility for our Continent. Mid-term review of the Transport White Paper published in 2001 by the European Commission*, COM(2006) 314 final, www. europa.eu/scadplus/leg (accessed 23 February 2011).

European Commission (2006e) *Global Europe: Competing in the World. A contribution to the EU's growth and jobs strategy,* http://trade.ec.europa.eu/doclib/docs/2006/october/tradoc_130376.pdf (accessed 23 February 2011).

European Commission (2007a) 'Steps towards a deeper economic integration: the internal market in the 21st century. A contribution to the Single Market Review', *European Economy*, 272, January.

European Commission (2007b) *Consumer Policy Strategy 2007–2013: Empowering consumers, enhancing their welfare, effectively protecting them*, COM(2007) 99 final, www.ec.europa.eu./consumers (accessed 15 April 2011).

European Commission (2007c) *A Single Market for 21st Century Europe*, COM(2007) 724, www.ec.europa.eu/internal_market (accessed 15 April 2011).

European Commission (2007d) *Reforming the Budget, Changing Europe. A Public Consultation Paper in View of the 2008/2009 Budget Review*, www.ec.europa.eu/budget (accessed 15 April 2011).

European Commission (2007e) *Agenda 2000*, http://ec.europa.eu/agenda2000/public_en.pdf (accessed 12 January 2011).

European Commission (2007f) *The Impact of a Minimum 10% Obligation for Biofuel Use in the EU(27) in 2020 on Agricultural Markets*, www.ec.europa.eu/agriculture (accessed 2 August 2010).

European Commission (2007g) *Limiting Global Climate Change to 2 degrees Celsius: The way Ahead for 2020 and beyond*, http://europa.eu/legislation_summaries/energy/european_energy_policy/l28188_en.htm (accessed 12 January 2011).

European Commission (2007h) *An Energy Policy for Europe*, Communication from the Commission to the European Council and the European Parliament, COM(2007) 1 final, http://ec.europa.eu/energy/energy_policy/doc/01_energy_policy_for_europe_en.pdf (accessed 12 January 2011).

European Commission (2009a) *Accompanying document to the 27th Annual Report from the Commission to the European Parliament on the Community's anti–dumping, anti–subsidy and safeguard activities*, Commission Staff Working Document SEC(2009) 1413, http://trade.ec.europa.eu/doclib/docs/2009/october/tradoc_145263.pdf (accessed 23 July 2010).

European Commission (2009b) *United States Barriers to Trade and Investment: Report for 2008*, http://trade.ec.europa.eu/doclib/docs/2009/july/tradoc_114160.pdf (accessed 23 July 2010).

European Commission (2009c) *European Competitiveness Report*, SEC(2009) 1657 final, http://www.eurosfaire.prd.fr/7pc/doc/1274338331_eu_competitiveness_report_2009.pdf (accessed 13 September 2010).

European Commission (2009d) 'Economic crisis in Europe: causes, consequences and responses', *European Economy*, 7.

European Commission (2009e) 'Five years of an enlarged EU', *European Economy*, 1.

European Commission (2010a) *Towards a Single Market Act For a highly competitive social market economy: 50 proposals for improving our work, business and exchanges with one another*, COM(2010) 608, http://ec.europa.eu/internal_market/smact/docs/single-market-act_en.pdf (accessed 2 November 2010).

European Commission (2010b) *Taxation Trends in the European Union*, http://ec.europa.eu/taxation_customs/resources/documents/taxation/gen_info/economic_analysis/tax_structures/2010/2010_full_text_en.pdf (accessed 3 November 2010).

European Commission (2010c) *EU Energy and Transport in Figures*, http://ec.europa.eu/energy/publications/statistics/doc/2010_energy_transport_figures.pdf (accessed 4 November 2010).

European Commission (2010d) *EU Citizenship Report 2010* http://ec.europa.eu/justice/policies/citizenship/docs/com_2010_603_en.pdf (accessed 4 November 2010).

European Commission (2010e) *A Strategy for Smart, Sustainable and Inclusive Growth*, COM(2010) 2020, http://ec.europa.eu/eu2020/pdf/ (accessed 29 October 2010).

European Commission (2010f) *Investing in Europe's Future, Fifth Report on Economic and Social Cohesion*, http://ec.europa.eu/regional_policy/sources/docoffic/official/reports/cohesion5/pdf/5cr_en.pdf (accessed 28 January 2011).

European Commission (2010g) *Statistical Annex of European Economy*, http://ec.europa.eu/economy_finance/publications/european_economy/2010/pdf/statistical_annex_spring2010_en.pdf (accessed 22 November 2010).

European Commission (2010h) *EU Budget 2009 – Financial Report*, http://ec.europa.eu/budget/documents/2009_en.htm (accessed 25 January 2011).

European Commission (2010i) *The EU Budget Review*, COM(2010) 700 final, http://ec.europa.eu/budget/reform/library/communication/com_2010_700_en.pdf (accessed 25 January 2011).

European Commission (2010j) *The Common Agricultural Policy after 2013: Your Ideas Matter*, http://ec.europa.eu/agriculture/cap-post-2013/debate/index_en.htm (accessed 18 November 2010).

European Commission (2010k) *The CAP towards 2020: Meeting the Food, Natural Resources and Territorial Challenges of the Future*, COM(2010) 672 final,http://eur-lex.europa.eu/LexUriServ/LexUriServ.do?uri=COM:2010:0672:FIN:en:PDF (accessed 18 November 2010).

European Commission (2010m) Europa Press Releases, 'Questions and answers on the revised EU emissions trading scheme', http://europa.eu/rapid/pressReleasesAction.do?reference=MEMO/08/796&language=EN (accessed 11 January 2011).

European Commission (2010n) *EU Energy and Transport in Figures, 2010*, http://ec.europa.eu/energy/publications/statistics/doc/2009_energy_transport_figures.pdf (accessed 23 December 2010).

European Commission (2010p) *Enlargement Strategy and Main Challenges 2010–2011*, COM(2010) 660 final, http://ec.europa.eu/enlargement/pdf/key_documents/2010/package/strategy_paper_2010_en.pdf (accessed 1 March 2010).

European Commission (various years) *The Agricultural Situation in the European Union*, Brussels.

European Council (2010) *Strengthening Economic Governance in the EU*, Report of the task force to the European Council, 21 October, http://www.consilium.europa.eu/uedocs/cms_data/docs/pressdata/en/ec/117236.pdf (accessed 30 November 2010).

European Council (2011) Conclusions, March 24/25, http://www.consilium.europa.eu/uedocs/cms_data/docs/pressdata/en/ec/120296.pdf (accessed 12 April 2011).

European Integration Consortium (2009) *Labour mobility within the EU in the context of enlargement and the functioning of the transitional arrangements*, Study carried out on behalf of the Employment, Social Affairs and Equal Opportunities Directorate General of the European Commission, http://ec.europa.eu/social/main.jsp?langId=en&catId=89&newsId=497 (accessed 8 July 2010).

Fagerberg, J. and B. Verspagen (1996) 'Heading for divergence? Regional growth in Europe reconsidered', *Journal of Common Market Studies*, 34: 431–48.

Faini, R. (1995) 'Migration in the integrated EU', in **R. Baldwin, P. Haaparanta and J. Klander** (eds) *Expanding Membership of the European Community*, Cambridge University Press, Cambridge.

Faini, R. and R. Portes (eds) (1995) *European Union Trade with Eastern Europe: Adjustment and Opportunities*, CEPR, London.

Faini, R. and A. Venturini (1994) *Migration and Growth: The Experience of Southern Europe*, CEPR Discussion Paper No. 964, Centre for Economic Policy Research, London.

Fanfani, R. (1998) *Lo Sviluppo della politica agricola comunitaria*, 2nd edn, Carocci, Roma.

Fennel, R. (1997) *The Common Agricultural Policy: Continuity and Change*, Oxford University Press, Oxford.

Fitoussi, J.–P. and J. Creel (2003) *How to Reform the European Central Bank*, Centre for European Reform, London.

Fontagne, L., C. Mitaritonna and D. Laborde (2008) *An Impact Study of the EU–ACP Economic Partnership Agreements (EPAs) in the Six ACP Regions*, http://trade.ec.europa.eu/doclib/docs/2008/march/tradoc_138081.pdf (accessed 18 February, 2011).

Frankel, J.A. (1997) *Regional Trading Blocs in the World Trading System*, Institute for International Economics, Washington, DC.

Frankel, J.A. and A. Rose (1998) 'The endogeneity of the optimum currency area criteria', *Economic Journal*, 108(441): 1009–25.

Frankel, J.A. and A. Rose (2000) *Estimating the Effect of Currency Unions on Trade and Output*, National Bureau of Economic Research Working Paper 7857, Cambridge, MA.

Frontex (2009) *General Report*, http://www.frontex.europa.eu/gfx/frontex/files/general_report/2009/gen_rep_2009_en.pdf (accessed 21 December 2010).

Gandolfo, G. (1994) *Corso di economia internazionale. Volume 1: La teoria pura del commercio internazionale*, 2nd edn, UTET Libreria, Turin.

Giavazzi, F. and M. Pagano (1988) 'The advantage of tying one's hands: EMS discipline and central bank credibility', *European Economic Review*, 32: 1055–75.

Giegerich, B. and W. Wallace (2010) 'Foreign and security policy: civilian power, Europe and American leadership', in **H. Wallace, M.A. Pollack and A.R. Young** (eds) *Policy–Making in the European Union*, 6th edn, Oxford University Press, Oxford.

Giovannetti, G. (2009) 'An overview of current globalisation, opportunities and threats', in **P. Della Posta, M. Uvalic and A. Verdun** (eds) *Globalisation, Development and Integration: A European Perspective*, Palgrave Macmillan, Basingstoke.

Goto, J. and K. Hamada (2002) 'Regional economic integration and Article XXIV of GATT', *Review of International Economics*, 7(4): 555–70.

Grabbe, H. (2002) 'EU conditionality and the *acquis communautaire*', *International Political Science Review*, 23(3): 249–68.

Grimwade, N. (2000) *International Trade: New Patterns of Trade, Production and Investment*, 2nd edn, Routledge, London.

Gros, D. (2007) *How to Make European Research more Competitive*, Centre for European Policy Studies, www.ceps.be (accessed 15 April 2011).

Gros, D. and S. Micossi (2005) *A Better Budget for the European Union: More Value for Money, More Money for Value*, CEPS Policy Brief No. 66, CEPS, Brussels.

Gros, D. and A. Steinherr (2004) *Economic Transition in Central and Eastern Europe: Planting the Seeds*, Cambridge University Press, Cambridge.

Gros, D. and N. Thygesen (1998) *European Monetary Integration*, 2nd edn, Addison-Wesley Longman, Harlow.

Grossman, G.M. and E. Helpman (1995) 'The Politics of free trade agreements', *American Economic Review*, 84(4): 833–50.

Grossman, G.M. and E. Rossi-Hansberg (2006) 'The rise of offshoring: it's not wine for cloth any more', Paper presented at the annual economic symposium organized by the Federal Reserve Bank of Kansas at Jackson Hole, www.KansasCityFed.org (accessed 15 April 2011).

Guay, T.R. (1999) *The United States and the European Union: The Political Economy of a Relationship*, Sheffield Academic Press, Sheffield.

Haas, E.B. (1958) *The Uniting of Europe*, Stanford University Press, Stanford, CA.

Hall, B. (2000) 'Immigration in the European Union: problem or solution?' *OECD Observer*, No. 221–2.

Hamilton, C.B. and L.A. Winters (1992) 'Opening up international trade with Eastern Europe', *Economic Policy*, 14: 78–116.

Hardy, S., M. Hart, L. Albrechts and A. Katos (1995) *An Enlarged EU: Regions in Competition?* Jessica Kingsley Publishers, London.

Harrop, J. (2000) *The Political Economy of Integration in the European Union*, 3rd edn, Edward Elgar, Cheltenham.

Hayes-Renshaw, F., W. van Aken and H. Wallace (2005) *When and Why the Council of Ministers of the EU Votes Explicitly*, EUI Working Papers RSCAS No. 2005/25, Robert Schuman Centre for Advanced Studies, European University Institute, Florence.

Healey, N.M. (1995) 'From the Treaty of Rome to Maastricht: The theory and practice of European integration', in N.M. Healey (ed.) *The Economics of the New Europe*, Routledge, London.

Heipertz, M. and A. Verdun (2010) *Ruling Europe: The Politics of the Stability and Growth Pact*, Cambridge University Press, Cambridge.

Hill, C. (1993) 'The capability–expectations gap, or conceptualising Europe's international role', *Journal of Common Market Studies*, 31(3): 305–28.

Hitiris, T. (2003 and earlier editions) *European Community Economics*, 5th edn, Prentice Hall, Hemel Hempstead.

Hix, S. (2005) *The Political System of the European Union*, 2nd edn, Palgrave, London.

Hoffman, S. (1966) 'Obstinate or obsolete? The fate of the nation-state and the case of Western Europe', *Daedalus*, 95(3): 862–915.

Hooghe, L. (ed.) (1996) *Cohesion Policy and European Integration: Building Multi-level Governance*, Oxford University Press, Oxford.

Horvàth, R. (2005) *Exchange Rate Variability, Pressures and Optimum Currency Area Criteria:*

Some Empirical Evidence from the 1990s, Working Paper 8/2005, Czech National Bank http://www.cnb.cz/miranda2/export/sites/www.cnb.cz/en/research/research_publications/cnb_wp/download/cnbwp_2005_08.pdf (accessed 12 November 2010).

Horvàth, R. (2007) 'Ready for the euro? Evidence on EU new member states', *Applied Economics Letters*, 14: 1083–6.

House of Lords (2004) *EU Development Aid in Transition*, http://www.publications.parliament.uk/pa/ld200304/ldselect/ldeucom/ldeucom.htm (accessed 18 February 2011).

Hudec, R.E. (1993) *Enforcing International Trade Law: The Evolution of the Modern GATT Legal System*, Butterworth Legal Publishers, Salem, NY.

Hughes, K. (2004) *Turkey and the European Union: Just Another Enlargement?* Friends of Europe Working Paper, June 2004.

IMF (1998) *World Economic and Social Survey*, Washington, DC.

IMF (2007) *World Economic Outlook*, www.imf.org (accessed 15 April 2011).

IMF (2010a and previous years) *Global Financial Stability Report*, http://www.imf.org/external/pubs/ft/gfsr/2010/02/index.htm (accessed 7 October 2010).

IMF (2010b) *World Economic Outlook*, http://www.imf.org/external/pubs/ft/weo/2010/01/pdf/text.pdf (accessed 7 October 2010).

Independent Commission on Turkey (2009) *Turkey in Europe: Breaking the Vicious Circle, Second Report of the Independent Commission on Turkey*, http://www.independentcommissiononturkey.org/pdfs/2009_english.pdf (accessed 9 July 2010).

International Organization for Migration (2010) *World Migration Report 2010, The Future of Migration: Building Capacities for Change*, http://publications.iom.int/bookstore/free/WMR_2010_ENGLISH.pdf (accessed 21 December 2010).

Irwin, D. (2002) 'Interpreting the Tariff–Growth Correlation in

the Late Nineteenth Century', *American Economic Review (Papers and Proceedings)*, 92: 165–9.

Italianer, A. (1994) 'Whither the gains from European integration?' *Revue Economique*, 20: 689–702.

Johnson, H.G. (1965) 'An economic theory of protectionism, tariff bargaining and the formation of customs unions', *Journal of Political Economy*, 73: 256–83.

Johnson, G.L. and C.L. Quance (1972) *The Overproduction Trap in US Agriculture*, Johns Hopkins University Press, Baltimore.

Josling, T. (2007) 'The WTO: What next?', *EuroChoices*, 6(2): 6–12.

Kahanec, M. and K.F. Zimmermann (2010) 'Migration in an enlarged EU: a challenging solution', in F. Keereman and I.P. Székely (eds) *Five Years of an Enlarged EU: A Positive-Sum Game*, Springer, Berlin.

Kandogan, Y. (2000) 'Political economy of eastern enlargement of the European Union: budgetary costs and reforms in voting rules', *European Journal of Political Economy*, 16: 685–706.

Kandogan, Y. (2005a) 'Power analysis of the Nice Treaty on the future of European integration', *Applied Economics*, 47(3): 1147–56.

Kandogan, Y. (2005b) *Trade Creation and Diversion Effects of Europe's Liberalisation Agreements*, William Davison Institute Working Paper No. 746, www.wdi.umich.edu (accessed 2 August 2010).

Kay, R. and R. Ackrill (2007) 'Financing social and cohesion policy in an enlarged EU: plus ça change, plus c'est la même chose?' *Journal of European Social Policy*, 17(4): 361–74.

Kemp, M.C. and H. Wan (1976) 'An elementary proposition concerning the formation of customs unions', *Journal of International Economics*, 6(February): 95–7.

Kenen, R. (1969) 'The theory of optimum currency areas: an

eclectic view', in **R. Mundell and A. Swoboda** (eds) *Monetary Problems of the International Economy*, University of Chicago Press, Chicago.

Kengyel, A. and T. Palankai (2003) 'Structural policy roles and directions', in T. Palankai (ed.) *Economics of European Integration*, Akadémiai Kiadó, Budapest.

Kindleberger, C.P. (1973) *International Economics*, 5th edn, Irwin-Dorsey, Homewood, IL.

Kindleberger, C.P. (1984) *A Financial History of Western Europe*, Allen & Unwin, London.

Kindleberger, C.P. (2000) *Manias, Panics and Crashes*, 4th edn. John Wiley & Sons, New York.

King, D. and C. Campbell (2009) 'The impact of the EPA on Caribbean economies: a structural analysis of four Caribbean economies, http://www.delbrb.ec.europa.eu/en/epa/one_year_on/EPA_conference_paper_Damien_King.pdf (accessed 18 February 2011).

Kinsella, S. and A. Leddin (2010) *Understanding Ireland's Economic Crisis Prospects for Recovery*, ebook, Blackhall Publishing, Dublin.

Koester, U. and S.M. Senior Nello, (2010) 'Pillar II: a real improvement of the CAP?' in **S. Senior Nello and P. Pierani** (eds) *International Trade, Consumer Interests and Reform of the Common Agricultural Policy*, Routledge, Abingdon.

Kok Report (2004) *Facing the Challenge: The Lisbon Strategy for Growth and Employment*, Report from the High Level Group chaired by Wim Kok, available at http://www.umic.pt/images/stories/publicacoes200801/kok_report_en.pdf (accessed 7 March 2011).

Korhonen, I. and J. Fidrmuc (2001) 'Similarity of supply and demand shocks between the euro area and the accession countries', *Focus on Transition*, Austrian National Bank, Vienna, www.oenb.at/en/geldp_volksw/zentral_osteuropa/eu_enlargement/2001_korhonenfidrmuc (accessed 12 November 2010).

Kreinen, M.E. (1972) 'Effects of the EEC on imports of manufactures', *Economic Journal*, 82: 897–920.

Krugman, P.R. (1990) 'Policy problems of monetary unions', in **P. De Grauwe and L. Papademos** (eds) *The European Monetary System in the 1990s*, Longman, London.

Krugman, P.R. (1991a) Is bilateralism bad?' in **E. Helpman and A. Razin** (eds) *International Trade and Trade Policy*, MIT Press, Cambridge, MA.

Krugman, P.R. (1991b) *Geography and Trade*, Leuven University Press, Leuven, and MIT Press, Cambridge, MA.

Krugman, P.R. (1993a) 'Regionalism versus multilateralism: analytical notes', in **J. Del Melo and A. Panagariya** (eds) *New Dimensions in Regional Integration*, Cambridge University Press, Cambridge.

Krugman, P.R. (1993b) 'Lessons of Massachusetts for EMU', in **F. Giavazzi and T. Torres** (eds) *Adjustment and Growth in the European Monetary Union*, Cambridge University Press, Cambridge.

Krugman, P.R. and M. Obstfeld (2011 and earlier editions) *International Economics. Theory and Policy*, 9th edn, Pearson, Boston.

Krugman, P.R. and A. Venables (1990) 'Integration and the competitiveness of peripheral industry', in **C.J. Bliss and J. Braga de Macedo** (eds) *Unity with Diversity in the European Economy: The Communities' Southern Frontier*, Cambridge University Press, Cambridge.

Laruelle, A. and M. Widgren (1998) 'Is the allocation of voting power among the EU member states fair?' *Public Choice*, 94: 317–39.

Lawson, N. (2008) *An Appeal to Reason: A Cool Look at Global Warming*, George Duckworth, London.

Layard, R., O. Blanchard, R. Dornbusch and P. Krugman (1992) *East–West Migration: The Alternatives*, MIT Press, Cambridge, MA.

LeSage, J.P. and M.M. Fischer (2008) 'Spatial growth regressions: model specification, estimation and interpretation', *Spatial Economic Analysis*, 3: 275–304.

Lindberg, L.N. (1963) *The Politics of European Economic Integration*, Stanford University Press, Stanford, CA.

Lipsey, R.G. (1957) 'The theory of customs unions: trade diversion and welfare', *Economica*, 24: 40–46.

Lipsey, R. (1960) 'The theory of customs unions: a general survey', *The Economic Journal*, 70: 496–513.

Lomborg, B. (2001) *The Sceptical Environmentalist: Measuring the Real State of the World*, Cambridge University Press, Cambridge.

Loureiro, M.L. (2003) 'GMO food labelling in the EU: tracing "the seeds of dispute"', *EuroChoices*, 2(1): 18–23.

Lucas, R.E. (1988) 'On the mechanics of economic development', *Journal of Economic Literature*, 22: 3–42.

Ludlow, P. (1982) *The Making of the European Monetary System*, Butterworths, London.

MacDougall Report (1977) *The Role of Public Finance in European Integration*, http://ec.europa.eu/economy_finance/emu_history/documentation/chapter8/19770401en73macdougallrepvol1.pdf (accessed 29 March 2011).

Marsh, J. and S. Tarditi (2003) *Cultivating a Crisis: The Global Impact of the Common Agricultural Policy*, Consumers International, London.

Martin, R. and P. Tyler (2006) 'Evaluating the impact of the Structural Funds on Objective 1 Regions: an exploratory discussion', *Regional Studies*, 40(2): 201–10.

Martin, S. (2007) 'Competition policy', in M. Artis and F. Nixson (eds) *The Economics of the European Union: Policy and Analysis*, 4th edn, Oxford University Press, Oxford.

Mattera, A. (1988) *Marché unique européen: Ses règles, son fonctionnement*, Jupiter, Paris.

Mayes, D. (1978) 'The effects of economic integration on trade', *Journal of Common Market Studies*, 17(1): 1–25.

Mayhew, A. (1998) *Recreating Europe. The European Union's Policy towards Central and Eastern Europe*, Cambridge University Press, Cambridge.

McKinnon, R. (1963) 'Optimum currency areas', *American Economic Review*, 53: 717–25.

McKinnon, R. (1996) *Default Risk in Monetary Unions*, Background Report for the Swedish Government Commission on EMU, Stockholm.

McKinsey Report (2009) *Pathways to a Low-Carbon Economy*, https://solutions.mckinsey.com/ClimateDesk/default.aspx (accessed 28 December 2010).

McMillan, J. (1993) 'Does regional integration foster open trade? Economic theory and GATT's Article XXIV', in K. Anderson and R. Blackhurst (eds), *Regional Integration and the Global Trading System*, St Martin's Press, New York.

Meade, J.E. (1962) *The Theory of International Economic Policy. Vol. 2: Trade and Welfare*, Oxford University Press, Oxford.

Messerlin, P. and C. Delpeuch (2007) *EPAs: A Plan 'A+'*, Groupe d'Economie Mondiale, Sciences Politiques, Paris.

Milward, A.S. (1984) *The Reconstruction of Western Europe 1945–1951*, Methuen, London.

Milward, A.S. (2000) *The European Rescue of the Nation State*, 2nd edn, Routledge, London.

Minsky, H.P. (1980) 'Capitalist financial processes and the instability of capitalism', *Journal of Economic Issues*, 14(2): 505–22.

Mitrany, D. (1966) *A Working Peace System*, Quadrangle Books, Chicago.

Molle, W. (2006) *The Economics of European Integration: Theory, Practice, Policy*, 5th edn, Ashgate, Aldershot.

Mongelli, F.P. (2005) 'What is European economic and monetary union telling us about the properties of optimum currency areas?' *Journal of Common Market Studies*, 43(3): 607–35.

Monnet, J. (1978) *Memoirs*, Collins, London.

Monti, M. (1996) *The Single Market and Tomorrow's Europe: A Progress Report from the European Commission*, Kogan Page, London.

Monti, M. (2010) *A New Strategy for the Single Market. At the Service of Europe's Economy and Society*, Report to the President of the European Commission, José Manuel Barroso, http://ec.europa.eu/bepa/pdf/monti_report_final_10_05_2010_en.pdf (accessed 2 November 2010).

Moravcsik, A. (1998) *The Choice for Europe: Social Purpose and State Power from Messina to Maastricht*, Cornell University Press, Ithaca, NY, and UCL Press, London.

Mueller, D.C. (2003) *Public Choice III*, Cambridge University Press, Cambridge.

Mundell, R. (1961) 'A theory of optimum currency areas', *American Economic Review*, 51: 657–65.

Mundell, R. (1973) 'Uncommon arguments for common currencies', in H.G. Johnson and A.K. Swoboda (eds) *The Economics of Common Currencies*, Allen & Unwin, London.

Navarro, L. (2003) *Industrial Policy in the Economic Literature: Recent Theoretical Developments and Implications for EU Policy*, Enterprise Papers No. 12, http://www.edis.sk/ekes/enterprise_paper_12_2003.pdf (accessed 2 February 2011).

Nelson, R.R. and S.G. Winter (1982) *An Evolutionary Theory of Economic Change*, Harvard University Press, Cambridge, MA.

Nerlove, M. (1956) 'Estimates of the elasticities of supply of selected agricultural commodities', *Journal of Farm Economics*, 38: 496–509.

Netherlands Bureau for Economic Policy Analysis (2007) *Expected Benefits of the European Services Directive*, http://www.cpb.nl/nl/pub/cpbreeksen/notitie/14nov2007/notitie.pdf (accessed 5 November 2010).

Neville Rolfe, E. (1984) *The Politics of Agriculture in the European Community*, Policy Studies Institute, ECPS, London.

Niebuhr, A., and F. Schlitte (2008) *EU Convergence and Enlargement: Does Market Access Matter?* HWWI Research Paper 1–16, Hamburg.

Nomura (2011) *Europe will Work*, http://www.nomura.com/europe/resources/pdf/Europe%20will%20work%20FINAL_March2011.pdf (accessed 24 March, 2011).

Nordhaus, W. (2006) *The Stern Review on the Economics of Climate Change*, Working Paper 12741, www.nber.org (accessed 28 December 2010).

Nugent, N. (2010) *The Government and Politics of the European Union*, 7th edn, Palgrave Macmillan, Basingstoke.

Nuti, D.M. (1994) 'The impact of systematic transition on the European Community', in S. Martin (ed.) *The Construction of Europe: Essays in Honour of Emil Noel*, Kluwer, Dordrecht.

OECD (2006) *Agricultural Market Impact of Future Growth in the Production of Biofuels*, OECD, Paris, www.oecd.org (accessed 19 July 2010).

OECD (2008) *Economic Assessment of Biofuel Support Policies*, www.oecd.org. (accessed 19 July 2010).

OECD (2010 and previous years) *Economic Outlook*, http://www.oecd.org/document/18/0,3343,en_2649_33733_20347538_1_1_1_1,00.html (accessed 7 October 2010).

Oksanen, H. (2010) 'Setting targets for government budgets under the EU Stability and Growth Pact and ageing populations', *International Journal of Economics and Business Research*, 2: 87–111.

Oksanen, H. (forthcoming) 'Persions and European integration', in A. Tovias and A. Verdun (eds) *Mapping European Integration*, Palgrave Macmillan, Basingstoke.

Olson, M. Jr (1965) *The Logic of Collective Action: Public Goods and the Theory of Groups*, Harvard University Press, Cambridge, MA.

Paas, T. and F. Schlitte (2008) *Regional Income Inequality and Convergence Processes* in the EU-25, HWWA, Hamburg.

Padoa Schioppa, T. (1987) *Efficiency, Equity and Stability*, Oxford University Press, Oxford.

Parsons, C.R., R. Skeldon, T.L. Walmsley and L.A. Winters (2007) 'Quantifying international migration: a database of bilateral migrant stocks', in C. Ozden and M. Schiff (eds) *International Migration , Economic Development and Policy*, Palgrave Macmillan and the World Bank, New York.

Pearce, D. (2003) 'Environmental policy', in M. Artis and F. Nixson (eds) *The Economics of the European Union. Policy and Analysis*, 3rd edn, Oxford University Press, Oxford.

Pelkmans, J. (2007) 'Mutual recognition in goods, on promises and disillusions', *Journal of European Public Policy*, 14(5): 699–716.

Pelkmans, J. (2010) *Single Market Revival?* CEPS Commentary, CEPS, Brussels, www.ceps.eu/ceps/download/3026 (accessed 3 March 2011).

Pelkmans, J. and H. Gremmen (1983) 'The empirical measurement of static customs union effects', *Rivista Internazionale di Scienze Economiche e Commerciali*, 30 (July).

Peterson, J. and M. Shackleton (2006) *The Institutions of the European Union*, 2nd edn, Oxford University Press, Oxford.

Pinder, J. (1995) *European Community: The Building of a Union*, 2nd edn, Oxford University Press, Oxford.

Pollack, M.A. (2005) 'Theorizing the European Union: international organization, domestic polity, or experiment in new governance?' *Annual Review of Political Science*, 8: 357–98.

Pomfret, R. (1986) 'The theory of preferential trading arrangements', *Weltwirtshaftliches Archiv*, 122: 439–64.

Portes, R. and H. Rey (1998) 'Euro vs dollar: Will the euro replace the dollar as the world currency?' *Economic Policy*, April.

Prescott, E. (2004) 'Why do Americans work so much more that Europeans?' *Federal Reserve Bank of Minneapolis Quarterly Review*, 28: 2–13.

Reinhart, C. and K. Rogoff (2009) 'Growth in a time of debt', *American Economic Review Papers and Proceedings*, http://blogs.wsj.com/economics/2010/01/04/reinhart-and-rogoff-higher-debt-may-stunt-economic-growth/ (accessed 3 December 2010).

Robinson, S. and K. Thierfelder (2002) 'Trade liberalisation and regional integration: the search for large numbers', *Australian Journal of Agricultural and Resource Economics*, 46: 585–604.

Robson, P. (1984) *The Economics of International Integration*, 2nd edn, Allen & Unwin, London.

Romer, P. (1986) 'Increasing returns and long run growth', *Journal of Political Economy*, 94: 1002–37.

Rose, A. (2000) 'One money, one market: the effect of common currencies on trade', *Economic Policy*, 30: 7–33.

Rose, A. (2002) 'The effect of common currencies on international trade: Where do we stand?' unpublished manuscript available at http://faculty.hass.berkeley edu/arose/RecRes.htm (accessed 2 August 2010).

Rose, A.K. (2008) 'EMU, trade and business cycle synchronization', http://faculty.haas.berkeley.edu/arose/EMUMeta.pdf (accessed 12 November 2010).

Sachs, J. and X. Sala-i-Martin (1992) 'Fiscal federalism and optimum currency areas: evidence for Europe from the United States', in M. Canzoneri P. Masson and V. Grilli (eds) *Establishing a Central Bank: Issues in Europe and Lessons from the US*, Cambridge University Press, Cambridge.

Salvatore, D. (2010) *International Economics, Trade and Finance*, 10th edn, John Wiley & Sons, New York.

Sapir, A. (2007) 'European strategies for growth', in M. Artis and F. Nixson (eds) *The Economics of the European Union*, Oxford University Press, Oxford.

Sapir, A., P. Aghion, G. Bertola et al. (2004) *An Agenda for a Growing Europe: The Sapir Report*, Oxford University Press, Oxford.

Scheller, H.P. (2006) *The European Central Bank: History, Role and Functions*, 2nd edn, www.ecb.int (accessed 15 April 2011).

Schiff, M. and L.A. Winters (2003) *Regional Integration and Development*, World Bank, Washington, DC, www.worldbank.org (accessed 2 August 2010).

Schimmelfennig, F. and U. Sedelmeier (eds) (2005) *The Europeanization of Central and Eastern Europe*, Cornell University Press, Ithaca, NY.

Schmitter, P. (1970) 'A revised theory of regional integration', *International Organisation*, 24: 836–68.

Schmitter, P.C. (2000) *How to Democratize the European Union – and Why Bother?* Rowman & Littlefield, Lanham, MD.

Schumpeter, J. (1975) *Capitalism, Socialism and Democracy*, Harper, New York (first published 1942).

Sellekaerts, W. (1973) 'How meaningful are empirical studies on trade creation and trade diversion?' *Weltwirtschaftliches Archiv*, 109: 519–51.

Senior Nello, S. (1984) 'An application of public choice to the question of CAP reform', *European Review of Agricultural Economics*, 11: 261–83.

Senior Nello, S. (1985) 'Reform of the EC agrimonetary system: a public choice approach', *Journal of European Integration*, 9: 55–79.

Senior Nello, S. (1989) 'European interest groups and the CAP', *Food Policy*, 2 (May): 101–6.

Senior Nello, S.M. (1991) *The New Europe: Changing Economic Relations between East and West*, Harvester Wheatsheaf, Hemel Hempstead.

Senior Nello, S.M. (1997) *Applying the New Political Economy*

Approach to Agricultural Policy Formation in the European Union, EUI Working Papers RSC No. 97/21, Robert Schuman Centre for Advanced Studies, Florence.

Senior Nello, S.M. (2002) 'Progress in preparing for EU enlargement: the tensions between economic and political integration', *International Political Science Review*, 23(3): 291–317.

Senior Nello, S.M. (2004) 'Cyprus and EU accession', in A. Landuyt (ed.) *Lo spazio politico nell'integrazione europea, Gli allargamenti della CEE/UE dal 1961 al 2002*, Il Mulino, Bologna.

Senior Nello, S. (2009) *European Union: Economics, Policies and History*, 2nd edn. McGraw-Hill, Maidenhead.

Senior Nello, S. and P. Pierani (eds) (2010) *International Trade, Consumer Interests and Reform of the Common Agricultural Policy*, Routledge, Abingdon.

Senior Nello, S.M. and K.E. Smith (1998) *The Consequences of Eastern Enlargement of the European Union in Stages*, Ashgate, Aldershot.

Siedentop, L. (2000) *Democracy in Europe*, Penguin Books, London.

Smith, K.E. (2001) 'Western actors and the promotion of democracy', in J. Zielonka and A. Pravda (eds) *Democratic Consolidation in Eastern Europe. Vol. 2: International and Transnational Factors*, Oxford University Press, Oxford.

Smith, K.E. (2003) 'The evolution and application of EU membership conditionality', in M. Cremona (ed.) *The Enlargement of the European Union*, Oxford University Press, Oxford.

Soloaga, I. and L.A. Winters (1999) *How has Regionalism in the 1990s affected Trade?* World Bank Policy Research Working Paper No. 2156, www.worldbank.org (accessed 2 August 2010).

Solow, R. (1956) 'A contribution to the theory of growth', *Quarterly Journal of Economics*, February, 65–94.

Spinelli, A. (1972) 'The growth of the European movement since the Second World War', in M. Hodges (ed.) *European Integration*, Penguin, Harmondsworth.

Srinivasan, T.N., J. Whalley, and I. Wooton (1993) 'Measuring the effects of regionalism on trade and welfare', in K. Anderson and R. Blackhurst (eds) *Regional Integration and the Global Trading System*, Harvester Wheatsheaf for the GATT Secretariat, London.

Stern, N. (2006) *The Economics of Climate Change*, www.hm-treasury.gov.uk (accessed 28 December 2010).

Stevens, C. (1990) 'The Lomé Convention', in K. Kiljunen (ed.) *Region-to-Region Co-operation between the Developed and Developing Countries: The Potential for Mini NIEO*, Avebury, Aldershot.

Stevens, C., M. Meyn, J. Kennan (ODI) and S. Bilal, C. Braun-Munzinger, F. Jerosch, D. Makhan and F. Rampa (ECDPM) (2008) *The New EPAs: Comparative Analysis of their Content and the Challenges for 2008*, Policy Management Report 14, ECDPM, Maastricht, http://www.ecdpm.org/Web_ECDPM/Web/Content/Navigation.nsf/index2?readform and http://www.ecdpm.org/Web_ECDPM/Web/Content/Content.nsf/0/0E4FD1DDEACB8E2DC12574180056C942?OpenDocument (accessed 23 February 2011).

Stiglitz, J.E. (2002) *Globalisation and its Discontents*, W.W. Norton, New York.

Stiglitz, J., A. Sen and J.P. Fitoussi (2009) *The Measurement of Economic Performance and Social Progress Revisited. Reflections and Overview*, http://www.stiglitz-sen-fitoussi.fr/documents/overview-eng.pdf (accessed 3 February 2011).

Swann, D. (2000) *The Economics of Europe: From Common Market to European Union*, 2nd edn, Penguin Business Library, London.

Sweeney, P. (ed.) (2008) *Ireland's Economic Success – Reasons and Lessons*, New Island, Dublin.

Swinnen, J.F.M., M. Negash and T. Vandemoortele (2010) 'Consumers and the political economy of European agricultural and food policies', in S. Senior Nello and P. Pierani (eds) *International Trade, Consumer Interests and Reform of the Common Agricultural Policy*, Routledge, Abingdon.

Taleb, N.N. (2010) *The Black Swan: The Impact of the Highly Improbable*, 2nd edn, Penguin, New York.

Tarditi, S. (1992) 'Esercitazioni', unpublished manuscript, Facoltà di Economia Richard Goodwin, University of Siena.

Tarditi, S., J. Marsh and S.M. Senior Nello (1995) *Agricultural Strategies for the Enlargement of the European Union to Central and Eastern Europe*, Study prepared for DG–1 of the Commission, Siena.

Taylor, J.B. (1999) 'An historical analysis of monetary policy rules', in J.B. Taylor (ed.) *Monetary Policy Rules*, University of Chicago Press, Chicago.

Tinbergen, J. (1952) *On the Theory of Economic Policy*, North-Holland, Amsterdam.

Tinbergen, J. (1954) *International Economic Integration*, Elsevier, Amsterdam.

Tondl, G. (1999) 'The changing pattern of regional convergence in Europe', *Jahrbuch für Regionalwissenschaft*, 19: 1–33.

Tondl, G. (forthcoming) 'A review on research in economic and social cohesion in the EU, the design of EU regional policy, and its implications', in A. Tovias and A. Verdun, *Mapping European Integration*, Palgrave Macmillan, Basingstoke.

Torres, F. (2006) 'On the efficiency-legitimacy trade-off in EMU', in F. Torres A. Verdun and H. Zimmermann (eds) *EMU Rules: The Political and Economic Consequences of European Monetary Integration*, Nomos, Baden-Baden.

Torres, F. (2008) 'The long road to EMU: the economic and political reasoning behind Maastricht', in S. Baroncelli, C. Spagnolo and L.S. Talani (eds) *After Maastricht: The Legacy of the Maastricht Treaty for European Integration*, Cambridge Scholars Publishers, Cambridge.

Torias, A. and A. Verdun (forthcoming) *Mapping European Economic Integration*, Palgrave Macmillan, Basingstoke.

Tracy, M. (1989) *Government and Agriculture in Western Europe 1880–1988*, Harvester Wheatsheaf, London.

Tracy, M. (1993) *Food and Agriculture in a Market Economy. An Introduction to Theory, Practice and Policy*, Agricultural Policy Studies, Genappe, Belgium.

Tracy, M. (2009) 'The Lisbon Treaty – decision-making and democracy? A commentary', http://lisbontreatycommentary. wordpress.com (accessed 22 April 2010).

Truman, E.M. (1969) 'The European Economic Community: trade creation and trade diversion', *Yale Economic Essays*, 9: 201–57.

Tsoukalis, L. (1997) *The New European Economy Revisited*, 3rd edn, Oxford University Press, Oxford.

Uvalic, M. (2002) *The Economies of South-Eastern Europe: From International Assistance to Self-sustainable Growth*, Bertelsmann Foundation Risk Reporting 2001/2002 South-Eastern Europe Economics and Reform Assistance Strategy Report, Gütersloh, Germany, www.stiftung. bertlesmann.de (accessed 27 January 2011).

Uvalic, M. (2010) 'Integrating the Western Balkans into the European Union: Overcoming the economic constraints', Paper presented at the 11th Mediterranean Research Meeting, Workshop 16, January 2010, European University Institute, Florence.

Vachudova, M.A. (2001) *The Leverage of International Institutions on Democratizing States: Eastern Europe and the European Union*, EUI Working Paper RSC No. 2001/33, Florence.

Varian, H.R. (2009 and earlier editions) *Intermediate Microeconomics: A Modern Approach*, 8th edn, W.W. Norton, London.

Vercelli, A. (2010) *Economy and Economics: The Twin Crisis*, DEPFID Working Papers 4/2010, Department of Economic Policy, Finance and Development (DEPFID), University of Siena, http:// www.aehe.net/crisis/economi-depfid-siena.pdf (accessed 7 October 2010).

Verdoorn, P.J. and A.N.R. Schwartz. (1972) 'Two alternative estimates of the effects of the EEC and EFTA on the pattern of trade', *European Economic Review*, 3: 291–35.

Venables, A. (2006) *Shifts in Economic Geography and their Causes*, Paper presented at the annual economic symposium organized by the Federal Reserve Bank of Kansas at Jackson Hole, www.KansasCityFed. org (accessed 15 April 2011).

Victor, J.C, V. Raisson and F. Tétart (2007) *Le dessous des cartes: Atlas d'un monde qui change, Vol. 2*, Editions Tallandier, Paris.

Vickers, J. (2009) *Competition Policy and Property Rights*, Department of Economics Discussion Paper Series, No. 436, University of Oxford, http://www.economics. ox.ac.uk/research/wp/pdf/ paper436.pdf (accessed 10 February 2011).

Viner, J. (1953) *The Customs Union Issue*, The Carnegie Endowment for International Peace, New York.

Wallace, H., M.A Pollack and R. Young (2010) *Policy-Making in the European Union*, 6th edn, Oxford University Press, Oxford.

Wang, Z.H. and L.A. Winters (1991) *The Trading Potential of Eastern Europe*, CEPR Discussion Paper 610, Centre for Economic Policy Research, London.

Wilhelmsson, F. (2006) *Trade Creation, Diversion and Displacement of the EU Enlargement Process*, www. nek.lu.se/NEKFWI (accessed 2 August 2010).

Williams, R.H. (1996) *European Union Spatial Policy and Planning*, Paul Chapman, London.

Winters, L. A. (1987) 'Britain in Europe: a survey of quantitative trade studies', *Journal of Common Market Studies*, 25: 315–35.

Winters, L.A. (1996) *Regionalism Versus Multilateralism*, World Bank Policy Research Paper 1687, World Bank, Washington, DC.

Winters, L.A. (2007) Introducing a global database on migrant stocks: American in Paris – but how many are there?' *CEPR Policy Insight*, No. 17, http://www.cepr.org/pubs/ policyinsights/PolicyInsight17. pdf (accessed 21 December 2010).

World Bank (2000) *The Road to Stability and Prosperity in South Eastern Europe: A Regional Strategy Paper*, World Bank, Washington, DC.

World Bank (2007) *Global Economic Prospects: Managing the Next Wave of Globalisation*, www.worldbank.org (accessed 15 April 2011).

World Bank (2011) *Migration and Remittances Factbook*, 2nd edn, http://siteresources.worldbank. org/INTLAC/Resources/ Factbook2011-Ebook.pdf (accessed 7 March 2011).

Wyplosz, C. (2006) 'EMU: the dark sides of a major success', *Economic Policy*, 21(46): 207–16.

Index

INDEX